THE GHOST*s* OF BLUE BELL HILL

& other Road Ghosts

THE GHOSTS OF BLUE BELL HILL

& other Road Ghosts

A case-centred study of Phantom Hitch-Hikers & Phantom Jaywalkers in Folklore and Fact

Sean Tudor

White Ladies Press

First published: 2017

A CIP catalogue record for this title is available from the British Library.

Layout and design by Sean Tudor.

ISBN 978-0-9957363-1-3

White Ladies Press

Ordering Information and Enquiries:

Special discounts may be available on quantity purchases by corporations, associations, educators, and others. For details, and for all other enquiries, email the publisher at: info@whiteladiespress.co.uk

Contents

Illustrations

Acknowledgements

As with any similar project, this book represents only the tip of the iceberg in relation to the mass of research and energy that goes into it. A significant proportion of this work—and by inference, of this book—would not have been possible without the input and assistance of a number of individuals and organisations. The author would like to extend his thanks to all of those who, over the years, have responded to or helped with his inquiries, or who have assisted simply by their interest and encouragement.

Particular thanks are due to the following: to Michael Goss, who so patiently answered all my questions and correspondence during the first faltering steps of my own researches, and without whose own book there would have been little foundation on which to establish my own work. Other authors I would like to extend my thanks to include the late Andrew Green, Dennis Chambers, Ted Wright, and Neil Arnold, who has contributed a number of leads and witness accounts that furnish this book.

Of the numerous witnesses and commentators, both public and private, who have accommodated me with their time, testimonies, recollections, anecdotes or other information, special thanks go to Bryan Wetton, to the family of Judith Lingham, to Ian Sharpe, and to all the witnesses who have given their experiences for the record, particularly those who have been willing to stand by their accounts with their real name: Ann-Marie Austin, John Arnold, Ryan Banks, Gillian Barry, Clare Bush, Neville Butteriss, Bob Fearne, Joy Gammon, Jacquie Hopkins, Renee Hughes, Glenn Jones, Anne King, Wendy Lang, Chris & Janice Leigh, Paul Lowing, Alan Matthews, Dan Mulford, Nick Norris, James Shoebridge, Richard Studholme.

Thanks also go to the following for their varied contributions or permissions in respect of Blue Bell Hill and other cases: Paul Abbott, Ian Baker, Daniel Barraclough, Phillip Baum, Audrey Brooks, Catherine Brown, Patrick Browne, Sharon Cornet, Brian Culver, Andy Doyle, David Elvy, Steve Everett, Rick Flynn, Georgina Gear, Rex Harvey, Helen Head, Peter Hedge, Edson Hendricks, Hannah Jackson, Michael Jennings, Richard King, Penny Lazell, Chris & Janice Leigh, Frank Lynch, Donna Maillie, Richard Marchant, Nick Morgan, Julia Nash, Nigel D., Nigel Nelson, Chioma Obiefuna, Peter Parvin, Andy Reeds, Samantha Steeden, Keith Scales, Mike Stevens, David Thomas, Jonathon Thomas, Ron Thomas, Stephen Watts.

And to the staffs of the libraries, past and present, of Maidstone, Chatham, Gillingham, Rochester; Medway Archives and Local Studies Centre (MALSC), the Kent History and Library Centre (Maidstone), the British Newspaper Archive (Colindale), the Folklore Society Library, Kent Police, and finally the journalists and staff of the KM (*Kent Messenger*) Media Group, whose reporting has been instrumental in establishing Blue Bell Hill's reputation in legend and fact.

In Memoriam: Belated thanks are extended to the following individuals, since passed, for their valued assistance to the author and contributions to the Blue Bell Hill story: Patrick Browne (d. 1998), Joe Chester (d. 2012), Andrew Green (d. 2004), Renee Hughes (d. 2005), Stephen Nelkin (d. 1998), Edward George (Pat) Sandford (d. 2016), James (Jim) Skene (d. 2013), Alfred (Jack) Woodger (d. 1994).

For permissions to quote from copyright material the author is grateful to: HarperCollins*Publishers* Ltd for permission to quote passages from *C.G. Jung: Memories, Dreams, Reflections* (Fontana Press, 1995) (edited by Aniela Jaffé), pp. 368–369, and from *Jung: Selected Writings* (Fontana Press, 1986) (edited by Anthony Storr, p.70, p.102 & p.218, and for its acknowledgement of no objection to the quotation of extracts from Michael Goss's *The Evidence for Phantom Hitch-Hikers* (The Aquarian Press, 1984), pp.2-3, pp.12-13, pp.91-92, p.95, p.100, p.102, p.104, p.106 & p.120; Daimon Publishers for permission to quote from Aniela Jaffé's *An Archetypal Approach to Death Dreams and Ghosts* (1999), p.30, pp.95-99, p.187; University of Minnesota Press for permission to quote from *Memoirs and letters of Oscar W. Firkins* (by Oscar W. Firkins, Richard Burton, Netta White Wilson) (1934), p.128; Taylor & Francis Group for permission to quote from Miranda Green's *Symbol and Image in Celtic Religious Art* (Routledge, 1992), p.187; Bob Hobbs at NA3T for use of photographic image no. VS02258-B (*see* Illustrations); KM Media Group for permission to use extracts and images from various KM Group newspapers (see Illustrations, Published History and Notes & References for details and attributions).

Finally, I would like to thank my wife, April, for her long-suffering patience over what seemed the never-ending project.

Dedication

In loving memory of my father, Michael Cornelius Tudor (1937–2006), and my uncle, John Edward Tudor (1944–2000), from whom I first heard the story of the Ghost of Blue Bell Hill. This book is dedicated also to all those who have lost their lives or whose lives have been irreparably altered by tragic events on Blue Bell Hill.

'We proceed, because we have begun; we complete our design, that the labour already spent may not be in vain.'

Samuel Johnson (1709–1784)

Introduction

For as long as there have been roads, lone travellers on the highways have encountered GHOSTS. Tales abound of ghostly highwaymen and cowled monks, of phantom soldiers and white ladies; even spectral animals and vehicles. Every culture preserves accounts of fearful meetings at lonely spots in the dead of night with a variety of supernatural entities, which vanish as suddenly as they have appeared, leaving behind shocked and frightened victims. Crossroads, in particular, were feared in the past as the haunts of ghosts, witches and evil spirits. In Britain, until 1823, they served as the burial places for executed murderers and suicides, whose bodies were additionally driven through with a stake as a kind of double insurance policy designed to prevent their disturbed spirits finding their way back to trouble the living.[1] Add to this centuries of accident, murder, and intrigue, and it is perhaps little wonder that our roads have achieved such a reputation for being haunted.

Such stories, of course, are seldom taken seriously today. While most everyone today knows something about ghosts, the prevailing attitude— certainly in western scientific culture—is one of denial, to dismiss them along with old wives' tales and other rural superstitions as vestiges of the same unreasoned fears and beliefs of our forebears.

And so it is with a much greater sense of shock and bewilderment that modern travellers report their own encounters with the same cast of supernatural characters that populate our histories and our folklore. In some cases, these events are more than fleeting glimpses of something unusual and therefore open to all kinds of interpretations, but compelling ones that allow little room for witnesses to doubt their experiences—as, for instance, where the 'ghost' appears to be a real flesh-and-blood person that steps out to collide sickeningly with the front of their vehicle; and where the police investigating have heard it all before.

As unbelievable as it may seem, this is precisely what happened at a busy hilltop location in Kent (UK) in 1992. In the space of just four weeks in October and November of that year, three different motorists reported knocking down a figure that ran into the path of their vehicle late at night on Blue Bell Hill, four miles north of Maidstone, Kent.

In the two most dramatic encounters, the figure of a young woman had stared calmly into the eyes of the driver as she was run over. Police investigations at the scene not only failed to find a victim, but no sign whatsoever of an accident, prompting their conclusion that these motorists must have encountered the famed Ghost of Blue Bell Hill.

The sightings—which, unbelievably, were to continue in the following months and to take on an even more bizarre twist—sparked a wave of press interest, which spread quickly to the national, and then the international stage. To date, the Ghost of Blue Bell Hill has been the subject of hundreds of newspaper, magazine and book features; it has been featured on a number of television programmes devoted to the 'paranormal', and has even found mention in the UK Parliament.[2] In all, Blue Bell Hill's ghost has come a long way from the seemingly apocryphal tale of local renown set in motion in the late 1960s and its humble beginnings in print, to stand (with some fifty well-attested sightings) as one of the more important modern examples of haunting on record; and arguably the foremost case of its kind in the world today.

By 'case of its kind', I refer to Blue Bell Hill's long-standing reputation as the haunt of a *Phantom Hitch-Hiker* (known in the United States as the *Vanishing Hitch-Hiker*). Since the late 1960s, Blue Bell Hill has been a place where it was said motorists could expect to encounter a lone female hitch-hiker—a young woman who, after seeking a lift home from a passing motorist, would vanish from the moving vehicle before reaching her destination. At least that is what rumours in the press and on the oral grapevine suggested. In fact, prior to 1992, no convincing evidence (to my mind, at least) involving a named, first-hand witness had been forthcoming—something that will have come as no surprise to folklorists who, with some justification, regard the Phantom Hitch-Hiker as simply an item of fashionable myth, a staple of 'modern' folklore, an urban legend.

In support of their position, folklorists are able to cite example after example describing the same pattern of events: a hitch-hiker (usually a female) hitches a lift from an unsuspecting motorist, asking to be taken home. During the journey, she would say little except to give the driver her address. Before reaching the destination, however, the motorist would discover to his consternation that his passenger had disappeared. Justifiably disturbed, but also intrigued, he would continue on to the given address, only to discover from the resident(s) that he was not the first to call about this girl—a girl who had died in a road accident a number of years previously.

This widely disseminated tale takes a form that is one of the most implausible one can imagine, even for a ghost story. It suggests that an apparently solid, three-dimensional figure—ostensibly a real person—is capable of interacting with human beings and the environment in a fundamentally real manner, and in a modern setting: the witness's own motor vehicle.

Even given the sometimes evidentially intriguing reports of other types of ghost, the hitch-hiking habit of the Blue Bell Hill ghost and her cousins worldwide, seemed a ridiculous proposition, belonging surely, as critics claimed, solely to folklore?

Be that as may, the report made by one motorist in 1974, to which the 1992 encounters would bear a striking similarity, suggested that *something* strange was going on at Blue Bell Hill. As they would again in 1992 (and after), journalists at that time lost little time in tying in this, and the rumours of a hitch-hiking ghost, with a fatal car crash on the Hill in November 1965, which claimed the lives of three young women, one a bride-to-be.

In many ways, it is understandable that the 1965 tragedy—particularly the death of a young bride-to-be from injuries sustained just hours before her wedding—should have become such a powerful and enduring source of interest, providing as it does a suitably tragic event behind the haunting. But was it really valid? Was it really the ghost of young woman who died there in a car crash in 1965? Or a ghost not yet identified? Or was something else at play?

Whichever the case, the cluster of reports coming out of 1992 certainly came as a surprise. Here was what amounted to a legend coming to life before us, with a determination not to be written off to disrespectful anonymity.

From the media's point of view, though, the story was a gift of sensationalism, and a timely respite from the gloomy overcast of economic recession and political tensions that dominated the news at the time. Perhaps this provides some small clue as to why the 'ghost' chose 1992 for its dramatic reappearance—as a product of our collective tensions? Or was it a response to the disturbance of the environment at the foot of Blue Bell Hill, which as of November 1992, was a sight to behold, with the widening of the M20 in full swing and the carnage wrought hereabouts on the countryside quite appalling? Some hauntings have been known to become active following alterations made to the structure of houses. Perhaps something similar was happening?

But who knew precisely why, after so many years of apparent inactivity—years occupied by, at best, vague or suspect reports, had the 'ghost' appeared back on the scene, and in so vital and forceful a manner? And why did its behaviour differ significantly from the hitch-hiking habit that was integral to the story's early and popular form?

This book traces the history of one particular 'road ghost', from legend to compelling fact. But in its investigation, and by drawing apt comparisons with numbers of similar cases, it also provides persuasive evidence for and a greater understanding of a phenomenon that, far from being an invention of folklore is, however it is defined, a real one, and which has been a feature of human experience throughout the ages.

From its early chapters, which set the scene and background to the case, we go on to examine the case's standing within the wider context of Phantom Hitch-Hiker accounts and the associated 'Spectral Jaywalker' or 'Phantom Road Accident' events that characterise the majority of the encounters at Blue Bell Hill. We then zoom in for a closer look at Blue Bell Hill itself, at the start of my own investigation, and an examination of the story's history and evolution through the printed medium. Chapter 8 looks at the sometimes sensational treatment of the case by the press and, for the first time, takes a properly objective view and presents the true facts and evidence relating to the primary focus of the media's interest and supposed origin of the haunting: the 1965 tragedy. Chapters 9 and 10 turn to the witnesses, the majority of whose accounts appear here for the first time. Not only does some of this evidence offer the intriguing possibility of real Phantom Hitch-Hiker encounters at Blue Bell Hill, but suggest that such encounters may pre-date the 1965 crash by a number of years, pointing for the first time to a different cause for the haunting.

More than once it has been suggested that Blue Bell Hill is the haunt of more than one ghost. But what should we make of reports that are identical in almost every respect save the specific description of the ghost? All over the world, case after case detail precisely the same pattern of events: of figures running out into the path of oncoming vehicles, giving the driver no chance to avoid a collision. Chapters 11 through 13 lead us away from the traditional view of the Phantom Hitch-Hiker and Blue Bell Hill's ghost as the spirit of a deceased person, and into the deeper waters of folklore. The bizarre hag-like apparition that began to feature in reports in 1993—and, in retrospect, the girl in white also—resemble more, in character and behaviour, the non-human entities and deities that populate our folk traditions and ancient mythologies and were said to be fearfully encountered at night by travellers on lonely highways. But were these real entities, appearing for reasons unknown, or symbols for something else dredged up from the dreamy realms of the unconscious?

Finally, Chapter 14 poses—and attempts to answer—the essential question: what are people really seeing at Blue Bell Hill, and in the many remarkably similar cases around the world? A range of theories and possibilities are examined, from the fashionable modern perspective of subjective experience—hallucination and confabulation—to the developing geocentric theory of anomalous phenomena, which looks at the ways we are linked and interact in body and mind with our planet and the forces that play across its surface.

As the reader will discover, there is a great deal more to Blue Bell Hill than simply a ghost story. But it is the story of the ghost girl and the real tragedies associated with it that have, and will, I suspect, continue to hold centre stage in our imaginations.

Before the turning point of 1992, the story of the Blue Bell Hill ghost was little distinguishable from the classic Phantom Hitch-Hiker of folklore. And in accordance with the contentions of folklorists, it looked as if there were little foundation to the story. Nevertheless, author Michael Goss[3] had recognised the wealth of anecdotal support for the case and dubbed the Blue Bell Hill phantom the 'uncrowned queen of British road ghosts'.

This book—the first full-length study of the case—finally marks her coronation, sovereign not only to British cases, but perhaps to road ghosts the world over.

This is the story of *The Ghost(s) of Blue Bell Hill.*

BLUE BELL HILL – PRINCIPAL SIGHTINGS LOCATIONS

Year	No. Witness -es	Principal Witness(es)	Date	Time	Des. Cat.	Loc.	Map ref.
1934	1 (M)	Jack Woodger	Winter	11 pm	1	D	**28**
1934	1 (F)	Renee Hughes	September	10 pm	6	H	
1957	1 (M)	Leon Posner	Spring	1 am	2a	C	**6**
1967/8	2 (M/F)	Malcolm Grant*	Not stated	Not stated	1	D	**24**
1967/8	1 (M)	Peter Leadbetter	Not stated	7.30 am	1	D	**23**
1968	2 (M/F)	Kenneth & Joan Gowers	Summer	Evening	1	A	
1968	1 (M)	Joe Chester	October	10 pm	2a	I	**8**
1968	1 (M)	Ron Thomas	November	4.15 am	2	O	
1969	1 (M)	David Smith	February	Not stated	4		
Late 60s	2 (F/M)	Wendy Lang	Oct. / Nov.	1 am	2	O	
1971	1 (M)	James Skene	Autumn	12 am	3/1	D	**25**
1972	2 (M)	Bob Vandepeer, Paul Clarke	Mid-year	Evening	1	G	
1973	1 (M)	Richard Studholme	Summer	12 am	1	G	**34**
1974	2 (M/F)	Gladys & Allen Painter	13 July	1 am	3	A	**11**
1974	1 (M)	Maurice Goodenough	13 July	12 am	3	A	**13**
Mid 70s	1 (F)	Joy Gammon	Not stated	12 am	2	A/I	**9**
1976/7	1 (F)	Ann-Marie Austin	Not stated	Not stated	2	C	**7**
1977	2 (M)	Steven Pope, Barry Collings	26 Aug.	12.40 am	2	G	**35**
1978	1 (M)	John Gear	Winter	6–6.30 pm	2	K	**26**
1979/80	2 (M/F)	'JST'	November	2 am	3	I	**6**
Late 70s	2 (M/M)	Neville Butteriss	November	1–1.30 am	3	B	**29**
1984	2 (M/F)	Darren & Christine Green*	Winter	10 pm–12	3	E	**32**
1984/5	1 (M)	Donald Gallagher*	September	9.30–10 pm	5	D	**27**
1987	1 (M)	Barbara Selwyn*	Autumn	10.30–11 pm	1/2a	A	**22**
1988	5 (M)	Nick Norris	Not stated	1 am	5	G	**36**
1990	4 (M)	Colin Eacott	Not stated	9.15 pm	5	B	**19**
1990	2 (M/F)	John Arnold	Summer	11–11.30 pm	5	A	**16**
1990	1 (F)	Clare Bush	18 Oct.	3 pm	2	H	
1990/1	4 (M/F)	James Shoebridge	January	12 am–1 am	5	E	**31**
1991	1 (M)	Nick Morgan	Mid-July	12.30 am	2a	A	
1992	1 (F)	Gillian Barry	January	1 am	2	A	**10**
1992	1 (F)	Jacquie Hopkins	25 Oct.	12.45 am	3/6	A	**14**
1992	1 (M)	Ian Sharpe	8 Nov.	11.50 pm	3	B	**15**
1992	1 (M)	Christopher Dawkins	22 Nov.	10.50 pm	3	C	**4**
1992/4	5 (F)	Ann King	Not stated	1 am	2a	N	**3**
1993	5 (M/F)	Rayburn* (family)	5 Jan.	12.05 am	5	F	**21**
1993	5 (M/F)	Maiden (family)	6 Jan.	12.40 am	5	F	**20**
1993	1 (F)	Paula Cooper	20 June	1 am	3	A	
1993/8	2 (F/M)	Joan Masters*	Winter	12 am	2	N	**2**
1994	1 (M)	Alan Matthews	September	11.45 pm	5	B	**18**
1999	2 (M/F)	Tracy & Simon Boon	Summer	7 am	2	A	**12**
1998	4 (F/M)	Janice & Chris Leigh	Autumn	Evening	8	M	**33**
2001	1 (F)	Janice Leigh	November	Evening	8	M	**30**
2008	1 (M)	Paul Lowing	Autumn	1.30–3 am	2a	N	**1**
2012	2 (M)	Dan Mulford, Ryan Banks	10 June	12.15 am	1/2a	C	**5**
2014	1 (M)	Glenn Jones	14 Feb.	6.50–7 pm	2	L	**17**

Description category (Des. Cat)

1. Hitch-hiker (female)
2. Passive female
2a. Walker
3. Collision (young female/unspecified)
4. Other – e.g. more than one apparition
5. Witch/Hag/Wizened old woman
6. Amorphous
7. Male figure
8. Hooded figure

17 **Young woman / Woman in white**

17 **Young woman - dark clothing**

17 **Old woman / dark figure**

Location

A. A229 Footbridge area
B. A229 Aylesford turn-off
C. Blue Bell Hill village
D. Lower Bell
E. Rochester Road
F. Kit's Coty Cottage
G. Veglios / Harvester (A229/M20 Jct 6)
H. Cossington
I. Upper Bell
J. Chatham Road - Kits Coty steps
K. Lower Warren Road
L. Warren Road
M. Westfield
N. Lord Lees
O. Bus stop – Salisbury Road

*** Denotes pseudonym (real name withheld on request)**

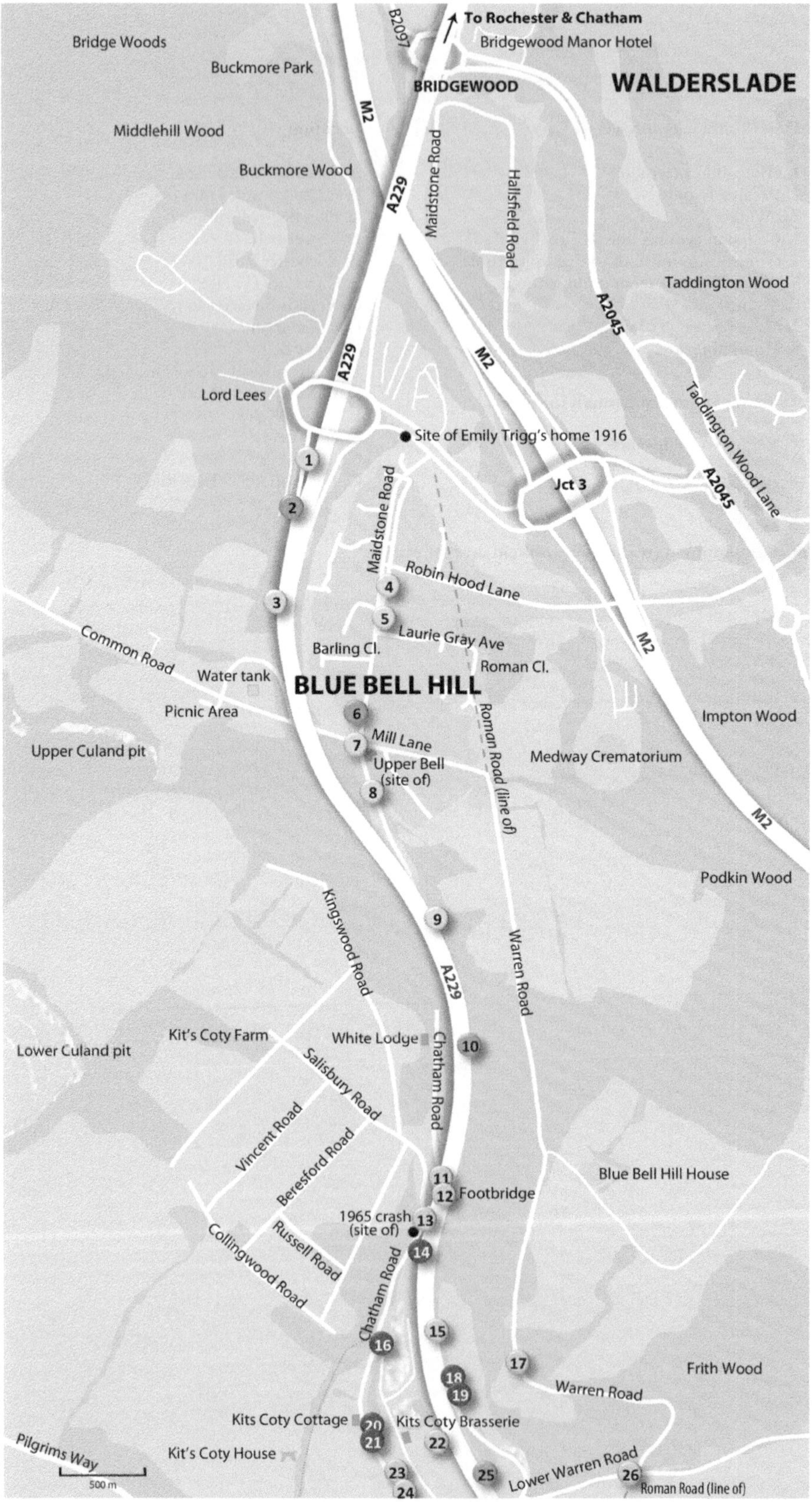
To Rochester & Chatham
Bridgewood Manor Hotel
B2097
BRIDGEWOOD
WALDERSLADE
Bridge Woods
Buckmore Park
Middlehill Wood
Buckmore Wood
M2
A229
Maidstone Road
Hallsfield Road
Taddington Wood
A2045
M2
A229
Lord Lees
Taddington Wood Lane
Site of Emily Trigg's home 1916
Jct 3
A2045
1
2
Maidstone Road
Robin Hood Lane
3
4
5
Laurie Gray Ave
M2
Common Road
Barling Cl.
Roman Cl.
Water tank
BLUE BELL HILL
Picnic Area
6
Roman Road (line of)
Impton Wood
7
Mill Lane
Upper Culand pit
Upper Bell (site of)
Medway Crematorium
8
M2
Podkin Wood
Kingswood Road
9
A229
Warren Road
Kit's Coty Farm
White Lodge
10
Lower Culand pit
Chatham Road
Salisbury Road
Vincent Road
Beresford Road
Blue Bell Hill House
11
12
Footbridge
1965 crash (site of)
13
Collingwood Road
Russell Road
14
Chatham Road
15
16
17
Frith Wood
18
19
Warren Road
Kits Coty Cottage
20
Kits Coty Brasserie
21
22
Pilgrims Way
Kit's Coty House
23
25
Lower Warren Road
26
24
Roman Road (line of)
500 m

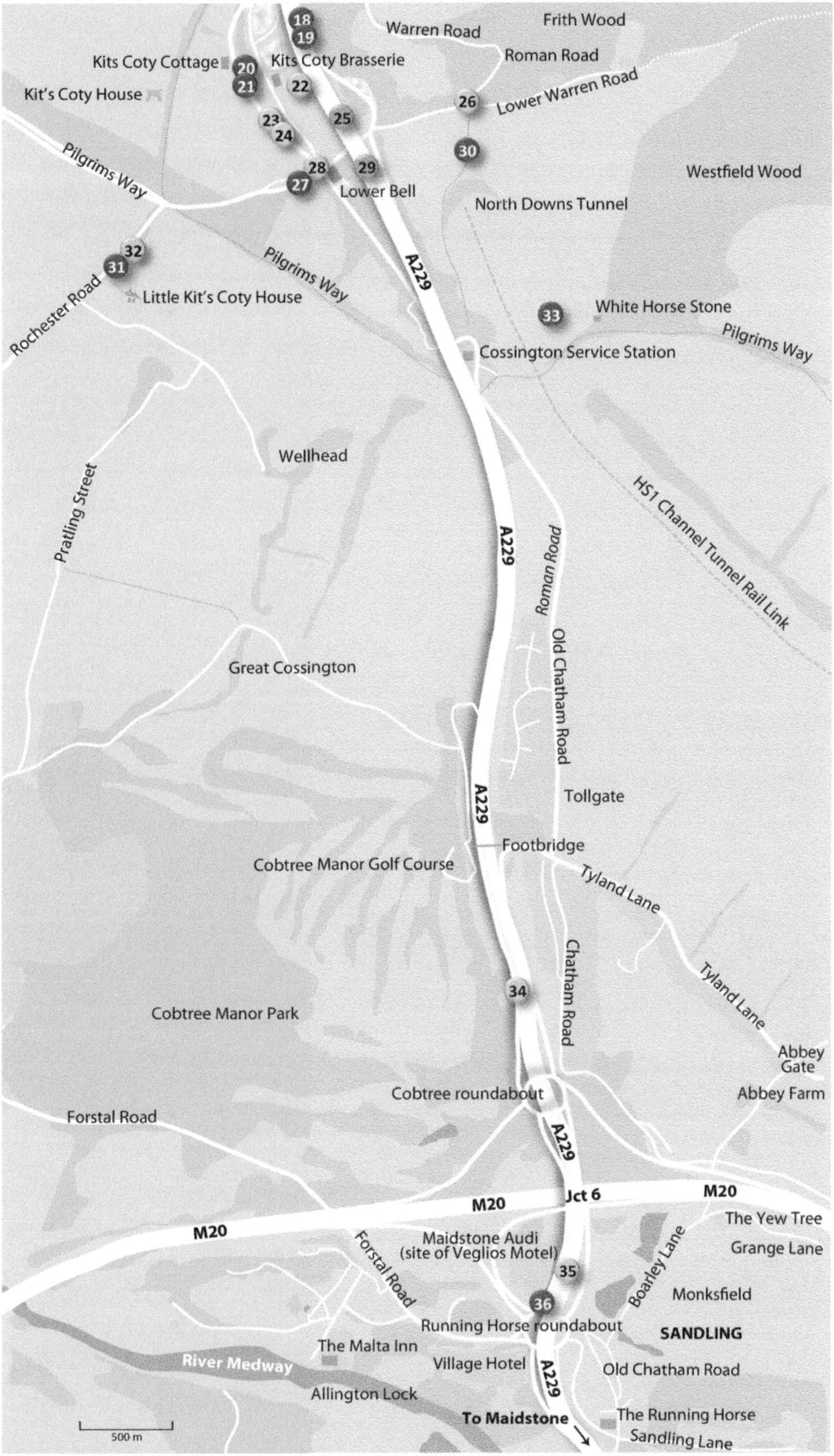
18
19
Warren Road
Frith Wood
Kits Coty Cottage
20
21
Kits Coty Brasserie
22
Roman Road
Kit's Coty House
26
Lower Warren Road
23
24
25
30
Pilgrims Way
28
29
27
Lower Bell
Westfield Wood
North Downs Tunnel
32
31
A229
Pilgrims Way
Rochester Road
Little Kit's Coty House
33
White Horse Stone
Pilgrims Way
Cossington Service Station
Wellhead
Pratling Street
HS1 Channel Tunnel Rail Link
A229
Roman Road
Old Chatham Road
Great Cossington
Tollgate
A229
Footbridge
Cobtree Manor Golf Course
Tyland Lane
Chatham Road
34
Tyland Lane
Cobtree Manor Park
Abbey Gate
Cobtree roundabout
Abbey Farm
Forstal Road
A229
M20
Jct 6
M20
M20
The Yew Tree
Maidstone Audi
(site of Veglios Motel)
Forstal Road
Grange Lane
Boarley Lane
35
Monksfield
36
Running Horse roundabout
SANDLING
The Malta Inn
River Medway
Village Hotel
Old Chatham Road
A229
Allington Lock
The Running Horse
To Maidstone
Sandling Lane
500 m

ONE

'GHOST GIRL SEEN AGAIN'

GHOSTS were about the last thing on Ian Sharpe's mind as he started down the A229 at Blue Bell Hill. It was shortly before midnight on Sunday 8 November 1992. Mr Sharpe, a 54-year-old coach driver, was on the last leg of his journey home to Maidstone in Kent, when, about halfway down the Hill, as he approached the turn-off for Eccles, Burham and Wouldham, the figure of a young woman appeared in front of him. Before he could react, the woman ran into the path of his car, turned quickly to face him and, with her eyes locked on his, fell beneath the bonnet. Horrified, he braked to a stop and shakily got out to take account of the accident.

'I honestly thought I had killed her,' he said. 'You can't imagine how it felt. I was so scared to look underneath, but I knelt down and looked straight through—there was nothing there.'[1]

Ian Sharpe
(KM Group)

Ian searched around about the car and in the bushes of the wide verge, but found nothing. He attempted to flag down two other cars for assistance, but when they didn't stop he continued on into Maidstone, making straight for the police station to report the incident. White-faced and 'shaking like a leaf, he told police that he had run over a woman but could not find the body. After listening to his account, in the course noting the spot on Blue Bell Hill where the incident had occurred, the police seemingly came to an immediate if presumptuous judgment by recounting to him the 'spooky legend' of the ghost said to haunt that stretch of road, no doubt adding to his sense of bewilderment.

Nevertheless, officers accompanied Ian back to the scene, and a search of the area ensued, which proved fruitless. There was no trace of the girl, and no sign of damage was found on his car, reinforcing opinion that he could not have encountered a real person. But he maintained that he had not been 'seeing things'. The girl had seemed perfectly real, not as he imagined a ghost to be.

The following day, Ian Sharpe was said to still be expecting the police to knock at his door to report the finding of the girl's body. It had been, he said, the

The A229 dual carriageway at Blue Bell Hill (looking south) as it appeared in 1992. Ian Sharpe first saw the woman in the road level with the road sign

'most scary' experience of his life.

Legend

It is probably no exaggeration to say that even before the *Kent Today*'s dramatic front page announcement on 10 November of the reappearance of the Ghost of Blue Bell Hill (and the unprecedented chain of events that was to follow, which began—publicly, at least—with Ian Sharpe's encounter), Blue Bell Hill's reputation for being haunted was known to the majority of residents of North Kent (and to a lesser extent throughout Kent and the rest of Britain). For more than a quarter of a century a mixture of rumour and newspaper reporting had fuelled suggestions that Blue Bell (*or* Bluebell)[2] Hill was haunted by the restless spirit of a young woman who died there in a car crash in 1965. But in spite of the evident popularity of the story, which had arguably attained legendary status, the notion that Blue Bell Hill might actually be haunted was probably one entertained by very few. And with good reason, for even aside to the reasoned or conditioned prejudices people hold against a belief in ghosts, the evidence in favour of Blue Bell Hill's phantom had never been particularly convincing, press assertions over the years notwithstanding. Published accounts had tended to be suspiciously vague in detail; or, in those few cases in which vital witness testimony had been included, failed to persuade that the subject of the encounter might indeed have been an apparition (by being observed to vanish or to perform some other trick in keeping with our expectations of them).

My own efforts over several years to locate credible witnesses through newspaper appeals and verbal prospecting had proven largely futile. In that time I heard numerous accounts in which probably explicable occurrences (rapping sounds on car window panes and interiors, sudden cold spots, engine failures, and so on) had taken on a more sinister meaning through awareness of the Hill's reputation—which, if nothing else, demonstrated the power that ghost stories (and this one in particular) could hold over the imagination. I had therefore learned to take much of what I heard about Blue Bell Hill with the proverbial pinch of salt. Anything remotely unusual occurring there seemed likely to evoke mention of the Hill's ghost. Even the press appeared to have finally grown weary of the tale. The last reference to the ghost appeared to have been made in 1980, when it was featured in a brief review of tall stories for the *Kent Messenger*.[3]

Consequently, by the start of 1992, I had all but come to the conclusion that Blue Bell Hill's celebrity had been founded more on hearsay and overzealous interpretation than any real evidence of genuine paranormal activity. All of this was to change, and dramatically so, the following November when a colleague brought to my attention reporter Emma Cooper's lead story ('Ghost Girl Seen Again') for the *Kent Today*.

In retrospect, it was probably inevitable that the case would eventually stimulate renewed media interest in some form, but never had I envisaged a time when it might again earn a national audience, as it had briefly in 1974 in what might previously have been regarded as its 'finest hour', much less that a vivid, credible account would finally come along.

The Achilles heel of the case had always been the lack of a 'complete' account: an unequivocal sighting supported by reliable named witness testimony and some form of independent corroboration. Ian Sharpe's account appeared to include all the important ingredients. A coach driver of 33 years' experience,[4] this was an individual accustomed to extended periods of driving who would not ordinarily be expected to be susceptible to hallucination or 'highway hypnosis'; nor a man, whose livelihood placed him in a position of responsibility for the safety of the public, given to wild public claims to an encounter with a ghost.

Whatever the true nature of Ian Sharpe's experience, it was clear that for him it had been a shockingly real experience. Evidently, the police had been sufficiently impressed with his report to accompany him back to the scene and, rather than dismiss his report, to conclude, apparently, that the only explanation was that he had encountered the Ghost of Blue Bell Hill—a conclusion that would inevitably find delight with the media.

In the days following his encounter, news of Ian Sharpe's experience spread to the national tabloids and beyond. Not since an uncannily similar experience by a Rochester man in 1974 had the haunting of Blue Bell Hill attracted such widespread media interest.

A Case of Dejà Vu

In the early hours of Saturday 13 July 1974, Maurice Goodenough, a 35-year-old bricklayer of Mooring Road, Rochester, rushed into Rochester Police Station in Cazeneuve Street, claiming he had knocked down a little girl on Blue Bell Hill. Police hastened with him back to the scene only to find the discarded car blanket (or tartan car rug)[5] with which Mr Goodenough had covered (or wrapped)[6] the injured girl, who he had carried to the roadside following the accident, which had happened around midnight.[7]

Goodenough told police that the girl had appeared suddenly in his car's headlights, forcing him to brake hard. But it had been too late to avoid running into her.

'The girl just walked out in front of me from the edge of the road,' he said. 'My car hit her with a hell of a bang.'[8]

Jumping out of his car, he found the girl lying in the road. She had a cut on her forehead and cut or skinned knees. One source included a feature that appeared in no other version of the incident: the girl was moving her head and had muttered 'Mummy' two or three times.[9]

Goodenough estimated the girl to have been about ten years old. She had shoulder-length brown hair, and was dressed in a lacy white blouse, white ankle socks and a skirt. He tried to wave down 'about four cars' but none stopped. So, unable to see a telephone box and of the opinion that it would be unwise to try to put the girl in his car, he left her by the roadside while he sped off to Rochester Police Station.

Thirty minutes later (*Chatham Standard; Chatham News*),[10] he returned to the spot with police officers, who immediately instigated a search for the girl on both sides of the steeply wooded Hill, which proved fruitless. The search resumed at dawn with the aid of a tracker dog,[11] but no scent trace, tracks or bloodstains were found, the effort by then hampered by heavy rain. Extensive inquiries, which included checks on local hospital admissions, failed to locate anyone answering the girl's description.

Aside from the obvious and natural concern for the girl's well-being, both the *Chatham Standard* and the *Chatham News* aired police fears that she may have been abducted: 'We would appeal for any parent whose child has some unexplained injuries like a bump on the head to contact us. We would also like to hear from anyone whose child is missing,' said a spokesman.

From his home in Rochester on the Saturday night, Goodenough was evidently confounded. He told *The News of the World* that he had definitely hit a girl and carried her to the side of the road. 'I'm not going mad,' he said. 'But where did she vanish? I'm still shaking from the experience.'[12]

If Maurice Goodenough was unsure what to make of his experience, the press evidently was not. From the start, the location of the incident and consequent failure to find the girl meant only one thing: the girl had to be a ghost. Apparent support for this contention (as would be the case eighteen years later with Ian Sharpe's encounter) lay with the inability to find any sign of damage to Goodenough's car, contrary to the reported force of the collision.

The similarity between Sharpe's and Goodenough's accounts is striking: both had involved a lone motorist travelling home late at night (around midnight—Ian Sharpe would later confirm the time of his encounter as 11.50 p.m.)[13] and involved the running over of a young woman or girl who had given little or no opportunity for the motorist to avoid a collision. Both had involved police in a futile search of the hillside after attempts to flag down passing cars for assistance had failed. Finally, both reports had attracted national press attention.

That Ian Sharpe's experience should compare at all to Maurice Goodenough's was both remarkable and ironic considering the latter's previous contextual standing in the Blue Bell Hill saga. The case had always been (and perhaps is still) best known as a *Phantom Hitch-Hiker* story—a universally disseminated tale, widely regarded as folklore, which describes the repeated habits of certain forlorn spirits with a penchant for hitch-hiking and vanishing from the vehicle en route. Such a one-off 'knock down' scenario, which differed significantly from the ghost's traditional behaviour, and clearly open to natural explanations, meant that Maurice Goodenough's experience had come to be viewed as an anomaly, conservatively dismissed as a possible paranormal event by objective commentators.

The circumstances of the Goodenough incident had certainly been unusual—no-one expects to encounter a child late at night at such a relatively remote location—but they were not totally inexplicable. And yet they had become rather easily woven into the fabric of the existing legend of Blue Bell Hill's ghost by the press, which brought the story to national attention, with three of the tabloids running it on 14 July 1974.[14]

The simplest and most rational explanation in this case—an errant child—was apparently quickly discarded by most media sources at the time in favour of the more sensational alternative—a conclusion based chiefly on the girl's 'disappearance'. Only the Chatham papers (*Chatham Standard*, *Chatham News*) refrained from committing entirely to a supernatural interpretation. Their published appeal by police for more information reflected proper concern for the plight of what was in all likelihood a real child who was still at large and probably in need of medical attention.

As it turned out, the gamble of the general press paid off. No child was ever forthcoming to invalidate their favoured interpretation.

There is more to be said for the Goodenough incident and the press follow-up of it, which will be discussed in a later chapter. Sufficient to note for the moment is that the incident that had revived and launched nationally Blue Bell Hill's reputation in 1974 had relied on the inability to *disprove* the case as a ghostly encounter rather than presenting evidence to support it.

Ian Sharpe's encounter, then, which was to spark the next big revival in the case (whose coverage, in fact, would far exceed that of Goodenough), appeared to offer final vindication for assumptions made about the nature of the girl Maurice Goodenough ran over in 1974.

On the face of it, the close conformity between the two accounts suggested that, finally, there might be some evidence of a real phenomenon in operation at Blue Bell Hill after all—unless this originated with the witness himself, based on prior familiarity with Maurice Goodenough's experience and the existing tales of the haunting; or with the press, who, in recognising the essential similarity between the two accounts, might be suspected to have employed a little journalistic license to reinforce the comparisons in the interest of good 'copy'?

Ian Sharpe's occupation, I thought, made it unlikely that he would risk his livelihood for the sake of a fleeting fifteen minutes of fame. Nor did I feel that he would necessarily possess the familiarity or temerity to mimic such a previously well-publicised account as Maurice Goodenough's in such exacting detail. Within the context of Blue Bell Hill's notoriety as a place where motorists were said to encounter a *hitch-hiking* ghost, a would-be hoaxer would perhaps have been more likely to simulate a disappearing passenger than a phantom road accident victim?

As for the possibility of journalistic artifice, there was reason to believe that Emma Cooper had based her 1992 *Kent Today* feature on one or two articles from the *Kent Messenger*'s own archives that similarly had only outlined the Goodenough incident. These sources, both penned by reporter Nigel Nelson in July 1974 in a follow-up to the Goodenough incident, had focused on the believed cause and identity of the ghost (a fatal car crash in November 1965 that claimed the lives of three young women) and were therefore concerned less with the specifics of the Goodenough incident itself, which had already been more than adequately covered by the *Kent Messenger* and other newspapers in the preceding week or so. Writing for the *Evening Post* (a *Kent Messenger* group newspaper; this issue dated 19 July 1974) and the *Kent Messenger* itself (26 July),[15] Nelson alone described the events leading up to the crash, and named one of the victims as the primary candidate for the ghost's identity, even interviewing her father.

With such a ready-made summary of the haunting readily available in the *Kent*

Messenger's own archives, was it likely that a deadline-tied reporter in 1992 would look any further than the Nelson articles? I thought not.

Emma Cooper's article echoed one in particular, allowing suggestion that it alone had formed the template for her 1992 article,[16] in which case she was in all probability unmindful of the closer comparisons to be made between Ian Sharpe's experience and the precedent found in Maurice Goodenough's—which was something that made Ian Sharpe's reported encounter all the more credible and impressive.

This was not to say that some purposeful alteration of fact had not taken place in the modern treatment. Ms Cooper's reference to Maurice Goodenough's victim as a *young woman* stands in bold contradiction to newspaper accounts of the day (including the Nelson articles) that described a youngster—'a little girl', 'a child', 'a young girl', 'a ten-year-old girl'—but it *is* in keeping with the ages of the 1965 crash victims, all of whom were in their early twenties.

In like manner, in 1974, reporters had dealt with the same disparity in the age of the 'ghost' to enable *that* story (the Goodenough incident) to relate more readily to the existing stories of the Blue Bell Hill phantom. The young woman or girl depicted in legend (by implication older than a mere child) found herself reduced in age in order to make a meaningful connection with the case at hand. Two of the 1974 sources (*The News of the World* and the *Chatham News*) further reinforced the connection by suggesting that motorists in the past had, in addition to seeing or giving lifts to a young girl, also knocked her down (although there is not to my knowledge a newspaper account before 1974 describing such a case).[17]

The propensity to look for meaningful connections or to distort facts to serve a particular belief or purpose is more than simply a journalistic trait, but one which to a degree characterises us all. In this sense, the distortion of minor points of detail—a young woman for a young girl (in the context of a ghost story probably regarded as harmless)—may be forgivable. In no way did it imply that Ian Sharpe's story as a whole was misrepresented.

As it was, fears to this effect were quickly dispelled in the evening of 11 November when Emma Cooper's version of events received corroboration from TVS (*Television South*)'s regional news programme *Coast to Coast*'s report on the incident. On-the-spot reporter Hugh Kirby related the same pattern of events given in the *Kent Today* article. More importantly, the report featured Ian Sharpe himself.

Ian described the way the woman's eyes had been fixed on his all the time as his car struck her and she disappeared beneath the bonnet. And he provided a description of the girl, which the *Kent Today* had failed to include in its report:

> She was 20-25. She had shoulder-length hair that was rolled inwards...at the shoulder. The front of her hair here was ruffled up. She had a roundish face, and big eyes...her eyes...she had gorgeous eyes.[18]

Ian Sharpe on TVS's *Coast to Coast,* 11 November 1992 *(TVS)*

Evidently the encounter had not been as ephemeral as the *Kent Today* implied. Rather than appearing suddenly in the path of Ian's car (something that had likewise been suggested in reports of the Goodenough incident), the woman in the TVS report had stepped out at the last moment, in a seemingly intentional act. If true, it helped to explain how Ian Sharpe had had time to absorb a fairly detailed impression of the girl's appearance, which included an estimated age that differed appreciably from that given by Maurice Goodenough.

Considering the setting—the open dual carriageway of the A229, which is well illuminated by overhead carriageway lights—it was difficult to dismiss Ian Sharpe's experience out of hand, particularly with the Goodenough incident standing behind it. Together they posed the exciting possibility that something genuinely anomalous could be occurring at Blue Bell Hill. But what, precisely? Could it really be (as the press supposed) that these motorists had encountered the ghost of a young woman killed here in a car crash in 1965?

Anniversary

As remarkable as Ian Sharpe's story was, it was made all the more so by the *timing* of his encounter, occurring as it had little over a week before the anniversary of the 1965 tragedy—a fact which, to the media, could only serve to reinforce claims that this crash—and, in particular, a member of that tragic party—lay at the heart of the case.

It is a matter of record that late in the evening of Friday 19 November 1965 two cars were in collision at Blue Bell Hill. Three of the four young women in one of the vehicles, a Mark 1 Ford Cortina, died from their injuries, one instantly. The fourth was seriously injured. The driver of the other vehicle, a Jaguar, was uninjured, and his companion, although badly hurt, was discharged from hospital a few days later.

One of the fatally injured women was a bride-to-be. Her wedding, scheduled for midday the following day, was never to take place. It had been too late to inform a number of the wedding guests, who dutifully gathered at the church in Gillingham the next day, only to be turned away.

In the early hours of that Saturday, surgeons were involved in a desperate struggle to save her life. But to no avail. Her injuries had been too severe, and she died five days later in the West Kent Hospital in Maidstone without ever regaining consciousness. She was unaware of the vigil that her fiancé had kept by her bedside throughout.

Unquestionably, the 1965 crash has provided a fitting and tangible origin for the haunting of Blue Bell Hill. We are inclined to assume a connection between sudden or violent death and hauntings. The 1965 crash—an incident that was well documented by local and county newspapers of the time, chiefly (and significantly) by *Kent Messenger* Group publications—satisfies our expectations perfectly in respect of location and manner of death, and it is therefore easy to appreciate how it might have become adopted as a focus for the ghost stories that appeared soon after.

But was the connection valid? Blue Bell Hill has been the scene of numerous fatal accidents over the years. If we were to accept the popular notion that the trauma-shock-unpreparedness of sudden death can somehow bind the spirit of an individual to the scene of their demise, then a number of fitting candidates for the identity of the ghost could be reasonably proposed. So how was it decided, and on what evidence, that the crash of 19 November 1965 was the source of the haunting of Blue Bell Hill?

As impressive as the close proximity of Ian Sharpe's encounter to the anniversary of this tragedy appears to be in evidential terms (one that also fulfils a tradition of ghostly behaviour which states the anniversary of death as the most likely occasion of the ghost's reappearance or re-enactment), it cannot be stated with any certainty that the two events are truly connected. The case otherwise relies not on firm circumstantial evidence, but on unsupported claims and supposition. Often overlooked, for instance, is that the identification of the crash and, in turn, a firm selection of a candidate from that tragic party for the ghost's identity was not made until 1974—*nine* years after the accident.

Printed references to the crash first appeared in July of that year during the press follow-up of Maurice Goodenough's strange encounter on the Hill. Three *Kent Messenger* group newspapers reporting on this incident (*Evening Post*, 15 July; *The Gazette*, 16 July; and the *Kent Messenger* itself, 19 July) highlighted a crash that had occurred on the Hill *eight* years previously 'at the same spot', resulting in the deaths of two young girls. Although imprecise in detail, there is little doubt that these papers refer to the 1965 crash and its *three* victims, correctly stated only in the *Chatham News* (a local independent) of 19 July.

In the *Kent Messenger* versions the identification of the crash was attributed to a police spokesman (unidentified) who described Maurice Goodenough's experience as the latest in a series of strange encounters that had occurred on Blue Bell Hill since that tragedy. *Kent Messenger* reporter Nigel Nelson followed up this clue and following 'a week of intensive investigation' he published his findings in the *Evening Post* (19 July). This article—'Drivers beware of the phantom on the hill' (an almost identical version of which was featured a week later in the *Kent Messenger* itself ('Spectre of Bluebell Hill', 26 July))—was to firmly establish the 1965 tragedy in the minds of the public as the cause of the haunting.

Although rumours and reports describing a phantom female had been in circulation since the late 1960s (the *Kent Messenger* version quoted the case's first researcher, 53-year-old Tom Harber, to the effect that he had first heard about them a year after the accident (1966)), this was the first time a specific origin for the haunting had been identified in print. In only two published accounts in the intervening years had an actual cause been alluded to, and these simply state that the girl was said to have been killed in a road accident—the latter (1968) adding that this had occurred 'some time ago'.[19]

Exactly why almost a decade should have elapsed before the crash became openly linked to the ghost stories, and on precisely what evidence, is still unclear. More certain is that its debut was a timely one, providing a convenient and compelling focus for the stories at a time when the case found itself under the spotlight of heightened press interest, which included coverage by three of the Sunday tabloids.[20]

Was there, then, any more to it than its apparent fulfilment of press needs to establish a logical and suitably tragic foundation to the stories? The police source suggested that perhaps there was. But whatever the legitimacy of the connection (which may have been fostered by police officials and/or private researcher(s)), once established, the crash thereafter became an integral, possibly inextricable ingredient of the Blue Bell Hill story. Indeed, it has become the *story* within the story, the tangible driving force behind it.

Bridesmaid's Dress

From a purely artistic viewpoint, it isn't difficult to appreciate how the 1965 crash has become such a powerful and enduring source of interest. The deepened sense of tragedy found in the death of a young bride-to-be just hours away from her wedding imbues the story with a special poignancy, fulfilling romantic notions of cruelly terminated love, which has made the Blue Bell Hill story particularly memorable, even captivating.

Spectre of Bluebell Hill

By Nigel Nelson

Could one of the girls who died in this crash be the disappearing hitch-hiker?

THE BIZARRE tale of the ghost of a young Rochester girl haunting a lonely stretch of Bluebell Hill has been resurrected again.

The phantom is rumoured to be 22-year-old Judith Lingham, who was killed with two other girls in a car smash there in 1965.

Ever since the crash nine years ago motorists travelling late at night have reported picking up a young girl who mysteriously vanishes from the car.

I spoke to Judith's father, retired merchant seaman, Mr Charles Lingham, 68, of Albany Road, Rochester. He said it was the first time he had been told his daughter was considered to be the mystery spirit.

My interview with Mr Lingham followed a week of intensive investigation into the baffling phenomenom which has intrigued Kent ghost hunters for years.

It begins on a cold, wet Thursday night in November nine years ago.

Judith was to be bridesmaid with another girl at her friend's wedding on the Saturday. The three girls had all been trying on dresses for the wedding and decided to meet the bride's fiance at a pub later that evening.

They never made it. Tragedy struck when their car spun off a treacherous Bluebell Hill bend and all three girls were killed.

Psychic researcher Tom Harber, 53, a blind switchboard operator at Oakwood Hospital, Maidstone, takes up the story.

"I first heard about it a year after the accident when people travelling from Maidstone to Chatham, generally after eleven at night, picked up a young girl by the side of the road thumbing a lift."

The girl would sit in the back of the car and then mysteriously disappear. And the same would happen to motorists going down the Hill: an apparition would take them for a ride.

Mr Harber added: "People travelling from Maidstone to Chatham would be flagged down by a girl who would want a lift to Rochester. This girl would not say much but she, too, would say she had been involved in a car accident."

Mr Harber believes he has received 14 authentic reports of this happening and there have been many other strange incidents.

The most recent was last Friday when motorist Maurice Goodenough, 35, a bricklayer, of Mooring Road, Rochester, dashed into Rochester police station to say he had hit a young girl on Bluebell Hill and wrapped her in a tartan car rug by the side of the road. But when police arrived there was the blanket but no girl – and not a mark on Mr Goodenough's car.

Yet police take the story seriously and even had tracker dogs out the next morning to look for an injured girl.

The appearing and disappearing girls may be a mystery to police but they are even more of a mystery to Judith's father.

He said: "What an extraordinary business. I'm astonished. My wife died last year and I'm still conscious of her presence but I don't believe in ectoplasmic ghosts that appear out of walls.

"I wouldn't like to say there are no such things, neither would I like to substantiate them."

REPORTS of ghosts on Bluebell Hill are now becoming a common phenomenom. And the reality of them is sometimes difficult to believe. But unfortunately the pictures here show that the accident which started those stories was all too real. It happened on November 19, 1965, when four girls were driving back from a friend's house after trying on dresses for the friend's wedding the following Saturday. The four girls were to meet the bride's fiance at the pub later that evening. But their car spun off a bend on Bluebell Hill. Three girls were killed and one seriously injured. And soon after this the ghost stories began.

***Kent Messenger*, 26 July 1974** *(KM Group)*

The most puzzling feature of the 1974 articles, then, is why the bride-to-be—as the almost perfect subject (from a story point of view), and 'logical' candidate of the three victims of the 1965 crash (as well as the primary subject of discussion on the oral grapevine in the late 1960s)—should have been overlooked in the identification of the ghost. Paradoxically, Nelson named one of the other victims of the crash, stating that the ghost was rumoured to be that of 22-year-old Judith Lingham of Rochester.

The source of the rumour, as for the crash itself, was never clearly identified, but henceforth this young woman became the main subject of interest and speculation for later writers and journalists who from time to time touched on the case.

A clue as to how Judith Lingham may have become identified with the ghost is to be found in Nelson's own articles. Credited in the *Kent Messenger* (26 July 1974, an expanded version of his *Evening Post* article) is the late Tom Harber. In it, Mr Harber described how, since the crash, motorists travelling between Maidstone and Chatham late at night (generally after 11 p.m.) had reported picking up a young girl who was thumbing a lift from the roadside at Blue Bell Hill—a girl who would subsequently vanish from the back seat of the car. Occasionally, before vanishing, the girl would say she wanted to be taken to Rochester, stating that she had been involved in a car accident.

Could the mention of Rochester as the destination of the ghost in Tom Harber's anonymous account (or, as has been speculated, Maurice Goodenough's own destination on the night of his encounter, his home in Rochester) have prompted Nelson to form an unconscious association with Judith Lingham, also from Rochester? Author Michael Goss observed that of the three fatal victims of the crash, Judith alone was pictured in one of the original crash articles in the *Kent Messenger*'s archives (*Maidstone Gazette*)[21]—which may again have forged an association.

Whatever the case (personal correspondence with Mr Nelson in 1990 failed to resolve the question, his involvement understandably too long removed and his notes no longer available),[22] it does not appear that the identification was founded on much more than hearsay. Needless to say, Judith's father was astonished at the suggestion that his daughter was haunting Blue Bell Hill.

The identification of Judith Lingham would not be the only source of confusion introduced in the work of Nigel Nelson. In addition to erroneously placing the date of the crash on a *Thursday*, he painted a somewhat different picture of the crash, furnishing his version with a hitherto unreported account of the fateful events leading up to the accident. In what Michael Goss would later refer to as 'these deviant facts', it was related how Judith was to have been a bridesmaid at the wedding of one of the girls the following day. They had been trying on dresses when they had decided to meet the groom at a pub later that evening. It was an appointment they were never to keep, as their car spun off a treacherous bend on Blue Bell Hill.

In providing such an attractive and tidy explanation for the haunting of Bluc Bell Hill, Nigel Nelson's articles would inevitably find favour in later years, in spite of their unsatisfactory features. Emma Cooper's article for the *Kent Today* would not be the first to focus on Judith Lingham or on Nigel Nelson's version of events (which were reproduced almost verbatim), but it would have the farthest reaching effects, since it was to serve as the blueprint for much of the media coverage that was to follow.

Of course, it is perfectly understandable that an existing archive source should be exploited, particularly where a fitting comparison could be made to the current story, as Emma Cooper had with the Nelson articles. The problem, however, with such time-honoured sources is that they often achieve a pseudo-credibility that frequently goes unquestioned in later years. Consequently, Nigel

Nelson's hastily researched findings which related the Blue Bell Hill haunting to the 1965 crash and to Judith Lingham were once again spread abroad in 1992, with arguably damaging effect—to the case itself, which had recently proven to be worthy of proper study, and to surviving relations of the deceased.

But, the media had decided that the 1965 tragedy—and Judith Lingham in particular—were at the heart of the case, and there would be little I could do or say to persuade them to treat this aspect with due caution and respect.

This was not to say that I had completely excluded the possibility that the 1965 crash and the sightings might be genuinely related—the near coincidence of Ian Sharpe's encounter with the anniversary of the accident was certainly intriguing—only that I would require a good deal more evidence before accepting that the connection (and indeed the phenomenon itself) might be valid after all. As it was, I had recently added to my files an account that would lend some support to both arguments. This was the experience described to me a fortnight *before* Ian Sharpe's encounter by a colleague by the name of Jacquie Hopkins.

A 'black shape'

Jacquie Hopkins' story, which I first heard on 26 October (the day after her experience), had certainly put me in mind of the Goodenough incident, but her description of a fleeting, shadow-like form she had run over on Blue Bell Hill sounded a little too ambiguous to be considered a possible ghostly encounter. Besides, as far as I was aware, nothing like it had been reported for eighteen years—and that episode, Maurice Goodenough's collision with a child, could not then easily be considered evidence of a paranormal event. But although not stated, implied by Jacquie's experience and her subsequent failure to find a rational explanation was the obvious association with the Hill's ghost—something I was not prepared to accept at the time, particularly from someone I knew.

Awareness of my research, or of Blue Bell Hill's repute, did not automatically disqualify Jacquie Hopkins from consideration as a possible witness to the Blue Bell Hill phenomenon, but it was, I thought, something to be viewed with caution. The power of autosuggestion—the unconscious influence of prior knowledge or belief over one's own perception (a worthy matter of consideration for every claimant)—could not be underestimated or ruled out.

It had been difficult to know what to make of Jacquie's experience. Clearly, it was something she perceived to be a real event, but it allowed no definite conclusions to be drawn. It was therefore more prudent to assign a 'rational' if not entirely satisfactory explanation—that, in the unfamiliar conditions of early morning, and perhaps with tired mind, she had misinterpreted effects of shadow and/or had unconsciously exaggerated a real but glancing collision with an animal, in spite of her insistence to the contrary. The account was duly noted, to be filed away and forgotten. Or so I had thought. Now, after the unexpected corroboration provided by Ian Sharpe, it commanded renewed interest.

It was between 12.30 a.m. and 12.45 a.m. on Sunday 25 October 1992 when Jacquie Hopkins, making her way home to Rainham, ran over a 'black shape' that appeared in front of her car (a powder-blue Suzuki jeep) on the northbound carriageway of the A229 at Blue Bell Hill. The incident occurred a stone's throw away over the carriageway from the spot where Ian Sharpe would meet his 'victim' two weeks later, just before the pedestrian footbridge that spans the five lanes of the dual carriageway here and its slip-road junction with a section of the Chatham Road. According to Jacquie, she was travelling at around 40 mph when the dark form, described as black and completely featureless, had appeared suddenly in her path.

'I felt the car shudder as though it had run over something, and I definitely heard a knock. I stopped almost immediately. I was quite badly shaken.'

Jacquie stopped her car at the intersection of the two roads, and got out to investigate. She searched around and beneath her car but found nothing to account for the incident. To check whether the object had been completely overrun and left further back on the carriageway, she retraced her path under the footbridge to where she estimated she had seen the figure. As she did so another vehicle approached from the south, illuminating the road fully as it passed, revealing nothing. Jacquie returned to her car, intending to check more carefully beneath it.

'I recalled that when I hit the object there had only been a single bump which I took to be the front wheels riding over it. There had been no second bump to suggest the back wheels had also ran over it. I thought that whatever it was must be caught beneath the car.'

Although the area of the incident is lit by carriageway lights, the underside of the vehicle remained in deep shadow. Not possessing a torch Jacquie got down on her hands and knees and tried to feel beneath the car as best she could. Shortly after, bewildered at her inability to find anything, she got back into her car and drove home.

'Because of the way it happened, at the time I thought I'd hit an animal, but later on when I got home I realised it couldn't have been an animal because I could see at least one-and-a-half to two feet of this sort of shadow in front of me and it did remind me of somebody going down, putting their hands up in the air.

'I spent a very sleepless night. I was up at about 7.30 a.m. again that Sunday morning to check my car over thoroughly. There was no mark on my car, no sign of any blood or anything on the wheels. I still couldn't sleep, so I went back indoors, got dressed, and drove back down to Blue Bell Hill.

'I searched the grass verge, and I even crossed the road by the bridge to search the other side in case I had hit something and it had gone across the road, but I could find nothing.'

Confronted with the lack of corroborative evidence Jacquie elected to try to forget the incident. Understanding of my interest in the Blue Bell Hill case, she briefly recounted the incident to me the next day without offering any opinion as to what it might have been. But she maintained that she had felt a bump—'not an impact as such'—as if she had ran over something which, because of its upright posture and height above the bonnet of her jeep (a significant point considering this to be above average waist level, around four feet), she believed had not been an animal and had certainly not been imagination.

'You really feel as if you've hit a person, really shaken up,' she said.

The vague form described by Jacquie Hopkins hardly compares to the young girl described by Goodenough or the young woman Ian Sharpe would encounter a fortnight later. Had it not been for the Sharpe incident, this alone would probably have disqualified her account from serious attention. As indeed I already had. As it was, aside from this contradictory point, Jacquie Hopkins' experience conformed remarkably well to the pattern I thought I could already see emerging initially out of a comparison of the Goodenough and Sharpe encounters.

In three separate named-witness accounts, lone motorists had undergone a broadly similar experience within the same general area of Blue Bell Hill, and at around the same time of night or early morning. In each case, there had been no damage to the vehicle, a fact attested to by police in the cases of Sharpe and Goodenough.

Fifty miles per hour might be regarded as an average speed for traffic on the A229 at Blue Bell Hill. This was the speed estimated by Ian Sharpe at the time of his encounter. Jacquie Hopkins, heading up the Hill, judged herself to be travelling at around 40 mph. If a collision had occurred with any sizeable object at such speeds, a great deal of damage would certainly have been sustained by both parties.

Jacquie Hopkins' encounter had occurred within sight of the scene of the Sharpe incident (less than 200 metres) and, it would transpire, very close to the scene of Maurice Goodenough's encounter. According to one source (and the only one to give an actual location, the *Chatham Standard* of 16 July 1974), this took place on the Chatham Road just before it joined the dual carriageway of the new A229—a spot less than 20 metres west of Jacquie Hopkins' encounter, on the other side of a narrow strip of woody undergrowth that today separates the two roads.[23]

Other sources of the time that mention a location do so only in terms of relating it to the 1965 crash. *The Gazette* (formerly the *Maidstone Gazette*) of 16 July 1974, for instance, places it 'at the same spot' as a fatal accident which occurred eight years previously[24]—an association, we might suspect, derived from the need to relate Goodenough's 'ghost' to a plausible cause rather than from any definite knowledge of the scene of the 1965 crash, which may or may not have been known by serving police officers or the press in 1974. However, in correspondence in 1998, PC Dave Elvy, whose father was one of the officers who investigated the Goodenough incident, placed the spot close to the current White Lodge access road (itself a former section of the earlier Chatham Road), seventy metres north of the junction and footbridge, thereby providing some corroboration for the *Chatham Standard* report.[25]

What is certain is that the precise scene of the tragic accident did not appear in print in 1974, nor indeed in any of the original reports related to the 1965 tragedy.[26] Later investigation would reveal that the 1965 crash (in the above source erroneously described as having claimed only two victims), widely taken henceforth as the source of the haunting, did indeed occur here, on the Chatham Road close to the current junction with the A229 and its footbridge (both of which had not then been constructed). This fact, established with certainty only after some time and effort, and known to very few) opened the intriguing possibility that the crash and the ghost stories that evolved soon after could conceivably be related after all.

Jacquie Hopkins could hardly have picked a better spot for her own encounter. Had the media been aware of her experience and its close proximity to the scene of the 1965 tragedy, it would undoubtedly have provided additional support for suggestions that the spirit of Judith Lingham was once again active on Blue Bell Hill.

As it turned out, the media found such in another, much more dramatic source. Precisely two weeks after Ian Sharpe's encounter (to within the hour), and barely before the furore surrounding his encounter had died down, incredibly, it happened all over again.

'Blue Bell Hill ghost seen again'

In what I thought at first might be a 'copycat' incident, another lone motorist heading for Maidstone, 19-year-old Christopher Dawkins of Coxheath, reported an experience that closely mirrored Ian Sharpe's, except that it had taken place further up the Hill, some distance away from the clustered group of encounters that preceded it, in the heart of Blue Bell Hill Village.

First again in print with the news was the *Kent Today* (23 November), which squeezed in a report at the foot of its front page. The article and the expanded versions that were to follow it, described a virtually identical scenario to Ian Sharpe's. The incident had occurred at 10.55 p.m. on Sunday 22 November, a few days after the 19 November anniversary of the 1965 crash.

Chris Dawkins

(KM Group)

Mr Dawkins, who was on his way home, was just passing the Robin Hood Lane junction in the village (southbound) when a woman reportedly wearing a red scarf suddenly ran into the path of his Toyota car and vanished beneath the vehicle.

In words remindful of Ian Sharpe's, Dawkins described the encounter: 'She ran in front of the car. She stopped and looked at me. There was no expression on her face.

'Then I hit her and it was as if the ground moved apart and she went under the car.

'I thought I had killed her because it wasn't as if she were see [sic] through or anything. She was solid—as real as you are.'[27]

Blue Bell Hill Village at Robin Hood Lane (left), scene of Chris Dawkins' encounter as it appeared in November 1992

In a state of shock, he got out to search for the injured woman, only to find she had vanished. At first assuming the woman had managed to run off without his seeing her, Dawkins found a nearby public telephone box and rang his father. After the call, he had second thoughts, it having occurred to him that the woman's body might be beneath his car. But he could not bring himself to look.

Upon his father's arrival, Dawkins broke down. His father promptly arranged to phone the police from the house of a village resident, Marian Warburton, who later attested to the distress the incident had caused the young man.

Police, who were likewise impressed with the integrity of the witness (as they had been with Ian Sharpe), searched the area but again found no trace of the woman, and no damage to the car. Their conclusion, once again, would be that the incident would have to be put down to 'you know what'—the ghost, which again, according to the *Kent Today*, was said to be that of Judith Lingham.

Mr Dawkins was apparently not reassured by this knowledge, but seemed resigned to accept this as the only explanation. Similarly, Mrs Warburton said the experience had changed her views on the subject, which until that night she had always dismissed. It was something she felt was bound to have an effect on the village as a whole.

As the news of the latest encounter went on to further excite the general press (particularly *The Sun*)[28] in late November and December of 1992, I was trying to decide in my own mind what exactly was going on. For most of its history the case had suffered for a lack of convincing eyewitness accounts. All of a sudden, sightings of the Blue Bell Hill ghost were like buses: you wait ages for one, and then three come along at once!

Putting aside interpretation at this stage, I concentrated on the encounters themselves. Verification for the published accounts was essential, particularly in the case of Chris Dawkins, whose experience would inevitably raise the greatest suspicions following the widespread publicity Ian Sharpe's experience had attracted. Letters to Messrs Sharpe and Dawkins, in the hope of checking their stories independently of the press versions, however, went without reply (not unexpectedly amidst the heat of press interest). While this would change in time, in relation to Ian Sharpe at least (I interviewed Ian early in March 1993), I was therefore initially forced to rely on the press versions.

The police involvement in both cases was rather easier to confirm, and proved a valuable source of independent corroboration for the encounters. If the authorities were treating these reports seriously and arriving at such unorthodox explanations as ghosts, then the credibility of the accounts would be bolstered.

In a telephone conversation a few days after Chris Dawkins' encounter, Inspector Dave Williams of the Maidstone constabulary told me that the police are obliged to follow up all reports made to them.[29] In the case of Chris Dawkins, the witness had been shocked and concerned; in his experience, he had certainly appeared to be genuine. The date and timing of the encounter were as reported.

While I had the opportunity, I asked Inspector Williams if he felt it likely that officers would be able to recall names and specifics of the 1965 crash, as claimed by two of the tabloids (*The Sun* and *Today*).[30] According to *The Sun*, police had told the witness that the ghost 'must' be bridesmaid Judith Lingham, who died in 1965 at the same spot (a physical impossibility also claimed by TVS's Hugh Kirby, who reported from the scene of Ian Sharpe's encounter on the southbound carriageway of the A229)—a section of road that did not exist in 1965). The answer, as I suspected, was 'no'. With a length of service of thirty years, only a handful of officers would have been in the division long enough to have been serving at the time of the accident or Maurice Goodenough's encounter in 1974, and it was doubtful if such detailed information would be on hand.

The truth, most likely, was that the attribution to a police spokesman seeks to add credibility to the favoured cause of the haunting by intimating that the police were familiar with reports of the ghost to the point of suggesting an identification—a situation which, contrary to its intention, ultimately proves to be detrimental to a case, simply because it is untrue.

A similar example featured in the *Psychic News* of 26 December 1992, in which psychic Nella Jones was quoted as saying that the ghost once stopped the car of a police inspector (unidentified) and, introducing herself as 'Judith', hitched a lift with him. After a hundred yards, she reportedly vanished when the officer turned to speak to her.

Unfortunately, unfounded reports such as this become too eagerly picked up and passed on and, often as not, progressively altered or 'improved' along the way. In this manner, what begins as rumour becomes popular anecdotal support for a particular belief or line of thought. For example, the 'police inspector' version subsequently appeared in a respectable author's book the following year as a statement of fact, and not clearly credited to the individual (Nella Jones) or the publication (*Psychic News*) where it originated,[31] showing that it is not always the mainstream press that is responsible for the propagation of such misleading 'facts', but unwitting writers and publications dealing with the paranormal also.

Psychic News had based its own report on Nella Jones's involvement with *The Sun*'s typically sensational and well-publicised 'investigation' of December 1992, in which Nella, during a visit to Blue Bell Hill, claimed to be able to sense the presence of all *three* of the 1965 crash victims (see Chapter 8). *The Sun*'s interest had been sparked on 24 November, when it published its own version of the *Kent Today* coverage of Chris Dawkins' encounter, which continued to link the encounters with the 1965 crash and to Judith Lingham—an interpretation, of course, that originated way back in 1974.[32]

Still, following Chris Dawkins' encounter, it seemed undeniable that *something* very strange was happening at Blue Bell Hill. Aside from its location and the added detail of a red scarf in his description of the woman, Dawkins' account conformed to the pattern of behaviour and timing I had first tentatively noted at the time of Ian Sharpe's encounter, which was both tantalising and puzzling. One of the few certainties of psychic phenomena (if this is what it all really represented, and which makes the subject difficult to study) is their very unpredictability. In this case, while derived from an admittedly small number of cases, the phenomenon appeared to adhere to a crude timetable and to exhibit a consistent, seemingly orchestrated pattern of behaviour:

- Each incident had involved a lone, homeward-bound motorist (two northbound towards Medway, the other two southbound towards Maidstone).
- In each case, a figure (three describing a young woman or girl) had stepped out in front of the vehicle, allowing the driver no opportunity to avoid her. Two of the motorists (Sharpe and Dawkins) had told of the way the woman had stared them in the face as their vehicles struck her and she vanished from sight under the bonnet.
- All had occurred 'around midnight' (as some will have noted, a time traditionally associated with supernatural occurrences, the 'witching hour'), defining a time frame for the encounters of between 11 p.m.–1 a.m.
- In all cases, no 'victim' could be found to account for the incident (Maurice Goodenough's, of course, had 'vanished' from the roadside before he returned with assistance).
- No damage was sustained to any of the vehicles, a fact attested to by police in three of the incidents.
- All had taken place on a weekend: Friday/Saturday (Goodenough), Sunday (Hopkins/Sharpe/Dawkins). Cynics may of course point out the possible significance of the weekend to such encounters, but in no case could drink be considered a factor.

A further observation that might prove to be of possible significance lay with the three encounters of 1992, which were separated from one another by almost exactly a fortnight—in the case of Sharpe and Dawkins (whose encounters proved to neatly straddle the anniversary date of the 1965 crash), almost *precisely* two weeks.

The unexpected pattern that came out of a comparison of the encounters on Blue Bell Hill, I was to discover, would recur in new accounts that came to light in the wake of the events of 1992, in both new encounters that appeared in the press in 1993 and thereafter, and in earlier ones that reached me privately. It would be a pattern that, in time, would also prove to be upheld in numerous similar examples worldwide—all of which supported my initial impression that this 'format' was a real, if improperly understood, feature of these encounters. It was something I felt might provide some clues toward determining what experiences properly represented, and possibly—just possibly—prove helpful toward predicting when and where they were most likely to recur.

For the moment though, the media clearly regarded these apparitional encounters as reappearances of the ghost of a young woman killed here over a quarter of a century earlier. Although the nonsensical behaviour of the phantom made this interpretation difficult to accept—the 'knock down' or 'suicide simulation' scenario seemed intended more to frighten and confound than to initiate meaningful communication—plainly there was something about Blue Bell Hill that was responsible for triggering such vivid and internally consistent experiences.

'Ghost' is an evocative word, popularly interpreted as a visible and often purposeful manifestation of the dead. But as F.W.H. Myers, one of the founder members of the Society for Psychical Research, pointed out over a century ago it is one that belies the complexity of the phenomenon, as well as being inappropriate, since phantoms of the living are also reliably reported. A more preferred term of modern parapsychology is 'apparition' —one that recognises the fact that people report such phenomena but without restricting itself to any one interpretation.

Whatever the reason for the unprecedented spate of activity by this particular 'road ghost' in October and November 1992, it had at least demonstrated that there was indeed a case to answer in the haunting of Blue Bell Hill.

TWO

A SPECIAL PLACE

> Blue Bell Hill can be characterized as one of those places that attracts to itself a canon of weird stories, just as a fallen tree will provide the focus for a growth of fungi.[1]
>
> Michael Goss, *The Evidence for Phantom Hitch-Hikers*

BLUE BELL HILL forms a high point along the chalk escarpment of the North Downs of Kent, located equidistantly (at four miles) between the Maidstone and the Medway Towns (a conurbation comprised principally of Chatham, Rochester and Gillingham). At 190 metres above sea level, the Hill commands wide and impressive views over the county town of Maidstone to the south, and westward across the Medway Gap (the break in the escarpment through which the tidal ribbon of the River Medway flows northward to join the Thames Estuary).

While the name Blue Bell Hill evokes images of a colourful and serene woodland landscape (of which it must undoubtedly have been deserving in its past),[2] it seems oddly incongruous against the backdrop of the busy and noisy motorway-grade highway (A229) that dominates the Hill today. Just as incongruous is the idea that the modern dual carriageway and its immediate environs could be the setting for a haunting.

Until relatively recently (early 1970s), the face of the escarpment at Blue Bell Hill presented a significant obstacle to travellers intent on a direct route from Maidstone to the Medway Towns, which had to negotiate a steep, meandering two-lane road that was rapidly proving inadequate to meet the traffic needs of the late twentieth century. The modern dual carriageway of the A229 has made this journey less taxing, but the impression the Hill must have commanded to the peoples of the past is largely undiminished.

The dominant feature of the Hill today is a deep road cutting that grazes the face of the escarpment at the point it begins a mile-long northward deflection from its approximately NW–SE trend. The 100ft (30m) chalk face here, at the junction with Lower Warren Road, is all that remains of former quarry workings

Blue Bell Hill from the A229 on the outskirts of Maidstone

The 'cat' simulacrum in the chalk cutting flanking the modern A229

beside the former Maidstone–Chatham Road that were exploited here to create a wide bench to accommodate the five lanes of the new A229.

Below its crown of trees the exposed chalk forms a vaguely animal-like simulacrum (which has been likened to a cat (or a horse) leaping over a rock)[3] — which, from the valley floor, combines visually with abandoned chalk pits[4] in the scarp face a little to the west to make Blue Bell Hill distinctive and easily recognisable. The attraction, however, is more than purely visual, for it is within the shadow of the sheer white walls of the road cutting here that the many of the encounters with Blue Bell Hill's ghost have taken place.

A Venerable History

Blue Bell Hill and its immediate environs have been a focus for human occupation and activity since before recorded history, long before the time of the Roman occupation when the first road was established here as a characteristically direct route to Rochester, where it joined the great Roman road of Watling Street. It is therefore not surprising to discover that over the course of its long history, the Hill has attracted to it a number of tales, many of a supernatural flavour. As author Michael Goss has pointed out, the stories regarding a road ghost are a quite recent addition to Blue Bell Hill's stock of legends and folklore, which are generally related to documented historical events or artefacts.

In many ways, the history that Blue Bell Hill has witnessed is the history of Kent itself. In addition to their significance to the history of the county, the events that have transpired near here have arguably been influential also in shaping the direction of the broader history of early Britain.

Kent has always been an important frontier to the continent of Europe, and consequently has experienced a number of raid and invasion attempts of variable success in its long history. This has been true even into modern times, with the Battle of Britain in the skies over the county in 1940 standing as the most recent defence of its shores—one that forced the cancellation of the planned German invasion.[5]

Many of the invasions of history that landed in Kent naturally proceeded westward and inland towards London, which was established by the Romans (as *Londinium*) and was a centre of steadily increasing importance long before it became recognised as a capital.

The physiography of Kent was very different in ancient times. The dense and virtually impenetrable Wealden forest (or *Andredesweald*)[6] that occupied the broad valley between the North and South Downs and extended into Hampshire, did not begin to be cleared until the ninth century. This meant that the rivers, the open and elevated lands and trackways (and later, surviving Roman roads) would have been exploited to their fullest.

The Medway, like most rivers, proved a significant obstacle to advancing armies. Fords were thus important strategic points, likely to be occupied and well defended. During the Roman Invasion of AD 43, commanded by Aulus Plautius, a flank attack by forces under Vespasian (a general later involved in the crushing of the Jewish revolt in Palestine in AD 66, and destined to become Emperor in AD 69) was decisive in setting up the defeat of the defending Britons, who retreated towards the Thames from their entrenchment on the north-west bank of the Medway, opposite Rochester. Vespasian's *Legio secunda Augusta* (Legion II Augusta) is believed to have crossed at the nearest upstream ford, Aylesford, or possibly Snodland. Today a ragstone memorial on the north bank of the river opposite Snodland's All Saints Church commemorates this event.[7]

Four centuries after the Roman invasion, in AD 455, a battle between British tribes and rebelling Saxon colonists from the Isle of Thanet (who were in actuality a mixture of Germanic tribes (Saxons, Jutes, and Angles) that, ironically, had been granted this land in return for defending Britain against incursions by the Picts and Scots) is said to have taken place near Aylesford, two miles south-west of Blue Bell Hill.

Bede, writing in the eighth century, dates the *adventus Saxonum vel Anglorum* (the 'Coming of the Anglo-Saxons') in the east of England to AD 449. In his most famous work, *The Ecclesiastical History of the English People*, he names eastern Kent to be the burial place of the Saxon chieftain Horsa, the brother of Hengist, who was slain in battle with the Britons, and to whom a memorial was said still to be in existence in his time.[8] A century later, the Welsh monk, Nennius, is more specific in placing the battle of AD 455 at *Episford* (Aylesford).[9]

One tradition (in all probability inspired by the later Anglo-Saxon Chronicle) maintains that after the battle, the Saxon leader Hengist raised his standard and was proclaimed king of Kent from a boulder actually on Blue Bell Hill. The White Horse Stone, a sarsen of Neolithic age, is visible today at the western spur of Westfield Wood, a little to the east of the A229's Cossington service station and separated from it by the line of the Channel Tunnel rail link. Hengist's standard is said to have carried the emblem of the white horse of Saxony, an emblem that Kent has adopted for its own.[10]

While the tradition remains alive with the current monument, the White Horse Stone is in fact one of two monoliths that have borne the name. Another, long since destroyed, and said to have been the original White Horse Stone, previously stood 'two hundred and eighty yards south-west' of the present monument. On its destruction, the name and the associated tradition is thought to have been transferred to the surviving one.[11]

The White Horse Stone (looking north)

Later writers have also placed the battle of AD 455 close to Blue Bell Hill. In 1766, Josiah Colebrooke, then Treasurer of the Society of Antiquaries, stated:

> It seems to be agreed by all historians, that this battle was fought near Ailsford, and it is most likely that it was on that plain which spreads itself on the hanging of the hill, and looks down upon Cosenton, in the boundary of Ailesford, there being no other place in that neighbourhood so open, and so fit for such an engagement.[12]

'Cosenton' (today's Cossington) lies half-a-mile south of the chalk cutting at Blue Bell Hill, and a little to the west of the A229. That a significant battle between the Saxons and the Britons took place somewhere near here—either on the plateau above the ridge, or in the valley immediately below (fords such as at Aylesford and Snodland were strategic points that any army would have to cross, as we have seen)—is certainly possible, even if archaeological support for the historical accounts is yet to be found.

Early English history at this time of emergence from the Dark Ages is sparse, contradictory and unreliable, and the order and even the outcome of these conflicts are disputed by the early British and Saxon annalists.[13] In the romanticised British accounts (which begin with Nennius in the ninth century), around six years after their initial settlement in Thanet the British king Vortigern ceded the kingdom of Kent to Hengist and his growing horde of warrior Saxon colonists in exchange for the hand of Hengist's daughter—a policy that raised indignation among his British subjects. Vortigern was deposed in favour of his son, Vortimer, who, with his brother Catigern, engaged the Saxons under Hengist and Horsa in four great battles in Kent: the first in Thanet, then at the river Darenth, from which the Saxons fell back to the river Medway. At Aylesford, the third battle, both Catigern and Horsa were killed and Hengist's army again was put to flight. Pursued by Vortimer to the place of the stone on 'the shore of the Gallic sea' (interpreted as Stonar, near Richborough), a final defeat of the Saxons compelled them to flee to their ships and retire for some years from Britain, to return only after the death of Vortimer.

According to Nennius, the British name for Aylesford was *Sathenegabail* (or *Saissenaig-Hobail*), on account of the overthrow of the Saxons here.[14] Lambarde (1576), however, gives the Saxon name *Angleford*, from 'the passage of the Angles, or English men.'[15]

If we were to accept the British version of events (at least as far as Aylesford is concerned) then the idea of Hengist raising a victory standard at Blue Bell Hill immediately after the battle seems more than a little doubtful. The Saxon accounts, however, tell a quite different story. The *Anglo-Saxon Chronicle* states that following their landing at *Ypwinesfleet* (Ebbsfleet, on the Isle of Thanet)[16] in AD 449 and their establishment here, the Saxon leaders, perceiving the weakness of their paymasters and the richness of the land, began to send for reinforcements from the continent, with the intention of taking up arms against their hosts in a conquest of Britain. The Chronicle states quite simply that *Aegels-threp* (Aylesford) was the *first* battle, in AD 455, after which 'Hengest obtained the kingdom, and Æsc his son.' In this event, it is reasonable to suppose that the Anglo-Saxon forces, marching westward along the great Roman road of Watling Street, may have turned south before Rochester to meet with the Britons, in which case they would quite possibly have made their way via the remnant Roman causeway at Blue Bell Hill.

After what is now a victory for the Saxons at Aylesford, Hengist and Æsc fought the Britons again in AD 456 or AD 457 at *Crecganford* (Crayford), killing 4,000 men and finally driving the Britons from Kent.

The only battle that the two traditions agree upon *is* the Battle of Aylesford. In the final analysis it is not important if this was the first conflict or the last, as they contest; or precisely when or where Hengist was finally established as the new king of Kent. Nevertheless, it makes a kind of sense that a suitably elevated place would be selected to make a declaration of kingship. What better place than the Hill overlooking the battlefield, and from which—fittingly—as one of the highest points of Kent, its new king could survey his prize?

What is not in doubt is that the tide of history would ultimately favour the Saxons. For as David Hume would observe, 'the progress still made by the Saxons prove that the advantage was commonly on their side,' and, 'continually reinforced by fresh numbers from Germany, [they] carried devastation into the most remote corners of Britain.'[17]

A Special Place

Nestled on the shoulder of Blue Bell Hill west of and below the haunted sections of road, stands Kit's Coty House, South East England's best known megalithic structure and Blue Bell Hill's claim to fame long before there were rumours of a ghost. The dolmen (or cromlech),[18] once described as 'the most perfect and handsome of all the structures of its kind in existence,'[19] has had its share of notable visitors. The diarist Samuel Pepys recorded his impressions of Kit's Coty House when he broke off a coach journey between Maidstone and Chatham to visit it on 24 March 1669:

> … and in our way back, I 'light out of the way to see a Saxon monument, as they say, of a King, which is three stones standing upright, and a great round one lying on them, of great bigness, although not so big as those on Salisbury Plain; but certainly it is a thing of great antiquity, and I [am] mightily glad to see it.[20]

In the nineteenth century, Kit's Coty House and the surrounding hillside became a favourite picnic spot of Charles Dickens.[21] In a letter to his friend John Forster soon after moving into Gad's Hill Place at Higham in 1857, Dickens remarked: 'I have discovered that the seven miles between Maidstone and Rochester is one of the most beautiful walks in England.'[22]

Some sources (based on local tradition) even place a scene from Dickens' famous first novel, *The Pickwick Papers*, on the road outside the Lower Bell Inn (the 'little road-side public house') where, it is has been argued, Pickwick and his companions try unsuccessfully to offload their lumbering horse during their enforced walk from Rochester to Dingley Dell.[23]

Although there is much earlier evidence for human activity in the area (terraced river gravel deposits at Aylesford have yielded Palaeolithic (Old Stone Age) flint artefacts alongside the remains of woolly mammoth and rhinoceros, some 10,000 years old), these stones, together with the collapsed jumble of stones comprising Little or Lower Kit's Coty House at the foot of the Hill due south of Kit's Coty House, plus the scattered remnants of other megalithic constructions, represent the first substantial evidence of habitation here and the earliest indication of a fascination—even a reverence—for Blue Bell Hill some 5,000 years ago,

Kit's Coty House: relict cromlech of a Neolithic long barrow (looking west)

at about the same time that Stonehenge and similar constructions began to appear across Europe and around the Mediterranean Basin.[24]

Kit's Coty House, comprising three massive upright stones and crowned by an even larger capstone, has been interpreted as the entrance (or false entrance) to a sepulchral chamber—a 'portal tomb'. The description is very apt. The imposing structure, with its facing pair of slabs of unhewn sarsen stone, each 2.4 metres tall and weighing around 8.5 tonnes, and its overhanging capstone 'lintel' of around 10.5 tonnes—looking like a giant lower-case Greek Pi (π)—does indeed resemble a grand entrance or doorway, but one designed for occasion rather than simply for passage. A fourth stone, irregular and less massive than the other three stands transversely between the uprights, comprising the 'door' to complete the picture.

Now standing alone at the edge of a field and, since the late 1880s, closely hemmed in by spiked metal railings,[25] Kit's Coty was originally joined by a rectangular earthen barrow that extended some seventy metres westward (on an east-west alignment) and was around fifteen metres in width. The mound, which was still evident at the time of the antiquarian William Stukeley's visit in 1722, may or may not have been flanked by a curb of smaller stones around its perimeter. Sadly, the mound has by now all but vanished.[26]

The name itself—Kit's Coty House (and its variants)[27]—has prompted much speculation regarding its origin. One rather doubtful seventeenth century offering is that Kit is derived from Christopher (Kit being a common contraction of the name), an old shepherd (or in other versions, a wandering vagabond) who used to shelter himself from the weather in the open chamber of the monument (*coty* or *cotty-houses* being an old term for 'hut' or 'small cottage', hence 'Kit's Cote, or Cottage').[28]

It is a different association, however, that has been passed down and popularly recounted, and it is a tradition that brings us back to the battle of AD 455. In that battle, Catigern (or Katigern), son of the British king Vortigern and brother of Vortimer, died in hand-to-hand combat with Horsa, brother of Hengist. Catigern is said to have been buried at Kit's Coty House ('Kit' having been derived from *Ket*, *Cat* or *Kat*). Although a number of historical sources erroneously describe the monument as having been erected over his grave in his memory (the structure is undoubtedly much older),[29] there is no major objection to the idea that this pre-existing burial chamber may have been selected as a fitting choice for Catigern's burial, at a spot near to the battlefield. But while this remains doubtful (no evidence of a burial has been found here, ancient or otherwise),[30] the association remains.

Sources as early as William Lambarde's *Perambulation of Kent* (1576)[31] relate the man to this monument. Camden's impressively titled *Britain, or Chronographical Description of the most Flourishing Kingdoms, England, Ireland and Scotland*, translated from its original Latin and printed in 1637, states:

> … and Catigern honoured with a stately and solumn funerall is thought to have been enterred neere unto Ailesford whereunder the side of a hill I saw foure huge rude hard stones erected two for the sides one traversall in the middle between them, and the hugest of all piled and laied over them in manner of the British monument which is called Stonehenge but not so artificially with mortice and

> tenets. Verily the unskilful people term it at this day of the same Catigern Keiths or Kits Coti House.[32]

But if we look at a different rendition of the name—Kit's *Coity* House—we can get a little closer to what may be the true meaning. Francis Grose, the eighteenth century antiquarian, made the following deduction:

> … and in Cornwall, where there are many of these monuments, those stones, whose length and breadth greatly exceed their thickness, are called Coits. Ket's Coity-house may then express—Catigern's house built with coits.[33]

A 'coit' is a 'stone', as in 'a coit's cast' ('a stone's throw').[34] In Cornwall today, such portal tombs are known as 'quoits'—as in, for example, Chûn Quoit, near St. Just, and Trethevy Quoit (St. Cleer).

Chûn Quoit, near St. Just, Cornwall

While this appears to quite neatly and reasonably account for the 'stone house' part of the name, who or what then does 'Kit' refer to, if not to Catigern? Another source provides a further clue in observing that other 'ancient tombs' possess similar names, citing Kitt's Hill (Cornwall) and Kite's House (Dartmoor) as examples.[55] To these we might add Kitt's (or Kit's) Grave long barrow, near Wilton in Wiltshire—which, like Kit's Coty, has had its name attributed to romanticised characters of relatively recent origin: either a highwaymen called Kit, who was hanged and buried there, or an old gypsy woman who died and was buried where she was found.[36]

It has been suggested that 'Kit' is a corruption of *kistvaen* (or *kistven*), which means 'stone chest' (a *kist* being a chest or cist). Kistvaens were burial vaults created by arranging four flat stones to form a box-like cell, over which a capstone was placed.[37] But before accepting what sounds like a plausibly complete explanation for Kit's Coty's name, we should consider that the term *kistvaen* is generally identified with relatively smaller Neolithic (New Stone Age) and Bronze Age structures that are sunken, grave-like, into the ground or sit low to the surface like raised tombs. Several good examples of kistvaens survive, particularly on

Dartmoor.[38] It is believed that these would originally have been covered with mounds of earth or stone cairns, and possibly surrounded by rings of stones.

Human remains have been found in a number of kistvaens, offering persuasive evidence that their singular purpose was to serve as graves—which is less than certain for the larger cromlechs and their chambers. In July 1822, a now lost kistvaen was discovered below Blue Bell Hill by farm workers around 300 metres north-northeast of the White Horse Stone. Dubbed 'Smythe's Megalith' (after the Maidstone antiquarian Clement Smythe who, with Dr Thomas Charles, excavated it before its destruction), the buried stone coffin gave up the skeletal remains of two individuals and fragments of a cinerary urn.[39]

Some sources confusingly relate Kit (or Kite) to *koit* or *koeten*,[40] thereby interpreting the word also as 'stone' or 'quoit'. Applied to Kit's Coty, this would render part of the name superfluous and rather meaningless, since 'Kit' and 'Coty' (Coit-y) would have the same meaning. More probably, the use of the word simply denoted an ancient site, a stone or a quoit, as the following seventeenth century source seems to suggest. We have already seen that Kit was a common contraction of Christopher. In William Cartwright's play *The Ordinary* (c. 1635), the character Christopher protests his introduction as Sir Kit with the following repost:

> My name is not so short; 'tis a trissyllable, an't please your worship: but vulgar tongues have made bold to profane it with the short sound of that unhallow'd idol they call a kit.[41]

Kit, then, could simply refer to an unhallowed (i.e. a pagan) monument. But before we move on, I wish to briefly look at one final—and to my mind, the most satisfactory—interpretation of Kit's Coty's name. 'Coit', as we have seen (at least in the parlance of the sixteenth to the early seventeenth centuries) meant 'stone', and was a term applied also to megaliths in antiquarian writings. However, the word *coit*, rendered variously as *coite*, *coet* or *coed* in the Celtic languages of Cornwall and Wales, also denoted 'wood' or 'forest'.[42] Thus, Kit's Coty might be translated as the 'quoit (stone, or conceivably, tomb) in the woods'.[43]

Furthermore, the Celtic word *cat* (or *Cath* or *Cad*) means 'battle'.[44] Thus Nennius names the site of one of King Arthur's legendary battles as *Cat Coit-Celidon*: the 'battle-wood of Celidon' (Caledonian Forest).[45]

Cat Coit...Kit's Coty? In this comparative light, Kit's Coty House becomes the 'battle-wood house', or the 'House in the Battle Wood'—a solution that brings us satisfyingly full-circle, to Kit's Coty as an adopted British name-memorial for the battle against the Saxons at Aylesford in AD 455.

Little Kit's Coty House, *aka* the Countless Stones (looking east toward the wood-shrouded Cossington springhead)

Folklore and Legend

Much of the air of mystery associated with Blue Bell Hill can undoubtedly be attributed to Kit's Coty House and its surviving family of Neolithic megaliths. The sheer antiquity of these stones (older than the pyramids of Giza) and the fact that so little is known about them or their builders, make them a natural subject of myth and folklore.

The antiquarian and writer Thomas Wright (1810–1877) attributed many of the legends and superstitions associated with them to the fearful reverence in which they continued to be held long after their original meaning and purpose had been forgotten. Thus, many Neolithic sites preserve similar traditions of the stones as the petrified remains of dancing damsels or soldiers, or associations with witches or the Devil himself.

'In France, as in England, and indeed most countries,' observed Wright, 'they are usually connected in the popular belief with fairies or with demons—and in England with Robin Hood.'[46]

Blue Bell Hill's stock of folklore fits this profile very well. One story attributes Kit's Coty House to an old woman who was carrying three loaves, one on her head and one under each arm, who, by some enchantment, became petrified in that position.[47]

A more sinister account is the claim that Kit's Coty was built by three witches who lived on Blue Bell Hill, who, unable to lift the capstone between them, called on a fourth witch to help them to complete the task. This particular legend was evidently well known in 1848 when it became the inspiration for a play, *The Witches' Stone, or the Battle of Blue Bell Hill*, at the Theatre Royal, Rochester.[48]

Kit's Coty House was to be the inspiration for another, later play. Published in 1932, *Kit's Coty: A Musical Fairy Play* depicts Kit's Coty as the door to Kentish Fairyland, which is accessible by the utterance of a secret password: 'Our Kentish fairies live under Blue Bell Hill,' a mother tells her children, where, in a cavern-like hollow in the chalk beneath Kit's Coty, the fairy king Oberon and Queen Titania hold their court in the Great Hall of Blue Bell Hill.[49] Whether this play was itself based on any folklore connecting Kit's Coty with fairies is by now impossible to say, but the play's theme is certainly in keeping with traditions from elsewhere in which cromlechs and similar Neolithic structures were known as 'fairies' tables' or 'fairies' grottos'.[50] Among other traditions related to Kit's Coty is the one that suggests that a personal object placed on the capstone on the night of a full moon will vanish if the monument is circumambulated three times.[51]

Thomas Wright's observation of 1861 also allows some sense to be made of the name of a road and a pub at Blue Bell Hill, which otherwise seem more than a little out of place. Robin Hood Lane, which proceeds eastward from Blue Bell Hill Village, once led to a farm of the same name.[52] Today, it passes Medway Crematorium and crosses over the M2 motorway to Lords Wood and Walderslade; while situated with its back to woodland off Common Road along the ridge of the North Downs west of the village, stands the 700-year-old Robin Hood public house (formerly the Robin Hood & Little John).

In this light, the association of popular folk heroes such as Robin Hood and King Arthur with ancient sites (and, as we shall see, the traditions of May Day) can be seen as another colourful thread that has become interwoven with the local fabric of folklore.

The collapsed remains of Little (or Lower) Kit's Coty House at the foot of Blue Bell Hill share a legend with at least eleven other Stone Age sites in Britain, including Stonehenge. Known equally well as the Countless Stones, it is said the stones cannot be counted to the same number twice. The 'Worthy Baker of Aylesford' placed a small loaf on each, and on reclaiming them, discovered one to be missing. In its place stood 'the Evil One'.[53] The localisation of such a familiar theme has implications in the later discussion of the Hill's ghost.

It was perhaps inevitable that a connection would be made in print at some time between Kit's Coty House and the modern ghost story, considering its close proximity to the haunted stretch of road. As subjects of mystery attached to the same area, the two are naturally identified as expressions of the same mystical aura that marks Blue Bell Hill as a 'special' place, instinctively identified as somewhere where strange experiences are apt to take place. The closing paragraph of an article in the *Evening Post* of 15 July 1974, for instance (one of the articles reporting on the Goodenough incident) states: 'Bluebell Hill runs across the sites of innumerable prehistoric graves, several of which are known to be connected with occult practices.[54] Individuals too have commented that they felt the stones 'had something to do with it' (i.e. the ghost).

The disturbance of burial places is regarded as taboo in many cultures. It is a convention in ghostlore that to disturb the remains of the dead is to possibly invite retribution from the spirit world. A number of Neolithic structures have undoubtedly been destroyed over the course of time on and around Blue Bell Hill. Before the 1850s, the Hill was described as being covered with sepulchral monuments and smaller cromlechs and circles, which led some to suppose that this immediate area was the burial place of a British tribe, a prehistoric necropolis.[55]

The original Roman road, represented today by a narrow tree-shrouded accommodation lane on the cliff top (Warren Road), is said, prior to 1844, to have proceeded through a continuous avenue of sarsen stones that led to a stone circle and scattered groups of flat-lying stones.[56] The aforementioned Thomas Wright investigated these in August 1844, taking a team to excavate beneath one of the stones. Under the slab, Wright found the mouth of a circular pit cut into the chalk, which was filled with flints. The local cottagers informed him that such stone-covered pits were frequently found on the Hill, and when a new road had been made a few years previously one of the pits had been exploited for its flints to a depth of ten feet without reaching the bottom.

'Comparing these pits with the one on the opposite hill at Ryarsh, which has at some remote period been completely emptied,' he noted, 'I am inclined to think that they have all chambers at the bottom, and to suspect that those chambers are of a sepulchral character. Perhaps after the remains of the dead had been deposited in the chamber, the entrance-pit was filled up, and a stone placed over the mouth to mark the spot.'[57]

A third cromlech is said to have stood somewhere between Kit's Coty and Lower Kit's Coty, but no trace of it now exists.[58] Another important stone known as the 'General's Tomb' occupied the same field as Kit's Coty House before it was blown up in 1867 by a farmhand, Thomas Costen, on the orders of the landowner, to remove it as a hindrance to agriculture.[59]

One of the few surviving megaliths, the aptly named Coffin Stone, a 4.4-metre long rectangular slab, lies below Blue Bell Hill, some 500 metres west-southwest of Kit's Coty House, at Great Tottington Farm. In 1836 several human remains, including two skulls, were reportedly found in association with it.[60] The Coffin Stone is associated with a jumble of buried stones that have been interpreted as the remains of a stone circle that once enclosed the spring at Tottington.[61]

It is apparent that this area, once known locally as 'Greywethers',[62] held some special significance for the builders of these monuments. While various interpretations have been made regarding the purpose of constructions such as Kit's Coty (for example, as sacrificial altars—'great stone scaffolds'—set up at sacred spots intended for public blood-letting in propitiation of the gods, or for divining the future),[63] modern opinions vary less markedly, noting them to be related genuinely to burial customs and/or to religious or calendrical purposes.

Many prehistoric sites support traditions of retribution for their desecration. Misfortune or death is said to befall the guilty, which seems to be a kind of supernatural insurance policy against disturbance, reminiscent of the infamous 'curse of the pharaohs'. Another suggests that the heavy stones were intended to imprison the spirits of the dead within their graves—an idea that dovetails to a degree with the paragraph in the *Evening Post* that implied that occult influences might have been unleashed by the destruction of the graves, or at least had tainted the atmosphere of the place so as to be conducive to hauntings.

History, Mystery and Apparitions

It is unlikely that the author of the *Evening Post* article of 1974 making this connection between Blue Bell Hill's ghost and its mysterious past would necessarily have known of the wider associations such sites have with apparitions and other strange phenomena. Nigel Nelson's observation would appear to be instinctive, much as the identification of the Maurice Goodenough incident with the ghost stories would later appear to have been justified.

In light of the above, it should come as little surprise that the literature records numerous examples of strange light phenomena (more frequently in the past termed 'fairy lights') and ghostly forms reported at these sites. Paul Devereux's *Places of Power*, for instance—a book that explores the strange energetic properties that some claim these sites possess—refers to a strange light phenomenon witnessed playing on the surfaces of Chûn Quoit in Cornwall, and a localised cloud-like effect captured in infra-red hanging over Kit's Coty House. (Others have recorded curious 'spirit mists' on night-time photographs, although these generally can be explained as artefacts of photography in cold conditions).[64]

Late one evening in August 2005, Jeff Coleman of Maidstone was driving down the A229 at Blue Bell Hill during a thunder storm. Along with lightning, he observed three flashing blocks of light over the field adjoining the White Horse

Stone. The next morning, he was amazed to see a crop circle in the same place he had seen the lights.[65]

The coincidence of particular phenomena at given locations in both folklore and fact poses the age-old chicken-and-egg conundrum: are the traditions based on the artefacts themselves as the inspiration for the eye-witness accounts and confabulated interpretations of unusual physical effects, or were the special energetic properties perceived at these spots the reason these sites were established where they are? Some would argue in favour of the latter, and cromlechs and other Neolithic sites may have been places where the world of the supernatural was thought to impinge on our own. In another parallel with Blue Bell Hill, Devereux has described 'odd' events associated with the 'spook' road that runs alongside the Rollright Stones, three miles north-west of Chipping Norton (Oxfordshire)—something that reinforces the association made between prehistoric sites and ghost traditions.[66]

Such lights bring these sites into consideration as places of natural power, where earth energies are concentrated and channelled. 'Ley lines' have grown steadily in popularity since the concept was first introduced in the early part of the twentieth century, particularly in New Age circles. These linear tracks which appear to link megalithic sites are believed by some to represent paths of force of

Coldrum Long Barrow, sighted on the chalk road-cutting at Blue Bell Hill

this elusive 'energy' (variously termed geomagnetic, Odic, or Chi forces), which flow in invisible channels over the landscape. They have been linked to the 'spirit paths', 'ghost ways' and 'fairy paths' of folklore, which knowing mortals were wary to infringe, and are said also to be followed aerially by UFOs.

Applied to Blue Bell Hill, a ley drawn from the megalithic long barrow of Coldrum at Trottiscliffe (aka *Trosley*)[67] five miles to the west across the Medway valley, appears to pass through Kit's Coty House, crossing the Chatham Road and the A229 near to where Ian Sharpe and Jacquie Hopkins had their encounters (and where later sightings would also be made).[68]

The alignment does seem to be a real one, but perhaps not for the reasons popularly supposed. Again, it was Thomas Wright who recorded his observations of large single stones scattered across the fields for some distance eastwards from Coldrum, which he related to a tradition among the peasantry that a continuous line of stones ran from Coldrum to Kit's Coty House.[69] In a later work, Wright stated his belief that these belonged to a long avenue that linked the two communities of megalithic remains.[70]

Alfred Watkins, who is credited as the discoverer of 'ley lines' in 1921, after noting the apparent alignment of prehistoric sites (many of which included 'ley' in their name), viewed them as serving a primarily practical purpose, as prehistoric trackways along which were placed confirmatory stone markers and sighting points. More substantial sites marked the intersections of leys, or the end-points of trackways sighted across a given distance, or astronomical alignments used for calendrical or other purposes.

In the case of Blue Bell Hill, Watkins, in his seminal work *The Old Straight Track*, points to it serving as a 'hill end' site, a terminal point in such an alignment, noting that the names of many hill sites incorporate 'bel' or 'bell' as a frequent word element. Thus, he noted, we have 'Bell Hill's in Dorset and Norfolk, and 'Blue Bell' as the name of a crossroads in Salop and a place with an inn in Kent.'[71] Following the lead of earlier workers, Watkins speculated that 'bell' could be derived from *Bel* or *Baal*,[72] referring to the pagan sun-god; or could mean 'ball' or 'globe', suggesting a sun alignment.

While Watkins may have been a little overzealous in his interpretation of the name Blue Bell Hill, as we shall see, some support of his idea is found in the name *Tottington*, the aforementioned farm below Blue Bell Hill, and in Watkins' observation that place names with 'tot' or 'toot' in them occurred frequently along his leys. Tottington is listed in the Domesday Book (1086) as *Totintune*, and was the manor in which Kit's Coty House stood.[73] A few nineteenth century writers interpreted the variants as derivations of the name of Celtic god *Taut* or *Teutates*, whom Julius Caesar equated with the Roman god Mercury, to whom stones (according to Caesar) were erected on eminences as guide markers over hills and along trackways.[74]

Hilltops would certainly have been important in the laying out of linear trackways, particularly across afforested valley floors such as the Medway Gap, where the line-of-sight afforded by the facing hilltops would have facilitated this. But historically they have also served another important function: as look-out points and for raising signal fires for purposes of advance warning. More recent opinion suggests that 'tot' may therefore be derived from *totian* (Old English) or *toten* (Middle English), meaning 'a look-out' place, a hill of observation.[75]

It has been observed, that there is a close association between Neolithic and Bronze Age barrows and the hilltop beacons of later times.[76] In Elizabethan times, for instance, the hills of southern England were famously employed in a network of beacons designed to work in relay to warn of the approach of the Spanish Armada. A crude map of the beacons of Kent at this time (1585) is featured in Lambarde's *A Perambulation of Kent* (1596 edition), which shows a number of sites flanking the Thames Estuary on the approach to London. Beacons in this network were sited at Chatham, Birling and at Shooter's Hill.[77] Blue Bell Hill appears not to have been so employed on this occasion, but it *was* to serve in the beacon alert system that was set up in 1803 in anticipation of Napoleon Bonaparte's planned invasion of England. [78]

It is very probable that these same sites employed beacons for similar purposes from prehistoric times. Watkins pointed out the usefulness of beacons as surveying tools; and, by his reference to Bel, conceded they may also have served ceremonial or religious functions—practices that later became syncretised in traditions such as the Beltane Fires.[79]

One of the four great festivals of the Celtic/Gaelic year, Beltane was a fire and fertility festival, ostensibly dedicated to the god Bel (known among the Continental Celts as *Belenus*).[80] It was the calendar opposite of Samhain (Hallowe'en), and marked the start of the bountiful summer, a festival of burgeoning life rather than of death and mourning. At this time, bonfires (hence *Bel-tein* (*teind* meaning fire or ember)[81]—*Bel's fire*) were kindled atop hills in symbolic appeasement of the god toward ensuring fruitful yields in crop and livestock and the health of individuals and the community. The festival was still commonly celebrated in Ireland, Scotland and parts of England on May Day (1 May) up to the nineteenth century. In a tradition recorded as observed still in late eighteenth century Stirlingshire, the unlucky selector of a blackened piece of a prepared oatmeal cake drawn from a bonnet (the Beltane bannock) that was passed around the circle was the person to be offered up in sacrifice to Baal (symbolically by this time, I would hope!).[82]

Beltane, like Samhain, was a 'thin' time, when the Otherworld drew near, and elementals and the dead could come forth to interact with the living. In Germany and in central Europe the night-eve of the festival is known as Walpurgis Night, when witches gathered in congregation or flew through the night.[83] According to some traditions, the lighting of the fires on the eve of the festival day (30 April) and the strewing of flowers were intended to ward off witches and other malignant beings from despoiling crop and produce,[84] while flaming wheels were trundled over fields to ensure their continued fertility.

In England, vestiges of the floral and agricultural aspects of the Beltane festival survive in rural life, in the May Day rites of Maypole and Morris dancing, and in the crowning of the white-attired May Queen.[85] In Kent, The Rochester Sweeps Festival, which was revived in 1981 by Gordon Newton, begins at dawn on 1 May at Blue Bell Hill with the Jack-in-the-Green awakening ceremony. Among the numerous Morris sides that gather to celebrate the event is Kits Coty Morris, a mixed Morris side from Maidstone (est. 1977), who see in the start of summer at dawn at Kit's Coty House.

The Jack-in-the-Green (represented by a tall cone of foliage crowned with a ring of flowers, out of which peers the face of a bearded man) has been identified with the Green Man, the archetypal spirit of woodland and of greenery, and sometime consort of the May Queen. Between the sixteenth and nineteenth centuries, the Jack-in-the-Green was paraded principally by chimney sweeps on May Day, their traditional holiday. Prior to this, the Green Man found expression through various traditions in the puckish guises of Green George, Robin Goodfellow (Puck himself), Jolly Robin, and Robin of the Greenwood (Robin Hood).

Robin Hood was a popular figure of May Day celebrations in Medieval England and Scotland, when the festival was sometimes popularly known as Robin Hood's Day. The two principal characters celebrated were Robin and Maid Marian, but other members of Robin's Merry band—Little John, Friar Tuck and Will Stukely—could feature prominently in the play enactments and games, the most famous being the pairing of Robin Hood and Little John (who, in the early ballads, vied with Robin himself in popularity).[86] At Blue Bell Hill, the name of the Robin Hood pub hints at similar festivities having taken place here in the past—an idea that is strengthened by the name by which it was still known until approximately fifty years ago: the Robin Hood & Little John.[87]

While they hearken back to a much earlier time, the contemporary celebrations of dance also recall the annual fairs that commonly took place at prehistoric sites, including Kit's Coty, up to the nineteenth century. These were often held on Christian feast days that fell on or near principal pagan 'quarter day' festivals (and which, it has been reasonably argued, they were designed to supplant). A surviving handbill (a poster or flyer) of 1809, for instance, advertises the Midsummer Annual Fair to be held at 'Kitts Cotty House' on 24 June. Among its di-

Kits Coty Morris celebrating Beltane and welcoming in the summer at dawn on 1 May at Kit's Coty House

versions were 'A Donkey Race For a Cheese' and 'Grinning Through a Horse Collar for Two Gallons of Ale' (the eccentric practice of facial contortion known better today as 'gurning').[88] 24 June marks the feast of the Nativity of St. John the Baptist, which follows the summer solstice by just a few days.

Another of the holy days when fairs were traditionally held was the Feast of the Ascension, forty days after Easter, which, taking place anywhere from the beginning of May to the start of June, makes it the closest to Beltane. It has been suggested that a fair may also have taken place in Kit's Coty field at this time.[89]

Against this backdrop of history and tradition, Blue Bell Hill, not unexpectedly, has its own traditions of hauntings. In common with a number of other battlefield sites, it is said that the battle of AD 455 is periodically re-enacted in silence, providing perhaps one of the earliest claims to a haunting associated—albeit loosely—with Blue Bell Hill. A more precisely located but no more elaborate anecdote involves the ghosts of Catigern and Horsa, who allegedly re-enact their mortal combat in 'unearthly silence' at Kit's Coty itself.

Another story associated with Blue Bell Hill describes the ghost of a murdering butcher who, mounted on his horse, is said to revisit the scene of his crime, a field several hundred metres behind the site of the now-demolished Upper Bell public house, where he murdered a youth who came to be known as the 'Blue

Boy'. The field where he met his end (since built over), located off Mill Lane, became known as 'Blue Boy Field'. Kent ghost investigator Frederick Sanders, who carried out a vigil in the haunted field in June of 1945 or 1946, dated the crime to 'about a century ago'. According to Sanders, the story of the 'Galloping Murderer' had been well known in the area up to thirty years previously, and several attempts had been made by groups of Rochester and Chatham youths to 'lay the ghost.' With the exception, however, of Sanders' own report of his late-night vigil, in which he describes the sound of heavy, laboured footsteps that approached the spot where he crouched (plus one intriguing account that reached me privately, which we shall return to in a later chapter), there appear to be no records related to actual events, nor sightings of this phantom.[90]

Quite possibly the story of the Blue Boy preserves distorted recollections of the highly publicised murder, on 4 March 1831, of 13-year-old Richard Faulkner Taylor of Strood, at Bridge Woods, between Rochester and Blue Bell Hill. His killer was another youth, from Rochester, who went by the name of John Any Bird Bell.[91]

John Bell (14), and his brother James (11), scraped a living with their father cutting wood and grubbing roots near the lime kiln at Blue Bell Hill (located below the familiar high chalk cutting) to sell at the market at Rochester or Chatham. They were accustomed to seeing young Taylor, sometimes accompanied by his young sister, make the fortnightly journey on foot to Aylesford to collect their father's Parish Relief entitlement. Their route took them via Stoney Lane, which left the Rochester-Maidstone road (the current B2097) to cut across Nashenden Valley and through Bridge Woods to Blue Bell Hill. On several occasions, they encountered the Bell brothers, and on one, on their return journey, they were met by them at the lime kiln at Blue Bell Hill, and John Bell, failing to persuade the Taylor boy to go alone with them into the wood, had walked part of the way home with them.

John 'Any Bird' Bell

On the afternoon of 4 March, Henry Lewington, a ship's warrant-officer onboard HMS Warrior at Chatham, was making his way from Chatham to the Blue Bell public house (the Upper Bell)—a journey he took frequently. On the way, between 9 a.m. and 10 a.m. he overtook Richard Taylor on the Hill, and walked with him as far as Bridgewood Cottage, where they parted. Later, between 12 p.m. and 1 p.m. he again met Richard Taylor coming up the road by the pub, accompanied this time by the Bell brothers, and they passed out of sight along the road.

Another witness, Mary Jones, wife of Corporal Jones of the Royal Marines, testified that she had seen the boys after 1 p.m. as they passed by her home at Bridgewood Cottage, about a quarter of a mile from the Blue Bell public house. The smaller boy, Taylor, stopped to pick up something before following the other two, who were proceeding along the Rochester road. This was the last time he was openly seen alive.[92]

Richard Taylor's remains were not found until 11 May, when a Frindsbury man, John Izard (or Isard), discovered the body close to a track in Bridge Woods on the north side of the Rochester–Maidstone road.[93] The body, later confirmed as Richard Taylor's by the boy's father, wore a cap, a blue jacket, brown trousers, and a canvas smockfrock.[94]

The trail quickly led to the Bell brothers who, on the day the discovery was made, were summoned with their father to the Blue Bell by Henry Lewington to be questioned before the constable of Burham parish. The constable refused to take the boys into custody, but with the discovery of the murder weapon, a knife (with which John Bell had slit Taylor's throat), and the circumstantial evidence mounting, the brothers were arrested on a warrant at Aylesford on 19 May by John Tupp, a constable at Chatham, who told them they had been apprehended on a charge of murdering Richard Taylor. Tupp escorted the pair up Blue Bell Hill on their way to Chatham cage (the town lock-up).[95]

During questioning before the magistrates at Rochester on 21 May, James Bell confessed their involvement, repeating his brother's admission to him during their journey to Chatham. The focus shifted to John Any Bird Bell, who confessed that he alone had performed the actual deed. That same day he was escorted on foot to Maidstone gaol by Chatham constable Charles C. Patterson, and on 29 July he was tried at the Summer Assizes at Maidstone for the murder of Richard Taylor.

At his trial, the confessions of both boys were read out, including John Bell's statement that it was his brother who had said to him prior to the murder: 'There goes Taylor down: let's kill him, and take his money; and let's lay him under them stones that you can't count over twice the same.' (A probable reference to the Countless Stones—Lower or Little Kit's Coty House—beside the Rochester

Road from Aylesford.) James had lent his own knife for the act.[96]

From his arrest, John Bell never protested his guilt and resigned himself to his fate. The jury found him guilty, but despite its recommendation for clemency on account of his youth and disadvantaged upbringing, the judge, Mr Justice Gaselee, sentenced him to be hanged, adding that afterward his body would be given over to the surgeons at Rochester for dissection. At this, Bell, who had remained stoic throughout the trial, 'dropped a solitary tear.'

John Any Bird Bell was hanged over the Turnkey's Lodge at the front of Maidstone prison before a crowd of eight or nine thousand people at around 11.30 a.m. on Monday 1 August 1831. John Bell was the first (and youngest) person to be executed outside the new prison, and the last ever child to be executed in Britain.[97] The case was one that had attracted national interest, and just the kind of event that would be expected to pass into legend.

The legendary Blue Boy, most recently recounted in Peter Underwood's *Ghosts of Kent* (1987)[98] has, over the years, faded into virtual obscurity, to be superseded by the arguably more popular and contemporary hitch-hiking phantom, about which tales began to circulate from the 1960s.

Other anecdotal accounts related to Blue Bell Hill include:

- At the turn of the last century, a swift one-eyed phantom on the Burham Common Road (which joins the Maidstone–Chatham Road at the site of the former Upper Bell public house).[99]
- The ghost of a headless horseman, and a full troupe of Royalist cavalry.[100]
- The ghosts of two mystery figures, both male—one at the site of the old Bridgewood gatehouse (now occupied by the Bridgewood roundabout complex), and another at Medway Crematorium in Robin Hood Lane (near whose junction with Maidstone Road in Blue Bell Hill Village Christopher Dawkins struck his phantom victim).
- The sound of galloping phantom horses.[101]
- A phantom stagecoach drawn by four white horses, which appears before midnight, around November. Appearing at the top of Blue Bell Hill it races down the Hill to disappear near the bottom. Seen initially as a fuzzy patch of light, the vision becomes clearer as it is joined by the sound of horses' hooves. After it fades, the dry, charged atmosphere that accompanies its appearance returns to normal.
- An old gypsy woman in dark clothing who appears on the old part of the Hill. The phantom, carrying what appears to be a basket (of pegs), reportedly roams about the roadside in the winter months.

- A procession of a Roman army with chariots on the Rochester Road between Blue Bell Hill and Aylesford.[102]

And undoubtedly, there are others. As meaningless as these anecdotes may be,[103] they serve at least to demonstrate that Blue Bell Hill has been no stranger to ghost stories; that it was perhaps readily receptive to a new and definitive story—one that was related to its most important modern feature: its road.

The Road

Thus far we have looked at the history and folklore of Blue Bell Hill without touching very much on its road. But it is the road that is in large part responsible for the village becoming established and is the setting for the modern ghost stories. Throughout its own long history, the road at Blue Bell Hill has witnessed its fair share of tragedy and intrigue—certainly enough to satisfy the proponents of untimely or violent death as a cause for hauntings. The last chapter outlined the popular cause of the ghost of Blue Bell Hill, a car crash in November 1965. The scene of the tragedy is located at the intersection of the former Chatham Road and the northbound carriageway of the present A229, near to Salisbury Road. The older route, which is preserved in several backwater sections parallel to the

Warren Road, the original Roman road surmounting the hill

Kitts Cotty House, near Aylesford, Kent **(1828), an engraving by Samuel Lacey from an original drawing by George Sidney Shepherd, showing the sometime inn *The Kit's Coty House* (left; now Kits Coty Brasserie) on the new road; and (right), the newly sited Lower Bell inn**

Kit's Coty House today (looking east)

A229 between Maidstone and Blue Bell Hill Village, today serves as a link road to the A229 for northbound traffic coming out of Aylesford, Eccles and Burham, and as an access road for residents of Kit's Coty Estate.

The construction of the modern dual carriageway, which now carries the designation 'A229', befitting its status as the main road between Maidstone and the Medway Towns, necessitated a massive earth-moving programme which has left little of the former Maidstone–Chatham road intact, and altered the character and appearance of the entire Hill. Consequently, Blue Bell Hill is today a very different place to what it was even at the time of the 1965 tragedy.

If at this stage we suppose, as the media have popularised, that the reports and rumours of Blue Bell Hill's ghost *can* be linked to the 1965 tragedy, the events of 1992 demonstrated that the radical disruption of the environment a few years following the accident had not discouraged it from manifesting, nor diminished the appeal the story holds for us. Indeed, the most convincing encounters have occurred sometime after the new road became established. Whether it is significant or not, the principal effect the new road has had on the stories (other than on the strength of evidence) is to mark a change in the ghost's behaviour: the late 1960s characterised by a hitch-hiking phantom, and the post-construction years by the by-now familiar 'suicide-intent' pedestrian.

The new road succeeds not one, but two earlier routes surmounting Blue Bell Hill. The original road, represented today by Warren Road, a tree-shrouded accommodation lane that runs over the hilltop east of and parallel to the current A229, marks the course of a Roman road that linked *Durobrivae* (Rochester) with *Portus Lemanis* (Lympne) on Kent's south coast. Proceeding southward along Warren Road, the route winds down the steep face of the Hill before resuming its characteristic straightness towards present-day Maidstone, where it continued via Week Street and Stone Street.

The road, possibly exploiting a pre-existing British trackway (as may the Pilgrims' Way, which crosses the modern road near to the Cossington service station and White Horse Stone) was established soon after the Roman invasion of AD 43, and its margins, and the Medway valley itself, were well settled by the close of the first century AD. The remains of Roman villas at nearby Eccles and at Maidstone have been dated to this time.

The remains of another at Blue Bell Hill (sometimes described as a temple or shrine) today lie buried in undergrowth on private land precariously close to the cliff edge flanking Warren Road. Excavations here in 1844 by Thomas Wright discovered 'extensive traces' of Roman buildings, including brick-flooring, broken tiles and pottery and traces of burnt wood and some human remains. Wright refers also to a Roman burial ground, discovered by a Mr Charles of Maidstone, and located several hundred yards north of this location.[104]

'Kits Coty House and Blue Bell', a sketch by F.G. Kitton, from a painting by J.J. Gegan, showing the 'new' road and Kit's Coty House around the start of the 19th century

The ancient road at Blue Bell Hill remained in use right up to the eighteenth century. By this time, the increasing burden of coaches, carts and heavy wagons, plus the great numbers of cattle and sheep driven along them, had left many of the county's principal roads in a ruinous state. At Blue Bell Hill, the problems were exacerbated by the steepness of the Hill. In the winter months, many of these roads could prove impassable.

Until this time, under common law, the responsibility for the upkeep of the highways (the major ancient roads) and the byways (all other routes) fell to the parishes through which they passed or served. At the beginning of the eighteenth century, a series of Turnpike Acts were passed in the interest of improving Kent's key roads. The turnpike system, which was administered by a number of Turnpike Trusts, was initially an unpopular one in many parts of the country since, for the first time, tolls were to be charged to traffic in order to finance the projects, with the given levy payable at a series of gates. The earliest Act for Kent, in respect of the road from Sevenoaks to Tunbridge Wells, was passed in 1709. The eleven-mile length of the Rochester to Maidstone road was granted its own Turnpike Trust in 1728, making it one of the earliest roads in the county to be turnpiked.[105]

The most significant alteration made at Blue Bell Hill was a major re-direction of the road to avoid the steep ascent at the southern end of Warren Road. The new route, which was established a short distance to the west in the last quarter of the eighteenth century (and certainly by 1801), ascended northward from the turnpike gate at what is now the Lower Bell crossroads, within sight of Kit's Coty

House. Hugging the side of the Hill, the road climbed to the hilltop at the Upper Bell Inn, and rejoined the Roman road just above Robin Hood Lane. The road was again altered and the gradient made less steep in 1824.[106]

With the construction of the new road, the steep section of the old Roman road represented by Warren Road became a backwater. The inns, the Lower Bell and the Upper Bell, which had developed as staging inns that served the burgeoning stage-coach industry in the seventeenth and eighteenth centuries, and which stood at either end of Warren road, were forced to follow the new road. In her book *A Steep High Hill,* which recounts the history of Blue Bell Hill Village, the late Edwina Kissick mentions an indenture of 1786 that records the new Upper Bell inn as having been 'lately built'.[107] Mudge's one-inch map of Kent of 1801 ('The First Ordnance Map') shows the Lower Bell still in its original position; [108] the move of the inn to its current position having not been made until around 1828.[109]

The coaching inns and staging inns that dotted the popular coach routes of the eighteenth and early nineteenth centuries were traditionally spaced around seven miles apart, where they served to refresh both passengers and horses—although this depended very much on the terrain. At Blue Bell Hill, the Upper and Lower Bell were located just a mile apart, and together provided an essential service on the steep, narrow road. The Upper Bell afforded an opportunity for Rochester-bound coaches to change horses after the arduous climb; while the very names of the paired inns hint at another important function—as a signaling system from one to the other. The narrowness of the old road (which would still be the case for the turnpike road) provided no easy means for the large four-horse carriages to pass one another. Neither could horses harnessed to a carriage halt readily or back up, especially uphill. To ensure the way was clear between the two inns, a simple bell system is said to have been

The pub sign outside the Upper Bell at the time of its closure

introduced to ensure that uphill traffic waited at the foot of the incline until the all-clear was given—hence the Lower Bell and Upper Bell.

Blue Bell Hill almost certainly owes its name to these two inns, and to the coaching trade that they served. While both in their time have been referred to simply as 'The Bell' or the 'Old Bell',[110] sources from as early as the 1759 have included 'Blue' in the inn's name, as in 'Upper Blue Bell', and 'Lower Blue Bell'.[111]

From around 1840, the Hill begins to be referred to as 'the Blue Bell Hill', and thereafter, with the development of the village inside the wedge formed by the old road and the new turnpike road, fully as 'Blue Bell Hill'.[112]

Prior to the 1820s the Hill had been commonly referred to as *Boxley* Hill. References to Kit's Coty House (and The Bell inn) make it clear that these do indeed relate to the area later known as Blue Bell Hill, which was then undifferentiated from the Boxley Hill that is today preserved in name on the North Downs a little to the east overlooking the village of Boxley itself.[113]

In the time of the old road and the early coaching days, Blue Bell Hill was little more than a waypoint on the way to somewhere else, to Rochester or Maidstone, and was characterised by open common land and woodland, the two inns, and a scattering of dwellings. In July 1775, the Hon. William Hervey (1732–1815) visited the Hill, recording the following entry in his journal:

> **July 8, Saturday**....From hence (Kits-Coty-house) we went to the top of Boxley hill, where [is] the single tree called the Blue bell from a hedge ale-house with that sign being near it.[114]

A hedge ale-house was a term used to describe an obscure roadside inn—a fitting description of the original Upper Bell inn, which was located at the top of Warren Road near to where it meets Mill Lane. This somewhat cryptic record seems to suggest the 'Blue bell' to have been a tree near the inn, and that an image of it, or of a blue bell, was depicted on a sign displayed outside the inn. A handful of 'Blue Bell' or 'Bluebell' inns today are named after the spring-blooming woodland flora, and show the lavender-blue flower on their signboards.[115] It would be quite reasonable to suppose (as is often assumed) that Blue Bell Hill derives its name in similar fashion. The common bluebell, however, can hardly be mistaken for a tree. Far more common are inns named *The Blue Bell* or *The Blue Bell Inn* which display blue-painted bells on their signs (or actual painted bells), as exampled by a number of former coaching inns and taverns around the UK. Good examples include The Blue Bell Inn at Annan (Dumfries and Galloway), and those sharing the same name at Levenshulme (Greater Manchester), Burslem (Stoke-on-Trent), Gretton (Corby, Northamptonshire), and Callow End (Worcestershire).[116]

The Upper Bell (c.2000). It was finally demolished in 2013

The Blue Bell was but one of a number of familiar and easily recognisable icons employed by the inn trade along the old pack-horse, stage and mail coach routes, and which had their origins in the medieval custom of identifying trades by simple symbols and signs that advertised their goods or services to a predominantly illiterate populace.[117]

Some signs suggested a trade or craft with which the inn was associated: the Coach & Horses, the Ship, the Plough, or the Blacksmith's Arms. Others perpetuated heraldic or historical emblems that were well known as signs for inns and hostelries, and which were made conspicuous by the use of bold colours to better catch the eye of drivers and travellers. Hence the Blue Bell finds itself in the good and ubiquitous company of the Red Lion, the White Hart, the Green Dragon, the Crown, the King's Head (or Arms), the White Horse, the Swan, the Black Bull; 'and many another old sterling English name',[118] and all their varieties in combination and colour.[119]

Blue symbols abound. In addition to the Blue Bell, there is the Blue Ball, the Blue Post, the Blue Boar, the Blue Lion, and the Blue Boy.[120] Coach companies also employed colours in their liveries to distinguish their coaches from their competitors; thus there was the 'True Blue', the 'Old Blue', and the 'Red Rover'.

The new Upper Bell inn was evidently still known as the 'Upper Blue Bell' at the time of the Gravesend naturalist and antiquarian Robert Pocock's visit in May 1822, when he took in the expansive view from the top of the house.[121] By the

1870s, the inn was being referred to on the Ordnance Survey's maps as the *Old Bell Inn*, and the area immediately west of the new road, along the Burham Common Road, as 'Upper Bell'. 'Blue Bell Hill' at this time described only the cluster of buildings near to the former inn site at the eastern end of Mill Lane, opposite Podkin meadow.

By 1908, the *Old Bell* had become the *Upper Bell* public house, and the name 'Blue Bell Hill' was being applied to the whole of the loosely extended village that had taken root along the Maidstone–Chatham road and a little way along Common Road. The founding of the village of Blue Bell Hill as we know it today essentially owes itself to this phase of growth, in which rows of workers' cottages sprang up in relation to the employment opportunities offered by the large chalk quarries below the Common Road. The Upper and Lower Culand pits, which were established in the 1890s to meet the increasing demands for lime by the brick and cement works at Burham and Wouldham, were at the height of their activity at this time. This period, and in particular, a tragic member of one quarryman's family would hold some later significance in the consideration of the identity of Blue Bell Hill's ghost, as we shall see.[122]

It is difficult today to imagine the relative remoteness and the accompanying dangers posed by the Hill in days past. In spite of its status, the road was sparsely travelled until the motor age. As late as the 1930s, private motor travel was still uncommon, and overall volumes of (mainly commercial) traffic were consequently low, particularly in the hours of darkness. Long before they were concerned about ghosts, wayfarers at Blue Bell Hill were more wary of it as the haunt of footpads and brigands, where the gradient made it a choice spot for preying on passing travellers.

In April 1725, for instance, four persons were robbed of money and jewellery on Boxley Hill (Blue Bell Hill) by three footpads with pistols.[123]

In July of that same year, a Mr Underdown, the Distributor of the Stamps for the County, was robbed of his money and was taken into the woods and bound while his attackers awaited further victims. When none were forthcoming, the robbers took his clothes (a coat, waistcoat, shirt and periwig) and released him.[124] And in April 1776, Edward Dunk, a sergeant in the West Kent Battalion, returning to Rochester from Maidstone, was accosted 'between the Old Turnpike and the lower Blue Bell' by a single footpad, who was disguised and carrying a large club, and who took from him a sum of fifty pounds and other valuables. The sources in this instance additionally provide a possibly important suggestion (by their reference to the 'Old Turnpike') that the new road (or at least work on it) had been established by 1776.[125]

In 1834, the foot of Blue Bell Hill was the principal rendezvous for a gang of the 'thimble-rig gentry', so-named for the classic three-cup-and-pellet trick that, by sleight of hand, they used to swindle passersby of their money and other valuables.[126]

John Any Bird Bell aside, footpads and other opportunistic petty robbers seldom inflicted serious harm to their victims. Sometimes, however, attempted robberies could go tragically wrong. On 10 August 1798, a loaded cart was being driven down 'Bexley Hill' by a Mr Large when two men leapt out of the hedge. The frightened horse lurched, throwing the driver to the ground on his face, and a wheel of the cart ran over him. A child travelling with him was thrown out of the cart, but fortuitously was 'received in the arms of a man on the hill' (presumably one of the robbers). The two were carried to the Lower Blue Bell, and a surgeon was summoned from Maidstone, but the young driver, who had been married just six days, died before his arrival.[127]

On another occasion, in the late 1840s, in an episode that prefigures the ghostly female hitch-hiker by some 120 years (not to mention variants of other transport-related urban legends), a butcher, John Wildash, of Ulcomb(e), near Leeds Castle, was travelling down the Hill when

> … he was stopped by a person in female attire, who asked him for a ride to Maidstone. When he consented, and the supposed female put her muff into the cart and he assisted her up; as soon as she was seated he saw, from a slight appearance of whiskers on the face, that his friend was a man, and with presence of mind he dropped his whip, and begged of his companion to get out and pick it up, as he did not like to leave his horse. The 'lady' got out, and he at once drove off at full speed to Sandling gate, where he examined the muff, and in it found two loaded pistols and a butcher's knife.

But John Wildash's luck was to run out. The same article of the *West Kent Guardian* that gave this account, reported that after thirty years of making his weekly trip on this road to attend the market at Chatham—in so doing having been robbed several times and narrowly escaped being murdered—he had finally lost his life here. On 22 January 1848, while descending Blue Bell Hill in the dark, he drove too near to the bank opposite Kit's Coty House, causing a wheel of his cart to ride up and overturn on top of him. He was found dead by a passing labourer, with the hub of the wheel resting on his chest. The man summoned assistance, and the body was conveyed to the Lower Bell.[128]

Ill fortune and tragedy could befall the vulnerable in other ways at Blue Bell Hill, as the following newspaper record for June 1793 attests:

> A few days since, a poor woman, far advanced in pregnancy, going from Chatham to Maidstone, was taken ill near the upper Blue Bell, and solicited assistance from that house, which refused her, and she was desired to walk on to the Lower Bell. Overcome with fatigue, she sat down near the top of hill, and was delivered of a fine child—for want of help, they both died immediately![129]

In September 1810 the body of a man, a Dartford shoemaker by the name of Saunders, who had been missing for eleven weeks, was found 'in a very putrid state' with a bundle by his side in Boxley Wood near to the Upper Bell. He had last been seen drinking beer and eating bread and cheese in the pub.[130]

And in 1859, on the evening of 29 January, 69-year-old spinster, Mary Hardy—'a woman of somewhat eccentric habits'—was found lying dead in a pool of blood in Mill Lane, not far from her home, again near to the Upper Bell. She had been visiting with a female neighbour about 9 p.m., and after a lengthy conversation, during which she had seemed unwell, she had left for her home, to be found a short while afterward in the road by a Mr Smith, a miller at the windmill. Despite her evident injuries—a severe lacerated bruise on her forehead—it was surmised her death had been due to a fall, and therefore of natural causes, and burial proceeded without the interest of the coroner. [131]

An indication as to how infrequently the old Roman road at Blue Bell Hill had become travelled by 1816 is found in the pitiful case of Ann Martin. On Sunday 22 September some young men had gone nutting in the woods near the Old Upper Blue Bell inn when they observed a woman lying beneath a tree, apparently asleep. They passed by without disturbing her; but on the Friday of the following week, they returned to the same area to continue their foraging, and were surprised to see the woman lying in the same position. One of the men approached the body, and to his horror, discovered her to still be alive, albeit in a most appalling state. Her clothes were rotten from long exposure, and maggots infested every area of exposed flesh, crawling over her in 'sickening quantities'—behind her ears, and between her fingers and toes, in her nostrils, and in her mouth.

With the help of two men from the Blue Bell, the woman was conveyed to an outhouse, where she was later treated by a Mr Browne, a surgeon from Rochester. The woman subsequently made good progress toward recovery, and later gave her name and how she had come to be in the spot. Some time back she had come from Lewes to be with an artillery soldier at Chatham Barracks, but had left him and decided to return home. Destitute of money, and exhausted when she came to Blue Bell Hill, she had lain down in despair to die. This had been on the Sunday prior to the one she was first seen, and therefore had lain there for eleven full days before she was discovered.[132]

Five years later, in October 1821, a woodman returning to his abode in the

The Maidstone–Chatham Road towards Blue Bell Hill, 1959 *(KM Group)*

The busy Maidstone–Chatham Road outside the Lower Bell, c.1965 *(NA3T photo)*

woods near the Upper Blue Bell was accosted by a man in a sailor's uniform, who told him he had been wandering the woods all day with the intention of killing himself. Believing the man to be insincere, and probably intoxicated, the woodman responded with pragmatic indifference, asking him why he had come there—and why, if he intended to kill himself, had he delayed so long to do it.

The man told him that the Devil had urged him to destroy himself, and he had spent the whole day looking for a suitable place to hang himself, but had changed his mind when God Almighty had appeared to him, and told him that his sins rendered him unfit to enter His presence. The woodman at this point tried to leave him, but the man followed, and insisted that he was telling the truth; that he had deserted his ship at Chatham and stolen a boat to come ashore with the intention of hanging himself, but God had dissuaded him. He could not, however, return to his ship for fear of severe punishment or hanging, and he had only a shilling to his name. The woodman declared that he had no money with which to help him, and went on his way. The next morning the man's body was found hanging in the wood. Evidently, he had been engaged and his fiancée had spurned him for another sailor, which had likely prompted his desperate final actions.[133]

The new turnpike road at Blue Bell Hill would serve as the major route between Maidstone and Rochester and the Chatham dockyards for virtually the next two centuries, until it was itself finally succeeded by the present dual carriageway, which was completed in 1972. An understanding of the exact form of the Maidstone–Chatham Road as it was known in the late 1960s is important in our investigation since it was on this particular section, between the Lower and Upper Bell inns, where the car crash of November 1965 occurred, and where subsequent rumours placed sightings of a female apparition.

While plans were already under way for a large scale improvement of the A229 by the end of 1965 (the project had first been mooted in 1963), the prospect did nothing to alleviate the day-to-day problems posed to motorists using Blue Bell Hill. A brief article ('Uphill work') in the Comment column of the *Kent Messenger* by then-News Editor Roy Plascott (September 1966) described the journey as 'a drag': 'It takes only one large lorry forced into a five-mile-an-hour crawl by the gradient to hold up scores of other vehicles. Most times it is too dangerous to pass. A breakdown blocking one side of the road can cause chaos.'[134]

Another article by Mr Plascott (13 October 1967) described in more detail the inherent frustrations of the journey: 'Every day hundreds of motorists are irritated and aggravated by the slow crawl up the long steep hill. And it is getting worse day by day. One morning this week the hardly-moving queue of vehicles stretched a quarter of a mile on the Maidstone side of the Cossington Service Sta-

The old: Chatham Road

And the new: the modern A229

tion. One could almost hear the teeth gnashing. What a way to start a day!'[135]

In July 1968, under a different column ('Talk of the Town') Plascott was again decrying the Maidstone–Chatham Road at Blue Bell Hill, making comparison to the old country train routes known as 'Bluebell lines' on account of their slowness, which enabled passengers to alight and gather bluebells and still have time to return to their compartments.[136] A rather amusing example of the hold-ups at Blue Bell Hill occurred in March 1970, when Kent was almost brought to a standstill by snow blizzards. On 4 March a man is said to have alighted from a bus at Bridgewood at the top of Blue Bell Hill, entered a café, ate a meal, and came out to re-board the same bus! [137]

Considering the volumes of daily traffic the road was expected to handle (a peak of around 18,800 per day in August 1966, projected to 42,000 by 1991), the road was inadequate and dangerous. Unlit, narrow, twisting and in need of repair, the Maidstone–Chatham Road at Blue Bell Hill was identified as a major trouble spot, the notorious scene of a number of accidents, occasionally proving fatal.[138] In poor weather conditions, the situation was exacerbated.

But dangerous as Blue Bell Hill could prove to be, the overriding reason for the upgrade was in the interest of improved traffic flow along this important link between the A20(M) and the M2, and between Maidstone and the Medway Towns. The first stage of the 'jam free recipe' for the Hill was begun in July 1970.[139] The work had been expected to take two years but on Saturday 26 February 1972 the new road was opened ahead of schedule without ceremony.[140]

In order to accommodate the new road and to reduce the dangerous mile-long 1-in-11 gradient to a more manageable 1-in-18, more than a million tons of chalk and earth had been moved. The local geography changed markedly as a result. The long established (and then still-working) chalk quarries and lime kilns located just north of the Lower Bell pub were demolished to create a wide bench for the dual carriageway's five lanes at this point (the inner of the three northbound lanes was intended as a crawler lane for heavy, slow-moving traffic). Much of the rubble from the excavations was used to build a ramp to support the lower reaches of the road south of the under-bridge over Lower Warren Road. The total cost of the project rose to around £1.75 million.

The route follows its predecessor along much of its length, but intentionally avoided the former course in places to avoid existing properties and residential areas. Thus, short sections of the former road are preserved, notably the stretch north of the Lower Bell crossroads, known today as simply as Chatham Road, which runs for around 600 metres before re-joining the dual carriageway as a slip-lane further up the Hill. The next original part of the road, the access road at White Lodge, adjoins Kit's Coty estate. Another is marked by the now disused slip-lane on the other (southbound) side of the carriageway that emerges from

Blue Bell Hill Village.

Blue Bell Hill Village today has had respite from the flow of heavy traffic for over three decades. But the first stage of construction—the major earth-moving phase—had not extended to bypassing the village. Thus, until the early 1980s traffic ascending the new fast hill route was forced into a residential bottleneck at the Upper Bell before emerging onto a roundabout system with options for the M2 motorway and the Medway Towns.

The second phase of the A229 improvement scheme began in 1983, when the dual carriageway was extended northward, cutting through the area formerly known as Upper Bell, bypassing the village on its western side, to run unbroken to Bridgewood. Still further changes, to the M2 interchange north of the village (as part of the A2/M2 widening programme between 2000 and 2003), and the subsequent closure (from 2003) of the southbound slip-lane onto the A229 at the Upper Bell pub (thus blocking through-traffic), has left the village quiet and, from a supernatural perspective, uneventful—but at some cost. With the bypass also went the through-trade, and the casualties of this loss of trade included a BP petrol station, the village post office, and the Upper Bell pub itself, which finally closed its doors sometime between 2003 and 2004 and was sadly demolished in 2013.[141]

With the improvement schemes Blue Bell Hill's traffic flow problems have been largely eliminated. The same, unfortunately, cannot quite be said of its safety record. Even before the work was completed the Hill had added another victim. In the first week of November 1971, amid frequent changes in the road layout as the scheme approached completion, a 21-year-old female from Frindsbury died when the van in which she was a passenger became involved in a three-vehicle pile-up on the Hill.[142]

The dangerous, sinuous gradient at the scarp has been eliminated, but no major highway can be expected to be completely safe. A function of improved traffic flow is an increase in traffic speed and, although the gradient is less severe on the dual carriageway, the 3.25-kilometre unbroken stretch of road from the summit of Blue Bell Hill to Maidstone allows vehicles to reach motorway speeds. Indeed, Roger Pen has aptly described the A229 here as '... a motorway in noise if not in name.'[143] Inevitably, and despite all precautions, accidents—many fatal—have and will continue to occur here.

The situation at Blue Bell Hill was not helped for a number of years by inadequate (in fact, nonexistent) lighting and a lack of barrier protection. A long overdue safety improvement scheme was implemented in 1988 to install overhead carriageway lights along the entire Blue Bell Hill to Maidstone stretch of the A229. *The Maidstone Star* announced its completion in November 1989 with the headline 'Lights all the way to Chatham', which described the switching on of the last kilometre of low-pressure carriageway lights along the road's central reservation. Other improvements involved the building of a central crash barrier to prevent out-of-control vehicles crossing the reservation, and the rigging of lights at the slip-lane intersections. In the five years to June 1989, there had been forty-six injury accidents along the unlit stretch of road, five of these fatal. Sixteen (and all of the fatalities) had occurred in darkness.[144] Whether it may prove to be significant, it is worth noting that the well-attested sightings of a ghostly figure on Blue Bell Hill have been under these favourable observational conditions. The illumination furnished by the overhead carriageway lights, together with the unobstructed view afforded by the wide dual carriageway, has provided motorists with a vastly improved sphere of visibility. Since it seems unlikely that the eye-friendly lighting is directly responsible for anomalous visual effects on account of their widespread use, we may idly speculate, perhaps, that Blue Bell Hill's phantom, stripped of its cloak of darkness is now more likely to be seen (contrary though this may be to expectations).

Whatever the merits of this line of thought, it has to be remembered that the ghost or ghost stories, whatever we take the phenomenon to be, originated in a more traditional setting—a dark, tree-shrouded stretch of the former Maidstone–Chatham Road. This supposedly haunted section of the old road (which includes the scene of the 1965 car crash) is preserved today north of the Lower Bell crossroads, where it serves today as a link road to the A229 for traffic northbound from Aylesford and Burham. It remains unlit, its diminished importance not warranting special lighting. The spooky ambience is therefore intact, and this section today provides the only opportunity to experience something of the road conditions of Blue Bell Hill prior to the construction of the new carriageway. If anything, the darkness here seems all the more oppressive today since it contrasts sharply with the well-lit slip-roads of the A229 which precede and succeed it.

The more supportable sightings may have shifted to the dual carriageway above and a little east of this neglected arc, but it is this section that lies at the heart of and epitomises the haunting(s) at Blue Bell Hill.

THREE

EARLY DAYS

Motoring on the road between Chatham and Maidstone one night at around 11 p.m., a man saw a girl in her early teens[1] thumbing a lift at the crest of Blue Bell Hill. She asked to be taken to Maidstone and during the ride mentioned her address in that town; speaking almost continuously in what the motorist felt was a state of high excitement, she also announced that she was to be married the next day. On reaching the outskirts of Maidstone her conversation lapsed and the driver was startled to discover she had unaccountably vanished from the car; he had not noticed the passenger door opening and had been keeping to a moderately high speed as they travelled. Although he gradually rationalized that the girl must have slipped out unseen when the car slowed down in heavy traffic, he was concerned about her safety and proceeded to the address which the girl had let slip during the conversation. Here he was told by the girl's mother that (X)—obviously identical with his talkative passenger—had been killed in a car crash on Blue Bell Hill. This tragic event had taken place on the eve of her wedding three years ago to the very day and hour he had met the Hitch-Hiker.

Composite version of the Blue Bell Hill story, by Michael Goss in his *The Evidence for Phantom Hitch-Hikers.*[2]

MY OWN INTRODUCTION to Blue Bell Hill's ghost came on 28 February 1981, the same day I moved with my family to Maidstone. Looking back, I find it interesting that the story should have featured so soon, but since it was related as we were driven up Blue Bell Hill for the first time, perhaps this was not so remarkable. And yet, hearing the story on that very first evening in Kent had a ring of fate about it considering my later involvement in the story.

That introduction could also be regarded as a kind of initiation to residence in this part of the county of Kent, for in the years prior to the widely publicised and genuinely peculiar occurrences on Blue Bell Hill in 1992, the story of the ghost girl of Blue Bell Hill had been largely confined to Kent, chiefly to Maidstone and the Medway Towns and their environs. There is, of course, no surprise in a reputedly haunted landmark achieving notoriety within its immediate neighbourhood. The surprise with Blue Bell Hill lay with the realisation as to how widely known the story was in the area—and by *story* I do not imply there was but a single tale in circulation, but suggest there was a simple and recognisable format to which the various versions conformed. My later estimates suggested that perhaps forty or fifty percent of the population were not only aware of Blue Bell Hill's repute, but could relate slightly varying versions of the same narrative: that of the disappearing female hitch-hiker. To my knowledge, no other ghost story had achieved the same degree of familiarity despite the superb historical sources that might have inspired them. There seemed to be something especially attractive about this particular tale.

As it was, I had only a passing interest in the story at the time. I had read of a similar tale in the story of 'Resurrection Mary', Chicago's own hitch-hiking phantom, who was said to hitch lifts from unwary motorists to her 'home', the Resurrection Cemetery in the city's South Side. Like Resurrection Mary, Blue Bell Hill's ghost—as another 'strange-but-true' story—sounded questionable to say the least. While I found it interesting that Blue Bell Hill had acquired its own rumours of such a phantom, I gave it little further consideration.

In time my interest would be rekindled after I had heard the Blue Bell Hill story repeated a number of times from diverse sources. Although I then had no proper appreciation for the ubiquity of such accounts, or for the consistencies in story point inherent in these popular tales, it began to become apparent that Blue Bell Hill's ghost, for what seemed an item of trivia, was unusually well known for 'just' a ghost story, and was evidently very durable. Essentially the same story came from quite different people, some of whom had grown up with it, which provided a clue to its age and testament to its longevity.

Part of the reason for the story's popularity possibly lay with the fact that unlike other supposedly haunted places like houses or churchyards, Blue Bell Hill is regularly visited in passing by large numbers of people in the course of their everyday business. Therefore the story would naturally feature widely because its setting is widely familiar. But that didn't begin to explain it. Other roads have reputations for being haunted. Why would this particular place gain such notoriety? Could it be because there might be more to it than mere hearsay?

Whatever the case might prove to be, it seemed that the ghost—or at least its rumoured presence on Blue Bell Hill—was real enough to some. I remember the admission of one person, who could otherwise be regarded as level-headed, who told me that he always took the precaution of turning aside his car's rear-view mirror when driving down Blue Bell Hill by himself at night. He had heard that the ghost girl had a penchant for sometimes appearing in the back seats of pass-

ing cars, and in spite of feeling somewhat foolish, he wasn't prepared to have it happen to him.

I have heard this particular anecdote from a few others, it appearing to be one of a number of minor variations associated with the story's basic theme (although such spontaneous back-seat apparitions are certainly not unheard of elsewhere), but it serves to demonstrate the power the ghost story has been able to exercise over the public imagination.

The Haunted Hill

The real impetus toward active research on my part came through my discovery of Michael Goss's *The Evidence for Phantom Hitch-Hikers* (1984),[3] which included a chapter ('The Haunted Hill') that was devoted to Blue Bell Hill. Goss's work confirmed both the content of the rumours in circulation on the oral grapevine, and—most importantly—provided a wealth of detail and references that at last pinned down the story and its possible origin to a specific time frame. Regardless of the merits of the case as a possibly genuine haunting, I could now see that the Blue Bell Hill story was not entirely apocryphal. It had some basis in fact.

The book highlighted the efforts of the late Tom Harber, a blind switchboard operator at the former Oakwood Hospital in Barming (Maidstone) and the pioneering researcher of the case. Mr Harber's interest in the story appears to have been inspired by the 1966 experience of a person known 'extremely well' to him.

The witness, who he interviewed less than twenty-four hours after his encounter, described how, after picking the girl up near the Lower Bell public house, she had talked of her wedding the next day as they drove towards Maidstone. Later (presumably after dropping her off uneventfully in the town), he went to the address the girl had given him to check on her safety, only to discover that she had died a year before on 'the very day' and at the same spot he had picked up the hitch-hiker. In this case, it seems the witness refused to believe that the girl he gave a lift to could possibly have been a ghost.

In due course, Tom Harber claimed to have traced and interviewed eleven further witnesses to the 'Week Street' girl (Week Street was then a busy road through the centre of Maidstone where, in other instances, the girl allegedly vanished),[4] including a Post Office driver and an ambulance driver (both unnamed).[5] Two of the accounts had featured more than one witness, but all described the same pattern of events, with the exception that in some cases the girl wished to travel to Chatham instead of Maidstone. According to Tom, the timings of the encounters also appeared to tally remarkably well, all occurring at 11 p.m. Each of the witnesses had initially taken the girl to be a real flesh-and-blood person, one who declared she was to be married the following day. While it was unusual for a young woman to be hitch-hiking by herself so late in the evening and from such an isolated spot, there was no reason to suspect (quite rationally) that she might be a ghost.

On the face of it, there appeared to be an impressive case for a hitch-hiking apparition on Blue Bell Hill. But as Michael Goss noted, acceptance of this rested on Mr Harber's testimony alone, since his witnesses (in one case at least, by request) remained anonymous, and their accounts were never committed to print.

'Though I stand to be corrected,' stated Goss, 'the first printed reference to the Blue Bell Hill haunt may have appeared in *The Gazette* (Mid-Kent's picture paper, a member of the *Kent Messenger* group) of 10 September 1968.'[6] While I would later be able to correct this statement by locating earlier references,[7] these in no way conflicted with Goss's supposition that the fixing of the rumours in print may have helped define the tale as it was later told.

The Lower Bell pub, at the foot of the Hill. The dual carriageway of the modern A229 passes on the tree-flanked ridge behind

Week Street, Maidstone, where the ghost girl was said sometimes to vanish. Now a busy pedestrianised route through the town

The version presented in this article described a very similar pattern of events to those described by Tom Harber's first witness: the girl is reported to wait by the Lower Bell, and thumbs a lift from a passing Maidstone-bound motorist. She chats busily throughout the journey until, 'somewhere in the vicinity of Week Street', the driver turns around to discover that his passenger has vanished.

'The story is always the same,'[8] remarked the author, implying that the story was unvarying, while carefully evading judgment as to whether this feature supported or refuted the reports as genuine paranormal events.

Tom Harber
(KM Group)

What was puzzling about the article was its reporting of Tom Harber's failure to locate a single witness to the ghost girl after a search of several months: 'I've made enquiries, but there's nothing you can pin down. I've kept asking for a description of the girl—and never got one.'[9]

Implied by this was that Tom Harber's search had begun in 1968, and by September of that year, he had failed to locate even a single first-hand witness to the ghost, let alone the round dozen he would later claim to have traced[10]—which evidently contradicted the

The Phantom Hitch-Hiker (*Evening Post* 19 July 1974) *(KM Group)*

stated date of his first interview, and (according to Goss) the reason for his involvement. Unless he was misunderstood or misquoted, it is difficult to imagine why Tom Harber should have been announcing a negative outcome to his inquiries in 1968 when he supposedly had detailed knowledge of at least one incident two years before.

According to Tom (as told to Goss), his 1966 witness had claimed his passenger had spoken excitedly of her wedding throughout the journey. But while the article painted a similar picture of a voluble young woman, there was *no* description of the content of her speech, and *no* reference to a wedding in the article. Since the versions heard by Tom Harber never themselves made it into print, it followed that the oral versions that *did* include reference to a wedding could not have been inspired by the early newspaper sources. Although printed reference would eventually be made (in 1974) to a car crash on Blue Bell Hill that involved the death of a bride-to-be, those articles paradoxically identified one of the *other* victims of that tragedy as the prospective ghost. And yet the bride-to-be continued to be favoured in many of the oral versions thereafter, possibly as she had before 1968.

I became intrigued with the Blue Bell Hill story initially out of curiosity regarding the mysterious bride-to-be. Why had she featured strongly in some of the oral accounts (after all, this particular version had survived intact for a number of years, until I first heard it in 1981) but not prominently in written accounts, and not *at all* in the earliest published versions?

If the bride-to-be and the impending wedding were genuine features of the earliest oral versions in circulation, then we might question why this very attractive elaboration on the essential story was rather perplexingly overlooked in the preparation of the published accounts.

As stated in the opening chapter, it is not difficult to appreciate the added value the death of a bride-to-be might have in terms of *story* point. The sense of deep sympathy that is naturally evoked in us would make the story memorable (thus ensuring its longevity), and her fateful and untimely death provides the perfect explanation for her return to the world of the living. 'She desperately did not want to die,' commented Tom Harber.[11] And Goss himself stressed the 'emotional or artistic rightness' of the idea of a tragically slain young woman futilely attempting to complete her last journey.[12]

The fact that the bride-to-be (or any association that was later made with the 1965 car crash) was not a feature of the early written accounts led to all sorts of questions regarding the origin of the story. Why, for instance, the discrepancy between Tom Harber's knowledge of the bride-to-be version in 1966 and his apparent public admission of finding no witnesses in 1968? Was the failure of the newspapers to report this aspect a function of its non-existence early in the history of the story, or because of the unwillingness of Tom Harber at the time to impart a possibly useful 'diagnostic' feature to the press, in spite of the interest it would generate?

The desire for answers to these questions would lead me into my own investigation—that, and the simple desire to find out more about the participants of this saga. Michael Goss had chosen to refrain from naming the victims of the 1965 car crash in his work. This was a laudable choice,[13] but all the same it was a little frustrating at this stage. I was curious to know who he was referring to when he described the 'bride-to-be', or the 'Rochester Girl'.[14] When I set out in search of the original archive sources referenced in Goss's book, I had no idea that it would lead one day to meetings and discussions with relatives of some of these people.[15]

What I discovered quite early on was that the inference that the rumours about a ghost may have been originated in 1968 was unfounded. The earliest published reference places the rumours of a hitch-hiking ghost back to at least December 1967, when the *Kent Messenger* printed a brief commentary regarding an account that had come to its attention as genuine, but which, on investigation, had proven impossible to verify.[16]

There is little cause to doubt, therefore, that Tom Harber may have heard such rumours and began his investigation in just the way he related it to Goss, in 1966. This determined, it left open the possibility that the earliest versions of the story, rather than acquiring fitting aspects of the 1965 crash later in its history (i.e. after 1974), may have had this association built in from the very beginning (even if this earliest printed account also omitted any reference to a cause of, or a prospective identity of the ghost). On this assumption, there may just *possibly* have been some justification for the later identification of the 1965 car crash as the cause of the haunting, regardless as to whether the reported encounters with a ghost thereafter were real or imagined. It explained to an extent how this popular version of the story had survived independently in the oral tradition to a slightly different and relatively less appealing 'official' account that was spread abroad by the local press.

Whatever the absolute truth of the matter, we will never know for certain. Tom Harber passed away a few years after Michael Goss interviewed him (in 1983), and long before I began my own research. What *is* certain is that Tom favoured the bride-to-be for the ghost's identity, for reasons we will examine in more detail later. We can be almost as certain that he kept his thoughts and opinions on this matter to himself, never declaring them publicly. This is a point worth remembering when we come to look in more detail for the reasons for the eventual identification of the 1965 crash as the cause of it all.

Michael Goss, aside from introducing and discussing the published history of the Blue Bell Hill case and providing an outline of the 1965 crash, had also pulled together some of the anecdotal support for the haunting. It seemed the ghost could be encountered at various points on the Hill. One resident (a young lady) told him that the Hitch-Hiker had been picked up at the bus stop near the top of the Hill (which I inferred to mean the stop on the Chatham Road near the Salisbury Road junction, rather than the stop then outside the Upper Bell pub further up the Hill in Blue Bell Hill Village) *and* by Medway-bound motorists on the dual carriageway.[17] Evidently, the ghost was not restricted to haunt the precise scene of her demise (which was believed at that time to be the crossroads at the Lower Bell).

This disparity in destination—*north* towards Chatham,[18] or *south* towards Maidstone—has been variously interpreted as evidence of the freedom of movement and will granted on the 'other side',[19] or as indicating the presence of *two* hitch-hiking ghosts, identifiable by character and habit. In these accounts garnered by another Maidstone researcher, Dennis Chambers,[20] the young lady who chats about an impending wedding is identified not as the bride-to-be but one of her companions. The bride-to-be herself is said to be silent (defying how her identification was made, and in contradiction to Tom Harber's picture of a chatty young woman).

According to Goss, Tom Harber believed that *all* of the accounts reflected the

The bus stop halfway up the Hill, and the location of the 1965 tragedy and the scene of Maurice Goodenough's strange encounter in 1974 (Chapter 7)

variable habits of a single ghost, the bride-to-be. In the instances where she wished to travel north, this was because this was the direction she was travelling on the night of her death (which, in fact, turned out not have been the case).[21] The journey south, he supposed, expressed her intention to be taken home (to Maidstone).[22]

Contrary to Tom's views, however, the double ghost hypothesis appeared to be lent some support by the reported sightings of Rochester man David Smith.[23] According to the *Evening Post* of 27 February 1969,[24] Mr Smith claimed to have seen, on several occasions, two pedestrians walking along the roadside at Blue Bell Hill, usually heading up the Hill on the pavement on the left. On two occasions they had vanished in full view, once when he was within a few yards of them as he drove up the Hill; on the other occasion when they walked into the path of an oncoming vehicle, which drove straight through them, leaving no trace.

Goss noted but passed over the obvious comparisons between this account and the Goodenough incident, regarding it as perhaps nothing but an interesting anomaly, since it featured no more. However, problematic as the account may be in terms of detail (Smith's phantom pedestrians are not even identified by gender), it is one that nevertheless finds familiarity through its overt similarity to the Goodenough incident, and to Ian Sharpe's and Chris Dawkins' encounters in 1992, and other incidents that would later come to light.

But the question as to whether there might be more than one ghost, or a single but very mobile one, ignored the fact that there was no very credible evidence for a ghost of any kind, David Smith's vague account and Tom Harber's claims to a number of witnesses notwithstanding. Only Maurice Goodenough's vivid encounter in July 1974 would begin to approach the degree of circumstantial evidence we might be looking for. But even if we were to blindly follow press assertions that this incident represented a genuine encounter with the Blue Bell Hill ghost (which certainly seemed unlikely at the time), the ghost's behaviour—allowing herself to be struck by the witness's vehicle—differed markedly to the accounts that depicted a hitch-hiking apparition.

If the evidence for a hitch-hiking ghost in the Blue Bell Hill case was so weak, why had the popular versions of the story developed in the way they had, and what was it about such stories that allowed them to capture the imaginations of quite wide numbers of people? These questions could only begin to be addressed after I had learned a good deal more about this very unlikely type of ghost.

Michael Goss had discussed the Blue Bell Hill case within the context of a category of apparitions known as *Phantom Hitch-Hikers*. If it was a revelation to discover that the Blue Bell Hill case had a number of parallels (besides Resurrection Mary), it was more so to discover the sheer ubiquity and uniformity of these tales. With so many very similar accounts appearing not only in the British Isles, but worldwide, it seemed that few, if any, could conceivably be true. Consequently, the task I came to set myself, of trying to determine whether the Blue Bell Hill case had any evidential basis in spite of its poor accounting in print, appeared to be doomed to failure from the very beginning. Be that as it may, a proper appreciation of the phenomenon would be essential to an understanding of how such a tale may have become established at Blue Bell Hill.

The next chapter delves a little deeper into the background and the peerage of this suspect, but fascinating class of ghost. In the process of examining the exploits of a sample of the Blue Bell Hill girl's ghostly cousins from around the world, we should be able to more properly assimilate the essential features of the story, and in turn come to a better understanding of the bizarre behaviour exhibited by the ghost in the many witness-attested accounts presented in this book.

FOUR

THE PHANTOM HITCH-HIKER

THE PHANTOM HITCH-HIKER (known in the USA as the *Vanishing Hitch-hiker*) is recognised by folklorists as nothing less than *the* classic transport-focused legend, a popular example of contemporary folklore—an *Urban Legend.*[1]

This 'returning-ghost' tale is one that is told the world over. Indeed, it has been said that wherever there are roads there are likely to be variations of the story.[2] Folklorists argue—and with good reason (and even aside from the subject matter, which proposes that apparitions can actually manifest to hitch rides from unsuspecting motorists)—that the ubiquity of the tale and its incorporation of a common set of easily recognisable narrative points or motifs, clearly designates the Phantom Hitch-Hiker as a creature of folklore. Typical of such legends, the Phantom Hitch-Hiker (or PHH) is a tale told as a supposedly *true* event, often by someone who qualifies this claim by reference to a witness one or two persons removed from themselves (who is customarily anonymous, or proves to be un-traceable), or to a news media source. But, we are told, true events are never so simple or invariable.

The plausibility of urban legends and their setting in contemporary history (the recent past) marks their distinction from traditional tales of myth and folk-lore—which is perhaps why we tend to accept them rather uncritically, particularly when the source of the story is a trusted acquaintance or the media (which, by and large, is not predisposed to the deliberate publication of fictional stories). Nevertheless, apart from the important difference in modern times that such tales are also spread by the media (and nowadays most rapidly and widely by the Internet), they are passed on in the same manner: by word of mouth. In other words, while the story is somewhat innovative compared to the public's concep-tion of the traditional ghost story, it belongs to the same 'oral tradition'.

Folklorists prefer to interpret urban legends as unconscious expressions of our common fears and neuroses, as explorations in the mind of various 'what if...?' scenarios. They are popular because they deal with bizarre, ironic or super-natural themes that invite us to temporarily suspend disbelief in order to milk them of their entertainment, moral, or cautionary value. Urban legends are told and retold in a variety of social settings, and by a cross-section of the population, who quite often fail to recognise that they *are* legends. Not surprisingly, a number of urban legends have found their way into books, television, music, and film. Blue Bell Hill's ghost, for instance, has itself inspired at least one fiction offshoot, and a music track.[3]

Much of the appeal of the Phantom Hitch-Hiker surely lies with the sympathy the story instils for the subject of the tale, the Hitch-Hiker herself—a young woman who has died in tragic circumstances and is forlornly trying to complete her last journey. But it is the 'punch ending'—the sudden and unexpected disappearance of the girl, and the motorist's realisation that he has shared his journey with a ghost—that gives the story its special power. And, most important of all, is its assertion that what is described *actually* happened.

Like other urban legends, the brevity and simple construction of Phantom Hitch-Hiker tales not only ensures that the essential elements are picked up and passed on (usually quite accurately), but also their ready relocation, anywhere and at any time, to local and familiar settings; the nuances of local detail thereby adding to the story's credibility and appeal. The physical setting, then, is likely to be well known to the audience. It is a place sometimes renowned for similar events, and the protagonist is someone known (if indirectly) by the narrator, and a person with whom the audience can readily identify.

Other conventions allow us, as is the folklorist's claim, to predict most variations of the story as they appear from location to location: The ghost—often, but not exclusively, an attractive young woman in white or light-coloured clothing—is, until her disappearance, taken to be a real person. Traditionally appearing on the anniversary of her demise (a victim of a road accident, a passenger or a wayward pedestrian), she attracts the attention of a passing motorist (frequently a lone driver, often male)[4] by various means: by waiting passively by the roadside or walking along it late at night, thereby encouraging the driver to stop and proffer a lift—or, in the classic situation, actively seeking a lift, thumb raised in characteristic hitch-hiker fashion.

Accepting the offer of a lift, the girl (as a matter of choice or circumstance) assumes the back seat of the vehicle (or its equivalent on a motorcycle, the pillion seat). After a short period of time, during which she gives her address, the girl grows quiet, prompting the motorist to look around, only to discover she has vanished. Shaken and perplexed, the driver continues on to the address given, only to learn that he is the latest in a line of motorists to bring the resident's daughter–sister–niece–granddaughter home.

Variations on the theme are plentiful. Sometimes the girl leaves a purse or a handbag on the back seat from which the motorist discovers her identity or her address, to which he then proceeds. At the destination, he may be shown or notice a photograph of the girl, pictured in the same dress in which the ghost had appeared.

In other, more elaborate versions, the motorist responds to his passenger's complaints of being cold and loans her an overcoat or sweater, and returns to collect it the following day. The person answering the door recognises the description as belonging to his/her daughter, a former tenant, and so on, and informs the disbelieving motorist of the familiar story, and directs him to the cemetery where the girl is buried. At the graveside he finds proof of the deceased status of his passenger (confirmed beyond doubt in some instances by the existence of a photograph set into the headstone)—and his loaned garment, neatly folded on the girl's grave. (Both of the above variations, incidentally, have been anecdotally related in respect of the Blue Bell Hill girl.)

With the above in mind, it is fair to say that the majority of Phantom Hitch-Hiker tales must be apocryphal. Wherever the familiar conventions appear piled on one another, and particularly where the protagonist is not forthcoming as a named witness, there can be little serious resistance to the argument that they belong solely to folklore.

But are all tales of this kind dismissible as folklore? The purpose of folklore study is less about determining whether such tales have any evidential basis, but to discern their patterns of dissemination, their internal similarities and variations, their genealogies, and above all, to ascertain *why* these stories are told—what purpose it is they serve in our everyday lives, particularly in our sophisticated modern times. That at least one genuine case may, in some instances, have provided the inspiration for the host of very similar accounts that become accepted and adapted as urban legends, is largely irrelevant. But I suspect that the majority of folklorists would tend to deny the existence of an archetypal event, or at least a traceable one, particularly in the cases with the more bizarre or supernatural themes.

Professor Jan Harold Brunvand, in his book *The Vanishing Hitchhiker: Urban Legends and their Meanings*,[5] points out that attempts to trace the originators of urban legends or to locate actual events to account for them, almost invariably prove futile.

While it is difficult to refute the idea that, as folklorists contend, Phantom Hitch-Hiker stories are but an old recipe served up in a new sauce,[6] is it possible that they are at least based on some modicum of truth? Might the popular versions represent romanticised distillates of one or more, admittedly rare, but true and originally more subtle and internally variable encounters?

The answer of the folklorist would appear to be 'no'. As we have noted, almost all of the characteristics of a typical Phantom Hitch-Hiker account can be anticipated, and this fact, coupled (in the minds of many) with the very impossibility of ghosts, renders them non-starters as far as their consideration as items of potential fact. Even where convention is broken—for instance, where a witness is named—it can be difficult to determine whether this might not simply represent a further bogus detail intended to reinforce its acceptance as a strange-but-true story. Michael Goss observes in his highly recommended analysis of the phenomenon, that whereas the repetition of particular anomalous events worldwide (he cites the commonality of poltergeist incidents)[7] has been used to support arguments favouring the existence of such phenomena, when it comes to apparitions, particularly those exhibiting a very specific mode of behaviour such as the Phantom Hitch-Hiker, the reverse seems to apply—undoubtedly a consequence of their patently artistic adornments.

Clearly, any honest evaluation of the Phantom Hitch-Hiker phenomenon must surely concede that most accounts are suspect. It is therefore a difficult prospect to separate apparently reliably reported accounts of hitch-hiking phantoms from their counterparts in folklore. But this is as it should be. Any account that lays claim as a genuine paranormal event should rightly be subjected to rigorous scrutiny before being accepted as such.

It has been suggested in the foregoing that the historical case of the haunting of Blue Bell Hill, in depicting a hitch-hiking phantom female, is far from unique. In demonstration of the cosmopolitan distribution of the motif, the following section outlines a selection of similar cases, which can be used to test some of the statements made above. Unlike the Blue Bell Hill case, in which I have attempted to verify all reported cases and facts, I cannot vouch for the veracity of the following accounts to the same degree. However, flawed as some may be in this respect, they demonstrate the recurrent features found in Phantom Hitch-Hiker and related accounts around the globe. The exercise, I hope, will prove useful in the forthcoming study of Blue Bell Hill's published history and will, perhaps, throw some light on the rather different behaviour exhibited by Blue Bell Hill's ghost in 1992 and in the numbers of witness-supported accounts that have come to light in the years since.

Resurrection Mary (Chicago, Illinois, USA)

The saga of Chicago's 'Resurrection Mary' (after the cemetery in Justice where she is reputedly buried, and her customary destination) is arguably the most famous phantom hiker tale of all. Here, in the city's south-west suburbs, so the story goes, a girl was killed in a motor accident on Archer Avenue while being driven home from the O. Henry Ballroom (later renamed the Willowbrook Ballroom). One version has Mary arguing with her boyfriend before being killed while trying to hitch a lift home. Having died with the argument foremost in her mind, she is said to repeat her fateful attempts at hitching on the anniversary of her death.

The main gate of Resurrection Cemetery on Archer Avenue in Justice, IL
(MrHarman CC BY-SA 3.0)

The incident is rumoured to have occurred sometime in the 1930s, but the girl, described as an 18-year-old blonde, blue-eyed Polish American, standing about five feet seven, and dressed in a white ballroom gown, has evidently been unable to come to terms with her demise, since she has reportedly been seen a number of times over the years (one source claims she has made more frequent appearances since the cemetery was renovated in the mid-1970s).[8]

Mary's favoured modus operandi, it seems, is to seek lifts from passing lone male drivers (or to force them on the driver by jumping into the vehicle uninvited), who are then guided to the gates of the cemetery where she vanishes. Her speech has sometimes been described as vague, as if confused. In one instance, she was initially suspected as having had 'one too many' to drink.

A variation on the theme involves Mary hitching a lift from a lone male who takes her home, and arranges to meet her for a date the following weekend. When the man turns up for the date, he learns that his would-be companion has been dead for some time. Whichever version is preferred, the consistent feature is that the motorist learns that his passenger is a ghost.

Resurrection Mary has her share of anonymous witnesses, but she has also been encountered by individuals willing to put their name to their story. In 1939, Jerry Palus met a young blonde at a dance, to whom he offered a lift home at the end of the evening. She accepted and directed him down Archer Avenue towards Resurrection Cemetery, where she asked him to stop the car. She told him that she had to cross the street there, and that he could not follow. Before he could respond, she was out of the, car and ran towards the Cemetery gates, where she vanished. At other times, she has either foregone the formality of exiting the vehicle in the conventional manner by passing right through the door, or has managed to enter the cemetery itself before disappearing (whether the gates are

'She was all in white, and her hair and the dress were flowing back like a stream away from her'

open or locked, of course). Palus apparently then understood why the girl had been so cold to the touch when he was dancing with her. Well...quite.

More persuasive, and of special interest on account of its similarity to events at Blue Bell Hill, is the experience in 1978 of Shawn and Geri Lape, who were driving past Resurrection Cemetery when a girl dressed in white ran out in front of their car.

'We are lifelong residents of Chicago and we know the legend of Resurrection Mary,' said Shawn. 'But no-one expects to hit her late one night coming home from their mother-in-law's. I didn't feel anything. There was no bump, no jar. Nothing. It wasn't like we hit a human.' The girl managed to complete her journey to the other side of the road, running towards the cemetery fence before which she vanished.[9]

'Mary' repeated this behaviour a decade later. In October 1989, friends Janet Kalal and Pamela Turlow-Wilson set out for an evening drive. They eventually found themselves driving past Resurrection Cemetery. As they did so, the figure of a woman rushed out in front of the car.

'She was all in white, and her hair and the dress were flowing back; it was like a stream, backwards, away from her, and I just saw this profile of a young woman. There was no impact; there was no bump to say that I had hit something. But

I know she had ran out—the young woman ran in front of my car, and I hit her. And yet, nothing. No impact, no sound, nothing.'[10]

These 'Spectral Jaywalker'[11] accounts, though appearing to be far removed in behaviour from the rather benign approach of the Phantom Hitch-Hiker, actually obey or share many of the conventions found in the typical or idealised Phantom Hitch-Hiker narrative, while at the same time lacking the romantic embellishments of the PHH itself that often prompt dismissal of the latter as a suspiciously fictional ghost. But more on this later.

Baltimore, Maryland (USA)

A girl hitch-hiker wearing a blue cocktail dress was picked up by two Baltimore City College students while driving down Route 40 East. Since they were on their way to a dance, they invited the young woman, described as blonde and attractive. She accepted, and they all went on to an enjoyable evening of dancing and socialising. At the end of the evening, which had turned cold, the students offered her a lift home. She again accepted, and one of the men gave the girl his coat to keep her warm. The journey was uneventful. They dropped her at her home, allowing her to keep the coat, which they would collect the following day. When they returned, an elderly lady answered the door. From their description of the girl the lady was able to tell them that this particular girl had died some ten years before. Naturally, the students were surprised, but could not believe the woman, despite the positive identification made through a match in the girl's name and description. The old lady was able to direct them to the girl's grave in a cemetery nearby, which would provide proof that what she said was true. Going there, they found the girl's headstone, and folded in front of it, the coat that had kept her warm the night before.[12]

Waterlooville, Hampshire (UK)

In November 1976, a man and his wife were driving down the Hulbert Road in Waterlooville, when the man saw a girl ahead, standing in the path of their car. The conditions were not good; daylight was almost out. It was apparent that his wife, who was driving, could see nothing. He cried out, but it was too late. He shut his eyes in anticipation of the impact. But there was none. When he later told his story to a workmate, the man discovered that this girl had been seen on other occasions. It was said that she came from a council estate in Havant called Leigh Park, and had been killed by a car while trying to hitch-hike from Waterlooville.

Another gentleman told the witness that he was once flagged down by a girl outside the cemetery on Hulbert Road. It was a wet evening, and he agreed to give her a lift to an address in Leigh Park. During the journey, the girl spoke very little. Arriving at the address, he turned to let the girl out, but found that she had vanished, the only evidence she had been there being a wet imprint on the seat.[13]

Uniondale (Western Cape Province, South Africa)

On Good Friday in 1980, 20-year-old André Coetzee was riding his motorcycle along the N9 desert road past Uniondale, some 200 miles east of Cape Town, in a search for a friend travelling from Johannesburg who he feared might run out of petrol in the Karoo desert—when, all of a sudden, he felt himself grasped around his waist, as if he had acquired a pillion passenger. Looking down, he was alarmed to actually see hands, and he then realised he had become subject of the attention of the ghost woman of Uniondale. 'Very, very scared', he felt an urge to get away from the area as fast as possible, and started to accelerate along the road. At around 150–160 kph, he suddenly felt three hard wraps on his crash helmet, and then 'she' disappeared, and the witness was left to bring his machine to a stop and find himself alone on the road.

Coetzee's experience stands as one of a number of ghostly encounters on the Uniondale to Willowmore road since a young woman died in a road accident here on Good Friday, 12 April 1968. Since then her ghost is said to wait at the Barandas turn-off on cold, wet nights for a lift.

Reports describing a blonde female hitch-hiker who mysteriously disappears from the pillion seats of other motorcycles have arisen in the years since the accident. An intriguing encounter occurred on 1 May 1976 when Anton Le Grange[14] from Oudtshoorn met a female hitch-hiker some thirteen kilometres from Uniondale. It was dark, around 7.15 p.m. The rain and cold prompted him to offer a lift to the woman, although she was not actually seeking a lift in the traditional manner. She was dressed in dark trousers and jacket; her hair, contrary to that depicted in rumour, was dark, and her face pale. The girl accepted the offer of a lift, giving the address to which she wished to be taken. It was shortly after pulling away that Le Grange thought to question the girl about the destination address, recalling that there was no such street in Oudtshoorn, his own destination. On looking over his shoulder, he found she had disappeared.[15]

The incident was duly reported to Uniondale police. The duty officer at the time, PC Snowy Potgieter, recalled that Le Grange had had been upset but sober, and agreed to drive out to the scene of the incident. On the way out there, the police officer (who was following in his own vehicle) witnessed the right-rear door of Le Grange's car open and close by itself. Le Grange reported that he heard a 'spine-chilling' laugh inside his car. (A slightly different version states that

(Rex Harvey)

Mr Le Grange was driving away from the police station when he heard a horrible scream inside his vehicle, in response to which he immediately turned back. Officer Potgieter then accompanied the witness on the way back to the scene of the incident, during which the door-opening event occurred.)

Officer Potgieter was of the opinion that he had witnessed a genuine paranormal occurrence. Le Grange believed the screaming to be the death cries of this woman, whom he later discovered was the victim of a 1968 road accident.

Le Grange's description of the girl revived some unsettling memories for Potgieter. At around 8 o'clock on the Sunday morning, he confronted a colleague, former police sergeant Pat McDonald, with the memory of a fatal accident of some years before. McDonald had been the first officer at the scene, where he found a Volkswagen Beetle off the road, and a girl lying on her back, her head propped against the embankment. The girl had died of head injuries.

After the Le Grange encounter had been featured in the newspapers a lieutenant in the South African Air Force came forward stating that the incidents involved his fianceé, 22-year-old Maria ('Ria') Charlotte Roux, who had been killed at around 4.30 a.m. on the morning of 12 April 1968 when their car had been blown off an embankment of the desert road near Uniondale by a freak gust of wind. A photograph of her, obtained from her mother by journalist Janie Meyer, was later shown to Le Grange—which, it is said, bore a close resemblance to the Hitch-Hiker. Remarkably, a police sergeant who attended the 1968 crash (who can only be Pat McDonald) apparently recalled that the victim to have been wearing dark green slacks and a navy-blue duffle coat—an impressive feat of recollection, if it is to be accepted.[16]

Another tantalising account concerns South African Army corporal Dawie van Jaarsveld who encountered the girl Hitch-Hiker two years later, at Easter 1978. The conditions were wet. At around 9.35 p.m., the Barandas to Willowmore Road was dark. As in the Coetzee incident, van Jaarsveld was riding a motorcycle. His destination was Louterwater, some 115 miles away, where he was to spend the holiday with his girlfriend. As he approached the isolated intersection, he saw a figure ahead on the roadside. He wasn't intending to stop, but as he made a turn to the right, she raised her arms as if to say, 'Oh no, aren't you going to stop?' Reconsidering, he stopped and offered her a lift, providing her with the spare crash helmet and an earpiece to listen to some music during the journey. The witness remembers telling the girl before they left to hold tight around his waist so that he could feel if anything should go wrong.

'After a few...say a kilometre or two, the bike had a twitch. I thought she fell off. A lot of things went through my mind. I turned around; I wanted to see if I still had somebody with me. There was nobody. I turned around. I went back with the motorcycle, [and I] looked to see if there was anybody lying in the road.'

Van Jaarsveld backtracked, swerving his motorcycle across the road so that the beams of his headlight might illuminate the girl, but all that he discovered was a repeat performance of the bumping sound. This, he discovered, was caused by the spare helmet which was now attached to the luggage rack. 'Then I got a fright...I saw the helmet. It was back on [the bike]; the earphone was just lying there (which was later found to be unusable, the adaptor jack somehow having been melted). And I just had to move off, because I realised then I didn't actually pick someone up.'[17]

Badly shaken, van Jaarsveld made straight for Uniondale, where he found the Petros café, which he entered in such a state that the proprietress immediately concluded that he had met the Phantom Hitch-Hiker. His description of the girl tallied with that given by others: not very tall, a girl with short dark (brunette) hair, wearing slacks and a jersey. He had no impression before her disappearance that she might have been a spirit, although it did feel strange.

One version states that Mr van Jaarsveld also later identified his passenger from a photograph of a road accident victim—the very same Maria Roux.

One of the theories that attempts to explain why the spirit of Maria Roux should not have found rest is that she is said to have been fast asleep at the time of the accident, and was therefore unable to prepare herself for death. Janie Meyer, the journalist who approached the girl's mother with the story following

Anton Le Grange's encounter, believes that Maria, who was in the process of finalising plans for her wedding (the couple's journey on the night of the accident had been with the intention of discussing their plans with Maria's parents in Riversdale) will carry on until she manages to reach her destination.[18]

Footnoting the Uniondale case is the suggestion that the area of the Barandas turn-off has a second ghost. On 30 October 1978, an eerily similar accident occurred here when a vehicle carrying another newly engaged couple mysteriously left the road and overturned. The 20-year-old female occupant was thrown from the car and died of head injuries.

According to the young lady's sister, a few months before her death, she had dyed her hair blonde and wore a white dress at the time of the accident—making apparent sense of the accounts that depicted the ghost girl with blonde hair and a white outfit rather than the usually darker hair and clothing of the original ghost.[19]

At around 9 p.m. on 19 May 1994, Roald Loots (47), a retired teacher of Bloemfontein, was on the long drive to Herolds Bay when, approximately ten miles outside Uniondale, 'suddenly a woman in a white sweater and white trousers stood in the middle of the road. She smiled and motioned me to stop.' Mr Loots stopped his car in the road, and then, inexplicably, he turned off the lights and fell asleep with his head on the steering wheel. About half an hour later, he was woken by the beam of a policeman's torch in his face. With shock, he recalled his encounter with what must have been the ghost woman, and realised the grave danger he had been in as heavy vehicles also used the road.[20]

But if the above account would seem to endorse the idea of a second ghost related to a more recent accident victim, the experience of Cradock residents Leonard Fraser and his wife Catherine, on Easter Friday in 1973, suggests a more complex picture.

'We were on our way to Oudtshoorn,' said Mr Fraser. 'At around midnight I stopped the car on the Willowmore–Uniondale road and got out to stretch my legs. The road was deserted when I got out but suddenly a figure dressed in a long white dress appeared beside me. I got such a fright that I dived straight back into the car and drove off. As I tore off down the road I could still see the figure standing there.'

'It was definitely a woman dressed in a long white gown,' said Mrs Fraser. 'The most terrifying thing was that I could see through her. I know people are going to laugh at me but what's true is true and I really saw her.'[21]

Some place rumours of a ghost girl along this stretch of road much further back than either tragedy, to as early as 1928.[22]

Bulawayo (Zimbabwe)

A female ghost reportedly terrorises motorists (usually male) along the Old Esigodini Road near Bulawayo by stopping them for a lift and then vanishing shortly afterward, leaving motorists terrified to offer lifts to females late at night.

Khumbulani Mhlanga stopped for a woman late one night on his journey out of town, but before he reached Hotel Rio at the Waterford turn-off, the woman was nowhere to be seen.

'I saw a woman stopping me and since it was already late I decided to help her out. When she got in the car we started chatting.

'I did not stop for her to disembark but after I had made a turn towards Waterford there was no-one on the passenger side where she was seated. Fear gripped me to a point where I failed to drive and at the same time I could not stop because I thought she could come back for me.'

Another witness, Tendai Shoko, came forward in June 2012 to claim that he had stopped for the woman on Old Esigodini Road near Bulawayo Country Club, between Hotel Rio and Bulawayo.

'The woman was extremely beautiful and I did not suspect that there was something wrong with her but as she approached the door to get inside, fear suddenly gripped me.' He decided to lock the doors.

'To my utter surprise she opened the door on the passenger side despite it being locked.'

According to the witness, the woman just sat in the car and never said anything or where she wanted to go. Shoku decided to drive off, while puzzling over his passenger's demeanor.

'Moments later, when I had gathered enough guts to ask her who she was, there was no-one on the seat,' said Shoku, who said the incident had given him the 'shock of his life'.

Manningdale resident Bathabile Ndlovu also claimed an encounter with the ghost: 'I stopped for her just after midnight at Leeside, but I got a shock of my life when she walked into the car without opening the door. She walked right through the car and came out on the other side. I will never stop for anyone again, lest I pick up a ghost,' she said.

The ghost is reported to have been tormenting motorists for more than a year.[23]

The Belchentunnel, Eptingen (Switzerland)

Switzerland's most famous Phantom Hitch-Hiker is the 'White Lady of the Belchentunnel'—an older woman, dressed in white, who haunts the hard shoulder of the motorway N2 near the entrance of a long road tunnel known as the Belchentunnel. When motorists stop to offer the woman a lift, she accepts but only wishes to travel to the other side of the tunnel. During the short journey she is said to exclaim that something terrible will happen. The motorist, turning to question her as to what she means by this, finds she has vanished.

Inquiries made to police have provided confirmation that reports of this nature were received from time to time, and that a number of fatal accidents had occurred in the tunnel, none of which could be connected with the ghost.

One encounter took place on 26 September 1983, when two women gave the ghost a lift through the tunnel. The woman had appeared pale and ill. When asked, the woman confirmed that she was feeling unwell and was grateful for the lift. During the journey, and again in response to one of the women's inquiries as to whether she was feeling any better, the woman replied that she wasn't, and that something awful would happen. The front passenger turned to face the woman, but found she had vanished from the back seats. With only two doors, there was no way she could have got out in the conventional manner. In a state of some shock, the women stopped at the earliest opportunity to search the car and call the police.[24]

From the above, it may be evident that some common features (other than the basic format itself) are shared by all. The female Hitch-Hiker, having died in a motor-related accident, is engaged in a repetitious re-enactment of her last journey, and/or search for the love and happiness she has been denied. Resurrection Mary had argued with her boyfriend, and was killed before she could make up. Maria Roux, in the Uniondale case, was engaged to be married, and was in the process of finalising her wedding arrangements (inviting comparison to the Blue Bell Hill case, in which a bride-to-be sustained fatal injuries on the eve of her wedding).

Several of the accounts involve cemeteries, either as the picking up or dropping off point for the girl Hitch-Hiker, or the place to which the motorist proceeds after the encounter where he finds proof as to the objective reality of the experience.

Some of the accounts are almost certainly spurious (Baltimore). Others seem contrived, but, unusually, name a witness (Jerry Palus's encounter with Resurrection Mary). Others are more intriguing (Uniondale; other sightings of Resurrection Mary; Bulawayo).

Another common feature is the girl's attire, usually white—a white evening dress, a white mackintosh (both, incidentally, have also been described of the Blue Bell Hill girl). In many of the cases in Western settings, involving Caucasian females, they frequently have fair hair—Resurrection Mary, the Baltimore girl, and some versions describing the Blue Bell Hill girl, among others.

With so many parallels in detail, between these accounts and the predicted elements of the folk versions, it is easy to appreciate how even named-witness accounts tend to fall before the contentions of folklorists. Like-for-like 'type' descriptions can only support this viewpoint. Interestingly though, the more detailed, and perhaps more convincing reports involve departures from these 'types'. While a reasonable deduction could be made to suppose that local changes of detail had been made to help the localisation of the story, it is intriguing that in certain cases particular details such as the style and colour of clothing and hair remain consistent from report to report, and that these are not necessarily white-attired blondes (quite naturally, of course, in different racial or cultural settings).

Perhaps the most obvious characteristic of these cases, and possibly overlooked for this reason, is that the hitch-hiking spirit is *female.* While it seems that the vast majority are female, there are cases in which male Hitch-Hikers have been encountered.

Stanbridge, Bedfordshire (UK)

In October 1979, Roy Fulton, a 26-year-old carpet fitter, met a Phantom Hitch-Hiker on the outskirts of Stanbridge, Bedfordshire. He had left a darts match in Leighton Buzzard at around 9.20 p.m., and was driving through Stanbridge along Station Road on his way home to Dunstable. As he passed Peddars Lane (on his left) he saw, approximately a hundred metres ahead where the street lights ended, a man at the roadside thumbing a lift. Fulton deliberately stopped short and watched the man as he walked toward his Minivan in the light of its headlamps. The man, about twenty years of age, wore dark trousers and jumper, and a white open-collared shirt. Opening the passenger door himself, he got into the vehicle. He did not speak, even when Mr Fulton asked him where he was going. Instead, the man raised his arm and pointed up the road, so Fulton assumed he wanted to go to either Dunstable or Totternhoe. A few minutes later, after the car had reached around 40 mph and about a mile down the road, the man had still not uttered a word. Fulton decided to offer him a cigarette, but on turning toward him he found the seat was empty. Stunned, he braked and checked the back seat, but finding nothing he turned back and drove away as fast as he could.

Fulton later described his passenger as totally real, very solid. There was no reason to suspect he was anything other than a normal human being. There had been nothing particularly unusual about him, except his complexion, which was pale, and his rather long face, which was topped off by a crop of short dark curly hair.

Station Road, Stanbridge, where Roy Fulton picked up a phantom hitch-hiker in 1979. (Looking north in the direction of Peddars Lane)

When the stranger had opened the passenger door, the interior light of the van came on as expected. The journey began, and there was no further communication between the driver and passenger. Fulton explained that he could not be sure exactly at which point the man had gone, but it must have been within a span of a few minutes. As anyone who has driven on country roads at night might appreciate, there may be little exchange with a passenger in the seat beside you, particularly if that person is unable or reluctant to talk—the latter being Fulton's explanation to himself as to why the man had pointed ahead along the road rather than declare his destination.

After he had absorbed the significance of the disappearance, fear gripped him, and he made off as fast as possible to his local pub in Dunstable, The Glider, where he uncharacteristically ordered a large Scotch, before proceeding to Dunstable Police Station to report his experience. A car was sent to the spot, and Fulton's statement taken without comment. Needless to say, nothing unusual was discovered. Mr Fulton did not go back out to the spot with them, and reportedly avoided the area at night thereafter. According to the *Dunstable Gazette* of 18 October 1979, it was rumoured that 'years ago' a young man had been run down and killed by a drunk driver while returning home from a party. His body had been discovered at the same spot Fulton had picked up the Hitch-Hiker.[25]

Borley, Essex (UK)

A similar experience to Roy Fulton's befell Jean Clarke, of Fobbing, Essex. Mrs Clarke, who had been a British spy in Germany before the Second World War, found that she had acquired a strange and unbidden passenger one winter's night in 1949 or 1950 during a journey to Bury St Edmunds:

> I was driving my shooting-brake, alone except for Buff, my cocker spaniel, on the Suffolk–Essex border. I got lost and pulled up to look at my map by the light of the dash-board. Suddenly, Buff, sitting in the back, began to howl. He was standing up, stretched out, staring at the front passenger seat. His fur was bristling. It was then that I saw, sitting beside me, a man dressed in a long, out-dated, cloak-collared fawn coat. I thought it strange that I had not seen him or heard him enter the car, but I had been deeply engrossed in the map.

The man then pointed forward, by which Mrs Clarke assumed that her strange companion wanted a lift. The atmosphere in the car had become very cold. She started off again, but they had not travelled more than forty yards before he motioned her to stop. 'Then,' said Mrs Clarke:

> … he just floated through the door. I thought he must have opened it silently while I was watching the road ahead. All the time the man was in the car my dog howled, his hair on end. Shortly afterwards I discovered that I was in the village of Borley, though at the time it had no significance to me, for I was in Germany before the war when Mr Price was investigating the Borley hauntings. It was only when I read of the headless coachman in the Sunday Express last week that I realised that it was quite possible it was he I had given a lift to. It had been too dark to see the man clearly. [26]

A38 Willand to Taunton, Somerset (UK)

An account that has been recounted more than once involves the A38 between Willand and Taunton in Somerset, where motorists have described encounters with a rather bedraggled figure of a middle-aged man in a long grey overcoat.

In 1970, Mrs Kathy Swithenbank of Taunton swerved to avoid the man, who was standing in the middle of the road, holding a torch. She had had no time to brake on seeing him, and he was no longer visible behind when she completed the manoeuvre. The publication of her account prompted others to volunteer their experiences. One lorry driver thought he had run into someone but when he got out to investigate, the figure vanished; while a motorcyclist is said to have broken a leg as a result of swerving to avoid a similar figure four miles west of Mrs Swithenbank's encounter.

The most interesting—and disturbing—encounter involved former long-distance lorry driver Harold Unsworth, who claimed a series of encounters with a seemingly well-educated grey-haired man in 1958. On three occasions, each at around 3 a.m. and in foul weather, he had given a man a lift from the Blackbird Inn on the A38 to Beam Bridge, by the Holcombe Rogus crossroads. The man was saturated; his curly grey hair fell almost to his grey or cream-coloured mackintosh, and each time he had been carrying a torch. During the journey, the man morbidly described the accidents that had taken place along the road in the past. The driver was more than relieved to discharge his passenger at his destination.

Although disturbed by the experience, Unsworth had no reason to suspect his passenger to be in any way ghostly—not, that is, until the following November. On this occasion, instead of the meeting ending with the man simply alighting at the usual bridge destination, he asked Mr Unsworth if he would wait while he collected some cases and then drop him off at another point further down the A38. Unsworth agreed, but after a wait of twenty minutes in which the man had failed to reappear, he continued on his way. However, three miles down the road, by Morgan's Transport café, he saw a figure in his headlights waving a torch. At first he thought it to be a motorist in trouble, but he quickly realised, to his astonishment, that it was the man in grey, who was shaking a fist at him.

The A38 at the Blackbird Inn, near Wellington, Somerset, near where Harold Unsworth picked up his sinister passenger in 1958 *(Phil Hussey)*

Unsworth realised there was no way the man could have got there so quickly. No other vehicle had passed him which may have given the man a lift. He tried to drive past him, but the figure leapt in front of his lorry. There was no sense of an impact. Unsworth braked to a halt. He jumped from the cab and ran back to see what had happened, only to see the man standing in the road again, shaking his fist and cursing at having been left behind. Then, as he watched, the figure turned his back on him and vanished instantly. Mr Unsworth, his hair suddenly standing on end, ran back to the lorry and drove off as fast as he could.[27]

Pluckley, Kent (UK)

A well-known haunted locality, the village of Pluckley, near Ashford, Kent, purportedly the most haunted village in England with twelve claimed ghosts, perhaps not surprisingly, has added its own Phantom Hitch-Hiker to its ghostly repertoire. In 1996, the television series *Strange But True?* related the unnerving experience of taxi driver Raymond Breakspear. Mr Breakspear was driving through the village after dropping off a fare at Headcorn, when he was flagged down by a figure at the side of the road. The time was around 2.45 a.m. to 3 a.m. Surprised, but not about to ignore the opportunity for a return fare, he pulled over, and the figure (a man) got into the back of the cab (appropriately for taxi passenger and Phantom Hitch-Hiker alike). Pulling away, Breakspear turned to ask where the man was going, assuming he would be heading either to Ashford or to Maidstone, but the figure had vanished. He had heard no sign of the door opening, neither had the interior light come on. There had been no way, he said, that someone could have got out without his knowledge.[28]

Aside from the difference that the Hitch-Hiker is male, the familiar format is generally adhered to. Why a female should be more commonly encountered than a male in these situations has been interpreted as having sexual connotations—that male drivers would naturally encounter female phantoms, and perhaps conversely. While this is a reasonable assumption as far as a folklorist viewpoint is concerned, it is not one that is upheld rigorously outside the folklore narrative. We will explore the possible reasons why the majority of Phantom Hitch-Hikers are female in more detail in a later chapter, but perhaps we should look more to the gender of the driver rather than the Hitch-Hiker to give some clue to why this apparent discrepancy occurs.

Few may dispute that lone night drivers are more likely to be male than female. The potential dangers related to women travelling alone are widely acknowledged. So much more significant is the advice towards caution for female hitch-hikers. Having established some probability that lone motorists are more likely to be male, it can be seen that this fulfils one requirement of the popular story. And if he were to come across a lone female hitch-hiker inappropriately dressed for the conditions, is not a male driver more likely to stop to offer a lift than not?

The significance of rainfall in these encounters should be obvious. It applies equally to cases which give little or no supporting evidence, e.g. where witnesses are named only in terms of occupation, and where other specific details are lacking—essentially the neat and well rounded versions perpetuated in urban legends—*and* those cases that are supported by corroborating detail that lends much to the credibility granted to the witnesses (the Uniondale case seems to be a worthy example). Here, rainfall becomes an almost necessary element of the experience, since the poor conditions weigh on the conscience of the motorist in favour of picking up a hitch-hiker where he might ordinarily avoid doing so. (A counter-argument, of course, is that some motorists, protective of their vehicle's upholstery, may regard the plight of a wet hitch-hiker less than sympathetically!)

In what we might call the 'folk' version, inclement conditions could be seen to be supportive of the story itself. In other words, it adds to the ambience of the tale, and a raconteur is more likely to include poor conditions than not. Michael Goss addresses this point: 'The persistence of the 'It was a dark and stormy night' type of opening through Gothic fiction and folk-equivalent right up to modern times is beyond critical dispute.'[29]

Whether for artistic reasons or out of realistic description, the dark, wet night element of many Hitch-Hiker cases can be used as a diagnostic tool (in addition to descriptions of dress, etc) to analyse the report for its factuality. Weather conditions for particular dates and times are objective details that can be checked more readily than many other aspects of a claimed real encounter. Such adds no corroboration to the encounter itself, but it provides additional support to the testimony if proven to be accurate. Conversely, where the conditions do not match those claimed, the discrepancy may lead us to re-evaluate the story as a whole, focusing either on the witness as the direct source of the information, or on an author or journalist bent on 'improving' the story for the benefit of his or her readership.

Certainly, some authors seem unable to resist the temptation to include them. An article that appeared in the *Kent Messenger* of 26 July 1974, includes the line: 'It began on a cold, wet Thursday night...'[30] The journalist, Nigel Nelson, was referring to the accident of November 1965 that has been popularly connected with the ghost of Blue Bell Hill, but the description of the conditions would appear to be instinctual rather than factual—although I have been able to establish that the conditions were not good that (Friday) night. Indeed, the *Chatham News* of 3 December 1965 reports that November of that year was particularly wet, with rainfall on seventeen days of the month.[31] Still, the relevance of rainfall to the original accident as a possible contributory factor is no reason for it to be evoked consistently in appearances of the ghost, unless it is supposed that similar conditions must be approximated in order for its manifestation to occur.

From the above accounts, the by-now familiar Hitch-Hiker theme should be recognisable. But in a few cases, the hitch-hiking habit appears alongside or even subservient to a different kind of behaviour, as demonstrated to good effect by Shawn and Geri Lape's experience outside Resurrection Cemetery; by the A38's 'Man in a Mackintosh', and, of course, by the incidents at Blue Bell Hill itself. The habit of stepping out or throwing oneself in front of a vehicle is a puzzling and, in its own way, more disturbing assault on the motorist's sensibilities than the discovery that their passenger has vanished en route.

The act of standing in the path of the vehicle features in some of the other accounts above. The motive (if any exists) seems to fail as an attempt at meaningful communication, as in the case of the hitch-hiking phantom and other purposeful ghosts. Rather, it appears to be aimed at inducing horror, for reasons we can only guess.[32]

Interestingly, the action appears to be integral in what we might consider to be the more convincing encounters—those providing specifics such as named witnesses, locations, dates, times, and so on, that we expect from 'real' situations.

We might speculate whether, had the motorist sufficient time or inclination to stop in these instances, the story might have ended similarly with a disappearing passenger? The question evokes some degree of conjecture, not least as to the possible origin of the Phantom Hitch-Hiker motif itself.

Earlier it was noted that Phantom Hitch-Hiker and the Spectral Jaywalker accounts actually share many of the same conventions. These can be summarised as follows:

- The ostensibly real, transport-focused apparition, often but not exclusively a young woman or girl attired in white or pale clothing (a staple not only of PHH apparel but of many other apparitions in popular tradition).
- The high incidence of lone motorists.
- The nonsensical behaviour and sudden disappearance of the figure (whether an accident victim or hitch-hiking passenger, the effect on the witness is the same).
- In the Blue Bell Hill case of 1992, the apparent conformity to the anniversary sub-motif.

Is it possible that the Phantom Hitch-Hiker story might have evolved from less fanciful but possibly more likely and evidentially acceptable encounters involving wayward ghostly pedestrians (which are certainly not uncommon in parapsychological literature)? Or are we limiting ourselves with such a view—that since these accounts are furnished with convincing sounding details that depart from the 'pure' Phantom Hitch-Hiker format, we automatically judge them to be more 'true' and dismiss the Hitch-Hiker aspects as embroidery on the 'fact'? If this is the case, then what becomes of cases like Uniondale or Stanbridge which are both convincing in detail and which apparently do not stray from the Phantom Hitch-Hiker format (or, as we shall see, the few first-hand accounts of Phantom Hikers given by motorists in the Blue Bell Hill case)?

Whether we are dealing with specific types of behaviour, or a combination of the Hitch-Hiker and Jaywalker motifs, we are left still with unanswered questions, not least of which is whether any of these reports in any way accurately describe real encounters with phantoms on our roads?

Variations

Phantom Hitch-Hikers belong to a wider set of ghosts which haunt our highways. Road ghosts take many forms, one of which has already been introduced in relation to the Phantom Hitch-Hiker—the would-be road accident victim, which is more commonly reported than its hitch-hiking counterpart. Certainly, these accounts are evidentially better supported.

One that bears similarity to the aforementioned A38 phantom is reported of the A12 near Hopton, Norfolk. The ghost of an old man, tall, with grey straggly hair, has been seen often, and has even been in collision with vehicles. On 2 November 1981, Andrew Cutajar saw the figure too late as it stood in the middle of the road. His vehicle passed through it and spun out of control onto the grass verge. A number of single car accidents have mysteriously occurred at the spot, and similar sightings have been made at various points along the A12.[33]

In addition to the shades of people, there are examples of phantom vehicles—carriages and carts, plus cars, buses and bicycles—in fact, just about every form of transport; even phantom sections of road.[34] It would seem that our roads are a common setting for haunting events, as if they were not busy enough.

If we accept that not all reports of phantom vehicles are spurious, it brings us to question our interpretation of what ghosts actually are, particularly those that suggest they represent the restless souls of the departed who have passed over in tragic or violent circumstances. How can inorganic materials be accounted for by this premise?

Some road ghosts might be classified as Phantom Hitch-Hikers although they differ somewhat from the familiar scenario. The appearance of a ghost in the back of a car has already been touched upon in reference to the Blue Bell Hill case, but an actual example is a different proposition. Footnoting its coverage of the Blue Bell Hill case, the *Sunday People* of 14 July 1974 related the experience of Derek Halliwell, a taxi-driver of Kendal, Westmorland. Mr Halliwell was setting out in an empty cab on one occasion when, in his rear-view mirror, he saw the figure of an older lady in the rear seat. When he turned, she had disappeared. A regular passenger provided the 'explanation' when he told of the crash involving the same cab two years previously in which an elderly woman had been killed.[35]

There may be a case for considering haunted taxis as a distinct and fashionable sub-category, for in November of the same year an almost identical experience came to light. In this, Brian Mohan was driving along the A6 to Stockport when he caught a glimpse of what appeared to be someone in the back of his cab via his off-side mirror. The rear-view mirror, he was startled to find, framed the image of a mature lady. Continuing on his journey, he took the opportunity to examine the image more closely. The figure remained, sitting still and upright. She was fifty to sixty years old, with long hair, and wearing a black overcoat, white blouse, and a black bow. He knew he had not stopped to pick up anyone since dropping off his last fare. But there she was. He decided he would have to stop, so he pulled in as soon as he could. When he turned round to pull aside the glass partition, he discovered that the woman had vanished. He checked the vehicle and street carefully, but could find no sign of her. For months afterwards, the black cab reportedly remained in the firm's yard. None of the drivers were prepared to take it out.[36]

Do we view the similarity in the above accounts as coincidence, or is there something else at play here? How do we account for essentially the same story occurring only months apart in adjacent counties? The answer might lie in part with the newspaper coverage which, in both cases, was national. Much of the believability comes from the details, particularly the named witness. There is less resistance to acceptance of an account if it appears that someone has willingly put their name to it. The handling and credibility of such material by newspapers will be subject to criticism within the context of the Blue Bell Hill case later, but for the moment let us briefly consider why our roads are apparently so haunted.

We live in age where travel by road is the most common form of conveyance. Despite man-made disasters that are singularly tragic in terms of loss of life such as aircraft, ship and rail disasters, death tolls on roads consistently outstrip these so as to represent the most common form of untimely and violent death. In October 1995, it was reported that the figure of half a million road deaths had been reached on British roads since records began. In the period 2002–2012, there were 2,377,122 reported casualties, which included 305,759 serious injuries and 29,744 fatalities.[37] Is it any wonder that roads and modern vehicles should be subject for hauntings? Where some accept a correlation between scenes of tragic death and hauntings, it is natural to expect such stories to come to light.

If only all road or vehicle hauntings were in some way connected with tragedy. However, this is simply not the case. In many encounters, there is no obvious cause for the sightings. It may be that they occur in the same manner as other haunting events where the ghosts appear in familiar surroundings—only, in the case of a vehicle, the haunted 'spot' is mobile, which seems to preclude it as a subject for a haunting since we usually regard such locations as fixed (e.g. buildings).

In the twenty-first century, commuting by private or public transport is a common and habitual practice. This in itself might provide us with a clue as to the apparent popularity of road ghosts in this day and age. It might be natural for confused 'spirits' to gravitate to the relatively mundane practice that occupied much of their time in life, such as travelling to work or returning home. Or their presence perhaps speaks more for the folklorist argument—particularly in regard to the Phantom Hitch-Hiker—which suggests that old and popular stories relocate themselves in space and time and, employing the modern trappings of the day, adapt themselves to remain in fashion.

Certainly, the advent of cheap and reliable transport would assist both in generating stories of spectral travelling companions (well versed in traditional folklore) and in spreading them far and wide. Is it coincidence that the account that I earlier suggested might serve as the modern archetypal Phantom Hitch-Hiker account (or at least, one of the better known)—Resurrection Mary—is said to originate in the 1930s, the same decade in which the motor car saw the beginnings of affordability with the masses?

FIVE

AGAINST THE LORE

FOLKLORISTS have been successful in classifying most variations of the Phantom Hitch-Hiker story, as we have already noted. One system of folklore classification, devised by E. W. Baughman—the Baughman Index —categorises a particular motif with a code, with each variation or elaboration of a motif represented by a suffix. The anniversary Hitch-Hiker, for instance, is described under E332.3.3.1(a); the meeting of a ghost on the road is E.332.2; the ghost that walks at midnight is E.587.5, and so on.

A more palatable system, devised by American folklorists Richard K. Beardsley and Rosalie Hankey from a study in 1942–43, classifies them under the letters A to D. Their conclusions were based on an analysis of seventy-nine cases gathered from across the United States. While they identified four distinct categories, distinguishable from one another by 'obvious differences in development and essence', the story was, they believed, essentially the same one, with the type A version serving as the 'original' story.

These types can be summarised as follows:

VERSION A: The classic address-giving Hitch-Hiker. A motorist (in the vast majority of cases, a lone male, often single) encounters a girl late one night standing alone along an isolated stretch of road. Accepting the offer of a lift, the girl assumes the back seat of the vehicle. Giving her address, the driver proceeds to the house, only to find on arrival that the girl has vanished. The occupant(s) of the house confirm that his description of the girl matches that of a daughter/fiancée, etc., who had been killed at the very spot he had picked up the girl several years before.

VERSION B: The prophesying woman. Encountered in identical fashion to the Version A Hitch-Hiker, it is here that the similarities largely end. The returning ghost theme is subservient to another: prophecy. Characteristically an old woman (sometimes taken to be a nun), the Version B Hitch-Hiker issues warnings of a coming catastrophe. In this instance, the Hitch-Hiker's vanishing act and/or the driver's subsequent discovery that his passenger could not have been a living person serves to further convince the listener of the veracity of the prediction.

VERSION C: Cases (with the exception of those showing a degree of contamination by certain features of the Version A story) in which the title 'Hitch-Hiker' is something of a misnomer, since a social venue—a dance, nightclub, or a bar—serves as the meeting place with the girl. As common an element as this may be, the defining characteristic of the Version C story is its ending at a cemetery. In common versions of the story, the girl's complaint of feeling cold is met with the motorist's loan of an item of clothing, for which he later returns. Disbelieving that the young woman he describes could have been a ghost, he is directed by the house's occupant to the local cemetery, where, folded neatly over the headstone of the girl's grave, he finds his jacket. In other versions of the story, the girl may request to be dropped off outside, or is discovered to have vanished after driving past a cemetery.

VERSION D: Where the Hitch-Hiker is associated with a higher order of being—an angel, a goddess, or some form of localised deity.[1]

In terms of our interest in the Blue Bell Hill case, we can more or less restrict our attention to Versions A and C, although the Version B and D characters have some bearing on the case, as we shall see.

From these outlines, we can immediately see how some of the cases described in the preceding chapter fit into these categories. Resurrection Mary is clearly a Version C Hitch-Hiker, while the most popular version of the Blue Bell Hill story, based on the information given thus far on her, can be categorised as a Version A—the 'purest' and most popular of the versions in circulation.

From their study, Beardsley and Hankey identified a number of other characteristics common to all or specific to particular versions, many of which will prove relevant to the study ahead:

- With a few exceptions, the Hitch-Hiker experience is a nocturnal event—that is, it generally takes place after dark. In a number of cases, the hour is 'downright late'. A few cases make specific mention of midnight as the time of the encounter.
- The weather, as we have seen, is usually poor, be it cold, wet, windy—'anything but pleasant'.
- The Hitch-Hiker is, without exception, female. Variations occur only with regard to age. Excluding those cases where no estimate of age is given, we find a distinct contrast between young females and old women, with the

young females forming the majority: 47 cases (59 percent) to 14. Outside of the inclement conditions that in many cases provide a logical reason to offer a ride to the Hitch-Hiker, this separation in age serves the same purpose, where it is the attractiveness of the girl, or the sight of an enfeebled old woman that prompts the driver to stop. Certain variants include additional reasons for the motorist to stop: the girl may have an armful of books; the woman, a heavy bag; and the old woman, a basket. Some of these items may be found in the vehicle after the Hitch-Hiker's disappearance, serving as objective proofs of the encounter.

- In the majority of cases (58 percent), the Hitch-Hiker appears to a lone man. The remainder of the time, the driver is accompanied by one or more persons, which may include his wife, his family, or other persons. The different versions show certain biases. Version A, for instance, shows a random variation of witness groupings, but a marked preponderance of single men. Version B—the prophesying woman—more often attracts the sympathy of a married couple or a family driving along the highway.
- The Hitch-Hiker's dress is never coloured, but may be black or white. The dress itself is usually quite conventional but may, in certain over-elaborate cases, resemble a shroud or the grave clothes of the deceased.
- The circumstances and time of the pick-up may vary according to which version is encountered. Version B is more likely to be met during the daytime, while Version C—the girl who is characteristically 'picked up' at a place of entertainment—is, for this reason, encountered exclusively at night. The Version A girl, we are told, is less particular about her timing, preferring to express her individuality through appearances mainly to lone drivers. Statistically, one can most often expect to encounter the Hitch-Hiker on the open highway. However, as befitting an urban legend, the street corner of a city is also popular. If, however, we take into account the versions proper, we find that Version B, for instance, is encountered only outside of a city. Since prophecy is also the exclusive domain of the old woman of the Version B (never a young woman), if we are looking for a prophecy, we should do well to heed Beardsley's and Hankey's advice and stay in the country.
- In most cases the title 'hitch-hiker' is an inappropriate one, since the Hitch-Hiker is offered a lift without actually asking for or appearing to expect one. The full title—Vanishing Hitchhiker, to take the American idiom—is particularly inappropriate as a description of the Version C since the girl is neither hitch-hiking nor vanishes at the end of the encounter.
- A noteworthy feature of many stories is the Hitch-Hiker's preference for travelling in the back seat of the vehicle, from where she can vanish unobserved. This feature is common to all versions except Version C, in which the

girl quite reasonably takes the seat next to the driver. Only in two of the cases collected by Beardsley and Hankey in which the Hitch-Hiker vanishes does the driver actually observe the disappearance. The greater majority of Version A Hitch-Hikers[2] vanish, compared to one third for Version B, and none in the case of Version C. Usually the fact of the disappearance stands without elaboration or reason. Confirmation of the driver's fears—the proof that his passenger was a ghost—is put off until the inevitable visit to the girl's former home. Sometimes, however, the Hitch-Hiker will vanish after crossing a stream or, more significantly, passing a cemetery, the circumstances of the disappearance in these cases bringing the driver to a premature realisation of what has befallen him.

- What distinguishes Version C from the other versions (at least in its uncontaminated form) is not only does it lack the disappearance, but it is the only version where the girl sometimes alights at a cemetery.
- The driver obtains proof of the encounter by various means. Frequently the source of this is the mother of the Hitch-Hiker or other relation, or a new resident of the girl's former home, but may include a host of other sources—the police, a neighbour, a shopkeeper.
- In a number of cases, the driver learns that his passenger suffered a violent death. Most commonly associated with Version A or its variants, around half of Beardsley's and Hankey's caseload of violent deaths involved automobile accidents, and in three-quarters of these (around 36 percent of the total) the Hitch-Hiker was killed at precisely the spot where she was picked up.
- Around 30 percent of the time, the Hitch-Hiker's appearance is a repeated one. In 10 percent of cases the Hitch-Hiker reappears on the anniversary of her death.
- Frequently the narrator will include or round up the story with some corroborative-sounding detail intended to bolster its acceptance as a true event. Thus, the address given will be said to have proven to be a real one, but the narrator will apologise for not remembering it. Or the witness will be said to have been driven insane or died as a result of the experience, and so on.

While Beardsley and Hankey acknowledged that the story contains features in common with or possibly derived from certain literary precedents (particularly the Version C), in their view the Vanishing Hitchhiker's strong dependence on contemporary features marked it as a modern contrivance. The motor car, the circumstances of the pickup (either through the hitch-hiking habit or a meeting at a dance or other informal social gathering), even the mistaken first impression the driver has that his passenger is, until her disappearance, a normal human female (a narrative point uncommon before the late nineteenth century), are all hallmarks of the modern tale, reflective of and functional only within the context of a modern urbanised culture.

Beardsley's and Hankey's data suggested the Version A probably originated sometime in the 1920s; the Version B they could date no further back than 1933, and was confined to the area around Chicago and the Midwest, while a characteristic example of the Version C—the version, ironically, with the most patent 'literary frosting', the girl who returns to her grave—was not heard before 1938.

Another telling feature of this modern tale—perhaps the defining one—is the reportorial style of narration itself. Told in the same factual, everyday fashion as modern items of news, and often included with the same, the Vanishing Hitchhiker tale is one apparently made for rapid modern means of news dissemination. Rather than slowly radiating outwardly from its point of origin, evolving on its way, it has the ability to spread swiftly and largely unaltered over great distances. Beardsley and Hankey, who clearly regarded the Vanishing Hitchhiker's origins as having been in the United States, noted that in less than a year one variant had made its appearance on opposite shores of the continent, and may well have spread abroad.

At the local level, the story may be treated in various ways. At the base level, we have the bare bones of the story. There is no attempt to localise or personalise the account by the teller, and all the expected elements of the relevant version are present. Very much like the lead off of a joke that might begin: 'Have you heard the one about...?' it is usually taken no further than its entertainment value and, unlike the personalised accounts, makes no specific claim to be true.

What we might call second-tier accounts are those that differ to those above only in that they are identified with a particular location. Although the majority of these are, in all likelihood, equally as doubtful, these personalised accounts best represent the folklore ideal, and are probably the most common form the stories take. In the course of conducting the early research for this book, I began to take note of the wide range of such localised accounts, both those circulating on the oral grapevine and those that had reached publication or been acknowledged by other authors. One concerned Detling Hill, two miles north-east of Maidstone, which claims an equally unenviable record of fatalities as Blue Bell Hill, including, in 1974, the death of a hitch-hiker. Another focused on Shooters Hill (Greater London), twenty-five miles north-west of Blue Bell Hill.[3]

Usually, having once settled on a particular location, the story tends to take root, and subsequently becomes incorporated into the oral and written fabric of the folklore of the area. Michael Goss noted during his investigation of the Blue Bell Hill case for *The Evidence for Phantom Hitch-Hikers* that the locals seemed to be very proud of *their* ghost.[4] Implied by this is its recognised value to the area through its contribution to its wider folk tradition, irrespective of whether the story could be proven to have any evidential basis.

There certainly appeared to have been a need for such a local attraction. In 1969, a journalist for the *Kent Messenger*, in a brief article entitled 'In search of news', decried the apparent lack in this part of Kent of appropriate 'silly season' stories with which to counter the boastful claims of holiday hosts:

> ... I find myself wondering if Maidstone is not lagging behind in the phenomena stakes.
>
> Think for a moment—what can you talk about by way of retaliation when holiday hosts start dragging out their Unidentified Flying Objects, their loch monsters and free-roaming menagerie abscondees. We have our giant sunflowers, to be sure. Who hasn't? We have our occasional farmyard strays; our truant cats and prodigal parrots. They really are pretty small fry, aren't they? Thank goodness for Tovil Treacle Mines, that's all!
>
> What we really need, of course, is a suitably conscientious poltergeist in the council chamber—that could do the town a great deal of good, no doubt. Or a properly elusive Mote Lake Monster—or a Medway Mermaid—or something. Anything.
>
> No? Oh well—has anybody heard any more about that puma that was roaming about in these parts a few years back?[5]

We can forgive the author of this piece (Alan Bignell) for not being particularly in tune with the 'Talk of the Town' (the standing title of the section in which the article appeared) and his seeming unawareness of the recent published history on such a phenomenon within his own newspaper group. Of course, it is easy to judge with hindsight, but in fact no less than five articles had been published in *Kent Messenger* Group newspapers on just such a sought-after talking point in the previous two years—the ghost of Blue Bell Hill. Indeed, the very same column under which Mr Bignell was writing was responsible for the first published reference to the case, which itself suggests that the story was making the rounds by word of mouth at least as early as 1967.

Reporter Nigel Nelson, who we met in the opening chapter, had made some connection between the ghost story and Blue Bell Hill's ancient sites, suggesting that the disturbance of ancient burial places during the construction of the new A229 might have somehow given rise to the haunting. Other authors have noted that some Hitch-Hiker cases are located at sites with similar historical or traditional associations. Resurrection Mary reputedly haunts a sacred and ancient Indian trail; at Newbury (Berkshire), apparitions plaguing the construction works of the controversial bypass were attributed to the English Civil War battles of 1643 and 1644; and the Stocksbridge bypass near Sheffield, scene of a number of fatal accidents and reports of a malevolent phantom since its opening on Friday

13 May 1988, reputedly disturbs the unhallowed burial place of a monk.

Could, I wondered, such an association (and/or an existing reputation for ghostly occurrences) have been the means by which Blue Bell Hill had attracted its own legend of a hitch-hiking ghost (in preference to other worthy local hill locations) at a time when such stories were beginning to enjoy something of a revival?[6] Or did the newspaper reporting reflect sincere but light treatment of rumours that were actually in circulation in the late 1960s—rumours (in light of the activity of 1992 and the accounts that followed) that may have had some solid foundation after all?

Certainly, the press has an important part to play in the propagation of such stories. One of the important questions we will look at in a little more detail later is just how the media balances its responsibility to *report* news against the temptation to *make* its own. In the case of the Blue Bell Hill phantom it was the press that, in later years, was responsible for linking the rumours of a ghost with a definite cause—the motor accident of November 1965 which, I have already intimated, may have simply been the right event at the right time, the convenient happenchance of fact with which to imbue the stories with credibility and meaning.

What we might call third-tier cases are the most intriguing, and from the point of view of folklore, the most challenging, since they are distinguished by being supported by first-hand eyewitness testimony. One of the tenets of the story according to Beardsley and Hankey is that the witness is never forthcoming. A line in the earliest reference to the haunting of Blue Bell Hill (the aforementioned 1967 *Kent Messenger* piece) demonstrates the point: 'But, we never got nearer than second or third hand...'[7] Many reports appear promising in the first instance, where someone will claim to know a person who has picked up the girl, but on attempted investigation, the lead evaporates: either the opportunity never arises to interview them, or the story turns out not to concern this person at all, but a friend, or a friend of a friend, who is too far removed from the teller to hold any realistic hope of contacting.[8] Friend Of *A* Friend stories (or *FOAF* tales) are a familiar aspect of Phantom Hitch-Hiker reports, and tend to support the contention of folklore that they are fictional.

What, then, should we make of accounts where individuals have actually come forward to claim such an encounter? Certainly, where the account supports all the major story points of the basic motif, and where the story arises in isolation, it is certainly prudent to apply caution, if not dismiss the whole thing. Some witness-supported reports seem simply *too* close to the romantically constructed ideal to earn our acceptance.

The experience of Jerry Palus that was outlined in the last chapter comes to mind. At face value, Palus's encounter appears to be virtually a textbook example of a Version C encounter, with the observed disappearance of the girl providing the proof of her ghostly status in place of the house-visit or the coat-finding finale at the graveside. It could be that Palus was sincere in his account (we must allow for that), but extraordinary claims do indeed demand extraordinary evidence, and without some robust corroborating support from other witnesses to the event, there is little to defend it against its fantastical elements (the girl's cold skin, and so on)—even though the Resurrection Mary case as a whole presents some strong indications that the legend is based on rather more than hearsay.

While the named-witness accounts too conform recognisably to Beardsley and Hankey's type versions, it may be significant that these vital accounts break the established conventions in several important ways. A few (e.g. Uniondale) include vital independent corroboration, from other witnesses and/or by verifiable record. Others, in a further departure from the folk type (in which the phantom hitch-hiker is exclusively female—a convention that is unswervingly upheld in first and second-tier examples), as we have seen, feature *male* hitch-hikers; even child ghosts.

Take, for example, the case of a lone female motorist who stopped to pick up a young male hitch-hiker in the winter of 1965. Mae Doria was driving along Highway 20 east of Claremore, Oklahoma, when she stopped to pick up a boy of around eleven or twelve years of age. The boy chatted throughout the journey, and when they arrived at Pryor, he asked to get out near a culvert.[9] The area was devoid of houses, so Ms Doria asked the boy where he lived, to which he replied 'Over there'. When she turned her head to look, the boy had vanished. In like manner to other witnesses, she stopped the vehicle immediately to check around it and up and down the highway, without success. Two years later she learned that a phantom boy Hitch-Hiker had been picked up at the same spot as long ago as 1936.[10]

Michael Goss has pointed out that in these 'truncated' accounts (which, paradoxically, appear to be the 'best' stories as far as detail and witness testimony is concerned) the behaviour of the ghost seems to defeat the aim of the motif itself, by either vanishing before an address is given[11] or by failing to provide any other proof of identity that might allow the witness to follow it up. This illogical and 'nonconformist' behaviour, noted Goss, brings the actions of these phantoms much closer in line with those described within the field of parapsychology.[12]

Despite a whole canon of lore that describes ghosts as purposeful spirits behaving in a more or less understandable manner, the majority of ghostly encounters (and this includes the Phantom Jaywalker) are more prosaic, lacking creative embellishment. The ghost appears suddenly, fleetingly, and vanishes as quickly, leaving witnesses reeling from their experiences.

Beardsley and Hankey, I believe, would not have been surprised by such variations. Rather, I am sure they would have readily accommodated them with new versions, regarding them, perhaps, as new variants of the motif that emphasise modern requirements for convincing-sounding detail over the romantic ideal.

For Beardsley & Hankey, the Phantom Hitch-Hiker was clearly a product of its time, a phenomenon that relied upon the contemporary modes of transport, social norms and modes of dissemination extant in 1920s and 1930s America. They predicted its eventual demise as cultural factors forced the story to continually adapt to a point where it would lose its relevance and identity. We can see an indication of this gradual evolution with Resurrection Mary. In a case arising in the decade following the renovation of Resurrection cemetery (in the 1970s), a cab driver apparently saw a girl (still dressed in a white dress, with black patent leather dancing shoes) standing outside the Old Willow Shopping Mall on Archer Avenue. Of course, after midnight in snow-swept January, the driver stopped to offer her a lift. Naturally, she wanted to alight at Resurrection Cemetery, where she vanished without being observed.[13] The location for the meeting—a modern shopping mall—is at variance with the traditional dancehall or ballroom that Mary might ordinarily frequent, but it is entirely in keeping with the adaptation the story might be expected to undergo if it were a folk-tale striving to maintain currency. (Of course, the ever-present alternative viewpoint is that it is the phenomenon itself that adapts to cultural changes for the same reason).

The Phantom Hitch-Hiker as a variant of ghostly encounter has persisted long past Beardsley and Hankey's expectations, but it does appear that the hitch-hiking habit finally peaked between the late 1970s and early 1980s, judging by the reportorial record. Most of the popular named witness versions (including those exampled in the previous chapter) date to this period, with few reported thereafter.

At the same time, reports of what at first appears to be an entirely different form of encounter, the Phantom Jaywalker (an arguably more shocking form of encounter so vividly portrayed in Ian Sharpe's and Chris Dawkins' experiences) have increased. It could be argued that the Phantom Jaywalker represents the story's continuing strive to present itself in a manner more befitting of modern times, by reflecting a very modern anxiety, in which becoming a victim or cause of accidental death is a more realistic everyday fear than the prospect of a spectral travelling companion. Perhaps. But if this is the case, the question that begs an answer is: what factors are involved in the shaping of the next form of the story and its simultaneous 'release' into the unconscious lives of ordinary people? Are these events attributable purely to psychosocial factors; or might something else be going on?

When we look closely at the Phantom Hitch-Hiker and the Phantom Jaywalker, it is apparent there is little indication of evolution from one motif to the other—rather, the two styles of encounter appear to happily co-exist in case examples (in Shawn and Geri Lape's experience outside Resurrection Cemetery, for instance). By contrast, it was only after Sharpe's and Dawkins' encounters at Blue Bell Hill in 1992 that I began to hear anecdotes displaying evidence of 'cross-contamination' between them—as, for example, in the rumour that the ghost girl had been run over and killed while hitch-hiking on the Hill.

Rather than showing signs of evolution from the Phantom Hitch-Hiker, then, the Jaywalker emerged fully formed to befall numbers of named witnesses at various locations in precisely the same 'scripted' fashion as its hitch-hiking relation. It has previously been demonstrated, I hope, that the two styles of event show a dutiful obedience to an underlying theme of spectral encounters on our roads, which can be traced back through our folk histories to early times. The behaviour of the 'ghost' in the witness-attested cases defies any attempt to rationalise them (as we seem to have a need to do, as expressed in our romanticised versions of the Phantom Hitch-Hiker motif)—which is why, perhaps, we find additional difficulty in accepting them.

For the diehard sceptic, the witness-supported account no more impresses than the folk versions. Often it is seen in terms of the claimant's desire for personal notoriety (a hoax), or it is otherwise dismissed as hallucination or autosuggestion. Part of the process of evaluating these accounts must include consideration of all the possible alternative explanations that critics would rightly have us examine before committing to a paranormal one. But to be properly objective, consideration of the latter possibility must be admitted also.

As a controversial and popular subject, the paranormal will always feature those disposed toward uncritical belief, plus hoaxers and charlatans. But it also features persons who most of us might judge to be truthful and reliable, who were not seeking their experiences, but who nevertheless step forward to tell their stories, with all the risks this entails. And we must remember, we are talking about what the witness *perceives* to be true, not a case for total objectivity. Witnesses are protected by their own psychological defence mechanisms to a degree, in that their initial reaction is often one of disbelief in the evidence of their own senses. People generally *do* tend to rationalise strange events as far as possible, preferring to either suspend judgment to preserve their own sense of reality, or to accept them and stand by their stories no matter what. Neither suggests a predisposition to uncritical acceptance of the encounter as portrayed in the folk version, but says something about how people react differently to experiences which challenge their personal belief structure.

The sometimes subtle consistencies between these rare witness-attested encounters (and they *are* rare—the cases presented in Chapter 4 are atypical in this respect), which only persons well versed in folklore and parapsychology would likely notice or find meaningful, seem to point to something deeper and more complex in operation that lies outside of individual consciousness, and possibly outside of the human sphere altogether. Folklorists, at least, might concede that the claimant must have either a detailed awareness of a typical Phantom Hitch-Hiker or Jaywalker story structure, or an unconscious talent for recognising that which constitutes the perfect road ghost tale.

While it may be difficult to accept the idea of ghosts—and hitch-hiking ones in particular—can we not also say that in respect of some cases for which the 'evidence' is relatively strong, that it also strains credibility to think that *all* cases are untrue, irrespective of the quality of that evidence? Such events are certainly improbable according to the current scope of knowledge, but are they necessarily impossible? Simple logic, after all, dictates that to *know* something is impossible requires one to know everything that *is* possible—in effect, to know everything. To the firm sceptic no amount of evidence or quality of testimony will be persuasive. But anyone who wishes to approach the subject without biased preconception may leave open the idea that the latter is at least possible, and that the event may have taken place largely as described.

Whether something similar to the preceding cases was operating at Blue Bell Hill was what I originally set out to find out—which began with the task of uncovering the early history of the case, in relation to both the Phantom Hitch-Hiker story with which it was popularly born, and the very real human tragedy said to be behind it.

SIX

THE OVERGROWN PATH

ALTHOUGH my interest in the Blue Bell Hill story had been revived by the discovery of Michael Goss's book in 1986, my own involvement would not begin for several years afterward—most likely following a repeat reading of his book, from which I gained a deeper appreciation for the story and its standing within the wider sphere of Phantom Hitch-Hiker tales.

More or less coincidental with this was the renewed appearance of published rumours regarding the proposed Channel Tunnel overland rail link. Early plans routed this high-speed link through Kent via the Boxley Valley and across the Medway Gap to London. The projected course of the line would take it uncomfortably close to the foot of Blue Bell Hill, where the proposed siting of what sounded like an extensive rail terminal (Mid-Kent Parkway), plus an electricity substation close to Kit's Coty House, threatened to obliterate the countryside near to the Hill's ancient monuments, which had otherwise largely survived the ravages of man and nature for over forty centuries.[1]

This threat to the vicinity provided further motivation to find out what I could about the story before the local geography became unrecognisable. My growing awareness of the popularity of the story of Blue Bell Hill's ghost indicated that it had rightfully earned a place in Kentish lore, and although I was not then sure if there would be very much to add to Michael Goss's work on the case, I determined that if the area of the haunting was to be effaced, the same should not happen to the story itself.

My first visit to Maidstone's public library in St Faith's Street in May 1989, however, was motivated primarily by curiosity regarding the identities of the participants and the circumstances of the 1965 car crash. For years the story had circulated as a typically impersonal Phantom Hitch-Hiker tale. Apart from the localised details that highlighted Blue Bell Hill as the picking-up point for the ghostly girl Hitch-Hiker, and the mention of her wedding, so cruelly thwarted on its eve, the story was indistinguishable from many other Hitch-Hiker tales.

KENT MESSENGER

Maidstone Gazette

TUESDAY NOVEMBER 23 1965 FIVEPENCE

MID-WEEKLY PAPER FOR

Maidstone Borough and the rural district council areas of Maidstone, Hollingbourne, Malling and Strood (part), including Aylesford, Boxley, Borough Green, Barham, Coxheath, Detling, East Peckham, Halling, Harrietsham, Headcorn, Larkfield, Lenham, Marden, Snodland, Staplehurst, Sutton Valence, West Malling, Wouldham, Wrotham and Yalding.

MINUTES after two girls died in the car crash on Blue Bell Hill late on Friday, staff photographer Mr. [illegible] Pollard took this picture of ambulancemen helping the injured.

Girls die in wedding eve smash

By Peter Rimmer

SURGEONS at West Kent Hospital, Maidstone, were fighting to save a girl's life on Saturday – the day she was due to be married.

Twenty-two-year-old Susan Browne came to England from Australia to marry an R.A.F. technician. On Friday she went on a wedding eve party but on the way home the Cortina in which Susan and her three friends were travelling was in collision with a Jaguar at Blue Bell Hill, Aylesford. Two girls were killed in the crash and two others seriously injured.

Patricia Ruth Ferguson, aged 23, of Dunfermline, Scotland, who was staying at Chaden Avenue, Gillingham, was killed instantly. Judith Lingham, aged 22, of Bank View, Albany Road, Rochester, died in hospital later.

Gillian Burchett, 20, of Howard Avenue, Rochester, the fourth girl in the Cortina, was also detained in hospital.

The passenger in the Jaguar, Sheilah Baird, of Curzon Road, Chatham, was seriously hurt but the driver, Mr. Harry Backhouse, aged 28, of High Street, Chatham, was released from hospital after receiving treatment.

Miss Browne had been staying at Woodlands Road, Chatham. Her fiance is Brian Wetton, aged 22, who is stationed at an R.A.F. Camp at Huntingdon. They were to be married at St. Mary's Roman Catholic Church, Gillingham.

Guests, who had not heard the tragic news were told when they arrived at the church for the wedding.

Yesterday Miss Browne was described by a hospital spokesman as "poorly." Mrs. Burchett as "fair" and Miss Baird as "quite comfortable."

JUDITH LINGHAM

Swim baths blamed for verrucae spread

MAIDSTONE Residents' Association has called for an end to the delay in replacing the town's ancient swimming baths, because many children are catching verrucae in the unhygienic conditions.

The £300,000 project for new swimming baths is not expected to start for six months, partly because of the Chancellor's cuts in public spending.

Mr. W. Betteridge, chairman of the association, told a reporter: "I know there is Government restriction, but I think there must be some action somewhere."

Treatment

He said that the verruca problem at the old baths was [illegible]. He knew of one girl who was unable to swim for [illegible] years. She developed one verruca and then had to several others.

"One of my own children suffered from a verruca for [illegible] months."

He said that children who caught verrucae had to have surgical treatment, which involved burning them out.

Mr. Alfred Westgarth, baths superintendent, told a reporter: "We recognise the fact that verrucae is present. Everything which can possibly be done within this particular building is being done to prevent its spread.

"The position will be improved in the new baths by compulsory footbaths."

Footnote: Verrucae are a kind of wart.

Frost stops trains

MAIDSTONE commuters were affected when early morning trains from the coast to London were 96 minutes late yesterday morning because conductor rails iced up outside Dover.

The 4.45 a.m. from Dover to Victoria was delayed, then the 5.16 a.m. from Dover to Charing Cross was held up. A diesel engine was called into action and took the two trains to Tonbridge.

Passengers from Ashford to Maidstone were also hit.

Black-out warning

AS snow fell in the Maidstone area yesterday afternoon, there were threats of an electricity black-out in the entire Maidstone district. Seeboard warned Maidstone police of the possible disconnection, depending on the demand for power.

Yesterday, Maidstone firemen had an alert about possible flooding of the Medway in the Allington region because of extra high tides.

Farmer fails in rate cut bid

A MAN who claimed there were gipsies all around his farmhouse failed on Monday in his bid to have its rateable value reduced from a proposed £102.

A spokesman for the Valuation Officer said he could not see any gipsies when he visited the area.

"There may have been some a mile away or in a wood nearby," Mr. L. P. Curtis added, "but I did not see them."

Mr. F. P. Hawkes, owner-occupier of Westfield Sole Farmhouse, Boxley, also complained of rubbish dumps affecting the value of the property, lack of streets and lights and also noted that the nearest letterbox was a mile away.

But the Valuation Court agreed that the proposed rateable value figure was "fair and reasonable" and let it stand.

Blaze at farm

HUNDREDS of apple boxes and farm machinery were badly damaged by fire which broke out in a building at Shingle Barn Farm, near Yalding Hill, West Farleigh, on Sunday afternoon.

Maidstone firemen had the blaze under control soon after 5 p.m.

Occupier of the farm is Mr Charles Knowles.

POLICE TELL OF BOYS THEFT GANG

BOYS as young as 11 were said by police on Friday to be part of a gang of thieves active in Maidstone.

This was disclosed at a juvenile court in Maidstone when two boys aged 11 and 14 were accused of breaking into a sports shop and stealing £[illegible].

Three other boys appeared in connection with the offence. Police said several others were involved. They opposed bail for one boy.

The cases, alleging larceny and taking and driving away scooters, were adjourned to December 3.

Page Guide

Maidstone Gazette **23 November 1965** *(KM Group)*

Goss's work provided the key to learning more about the story, both the case for the haunting and the very real and tragic human story behind it. His book helpfully listed a number of newspaper articles that outlined the essential history of the case, including coverage of the 1965 crash.

On viewing these sources, those about the ghost revealed little that had not already been discussed by Goss. More revealing were two front page articles that described the 1965 car crash. Both the *Maidstone Gazette* (23 November)[2] and the *Kent Messenger* (26 November)[3]—both penned by Peter Rimmer—included photographs of the two-car crash, which had been taken 'within minutes' of the accident by *Kent Messenger* photographer Mike Pollard (who happened to be passing by that evening).

The images showed a Jaguar buried in the side of a Mark 1 Ford Cortina,[4] with police and ambulancemen in attendance. The road and kerb (onto which the Cortina had been shunted), damp and slick judging from its reflectivity, was covered with fragments of glass and debris. At centre-left of the picture, at the limits of the flash-illumination of the photograph, was a bus stop sign, a feature that would later prove helpful in identifying the scene of the accident.

The *Maidstone Gazette*'s article ('Girls die in wedding eve smash') reported how, the previous Saturday, surgeons at Maidstone's West Kent Hospital[5] had been engaged in a fight to save the life of one of the young women on the day she was to have been married. The young woman, who was named as Susan Browne (22) [sic],[6] reportedly came from Australia to England to marry her fiancé, a technician with the Royal Air Force.

According to the paper, on the evening of Friday (19 November), she and three friends had been out on a wedding-eve celebration when, on their way home,[7] their Cortina collided with a Jaguar at Blue Bell Hill, Aylesford.[8] Two of the girls in the Cortina were killed in the crash; the other two seriously injured. The two girls who died were Patricia Ruth Ferguson (23) of Dunfermline, Scotland, who was staying in Gillingham (reported to have been killed instantly), and Judith Lingham (22) of Albany Road, Rochester, said to have died later in hospital.[9]

The fourth member of the Cortina party, Gillian Burchett,[10] was detained in hospital, and was said to be in 'fair' condition a few days later.

The occupants of the Jaguar both survived. The driver, a 29-year-old Chatham man, was released from hospital after receiving treatment, while his passenger, reported to be seriously hurt, was detained and was later described as 'quite comfortable'.

Miss Browne, who had been staying at Woodlands Road, Gillingham,[11] had been due to marry Bryan Wetton at St Mary's Roman Catholic Church, Gillingham.[12] Guests, who were unaware of the tragedy, were informed when they arrived for the wedding. On the following Monday her condition in hospital was described as 'poorly'.

The following Friday, Peter Rimmer's second article for the *Kent Messenger* ('Prelude to grief...') reported that bride-to-be Susan Browne had died on Wednesday (24 November), five days after the accident which had claimed the lives of two of her friends. The article otherwise outlined the circumstances and details given by the *Maidstone Gazette*, adding only that formal evidence of identification had been given at an inquest the previous day. The hearing was to be adjourned for two months to allow police investigations to be concluded.

The rest, as they say, is history. In 1974, the crash would be firmly linked by other *Kent Messenger* Group articles to legends that described a ghostly girl Hitch-Hiker on Blue Bell Hill. The subject of their suppositions regarding the identity of the ghost (as related in some detail in Chapter 1), however, would focus not on the particularly tragic bride-to-be, a young woman in the high emotional state on the eve of her wedding, but, confusingly, on one of her companions, Judith Lingham, whose picture appeared as an inset in the *Maidstone Gazette* article.

According to Michael Goss, rumours surrounding the ghost had started soon after the 1965 tragedy, first coming to Tom Harber's attention with his 1966 witness. The information provided by this person, although sadly lacking in all but essential detail, clearly implicated the bride-to-be as the ghost—a ghost, if the 1965 crash connection was valid (and at this stage there were no firm grounds to question it), whose name was now known to me.

Viewing the crash articles in the library archives intensified my interest in the case. The more complete knowledge of the crash and its unwitting participants—particularly the bride-to-be—added a sense of poignancy to the story that was only suggested by the anonymous version (but which is fully in keeping with the love-transcends-death theme that runs through a number of Phantom Hitch-Hiker and other supernatural tales). And in a manner, the ghost story's suggestion that one of the victims of this crash had survived bodily death to pitifully haunt the scene of her death deepened the fact of the tragedy itself.

The pathos of the 1965 crash and its wedding-eve victim (identified through genuine implication, or by deliberate selection for this very reason) complements the format and requirements of the classic Phantom Hitch-Hiker tale so well that it is little wonder that their combination has produced such a powerful and memorable story, irrespective almost of the 'real' encounters that would come to light in time.

The deepened sense of tragedy found in the death of a bride-to-be is something that rarely goes without comment, and not only by writers of the supernatural. *The Gazette* (formerly the *Maidstone Gazette*) of 18 February 1975, for instance, describes the death of a young bride-to-be in a near-midnight crash at another hill location, Sutton Valence, near Maidstone.[13] Similarly, the *Kent Messenger* of 20 October 1967 reports that a jury at the inquest on the death of a young man was told by his fiancée that they had planned to make enquiries about getting married the day after the fatal car crash.[14] But although worthy of comment, observations of the tendency to make particular note of these wedding/tragic death correspondences add nothing to the weight of evidence necessary to persuade us that in the Blue Bell Hill case the 19 November crash was not simply someone's conveniently located and inspired selection.

Of interest in the crash articles were a few points which either through their absence or in point of detail differed somewhat with Tom Harber's collected accounts and opinions. For instance, in neither of Peter Rimmer's articles was there reference to the time of the crash. Although the crash photographs from both newspapers clearly showed the accident to have occurred at night, only the *Kent Messenger* actually relates this fact, stating that it had occurred 'late on Friday night'. Tom Harber's 1966 witness had reputedly encountered the ghost on the anniversary of her demise. Did her adherence to the anniversary date (by now familiar to the reader from the previous chapters) relate—if not to the actual moment of her death—then to the precise time of the traumatic incident that had effectively killed her? According to Goss, all twelve of Tom Harber's witnesses had encountered the ghost after 11 p.m. Was this an oblique reference to the presumed (or known) time of the crash?

The precise time of the crash was not something of critical significance, unless one considered that if it had occurred at around 11 p.m., the ghost, according to the accounts given by Tom Harber's witnesses, exhibited a propensity to take her reappearance on the anniversary of her death almost too literally. (It may be recalled that the encounters of 1992 also occurred around 11 p.m. or after.)

Probably the most significant point to note was that the bride-to-be was said to have come from Australia to marry her fiancé—a fact that rather countered Tom Harber's stated belief that she came from Maidstone. Furthermore, if she was residing in Gillingham during her stay (erroneously given as Chatham in the *Kent Messenger*'s reports) as the press accounts stated, it made it even more difficult to understand how Maidstone (specifically the Week Street/County Hall area of that town) had become the favoured destination for the ghost girl. Goss himself mused over the motivation a homeward-bound spirit might have for heading for a place that was not her home. Although I was to turn up material that at least suggested how Tom Harber may have come to associate the ghost with Maidstone (which will be examined shortly), the fact that the bride-to-be plainly was not from that town tended to cast doubt on accounts which included it as her home destination (even if their close adherence to the Phantom Hitch-Hiker format had not already done so).

As a registered blind person, the true or suggested nationality of the bride-to-be was something that could conceivably have escaped Tom Harber's attention. If there was really anything to the stories given by his anonymous witnesses—that they had genuinely encountered a girl who behaved in typical hitch-hiker fashion and who was intent on being driven to Maidstone, it suggested that the ghost either had some obscure reason for choosing that town, or the whole thing had nothing to do with any of the 1965 crash victims.

These questions were part of the reason I came to undertake my own investigation—these, and the fact that Michael Goss (quite unintentionally, I am sure) had thrown out a challenge in his book when he suggested that *The Gazette* of 10 September 1968 (see Chapter 3) was the earliest published reference to the case. I reasoned that if rumours were circulating in the area as early as 1966 (as suggested by Tom Harber's first witness), then the local press may have picked up the story at about this time or soon after—which was indeed the case.

By far the most useful resource, however, would be the general public. Conceivably, out there still were some of Tom Harber's original witnesses, who might yet be willing to commit their accounts to the record. The one informant Tom contacted on Michael Goss's behalf in 1980 declined to be interviewed, and Tom rightfully respected his wish to remain anonymous.

In an attempt to locate these and other possible first-hand witnesses in these years before the Internet, I sent letters of appeal to various local newspapers.[15] Alas, none of the replies delivered the first-hand testimony I had hoped for. Nevertheless, these sources did provide some additional background and anecdotal material on the case.

An account described in one of the letters would prove to have some relevance much later in the research, through its overt similarity to Jacquie Hopkins' experience (and similar accounts from elsewhere). In reply to my appeal in the *Maidstone Star* of 25 January 1990,[16] Mrs Renee Hughes, of Barming, Maidstone, described an unusual experience she had had at Blue Bell Hill in 1934—providing the first, if tentative, suggestion of unusual events on the Hill much earlier than 1965:

> Reading your account of the 'Phantom Hiker' took me back to something that has always remained unexplained to me. As a keen cyclist, often in the evening I would ride (on my own) to Chatham. I would meet a friend there, and then return via Blue Bell Hill to Pine Grove [Boxley Road, Maidstone]. One night I left Chatham at about 9.30, and I think it must have been in September, as it was dark and my cycle lamp was lit. I was free-wheeling down the hill and, in those days, there was very little traffic at night, when I thought I saw a dark cloud cross my path. The next thing I knew I was laying on the ground beside my bike. I felt a bit

> shaken, but I examined my bike; it was unmarked, and the lamp still on, so I resumed my journey...[17]

Mrs Hughes added that she was an experienced cyclist. This was the only occasion that she ever fell off her bicycle, and no other incidents befell her on subsequent journeys to Chatham. The incident remained a mystery.

The 'encounter' had taken place 'halfway' down the Hill from the Lower Bell public house (somewhere in the region of the Cossington section of modern day Blue Bell Hill). The 'cloud' or whatever it was had come from above, falling across her path. Picking herself up, Mrs Hughes found nothing on or about the road to account for the incident. It was many years before she would hear of Blue Bell Hill's reputation for being haunted. Interestingly, her earliest recollection of a ghost associated with the Hill was not related to a hitch-hiking female, but the figure of a man in a snow storm—a tale Mrs Hughes believes she had heard in the 1950s.[18]

One of the other letters had more of a direct bearing on familiar aspects of the story. Mrs G. Beever, of Sheerness, related that in-laws of hers had lived at Blue Bell Hill for twenty years. On occasion, the voice of a woman could be heard in the still of the night calling the name 'Johnny'. 'It was said that one of the girls that died in the accident was to be married the next day to a boy called Johnny.'[19]

Although this anecdote is meaningless in itself—it cannot be related to the 1965 tragedy or anyone associated with it (although it is redolent of John Leyton's atmospheric 1961 hit 'Johnny Remember Me', a song about a girl whose plea to be remembered could still be heard by her boyfriend sighing in the treetops a year after her death)—it at least demonstrates how particulars of the case—here, vague reference to the 1965 car crash and next-day wedding of one its victims—become subtly altered through rumour and/or hazy recollection of real or reported events.

Such would prove to be the case with further anecdotes I would hear in time. One account demonstrates how aspects of the published history of the case could be confused, in this case combining the traditional hitch-hiking behaviour of the ghost with the 'knock down' scenario popularised by Maurice Goodenough's well-publicised encounter: a motorist, having knocked down a young girl late one night on Blue Bell Hill, picks her up and carries her to his car, where he places her on the back seats, from where, of course, she vanishes.

Another variation (one I have heard more than once) suggested the ghost to be that of a hitch-hiker who was knocked down and killed on the Hill—an attempt perhaps to justify the hitch-hiking behaviour of the ghost, or an example of imperfect recollection of an actual incident?[20]

In a later telephone conversation, Mrs Beever related two incidents describing encounters with the hitch-hiking ghost by individuals (anonymous, of course) living in the immediate Blue Bell Hill area.

The first, dating to around 1969, involved a man who worked at the Aylesford Paper Mill (formerly Reeds, now known as Aylesford Newsprint). Driving home in the rain he passed a young woman waiting at the bus stop located near to the current footbridge over the A229 at Blue Bell Hill, close to the turn-off for his destination. Reaching home moments later, his conscience pricked him, so he turned around and went back to offer the girl a lift home. The girl got in the back seat of the car, and said very little throughout the journey (her destination unspecified). At some point along the way, the motorist discovered his passenger to be missing—something that so disturbed him that he reputedly wound up receiving treatment at Oakwood Hospital, Barming (a former psychiatric hospital in Maidstone—prompting some speculation that Tom Harber may have first heard the story through his capacity as a switchboard operator at this hospital).[21]

The second account involved a motorcyclist who, on picking the girl up, established that she lived in Gillingham. When they arrived at the destination road, he turned into it only to feel the girl slip off his motorcycle, but when he stopped he could find no trace of her. Mrs Beever speculated that this (undated) encounter may have marked the girl's last hitch-hiking journey, since she had finally succeeded in reaching her destination.[22]

Later, in 1992, a resident of Blue Bell Hill Village related a further incident involving the hitch-hiking girl. Around 1972, a friend of his parents was witness to a passing motorist who stopped off at the Upper Bell pub for a stiff drink (a scotch) after picking up a girl who had vanished from the passenger seat of his car.[23]

Another—lifelong—resident of Blue Bell Hill Village, and former employee of the Bridgewood café (which, until it fell casualty to road layout alterations in 2002, was located at the top of the Hill near to the former Bridgewood roundabout) told me of an occasion in the middle to late 1960s when a lorry driver had entered the café claiming he had just given a lift to a girl who had asked to be taken to Eccles (a village a mile south-west of Blue Bell Hill), [24] but who had vanished when he reached the village.

All of the above accounts, characteristically deficient in detail (particularly in regard to witness identities), are quite typical of Beardsley and Hankey's Version A Phantom Hitch-Hiker. Only in the last instance can the narrator personally vouch for the actual existence of the claimant, even if she knew him only by sight, and only from this one occasion. The existence of a claimant, however, says little for the veracity of the story itself.

As we noted in the previous chapter, the above accounts correspond with the period of peak popularity of the Phantom Hitch-Hiker in the press, and we can rightly question which influenced which. Disregarding a peculiar incident in 1977 involving a mystery female standing at the bottom of Blue Bell Hill (who was not attempting to hitch-hike, and did not enter the car),[25] only one published account after 1970 describes an encounter with a female hitch-hiker on the Hill and this, involving guitarist Richard Studholme around 1973, suggests he may have been the subject of a hoax based on the Phantom Hitch-Hiker theme.

Several named-witness Hitch-Hiker accounts were to reach me privately in the years that followed (these also dating to the 1960s and early 1970s—see Chapter 9), but at this time the case was offering little serious resistance to the idea that it too was simply a reflection of press interest in the story at this time—a story that would, in time, inevitably fall out of fashion, particularly in the years following Maurice Goodenough's encounter in July 1974 in which a different behaviour was reported (and subsequently repeated).

It is interesting to note that of the two accounts above that mention a destination, only the one involving the motorcyclist identifies a town (Gillingham) that holds a proven association with any of the victims of the 1965 crash. Gillingham first enters the published history of the case in 1974 when, perhaps, it was adopted as a means by which the newly-identified 1965 crash (and in particular, the bride-to-be) could be linked to the existing ghost stories. The fact that this town appears in an account laying claim to having taken place in the late 1960s (when, according to local newspaper accounts, *Maidstone* was the favoured destination of the ghost girl), suggests that either it was a genuine feature of the account as originally told (Mrs Beever maintains that it happened to someone known by sight to an acquaintance of hers—a *FOAF* situation, admittedly), or this detail (and perhaps the account itself) originated much later, probably in 1974 or thereafter.

A motorcyclist who gives a lift to the girl, and Gillingham as the girl's destination, are combined features that appear in three *Kent Messenger* Group newspapers reporting on the Goodenough incident in July 1974 (the *Evening Post* of 15 July; *The Gazette*, 16 July; and the *Kent Messenger* itself, 19 July). These again suggest that the newspaper reports were the inspiration for an oral version which unconsciously united two separate outlines to form the account as given, which was subsequently attributed to the 1960s. (For completeness, the Gillingham address—mentioned only in the *Evening Post*—is noted in relation to a motorist rather than a motorcyclist). Given the nature of the story and its propagation in rumour, it is easier to accept this as the explanation than suppose that had Gillingham been a feature of real 1960s events or rumour, it had somehow managed to escape the attention of the press until 1974.

Another letter of note was from Maidstone researcher and lecturer Dennis Chambers, whose own findings had found brief mention in Goss's book. Having seen my newspaper appeal, Dennis wrote to offer some help with my research.[26]

Dennis's letter referenced notes and cuttings he held on the 1965 crash, and to the subsequent sightings of two of the three girls who perished, which was something that tallied with the information attributed to him by Goss.

At a later meeting, and described in a copy of his notes on the case, Dennis reiterated his belief that two of the victims of the 1965 crash were haunting Blue Bell Hill. He related how drivers travelling from Maidstone to Rochester would stop to pick up a girl who asked to be taken to Albany Road in Rochester, stating that she had been involved in an accident. Taking the back seat of the car, the girl would remain silent, and be discovered by the motorist to be missing on arrival at the address. Owing to her disappearance, drivers were naturally concerned, some suspecting that she had somehow fallen out of the moving vehicle. Others (which included representatives of the local press) were said to have proceeded to the Albany Road address[27] and had spoken to the parents of the girl, who was said to be 22-year-old Judith Lingham—whose description, apparently, matched that of the ghost girl so closely that there seemed little doubt that they were one and the same.

During the course of his enquiries, Dennis claimed to have uncovered evidence that one of the other women from the 1965 crash had put in appearances at Blue Bell Hill. Although he conceded that there was no definite proof, he stated that this girl was believed to be the bride-to-be, who reputedly waits at the bottom of Blue Bell Hill, near to where the A229 joins the M20 (Junction 6). As with Judith, she hitches lifts from passing motorists, claiming to have been involved in a serious road accident (although it was said that she doesn't always speak), and similarly vanishes before her destination is reached. On account of the number of visits Mr Lingham (Judith's father) had received from motorists alleging to have picked up his daughter, and the toll such reports had taken on his family's health, he had apparently threatened to have a service of exorcism conducted at Blue Bell Hill which, as far as Dennis was aware, was never carried out.[28]

Supplementary notes, which were to prompt further clarification, included details that were at variance with the outline above, or with particulars relating to the 1965 crash given in the newspaper reports. In these, the two candidates for the ghost appear to have been confused. Here, it is the bride-to-be who sits silently in the rear of the vehicle after asking to be taken to her home in Rochester, and who disappears in the vicinity of Rochester Aerodrome. The other girl, said to have lived at Aylesford, and described as 19–20 years of age, pretty, and wearing a headscarf, [29] heads for Maidstone, and chats all the way into the town, saying there had been an accident and she had to inform the prospective bridegroom. She vanishes in the County Hall area (at the head of Week Street).

Finally, Dennis told me of a television programme he had been involved in

Albany Road, Rochester, where in some versions Blue Bell Hill's phantom hitch-hiker wished to be taken. Judith Lingham's former home, Bank View, stands at the end of the row of houses

some years before, in which the makers[30] had reconstructed a motorist's encounter on the Hill with the hitch-hiking ghost. Although the accounts furnished by Dennis stated that the girl tended to vanish before reaching her destination, the finished reconstruction included what we can now recognise as a Version C Phantom Hitch-Hiker finale—with the motorist's overcoat found laid on the girl's grave (which, according to a different source,[31] was located in Sutton Road Cemetery, Maidstone, in keeping with the girl's assumed identity with that town).

While he had admitted to failing to find proof that the second ghost was that of the bride-to-be, Dennis seemed quite sure that the main subject was Judith Lingham—an identification, of course, which was in accordance with the suppositions made by Nigel Nelson in 1974. Since motorists had reputedly visited Judith's home address in Albany Road (a 'fact' given in various newspaper reports) and the apparent match between her description and that of the ghost girl, Dennis appeared to be satisfied that the girl wishing to be taken to Rochester was in fact this young lady. However, as we have noted, the address-giving ghost, the anonymity of the witnesses, and the girl's preference for travelling in the back of the vehicle, are hallmarks of the stereotypical Phantom Hitch-Hiker tale. These accounts, therefore, like those above, could not in themselves be accepted as proof of real events or identifications.

The possibility that real encounters had occurred in a fashion that conformed to a precedent of folklore, however, could not be entirely ruled out; only that it seemed most unlikely. To even begin to accept the proposition of a hitch-hiking ghost would require persuasive evidence, not anecdotes, as interesting as they might be.

The testable features of the story, I suspected, would tend to negate the case for a haunting rather than strengthen it, as indeed had already proven to be the case on a few points—and as demonstrated by my own failure to find actual first-hand witnesses, and the problems in identifying any of the 1965 crash victims with the Maidstone Girl. One of the testable features of Dennis Chambers' account would be whether a motorist had ever knocked on the door of Judith's former home claiming to have given her a lift there. I would later establish with one of Judith's sisters that this had never occurred.

To evaluate the case objectively, it followed that I would have to find out as much as possible about the supposed haunting *and* the 1965 crash and its victims (assuming, of course, a supportable connection between tragic death and ghostly manifestations). The ghost reports would need to be compared and contrasted to the facts behind the crash and vice versa to discover if they were in any way related. If this were the case, there should be some definite supporting evidence: named witnesses, careful descriptions, plus dates, times and locations.

Some of this detail, I felt, might only be obtained from relatives of the deceased. On this point, I decided that I would consider trying to contact any of them *only* if the research should throw up evidence that strongly implicated their loved one (which I thought was extremely unlikely). I had no intention of causing offence to anyone connected with the unwitting victims of the 1965 tragedy, or any of the other candidates that have come to be considered in the unfolding story of Blue Bell Hill's ghost.

At the same time, I felt it important that the truth behind a story that had fairly captured the imagination of the public should be made known, whatever its outcome. I came, therefore, to view the investigation as being divided between the ghost stuff, and the circumstances leading up to and including the 1965 accident itself.

Investigating the Blue Bell Hill case was to prove analogous to the proverbial patterned rug, whereby a tug on a single thread may change the whole pattern. While it would have been more proper to detail and discuss my subsequent findings from both avenues as they came to light, such an investigative style (while of interest to some) would unnecessarily complicate the picture. Therefore, for the sake of simplicity and clarity, the two principal lines of enquiry are treated separately in the chapters that follow.

SEVEN

PUBLISHED HISTORY 1967–1980

Part 1: Birth of a Legend (1967–1970)

Hitch-hiking Spirit

The earliest published reference to Blue Bell Hill's ghost appears in the *Kent Messenger* of 8 December 1967, in what was a regular local interest column ('Maidstone Comment') penned by then-District Editor Roy Plascott.[1]

The brief article (if it can be called that) describes nothing less than the classic Phantom Hitch-Hiker tale: Driving down Blue Bell Hill towards Maidstone late one night, a man saw a young woman standing by the bus stop at the bottom (presumably the one then outside the Lower Bell). Knowing that the last bus had long gone, he stopped to offer her a lift. Since the man had someone in the car with him, the girl was forced to climb into the back of the car.

The late hour prompted the driver to take the girl all the way home, and she gave her address in the Mote Park area of Maidstone. When the vehicle reached the house, the two men were astonished to discover that their 'fair' passenger had vanished. The vehicle had neither stopped nor slowed long enough for the girl to get out.

The 'pay-off' of the story, as Plascott termed it, was that, on calling at the house, a man answered and, after listening to their story, reported that the two men were not the first to have called about the girl, whom he believed to be a former resident who had been killed in a road accident.

Plascott stated that the story had been reported to the *Kent Messenger* as genuine and, as a result, some time had been spent checking it out, but with predictable lack of success. The endeavour failed to get any closer than second or third hand.

Then, apparently, another call was received from someone claiming to have picked up a girl wanting a lift to East Malling…

'It sounds very much like one of those tall stories which occasionally go the rounds' was the astute conclusion of the writer, who also made note of its proximity to Christmas, a time traditionally associated with the telling of ghost stories.

Save for the fact that the motorist is not alone, all the expected features of the Version A Phantom Hitch-Hiker encounter (recognised as the 'purest' form of the story) are embodied in this article. Although a popular aspect of such stories, the lone motorist is not an obligatory requirement. In this case the driver's companion, by occupying the front passenger seat, provides a logical reason for the girl to assume the rear seat of the vehicle, from which, according to convention, she can safely vanish unobserved.

Appearing as it did, untitled, in a rather inconspicuous side-column of the *Kent Messenger*, it is difficult to believe that this piece in itself made any great impression on public awareness (indeed, it seems to have been completely overlooked since its original publication). Rather, it appears—as is the claim of its author—to reflect rumours that were genuinely in circulation in the Maidstone area at the time.

The mention of East Malling (a village four miles west of Maidstone) as an alternative destination for the ghost girl is noteworthy. Unless it was thrown in for good measure in order to demonstrate the free-floating nature of unfounded rumour, it suggests that Maidstone had not yet become fixed in the public consciousness as the girl's home town. This identification was undoubtedly reinforced thereafter by the press treatment which, in this case, described a particular part of Maidstone—the Mote Park area—which, in reality, describes a relatively large area of the town. The roughly rectangular 550-acre park, whose north-west corner impinges on the town centre, has an area approaching 10 percent of the total area of the town area, and is today surrounded on all sides by residential areas.

Five months later, in the *Kent Messenger* of 10 May 1968 (but this time in his 'Talk of the Town' column), Roy Plascott found himself reporting on the ghost girl again. In 'Hitch-hiking spirit', he observed that the rumour regarding a ghost waiting at the bottom of Blue Bell Hill—which had been widespread in the Maidstone area several months earlier—was once again in circulation.[2]

This article marks Tom Harber's debut in the published history of the case and his original appeal for further information about the ghost. Plascott reported that during that week Mr Harber, a telephonist, had heard the story repeated on three separate occasions during the course of a single day, prompting him to decide to pursue the rumour to its source—'if indeed it is a rumour', he added. The article further suggests that Tom first heard the story and began his investigation in 1968, in conflict with his later claim to have originally heard it in 1966 (see Chapter 3).

The writer outlined the same pattern of behaviour of the girl described in his 1967 piece: motorists picking her up at the bottom of the Hill and taking her to the given address (not openly stated, but implied to be in Maidstone) find on arrival that she is no longer there. For the first time, however, reference is made to a supposed cause of the haunting. The ghost is said to be that of a girl who died in a road accident 'some time ago'. Whether such represents an early reference to the 1965 crash or is simply a logical inference made to account for the ghost can only be conjectured. No further reference to a cause is made until 1974, when the 1965 crash became openly linked to the stories.

Once again, Plascott rounded off his article in a manner that further suggested he had a definite insight if not familiarity with the workings and structure of urban legends: 'I wish Mr Harber luck. Up to now the rumour has always concerned 'a friend of a friend'. Perhaps he can nail down that someone.'

Four months later the *Evening Post* (9 September) and *The Gazette* (which ran a virtually identical version the next day) were reporting Tom Harber's failure to locate first-hand witnesses to the ghost girl after months of investigative effort. Both articles reported that since his appeal the previous May, Mr Harber had received dozens of telephone calls from people eager to talk to him about the Blue Bell Hill ghost and others. Around thirty of the estimated ninety calls had concerned the Blue Bell Hill girl, but all had related second-hand information. No-one had been forthcoming with a description of the girl.[3]

Both articles relate the familiar story of the girl Hitch-Hiker, but with a few important differences. While still awaiting her lift by the side of the Maidstone–Chatham road at the bottom of Blue Bell Hill, the girl is now said to chat to the driver during the journey into Maidstone. Whether in this conversation she gives her home address goes without comment and, in any case, proves to be irrelevant. No longer content to wait the few minutes it would take to reach the closest outskirts of Mote Park, she now vanishes near Week Street—an equally familiar but more precisely defined (and therefore preferential) town feature, that provides familiarity and thus plausibility to the story.

The story takes an abridged (some would say, degraded) form over that of the address-giving ghost who vanishes on arrival at her home. The girl's abrupt or premature disappearance in this case, which occurs before she has given her address (contrary to most similar oral versions), deprives the motorist of the opportunity to proceed to the house where he obtains proof of her deceased status from the resident(s).

Considering the well-supported accounts that were to make Blue Bell Hill's ghost front page news in *Kent Messenger* Group newspapers in 1974 and 1992, it is ironic that the story's roots should be found in an absolutely typical Phantom Hitch-Hiker tale—a tale, from its stylised construction and content, we have learned to view with some suspicion.

Thus far, the early published record provides little resistance to the idea that the story of Blue Bell Hill's hitch-hiking ghost girl represented just another transplanted Phantom Hitch-Hiker story, which may have become established in relation to the Hill for reasons proposed in the previous two chapters. Not least of these is the one which suggests that PHH tales tends to take root at places with an existing reputation for strange or supernatural occurrences where, perhaps, in cuckoo fashion, they displace the resident tale(s). It isn't difficult to imagine how fragmentary or nonsensical rumours might give way to or find expression in an introduced Phantom Hitch-Hiker narrative. Aside from its artistic qualities and ready adaptability, the story extends a much sought-after sense of logic and purpose to the ghost's manifestations. As Michael Goss noted, not only does it concur with popular notions of what ghosts are purported to be (the spirits of the dead), and how they come to be (arising from sudden or violent death—in Phantom Hitch-Hiker accounts, commonly found in a motor accident), but the story accounts for *why* they appear—in this case, to complete an unfinished journey home, or to search for the betrothed they have left behind. (On the latter point, it might be supposed that the elevated emotional state of the victim at the time of her death—demonstrated to best effect by Blue Bell Hill's tragic bride-to-be—contributes equally to the 'how' of her appearances as to the 'why').

The later history of the Blue Bell Hill case certainly suggests that the original rumours of a haunting may have had some basis in fact, even if their outward expression through the newspapers came in the form of an apparently fanciful Phantom Hitch-Hiker tale—something that would inevitably find favour (particularly with the press) over similarly vague or anecdotal but aesthetically less satisfying accounts.

All of the above is speculation, of course, but it may go some way toward explaining why the next published account describing ghostly encounters at Blue Bell Hill—David Smith's spectral jaywalkers—attracted relatively little attention, in spite of its status as the first (and only pre-1970) account involving an actual named witness. The account appears only in the *Evening Post* of 27 February 1969,[4] failing even to be duplicated in the following Friday's *Kent Messenger*.

The press appears to have not quite known what to make of Mr Smith's report. In departing from the expectations and formula established by earlier reports of a single hitch-hiking ghost, his account describing *two* ghostly pedestrians evidently failed to make anything like the same impression as the popular story on press and public alike. The account finds no further mention in the published history—unless we consider the remarks regarding pre-1974 Phantom Jaywalker encounters made at the time of Maurice Goodenough's encounter (found in *The News of the World*, 14 July 1974; *Chatham News*, 19 July 1974) to be vague references to it.[5]

Perhaps David Smith's story may have fared better had it included some descriptive detail that would have enabled it to be more clearly related to the familiar story of the girl Hitch-Hiker, but other than the fact that his two walkers appeared to be 'quite earthly and solid' both figures go undescribed, even to establishing their gender. On top of this, we are given no clue regarding the precise locations or timings of the sightings. Unfortunately, Smith is a common surname and my attempts to trace the witness in the hope of resolving some of these questions faltered against this obstacle.

The concluding paragraphs of the article return to what is described as the 'more mysterious' (certainly the more familiar) case of the hitch-hiking ghost girl. Perhaps the mystery surrounded the fact that by 1969, and in spite of the persistence of the story, still no-one had come forward to claim such an encounter, and the girl's identity—indeed, her very existence—remained problematic.

The brief outline of the girl's alleged activities given at the foot of the article is, in principle, no different to that found in earlier versions. However, after repeated appearances at the bottom of Blue Bell Hill, the girl is now said to wait for her lift to Maidstone at the top of the Hill. Motorists, who have noted nothing unusual about her appearance when they stop to offer her a lift, continue on into the town but, when answering the girl's request and they come to let her out at Week Street (no longer in the *vicinity* of Week Street, it may be noted), they find she has vanished.

Following the rather different picture of the haunting painted by David Smith's account, the case received no further press attention for almost two years, and featured then only as a lead-off for an appeal for readers to send in their own ghost stories for which the author, John Huffam, was offering two guineas for what he considered the most fascinating. Writing in his 'Listening Post' column for the *Evening Post* on 9 December 1970,[6] Huffam declared that the girl phantom of Blue Bell Hill—'that old chestnut of a ghost story'—had come out of hiding again. During the previous week he had heard at least two uncorroborated stories of motorists giving lifts to the 'now celebrated' girl Hitch-Hiker—a girl with a habit of vanishing shortly after being picked up.

Huffam speculated whether the massive earth-moving programme and heavy road works in the area (the preparation for the building of the phase I section of the dual carriageway of the A229, initiated barely five months earlier, in July of 1970)[7] may have shaken up the spirit world, or whether it was the onset of Christmas again, with its eerie ambience, that had prompted the revival of the story.

Although in all probability intended as a throwaway remark, Huffam's comment regarding the possible significance of the earth-shifting programme is nevertheless of interest. It might be recalled from Chapter 2 that the levelling of the terrain to facilitate the construction of the new road necessitated the removal and redistribution of approximately a million tons of material, which was certainly a huge undertaking by most road-building standards.

Significant modifications to the road network above and below Blue Bell Hill have taken place in the intervening years. In the early 1980s an extension of the dual carriageway at the top of the Hill finally enabled the A229 to bypass Blue Bell Hill Village. The road complex north of the village was more extensively modified between 1999 and 2003 as part of a major widening of the A2/M2 motorway through the Nashenden Valley—which itself coincided with the construction of Section 1 of the Channel Tunnel Rail Link and the North Downs Tunnel, which carries the route beneath Blue Bell Hill.[8] But before this, in 1992, the most significant work in the area since 1972 was the widening of the M20 motorway and the associated modifications to Junction 6 at the foot of the Hill. This £70 million project, which began in the spring of 1992, was in full swing by November of that year, at the time of Ian Sharpe's and Chris Dawkins' encounters.[9] Parapsychology records cases involving outbreaks of poltergeist activity and other ghostly phenomena that have reportedly come about as a result of renovation or alteration to the physical environment. Could a similar mechanism be responsible for triggering the phenomenon at Blue Bell Hill? The question is one we will return to.

For the record, it is worth noting that John Huffam's appeal resulted in no further information regarding the Blue Bell Hill ghost.

Part 2: 1974–1980

The Goodenough Incident revisited

1974, of course, was the year of Maurice Goodenough's encounter with a mystery child on Blue Bell Hill. The incident, which was outlined in the opening chapter, both renewed the interest of the local press in the case after a number of years of apparent abandonment and, for the first time, attracted the attention of the national tabloids. Altogether, including the three Sunday tabloids, the incident inspired ten newspaper articles,[10] making it the most widely publicised event in the history of the case, to be surpassed in time only by the publicity surrounding the events of 1992.

Passing over David Smith's testimony regarding two ghostly pedestrians in 1969, this was the first time an actual witness had come forward to claim a strange encounter on Blue Bell Hill—although at the time, Mr Goodenough had no idea that his concerned flight to Rochester Police Station to report a collision with a young girl would embroil him in something as bizarre as a ghost story. As we have seen, the location of the incident and the subsequent failure of the police to locate the child that Goodenough claimed to have hit that July night led the press to conclude that he had encountered the legendary girl phantom of Blue Bell Hill—a conclusion that overlooked the patent discrepancies in age and behaviour between the girl and the female Hitch-Hiker, and one apparently arrived at before police could properly conclude their inquiries.

Viewed in isolation, before the remarkably similar accounts given by Sharpe and Dawkins in November 1992 that were to prompt its re-evaluation, the Goodenough incident provides few clues to justify the rather extreme conclusions arrived at by the press at the time. As Michael Goss pointed out, both Goodenough and the police (as demonstrated by their respective actions) clearly viewed the accident as a real event involving a normal flesh-and-blood human being. It was the subsequent press reporting that first suggested a supernatural interpretation.

It goes against accepted sense to suppose that a phantom might be capable of attaining, albeit temporarily, all the physical characteristics and capabilities of a normal, live human being—weight, form, skin texture and warmth, speech, and the ability to sustain visible injury—that Goodenough must have noted (or failed to note the lack of) in removing the girl from the road. It is much easier, certainly more rational, to believe that the girl was exactly what she appeared to be: a child accident victim who had absented herself from the scene after Goodenough, unsure of her injuries, had left to seek help. Quite what a child should have been doing alone at such an isolated spot so late at night is another matter.

Goss noted one possibility considered at the time—that the girl may have been on the run, perhaps from a local child care centre. Only three months earlier, in April, two 11-year-old girls on their way to Chatham had been intercepted by police at Blue Bell Hill after absconding from a Maidstone school.[11] Goss theorised that during the hiatus between Goodenough's departure and his return with the police, the girl may have crawled or walked away, her injuries perhaps only superficial, or at least not as severe as the motorist imagined.

Fear of apprehension, absconder or not, would certainly provide sufficient motivation for a child to leave the scene as soon as she was able. However, the converse—the fear that *no-one* was coming back for her—would also explain why she may have been encouraged to help herself. It is not difficult to sympathise with the thoughts of a young girl, lying injured in the dark by the side of the road. Goodenough's hasty departure may have given her the impression that she was being abandoned—an impression that would have turned increasingly to certainty the longer she remained there.

Most sources imply that Goodenough's return with the police was not long delayed, suggesting that following his report to them in person at Rochester Police Station, they rushed with him to the scene (which the *Chatham Standard* of 16 July places on the Chatham Road a little before it joins the new A229).[12] Only the

The probable scene on the Chatham Road of the 1974 Goodenough incident, and the location also of the fatal crash in 1965 involving a bride-to-be. Facing south from the footbridge at the road's junction with the modern A229

Chatham News (19 July 1974) provides an actual time estimate for Goodenough's round-trip: thirty minutes—certainly a more realistic estimate given the distance from the accident scene to the police station in Cazeneuve Street, Rochester (a little over five miles).

Thirty minutes—ample time, one might think, for the girl to assess her own condition and, even allowing for her injuries, to be well away from the scene before the police arrived. It is not unreasonable to imagine, as Goss suggested, that the girl may even have reached a safe refuge before the police search commenced. At very least, he observed that the protection offered by the darkness and the heavily foliated terrain, could have meant she easily evaded detection during the search, which ensued after some time with a tracker dog.

There is some question regarding the means by which Goodenough first reported the incident. The commonly accepted view is that following failed attempts to wave down passing vehicles for assistance, and out of sight of a telephone box, Goodenough drove to Rochester Police Station, arriving there (according to Goss) at 12.15 a.m. However, later inquiries with various Kent constabularies made by Michael Goss produced contradictory accounts. One, to the Divisional Superintendent at Maidstone's Divisional Headquarters in 1980 (admittedly made after records relating to the incident had been destroyed.[13] This version is therefore dependent on the memory of an individual) suggested that Goodenough first reported the incident by telephone—a view that concurred with Tom Harber's understanding of events. According to this premise, it was only after he had returned to the scene and found that the girl had vanished that Goodenough drove to the police station, fearful that an injured child was wandering about the countryside.

According to Tom Harber, who later interviewed him, Goodenough believed the girl might be concussed, and was horrified to think she might die.[14] If this were the case, we might question what Goodenough told the police, and what their initial response might have been for him to feel that a trip to the station was warranted after discovering the girl to be missing. Should not help have been despatched immediately upon receipt of his call?

A simpler and more realistic explanation is given by David Elvy, one-time police officer for the Blue Bell Hill locality, and one of the officers engaged in the investigations there in 1992. Ironically, Mr Elvy's father, a former sergeant at Maidstone Police Station, was involved in the 1974 investigation, and was in fact the officer who organised the party to accompany Goodenough back to the scene (which he placed as near the White Lodge access road, just off the modern A229 a short distance north of the slip-road) following a referral from Rochester Police Station. According to Mr Elvy Snr., the public telephone at the top of the Hill was not working,[15] forcing Goodenough to drive on to report the incident in person.

Whatever the case, had the child made her getaway while Goodenough was away, it stands to reason that by the time he returned to the scene and then set about driving to Rochester, she would have had appreciably more than thirty minutes in which to make her escape.

On their arrival at the scene the police found only Goodenough's abandoned car blanket. An immediate search of both sides of the hillside revealed nothing, and the search was extended to include door-to-door inquiries. One Blue Bell Hill resident who later spoke to Michael Goss recalled being asked by police if her daughters were indoors. Another resident, living in Queenswood Road on Kit's Coty Estate, recalled the systematic check of all houses in the area in the early hours of that morning. Posed the same question as the lady above, this man allowed the police into his house to prove that his ten-year-old daughter was at home and asleep.

After some time (at dawn, according to three sources) ,[16] a tracker dog was brought in to continue the search, by which time the effort was reportedly hindered by heavy rain (*The Gazette*, 16 July). Not surprisingly given the conditions, no tracks or bloodstains were found. Subsequent checks on local hospital admissions failed to produce anyone matching the girl's description.

The absence of a tangible trace or any kind of lead would be seen by the press as evidence that the girl was something other than entirely human—a ghost. However, the lack of blood, tracks, or even a scent trace on the car blanket which had covered the girl allows no definite conclusions to be drawn, as Goss confirmed when he sought expert opinion on the matter from the Essex Police Dog School. Chief Inspector Clark stated that tracking with a dog is not as straightforward as is widely assumed. In this case, the search—with only a single dog (not the tracker dogs reported by the newspapers—a fact established by Goss) proceeded in less than ideal conditions, and again, according to newspaper sources, sometime after the girl had vanished. The scent, if present at all, would not necessarily be strong, and would deteriorate rather quickly. It could easily be masked by or confused by scent given off by the human searchers at the scene and the roadside environment itself, with its residuum of traffic-related traces and odours. And, of course, there would be no guarantee that a usable scent obtained from the blanket could be tracked with any success.[17]

With the outcome of the police investigation proving inconclusive, the incident naturally became subject of free press conjecture regarding the girl's true nature and identity. Other than the *Chatham News*,[18] which at the close of its report aired police fears for the girl's condition and safety (something which continued to demonstrate the seriousness with which the police were treating the matter), the majority of the press coverage of the incident during the forthcoming week shows little regard for the plight of a missing child in its almost unrestrained eagerness to relate the incident to the girl Hitch-Hiker of rumour and legend.

Paradoxically, these sources suggest the police themselves contributed to the supernatural furore. A spokesman revealed that they had investigated many strange reports from motorists since the deaths of two[19] girls in a crash on the Hill a number of years earlier (given variously as '1967', 'eight years ago', or in the case of the *Chatham News*, '1965')[20]—a 'clue' that would lead reporter Nigel Nelson to identify and, for the first time, name the 1965 car crash and Judith Lingham in connection with the case.

On one occasion, according to *The News of the World* (14 July), which attributed the information to the police spokesman (said to be based at Maidstone), a group of people stopped to pick up a young girl. She sat in the back of the car and, after giving her name and address, just disappeared. They later went to the address where they met a couple who confirmed that their daughter had been killed some years previously on *Bluebird* Hill ...

Essentially the same story, less clearly assigned to the police spokesman but more correctly to Blue Bell Hill, appeared in the *Evening Post* the following day

(15 July). In this, it is a single motorist who picks up the address-giving ghost, who vanishes from the back seat before reaching the stated address in Gillingham, to which he inevitably proceeds after the encounter. Other motorists and a motorcyclist had apparently reported similar encounters with a young female hitch-hiker on Blue Bell Hill.

The *Chatham News* adds that motorists had on occasion also knocked down a teenage girl who subsequently vanished. However, as we have observed previously, it is surely significant that no reference to such a case exists prior to Maurice Goodenough's experience in 1974.

Following the scale of the police search and with the whole affair rapidly turned by the press into what Goss described as a 'ghostly mystery', it is hardly surprising that no-one—the parents or guardians of the girl—came forward to offer an explanation. Taking all into account, the real mystery behind the incident appeared to be how it could so readily be blown out of all proportion by the press.

In 1990, a snippet of information came to light which at long last held some promise of offering a solution to the Goodenough affair. At very least it reinforced suspicions held by some for years that the girl's identity was known or suspected by some local residents. Mrs Beever of Sheerness, who we first met in the previous chapter, told me that a young girl was known to frequently stray from her home in the Blue Bell Hill area. Known to whom, though, was not forthcoming.[21]

Could this conceivably be the solution to this particular mystery? It seemed so at the time. If so, there was the possibility that the girl or her parents could be traced for confirmation, and the whole matter regarding ghosts finally laid to rest. Quite frankly, though, I had made no attempt at verification by the time of Ian Sharpe's and Chris Dawkins' encounters in 1992 when, suddenly, this perfectly logical explanation was cast into some doubt.

However, it is worth considering the implications of discovering with certainty that the girl Goodenough ran into that night really *was* a normal human child. What would we then make of the later reports that so closely mimicked his encounter—namely those of Sharpe and Dawkins? Since it seems highly improbable that similar events involving an equally elusive young woman would coincidentally be played out at the same location years later, or that Sharpe and Dawkins could have been subjects of a hoax (the improved observational conditions at both locations and prompt searches for the victim by both drivers precludes the possibility of an unobserved escape), we would be forced to consider that their experiences may have in part been stimulated by an unconscious recollection or knowledge of the sensationalised newspaper coverage of the Goodenough incident. Either that—or a real phenomenon had for some reason chosen to pattern itself on an event which, although non-ghostly in nature, happened to coincide with popular expectations.[22]

How and why such should spontaneously translate itself into essentially identical and convincing personal encounters years later—which, in this scenario, would be based on a false belief that the location was haunted—defies easy explanation, but it would have to be considered an important factor in such experiences. The possibility that vivid hallucinatory experiences might form the basis of many assumed hauntings—whatever the precise mechanism—is something that is examined in detail in a later chapter. Certainly, in cases such as Blue Bell Hill which, as we shall more properly see later, supports some evidence of a truly anomalous phenomenon, a hallucinatory component cannot reasonably be disputed. This is not to say that the percipient imagined the whole thing, merely that the interaction of the mind with some extrinsic triggering process forms a necessary part of the experience.

A common feature of the encounters at Blue Bell Hill has been the impression of each driver that he or she had hit a real person—an action which, as has been previously pointed out, should have resulted in some damage to their vehicle and have been quite devastating, if not fatal, to a real human casualty. The failure to find *any* sign of damage or physical trace suggests that the subject of the collision could not have been real, at least as far as our understanding of reality is concerned.

Michael Goss's evaluation of the Goodenough incident questioned the speed of Goodenough's car at the time of the collision. As he noted, the superficiality of the girl's injuries—a cut to her forehead and skinned knees—were not inconsistent with a relatively low speed that may have resulted in little or no damage to the vehicle itself. Although most sources make no mention of whether he had time to brake before the collision, the *Sunday People* article differs, suggesting that Goodenough braked hard on sight of the girl, in which case his speed would have been reduced appreciably before actual contact.

Nevertheless, we might agree with Tom Harber, who told Goss that he thought the girl would have been thrown to one side as a result of the collision, not fallen immediately in front of the vehicle where Goodenough is said to have found her. The point, although seemingly inconsequential, gains in significance when we recall the descriptions given by Ian Sharpe and Chris Dawkins, both of whom reported a broadly similar effect: the young woman, instead of being thrown over the top of the vehicle or to one side from the force of the impact, vanished beneath the bonnet in a decidedly unnatural fashion—melting from view, all the time with her eyes calmly fixed on the driver. In Ian Sharpe's case, where we have a definite speed estimate (around 50 mph) his victim should most certainly have been thrown over the vehicle and have caused significant damage to the vehicle, if not serious harm to the driver himself.

The calm gaze of the girl reported by Sharpe and Dawkins is strongly remindful of a description given in another road ghost account, which took place two miles outside Llanidloes, Powys (Wales). In May 1973, school headmaster Bill Hopkins found himself unable to avoid a collision with a woman who stepped out in front of his vehicle as he approached an old and apparently notorious railway bridge (known as the Red Bridge) on the road to Newtown. In a strikingly similar description to that given by Ian Sharpe, Hopkins told of the way the woman had looked straight at him with a *sorrowful* expression as his vehicle passed through her.[23]

The newspaper coverage of the Goodenough incident uniformly states that his victim appeared as if from nowhere before his vehicle—a description that undoubtedly supported the contentions of the press—after all, ghosts habitually appear and disappear, but possibly also an accurate impression related by the witness? The shocking nature of a sudden and unexpected encounter at a late hour might very well have left the witness with the impression that the girl had appeared spontaneously. However, Tom Harber's interview with Maurice Goodenough suggested that the girl did not run into the road, but seemed to spring out of the earth. Notes made by Michael Goss from his discussions with Tom add that the girl appeared to emerge from *under* the car.[24] This apparent response to passing vehicles would be a feature that would recur in later reports at Blue Bell Hill (see Chapter 9). Interestingly, Chris Dawkins' printed comments in the *Kent Today* of 24 November 1992 describe his victim's disappearance in similar terms: at impact, it was as if the ground had moved apart and the female figure vanished beneath the car.[25]

Such minutiae, together with the broader consistencies in behaviour, begin to speak for something genuinely anomalous at play—something that is not rooted entirely in the mind of the percipient. Michael Goss learned from a local resident that only a matter of months after the Goodenough incident the police received a similar report from another man. This incident attracted no press attention, and it seems that in this case the police suspected a hoax.[26]

However, from the perspective granted the case in 1992, Maurice Goodenough's experience can be seen to clearly fit a pattern of events on Blue Bell Hill which, rather discouragingly from his point of view, raises the real possibility that (and as the press claimed at the time) he had encountered a ghost. As we shall see, the publicised encounters—Goodenough, Sharpe, and Dawkins—are not the only well-attested reports describing a similarly behaved phantom female associated with Blue Bell Hill. But for the moment, let us stay with the discussion of the Goodenough incident.

If we were for a moment to accept the popular interpretation of what a ghost is purported to be—the spirit of a departed person—we inevitably run in to the problem of reconciling Goodenough's ten-year-old victim with the young woman described by Sharpe and Dawkins.

Tom Harber apparently had no problem identifying the girl with one of the 1965 crash victims. He pointed out to Michael Goss that Goodenough's estimate of the girl's age was made under fraught circumstances on an unlit stretch of road (but presumably partially illuminated by his car's headlights?). Tom believed that Goodenough's estimate of the girl's age may have been based on two factors: her diminutive stature, and her attire. Her white ankle socks in particular, he observed, may have given Goodenough the impression that she was a schoolgirl. Goss himself points out that they were also a fashionable item of dress among teenagers in the 1960s.

Tom undoubtedly favoured the bride-to-be as the ghost. Her identification, said Goss, rested on descriptions he had gleaned of the girl Hitch-Hiker. The bride-to-be, Tom claimed, was a small person, apparently youthful in appearance—something upon which a number of his witnesses had remarked. On the night she died, she had been dressed 'youngish' and had been wearing white ankle socks.

Quite how Tom might have come by this information, however, is not known. I stated earlier that the bride-to-be was not from Maidstone as Tom appears to have believed (at least initially), but from Australia. I later established that she was on only her second trip to England (for the occasion of her marriage) when she died. She had no relatives in Britain. To my knowledge, therefore, no record accessible to the public existed in the UK that could have provided such information. The newspapers reporting on the 1965 crash provide no descriptions or other pertinent specifics relating to the victims—such would hold no relevance in the reporting of the crash itself, although two of the party—but *not* the bride-to-be—were pictured in Kent newspapers.[27]

The only possible source of this information (aside from friends or relatives of the other deceased, or the surviving member of the party—and there is no evidence to indicate that Tom attempted to contact them) would have been the public inquest of the 1965 tragedy, which was held in March 1966. In this case, even if Tom first heard the story very early in 1966, it is unlikely he could have gathered sufficient information to identify the crash and its bride-to-be in time to attend the inquest of the accident. Indeed, our earlier examination of Tom's early involvement in the case almost certainly rules this out. Other than through a romantically inspired identification with the ill-starred bride-to-be, it is therefore difficult to see how Tom Harber came to so definite a conclusion.

Tom's comments regarding the apparent youthfulness of the ghost girl, however, has found some support in a convincing double-witness encounter (*c.*1985)

I would later hear. In this case, a couple who were confronted with the sight of a girl dressed in a light top and white ankle socks one night on the Rochester Road at the foot of Blue Bell Hill (see Chapter 9 for the full account) estimated her to have been in her early teens.

In the absence of the witness himself (Goss states that the negative aspects of the publicity surrounding his encounter eventually forced Goodenough to refuse to talk about his experience),[28] it is impossible to confirm the estimated age of the girl, although there is no reason to suspect that it was not accurately reported.

Intriguingly, an account given by one of the police officers involved in the investigation gives a different estimate—one that compares more favourably with that given by both Sharpe and Dawkins and the age band of the 1965 crash victims, as well as presenting a picture of the incident that is somewhat at variance with the published versions.

In his book *One Dog and her Man,*[29] retired dog handler Ted Wright's memoirs of his work with police dog Bess (a black Labrador) for the Kent County Constabulary, Ted recounts how, in the early hours during one particularly busy night shift (and therefore not at dawn), he and Bess were called out to Blue Bell Hill to search for a missing accident victim. Although neither the year nor the motorist's name is given, there is little doubt from his description that he is referring to the Goodenough incident of July 1974.

On arrival at the scene, Ted took minimal details from the Inspector before directing Bess to a car rug that lay spread out on the grass verge. Scent detected at the rug led back only to the assembled gathering of police officers and ambulancemen. Checks round about the rug revealed nothing. Bess failed to pick up the human scent they were looking for, although she had no problem finding Ted's van keys that he subsequently dropped into the grass to act as a control.

Ted relates how they listened to a very strange story from a motorist, who had been driving up the Hill when a lady had stepped out in front of him. Having no time to take evasive action, he struck the woman with such force that she was thrown clear over the car and landed in the road behind.[30] When he went to her, the motorist found her to be bleeding badly. Fetching a car rug from the boot of his car, he gently placed the lady on it and carefully moved her to the safety of the grass verge. With the road deserted at that hour, he drove straight to Rochester Police Station to report the accident and to obtain help. When the emergency services arrived at the scene with the motorist, there was no sign of the lady, and no trace of blood. The damage on the man's car had also apparently disappeared. In the words of Bess, from whose point of view the book is written, the piece concludes with: 'Had I been trying to track the infamous Ghost Lady of Bluebell Hill?'

Seeking confirmation of the details of his account (particularly the estimated age of the woman) I managed to get in touch with Ted late in September 1994. First of all, he confirmed that the incident he had attended had indeed taken place in 1974. Although quite naturally he could not remember the name of the driver, the incident itself was still clear. He had been called out to the scene between 2.30 a.m. and 3.00 a.m. It was still dark. Ted placed the location on the old part of the Hill, 'about halfway up', in the region of the bend occupied by Kit's Coty Cottage (a few hundred metres below the junction with the A229). It was not raining, at least not at the time Ted conducted his search, which refutes the idea that scent from the victim or her tracks could have been obliterated before the police arrived.[31]

As Ted indicated in his book, Bess (who he described as an outstanding dog) *did* detect scent on Goodenough's car rug, but it only led back towards the road (no trace at all was found in any other direction away from the spot)—from where, of course, Goodenough had moved the woman in the first place. A possible scent trace given off by the woman would therefore have been confused or masked by that of Goodenough himself, and subsequently the police investigators who would have inevitably approached the article from the same direction.

Something that *did* strike Ted as odd was the arrangement of the car rug. It lay quite literally on top of the grass. There was, he said, no indentation, no impression in the grass beneath to suggest it had borne the weight of a body. Conflicting with newspaper versions which suggest Goodenough carried his victim to the grass verge and then covered her with his car rug (in which case, the discarded rug might well be found lying 'on top' of the grass), Ted said that he had in fact laid the rug on the road next to the woman (who was quite definitely described by the motorist as a young woman) and then carefully rolled her onto it before proceeding to kind of drag her carefully to the safety of the verge.[32] Inevitably, some sign of disturbance or crushing of the grass beneath the rug and on the perimeter of the grass strip nearest the road should have been evident.

Goodenough's initial reaction was described as distraught. However, when the police search revealed absolutely no sign of an accident, let alone the fatality they expected to find, Goodenough's state of panic turned to confused embarrassment. With no lead to go on, the investigation was wound down fairly quickly.

Finally, Ted remarked on certain 'inconsistencies' in Goodenough's behaviour noted by officers at the time. In parallel with my own thoughts on the matter, they were puzzled as to why he had driven like 'hell's bells' to Rochester Police Station when at the top of the Hill, in Blue Bell Hill Village, the police house had been open, with light showing. Plus the fact that there was a telephone kiosk there, which Ted himself ascertained was in working order. However, it is entirely possible that Goodenough was unaware of their existence, or that they were overlooked in his blind panic following the accident. Under the circumstances, he likely decided that it would be quicker to drive directly to a place where he was sure help could be obtained rather than waste time searching for a phone.

The most valuable aspect of Ted Wright's information, of course, is the revised age estimate of Maurice Goodenough's victim—not a child as reported by the newspapers, but a young woman. If we accept this as the true estimate given by Goodenough, Ted's version eliminates a major discrepancy between the Goodenough incident and the later reports, providing a consistency to the sightings not before realised.

We have noted that Tom Harber believed the ghost to be that of the bride-to-be. Others, of course, had different ideas concerning her identity. As we are by now familiar, the *Kent Messenger*'s Nigel Nelson named another member of that crash party as the ghost: 22-year-old Judith Lingham.

In his article for the *Evening Post* of 19 July 1974, Nelson stated that while Kent ghost hunters were busily following up the latest mystery, he interviewed the 'ghost's' father, retired merchant seaman Charles Lingham. Mr Lingham was understandably amazed at the suggestion that his daughter might be haunting Blue Bell Hill. According to an expanded version of the article which appeared in the *Kent Messenger* the following Friday (26 July), he said that it was the first time he had been told that his daughter was considered to be the 'mystery spirit'.

Precisely how the identification of Judith Lingham came about is still a matter of speculation. A few possibilities were discussed in the opening chapter, where it was supposed that an unconscious link may have been forged by Nelson between Judith's home (Rochester) and the destination of Maurice Goodenough, also in Rochester; or that a photograph of Judith featured in the *Maidstone Gazette* of 23 November 1965 had focused his attention on her.

Apart from informing Mr Lingham of the existence of rumours surrounding his daughter, there appears to have been little to gain from Nigel Nelson's interview with him. However, it is possible that Nelson gleaned his 'bridesmaids' version of the 1965 crash and the events leading up to it from Judith's father, relying on his recollection of the events of that night. Support for this idea is found in correspondence with Mr Nelson in 1990, in which he indicated that his information probably came from a mixture of police sources, Judith's father, and *Kent Messenger* files, although his recollection was necessarily hazy after so many years.[33]

In that same correspondence Mr Nelson told of how the Goodenough story first came to light, and how he was led to formally identify the 1965 crash. At the time he was crime reporter for the *Evening Post*. During the routine police calls one morning, the duty inspector at Rochester Police Station (who Mr Nelson remembered only as 'Fred')[34] told him that a motorist had dashed in to say he had hit a young girl on Blue Bell Hill and no trace of her had been found. Fred found the whole thing so strange he mentioned to Nelson the 'old tale' of the ghost of Blue Bell Hill, prompting him to try to find out the real story behind it all.

Nigel Nelson's articles bring Tom Harber back into the picture, quoting him in respect to the background of the case. It is in these articles that we learn from Tom the timings of the encounters: generally after 11 p.m. By this time, it seems, Tom's collection of what he believed to be authentic reports had grown to fourteen, although no detail relating to any is to be found in Nelson's articles. Recounted instead is the familiar story of the hitch-hiking ghost, described here as 'a young girl'—a description clearly designed to match Maurice Goodenough's recent report. However, contrary to earlier newspaper accounts that quote Tom Harber and which almost consistently report the girl's destination as Maidstone, the girl is now said to seek her lift in the opposite direction, towards Chatham (although it is added that the same had happened to motorists heading down the Hill). Motorists driving up the Hill would be flagged down by a girl who claimed to have been involved in a car accident, and who wished to be taken to Rochester.

The inference of the last sentence is clear: that Judith Lingham, named in these same articles for the first time—and the only one of the deceased from the 1965 crash party to hail from Rochester—was likely to be the ghost. However, we must surely be suspicious of the fact that it was only with the identification of the 1965 crash that the Medway Towns (where all the victims were residing)—in particular, Rochester—began to feature in the apocryphal accounts in preference to Maidstone, which until then had been the established destination of the ghost girl.

It is curious that this information should be ascribed to Tom Harber who, as we have seen, previously considered Maidstone to be the ghost girl's home town. What prompted his apparent change of mind regarding the girl's destination? I suppose it is possible that a few of Tom's later accounts involved a girl intent on travelling to Medway rather than to Maidstone. The other—more likely—possibility is that the attribution reflects a journalist's attempt to establish credibility for his supposition through credit to a supposedly authoritative source—an 'expert' or 'psychic researcher'. However, Tom Harber told Michael Goss in 1980 that the identification of Judith Lingham did not originate with him.[35]

Considering the small flood of sightings in 1992, it is difficult at least to argue with Nigel Nelson's conclusion in his article for the *Evening Post* of 19 July 1974: 'Whether it is Judith or not, it's quite clear that someone or something is making its presence felt on Bluebell Hill.'[36]

A Phantom Thrill on *Blueberry* Hill

Apart from passing references made in two articles on ghosts in the *Kent Messenger* (in August 1974, and January 1975—the former briefly outlines the Goodenough incident; the latter reports on the making of a half-hour programme on ghosts by a film crew from Southern TV, who are reported to have gone to Blue Bell Hill to film a reconstruction of a motorist's encounter with the Phantom Hitch-Hiker)[37]—the Blue Bell Hill case received no further attention from the local press until 1977.

Meanwhile, in May 1975, an account appeared in an independent source, the popular weekly magazine *Reveille*.[38] The article related the experience of pop musician Richard Studholme.[39] According to the article, the incident occurred just after midnight as Mr Studholme was making his way back to London after a night's work at Rochester. As he began his run down *Blueberry* Hill (described as four miles to the north of Maidstone, and therefore clearly meant to be Blue Bell Hill) his attention was drawn to a hitch-hiker thumbing a lift.

He stopped the car and the girl came running over. She asked for a lift to West Kingsdown, approximately twelve miles west of Blue Bell Hill, and since it was along his way, Studholme agreed. He took the girl's case from her and put it in the car. The girl got in and he set out for West Kingsdown.

During the journey the girl said very little, although she did ask Mr Studholme if, after dropping her off, he would call at her parents' house in Swanley to deliver a message. 'I agreed to tell her parents that I had given her a lift and that she was well,' he said. 'She gave me their address and I dropped her off at West Kingsdown.'

When he got to the house, though, the man who answered the door informed him that it could not have been his daughter he had given a lift to since she had been killed in a road accident two years previously, 'at the very spot' Studholme had picked her up.

Mr Studholme's reaction to this news was to conclude that he had been the subject of a cruel hoax, in spite of the fact that his passenger had apparently been dressed in clothes similar to those worn by the dead girl the night she died. There had been nothing unearthly about her; quite the contrary, in fact. He recalled touching her; he had taken her bag from her and helped her into the car. 'There was nothing unusual about it. No peculiar sensations like coldness,' he commented.

Some months later, however, he read in a Kent newspaper about other strange happenings at the spot, at which point he began to entertain the idea that he might himself have given a lift to a ghost.

I GAVE GHOST A LIFT, SAYS POP STAR

POP musician Richard Studholme is convinced that he once gave a lift to a ghost hitch hiker.

The incident happened just after midnight when he was on his way back to London after a night's work at Rochester, Kent.

The hitch hiker thumbed his car as he began the run down Blueberry Hill, four miles north of Maidstone.

Richard says he stopped the car and the girl came running over.

"She asked me if I would drop her at West Kingsdown. It was on my way, so I agreed," says 19-year-old Richard, who is lead guitarist with the pop group, Chicory Tip.

Richard took the girl's case and put it in the car. She got in and he drove her to West Kingsdown.

"During the journey she said very little," says Richard. But she did ask him if he would call at her parents' house at Swanley farther along the route to London.

"I agreed to tell her parents that I had given her a lift and that she was well. She gave me their address and I dropped her off at West Kingsdown," he says.

But he was in for a shock when the girl's father answered his knock.

"He told me I couldn't have given his daughter a lift because she had been killed in a road accident two years earlier at the very spot where I picked her up," he says.

Richard at first believed it had been a cruel

Richard Stodholme

she was killed. "It wasn't until some months later that I read in a Ken newspaper of other strange happenings at the spot that I began to believe I had driven a ghost in my car," says Richard.

"I actually touched the girl. I took her bag from her and helped her into the car. There was nothing unusual about it. No peculiar sensations like col ness," recalled Richard.

The mystery hitch hiker has been picked up a number of times since at the same spot. And other drivers have called at the address in Swanley, just like Richard.

In fact, Richard's girlfriend, Ann-Marie, has a brother in the local police force. Recently a driver reported that he had hit a girl on the same road, covered her body with a blanket and rushed for help.

Richard Studholme's encounter, as reported by *Reveille* magazine (c.1975)

It is almost certain that these 'strange happenings' refer to what was in fact a single incident—Maurice Goodenough's experience in 1974. Only that incident had achieved the degree of publicity whereby a newspaper report was likely to have been seen by Studholme. The article itself adds that the brother of Mr Studholme's girlfriend, Ann-Marie, who was a police officer in the local force at the time, stated that a driver had 'recently' hit a girl on the same road and covered her with a blanket before rushing for help (which can only be Goodenough's encounter).

The coverage of Richard Studholme's encounter naturally resurrected vague tales of the hitch-hiking phantom, which may have given rise to the impression that there had been a number of similar 'happenings' there—even, as the article's unidentified author intimates, that the Hitch-Hiker had been picked up a number of times since at the same spot. And in requisite fashion, the writer attempts to further underpin the supernatural interpretation by suggesting that other drivers had also called at the Swanley address—although, of course, no evidence or source is given in support of this claim.

It is impossible to make any kind of valued judgment regarding Richard Studholme's experience on the basis of a single, perfunctory source such as the *Reveille* article. If it were not for the named witness, it would be easy to dismiss the story simply on account of its close resemblance to the formulaic Phantom Hitch-Hiker script. However, both Michael Goss and I subsequently established that the event *did* take place largely as described. At the time of Goss's investigation, Studholme himself was unavailable for comment, having taken up residence in the USA. In his absence, Goss contacted a person close to him, who confirmed the story and assured him that Studholme would not have made up such a story. We might reason that if he had, we would not expect to find the girl and her 'disappearance' described in such natural terms, nor the incident written off as a hoax by the witness himself.

My own attempt to contact Mr Studholme for verification of the incident was more successful. My brief telephone interview with him in the autumn of 1994 confirmed that the incident *had* happened—although, interestingly, not quite as described by *Reveille*.[40]

The article had neglected to state the date or year of the encounter, only that Mr Studholme was convinced 'he once' gave a lift to a ghost. Reasonable estimates based on the limited information contained in the article suggested it had occurred some months before Maurice Goodenough's encounter in July 1974. Studholme himself estimated it to have been around 1973, sometime during the summer. Understandably his recollection of what to him at the time was a puzzling but otherwise not highly significant event, was less than perfect after so many years. However, the essentials of the matter—which, incidentally, he still believed to have been a hoax—were still clear to him:

He was, in fact, heading *up* Blue Bell Hill on his way back to London (via the M2) after a gig at The Mitre pub in the Corn Exchange, Maidstone (which is in the opposite direction to that stated in the article). It was late, around midnight. He stopped to pick up the girl at the bottom of the Hill (he could not recall the precise spot, pointing out that the Hill has changed a lot over the years—only that it was much further down than the Lower Bell). Asking her where she wanted to go, he was surprised to find she only wanted to be taken to the top of the Hill. (Where the West Kingsdown/Swanley connection came from he had no idea.) Nevertheless, he obliged her, and dropped her off at the site of the old petrol station near to the former Bridgewood roundabout north of Blue Bell Hill Village—but not before she had asked him if he would go to her house to report on her safety.

The petrol station on Maidstone Road (since demolished) near where Richard Studholme dropped off his hitch-hiking passenger in 1973

The girl gave an address in the Walderslade area, which Studholme said he wrote down and kept for years afterward (but is now unfortunately lost). Not especially familiar with the area, he could not now hazard a guess as to even the approximate whereabouts of the house.

Exactly why he agreed to go at that hour begs an answer. It might seem a little irregular to pay a visit to a house after midnight simply to report on a girl's well-being. It would be different, of course, had the girl given the impression of being distressed or in trouble, but this doesn't appear to have been the case. As it was, we can assume that the fact that Studholme lived in London made it impractical for him to delay the visit until a more sociable hour. We might also assume that the house was not equipped with a telephone—surely a more logical and convenient means of relaying the message. Whatever the justification for his impromptu visit, Studholme broke off his journey home and made his way to the address via Robin Hood Lane, which proceeds eastwards out of Blue Bell Hill Village and into Walderslade.

Even before arriving at the house, the rather nonsensical nature of Studholme's visit must surely have occurred to him. After all, he had nothing to tell the occupants other than that he had given a lift to their daughter and that she was well. If he was feeling in any way awkward at the thought of having no relevant information about the girl when he knocked at the door—a contact number or an address; a promise from her that she would get in touch soon—he must have felt immeasurably more so when it was answered. Studholme told me that the man who came to the door had been 'very upset' by the news. His daughter had been killed on Blue Bell Hill (according to the article, two years earlier). At this point, Studholme decided he had been the victim of a distasteful joke, that the girl had directed him to a household she knew had not long ago lost a daughter.

Certainly a hoax is the most plausible explanation for Richard Studholme's experience, but even this has its difficulties. Why should it have been perpetrated at a time when the Blue Bell Hill case was not especially well known? Of course, stories of a ghostly female Hitch-Hiker had been subject of rumour and occasional newspaper reporting for some years, but its popularity only really grew out of the widespread coverage surrounding the Goodenough incident, which, by Studholme's estimate, was to take place the following year.[41]

What should not be overlooked is that a hoax is quite an elaborate and risky undertaking, particularly for a young woman out alone late at night. Its success would depend on the subject both agreeing to visit the given address, and his subsequent reporting of the incident to the authorities or, preferably, the media.

On the other hand, it seems plainly incredible to consider the alternative: that the girl may have been a bona fide hitch-hiking phantom—one that was acting according to conventions familiar to us from folklore.

Precluding this possibility, it would seem, was Studholme's failure to note anything ghostly about the girl. Indeed, her departure had been in an entirely conventional manner. However, it might be recalled that, traditionally, up until the point of her disappearance, the Phantom Hitch-Hiker is taken to be a normal human being. Michael Goss further reminds us that in Version C accounts the girl does not vanish in the dramatic and unexpected fashion of the Version A Hitch-Hiker, but simply leaves the car at her destination—her home or, 'even better, the cemetery'.[42]

The cemetery as destination is undeniably a very melodramatic touch to a story, one bound to inspire scepticism. Yet it seems to be a genuine feature in at least one example we have seen—the experience of Shawn & Geri Lape in the case of Resurrection Mary (Chapter 4). Might it not also be significant, therefore, that Chris Dawkins' collision with a young woman in Blue Bell Hill Village in November 1992 occurred just as he was passing the entrance to Robin Hood Lane? The woman had appeared from the left side, from the direction of Medway Crematorium, which is located 300 metres along Robin Hood Lane. The idea seems far-fetched, but it is difficult to think of another reason why Dawkins' sighting should be so far removed from the clustered encounters further down the Hill (although we might consider that Judith Lingham's funeral took place here on 29 November 1965.[43] And, in fact there is one other, which we shall consider later).

Richard Studholme's encounter, then, appears to combine elements of Beardsley & Hankey's Version A and Version C Hitch-Hikers. Unlike the folk versions, however, it leaves us up in the air, uncertain as to what he really did encounter. The *Reveille* article suggests that his passenger had been dressed similarly to the man's daughter on the night she died, which is certainly a step towards the proof of the girl's identity and status that is found, for instance, in a motorist being shown a photograph of the dead girl. But the suggestion is not further developed, leading us to suspect that this material was probably contributed by the author as another means of reinforcing the story's ghostly countenance. The account therefore falls short of the unsettling but tidy conclusions found in most folk versions.

Aside from the fact that the account breaks two conventions of the popular tale (by providing a named witness instead of the traditionally anonymous or untraceable protagonist, and its unsatisfactory ending), there is little to distinguish Studholme's story from the standard folk narrative. Like it, there is little testable detail that might enable us to resolve the issue either way: we have no description of the girl (something that would prove useful by comparing it to descriptions given by other witnesses or to known crash victims), and only the crudest idea of the location of the given address.

One feature, however, that might be tested is the reputed death of the man's daughter on Blue Bell Hill, said in the article to have occurred two years prior to Studholme's encounter. Stepping back two years from 1973 (a year itself dependent on the reliability of the witness' memory concerning the event) brings us to 1971. On 5 November of that year the *Kent Messenger* reported the death of a 21-year-old woman in West Kent Hospital, Maidstone, following a three-car pile-up near the bottom of Blue Bell Hill. The tragedy, which had occurred some 400 days into the construction of the new A229 dual carriageway, was attributed to the confusion caused to motorists by the constant changes made to the road layout that were necessary to keep traffic flowing smoothly.[44]

The correlation seems quite impressive (even, in the wider perspective of the case, down to the November date of the crash)—that is, until we note that the victim lived at Frindsbury, not Walderslade, thereby making her an unlikely candidate for Studholme's ghostly passenger, genuine article or impostor. Besides, a source crash in 1971 could hardly explain the supposed sightings and rumours of a ghost in the middle and late 1960s. Mostly likely, it is simple coincidence. Death crashes, while not very common at Blue Bell Hill, inevitably did (and do still) occur here. Earlier that same year, for instance, in April, a lorry driver was killed when his vehicle ran off the road and hit a 27-ton earth-moving vehicle.[45]

Richard Studholme's experience therefore remains open to interpretation, although on the limited information available to us, the sensible conclusion would be to agree with the witness' own assessment of the incident. Only Mr Studholme's passenger, if she was a hoaxer, holds the answer to this particular mystery.

Nevertheless, certain features *do* fit the pattern that appears to characterise encounters at Blue Bell Hill—the timing and location of the incident, for instance. 'Around midnight'—say, between 11 p.m. and 1 a.m.—describes the timing of all the incidents we have examined so far, and the majority of those we have yet to look at. And the location, the bottom of Blue Bell Hill, features in two other sightings of mystery figures, including the one we will look at next.

Brief Encounters

After a few years of quietude, the case was reactivated in 1977 by an article in the *Evening Post* of 30 August. 'Two in 'haunting' encounter on Blue Bell Hill' describes the brief encounter a driver and his passenger had had with a mysterious woman in white in the early hours of the previous Friday (27 August).[46]

Lloyds insurance brokers Barry Collings, from Welling, and his passenger, Steven Pope, of Erith, had just turned off the M20 on to the A229 at the foot of Blue Bell Hill (on the outskirts of Maidstone) at around 12.40 a.m. when the headlights picked out the figure of a young woman standing by the roadside opposite the Veglios Motel (long since demolished to accommodate part of the M20 widening/Junction 6 interchange improvements, and now occupied by an Audi dealership).

The girl was very attractive. She wore a white evening dress and had a vanity bag (or clutch handbag, according to the *London Evening News*, which briefly recounted the incident on 12 September).[47] The dress appeared to be in some disarray which made them think she might be in some trouble. They pulled up to ask her if she was alright, and if she wanted a lift, but the question was met with a mute response.

'She didn't say anything, just smiled,' said Collings.

Then the pair of them noticed that although it was a blustery night, the girl's loose blonde hair was undisturbed, and everything about her appeared to be still. Uneasiness dawning on him, Pope whispered in disbelief: 'It's a ghost', and they quickly drove off.

At the time neither man had believed in ghosts, but later that day, after recounting the incident to colleagues, they learned for the first time about Blue Bell Hill's reputation for being haunted—which, said the article, dated back to 1965 when a bride-to-be and two companions had been killed in a crash there.

The most important question to ask about the Collings–Pope encounter might be what exactly it was about the girl that convinced two presumably stable and reliable individuals that she was a ghost?

The uncommon sight at that hour of an unaccompanied, inappropriately dressed female standing passively by the roadside might in itself have given rise to suspicions that there was something odd about her. Add to that the further incongruity of her unnerving reply to their offer of a lift: her untroubled smile which, given the girl's dishevelled appearance, must have stood in distinct contrast to their expectations—and the men might be forgiven for concluding that she was something other than a normal human female. However, these factors alone hardly justify such a claim. Although it would certainly be unusual to select this particular spot when the forecourts of the Veglios Motel and the Running Horse pub[48] were available nearby, it is not inconceivable that someone should be genuinely awaiting a lift here, even a lone female—or that she really had been in some trouble in spite of her contrasting response, in which case the men's hurried departure may have ignored some responsibility for her welfare.

The observations that appear to have persuaded the two men that the girl was a ghost—the unnatural stillness about her; the appearance of her hair seeming to be undisturbed by the blowy conditions—as Michael Goss noted, are details that might be dismissed by critics as the imaginings of witnesses already spooked by the unusual circumstances of their meeting. But was this all there was to it? Unfortunately, Pope and Collings did not stay long enough to find out one way or the other. We can only assume that had they any doubt the girl was a ghost (which I'm sure they would have preferred to do—people, as a rule, do tend to rationalise their experiences as much as possible), they would have remained long enough to properly ascertain her condition.

Equally as subjective, but clearly comparable to the experience of Pope and Collings is the sighting by Mrs Ann-Marie Austin and a female friend, also of a passive female figure dressed in white late one night on Blue Bell Hill. It is interesting in that Mrs Austin appeared to be unaware of the Pope and Collings story, and yet she reports a similar impression of unreality about the woman she saw standing by the bus stop near to the Upper Bell public house in Blue Bell Hill Village at about the same time, around 1976 or 1977.

Passing the woman on their way out of the village towards Maidstone, Mrs Austin remarked to her friend that she thought she was seeing a ghost. The woman's appearance, she said, made her shudder. She had long hair, and her face was 'deathly white'; it appeared to be 'unreal', without proper substance. The woman was still there as she looked back. Unfortunately (for us), Mrs Austin turned down the opportunity offered by her friend to go back to find out for sure. Mrs Austin wisely tempered her view of her encounter with the fact that she knew about Richard Studholme's encounter. As a former girlfriend of his, she conceded this may have had some influence upon her own interpretation. Like the Collings–Pope encounter, critics could reasonably come up with a credible alternative to a ghost as explanation, citing perhaps the bus stop and/or the pub as reason enough for the woman's presence there—although this section of the road has featured in other accounts.

Returning to the experience of Pope and Collings, it is worth noting that the location of their encounter—the bottom of Blue Bell Hill (although this spot is around a mile-and-a-half from the scene of Ian Sharpe's or Maurice Goodenough's encounters), was to be the scene of a subsequent sighting—though not of a young woman, but the diminutive figure of a bizarre 'gypsy woman' (see Chapter 11), as well as the place where Richard Studholme had stopped to pick up a young woman a few years previously. Although the wording of the *Evening Post* suggests that the men had come onto the A229 southbound (where they would almost immediately have found themselves directly opposite the Veglios Motel), the later summary given by the *London Evening News* actually states they were heading *up* the Hill—the same direction as Studholme. The possibility that a mischievous hoaxer might have been out again to dupe still more motorists, while not impossible, is possibly as difficult to accept as the idea that she was a ghost.

As the reader will have noted, in addition to the classic circumstances of the meeting, the description of the girl—white dress, blonde hair—is quite typical of the female Hitch-Hiker commonly encountered in folklore. Only the witnesses themselves can tell us if it is a true one, or one perhaps contrived to some degree by the author of the article. We can only ponder what may have happened had the young woman accepted Pope and Collings's offer of a lift.

Full Circle

Although it is quite possible that the Blue Bell Hill haunting found mention in the intervening years, the final local press account I have from this period is found in the pages of the *Kent Messenger* of 26 September 1980.[49] Appropriately, it ends in the manner of its published origin way back in December 1967, with a cursory treatment by Roy Plascott, who outlines essentially the same apocryphal story he told in that newspaper's 'Maidstone Comment' all those years ago.

'What a story—if it's on the level!' uses the Blue Bell Hill ghost as a prime example of the kind of outlandish tale (what we would today call an urban legend) that news people hear from time to time, and which, as implausible as they may sound, just might be true and they are therefore duty-bound to check out: 'It had all the markings of a first rate off-beat news story. If only it were true.'

Before 1992 and the events that catalysed the coming forward of other people with their own strange experiences at Blue Bell Hill, the words used by Plascott to open his article might have served as a fitting summary and epitaph to the case as a whole at that point. Although certain incidents—notably, the experience of Maurice Goodenough—hinted at something strange going on at Blue Bell Hill, any objective study of the case could only confess to disappointment. Lacking was even a single unequivocal account to seriously suggest that the Hill might indeed be haunted, let alone one that clearly pointed to a definite cause and identity for the ghost.

EIGHT

PRIMARY CANDIDATES

The wind doth blow today, my love,
And a few small drops of rain;
I never had but one true-love,
In cold grave she was lain.

*

'Tis down in yonder garden green,
Love, where we used to walk,
The finest flower that ere was seen
Is withered to a stalk.

From *The Unquiet Grave* (Anon)

On the evening of 14 December 1992 I met with members of Judith Lingham's family to discuss the recent sightings at Blue Bell Hill (by Ian Sharpe and Chris Dawkins) and the sometimes sensational press coverage they had generated.

After years of rumour and ambiguous press reporting, I hadn't expected to hear of anyone actually encountering the ghost. So it had been with no small surprise, and with some doubt, that I first greeted the news of Ian Sharpe's experience, which I first heard from a colleague the morning after the news release. Naturally, I was eager to find out more about the encounter (which, at the time, I felt resembled Maurice Goodenough's experience of 1974 a little *too* closely) and, hopefully, to arrange an interview with Ian.

At the same time, I felt that I should do something to try to inject some restraint regarding the connection that had once again been made with the 1965 crash, and with Judith Lingham in particular. As impressive as the proximity of Ian Sharpe's encounter to the 1965 crash anniversary had been, there was little in the way of firm evidence to support the identification.

And so, the day after the *Kent Today*'s front page splash (11 November 1992), I called in at the *Kent Messenger*'s Middle Row offices in Maidstone in the hope of talking to the reporter, Emma Cooper. By chance, Emma was in the office and came right out to talk to me. Coincidentally, she was in the process of writing up the following Friday's *Kent Messenger* version of the incident, and naturally fixed on my research as something she could use. At the end of the conversation she offered to include a brief appeal for other prospective witnesses to write to me, to which I of course agreed.

One of the letters I received in response to this appeal was from Judith Lingham's youngest sister, Catherine.[1] The letter noted somewhat wearily the reopening of interest in the subject of the Blue Bell Hill ghost. But sufficient time had passed for the family not to be upset by reports of supposed sightings of Judith, except where the facts were wrong or the story sensationalised. Catherine was interested to know what I had discovered about 'this apparent ghost'. Following a lengthy letter in reply, it was decided that it might be interesting for us to meet.

At that meeting, it was acknowledged that the 1965 crash would probably never be completely dissociated from the story of the Blue Bell Hill ghost. It was, after all, the only viable 'cause' that had until then been identified, without which the sightings lacked any logical foundation. But, it was hoped that publication of the facts might encourage the press and subsequent writers to abandon much of the unfounded and inaccurate material that had been perpetuated over the years.

Judith's sisters were very helpful in confirming a few of my own suppositions, as well as much of the new material I had gathered from other newspaper sources and official records. My research had revealed an account of the crash that differed in detail even to that described by the *Kent Messenger* in 1965, plus a different location for the accident than had thus far been presented. But in addition to trying the case for the 1965 crash connection, this material—the redressed facts—was to prove particularly useful in combating some of the sensational claims and statements of various publications, notably the national tabloid, *The Sun*.

Even before the meeting took place, press interest in the case had flared up again with a second sighting of the ghost, by Chris Dawkins, on 22 November. Close on its heels, on 26 November, *The Sun* published a sensational double-page feature on the haunting and the 1965 crash.[2] In spite of its bold claim to represent the facts surrounding the 1965 crash, the article contained some significant factual errors, plainly sourced from original newspaper accounts of the tragedy.

There had also been some attempt to contact the crash's only survivor, Gillian Burchett, for comment. As it was, the newspaper succeeded only in getting in touch with her father, who said that the matter was still too painful for his daughter to talk about. In all, the article represented the kind of journalism this book aimed to moderate.

A *Sun*-sational day

In the week following Chris Dawkins' experience, *The Sun*'s Mike Ridley took one of Britain's 'top' psychics, the late Nella Jones,[3] to Blue Bell Hill. During her brief sojourn on the Hill, Nella (who had gained some fame from her involvement in the Yorkshire Ripper case from 1979 until the arrest of 35-year-old Peter Sutcliffe in January 1981) reportedly gained impressions of all *three* victims of the 1965 crash, prompting her to claim that she had never been to a place that was so haunted.

Starting out at dusk, the party—Nella, Ridley, and photographer Terry Richards—had hardly arrived, having walked only forty-four paces, when Nella stopped to report picking up her first impressions of the ghost (one wonders whose job it was to count Nella's footsteps, and quite what relevance this had, besides melodramatic effect). Nella described an icy cold feeling in her back, and a pain that extended from her left hand up her arm, which she interpreted as the girl's memory of her injuries.

Nella then turned around and began walking down the Hill towards the Lower Bell pub (a description that places the location as the Chatham Road above the Lower Bell crossroads). In a voice 'barely more than a whisper', she declared that the girl had not walked into the path of a car (a comment that demonstrates that she was aware of the style of the recent encounters), but had been *inside* a car—a car that had been heading down the Hill, and which had gone out of control after its driver had been dazzled by the headlights of an oncoming vehicle.

'She's here...she's here. I can feel her presence,' she said. The girl had been in a car that had been crushed. Nella could see and hear the twisting of metal. Then she sensed that there had been other girls in the car, prompting the reporter to note proudly that they later discovered that THREE young women had died in the 1960s 'when their Ford Cortina careered off this road'—a 'fact' that was readily obtainable from local newspaper archives, in this case very likely taken from one of Nigel Nelson's articles for *Kent Messenger* Group newspapers in 1974. Only Nelson's version of the 1965 crash states the car swept off a bend (whereas in actual fact the two vehicles in the accident collided and came to rest together on the side of the road).

One of the girls, Nella said, did not die immediately. Described as very pretty, not very old, with shoulder-length fair hair and dressed in dark clothes and wearing a pretty red scarf, this girl was on the other side of the road, and was not tied to one spot. 'She is here and there,' she said.

Again, punctuating the report with a bold-typed statement of FACT, Ridley announced that the driver of the car, Susan [sic] Browne, had lived for five days after the crash—which is true. He neglected or failed to note, however, that in fact *two* of the women had not died right away—the bride-to-be, and one who had died an hour after admission to West Kent Hospital in Maidstone.

Compounding the oversight with another erroneous statement, Ridley announced that Patricia Ferguson had been killed instantly, while front seat passenger Judith Lingham died the following day—which is the way it was originally reported by the *Kent Messenger*[4] and the *Maidstone Gazette* in the first reports following the accident in November 1965.[5] In truth, it was the other way around—a fact supported by later articles reporting the findings of the inquest on the crash (in March 1966), and by official records.[6] The discrepancy in the original *Kent Messenger* reports can be attributed to the understandable difficulties of 'on the spot' reporting.

Furthermore, it is difficult to relate Nella's sketchy description of the first girl to the bride-to-be, or to either of the other victims of the 1965 crash. All three were certainly young, in their early twenties. And it must be conceded that the description of fair hair could conceivably relate to the bride-to-be. In the earliest of the available photographs of her (1963 or earlier), she does appear to have had light-coloured hair, but in those taken nearer the time of her death, her hair was noticeably darker, perhaps light or medium brown.[7] Beyond this, there is little else to connect Nella's impression with the 1965 crash victims, and this detail must therefore remain inconclusive.

Having said that, fair hair *is* a characteristic reported in several encounters with the Blue Bell Hill girl—in the description given by Collings and Pope for instance, and in an account I received in 1992 in response to the *Kent Messenger* appeal (which is recounted in the next chapter). Interestingly, it also features in Ian Sharpe's and Chris Dawkins' descriptions. When I interviewed him in March 1993, Ian described the girl's hair as shoulder-length and fair, which contradicted the description attributed to him in the *Kent Messenger* of 13 November 1992.[8] This, Emma Cooper's second article, was the only source to include a description of the girl, stating that she had 'shoulder-length brown hair, curled under at the ends', adding also that she wore a white coat. Chris Dawkins had read Emma Cooper's description (which very possibly arose from a confusion with Maurice Goodenough's description of the girl—who, according to newspapers of the time, had shoulder-length brown hair), and yet he would later state following his own encounter nine days after Ian Sharpe's that the girl had long blonde hair (although this detail was not reported in the newspapers).[9]

Nella then focused her attention on what appeared to be a *second* ghost. After commenting that most of the Hill appeared to be 'utterly haunted' by these girls, she observed that one of them (who goes undescribed) was walking down the Hill towards them: 'Oh God, she is getting close. She knows we are here. This poor girl is here every night.' Nella sensed that there was a connection with dockyards or ships. Once again, with what appears to be another impressive 'hit', Ridley's insert commentary (which is almost certainly taken from the *Chatham News* of 26 November 1965)[10] revealed that Judith's father, Eric Lingham,[11] was a chief steward on a liner that had left for Hong Kong only two days before the accident. The news of his daughter's death had been relayed to him by radio.

But while this association is valid, it may not be quite as significant as it appears. Until its closure finally came about in 1984, the Royal Navy Dockyard at Chatham was the largest employer in the Medway area, with a workforce of around 7,000. It was not improbable, then, that someone picked at random from the Medway area may have had some association with the dockyard. In this case, for instance, it is worth noting that Patricia Ferguson's father was a former head of departments at the Dockyard Technical College.[12]

However, if we were to concede the possibility of some genuine ability on Nella's part, it is also well to note that there is a more fitting crash candidate with connections with ships and dockyards. In August 1976, three people were killed in a triple car crash—on a Friday—at Blue Bell Hill, on the dual carriageway some 200 metres north of the Aylesford slip road (approximately where Ian Sharpe had his encounter in 1992). One of the victims—the only female—was a 24-year-old WRNS secretarial officer based at Chatham Naval Base.[13] Now, I am not for a moment suggesting that this accident might be a possible origin for the haunting. It had, after all, occurred two years after the Goodenough incident, and many years after the original rumours of a ghost, but it might serve as a lesson that if we are to accept untimely death as a cause of hauntings, we should consider *all* possible candidates.

Confusingly, given that two apparently distinct personalities had been identified—the girl across the road, and the one described walking down the road towards them—Nella is then credited with having contacted a SECOND ghost. Surely Ridley meant a THIRD? No. The discovery of the third was to follow shortly afterward. The inference here is that the two descriptions above referred to just one girl, although clearly this could not be the case. Judith Lingham did not die five days after the crash, and the reference to Eric Lingham's maritime occupation would obviously be meaningless to an identification of the bride-to-be.[14] This second ghost, who was distinguished by her 'different vibration rate', purportedly kept talking about her mother. Nella asked repeatedly who 'Ann' might be, but an answer, even from Ridley, was not forthcoming. As it is, the name holds no immediate family association for any of the 1965 crash victims (unless we consider it in relation to the second syllable of the true rendition of the bride-to-be's name, Suz-anne). Like the description, however, whether it might have any significance for any other tragic victim is another matter.[15]

Next, Nella's 'highly-developed sixth sense' picked up the third and, it was said, the most tragic victim. This girl, who was reputedly in search of her lover, shied away from them, staying back up the Hill. Not fully aware that she was dead, she was said to be waiting for her boyfriend, who, Nella tells us, had later married and had children. She didn't love him anymore. She just wanted to see him, and was unlikely to leave until she had done so. At this stage, Ridley introduces further confusion by relating this personality to bride-to-be Susan Browne (correctly described as an orphan), who was to be married the next day.

It has previously been noted that Ms Browne, whose fatal injuries had been incurred so close to her wedding day, could indeed for this reason be regarded as the most tragic figure of the crash party. But hadn't she already been identified with the first entity? The contradiction passes unnoticed as Nella went on to sense blood in the middle of the road. She was unsure from whom it might have originated. 'It's odd,' she comments—a somewhat naïve comment to make, perhaps, in view of the fact that she was dealing with a fatal accident. Or was Nella sensing something to do with Maurice Goodenough's victim, struck by him on this same stretch of road and, according to Ted Wright, found to be bleeding badly? Nella felt sure that the unusual amount of paranormal activity signified that it must be the anniversary of the event, and predicted that this would not be the end of it—that the girl (now back to the singular) was not going to go away.

Then, the grand finale. Walking back up the Hill, Nella again stopped suddenly to look out over the fields, where, the article states (again, inaccurately) the car came to rest. Nella's voice rose and she shuddered: 'She's walking right through me. She is here. This has got to be sorted out so these girls can be in peace. I must come back on a Friday. Friday is very significant.'

Mike Ridley's final FACT revealed that it was almost twenty-seven years to the day since the tragedy. Further investigations revealed that the crash had, in fact, happened on a foggy...Friday night.

No other source on the Blue Bell Hill ghost can quite match *The Sun* for sheer drama, including *The National Enquirer*, which published its own version of the events in December 1992.[16] Some of the details attributed to Nella Jones certainly appear to be impressive. Ridley had found a number of meaningful correlations in his brief research on the circumstances of the 1965 crash: the accident, of course, *did* happen on a Friday. It *did* involve a party of young women killed in a crash with another vehicle after the other car's headlights had dazzled the driver of the Cortina (which, incidentally, *had* been heading *down* Blue Bell Hill, contrary to the direction suggested by the original newspaper coverage of the crash). And one of the party—Judith Lingham—did have a ships and dockyards association, through her father. And their visit *was* close to the anniversary of the event.

All of these details, however, are readily obtainable from the original articles on the crash held in local newspaper archives and, as we have seen, some are certainly open to interpretation. More significantly, most had recently found new light in reports describing the Sharpe and Dawkins incidents—which, of course, is how *The Sun* came by the story in the first place.

Certain details even allow the identification of specific source articles. The cause of the accident, for instance—the dazzling of the driver by the lights of an oncoming car—is described in exactly these terms by the *Chatham Observer* of 25 March 1966, one of the articles that reported on the inquest on the crash.[17] That same article had also stated the correct destination of travel at the time of the accident (which is contradicted in *The Sun* article by an inset panel ('Survivor's Silence') which states that the girls were returning to Rochester from Maidstone after a final fitting for their wedding outfits—the Nelson version of events prior to the crash). Similarly, the *Chatham News* (26 November 1965) serves as the source of information regarding Judith's father, Charles E. Lingham, as well as the fact that the bride-to-be was an orphan.[18]

In essence, Mike Ridley's article contains little that cannot be found in original newspaper accounts or cannot be refuted by a thorough knowledge of the true facts of the 1965 crash. Which leads us to question just how impartial and objective the investigation and the reporting of it actually were. How much did it rely on prior knowledge or research of the case, on the part of Nella and/or Ridley? To what degree might Nella's on-the-spot impressions have been adapted to fit the circumstances and details of the 1965 crash and its victims later (as claimed) discovered by Ridley?

I found it difficult to believe that Nella could have been without even a superficial knowledge of the case beforehand. Then living in Bexleyheath, Kent,[19] and considering the nature of her business, it is possible she may have had some prior awareness of the case even before her involvement with *The Sun*. Alternatively, she may have picked up something of the story during the previous fortnight from the regional press, television, and tabloid coverage of Ian Sharpe's encounter. Most likely, however, is that some background detail featured in conversation on the way to or during the visit at Blue Bell Hill—which would be perfectly understandable in the informal atmosphere of an 'investigation' such as this (whose purpose, let us remind ourselves, was to sell newspaper copy, not to act in a detached, impartial manner).

Mike Ridley tells us early in the article that it was getting dark when they began their investigation, dusk fast becoming dark. And yet, Terry Richard's sepia-toned photograph of the Chatham Road which supports the article's headline clearly shows it to have been taken in full daylight—around 1 p.m., judging by comparative photographs I took from the same spot a few days later.[20] An estimate of early to mid-afternoon for *The Sun* picture, therefore, does not seem unreasonable. Unless Richards had arrived a couple of hours ahead of Nella and Ridley (in which case, his presence there at dusk seems superficial), or his photographs were taken on a different day, it seems reasonable to suppose that the three of them had been at Blue Bell Hill for some part of the afternoon. This being the case, surely they couldn't fail to have spoken about some of the background details?

Nella's comment early in the article that the girl had not walked into the path of a car but had been inside one, certainly suggests some prior familiarity with the recent press accounts that reported the jaywalking habit of the ghost. Few sources repeating the story failed to include the 1965 crash by way of explanation for the haunting. Reinforcing the point is the reference to the ghost's 'pretty red scarf'. But for the description of the girl given by Chris Dawkins only a few days before, which—for the first time in print—featured a red scarf, Nella Jones's information might have been disregarded as an anomaly. Instead, it becomes highly significant—although not for reason of its apparent correlation with a detail given by an eyewitness (which inevitably found its way into the few tabloids that ran the story—one of which, not surprisingly, happened to be *The Sun* on 24 November),[21] but because it would appear that Dawkins was misreported. Dawkins later told David Thomas (a researcher representing paranormal research group ASSAP, who started a parallel investigation of the case in 1992), that a red scarf had *not* featured in the description he gave of the girl.[22]

Such might serve as a cautionary lesson regarding *The Sun*'s presentation. As might the fact that *The Sun* went on to make further capital from the story in the days that followed. On 27 November (the day after the double-page feature) the paper published a scaled-down reprint of Terry Richard's photograph of the Chatham Road, highlighting a shape in the hedgerow further down the Hill after readers had phoned in to say they could see a figure among the trees. Iris Stewart of Croydon, Surrey, said she could clearly see the ghost, with her arms outstretched and wearing a long dress. 'Is this the ghost of Blue Bell Hill?' asked the accompanying caption.[23] Predictably, the answer is 'no'; it proving to be nothing more than an effect of light and shadow in the foliage, coupled with a sign-post.[24]

The following Wednesday (2 December), after Nella's 'psychic revelations' at Blue Bell Hill, *The Sun* was inviting readers to join her as she went sparring with the spectres of Britain.[25]

Before leaving this critique of *The Sun*'s hyperbolic treatment of the case, and ignoring the small faux pas of Nella's reference to a red scarf, it has to be noted that attesting to some belief in Nella's abilities are the personal accolades she received from the police, who she helped on a number of occasions. I accept that some individuals seem to possess the ability to give accurate if often trivial details concerning events and persons which appear to have no obvious or natural source. On this basis, I would be willing to accept that the information attributed to Nella came to her just as described—assuming, of course, that it could have been determined that she was in no way exposed to details of the case beforehand.

In an interview for LivingTV's *Scream Team* in 2002 (in which I was also featured), Mike Ridley stated that he had given Nella Jones no prior information before taking her to Blue Bell Hill, and that the discovery of the correspondences with the reported details related to the accident came from investigation afterward. For Ridley, this was the turning point, which made him feel that there might be something to it, where beforehand he had, by his own admission, not taken it seriously at all. [26] However, I stand by my earlier comments, particularly in reference to Nella's likely prior awareness of Blue Bell Hill as a reputedly haunted location—which doesn't overlook that *The Sun*'s involvement itself came via a press agency referral of the regional newspaper coverage, which in its reporting of Ian Sharpe's and Chris Dawkins' encounters, of course, made reference to the 1965 tragedy.

The essential question is whether such abilities represent genuine contact with the dead, or a keen intuitive faculty aided perhaps by selective cold reading? One problem area lies with the level of detail that comes through. Too rarely do we receive precise details or meaningful messages that we might reasonably expect if the medium really were in communication with the dead. Descriptions are characteristically vague, and different psychics seem rarely to report the same information.[27]

Nella Jones's involvement in the Blue Bell Hill case differs little. For instance, the article gives us the impression that she could actually *see* the girls—in which case, a little more descriptive detail might reasonably be expected. As it is, aside from Nella's description of a young fair-haired girl (which, as we have seen, does hold some significance within the context of eyewitness accounts at Blue Bell Hill, as well as a common feature of the classic Phantom Hitch-Hiker tale), we learn nothing that could not be found in the newspapers—which would explain, perhaps (among other things), why both Nella Jones and Mike Ridley were not able to identify the correct scene of the 1965 crash.

Whatever the truth behind Nella Jones's information—prior awareness, journalistic embellishment, or genuine psychic ability—she would be proved right in one respect, when she said that these events would not be the end of it. Just seven weeks later, it was off again—although this time it was not a young woman reported on the Hill, but something far more bizarre and frightening (see Chapter 11).

The Emerging Path

One of the first important discoveries I was to make regarding the fateful events of 19 November 1965 was that the initial newspaper reports on the crash were in error over the deaths of Judith Lingham and Patricia Ferguson, which probably owed itself to some initial confusion of their identities on admission to Maidstone's West Kent Hospital. In any event, what was reported (and which has been perpetuated ever since) is that Patricia was killed instantly, and Judith died the following day. The mistake first became evident from a brief report on the inquest findings in the *Kent Messenger* of 25 March 1966.[28]

At the inquest, held the previous Wednesday (23 March), the coroner, Mr G. H. Coombe, was told that the death of 22-year-old Judith Lingham was probably instantaneous. Patricia Ferguson, 23, died an hour after admission to the West Kent Hospital. The bride-to-be, Susan [sic] Browne, 24, described as Australian-born, died five days later.[29] The hearing had been postponed for several weeks in the hope that the fourth member of the party, Mrs Gillian Burchett, might have recovered sufficiently to give evidence. But, four months after the accident, she was still in hospital and unable to do so. There had been no independent witnesses to the accident. The jury returned a verdict of 'Accidental death' on all three women.

At the time of my finding of the inquest reports (March 1990), the fact that it was actually Judith Lingham who had died on Blue Bell Hill seemed to make some sense out of the press accounts which, in 1974, had first proposed her for the ghost's identity. Although the reasons for the identification were never stated, it did appear at this early stage in the research that the press—specifically the *Kent Messenger*'s Nigel Nelson—may have made the right selection after all. If there really was anything to the idea that the ghost of a person is most likely to haunt the spot where he or she died, then Judith, as the only one of the three girls to actually perish on the Hill, was surely the prime candidate.

For the first time, the occupations of the 1965 crash victims were given: Susan Browne was a shorthand typist; Judith Lingham, a secretary; and Patricia Ferguson, a school teacher—superfluous information, perhaps, but valuable in beginning to build up a picture of each personality in this tragedy. I had learned elsewhere that ostensibly trifling details could take on greater significance later in the investigation, or when viewed in a wider perspective. In this case, such minutiae just might prove useful in aiding (or countering) an identification of one of these women, if ever a reliable claim to a meeting with the ghost should emerge. At very least, these personal details reminded me that I was dealing with real people and situations, not merely names off a printed page. And sometimes, they would serve as clues that would lead to new sources of information.

One such detail was that Ms Browne was said to be from Upwood, a village in Huntingdonshire (now Cambridgeshire), which was a little puzzling at first. I had learned very early on that she was Australian, and that she had come to England to marry her RAF technician fiancé, and had been staying at Woodlands Road, Gillingham. So, where did Upwood come into the picture? The *Maidstone Gazette*'s report on the crash (23 November) had mentioned that her 23-year-old fiancé was stationed at an RAF camp in Huntington. Upwood, nine miles north of Huntingdon, lies close to two airfields, Wyton and Alconbury.

The Upwood connection suggested that the bride-to-be had not come to England (and directly to Gillingham) immediately prior to the wedding (which seemed to be implied by the original *Kent Messenger* report on the crash), but had spent some unspecified time at Upwood, quite naturally in the interest of being near her fiancé. Her stay in Gillingham therefore (unless it represented a recent move) seemed most likely to have been a temporary arrangement for the wedding, due to take place the day after the accident. Indeed, I later established that the Woodlands Road address was the home of her fiancé's sister.

The Upwood link was to find verification in a brief report on the front page of the *Hunts Post* of 25 November 1965.[30] While it failed to make mention of Upwood itself, the report confirmed that Ms Browne's fiancé, a Junior Technician, had been based at RAF Wyton, just north of Huntingdon. The wedding, it said, had been called off after his 24-year-old Australian bride-to-be, *Suzanne Brown* [sic], from Adelaide (South Australia), had been seriously injured the previous Friday.

This spelling of the bride-to-be's name I would later find, was almost correct—it in fact being *Suzanne Browne*, as established from official records.[31] That same documentation—the victims' death certificates—proved invaluable in corroborating the other details contained in the *Kent Messenger*'s inquest article and the *Hunts Post*—the ages of the victims, their occupations, addresses (which, for Suzanne, at the time *was* at Upwood), and when and where each had died. These records proved to be the only means of verifying the details of the report: that Judith Lingham had indeed died on Blue Bell Hill, on 19 November, followed by Patricia Ferguson on 20 November in West Kent General Hospital, Maidstone. All three victims had died of multiple injuries and shock as a result of a collision between two private motor cars on 19 November 1965.[32]

In the early versions of the story, it will be recalled, it was Maidstone that was the girl Hitch-Hiker's former home and destination—a bride-to-be in some versions heard by Tom Harber. The Maidstone connection had been rather easily dismissed by the revelation that the bride-to-be of the 1965 crash, Suzanne Browne, who Tom believed to be the ghost, was an Australian staying (or, in the *Kent Messenger* version, living) in Gillingham.

In turn, the fact that Suzanne was living at the time at Upwood meant she had no significant ties with Gillingham either. Of course, this in itself didn't preclude the possibility that her ghost might wish to be taken to that town, which, as we have seen, became the ghost girl's preferred destination in some later accounts (it could be argued, for instance, that it was her desire to get back to the Woodlands Road address—which was, after all, her last 'home', as temporary as it may have been). But it did rule against those accounts which, in accordance with the classic folk version, might have motorists proceeding to a meeting with the girl's relatives at her former home.

With the classic plot with respect to the bride-to-be so weakened, did this provide a possible further clue (to add to those discussed in preceding chapters) as to why Judith Lingham came to oust Suzanne Browne from the ghostly top spot? After all, Judith was the only one of the three victims (judging from the original newspaper accounts) to have clear links with the area. Patricia Ferguson was said to be from Dunfermline, in Scotland, and, like Suzanne, staying in Gillingham. Later investigation revealed that she was born in Gillingham, and was living and working in the area.[33] Judith, however, had a permanent address in Albany Road, Rochester, which later featured in some apocryphal accounts.

With the discovery of the inquest findings there appeared to be little to add to the circumstances of the 1965 crash. All that remained was to follow up some of the detail, the most important of which was to determine, if possible, the precise location of the accident. The reader needn't be reminded of the time-honoured relationship between scenes of death and hauntings. The Phantom Hitch-Hiker is frequently said to be encountered at the very spot where she died. Although later accounts described the Blue Bell Hill girl as appearing at or seeking lifts at various points on the Hill, the earliest versions of the story had her waiting at the foot of the Hill, by the Lower Bell pub.

In apparent support of this particular convention was Michael Goss's identification of the Lower Bell crossroads as the scene of the accident. Goss's research had given me little reason to question his findings and conclusions—and indeed, one source (the *Chatham Standard* of 23 November 1965) indicated that the crash occurred 'near the Lower Bell'.[34] However, I found it difficult to reconcile the crossroads location with the crash scene pictured in the newspapers, which showed the girls' Cortina shunted onto what appeared to be (at least within the frame of the photograph) an unbroken length of pavement backed by foliage. Not that this point was of any great significance. The precise spot at which the collision had occurred could well have been some small distance removed from the crossroads itself without invalidating the associations made with it. What began to persuade me that the crossroads was *not* the true scene of the accident came from another feature of the crash photographs—a bus stop pictured immediately behind the vehicles. This was the only feature that offered any degree of traceability. If it could be established where on Blue Bell Hill the bus stops had been located in 1965, then the precise scene of the accident might be determined—and, in turn, if the folk tradition was upheld and on the assumption that there was any foundation to the story, where encounters with the ghost were perhaps most likely to occur.

With this in mind, I wrote to Maidstone and District Motor Services (buses) at Chatham. In reply, I received a letter and location map from Traffic Assistant Richard Lewis. Although Mr Lewis had been unable to produce actual records of bus stop locations for as long ago as 1965, he had spoken to a colleague with a long-standing knowledge of the area. I was reminded that this was before the dual carriageway had been built. However, it was thought that the bus stops would have been in virtually the same locations as at present, with the exception that they were located on both sides of the road at that time. Hence, there were stops outside and opposite the former Upper Bell pub; and on the Chatham Road adjacent to and opposite Salisbury Road, with the current 'up' stop at essentially the same location; and finally, outside and opposite the Lower Bell, with the current 'up' stop, again, located near its original position.[35]

Of the three locations, the stop near to Salisbury Road seemed the most fitting. Not only was the road at this spot closely bordered by trees and scrub consistent with the crash photos, there were other reasons to recommend it. The bus stop at the top of the Hill, for instance, had been mentioned as a probable picking-up point for the girl Hitch-Hiker. And, in his version of the 1965 crash, Nigel Nelson—while failing to mention that it had involved a collision—*had* stated that the girl's Cortina had swept off a bend—which I thought might have been part of the truth.

It was difficult to imagine the Cortina sweeping off a bend while travelling uphill (the reported direction of travel (homeward) in most accounts), unless it had done so in an attempt to avoid the collision with the Jaguar. What made more sense came from the discovery that the Cortina had, in fact, been heading *downhill*, toward Maidstone. The source of this new information, the *Chatham Observer* of 25 March 1966,[36] provided a more detailed report on the inquest than the *Kent Messenger*'s, including the circumstances of the crash itself.

In 1965, the slightly sinuous and steepening section of road at this location was the most dangerous feature of the Maidstone–Chatham Road at Blue Bell Hill—as attested by individuals familiar with the 'old hill'. Where a road is steep, even minor deflections in its course may hold dire consequences for the unwary driver. The Salisbury Road section marked a point where the road veered from its more or less southerly direction to describe a slight but treacherous curve to the left. A little further down the Hill, at Kit's Coty Cottage, the road made a more

The view (south) from near to the entrance to Salisbury Road towards the present bus stop, just visible at the apex of the curve

pronounced, sweeping left bend on the gradient that descends to the Lower Bell crossroads. This bend (which is preserved today) was notorious as the scene of a number of accidents involving vehicles sweeping off the road (accounting for why it may have become assumed by some as the scene of the 1965 tragedy).

In time, I was able to prove that the section near to Salisbury Road was the correct scene of the 1965 crash. When I met them in 1992, Judith Lingham's sisters were able to confirm this location as the scene of the crash, and that the girls had indeed been heading towards Maidstone. Further support for the general area of the crash came in 1994 when I managed to contact an actual eyewitness to the aftermath of the crash, former police officer Peter Parvin, who was, in fact, the first officer to arrive at the scene that night.

The only remaining detail to ascertain was the whereabouts of the church where the wedding was to have taken place. A key element of the story of the Blue Bell Hill ghost—one that made it particularly memorable —was the next-day wedding of the bride-to-be. While finding the church was largely to satisfy my own curiosity, attached to it was the hope that it might still hold marriage preparation papers that would confirm the intended date of the wedding, which was all part of the documentation process. Newspaper sources had given the church as 'St. Mary's Roman Catholic Church, Gillingham'—which proved to be something of a misnomer. The church's formal name turned out to be 'Our Lady of Gillingham', in Ingram Road, Gillingham, which I found was also known locally as St. Mary's ('Our Lady' and 'St. Mary', of course, being one and the same). A reply to an initial letter of inquiry established that the church archives did indeed preserve marriage preparation papers for Wetton and Browne, but the parish priest, Father A. Kinnane, was understandably reluctant to give out more information until he had had a chance to discuss the matter with me.[37] But following a subsequent telephone conversation in which I restated the aims of my research, and with assurances that no material would be used in detail, arrangements were made to view the papers.

Those papers consisted of the couple's prenuptial inquiry forms, which were essentially their application to be married. In addition to confirming the proposed date of the wedding—Saturday 20 November 1965—I noted a few details that confirmed some of the newspaper reports. For instance, they confirmed that Suzanne Browne was Australian. Born in Port Pirie, South Australia, prior to coming to England she had lived in Blair Athol, a suburb of Adelaide. At the time of her application, in September 1965, she had been at her current address (in Upwood) for two months (i.e. since July). (One of the reports on the inquest (*Chatham Standard*, 29 March 1966) indicated she had arrived in Britain in May).[38]

As useful as some of this information proved to be, attached to the inquiry forms was something that was far more arresting, and poignant. This was a letter by Ms Browne herself to Father Arthur Porter, then parish priest of the church.[39] Dated 28 September 1965 and handwritten in blue ink, it asked Father Porter if he would be available to marry her and her fiancé, Bryan, on 20 November, at 12 noon. Holding that letter, it was sobering to realise that in a little less than two months from that date, bride-to-be Suzanne Browne, so obviously full of life and aspirations for her future would, along with two of her friends, be dead.

At the time of my visit with Father Kinnane in February 1992 the Blue Bell Hill story had appeared to be little more than folklore, albeit one that relied on a tragic real-life event for its potency. Checking out the facts behind the 1965 crash and its victims was more a matter of verifying story point than a serious investigation into the possibility that any of these young women might actually be haunting Blue Bell Hill.

Just eight months later, all of that changed. With Ian Sharpe's and Chris Dawkins' widely publicised sightings on 8 and 22 November 1992, plus those that came to light in their wake, it was becoming increasingly evident that the Blue Bell Hill story was far more than the transplanted folktale it had appeared to be, but a seemingly bona fide haunting, and one that naturally re-implicated the historical cause, the car crash of November 1965. The media, of course, needed little persuasion in supposing the 1965 crash to be responsible for the haunting, and Judith Lingham as the primary candidate for the ghost's identity—a conclusion based principally on the November dates of the Sharpe and Dawkins encounters and pre-existing articles that named Judith.

While I still felt there was good reason to question the renewed connection with the 1965 crash, I had to concede the possible significance of the November dates. What I had found out thus far about the crash and its victims allowed for adequate criticism regarding the accuracy of the press reports, but had not yielded a very great deal of specific information—descriptions, photographs, and so on—that might settle the matter one way or the other. Therefore, while I sought to arrange interviews with Ian Sharpe, Chris Dawkins, and other witnesses who had now been encouraged to come forward, I set about trying to gather as much additional information on the 1965 crash victims as possible, a task that was promisingly aided from the start by Judith's family.

I was to find that what I had already learned about the crash and its victims hardly scratched the surface. The 1965 tragedy would prove to be an exceptionally well reported incident, carried in additional district newspapers (which would prove to be both detailed and largely accurate) and on the front pages of the London evening papers and by a number of the daily and Sunday nationals. News of the tragedy—and, in particular, of the plight of the bride-to-be—would also (by virtue of the Australian Associated Press in London) be reported in Australia, in Suzanne Browne's home city of Adelaide.[40]

Assembled from these and other sources (which include one of the police officers who was in attendance at the accident, the bride-to-be's brother and the prospective groom himself), what follows is the full story of the 1965 tragedy.

'Look out, Sue...'

Suzanne Ingrid Browne was born on 17 June 1941 in Port Pirie, South Australia. She was the eldest child of Patrick Sylvester Browne and Ingrid Alice Browne, the proprietors of The Globe Hotel in Solomontown, a suburb of Port Pirie. On the death of their mother in January 1946, Suzanne and her younger brother Patrick found themselves orphans, their father having died the year before. The responsibility for their care fell to their father's brother, John (Jack) Browne, who arranged for them to stay with a second cousin, Mary White, in Lettie Street, Blair Athol, in the north suburbs of Adelaide, the beautiful 'City of Churches' and capital of South Australia.[41]

Suzanne was educated at Rosary School, the local Catholic parish school in the suburb of Prospect, and was a regular member of the Church community, occasionally playing the organ at church services. She later went on to St. Aloysius College, Adelaide, before training as a pre-school kindergarten teacher at

Adelaide Teachers College. Between 1960 and 1962 she worked with the Kindergarten Union of South Australia. She is later credited as having been on the editorial staff of the *South Australian Countrywoman*.[42]

'Suzy', as she was affectionately known to family and close friends, was described by her brother as a vibrant young woman, intelligent, independent, and possessing of a great sense of humour.[43]

In 1963, the lure of the 'old country' brought her to the UK, to London, and she based herself in South Kensington among the growing community of other expat Australians around Kensington and Earls Court. The experience proved a taster that was to see her plan a return trip early in 1965, accompanied by three friends, that was to include a tour of Europe in the itinerary. On her return to Adelaide, she took up a position as a laboratory secretary in the Adelaide Children's Hospital.

Suzanne Browne met her fiancé, RAF photographer Bryan Wetton, at an ESU (English Speaking Union) gathering in Adelaide in September 1964. Bryan, of Toronto Road, Gillingham, was stationed at Edinburgh RAAF Base near Elizabeth (to the north of Adelaide) during his overseas posting with the No.4 Joint Services Trials Unit (4 JSTU) Australia from January 1964, where his role was to document the trials of Britain's new Cold War nuclear deterrent, the Avro Blue Steel guided missile at the Woomera Rocket Range.[44]

The couple became engaged shortly before Bryan's stint in Australia came to an end with the winding down of the Blue Steel trials in the first half of 1965.[45] With plans to marry later that year in England, Suzanne departed from Port Adelaide aboard the SS Aurelia in April 1965. She was accompanied by three friends also intent on a working holiday in England. One of the girls would later be at the hospital with Suzanne after the accident.[46]

After seeing them off, Bryan remained in Australia for another two weeks before the RAF finally flew him home courtesy of BOAC in the first week of May 1965. A couple of weeks later, the girls' ship arrived at Tilbury (Thurrock, Essex). Bryan, still on embarkation leave before taking up his new posting at RAF Wyton, near Huntingdon (Cambridgeshire), and accompanied by two fellow servicemen friends, was there to meet them. Together they escorted the girls to their booked accommodation at the ESU in London's West End.

The father of two of the girls, twins Ann and Helen Gosling, had been in the motor industry and had arranged for Suzanne to inspect suitable second-hand cars at a Rootes showroom at Piccadilly. Suzanne picked out a Mark I Ford Cortina, which was to be used for their European trip, on which they were to embark the following Tuesday.

That weekend, Suzy, accompanied by the fourth member of the group, Pam Jones, drove down to Gillingham to see Bryan, where they also met his mother.

Suzanne Browne
(Bryan Wetton)

Patricia Ferguson
(Chatham Standard)

Judith Lingham
(KM Group)

Bryan Wetton (Aug. 1964)
(Bryan Wetton)

That evening, following 'a heartbreaking parting', Suzy drove back up to London before all four left together for the Continent. Shortly after, Bryan took up his post at RAF Wyton. During their separation, the couple corresponded frequently, so that soon the whole camp at Wyton knew of the romance.

Suzanne Browne was an experienced and competent driver. The party's tour of Europe was to take them through France to Spain, and then on to Italy. The full round trip would clock up approximately 10,000 miles before their return in July. It was while they were in Spain that news reached Suzanne that was to prompt her to return temporarily to the UK. One night in June, Bryan received a phone call informing him that his mother had been taken seriously ill and was in hospital. Bryan was granted compassionate leave and journeyed down to Gillingham, where he was met by two of his close friends, Peter Howes and Tony Stone, who drove him to Medway Maritime Hospital to see her. Her condition was very poor, but when it seemed not to be worsening, Bryan returned to Wyton. The following Saturday (20 June), however, he learned that his mother had passed away. Suzanne, who had been made aware of his mother's illness, and was telephoning every day, promptly flew back to be with Bryan. After a week she rejoined the others in Italy.

Suzanne and her companions finally arrived back in England in July. The other girls had arranged accommodation in a flat at Queen's Gate, back in Kensington, while Suzanne and Bryan set off for RAF Wyton, where Bryan had arranged for Suzanne to stay temporarily on the base's married patch with friends of his until suitable accommodation could be found. Suzanne resourcefully found employment as a shorthand typist, and in August, a place to stay, at Upwood House, Upwood, which she set about making into a home in the months leading up to the wedding.

As their plans developed for the wedding, the couple decided they would rather return to Adelaide than live the life of an RAF married couple. Bryan made arrangements to purchase his discharge (which was to take place in December), and they made plans to return to Adelaide in the New Year, where they intended to set up a photography business. Their passage back to Australia—a 'honeymoon' cruise—had been arranged for 13 January 1966.[47]

Weekends were generally spent down in Gillingham. Bryan, who had grown up in the town, had been part of a small social group that met regularly at the Good Companions Club ('GCs'), a venue at the top of Star Hill, in New Road, Rochester.[48] Other members of the regular 'gang', which came together for weekend dances, parties and excursions, included Bryan's close friends from his school days, Peter Howes, Tony Stone and Tony Bunting; and the girls they met up with: Pat Ferguson (who was the girlfriend of Tony Bunting), Dee Smith, Rosemarie Jones, Judith Lingham, and Gillian Burchett. Suzanne was the newest

Back row (left to right): Judith Lingham, Gillian Burchett, Pat Ferguson. Front (right): Bryan Wetton, Suzanne Browne. From a photograph taken just weeks before the fatal crash *(Bryan Wetton)*

addition to the group.

The wedding itself was to take place at the small Roman Catholic Church of Our Lady of Gillingham in Ingram Road. The ceremony was arranged for midday on Saturday 20 November 1965. For the week before the wedding, Suzanne stayed with Bryan's sister in Woodlands Road to enable her to make the final preparations.

Bryan recalls that Father Porter 'took to Suzy like a storm' and in his grief was unable even to speak to him after the accident, and could not bring himself to remove the flowers from the altar that Suzy had prepared so lovingly on the Friday afternoon.[49]

Contrary to the claims of some press reports, the early part of that fateful evening of Friday 19 November—as close friends were keen to point out—was not spent out at a 'hen party' or simply on the trying on of bridesmaids' dresses. Instead, the girls had been engaged in final preparations for the 80-guest reception at the Prince of Wales Hotel in Chatham.[50]

Patricia Ruth Ferguson (23), a friendly, popular teacher at Fair View Junior School, Wigmore, and a member of Rainham Amateur Theatrical Society, was the girlfriend of Bryan's Wetton's friend and best man, Tony Bunting; her association with Suzanne clearly coming from that relationship.[51]

Judith Margaret Lingham,[52] a 22-year-old London stockbroker's secretary, and former Gravesend Grammar School girl, was, in the words of her sisters, 'zany': an easy-going, happy-go-lucky girl. Judith sat on the committee of the Good Companions Club, through which she may have at first become friendly with 20-year-old Gillian Burchett, who lived just a few streets from her.

Peter Howes, who was to have given the bride away, later said: 'Gillian Burchett and Judy Lingham had spent most of the evening at Gillian's flat in Borstal,

The Church of Our Lady of Gillingham (aka St. Mary's), Ingram Road, Gillingham

getting ready for the party.

'Sue and Pat Ferguson had been to one or two places trying to find some of the men who had gone out for a quiet drink with the groom and then they joined the other two at Gillian's flat.

'All four left there in Sue's car at about 10 p.m. and looked in one or two places we might have been, and were just on their way to a place outside Maidstone [The Running Horse, at Sandling, or possibly The Malta] for a final look' [when the accident happened].[53]

In a later statement, taken for the inquest while she was still in hospital, Gillian Burchett confirmed this time for their departure. She told the inquest that in the course of their search she and the other girls had gone out in the car at around 10 p.m. She, Judith and Patricia had had one drink each; Suzanne, who was driving, had a tomato juice.[54]

The conditions out that night were far from good. A newspaper weather forecast made that day for the weekend ahead predicted that it would be: 'Cloudy, misty, with outbreaks of rain, becoming colder with a possibility of rain or sleet'—a forecast that would prove perilously accurate.[55]

Blue Bell Hill was shrouded in a misty drizzle as the girls began their descent towards Maidstone, with Suzanne at the wheel. Beside her, in the front passenger seat, sat Judith, with Patricia and Gillian in the back; Gillian on the offside, behind Suzanne.

The Running Horse at Sandling, Maidstone

During the journey the girls chatted to one another, with the exception of Suzanne who, concentrating on her driving, wasn't saying very much. Approximately halfway down the Hill, Gillian had the impression of what appeared ahead of them to be two extremely bright, dazzling headlights.

The car then seemed to swerve to the right and, seeing Suzanne turn the wheel, Gillian quickly remarked to her: 'Look out, Sue, we will be running out of road.'[56] She remembered nothing else.

Taking the full force of the impact, on the Cortina's nearside, were Judith and Patricia. The girls' car was shunted onto the strip of pavement on the road's west side, with the Jaguar buried in its side, its rear end slewing around anticlockwise as they came to a stop.

At the inquest the following March, the driver of the Jaguar, Mr Harry Backhouse, of High Street, Chatham, testified that he and his companion had been on their way back to Chatham after a meal at Hollingbourne. He was travelling with dipped headlights at around 30 mph, when he saw the girls' Cortina coming around the corner. From that moment, he 'just knew' what was going to happen. The car showed no sign of altering course; it had looked as if it were out of control, although it was travelling at no great speed, which he estimated to have been no greater than 30 mph to 40 mph. Faced with the sudden and imminent prospect of a collision, he simply froze. Similarly, his passenger told the coroner that on seeing the other car's headlights, she had thought to herself: 'This car is going to hit us.'[57]

PC Peter Parvin commenced his shift on the night patrol at Maidstone Police Headquarters in Sutton Road at 10 p.m. It was possibly 10.30 p.m. when the call came through from the operations room with the report of the accident. The few newspapers to assign a time to the crash put it a little later (excepting one source), at 10.45 p.m. or 11 p.m.—which is certainly more consistent with the girls having visited one or two pubs before deciding to head for Maidstone.[58] Parvin and fellow officer Ted Gilbert immediately set out for Blue Bell Hill. When they arrived at the scene, as Parvin later told the inquest, they found a Jaguar 3.4 embedded in the side of the Cortina. Resting on the nearside of the road, it was still in third gear, having achieved no great distance or speed after turning onto the Chatham Road from the direction of Aylesford (at the Lower Bell crossroads). Three of the four women had been removed from the wreckage and were lying on the grass verge, unconscious. The fourth, still in the rear of the vehicle, was still conscious but in great pain.[59]

Mr Parvin said that the left-hand bend in the road presented to Maidstone-bound traffic at that time tended to push vehicles over to their offside, an effect that would have been exacerbated by the wet conditions. The accident could thus be viewed as a chance collision between two vehicles in inclement conditions on a dark and treacherous section of a notorious hill route.

Judith Lingham was killed instantly in the collision. Patricia Ferguson died approximately an hour after admission to West Kent Hospital, Maidstone (where all the casualties were taken), early on what was by then the day of the wedding, 20 November.

Meanwhile, the men returned home unaware of the accident. Bryan was staying overnight with his best man, Tony Bunting, at his house in Chada Avenue, Gillingham. At around 2 a.m., they were awakened by a loud knocking at the door. Answering it, they found Bryan's sister, Pearl, who told them that the police had informed her of an accident involving the girls that had taken place at Blue Bell Hill. There was no further information. The pair immediately drove around to Peter Howes' home in Larkfield Avenue to collect him and share the news, and all three then drove 'pell-mell' to West Kent Hospital, in Marsham Street, Maidstone.

On arrival, the emergency team took Tony aside to break the news that his fiancée, Pat, had not survived. Suzanne, meanwhile, was reported as undergoing emergency surgery, and Bryan waited anxiously outside the operating theatre for news.[60]

When the three regrouped they learned that of the four in the car, Pat and Judy had died. Suzy had been critically injured, and Gillian had suffered considerable injuries.

When Bryan finally saw Suzanne she was lying peacefully but was not conscious. He was to hardly leave her bedside over the next five days, and was there when, later that day, guests who had not heard the news began to arrive at the church only to be turned away by friends of the couple. Sobbing, one commented: 'It's terrible...Suzanne is such a lively girl.'[61]

Also in attendance at Suzanne's bedside that weekend was Father Gregory Moore, a Roman Catholic priest from Maidstone, who had been called in following the accident. On the Sunday, he led the morning mass in prayer for the couple at St. Francis RC Church in Week Street.[62]

Described as 'very poor' after the operation, Suzanne's condition remained critical in the coming days until, on the afternoon of the following Wednesday (24 November) and without ever regaining consciousness, she finally lost her fight for life.

The following day, it was announced that Suzanne's body would be flown home to her uncle and brother in Australia for burial in her home town of Adelaide.[63] Her brother, Patrick, who had been kept apprised of her condition on an almost hourly basis by her fiancé, had readied himself to fly to England immediately on receiving news of the accident. But before a passport and airline schedules could be arranged, Suzanne had died. Her body was flown home in the week following her death—the same week in which the funerals of her two friends took place in Kent.

Suzanne Browne, the tragic bride-to-be, rests in the bright parkland surroundings of a beautifully kept cemetery a mile from her former home in north Adelaide.[64]

While the renewed phase of research undoubtedly succeeded in revealing a more complete account of the 1965 tragedy, at the same time it failed to provide very specific descriptive detail for each victim (which could only really be gained from their relatives—an intrusion difficult to justify without very much more than the impressions of the ghost girl gained by witnesses). But then, considering the fleeting nature of most encounters, such information could well be regarded as extraneous anyway. What it *did* produce was something arguably more helpful: photographs of each of the victims that accompanied certain newspaper articles that reported the accident.[65] Taken initially from microfilm sources, however, these were not of especially good quality and, as it turned out, were to find little recognition with those witnesses that viewed them. Only in one case would a positive identification be made, and this with qualification (something that prevents me from naming either the witness or the subject of the identification).

As we have noted, a feature of some of the witness descriptions was the fair hair of the girl—which, of course, had also featured in Nella Jones's sketchy description of one of the girls. These images of the crash victims suggested that all three to have had medium or dark hair. In 2001, however, I was to receive photographs from the groom, Bryan Wetton himself. In some of these, his fiancée, Suzanne Browne, does indeed appear with light or blonde hair—which is a point to be conceded. It is also possible to gain an impression of the height and build of each of the girls; Judith and Pat appearing to be of slight build, and Suzanne of medium build.

Even so, taking all into account, we are left still with little on which to arbitrate, and the evidence for or against an identification of any of the victims rests on little better than this. Rather, the fair-haired girl-in-white and her behaviour bear closer resemblance to the classic folk-type—which is something to bear in mind when we come to discuss the possible causes of the haunting.

On top of this, what at first seemed to be impressive support for the 1965 crash connection—and here, I'm thinking of the date, time, and in a few cases, the location—began to appear less significant the more accounts I gathered. Although the timings of the encounters were to remain broadly consistent—between 10.30 p.m. and 1.00 a.m.—the locations where one could expect to encounter the ghost would vary considerably up and down the A229, with sightings separated by anything up to two-and-a-half miles, which naturally strains our concept of what defines a haunted place.

Most significantly, at least one account (if accepted as part of the Blue Bell Hill phenomenon) would seem to vindicate the claims of some commentators that the ghost girl was active many years before 1965—in fact, at least as far back as 1934, as we shall see.

NINE

THE WITNESSES: 1992-1996

'They were knocking them down, they were picking them up...'
Tom Harber[1]

IAN SHARPE'S and Chris Dawkins' encounters in November 1992 did more than reopen the real possibility that Blue Bell Hill was the scene of a genuine haunting. They also provided a focus and means by which the experiences of others were to come to light. While a few of these arrived in response to my appeal for further witnesses in Emma Cooper's *Kent Messenger* article of 13 November 1992, many, ironically, were to arise from 'friend-of-a-friend' situations—only in this case, the witnesses were not to prove inaccessible or untraceable. And, with a few exceptions, these persons were willing to put their names to their experiences.

It is important to add that by no means can most of the individuals whose accounts follow be accused of jumping on the publicity bandwagon. But for the renewed attention granted the case by Sharpe and Dawkins, and their introduction to my special interest in the case, it is questionable whether many of these accounts would have come to light at all. To avoid possible future publicity, some requested that I not use their real names—which, while disappointing, is something I both understand and respect. Substituted names used in accordance with this request are indicated by an asterisk (*).

As I gathered these reports, in so doing noting a number of similarities between them, in points of detail or in the behaviour of the girl, my thoughts echoed the words of the late Tom Harber, who, in his second conversation with Michael Goss, said: 'I have never found such a well-tallied set of accounts.'[2]

Ian Sharpe & Chris Dawkins (November 1992)

Probably the most important witness I was to talk to, on account of his much-publicised encounter, was Ian Sharpe himself. The interview came five months after his encounter, in March 1993, by which time media interest in the story had largely waned. After his experience, Ian said 'the telephone never stopped'—which said something for the resourcefulness of certain parties since Ian's telephone number was unlisted. Little wonder that during this time Ian chose to ignore my letter. But, following the publication of a magazine article in which we were both featured, Ian finally agreed to an interview.[3]

Ian's own version of events proved to be slightly different to those reported in the newspapers and elsewhere. And, of course, it was far more detailed and vivid. Rather than appearing before him, as many newspapers had suggested, Ian noticed the girl some distance ahead, standing in the centre of the outside lane of the road. Taken from that taped interview, Ian recounts his experience of 8 November 1992:

Ian: This was at exactly ten-to-twelve at night. I know it was the time because I'd just looked at my watch. I'd lit a cigarette up and come [sic] out of the Blue Bell Hill slip-road from the village, coming down the Hill. I'd just had a puff when I saw this woman, and I thought, 'Oh, she'll go back; she won't come across'. But then she just ran straight in front of the car [from the right], and I hit her on her left side...and her head was facing this way; she was looking at me all the time.
Q: Did it seem she was aware of what she was doing? It wasn't like she was unaware of the car?
Ian: Well, I don't know. It all happened so quick[ly]. I mean, this all happened in a few seconds.
Q: But it happened where the press indicated, just before the Aylesford turn-off?
Ian: That's where it was. You know that big sign? It was just a few yards in front of that.

At the time I went into the police station [Maidstone] I still thought that I'd knocked a woman over. I don't believe in—I never have believed in ghosts. My impression of a ghost is something you can see through, all white or pale. But this was a...a woman, and her skin was normal, and her eyes...she had big eyes, really big eyes.
Q: The press, of course, were quick to identify the ghost as that of 22-year-old Judith Lingham, who died on Blue Bell Hill in 1965—an identification that, in a number of articles, was attributed to a police source. Would the police have identified her to you?
Ian: No. All that was said was, 'Oh, you just hit the ghost of Blue Bell Hill'. And that was the first—
Q: What, as soon as you went into the police station?
Ian: No, when we went back up there. When we went back up there the police who came up with me said, 'Oh, you just hit the ghost of Blue Bell Hill'. After we

The location of Ian Sharpe's encounter, as it appears today

came back down [they said], 'We've got to put it down as another sighting of the ghost of Blue Bell Hill'. But no name was mentioned whatsoever.

Q: Is it true that they did a sketch based on your description?

Ian: What, the police? No. It was the *Kent Messenger*. What was going to happen was this: an artist was going to come to see me and I was going to describe this woman and he was going to do a sketch of her and then show it to me, and say, 'Is that what you saw, or is that not what you saw?' And I'd just about had enough of it—I said no, look, I can tell you over the phone what she was like. She was a normal woman, roundish face, she had shoulder-length hair that rolled inwards at the [shoulder]...and she was fair haired. She was wearing a light-ish coat [described later as a 'mushroomy' colour; a light-coloured coat with a long V-neck reminiscent of the 'Duster' coats of the 1950s or 1960s, with a light blouse or roll-neck underneath]—whether it was a mac or whatever, I didn't notice; all I can remember is the upper part of it. Now whether it was full-length I can't remember. But her face...I can still see her face now.

Satisfied that they were not dealing with a real traffic casualty, the police interest in the matter was closed. Ian, however, was still in a state of shock, literally shaking, so much so that he was unable to drive. As one of his sons told me, members of the family had to collect him and his car from the station.

Ian: You know, when I went to the police, I was convinced I'd knocked somebody over. I was *convinced*. I said to my wife, 'The police are going to be up tomorrow to report that they found a body up there.' But then the police told me that if you hit somebody doing fifty miles an hour the front of your car would have been caved in. She wouldn't have gone under it; she would have gone up and over the top. When you're going to hit somebody, you don't think of anything like a bump. All you know is: I'm going to hit her, I'm going to hit her.

Q: Did you actually try to swerve? Did you have time?

Ian: I didn't have time! I was doing fifty miles an hour.

Q: Was it almost as if she was waiting for you to come down, before running out? Was there the impression that she was timing it?

Ian: I don't know. I saw...well, you've got the two lanes there; you've got the crash barrier in the middle, and she was two yards or so from the crash barrier [approximately a third of the way into the outer lane]. And I was on the left-hand lane going down, and I saw her and, for a split second you think: 'Oh, she'll go back—she won't come across'. And then she was sort of like this [Ian assumed a standing, side-on pose, head turned to look over his left shoulder], and she just came in front of me. And there was nothing I could do—except, gripping the wheel, brakes on, and, you know, from fifty miles [an hour]—what the actual speed of impact was, I don't know, but it just happened so quick[ly].[4] But all that I can remember is her looking at me like this. And I'll always remember those eyes.

Q: Her expression—it wasn't distraught?

Ian: No.

Q: Were you the only one on that stretch of road at the time?

Ian: Two cars came down behind me. The first car I flagged—I slowed him down, but he just slowed right down to where I was, looked at me, and went. And then another one came down and he just went. They must have thought I was a drunk or something—I was in a state of shock wandering about the road. And then I went down a bit further and there was a lorry parked, but the driver—it was a Safeway's lorry in the slip-road—he was asleep. And I thought, 'Oh God, what am I going to do?' You know, I still thought it was a woman; I've got to report it. And having reported it, well, that would be the end of it.

Q: Well ordinarily, you wouldn't really want to leave the scene?

Ian: Well, that's it. But there, you have no phone, nothing. So I thought, 'I've got to report [it].' So I went in and reported it, come home here; I had a couple of brandies, still shaking like a leaf, and I just naturally thought that would be the end of it. But then it all blew up from there.

Q: Have you been up the Hill since, on your own?

Ian: Well, the next day I was off work. And the following morning I had to be at

work at 5 o'clock. I waited at the bottom of Blue Bell Hill for another car to come [along], and I followed him up the Hill. Now I never come down that way of a night-time on my own. I always go round Snodland and back that way.
Q: Did you feel afterward, when you had a chance to reflect, whether you were picked out personally, for any reason?
Ian: I don't know; I just don't know.
Q: Or was it sheer bad luck, from your point of view?
Ian: I think I was there at the right time—if it hadn't been me, it would have been somebody else, maybe. I honestly don't know.

In October 1994, Ian repeated his experience before an audience of millions on the BBC's *Out of This World*, a one-hour television special on the Paranormal, hosted by Sue Cook and featuring experts Dr Susan Blackmore and the late Dr Lyall Watson.[5] As one of four stories, the Blue Bell Hill case received barely ten minutes of air time, with most of that taken by drama reconstructions of Ian's and Chris Dawkins' encounters, followed by a few minutes of analysis. The presentation itself is perhaps best passed over without comment. What I was impressed with was that nearly two years after his encounter, and well over a year after my interview with him, Ian's story was absolutely unchanged. He described his experience in exactly the same way, and repeated the same details as he had to me, adding only that the girl had worn a jumper or roll-neck beneath her light-coloured coat.

Also of value was the testimony of two police officers involved in the investigation, PCs Roger Ginn and Steve Nelkin, particularly the former, who confirmed what Ian had said regarding the conclusion of the police following their investigation: 'Once we were satisfied there was no sign of an accident, no damage to his car, and particularly in view of where it had occurred, we just had to write it off as another sighting of the Blue Bell Hill ghost.'[6]

The programme also provided the opportunity to hear Chris Dawkins' account from his own lips. To refresh the reader's memory, his encounter had taken place in Blue Bell Hill Village on 22 November, at around 10.55 p.m. The girl had emerged from between parked cars (on the road's east side) to run out in front of him. As he struck her and she fell in front of his car, she looked right into his eyes—according to the actor's portrayal in the reconstruction, smiling as she did so.

Chris checked beneath and between the row of parked cars, and finding nothing he began to panic, convinced by now that the girl must be trapped beneath his car. Too afraid to investigate himself, he telephoned his father to report his fears that he had killed someone.

Chris's father, Graham, reported that once he had managed to calm his son down over the phone and got him to talk lucidly, he realised that something out of the ordinary had taken place. At Blue Bell Hill, he found Chris waiting inside the car. At Chris's insistence that the girl must still be underneath, he got down to take a look and, of course, found nothing. He then set about contacting the police.

Darren and Christine Green (c.1984/5)

The next account is a little unusual in any case of ghost-seeing, in that it involved more than a single witness—which, if we exclude any criticism of cross-contamination between witnesses that might be levied by some commentators, does suggest that some aspect of the phenomenon is objective in nature. Certainly the couple in this case, Darren and Christine Green* of Maidstone, would dispute any accusation that they had imagined or hallucinated the girl they feared they were about to hit late one winter's night at the foot of Blue Bell Hill.

The Greens' experience took place before they were married, around 1984 or 1985. Estimated time of night: between 10.30 p.m. and midnight. There was no other traffic on the road, which is unlit. They had just come off the A229 southbound at the Aylesford turn-off at Blue Bell Hill (which is actually signposted for the villages of Eccles, Burham and Wouldham)—a route that would bring them westbound under the dual carriageway and past the Lower Bell towards Aylesford (where Christine then lived)—when, as their car (a Fiat 127) came out of the bend at the bottom of that stretch onto Rochester Road, suddenly in the road before them was the figure of a girl.

As in Ian Sharpe's encounter, it was to be over very quickly. Darren immediately stamped on the brakes, but with no time to manoeuvre, both braced themselves for the inevitable collision—which never came. Neither could recall at which instant the girl was no longer there, only that as they passed over the spot she was nowhere to be seen.

Darren brought the car to a stop and checked the road by engaging his reversing lights to light up the hedgerows, which he described as dense and unbroken at that spot. The road was deserted all the way back to the bend. Understandably, neither wished to get out and investigate.

In spite of the brevity of their sighting, the couple managed to give a fairly detailed description of the girl. It is one that holds some familiarity: she was dressed in a white top and wore white ankle socks (both clearly noted because of the amount of light they reflected). The colour or shade of garment covering her lower torso was not recalled, only that it was knee-length or ended just above the knee, since her bare lower legs were visible. Like her skirt, the colour of her hair was not memorable, only that it was not fair. Altogether, her dress was suggestive of a school uniform, which may account for their estimate of her age as 'in her teens'.

The description could have been given by Maurice Goodenough. However, the couple maintained that at the time neither was very much aware of Blue Bell Hill's ghost, let alone Goodenough's 1974 encounter.

Later, Christine's mother had related one version of the story, but this told of the girl Hitch-Hiker who, on vanishing, leaves her jacket behind in the vehicle. Christine in particular was quite taken aback when, after my interview with the couple, I produced copies of Goodenough's reported description of the girl he had hit in 1974.[7]

A year later, in December 1993, I had the opportunity to interview them for a second time. The value of this was twofold. A second interview allows the researcher to check to see if any inconsistencies have crept into the account. Secondly, it enabled their account to be presented in their own words:

Darren: We were going down the Hill, and we'd just gone around that sharp left-hand bend, where there's a junction—
Q: The Burham turn-off?
Darren: Yes. And we'd gone down there—I don't know, a little way—it was be-

Rochester Road looking back towards Blue Bell Hill, where Darren and Christine Green drove through the figure of girl with white ankle socks

fore the stones [The Countless Stones or Little Kit's Coty House, located in a field just off the Rochester Road 200 metres further down, on the left], so it was in that stretch there.

Christine: It was on the left-hand side, she ran out from the left.

Q: She stepped out?

Darren: No, she was just there.

Christine: No, it was just there, wasn't it—there, as in front of the car.

Q: So, in that left-hand lane?

Christine: Yes.

Darren: But the thing was, I must have had the lights on high beam, because there was nothing else there. Normally, if someone is standing in the distance, they show up, don't they? You see somebody in the distance, and then you slow down or whatever—but this didn't, it was just there, so one minute there's nothing, next minute it's in the headlights and you've sort of passed it.

Q: How long would you estimate the sighting lasted?

Christine: It would have been seconds.

Darren: Well, I hit the brakes, but I hit the brakes after we'd gone— y'know, if it had been an actual solid figure, it would have been gone down the road.

Christine: It was enough for both of us to recognise, 'Oh my God', you're gonna hit it, and that's it, and it's happened, and it's gone.

Q: But it was a person?

Darren: Yeah, definitely. You could see features and everything.

Q: Because, I know before you gave a description—which was a light-ish top and white ankle socks—that you remarked on?

Darren: Yeah, very much so, because that sort of stood out—the schoolgirl/teenager type.

Q: Any estimate of height above the bonnet, that you can recall?

Christine: It definitely wasn't a child, was it?

D: No, I would say it was a thirteen or fourteen-year-old; I don't know, sort of five foot, something like that.

Q: Hair style, length?

Christine: Blonde hair, was she?

Darren: I was just going to say dark. I'm sure it was fairly dark, sort of three-quarter length, not short, not cropped or anything—down to shoulder-level.

Q: What about orientation to you?

Darren/Christine (in unison): Face on. Straight on.

Q: Almost as if it appeared in front of you?

Darren: Yeah, it was just straight there. There was no mistaking or anything. Y'know, we just sort of went 'bang', straight through it.

Christine: I'm sure I screamed; I remember shutting my eyes because I thought

that we were going to hit it—so you see it, and you react, and I'm sure I shut my eyes.
Darren: I skidded all the way down the road to a halt, and we both looked behind, and there was nothing in the road at all—y'know it took the car quite a while to stop because of the speed I was going [estimated at around 60 mph].[8]
Q: No impression of impact?
Darren: No. No, nothing. There was no noise, or anything.
Q: And you went through the spot she was on?
Darren: Yeah, straight through it. There was no way anyone could have moved out the way.
Q: Do you know what the weather conditions were at the time?
Darren: Fairly good, I think.
Q: So, again, we're not talking about fog banks or anything?
Darren: It was dry. No, nothing like that, because it does get like that down there. You say about the white ankle socks, they were definitely—
Christine: That's what sticks out in my mind more than anything.
Darren: They really stand out, a hell of a lot.
Q: Whatever it might be, anything light is going to get picked out, isn't it?
Darren: Yeah, they really stood out.
Q: Last time, I was trying to establish the length of skirt or dress portion, and I know you were a little bit vague on that. Was it because of the fact that if it was dark you wouldn't have the contrast, the reflectivity?
Darren: I seem to remember with the ankle socks you could see quite a bit of the legs, so it would have been knee-length or something, or just above the knee.
Q: So, bare legs?
Darren: Yeah.
Q: What time of night would this have been?
Christine: We reckoned it would have been somewhere between eleven and twelve?
Darren: Probably. It was definitely after half-ten—so, say, half-ten to twelve, that sort of time.

(At this point the couple was shown photographs of the 1965 crash victims. None inspired any recognition).

Q: Do you think that if you saw this girl again, you would recognise her?
Darren: If the person was dressed in the clothing and everything else again.
Christine: I didn't take much account of features.
Darren: You have certain details there: the legs, the ankle socks—that sort of thing; to a certain extent the shape of the hair, and the style of it all, I think…was

back, I don't know, in the fifties or something; it wasn't anything modern day. Because, the shoes, I think, had, like, the buckles across. It's difficult.

Q: Your impression was you saw a girl and she's suddenly not there.

Darren: It's an eerie feeling afterwards, isn't it?

Christine: Oh, yeah.

Darren: You do get the feeling that it's a ghost, but whether that's because you can't put it down to anything else.

Q: Did that come out of discussion between the pair of you, or did you both know instantly, you think, that that was the only explanation?

Darren: It was weird. As soon as we hit it I knew there was something strange, because there wasn't a bang, there wasn't a thump, or anything.

Christine: Yeah, afterwards we thought it must have been a ghost.

Darren: We just skidded to a halt, and looked around, and you knew straight away.

Q: Do you recall if she came all the way up to the bumper? I mean, would it be a case of actually arriving directly at the spot she's at when she disappears, or did she disappear in your beam before you got there?

Darren: No, No. She disappeared when we hit her.

Q: Any question on how she disappeared?

Darren: No, she was just gone—just gone, instantly. Y'know, I suppose you close your eyes waiting for the impact or whatever…it happened that quick that you were looking out the back window to see whether you had actually knocked her flying over the top.

Christine: When you first saw her, you didn't think at that moment, 'God, there's a ghost'.

Darren: It was a solid figure.

Christine: The thought was: there's a girl in the road, and also in your mind is: what is a girl doing in the road, dressed like that, at this time of night? But it's not until afterwards, where it was apparently gone, that you think, gosh, it must have been a ghost.

Q: And at that time, you hadn't heard of the ghost particularly?

Darren: No, we never thought about it.

Q: I understand that it was only when I showed you the articles or a transcript of the description from '74 that it meant much to you?

Christine: Yeah, yeah. We didn't really know—or I didn't really know anything about it at all before.

Darren: We knew of the rumours.

Q: Do you have opportunity to go back that way of a night very often?

Darren: Basically, we avoid it, don't we? We don't go that way. If we've got no call to go that way, we won't go that way just for the sake of it.

When asked if they felt their encounter had anything to do with them personally, they both answered 'no'.
Q: So it was just that you were the first vehicle that came along?
Darren/Christine: Yes.

Gladys and Allen Painter (July 1974)

If Darren and Christine Green's experience attests to something seemingly objective about the Blue Bell Hill phenomenon, the following case only reaffirms the subjective aspect, suggesting that some people are perhaps more likely to see apparitions than others.

One of the early letters I received back in 1992 in response to the *Kent Messenger* appeal following Ian Sharpe's experience was from Mrs Audrey Brooks of Maidstone. Mrs Brooks was not claiming a sighting herself, but told of the experience of her late mother, Mrs Gladys Painter, who had died only a month before Ian's encounter. It was an experience that evidently impressed her deeply, and was often a subject of discussion in the years that followed. That experience is best summarised by Mrs Brooks herself:

> We used to get a visit from our parents weekly. They came from Gravesend.
>
> We had the *Kent Messenger* here with the story of the motorist who ran down the girl and covered her with a blanket. I believe the police had tracker dogs to see if she had crawled into the undergrowth. I am not sure what year that was.
>
> Anyhow, when my mother visited me I said to her, 'Well, the ghost has been out on Bluebell Hill again, then.'
>
> She said: 'What do you mean?'
>
> I picked up the paper, and both my mother and stepfather were white with shock.
>
> I said: 'What's the matter?'
>
> My mother remarked: 'When did that happen?'
>
> It so happened that my mother knew nothing about the ghost of the Hill, but the night previously to her being knocked down (the ghost, I mean), they had left my house late, and were travelling up Bluebell Hill, when my mother screamed she saw this girl running right into the path of their car.
>
> She shouted: 'Allen, you'll kill her'. She grabbed the steering wheel.
>
> My stepfather never saw a thing, but my mother described her so vividly.
>
> She definitely saw her. She said she had long hair and a white dress.[9] She often mentioned the sighting. It happened definitely the night before the motorist who thought he had run her down.[10]

The 'motorist who thought he had run her down' clearly refers to Maurice Goodenough—which meant that Mrs Painter's sighting took place in July 1974; according to her daughter, just the night before Goodenough's.

Such would not be the first time that sightings on the Hill would be so closely related. In fact, in the interview with Mrs Brooks that followed, it transpired that these two incidents may have been more closely related still:

A: According to my mother, they were going up the Hill, and she started screaming because this girl ran out, and she kept saying: 'Stop Allen, stop. You'll run her down.'

And he said: 'There's nothing there; there's nothing there.'

As they got closer, she just pulled on the wheel because this girl just stood in the road and faced them. She saw her run out at some distance. It wasn't a sudden thing. She didn't just suddenly appear—she saw her run out. And she faced her, and they got nearer, and then that's when she pulled on the steering wheel.
Q: Because it was obvious your stepfather wasn't going to avoid the girl?
A: He wouldn't stop. She was so worried he wouldn't stop. And he said: 'Nothing there, nothing there'—and she was really upset about this.
Q: And he didn't have any prior knowledge of the ghost? It wasn't that he was saying 'there's nothing there?'
A: He never saw it. He said there wasn't anything there. He didn't see it, and she did. She would have seen it on the Friday to the day of that man covering her up in the blanket—that was the night before.
Q: Would it definitely have been a Friday?
A: It was a Friday. I'm pretty certain it was a Friday.
Q: And this would be on the new road, of course?
A: It was going up Blue Bell Hill, there's a little side road of the old Hill. It was just beyond there [on the main carriageway of the A229, fractionally above the entrance to the remnant section of the Chatham Road for White Lodge, as ascertained later in the interview].

A: She certainly saw it. She described this girl: 'I'd know her again,' she said, as if she was—she spoke as if she was a real person: 'I'd know her again, if I met her, I'd know her again.'
Q: Did you get the impression that your mother felt that they'd been—or she had been selected specially, or [was it] just pure chance that they had come along at that time?
A: I don't really know.
Q: It's something I've asked other people, other witnesses.
A: I don't know. She could just see it. She saw her from head to toe. When I told

them the next Friday about it, they truly had no idea there was such a phantom: 'Oh, didn't you know about the ghost on the Hill?' 'No'. And they truly didn't. Allen looked at her and he was as white as a sheet.
Q: *He* was?
A: He was white, and she said: 'There you are Allen,' she said. 'I told you. There was something on the Hill. I told you what she was like,' and he… I went and made him a cup of tea, because he had a bit of a row with my mother, because she nearly caused an accident. She screamed at him and told him off first, then pulled the wheel, and he said: 'Don't you ever do that again!'

She said: 'I wouldn't, but you ran her down.' He wouldn't get out and have a look. He told her it was a load of old rubbish, but she wouldn't have it and, of course, the next Friday it all came out. She was so relieved to know she was right.
Q: Do you know whether the swerve would have avoided the girl, or whether she just wasn't there?
A: Well, they certainly swerved, because my mother did pull on the wheel. Whether she pulled right or left I'll never know. Probably there wouldn't have been an accident, with my mother doing that at that time of night, because there wasn't a lot of traffic about, I think. But had there been—I mean, my mother has never done that in her life before—but she just wanted to avoid the girl. She saw her run out, certainly before they got there.
Q: Do you know from which side of the road?
A: I think she came from left to right. She saw her run out, and then she turned, because as soon as my mother saw her run out, she started screaming, telling Allen to 'Stop, stop. You're going to run her down,' and Allen saying, 'What are you on about? What are you on about?' And as they got really close up, she pulled on the wheel—so perhaps my mother thought she'd avoided her. But she was in such a state, my mum.
Q: Did your mother ever describe an expression, any facial details?
A: She looked straight at her. 'I'd know her again', she said. She had big eyes.[11] She said she looked straight at her, and she had longish hair, she said it was sort of light, but then taking into consideration the [poor] light—I think she said light hair, and she had—she didn't really say a dress, she said she had a white—definitely white—blouse, and a light skirt, and it was long...longish. But she saw her complete.
Q: Did she see shoes or anything about the lower legs?
A: Head to toe. There was not a part of her legs or anything missing — it was like a person from head to toe. I don't know…she probably had shoes on or something. She certainly—because, I said to her, 'Was her face there?' and, 'Was she all complete?'

The northbound carriageway of the A229, scene of Gladys and Allen Painter's sighting in July 1974. The entrance to White Lodge access road is just above the car on the left

'Oh yes, from head to toe,' she said. 'She was just a person.'

My mother saw her run out, and then she turned and faced her.

Q: That's exactly what happened with Ian Sharpe.

A: Really?!

Q: That wasn't stated by the press. They said the girl just appeared.

A: Really? Well, that's interesting. Well, I never—because she wasn't just standing there. She actually ran out and turned and faced…because my mother said: 'She just looked at me', and she really thought she was a real person.

The conversation came round again to the date of Mrs Painter's sighting, with Mrs Brooks reiterating that it took place the night before Maurice Goodenough's 'accident':

Q: Is it possibly the same night, I wonder, because some sources reporting on Goodenough's experience state the early hours of Saturday morning; others, late on Friday night?

A: Oh.

Q: Now, they [press sources] give a time of 'around midnight'. Some say slightly

before, some after, so it's a Friday or Saturday, depending upon your point of view.
A: Oh, I see.
Q: So it's quite conceivable it was the same night?
A: Oh, it probably is, then. Mm, well I'm saying Friday night. Well, it would have been after midnight, so it would have been Saturday, wouldn't it. I never thought about it. I was thinking my mother left me on a Friday.
Q: Wouldn't it be intriguing to think the two events might tie up: that this fellow Maurice Goodenough knocked her down, and of course, he left to find the police, and when they all came back, the girl was gone, to perhaps trot across the road in your mother's path?
A: Yes, it would be a Saturday, actually.
Q: We're talking about midnight or thereabouts—around about midnight on this Friday night. So, you're mother and stepfather left here [Maidstone] about half-midnight, you say, to one o'clock?
A: Yes.
Q: So by the time they got up the Hill, it could well have been a combined incident.
A: It was always…they never used to leave our house until about midnight. They'd keep looking at their watch saying: 'We must go, we must go...' and it was always about midnight when they went.
Q: Was there any estimate of age that you remember, of this girl?
A: Oh, she was quite youngish, my mum said; quite a young girl.
Q: Actually young or young-looking?
A: She just said youngish. I don't know.
Q: According to newspaper reports of the Goodenough incident, the girl was about ten years old. That was his estimate.
A: Oh no, not as young as that, I wouldn't think. Not a child, because she would have said a child. She said a young person.
Q: Shoulder-length brown hair—again, depending on light conditions, possibly; white blouse, white ankle socks, and a skirt. That's why I asked you if there was any recollection of anything below the knee.
A: No, she never said anything like that. She just said she was a complete person from head to foot. There was no part missing.

With regard to the press's identification of the 1965 crash as cause, made at the time of Maurice Goodenough's experience:

A: I've always had in my mind that that girl was not to do with that accident, because I heard of the Hitch-Hiker much, much earlier—in fact, when I lived in

Rainham [before 1963], and I've always thought that when they talk about the ghost of the Hill it was before that car crash.
Q: That would be very useful to find out for sure. How would you have heard about it? Would it be rumour, or do you think it could be related to press accounts?
A: In my mind—when I've seen about the ghost of Blue Bell Hill and this accident, I've thought, 'Well, no, it was before that.' Well, I lived in Rainham; then we moved to Maidstone in '62...about '62.
Q: So if you did hear it around then, then you certainly did hear it before the crash.
A: Yes, there was a Hitch-Hiker long before that crash. No matter how much you can read of this, I think people who genuinely see it—I don't think you could imagine you saw that. I mean, the shock I saw on mum and Allen's faces the following week when I mentioned it, I knew they didn't know about the ghost of the Hill. I could see that they were shocked. You can't make it up like that.
Q: And I think the police saw that with Ian Sharpe and Chris Dawkins— the fact that their reaction was so extreme, they knew they weren't having their leg pulled.
A: Yes. I think it certainly does something to you. You couldn't say, 'Oh, yes, I've seen it', you couldn't say that. You've got to be a certain person to see this. Not everybody can see this, obviously, from mum and Allen.

My mother often said...well, it haunted her. She never stopped talking about it, and—it was about last year, I think—she said: 'I think I ought to write it down'. I said: 'Well, I think you should.'

Y'know, I wish she had. I do wish she had.

When I later contacted Mrs Brooks' stepfather, he regretted that he could remember so little of this particular incident. It wasn't something to which he attached any significance, even when he and his wife saw the newspaper article the following week, since he saw nothing himself, nor had there been any physical contact with the car. However, he does recall his wife's exclamation that she could see a person walking in the road, which caused his foot to reflexively jump to the brake. He began to slow down, but seeing nothing in front or behind, he proceeded up the Hill. At the time he had been more concerned with the heavy traffic around them, and the poor conditions, which he described as teeming down with rain.

Bob Fearne (*c.* November 1967)

Bob Fearne's experience on Blue Bell Hill occurred sometime between 1965 and

1967 while driving a lorry from Faversham to New Ash Green. His memory was understandably hazy regarding specifics after so long, but he remembered that it was a Wednesday, and the conditions were 'dark, dusky'—around 4.30 p.m. or 4.45 p.m. in the afternoon (at 'around about this time of year'—November). He believed it may have been raining.

Pin-pointing the equivalent spot on a modern, unmarked map of the Hill, Bob identified the location of his sighting as the footbridge/Chatham Road intersection—which is coincidental with the bend on the former route that was the scene of the 1965 crash. As he rounded that bend (southbound), in the 'middle of the bend' was the figure of a woman on a bicycle, a blonde dressed in what he took to be light-coloured shorts and a blouse. She was not showing any lights. He immediately swerved around her, trying to get the vehicle back over to the left before uphill traffic appeared around the bend. He was sure he had missed her. The cab of the lorry veered around, and he found himself cursing her.

At a café stop further along his route ('The Jungle Café', Wrotham Heath), he had opportunity to talk to his fellow driver and friend who had been following right behind in his own lorry. This gentleman (unnamed) had seen Bob swerve, but hadn't seen any reason for the manoeuvre. Certainly, there had been nothing in the first lorry's wake as he himself passed the spot. Rounding off the episode in a manner reminiscent of the classic PHH ending, a lady working at the café then told him about the girl who had been killed there months or years before.

At the time of my brief interview with him (ten days after Ian Sharpe's experience, in November 1992), Bob shuddered still at the thought of that news, stating it made the back of his neck tingle. He had no knowledge of Ian Sharpe's experience, and no real interest in the story as a whole.

Bob Fearne's sighting stands out in Blue Bell Hill's ghostly repertoire (if indeed it was such an event) by the unusual feature of a bicycle. Interestingly, other road ghost cases have depicted vanishing cyclists, including those who have fallen under the wheels of passing vehicles. The A12 between Essex and Norfolk, for instance, is the setting for several encounters involving a man on a bicycle. On 9 August 2001, Phillip Baum and his wife were travelling north on the A12 between Ipswich and Lowestoft at around 10 p.m. when, as they approached the junction with the A1145 to Beccles, a cyclist suddenly pulled out right in front of their car.

Mr Baum takes up the story: 'I was travelling at 60 mph and could not stop in time. The cyclist turned and smiled at me as I hit him. There was a large impact. Immediately after I stopped I got out of the car. There were vehicles by this time slowing down behind me. I checked all round the car for the cyclist. I looked underneath the car; there was no sign of him—not even any sign of the pushbike he was riding. I ran back to ask the people in the car behind me if they'd seen anything; they hadn't.

'My wife phoned the police for them to check the area, in case the cyclist was thrown to the side of the road somewhere. They found no sign. There was no damage to my car, even though I had felt a large impact.

'The police told me that this incident wasn't the first, and probably won't be the last. They claim that there is a ghost which haunts this stretch of the A12.'[12]

In 2004, I received a similar report for the B1389 in Witham, Essex. Before the A12 bypass was built to loop around the town, the London–Colchester road ran through it. The town road is today designated the B1389. Steve Everett was driving to work at around 6.30 a.m. in February 2004, when, near the Eastways Industrial Estate, he saw a 'rough looking man' at the side of the road with a bicycle.

The man wore a parker jacket, old trousers, a jumper and shoes. As Steve approached at about 30 mph, the man seemed as if he were waiting, looking up the road in his direction. But as soon as Steve drew level, the man walked straight out in front of his car...and vanished. [13]

Richard Marchant had an experience involving an apparition of a cyclist near Sandling, at the foot of Blue Bell Hill, one misty morning in December 1968. Richard, of Gillingham, was driving his Isetta westward along Grange Road and had just turned left into Boarley Lane, southward in the direction of The Running Horse Inn, when he saw a cyclist in front of him, crossing the road from his right, where there was a wooden fence with no apparent openings.

'At that time, in 1968, there were huge elm trees along the fence, about ten feet apart. The cyclist was just a black outline in my dipped headlights and moved in slow motion. His wheels were at least three inches below the level of the road, the rest of him was faceless and I could see through his body. On the left of the road was a huge hedge into which he disappeared. I continued towards the spot and looked along the hedge to see if he reappeared, but as there was no lighting at that spot I could see nothing.'

The figure wore what appeared to be a cloak, which was quite visible, leaving only half of the rear wheel visible.

'I have to stress,' said Richard, 'that there was a stout wooden fence along the road at that time, some three feet in height and in good condition. I inspected it at the time. This apparition must have been formed some years before 1968 when the fence either had a gate, an opening or didn't exist, because the figure came straight out of it.'

The lane has altered from how it appeared in 1968. The hedge, trees and the original fence are no longer there, but the spot itself, bordered on its east side by low post-and-rail fencing near to the Yew Tree pub, is preserved today immediately south of the line of the M20, which bridges Boarley Lane just east of Junction 6.[14]

There are possibly a number of pedal cyclists who have been injured on Blue Bell Hill over the years. Only one historical fatality, however, has turned up in the news archives. On the evening of Friday 5 September 1908, Thomas Kempster, 32, of Maidstone, a telephone wireman for the General Post Office, was cycling down Blue Bell Hill—'one of the steepest and most dangerous in Kent'—when he 'dashed into a van, was terribly injured, and died shortly afterwards.'[15] Stefano Riggoli, a caterer, told the inquest at the West Kent Hospital, Maidstone (where Mr Kempster died the day after the accident) that he and his wife were driving up Blue Bell Hill in their horse-drawn trap at about 7.30 p.m. when, 'near the bend of the centre of the hill' (a probable reference to the bend at Kit's Coty Cottage) they saw Mr Kempster 'riding down the hill as if he had lost control of the machine'. Before Riggoli could react, Kempster hurtled into the shoulder of the horse, and fell beneath the trap. The injured man was removed to West Kent Hospital, where he later died. The inquest, which concluded with a verdict of accidental death, noted that at the top of the hill there was a notice stating it was dangerous for cyclists.[16]

The description of the location—the steep section of road above the Lower Bell—places the accident some distance (a little over a mile) from the vicinity of Richard Marchant's encounter, but in terms of the history of the Hill—and Bob Fearne's experience—it is noteworthy all the same.

Paula Cooper (June 1993)

The next case playing according to what I have called the 'knock down scenario' came several months after the media fuss over Ian Sharpe's and Chris Dawkins' experiences (and those that followed not long after—see Chapter 11) had died down. First again with the news was the *Kent Today*, which, on 23 June 1993, in another article by Emma Cooper, reported the experience of 24-year-old Paula Cooper (no relation) of Walderslade—which, according to the author, backed up theories that the ghost of a woman killed there in a three-death crash in 1965 was still haunting the place.

Paula had been on her way home in the early hours of the previous Sunday morning (20 June) after a night out with friends in Larkfield, Maidstone. She was driving up Blue Bell Hill when somebody suddenly ran out in front of her:

'It felt like I went over something, I really thought I had hit the person.'

She stopped the car and looked around, but she could see nothing. Being 1 a.m. and by herself, Paula did not get out to investigate. Instead, shaken, she drove to Chatham Police Station to report the incident. All of a sudden it hit her when she remembered about the ghost. The police investigation revealed nothing at the scene, and no sign of damage to Miss Cooper's car.

'I really don't know if it was the ghost, but I was wide awake when it happened,' she said.

Paula's experience was said to be similar to several other incidents in the years since the 1965 crash, two occurring the previous November, around the anniversary of the tragedy.[17]

Paula, it turned out, worked within the *KM* Group, and was well known to Emma Cooper, which perhaps raised some suspicion. Emma, however, assured me that Paula was truthful and reliable, and had been genuinely frightened by the experience. The incident had taken place on the dual carriageway at the point where the Chatham Road joins the A229—a location that will now be familiar to the reader. The witness could not determine whether the figure had been male or female, only that it wore a 'white shirt'.[18]

According to the article, the police had investigated the scene following Paula's report to them at Chatham Police Station. Seeking verification, I called Chatham Police Station. I was referred from there to Control at Rochester, who, curiously, could not confirm a report or the despatch of officers to that location early on Sunday 20 June.

So, was this a late attempt by the *Kent Today* to recapture some of the thunder generated by their coverage of the Sharpe and Dawkins encounters of the year before, or a genuine event? The reader is left to decide.

Stefanie Savage (1996?)

On 1 November 1996, the *Daily Mirror* reported that the ghost of Blue Bell Hill had claimed another victim. The brief account told the story of 18-year-old Stefanie Savage, whose insurers, it reported, had been saddled with a £3,000 repair bill after she swerved to avoid a figure that appeared in the road in front of her.

'I was driving there, as I have many times, when something or someone seemed to run out in front of me,' she said. 'I swerved to avoid it, wrote off the car, and demolished three garage petrol pumps.'[19]

The publication date hints at it being a Hallowe'en-related column filler, probably based on a regional newspaper report. Alas, I have been unable to locate the potential local source. Likewise, I failed to identify a report of an accident involving such a crash at either of the petrol stations at Blue Bell Hill around the same time. (The only record of such an incident—at the Cossington service station—in which a 21-year-old woman crashed into and demolished a petrol pump, which sparked into flame—was in February 1975.)[20]

As it is, Stefanie Savage's reported encounter provides little meaningful information, even as to the gender of the figure, so her account must be passed over without further comment.

Parallels

The encounters at Blue Bell Hill are far from unique. They find familiarity in a number of very similar events elsewhere. In fact, they appear to be the most common form of road ghost, easily outnumbering accounts involving Phantom Hitch-Hikers, with which they are often associated. We looked briefly at two examples in Chapters 4 and 7, in the experiences of Shawn and Geri Lape in Chicago, and of Bill Hopkins outside Llanidloes, Wales, and noted the variations on this essential theme, as illustrated by Phillip Baum's and Steve Everett's experiences.

Another of noted similarity to events at Blue Bell Hill, albeit again with a small variation on the theme, and which again supports the idea of the phenomenon being a real one—which, like the PHH, behaves according to a clearly defined 'script'—is the experience of Peter Leslie of East Finchley. According to the *Hampstead Local Advertiser* of 17 October 1985, Mr Leslie was driving along the A41 towards Stanmore at around 6 p.m. on Sunday 13 October, when 'all of a sudden' a man with a Doberman dog appeared before him. Registering the unavoidable impact, the witness saw both figures go over the car (a description comparable to Ted Wright's version of the Goodenough incident). In his rear-view mirror, Leslie could see the pair lying in the road behind as he brought his car to a screeching halt. He could also hear the man's screams and a dog's whimper, but when he got out of the car there was no sign of either. Mr Leslie, in a state of shock, telephoned the police, who checked the scene but were unable to find any evidence of an accident. The car, of course, showed no sign of damage.[21]

Switching to the United States, we see the same scenario played out outside Easton, Connecticut's Union Cemetery. Two witnesses have described their encounter with the ghostly 'Lady in White', who has haunted the locality since the 1940s. Of the other cases presented here, the descriptions and the actions of the apparition bear the closest resemblance to the Blue Bell Hill phantom outside of the UK.

Glen Pennell's experience took place one night in 1993 when he responded to a call to three power transformers that had blown up next door to the cemetery. With him was a police officer. As they drove past the front of the cemetery, the officer suddenly screamed: 'Watch out!'

Standing in the middle of the road ahead was a woman dressed all in white. Pennell applied the brakes immediately, but could not stop in time, and the truck hit her. The woman was thrown over the hood of the truck, and then recoiled back to the ground in front of the vehicle. Jumping out to take a look, there was no sign of the woman.

'There was no blood, no clothing, no body. There was nothing,' said Pennell.

Rod Vecsey encountered the lady in white one night in July or August of 1990 during a homeward journey that took him past the cemetery between 12.30 a.m. and 1 a.m. His experience began with the strange feeling that someone was sitting next to him in the car. Glancing across, he was confronted with the apparently solid figure of a man in a small brown crumpled hat and a little scruff on his face. He looked away and then back, and the figure was gone. But when he looked up, he saw the woman in the road. She was sixty or seventy feet ahead, but as soon as Vecsey stepped on his brakes, she came forward to right in front of the car, where she raised her arm toward him in a gesture—not to stop exactly, but almost imploringly. Like Bill Hopkins' experience near Llanidloes, the figure went through the car before it vanished, leaving the witness with an impression of sadness so strong he began to cry.[22]

Back in the UK, there is the experience of Birmingham plumber David Bingham in the early part of 2 January 1996.

Mr Bingham, 30, reported to police that he had hit a pedestrian with his van as he drove past the Birmingham City Cemetery, in Moor Lane, Witton.[23] The incident happened at 12.50 a.m. while he was out on 24-hour call. The figure—a man—had appeared in front of the vehicle. Stopping immediately after the collision, Bingham found no trace of an injured person, or blood, or damage to his van. 'Badly shaken', he reported the incident to Queens Road police. Officers investigated but found no sign of an accident.

A police spokeswoman said: 'This isn't the first time that ghost sightings have been made in the area. This gentleman is convinced that he has seen a ghost and is really quite upset. He was as white as a ghost himself and really shaking.'[24]

Mr Bingham himself, who spent the day following the incident recovering from it, said: 'I didn't believe in ghosts but this has really made me think again. I'll never forget the man's eyes staring at me before I hit him. There was definitely someone there. The only explanation is it was a ghost.'[25]

Coach driver's ghostly collision

by Sally Yonish

A COACH driver says he is still reeling after colliding with a ghost.

Keith Scales, 53, went round a bend in White Hill, Wye, on his way to work at 6.45am last Friday, to find a woman standing in the middle of the road.

She rolled over his bonnet and he jumped out of the car to see if she was injured but could not find her.

On arriving at Poynters Coaches, in Churchfield Way, Wye, Mr Scales phoned the police, who searched the area and nearby woods but could find no trace of the woman or any blood.

Nevertheless, Mr Scales insists that the accident occurred and remembers the woman, who was blonde, aged between 30 and 35 and wearing a long, dark coat, smiling at him just before the collision.

He said: "I definitely hit her. I felt the thump on the front of my motor.

"She didn't try to get out of my way but just looked at me and smiled as I hit her. She bounced over my bonnet and disappeared.

"I was shaking like a leaf. I got out of my car to look for her and went right up the bank but I couldn't find her."

Villagers have previously reported seeing a ghostly white female figure in that area.

"She just looked at me and smiled as I hit her"

Mr Scales, from Sheppey, a driver for the past 32 years, never used to believe in ghosts but this incident has made him think again.

"I used to think ghosts were just a fantasy but I don't any more," he said.

Barry Poynter, who runs the company with his father, John, said: "Keith is a very steady guy who has been all over the world.

"He is adamant it was not a deer that he hit.

"Over the years there have been a number of stories about ghosts on White Hill but no one I know has ever seen one.

"This is the closest I have come to it.

"The police say there have been several similar instances."

John Rogers, former chairman of Wye Parish Council, said: "Years ago there was a white deer in King's Wood and I saw it while drivng along White Hill. That could be what Mr Scales saw."

MYSTERY BUMP: Keith Scales and the damage caused to his wing mirror 5A/6665E/00

(KM Group)

Returning to Kent, to a case not far removed from Blue Bell Hill in setting or description, the next account is one also that is eerily reminiscent of Ian Sharpe's experience on Blue Bell Hill (down even to the witness's occupation, his own words, and the press handling of the affair), bringing out fully the idea of a 'script' to which these events appear to conform.

The incident took place at 6.45 a.m. on Friday 6 January 2000. Keith Scales, a 53-year-old coach driver, was on his way to work at Wye, near Ashford. Mr Scales' southbound route routinely brought him down White Hill, an eastern extremity of the same chalk escarpment of the North Downs that comprises Blue Bell Hill, which lies 25 miles to the west. The road here, narrow and bordered by woodland and high earthen banks, makes a lonely, sinuous descent.

Rounding a left bend, Mr Scales was confronted by a woman standing in the middle of the road. It was too late to avoid her. His car struck her and she rolled over the bonnet and vanished from sight.

'Shaking like a leaf', he jumped out to see if the woman was injured but he could find no trace of her. He even climbed the high bank at the roadside in case she was thrown up there by the collision.

Continuing on to his workplace, Mr Scales phoned the police and two officers, a PC and WPC, came out from Ashford Police Station to investigate. A search of the scene and the nearby woodland revealed nothing. But Mr Scales was insistent that the incident had occurred. He described a woman, aged thirty to thirty-five, with shoulder-length blonde hair and dressed in a long, dark overcoat.

'I definitely hit her, he said. 'I felt the thump on the front of my motor. She didn't try to get out of my way but just looked at me and smiled as I hit her. She bounced over my bonnet and disappeared.'

In an unusual departure from most accounts of this type, Mr Scales' car was found to have incurred some damage—a broken offside wing-mirror—although it could not be ascertained that this damage was not there beforehand.

As always, while the witness previously knew nothing of White Hill's reputation for being haunted (having moved to the Isle of Sheppey in 1998), local people were already familiar with the hill's ghost. After Keith Scales' experience, a lady passenger on his coach told him the same thing had happened to her.

White Hill, as it appeared around the time of Keith Scales' encounter in January 2000

Subsequent to the *Kentish Express* report, I contacted the journalist, Sally Yonish, and a little afterward, the witness himself. Mr Scales confirmed the details of the report, and, in response to questioning, was able to provide further information on his encounter: His speed, as he hit the woman, he estimated at around 20 mph, which, judging from my own visit there, seemed reasonable for a car cautiously negotiating the bends on that stretch of road. The woman was stood with one arm 'tucked in'; the other rested casually on her hip. After the police officers heard his story, the PC said: 'I deal in facts'—to which Mr Scales replied with something like: 'I'm giving you the facts. I'm telling you I hit someone.' The WPC whispered to her colleague: 'I told you it was the ghost.'

Mr Scales also subsequently heard that the bottom of the hill (before it meets the A28) is reputed to have a phantom female that walks into the path of vehicles.

One possible reason for the ghost's appearances was proposed by colleagues of Mr Scales, who recalled the murder of a woman by her husband there 'eight to ten years ago'. But irrespective as to whether a tangible real-life tragedy might be identified and linked with any confidence to the sightings, the fact remains that encounters of this kind bear more relation to one another than to any single, isolated 'cause'.[26]

We stay in Kent for one final example, which is set, in fact, on the A229—the same road as at Blue Bell Hill—but some fifteen miles to the south. In the early hours (around 2 a.m.) of Saturday 26 June 1999, Bob Prowse (brother of actor Dave 'Darth Vader' Prowse) was on his way home to Hawkhurst from Maidstone, when, passing through the village of Hartley, and near to the junction with the B2085, the headlights of his Ford Probe picked out a figure in the road ahead.

Mr Prowse swerved to avoid the figure and brought the car to a stop, but there was no-one there. He even reversed the car to the spot where he had seen the man, but was too 'spooked' to get out. The figure—a man—who he saw for only a 'brief second', was around 6ft 2in tall, and had *blonde* hair.[27] The man, who he described as 'blueish', '...was just standing there[,] not moving[,] with his arms at his side, almost as though he was standing to attention.'

Mr Prowse expressed concern that his speed at the time (around 60 mph) could have resulted in him crashing and being killed. At least one fatal accident is said to have occurred at the spot that same year.[28]

Hitchin' a Ride...

We now come to what are, in light of the discussion earlier in this book, the most 'troublesome' witness cases—those involving a vanishing passenger: the Phantom Hitch-Hiker.

A disappearing road accident victim is one thing—where, in spite of the quality of the evidence or the veracity of the witness, it is possible to come to any number of possible interpretations based on what is generally a sudden and rather fleeting encounter with a figure in the road that has no proven substance. A more prolonged meeting in close proximity with what to all intents and purposes appears to be a normal human being that subsequently vanishes, is something else entirely—one that poses a far more serious challenge to our belief structure, particularly where it behaves in a manner faithful to the popular folk versions.

While such encounters are bound to raise doubts, with respect to the integrity of the witness or those instances in which the mysterious passenger has left the vehicle in the conventional manner, at the same time these accounts might stand in vindication for what Tom Harber was claiming for the Blue Bell Hill case all those years ago.

Malcolm Grant (1967/8)

The first—and briefest—tale in this bunch is that related by an Aylesford businessman, Malcolm Grant*. Although his real name has previously been given in a printed feature, he told me that this had been against his wishes, and he would prefer for it not to be repeated here, chiefly out of consideration for the former girlfriend who shared and was greatly upset by the experience.

Mr Grant's story came to light when, having read about Ian Sharpe's encounter, he telephoned Ian out of sympathy early in 1993. It just so happened that a journalist was at Ian's house at the time, and naturally picked up on the incident. My short conversation followed when that journalist put me in touch with him. Undoubtedly wary at the prospect that his experience might attract further unwanted attention, Mr Grant was a little reticent about talking at any length, accounting for the brevity of the account given here.

The brief encounter took place around 1967 or 1968 while he and a girlfriend were travelling southbound towards Maidstone. A young woman flagged down the car from the roadside above the Lower Bell. Mr Grant stopped to offer her a lift, and she got into the back of the car. He turned to ask the girl where she wanted to go…and she had vanished. The encounter was over that quickly. In his own words, his girlfriend became 'absolutely hysterical' at the girl's disappearance.

As it stands, there is very little to separate this encounter from scores of other PHH accounts. We have no precise idea of the year, the season, the time, or even if it was night or day, and no description of the girl.

The witness's desire for anonymity is to be respected, and through the circumstances that it came to light, speaks much for its authenticity. Unlike some accounts, the witness was not courting publicity—in fact, he was anxious to avoid it. However, at the same time, it has to be accepted that this does nothing to persuade the reader (or the folklorist, for that matter) that the event happened to a real person or persons. In further fulfilment of the convention that declares witnesses to be either anonymous or untraceable, is that when I later tried to contact Mr Grant for a more detailed description of his experience (admittedly more than a year later), I found he had moved.

But before we dismiss his story altogether, it is well to remember that where the event took place—near to the Lower Bell—was the setting for the earliest published encounters, and for another Hitch-Hiker account that we have yet to examine.

James Skene (1971)

In 1994, I first heard an account that stands as perhaps one of the most important in the entire Blue Bell Hill saga, not least because it might serve to illustrate the connectedness between the 'knock down' habit (also dubbed the 'Spectral Jaywalker', 'non-existent road accident', or 'suicide simulation') and Phantom Hitch-Hiker encounters. It is also one which was told by a witness who was willing to put his name to his experience.

James Skene
(KM Group)

The incident—which the witness first recounted to me by telephone interview and later for the *Kent Messenger* in 2003[29]—occurred in the autumn, around 1971.

James Skene, of Farleigh Lane, Barming, near Maidstone, was at that time a District Inspector based at Gravesend bus depot. It was just after midnight, 'coldish' and damp. He had just come off a long day's work which, by his own admission, had left him a bit tired. He was on his way home to Maidstone when, driving down Blue Bell Hill, a girl suddenly appeared in front of his car.[30] Whether she stepped out or simply appeared in his path, he could not recall after so long, only that she was suddenly there and he had to swerve to avoid her. If he hadn't made the manoeuvre, he said, he was sure he would have hit her.

Mr Skene said he was not going very fast, estimating his speed at around 40 mph. He veered around her and pulled up, intent on scolding her for nearly causing an accident. But when he pushed the passenger door open, she was suddenly in the car (i.e. jumped in uninvited). She asked to be taken to Chatham. He was heading for Maidstone. He started to point out that she was on the wrong side of the road but, on reflection, he decided to turn the car around. She had brown hair, and wore a dark grey or black dress, which appeared to be velvet, and quite unsuitable for the conditions.

Although the girl did not seem to be flustered, confused, or in any way troubled, Mr Skene's first thoughts were that she might be in some trouble, making some sense of her presence at the spot at that hour by supposing she had had a bad experience in another car and jumped out. Not best pleased at the prospect of taking her all the way to Chatham, he nevertheless felt that if he had kicked her out, she may have ended up in 'more bleeding trouble'. In any case, he said, 'She just sat there.'

Resigned to the task, he turned the car around at the Lower Bell and drove the girl to Chatham, where he dropped her off outside 'the old Chatham cinema'.[31] He could not recall the precise reason she chose to alight there—whether she asked to be let out there, or if that was simply as far as he was prepared to take her. As far as he could remember, she said nothing after asking to be taken to Chatham.

The street where he dropped the girl was lit. On the corner was a gateway with a foldaway metal trellis gate, which was closed in place. After letting her out (again, he could not recall whether she opened the door herself; only that he didn't assist her), he reversed around the corner to turn the car around, and noticed in the process that the girl had gone—but there had been nowhere for her to go.[32]

Thinking her disappearance odd, Mr Skene nevertheless thought no more of the matter at the time, having no knowledge of the Blue Bell Hill ghost. The most widely publicised encounter—Maurice Goodenough's, in 1974—was still a few years away), and it was only then that he came to ponder the incident.

Mr Skene had encountered the girl near the bottom of the Hill. Exactly where, again, he could not recall. The length of time that has elapsed is one thing. Another point to bear in mind is that in 1971 the construction of the new dual carriageway was in mid-phase. He only knew that it occurred after the crest of the Hill, on the way into Maidstone, somewhere in the region of the Lower Bell, possibly on a section of the new carriageway.

The girl was estimated to be in her twenties. There was nothing unusual about her. In a departure from most folk versions that describe a pretty girl in white, Mr Skene said she was 'not stunning, not attractive—a plain girl'. He recalled nothing about her attire other than the dark dress—i.e. nothing comparable to the white blouse reported in the later encounters involving Goodenough, Green, and Sharpe—and nothing relating to the colour or style of her hair. The only other thing he could remember is something of her height and build: not a large person; neither fat nor thin (medium build).

When I spoke to him, Mr Skene still found it difficult to accept that he may have given a lift to a ghost, although he said he maintained an open mind on the subject. However, he did add that if he had had any knowledge of the story at the time or any inkling that she might have been a ghost, he would probably have scarpered!

Analysing it in folk terms, James Skene's story clearly falls into the Version A category of Phantom Hitch-Hikers: a young woman, seeking her lift late at night from an isolated spot, attracts the attention of a lone male driver who she 'persuades' to stop and to give her a lift to a given destination where, upon being let out of the vehicle, she promptly vanishes—according to the custom—without being directly observed.

In detail, the encounter departs from the folk version, while in other respects it exhibits characteristics found in other cases. The most obvious difference is the omission of a satisfactory ending—no onward journey to meet bereaved relatives, or other means (other than the later discovery that the location where the girl was picked up has a reputation for being haunted) of establishing that the girl was a ghost.

Of particular interest is the manner by which the girl attracts her lift. Not willing, apparently, to risk being overlooked or ignored by waiting passively by the roadside or thumbing a lift, she steps into the path of the driver, giving him little or no opportunity to avoid her—a scenario that we have seen a number of times already at Blue Bell Hill. Only, on this occasion, the driver doesn't hit her or manage to swerve around her and continue on his way, but stops the car to chide her for her foolishness—an action that is perhaps responsible for converting a 'knock-down' episode into a Phantom Hitch-Hiker encounter.

Having successfully stopped the vehicle, the girl further ensures her lift by jumping into the vehicle uninvited (a behavioural trait, it may be recalled, also claimed for Chicago's Resurrection Mary.) In this case, there is no excuse to take the back seat. The girl remains in view in the front passenger seat—a fact that may account for the distance she manages to travel, there being no opportunity for her to vanish unobserved until the driver has let her out and is engaged in turning the vehicle around—a non-routine task that possibly breaks the 'spell' of the encounter. Otherwise, we have a typical loose-ended Hitch-Hiker account, one that has broken free of some of the stereotypical trappings of the folk version to permit consideration as a potentially genuine PHH account—although, strictly, based chiefly around doubts about the girl's claimed 'disappearance', it must be regarded as inconclusive.

In many ways, the above incident resembles and is subject to many of the same criticisms and comments as the experience of Richard Studholme (Chapter 7), which I shall not repeat here. Suffice to say that, judging the witness to be truthful and reliable, and in light of the wider pattern of events and history of encounters on Blue Bell Hill, the *possibility* that the incident involved either a real hitch-hiker who happened to be stranded at Blue Bell Hill (and who gained her lift at great risk to herself, and in a manner identical to later 'ghostly' incidents—which could not then be easily anticipated), or another sophisticated hoax (whose intention in this case, judging from the total lack of publicity, failed) seems almost as preposterous as a ghost actually hitching a lift.

What is certain is that, ghost or hoax, the Skene episode fails in its supposed intention. Whereas we find with the accounts in this chapter (including the other hitch-hiker account) as great a difficulty relating them to the victims of the 1965 tragedy as those of Sharpe and Dawkins, James Skene's encounter is virtually unique in offering a prolonged opportunity for gathering the kind of detailed personal information about his passenger, both descriptive and from conversation with her, that we might be looking for. And yet we find that it, likewise, fails to do so. The 'ghost' fails in its presumed attempt at meaningful communication, and the assumed hoaxer fails to make any connection with (or capital from) the popular legend. Mr Skene, according to the *Kent Messenger* report, says simply: 'We didn't speak [during the journey].'[33]

James Skene's account, however, does suggest a description that, in terms of the girl's build ('medium') *could* be made to fit one of the victims of the 1965 crash—the bride-to-be—but that is as far as it goes. If anything, it (along with Malcolm Grant's encounter) paints a more confusing picture, since neither of the stated destinations—Chatham or Maidstone, as we have previously noted—finds any meaningful connection to the victims, and are noteworthy otherwise only as the principal towns at either end of this stretch of the A229.

With these accounts we are, in a sense, brought full circle, to the case as it stood in the late 1960s, with the variations in destination reported by Tom Harber's anonymous witnesses. We may have advanced to a point where the premise of a genuine haunting is more supportable, but the case overall falters in the pursuit of the satisfying 'explanation' found in the time-honoured 'cause' of that period.

Any criticism regarding the possibility of hoaxing would seem to fall apart with the final account garnered in this period, which is recounted in the next chapter. It is also one which casts the gravest doubts on the 1965 crash connection, taking place as it did way back in 1934, while (for the moment accepting that the ghost is what it is generally supposed to be—the restless spirit of a deceased person) suggesting another fitting candidate for her identity.

TEN

THE WOOD MURDER

Jack Woodger was a lifelong resident of Blue Bell Hill.[1] Long retired when I interviewed him in November 1993, from 1929 and for some forty-three years Jack worked at the Aylesford Paper Mill on a rotating shift pattern. His journey to and from work routinely took him via the Maidstone–Chatham road at Blue Bell Hill. It was on his homeward journey one night after an evening shift in 1934 that he came across a young woman standing in the road outside the Lower Bell:

Jack: What I said to ____ some considerable time ago, is the fact that in 1934—a long time before this girl was actually supposed to have been killed—I was coming off work at 2–10 [p.m.], and I'd got a motorbike, and as I come up round by the Lower Bell there was this girl stood in the middle of the road, and she wanted to go to Burham.
Q: Burham?
Jack: And so I took her along the old Pilgrims' Road to Burham, dropped her off by the church, or by the school as it was then, and she said she lived down the road, on the right [in Church Street]. But as she got off the bike and went down, I turned around to come back home, she disappeared. Well, who it was, what it was, I don't know. But that's the only time I had any personal [experience on the Hill]. But that was 1934—way before any of these people—the ghost, you know.
Q: I appreciate that it's a long time ago, but you say she disappeared? Yet might she have ducked into a doorway or passageway?
A: Well, this I don't know. But when there was all this talk about the ghost and whatever all around here, it suddenly made me wonder whether I'd seen one.
Q: Sure. You say she was standing in the middle of the road, though?
A: Well, I suppose I surmised she got off the last bus from Maidstone to Chatham, and she was lost; she'd got to go to Burham, and it was a hell of a way for anyone to walk it, at that time of night [a bit over a mile]. So that's all I can tell you about that.

The crossroads at the Lower Bell. The pub is out of view to the right. Jack Woodger's homeward journey brought him up the hill from the left

Q: Strange that she was waiting *in* the road, though, isn't it—rather than on the verge?
A: I suppose she stood in the middle of the road, like—in those years, it was very, very quiet, very dark; no traffic about hardly. She saw me coming up from Aylesford, I suppose, so to be safe, instead of standing on the path near the edge, she stood in the middle of the road, thinking she'd be safe if anyone was to attack her. She might have had that in mind. But I just stopped and asked her what the trouble was. She said she'd got to go to Burham, so I said, 'Well hop on and I'll take you there'—which I did, and I didn't give it any more thought.
Q: On the back of your motorbike?
A: I had a motorbike. I had a 350-BSA.
Q: Would you have any idea of clothing at all?
A: No. I was more concerned with getting home and getting asleep.
Q: Right, sure. To recap: where precisely was the girl standing?
A: [I guess] she'd come up from Maidstone, and she had to get off here because she wanted to go to Burham.
Q: So she was waiting opposite the Lower Bell?
A: She was waiting outside the Lower Bell.

Church Street, Burham, where Jack Woodger dropped off a hitch-hiking female in 1934. The 'new' church stood on the right

Q: So you really had to go out of your way to go to Burham?
A: It didn't take me long, not on a motorbike.
Q: What time of year was this?
A: In the winter time. It was pitch black. And in those days, there was hardly any transport about at all. All you saw coming from Maidstone on the Maidstone–Chatham road of a night was probably the headlights of the last bus from Maidstone to Chatham.
Q: About what time would that be?

A: Five-to-eleven it left the depot. This person that I picked up, she'd got what appeared to me to be an American accent, but other than that, I don't know. As I say, it was in 1934.

At this point, Jack's wife (who, for the sake of the interview, we'll denote as 'B'), who we met very briefly and anonymously in Chapter 6, told of some of the claimed encounters she heard in the 1960s while working at the Bridgewood Café,[2] a little north of Blue Bell Hill Village:

B: I worked at the café, for nearly fifty years. This lorry driver came in at this particular time and he was talking over his cup of tea, and he said: 'Last night I had a funny experience,' and I said, 'What was that?' and [he said that] this girl had flagged him down; he took her home and when he opened the door of his cab, she was gone. And I said, 'Well, I can only suggest you change your pub!'

Q: What year was this?

B: That was from the beginning of this ghost lark. And then we had another one come in and tell us the same story—1968 probably, something like that. And he seemed genuine enough. He was coming up the Hill, and this young lady flagged him down, and she wanted to go to Eccles, I think he told me, Eccles. And a little while later another one came in with the same sort of story.

Q: Did that make you think, the second one?

B: No, not really. I'm yet to be convinced. [But] these lorry drivers, they were very convinced that they had picked this girl up, and this first one that told us about it, he said: 'I took her there; I opened the cab door for her; I knocked on her parents' door; I looked round and she'd gone.' I don't know whether he said her mother or father answered the door, and he said: 'Oh, I just brought your daughter home, but I don't know where she's hopped off to.' And they said it couldn't be their daughter, because she got killed on Blue Bell Hill such and such a time ago. He said: 'Well that's where I picked up her up.'

Q: And this is probably Eccles?

B: Yes, she lived at Eccles, as I understood.

Q: Have you any idea of what time the lorry drivers were passing through?

B: It was night-time. Never did hear the girl's name—who she was—only that she came from Eccles. It was Eccles to me, anyway. Jack said this person he saw wanted to go to Burham.

Q: Which is the same area [the villages of Eccles and Burham are close neighbours, separated by less than half a mile].

B: All the same isn't it, intermingled there.

Q: The only possible connection I've come across with a reference to either—Burham, in this case—is a murder case. In 1916 a local girl was found murdered at the top of Blue Bell Hill. She lived at Providence Row, Blue Bell Hill—[3]

B: Ah, you're thinking of Mr Trigg's daughter?

Q: Yes, Emily Trigg.

B: Yes, that was down the Rochester Road. And my neighbour, who used to live next door to me, she and her father were blackberrying and found her. She worked in Rochester, like they used to, in servicing [domestic service].

Q: Right, that tallies with some of the accounts I've read. Now, I've tried to place the scene of the murder. One of the original newspaper reports on the inquest states that the body was found close to the Rochester Road, in Bridge Woods, some 200 to 300 yards from its junction with the Maidstone–Chatham Road,

which is the current Bridgewood roundabout.[4] Of course, it's all changed up there now.
B: Well, I don't know. There's still a bit of wood and the site they did the blackberrying.
Jack: That bit of wood where they found her is still wood. [Described as the thin strip of woodland preserved between the Rochester Road (B2097) and the M2 motorway.]
B: A Mr Jennings found her. My neighbour—she was a young girl then, Miss Jennings—and he, they were blackberrying, and they came across her.
Q (to Jack): Now, the road where you dropped the girl would be Church Street in Burham, wouldn't it?
Jack: Yes.
Q: That's the little narrow one that goes out to Wouldham, isn't it?
Jack: Yeah, that's right.
Q: Which is very interesting, since Emily Trigg's remains were buried in Burham churchyard, which is a connection that makes some sense. Is Burham Church still there?
B: I don't think it is. Didn't they demolish Burham church?
A: No, they did away with the school.
B: Ah, but what about the church?
A: I don't think the old church is there.
Q: So the churchyard is gone, of course, as well?[5]

The story of the murder of Emily Trigg was something I had been aware of and had considered since it was first brought to my attention by a colleague who had read about it in an old, locally published booklet, *Crimes That Shocked The Medway Towns.*[6]

Brutal murder is, of course, a popularly accepted and time-honoured cause of hauntings, particularly (as in this case) where the murderer was never brought to justice. What better candidate, then, than a young woman who had lived at Blue Bell Hill, and had been found murdered at Bridge Woods at the top of the Hill?

Far from proving that the murder of this young woman is ultimately the origin of the haunting at Blue Bell Hill, the case, as described by the original newspaper coverage of the investigation and the inquest,[7] does contain some very interesting, and possibly significant, details.

Servant Murdered in a Wood

The inquest, which opened at the Town Hall, Chatham, on Monday 25 September 1916, was told that Emily Trigg's remains had been discovered on the afternoon of the previous Thursday (21 September).

The find had been made by John Jennings, a greengrocer of 66 King Street, Rochester, at Bridge Wood, in the parish of Wouldham, by the Rochester–Maidstone Road (today's B2097). Described as a lonely spot, where the road cuts through woodland, Mr Jennings had entered the wood via a track on the road's south side at around 6.10 p.m. to gather blackberries with his two children. On the return to this track, between twelve and twenty yards from the road, Jennings saw something hidden in the undergrowth. Approaching it, he was horrified to discover a human skeleton—which, by its long hair, he deduced to be that of a woman. The only items of clothing observed were shoes and stockings.[8]

Emily Trigg
Chatham News
(30 Sept. 1916)

At the sight, Jennings hurried out onto the road, and alerted a soldier who was passing with a young lady. Inspecting the remains, the soldier pointed out a necklet around the neck. Between them, they alerted the

The Rochester–Maidstone road (B2097), facing toward Rochester. The strip of woodland on the left, formerly known as Coal Pit Bank, is one of the locations where Emily Trigg's remains were said to have been found

authorities.

On his way home to Rochester, Jennings met a farmer by the name of Eldridge, who told him that a young woman from Blue Bell Hill was seen walking up the road with a soldier about six weeks previously, and had not been seen since.[9] The Coroner, Mr C. B. Harris, dismissed this particular detail as hearsay.

John Jennings
(Michael Jennings)

Police Superintendent A. E. Rhodes told the inquest that following the news of the discovery on the evening of 21 September, he despatched a constable to the spot to keep guard over the remains until morning. In a line that, for different reasons, would be appropriate more than seven decades later, the *Chatham, Rochester, and Gillingham News* of 30 September stated that Constable Blundell '... probably spent a weird and weary night, but police officers get accustomed to strange experiences and are not fearful of gloom and shadows.'[10]

At 8 a.m. the next morning, Supt. Rhodes proceeded to the spot with Detective Inspector Cochrane and Police surgeon Dr H. J. Bryan, which was about half-a-mile north of the junction of the Rochester–Maidstone and the Chatham–Maidstone roads (today's junction between the B2097 and the A229 at Bridgewood—a location previously known as Bridgewood Gates after the turnpike gates that formerly stood here (see Chapter 2)). This places the site today on the south side of the road a little south of Laker Road, below Rochester Airport. (Another source, it must be said, states the location to have been only 200–300 yards from the junction).[11] The *Kent Messenger* of 14 October 1916 is more specific about the location, naming it as Coal Pit (or Coalpit) Bank, a narrow strip of woodland skirting the Rochester–Maidstone road that largely survives today between the old turnpike road and the shoulder of the M2 motorway, approximately where the Rochester–Maidstone milestone still stands.[12]

On inspection of the remains, which were found lying parallel to the road, the police immediately suspected foul play. The body lay face down, and had been crudely covered over with cut grass about two feet in length. The left arm was outstretched, and the right was folded under the body. A white glove covered the right hand. Still fixed in the hair was a side-comb, and around the neck was a gold-coloured necklet, attached to which was a pendant containing a bullet upon which a cross had been engraved.[13] The sole of the left shoe was worn down, indicating that the body had been dragged a small distance. A hat, ornamented with pink roses, was found close by.[14]

36 Maidstone Road, Rochester, where Emily Trigg worked as a domestic servant, and from where she left on her last journey on 6 August 1916

Lodged between the teeth was found a strip of calico (muslin cotton) fabric. When it was removed during a more detailed examination of the remains at the mortuary at the Brook, Chatham the following morning (23 September), it was found to have a small bone adhering to it. This, the police surgeon, Dr Bryan, identified as the hyoid bone, which sits at the base of the tongue, and indicated that the material had been pushed far back into the mouth.[15]

While further investigations were still to be carried out, the discovery of the distinctive pendant led Detective-Inspector Cochrane to immediately associate the remains with the description of a young woman that had been forwarded to Chatham by Rochester Police, who had been reported missing since 6 August.

Emily Maria Trigg, a 20-year-old domestic servant, who was employed by a Miss Catherine Cooper, had left her employer's address at 36 Maidstone Road, Rochester at around 3.15 p.m. on 6 August to make her customary Sunday afternoon visit with her mother, Mrs Kate Trigg, at Providence Row,[16] Maidstone Road, Blue Bell Hill.

Mrs Trigg, a quarryman's widow, said her daughter had to pass by Bridge Wood on her way home from Rochester. Emily visited her regularly. She generally walked, usually arriving home soon after tea. Emily's younger sister, Edith, said: 'She was very happy in her place, and had two evenings off every week. I often met her, and she always came by the main road. It took her about three-quarters of an hour to walk'.[17]

On 6 August, Mrs Trigg had looked out for Emily, but when she failed to arrive, she knew that her mistress was entertaining some wounded soldiers at the house on the Monday and assumed that Emily had perhaps been kept at work.[18]

Likewise, when Emily failed to return to the house in Rochester by 9 p.m. that evening, Miss Cooper had not been overly concerned since, on a previous occasion, she had stayed over until the following morning when it had rained.[19] The first occasion either had any clue that Emily was missing was on the Tuesday morning following, when her mother arrived at Miss Cooper's with some clean clothes for her. They promptly informed the police, who circulated Emily's description, but no attempt was made to search for her along her known route.

The police description of Emily, who had turned twenty on 11 March, was as follows: 'Height, 5ft; hair, light brown; eyes, brown; blue costume; white hat, trimmed with roses and pieces of black velvet.'[20]

Speaking later to a reporter, Mrs Trigg furthered the description of her daughter, describing her as a quiet and modest girl, and of medium build. She sometimes had a comb in her hair, wearing it at the back. She had last seen her daughter on Thursday (3 August).

Miss Cooper described her as a very pretty girl, who had been in her service about ten weeks. 'And she was such a respectable and quiet and nice girl.'[21]

The police investigation continued on the Saturday morning (23 September) after the discovery with an extensive search of the surrounding woodland. On the edge of the woods, close to an open field, they found the girl's clothing, which had been roughly bundled up. 'All the garments had been ripped and torn; and appeared to have been removed from the body with considerable violence.'[22] A portion of the undergarments noted as missing corresponded with the material found in the mouth.

Other personal effects were found in the woods on the opposite (north side) of the Maidstone road. These included a leather handbag containing a small green leather purse, handkerchiefs and other sundry items, and, five yards away, a glove (which matched the one found with the remains) and a piece of linen, which was also later established as belonging to the undergarments. The bag also contained a photograph of a soldier, identified as Private George Harris of the Queen's Royal West Surrey Regiment, with whom Emily had been 'walking out', and a letter addressed to 'Miss Emily Trigg, 36, Maidstone-road, Rochester', which was postmarked 5 August, and from a Mrs Howard of Bromley, with an offer of employment. Mrs Trigg later confirmed all of the items as having belonged to her daughter.

But even before the discovery of the other items, the item that had conclusively identified the remains as those of Emily, was the necklace and pendant that Mrs Trigg had had made for her, and which she had immediately recognised when they were shown to her on the day Emily's remains were recovered. Fashioned around a German bullet that had been carved into the shape of a cross and sent home by Mrs Trigg's son William (one of three sons fighting in France) as a present for his sister, it had been made for Emily just before the wedding of her fourth brother the previous April.[23]

Emily's plain blue dress (a blue cloth jacket, and matching skirt), last worn by her on her fateful last journey, had also been made for that wedding.[24]

According to one source (*Chatham News*, 30 September)[25]—which attributed the information to Emily's employer, Miss Cooper—Emily had been engaged to be married. Her young man, George Harris, had been wounded in France and was recovering in hospital in Shoreham. Mrs Trigg said he had been 'just like one of the family', and was at the time still in hospital after being brought back wounded from France.[26]

Emily's sister, Edith, then fifteen and still at home with her mother, apparently concurred with this belief. She said, 'Em was a darling girl, and never spoke to anyone but her young man. She was very fond of him, and expected to get married when he got better.' He had given Emily his Army badge, which she wore as a brooch, which was found close to where she was discovered.[27]

For someone missing for only six weeks, Emily Trigg's remains were in a surprisingly advanced state of decomposition, having been reduced virtually to a skeleton. Dr Herbert Bryan told the reconvened inquest on 9 October that while this was unusual, it had to be remembered that the weather had been very wet. In the absence of bodily tissues, the precise cause of death could not be medically determined with any certainty, although it was otherwise clear from the circumstantial evidence that the victim had been criminally assaulted.

The Coroner asked, 'Does it look like another person in it?'

Dr Bryan: 'Everything points to that, but there is no medical evidence to show that.'[28]

A fortnight before her disappearance, Emily had accompanied her sister to the bus terminus at the Military Road, Chatham, to see her on her way home to Blue Bell Hill. There she had met a soldier, who had spoken to her and walked with her back to her employer's address in Rochester. He had asked her what she did for a living. When she answered that she was working, he admitted that before the war he had had 'no need to stoop to pick up a stick.'

As they had walked, he had asked her if she 'intended to be faithful to her boy', and she had replied, 'Of course I do.'

The man had laughed, remarking, 'You never can tell.'[29] He then asked her what time she had to be in, and she said 'eight o'clock'. 'If your missus is cross with you,' he told her, 'you can come back to me.'[30]

THE KENTISH WOOD MYSTERY.

Emily Trigg (back), with her mother and younger brother. *Daily Mirror* (25 Sept 1916)

Miss Cooper recalled that on that Thursday evening Emily had asked her if she had seen her talking to a soldier at the gate. She had replied that she could not be sure it was her, but she had seen a soldier. Emily had told her of the meeting at the bus terminus, and that she had not liked to be seen with him, as he was a gentleman and she was only a country girl. Miss Cooper later told the Coroner that she had been unable to tell the rank of the man, only that he was tall and wore glasses. She had reminded Emily of the foolishness of allowing strangers to talk to her, but had later heard from 'one who knew Emily very well' that there had been some talk of her meeting this same soldier again on 6 August—the day she disappeared.[31]

On that day, however, she had seen Emily leave the house and turn out of the gate to her right in the direction of her home. She had been alone then.

The *Chatham Observer* (30 September) added that the police had been unable to ascertain that she had met any man on the Sunday afternoon. When last seen she had been 'a long way up the Maidstone-road, and quite alone'.[32]

The findings of the inquest, which were announced on 9 October 1916, were non-committal. Although the evidence pointed to foul play, the subsequent investigation had come to nothing. The advanced decomposition of the body did not allow for the cause of death to be established with certainty. It was therefore decided that, in the absence of any further developments such as a confession, it would not be safe for the jury to formally arrive at this conclusion. The jury, therefore, returned a verdict of 'Found dead.'[33]

Emily Trigg's remains were quietly laid to rest in the churchyard of St. Mary's, in the parish of Burham (the parish covering her mother's residence at Maidstone

Church Street, Burham from Blue Bell Hill. The original church of St. Mary's is visible at the apex of the river bend

Road, Blue Bell Hill) on the afternoon of Saturday 7 October 1916. In attendance were her mother and sister, and two of her brothers, plus other relatives and a handful of friends and neighbours.[34]

Before we go on to look at how the tragic case of Emily Trigg relates to the reported phenomena at Blue Bell Hill, there is a postscript to the story, which the newspapers reported in the weeks following the closure of the inquest.

On 21 October 1916, the *Chatham Observer* reported that there had been a dramatic development in the case of the Wood Murder. At the County Police Court the previous morning (Friday), Charles B. Hicks, a bombardier in the Royal Garrison Artillery (RGA), stationed at Winchester, '... was charged on suspicion with being concerned in feloniously, willfully and of malice aforethought killing and murdering Emily Maria Trigg, at Wouldham, on or about August 6th'.[35]

Detective Inspector Cochrane reported that he had met the prisoner at Winchester on Thursday and, after cautioning him, had informed him that he would have to return to Chatham with him on suspicion of being concerned in the murder. Hicks had made no reply.

At Chatham, when asked if he had anything to say against his remand, Hicks simply stated his innocence, claiming he had been brought there by mistake. Det.-Inspector Cochrane's request for the prisoner to be remanded until the following Tuesday was granted.

When it reconvened on the morning of Tuesday 24 October, the Police Court was crowded in waiting anticipation of further police evidence. But when Supt. Rhodes addressed the bench, it was to announce that their questioning of the accused during his time in remand had resulted in all doubts being satisfactorily answered, and the police had no further interest in bringing a case against him. In consequence of this unexpected reversal, the Chairman promptly acquitted Bombardier Hicks, who then left the court with his friends.[36]

Quite what the content of the initial doubts were that had led the police to actually charge Hicks with Emily Trigg's murder we shall probably never know. The *Kent Messenger* of 28 October 1916, however, adds that suspicions had initially been aroused by comrades after hearing something the defendant had said in his sleep,[37] but the police presumably had something more solid than mere hearsay to warrant the formal charge brought against him. As it was, the police were satisfied that Hicks could account for all of his movements on the day of the murder, and there the matter rested.

On paper, Emily Trigg might be the perfect candidate for the Ghost of Blue Bell Hill. Her connections with Blue Bell Hill, the manner of her death, and the interment of her remains at Burham, make some sense of Jack Woodger's experience years before the accepted framework for the haunting, but in detail the affair holds some interesting comparisons with the case as a whole. Emily's description, for instance: her age and appearance—a pretty young woman; her height and build; the colour of her hair; even her dress, are all features that are certainly consistent with aspects of one or more witness descriptions of the ghost girl.

The case of Emily Trigg also shows some clear parallels with details relating to the 1965 crash victims. As a residential maid working in Rochester, Emily could easily stand in place of Judith Lingham as the 'Rochester Girl', while the dress she was wearing at the time of her murder (made for her brother's wedding), and her own purported engagement (making her a bride-to-be), invite comparisons to the 'bridesmaid's dress' feature and the bride-to-be of the 1965 case.

As a lifelong resident of Blue Bell Hill Village, Emily had a strong connection with the haunted locality itself—and one prominent encounter with the ghost was to take place near to her former home.

Finally, we have the fact that Emily's murder remained unsolved, and her assailant (or assailants)[38] escaped justice—which (accepting for a moment a connection between violent, unrequited death and ghostly manifestations) we may suppose might give reason for Emily's restless spirit to appear at places that held strong emotional significance for her—her home, the scene of her demise, and the village (Burham) where her remains were finally laid to rest. Even the conclusion of the inquest might be seen to contribute to the injustices connected with her death, where in spite of overwhelming evidence that she had been assaulted and murdered (or at very least purposely left to die, with a rag forced down her throat), the Coroner ruled that conclusion as unsafe, opting instead for an open verdict.

The lift given to the girl by Jack Woodger from the Lower Bell to Burham would, in this case—and in true Version C Hitch-Hiker style—represent a return to her place of burial. Recalling his experience, Jack Woodger had dropped his passenger off in Church Street, outside the church itself. Characteristic of a variation of the Version C ending, he did not witness her disappearance. The Church of St Mary the Virgin,[39] built in the Victorian gothic style, had, until it was demolished in 1981, stood at the head of the street, on the corner with Rochester Road.

Whether Emily's remains were laid to rest in the churchyard here is by now difficult to say, but it seems doubtful. The church was of significant size, and the plot (now occupied by private housing and the war memorial) is narrow, suggesting only marginal space for a graveyard.

This facility, for burials, was served by an earlier church of the same name. Less than a mile from the present village, the original medieval Church of St Mary the Virgin (which was known locally as 'Burham Old Church' to distinguish it from the 'New Church') still stands on the northern bank of the River Medway, at a crossing point used by the pilgrims on their way to and from Canterbury.

With the completion of the New Church in 1881 in the relocated village that was developing on the higher ground along the Rochester Road (where it was in closer proximity to a new source of employment—the quarries and works of the burgeoning cement industry (see Chapter 2)), use of the Old Church gradually declined. Regular services ceased there in 1919 and, apart from its occasional use as a funerary chapel, the church and its grounds fell steadily into neglect. By 1920, the buildings were described as devoid of fittings. Repairs carried out by a charity, the Friends of Friendless Churches, maintained the church until 1956, when it was reopened for occasional services. But by 1973, the burden to the parish of maintaining two churches resulted in it being declared redundant, and its care passed to the Redundant Churches Fund (now the Churches Conservation Trust).[40] Even so, the churchyard remained (and remains still) in occasional use for burials, and it is very likely that this is where Emily Trigg was buried (and where her father, John Trigg (d. 1912), and mother, Kate (d. 1921), were most likely laid to rest). No markers or cemetery records survive, however, to be certain of the matter.

The isolation of the Old Church today can be appreciated from the southern end of Church Street, where it abruptly gives way to open countryside, and slopes

The site of the former post office and entrance to Laurie Gray Avenue, Blue Bell Hill Village—the location of a former home of Emily Trigg, and of encounters with a ghostly young woman

away toward the river. From here, the church sits below to the south-west, in detached seclusion against a loop of the river. By day, the spot is a lonely one; a little-visited backwater. By night, it is plain eerie, quiet and still; the churchyard an inky void cut out of the gloom by an overgrown picket fence—the perfect backdrop to operate on the imagination within the context of a ghost story.

Then there is Emily's customary visit with her mother at Blue Bell Hill on Sunday afternoons, and, of course, her disappearance on that day. Although probably not highly significant, we can note that four encounters (Hopkins, Sharpe, Dawkins, and Cooper) also occurred on a Sunday.

Chris Dawkins' encounter in Blue Bell Hill Village in November 1992 was to find additional significance. The village has been the scene of two other reported encounters: Ann-Marie Austin's sighting in 1976 or 1977 near the Upper Bell pub (Chapter 7), and another we will look at in Chapter 12. Chris Dawkins' experience—the more dramatic of the three—occurred as he passed Robin Hood Lane (on his left) on his way home late on Sunday 22 November 1992, when the girl ran from between parked cars and vanished beneath his car.

This places the collision virtually outside the former Post Office at 571 Maidstone Road (now a private residence). In Chapter 7, the possible significance of the proximity of Medway Crematorium, in Robin Hood Lane, was considered both in terms of cemeteries as the sometime destination of the Version C Phantom Hitch-Hiker, and as the venue for Judith Lingham's funeral in November 1965.

It may be more significant, however, that this spot marked a former home of Emily Trigg. Between 1901 and 1911, as the censuses of those years record, the Trigg family, headed by John Trigg, a chalk worker, lived on Maidstone Road, Blue Bell Hill, in the vicinity of the village Post Office. In 1901, the family numbered ten. Emily, then five years old, was one of three sisters and five brothers living at home.

The cottages are long gone, but it is possible to say where the Trigg home stood, thanks to an Inland Revenue property valuations survey that was carried out in 1909–10, and the annotated 1:2500 scale Ordnance Survey maps (1908 edition) used by the surveyors. On these large-scale maps, the ledger reference for each property, giving the head of the household, is marked, enabling the precise location to be determined. The entry for John Trigg, for instance, is 920.[41] The cottage was the next but one from the Post Office, on its south side, and would have stood approximately where the entrance to Laurie Gray Avenue is now located. This area is given on the Inland Revenue records as 'Upper Bell'; in the 1901 Census as 'Burham Hill', and in 1911 as 'Blue Bell Hill'.

While a significant correlation, this, however, was *not* the Providence Row given as Emily's home address by the newspapers in 1916. Kate Trigg, Emily's mother, was reported to be resident at 3 Providence Row, Maidstone Road.[42] Providence Row referred to a set of five cottages situated at the north end of the village, between the Bridgewood Cottage public house and the Zion Mission Hall (chapel). All have fallen victim to redevelopment of the area over the years. Providence Row stood approximately where a section of dual carriageway in the A229/M2 interchange north of the village crosses the line of the old Maidstone Road between the present northern limit of Blue Bell Hill Village and Hospital Lane Dental Clinic.[43]

Emily's father, John Trigg, died in 1912 at the age of fifty. It is possible that after her husband's death, Mrs Trigg was obliged to relinquish the cottage, or chose to move to another part of the village. In 1891, five years before Emily's birth, the family had lived at 1 Bridgewood Cottages, next to the 'Bridgewood Beer House' (the Bridgewood Cottage). Mr Trigg was at that time a general labourer.[44]

Two of the Triggs' neighbours, James Broomfield and Frederick Greenfield, were still resident here in 1901, when the census records both as living at Provi-

Bridgewood Cottage public house, Blue Bell Hill (*Simon Pujuz CC BY-SA 2.0*). **Emily Trigg's last home stood to the left of the pub (now demolished)**

dence Row rather than Bridgewood Cottages—so it would seem the row had taken on a new name in that time.[45] The cottages at Providence Row, then, would have been familiar to Kate Trigg had she returned there as a widow after 1912. We will not know with absolute certainty which was Kate Trigg's (and therefore Emily's) last address until the 1921 Census is released in 2021.

But, in either case, we can say that the scene of Chris Dawkins' encounter was not very far away from Emily's home.

Another incident—Richard Studholme's encounter in 1973, in which his female passenger wished to be dropped off at the top of the Hill, on the Maidstone Road immediately before the Bridgewood roundabout—might serve, in broad observation of the Version C habit, as a return to the scene of her demise, a little way down the B2097 Rochester Road, north-west of this spot. (In this instance, however, it may be recalled that Mr Studholme was directed to an address in the Walderslade area, and suspected afterward that he had been the victim of a cruel hoax (see Chapter 7)).

Further (albeit tentative) links to Emily are found in several reports.

Paul Lowing, of Robin Hood Lane, Walderslade, saw a young woman in a white dress and white hat walking along a slip-road of the northbound A229 in the early hours of one autumn morning in 2008. The slip-road, which runs onto

The A229 toward the Lord Lees interchange and the M2—scene of several sightings of a young woman in old-fashioned costume

the double-bridge interchange of the Lord Lees roundabout immediately north-west of Blue Bell Hill Village, provides options for the M2, Buckmore Park, Borstal and Rochester. Paul, a driver for the Royal Mail, was returning to the Royal Mail depot at the former Fort Bridgewood site (on the B2097 Maidstone Road, Rochester) in his articulated lorry when he saw the woman walking up the cycle path along the margin of the road at the crest of the Hill. The location is an unusual one to see a woman walking alone, particularly at that hour, sometime between 1.30 a.m. and 3 a.m. As he passed her, Paul looked back in his side mirror, but in that moment she had vanished. The whole sighting lasted less than thirty seconds, but long enough for Paul to gain a sure impression of her attire: simply a dress, just below the knee in length, and a hat. She had no overcoat, scarf, or other means of protection against the conditions.[46]

A similar sighting was made at the same location by five women travelling along the same stretch of road at approximately 1 a.m. sometime between 1992 and 1994. Ann King, who was driving, was returning home to Gravesend with friends after a night out in Bearsted, Maidstone. At the top of the Hill, the A229 then offered a shorter length of slip-lane here onto a simpler interchange of roundabouts with options for Chatham and the motorway. On the approach to this, on the A229 itself, the party of women saw a figure of a young woman walking northward on the verge pathway, close to the grass and scrub bank. The figure was slim, and wore a long, light-coloured dress of old-fashioned style, comprised of a tight bodice and a long skirt which extended 'to the floor'. She wore a white hat with a floppy brim, and carried a handbag or a basket over her arm. She was walking along quite casually, as if she hadn't a care in the world.

The surprising sight of a woman walking alone at that spot at that hour prompted speculative remarks from the car's occupants, the first impression being that she was walking home from a fancy dress party ('fancy being out like that on your own'), or she might have broken down, and perhaps they should stop and offer her a lift. They passed her in seconds, but as they did so, she didn't look up or turn her head, but continued on, staring ahead. One even joked, 'perhaps it's a ghost'. A moment later, Ann checked her mirrors; two of her friends also glanced back, but there was no sign of the woman.

Ann told me that she has been a resident of Gravesend for most of her life, and had worked in London. She hardly ever travelled to east Kent, and had only been to Maidstone three or four times. Consequently, she (and her friends likewise) had not even heard of the Blue Bell Hill's ghost at the time (which is not surprising, since before 1992 the Hill's reputation had faded in local knowledge since its heyday in the late 1960s and early 1970s and was only just beginning to become well known again publicly).[47]

The location of Paul Lowing's and Ann King's sightings lies between 150 and 300 metres (500–1000 feet) south-west of the site of Emily Trigg's former home at the north end of Blue Bell Hill Village, which may (or may not) be significant. The spot, in 1916, would have been a part of Lord Lees, an area of woodland on the eastern flank of Bridge Woods, which ran right up to the western margin of the village—hence is not a spot likely to have been frequented by pedestrians, Emily included. But then we have seen that similar ghostly figures have also been encountered on the dual carriageway of the modern A229 further down the Hill, which likewise suggests that they are not constrained to familiar locations, but are capable of interacting with features (the modern road) which did not exist in their time.

Anecdotes involving a similar figure came via author Neil Arnold, who, following a talk in March 2011, was approached by a woman who recounted her husband's sighting of six years earlier (2005). The lady herself, who unfortunately did not leave her name or contact details, admitted to being sceptical but conceded that her husband had been 'freaked out' by his experience, which happened at around 6.30 a.m. one morning as he drove his tarmac lorry up the Hill. In the vicinity of the current Shell petrol station (which was built around 1993 opposite the Aylesford turn-off), he saw '… a woman in a whitish dress [and] wearing a white hat' walking up the verge. He drove past her, thinking it odd to find her there, but when he looked in his mirrors, she was gone.[48]

The Nashenden Valley, dominated today by the M2 motorway, and bounded on its north side by the tree-shrouded B2097, where Emily Trigg's remains were found in 1916. Bridgewood roundabout (formerly Bridgewood Gates) is located at top-right of the picture

Behind the Shell petrol station (on its west side), the Old Chatham Road and Chatham Road form parallel arcs that merge further up before joining the modern A229 dual carriageway. The inner arc (the older remnant) leads past Kits Coty Brasserie (the former Kit's Coty House—the Georgian manor house, not to be confused with the ancient monument of the same name) and Lower Bell Industrial Estate.

The outer arc is distinguished by Kit's Coty Cottage, situated on the apex of the bend. This was the location of another sighting in the winter of 1991 or 1992. The brief account, again received by Neil Arnold, came from a gentleman who gave only his first name, 'Chris'. Chris and his wife had turned onto the Chatham Road at the Lower Bell at around 10.30 p.m. It was quite a foggy night. About halfway up the Hill, in the vicinity of the cottage, they both saw, on the left side, a young woman walking slowly up the road. She occasionally glanced toward the road. She wore an 'old fashioned' greyish dress, and had 'longish hair', but as they passed her they heard the sound of a crash, and there was afterward no sign of the girl.

No mention is made as to whether another car had passed them to account for the crash, but the inference is that it was a real one that happened nearby (presumably on the A229 a short distance away) as the witness afterward '…

wondered if the crash had been caused by the girl'.[49] This location, not far removed from the scene of Ian Sharpe's or Maurice Goodenough's encounters would become the focus for repeated encounters of a quite startling kind a couple of years later (see Chapter 10).

For the time being, we can note the similarities to Gladys Painter's description of the girl (long hair and a white dress) that she had seen on a nearby section of the Hill in 1974; to Pope's & Colling's description of the young woman they had met at the foot of the Hill in 1977 (white evening dress and blonde hair), and to Chris Dawkins' description of the girl (long blonde hair) in 1992—perhaps less a recognisable description of Emily Trigg than the ubiquitous lady-in-white of PHH lore, but noteworthy all the same.

Returning to the top of the Hill, in 2010 I corresponded with a lady from Northampton who, posting as 'oldsunset' on the Kent History Forum, had submitted her daughter's experience in January of that year. She said:

> Personally I don't believe in ghosts but my daughter, 30, does; and when we had the snow recently she rang me up very excited. Her fella and her [sic] were stuck in their car at the roundabout [at the] top of BBH as they were trying to get home to Walderslade Woods, where they live. Looking out of the window, [there] was deep snow to her left, on the verge. She was watching the snow falling on it out of boredom—it was fresh and pristine. Suddenly, footprints—*deep ones*—ran across the snow and turned and faced her window. She screamed. Her fella jumped out of the car and went round to her side of the car. [There was] no person in sight, just footprints, as if someone had run up to the car window and looked in at her. No prints led away from the car either; they just vanished. Her fella was shocked; everyone was still stuck in their cars, and there were no pedestrians in sight, and it wasn't really dark; only about 5 p.m.[50]

The location was established as the top of the off-ramp of the M2 at Junction 3, where the roundabout forms an oval over the motorway, providing options for Walderslade and Chatham on the north side, and Blue Bell Hill Village and Maidstone on the other. It was not possible to state whether the footprints indicated a male or female 'presence', only that the impression formed by the witness was that they had stopped beside the car, '… as if the person stayed there.' This location is quite close (again within 300 metres) to Emily Trigg's former home. However, since we can make few further deductions from this episode, the account must be taken at face value. Of further note only is that this slip-road (assuming it to be the one off the eastbound carriageway of the motorway, which was constructed as recently as 2002 as part of a general widening and improvement of the M2) begins at the point where the Maidstone–Chatham road formerly crossed the motorway. Prior to the construction of the motorway in 1963, which introduced a cutting here, the road ran over level ground from the northern end of Blue Bell Hill Village, near to Emily's home, northward to Bridgewood, where it divided. In 1916, the road was flanked on either side by woodland almost all the way to Bridgewood, presenting quite a different aspect to the area to that known today.

Today, this section of the A229 Maidstone–Chatham road is displaced westward to line up with the dual carriageway that bypasses Blue Bell Hill Village, and the former route—the one regularly used by Emily, and where the café that Mrs Woodger worked in the 1960s was located—has, on the north side of the motorway, become an extension of Hallsfield Road.

This is not, however, the only instance of a connection with the M2 immediately north of Blue Bell Hill. Years previously (prior to 1993) it had been suggested that the ghost girl had been sighted on the motorway itself. The source of this snippet, the late paranormal investigator and writer Andrew Green, told me this had been related to him by a member of the Thanet Psychic Research Society.[51]

Again, we find some relevance in terms of what we know of Emily Trigg's plight. At Bridgewood, the Rochester road (the current B2097) splits off the main road to run north-westward along the edge of the Nashenden Valley. In Emily's time, the floor of this chalk valley was occupied by pasture that was flanked by woodland. A track across the valley bottom through woods and fields, known as Stoney Lane, was often used as a shortcut by persons travelling between Rochester and Blue Bell Hill—but the dangers posed by this route were well known. This was the area where, in 1831, John Any Bird Bell accosted and murdered Richard Faulkner Taylor at a spot not far removed from where Emily Trigg's remains were found (see Chapter 2); and where, as recently as 1950, a Walderslade woman (ironically by the name of Mrs Mary Hicks, a namesake for the accused in Emily Trigg's case) was attacked and robbed when taking her regular shortcut through woodland between Bridgewood and her home, and left with severe head injuries.[52] With good sense, Emily is said to have kept to the main roads—even if her own route may have been tragically predictable.

While Andrew Green's anecdote led no further, echoes of this rumour are found in other anecdotal accounts that were to come from disparate sources. The aforementioned Neil Arnold, then of Chatham, wrote to *Fortean Times* magazine in March 1998 to report that a relative of his (un-named), while driving along the M2 towards Chatham in daylight the previous September, had seen a 'bridesmaid' standing in the foliage beside the motorway.[53]

One other correspondent also places his sighting of a similar figure in the woody margins of the M2 above Blue Bell Hill. Colin Field, who first wrote to me at the start of 2002, reported that, on two occasions in the early 1990s—both at dusk, around 6.00–6.30 p.m.—when driving westbound along the M2 from Thanet to his home at Shorne, he had seen '… a rather large woman with reddish hair wearing a conventional bridal gown standing in the trees just before the slip road which leads down to the A229'.

Seeking further information in 2010, Colin, by now living in North London and retired after thirty years as a probation officer, was able to pin-point the spot more precisely, which he gave as the woods just before Buckmore Park (partly occupied by a go-kart track). Both sightings had been fairly fleeting, but the dress appeared to have been a veil and train. 'Even now I can recollect the incongruity of the figure which on both occasions was quite motionless'.

In re-describing the figure, which he gave as 'squat and stocky, almost like a man in drag', Colin was struck with the notion that perhaps it was indeed a man in a dress: 'All sorts of things apparently went on in the woods further up the M2 near Shorne.' Cases brought to court, he commented, would occasionally mention the wearing of women's underwear, but never a wedding dress! As Colin sensibly concluded, he could not be certain that his sightings of the figure qualified them as sightings of the ghost. 'But I did see it,' he said.[54]

Other anecdotes provide further suggestive links between Emily Trigg and ghostly sightings along the route of her fateful last journey. A couple in the early 1970s who were driving toward Borstal and Rochester on the B2097 saw, in their car's headlights in the vicinity of the milestone (see p. 228), a young woman in a long, pale dress walking along the verge toward them on the opposite side of the road. It was around midnight, and concerned for her out alone at that hour, they decided to turn the car around to go to her assistance, but despite driving up and down several times, they could find no trace of her.[55]

Prudence is perhaps best applied to this anomalous collection of accounts, both in terms of relating them to the sightings at Blue Bell Hill itself, and to the case of Emily Trigg—whose connection, after all, largely rests on Jack Woodger's account alone.

In the latter case, if it is valid, we may wonder at the apparent absence of other reported sightings or rumours associated with Emily in the decades since her death, near to either her home or the place where she died. Part of the reason may, perhaps, be attributed to the lack of regard for ghost sightings in the printed media of this period, but we find a similar absence also in the oral record. Nevertheless, it is of some interest that among the above accounts we find descriptions of a young woman in old-fashioned dress when witnesses may otherwise have been expected to describe a figure in clothing more in keeping with the victims of the 1965 tragedy. In them we also find an apparent blurring of the boundaries between the two purported 'causes': the girl in old-fashioned attire turns up at locations normally associated with the 1965 crash victim(s)—the middle part of the Hill, in the vicinity of the Lower Bell—while the bridal dress, symbolising the impending wedding of one of that party, is noted at locations more readily associated with Emily Trigg (the top of the Hill).

Ultimately, as with the 1965 crash victims, any attempt at a positive identification with Emily Trigg is meaningful in only a few respects, failing equally to account for some of the broader variations in detail found in the various witness accounts. For instance, in the three Hitch-Hiker accounts we have examined—Jack Woodger's, and the two in the previous chapter—while each focuses on the Lower Bell section of Blue Bell Hill as the place the girl is encountered (which, as pointed out in the first example, does at least correspond with the earliest accounts of the haunting), the destination varies markedly: Maidstone (presumably); Chatham; Burham. If we were to take into account the various anecdotal accounts, we could add a number of other destinations: Rochester, Gillingham, Eccles, Aylesford, East Malling, and Blue Bell Hill itself—which makes the whole thing rather absurd.

But this is perhaps overstepping the mark to a degree. An identification of *anyone* presupposes that we are dealing with a case of survival—that the ghost is that of a deceased person, who has either returned or has failed to 'move on' for some indefinite reason. In fact, none of the cases we have looked at definitely points to this as the explanation. All we can say is that, collectively, these encounters point to something out of the ordinary happening at Blue Bell Hill, of which continuance beyond death is but one possible explanation.

The encounters that speak most in favour of this—those involving a vanishing hitch-hiker—are, of course, also the ones most open to criticism, both in terms of interpretation (in one case only—Malcolm Grant's—was the girl clearly not able to get away unobserved and by inference a ghost—and here, valuable supporting detail, and the witness himself, are absent), and in their close adherence to an oft-found motif of folklore.

Any criticism on this basis is surely valid, but viewed within the wider context of encounters at Blue Bell Hill, they clearly fit the same pattern identified in the 'knock down' cases, taking place at essentially the same time of night (typically late, around midnight), often at the same locations (in two cases, with the girl, in like fashion, standing in the middle of the road), and ending in a similar manner with the unobserved disappearance of the girl (which, in the 'knock down' case, is beneath the vehicle).

In his book, Michael Goss states that a world of difference exists between the habits of what he calls the 'Spectral Jaywalker' and the Phantom Hitch-Hiker, but not infrequently the two motifs can be found in the same road ghost story cycle.[56] While I disagree regarding the extent of their differences (in Chapter 4, I drew attention to their *similarities*, suggesting that the two are not disparate themes, but aspects of the *same* phenomenon), the case at Blue Bell Hill certainly bears this out. The best example of this must be James Skene's experience which, as in the A38 Man in the Mackintosh case (Chapter 4), seems to combine elements of both.

I have stated previously that witnesses' descriptions of the ghost girl— her general appearance and behaviour—resemble less any given identity (whether it be any member of the 1965 crash party, Emily Trigg, or any other person tragically killed on or near the Hill) than the classic Phantom Hitch-Hiker folk type (I need not remind the reader of, say, Ian Sharpe's description of the girl to illustrate this)—which would perhaps be easier to explain if we were not confronted with the testimony of a number of credible first-hand witnesses. The point raises some very pertinent questions regarding the reality of these events, and their relationship to folklore. Are we seeing, by some mechanism, fact mirroring supposed fiction? Or are we looking at a consistent and long-standing phenomenon upon which a body of folklore was subsequently founded? The question gains in standing as we come to examine the next twist in the Blue Bell Hill saga.

ELEVEN

HEKATE ON THE HILL

The Hag is astride,
This night for to ride;
The Devill and shee together:
Through thick, and through thin,
Now out, and then in,
Though ne'er so foule be the weather.

A Thorn or a Burr
She takes for a Spurre:
With a lash of a Bramble she rides now,
Through Brakes and through Bryars,
O'er Ditches, and Mires,
She followes the Spirit that guides now.

No Beast, for his food,
Dares now range the wood;
But husht in his laire he lies lurking:
While mischeifs, by these,
On Land and on Seas,
At noone of Night are a-working.

The storme will arise,
And trouble the skies;
This night, and more for the wonder,
The ghost from the Tomb
Affrighted shall come,
Call'd out by the clap of the Thunder.

Robert Herrick, 'The Hag', 1648[1]

On the afternoon of 19 January 1993, I received a call from Claire Ogley of the *Kent Today*, who asked me if I had ever heard of the ghost of an old woman being sighted on Blue Bell Hill. Replying 'no', I asked her what *she* knew. It transpired that I had been missing the latest shenanigans playing out on the Hill. What Claire described—a menacing witch-like apparition—sounded too bizarre, too fairytale-like to possibly be true...except that a family, very much frightened by their experience, had come forward to say it had happened to them.

A few days later, my inability to account for the latest sightings was reported in the *Kent Today* under the heading 'Blue Bell Hill spectre puzzles historian' (22 January).[2] The article stated that three people had contacted the *Kent Today* to report seeing an old wizened figure walking slowly across the A229 Maidstone–Chatham Road late at night. The first to see the figure, Angela Maiden, of Wallace Road, Rochester, was said to still be in a state of shock, and had since seen a vicar, who was reported to have placed a protective aura around her.

Another witness, Diane Rayburn*, of Gillingham, contacted the newspaper after reading about the experience of Mrs Maiden and her family to report that she and her own family had been similarly terrified when they spotted the figure in deep fog the night before. At the sight of the figure, they all turned icy cold; her husband, at the wheel, simply froze. Mr Rayburn afterward stopped a police car to report the sighting, but on arrival they found nothing.

Mrs Rayburn's description matched that given by Mrs Maiden: 'It had an old face and blonde hair with horrible eyes and no lips. But instead of a cloak, it was wearing a kilt.

'At first we thought it was a man dressed up but now I don't know what it was. It stood on the side of the road and was beckoning us with a bunch of heather in its hand but I'm sure it wasn't a gypsy.'

Mrs Rayburn's brother-in-law drove up the Hill some ten minutes afterward, but saw nothing unusual.

Footnoting the article were references to two previous *Kent Today* articles on the subject, also by Claire Ogley, dated 8 and 14 January.

The first ('Wizened road horror is ruining our lives') described how the Maiden family were desperately hoping to prove their terrifying sighting in deep fog on Blue Bell Hill was the work of a cruel hoaxer. Angela Maiden was reported to be unable to sleep following the sighting, which took place at around 12.45 a.m. the previous Wednesday (6 January) as she, her husband, and her 64-year-old mother were returning home from a night out.[3]

It was her husband, Malcolm (who was driving), who first sighted what he thought was a haggard old woman in old-fashioned clothes walking slowly across the northbound carriageway, about halfway up the Hill. As they approached the figure, and slowed down in the foggy conditions, Mrs Maiden at first thought that it was someone in fancy dress. The figure stopped in the middle of the road, with its back to them. But as they slowly passed it, with it only about a foot away from the window, it turned and hissed at them.

Caricature rendering of Angela Maiden's sighting (from 'Wizened road horror is ruining our lives', *Kent Today*, 8 January 1993) *(KM Group)*

The terror, according to Mrs Maiden, was unbelievable. It left the three of them speechless, and with an overwhelming sense of evil and horror.

'It was very small and wizened. The eyes were very close together; small and round and black, and the mouth was thin-lipped.'

Mrs Maiden said they would have been able to tell if it had been a mask or make-up.

'Then it began to sneer. It had an enormous mouth which was totally black and then it hissed and lifted its arm and began shaking twigs at us as if it was putting a curse on us.'

The hissing sound, which was very loud, seemed to fill the car as Mr Maiden tried frantically to find the gears, all this seeming to happen in slow motion. As he finally managed to pull away, the figure seemed to disappear.

The Maidens reported their sighting to the police at the first opportunity, and were apparently told that there had been two or three similar calls that night, although none had been logged.

PC Jonathon Thomas of West Malling Police (under whose jurisdiction Blue Bell Hill fell) said that a thorough search of the area was made, but no-one or thing was found to account for the incident. If it were a hoax, he said, apart from making people's lives a misery, the culprit had put both himself or herself and others at risk; but '… as for the truth behind it—who can tell?'[4]

Angela Maiden returned to the spot the following day to ask a woman living in a nearby cottage if she had seen or heard anything strange that same night, but the woman, who was frightened, did not wish to hear what they had seen.

In response to the *Kent Today*'s subsequent appeal for other witnesses to the old woman to come forward, taxi driver Colin Eacott contacted the newspaper; his story appearing in the 14 January issue.[5]

Mr Eacott, who worked for a Chatham cab firm, claimed that he saw the same old woman, dressed in old-fashioned clothes, on the southbound carriage-way of the A229 at Blue Bell Hill in the winter about two years earlier. Disbelieving in ghosts, he too at the time explained it away as a hoax, but the Maidens' sighting caused him to reconsider. He had not told anyone beforehand on account that people might think him 'cranky'.

His sighting took place at about 9.15 p.m. He was taking 'four lads' to the Great Danes (Hotel) near Hollingbourne,[6] when he saw the figure 'just before the Aylesford turn-off.'

Everyone in the car thought it was someone in fancy dress, and the youths started calling names out of the window. At first, he thought it must be an old lady, but then he questioned who in their right mind would be walking down there in the pouring rain.

'She was wearing a black cloak and a long hat and walked with a stick. You couldn't see the face at all.'

Colin's passengers urged him to stop the car, while continuing to shout at the figure, which failed to induce it to turn round. 'Then,' the article states simply, 'it disappeared.'

While it was true that I was initially at some loss to explain these new encounters, I very quickly saw that they had much in common with other encounters on the Hill in terms of location, timing, and even in the behaviour of the 'apparition', and with a few other cases in the literature. However, before I could offer comment, or even speculate about what these sightings might represent, it was important to find whatever corroboration for them that I could, of which the testimony of the witnesses themselves would be the most valuable.

The most important feature of these accounts—described in two of them—was (if true) the directly observed disappearance of the figure. In consideration of this, plus the duration of each encounter, and the fact that these were all collective sightings involving more than two witnesses in each case, the sightings of the old woman, ironically, promised to be far less ambiguous than many involving the ghost girl.

In practice, gaining that corroboration would prove to be more difficult than I had anticipated. In the Maidens' case, several letters went unanswered—quite probably, and understandably, for the same reasons Ian Sharpe and Chris Dawkins had failed to reply months before.

The Rayburns' story initially fared no better. I turned to Claire Ogley to see if she could put me in touch. Alas, all Claire could add was that the Rayburn's sighting had occurred late at night in the footbridge area of the Hill (which would, in fact, turn out to be incorrect). The breakthrough came over a year later, when television researcher Daniel Barraclough, who was investigating the Blue Bell Hill case for a possible slot on London Weekend Television's paranormal series, *Strange But True?*, managed to contact both the Maidens and the Rayburns via the *Kent Today*, with both agreeing to some involvement in the programme.

With solicitous regard to the possibility for offence that a televised discussion of the appointed cause of the haunting (the 1965 crash) might cause to relatives of the victims, the programme's producers decided to restrict their attention to the sightings themselves, with some reference to Blue Bell Hill's history and folklore. Mr Barraclough kindly sent me a transcript copy of the notes he made during his initial interview with Angela Maiden, and, following the programme's withdrawal from the story shortly afterward, he put me in touch with the Rayburns.

Both accounts were to show that while the newspaper versions had conveyed the essential facts and impressions of the sightings, they had not, as we have come to expect, given the whole story:

The first thing to say about Angela Maiden's story is that the event was deeply disturbing to her. She did not sleep for three or four days afterwards, and remained traumatised for a year afterward. A midwife by profession, Mrs Maiden was a practical woman not easily fazed by events. Nevertheless she said that every time she closed her eyes she really felt she had had an evil curse put on her.

The encounter took place, as reported, at approximately 1 a.m. on Wednesday 6 January 1993—*not*, however, on the A229 dual carriageway, as the *Kent Today*'s article implied, but on the old road, now termed simply Chatham Road.

There were five people in the car: Mrs Maiden, her husband (who was driving), her mother, her young daughter, and a family friend. The daughter was asleep, but everyone else witnessed the event.

They had come up from Aylesford, turning left onto Chatham Road at the Lower Bell crossroads—a route that would bring them onto the northbound dual carriageway further up the Hill. It was a dark, frosty night. Observational conditions were therefore ideal, far from the foggy conditions described by the *Kent Today*. They were just turning into the bend occupied on one side by Kit's Coty

The bend of Chatham Road, scene of the Maidens' and Rayburns' encounters in January 1993

Cottage when they saw a figure start across the road towards the house.

'At first I thought it was [somebody in] a fancy dress costume. It was wearing a long dress, very old-fashioned, that stopped mid-calf. It had a tartan shawl round the top and a bonnet with a brim.'

Mrs Maiden remembers remarking to her husband, 'Somebody's playing a prank.' But then the car's headlights fully illuminated the figure.

'It was like when you trap a rabbit in your headlights. It stayed dazed, hunched over without looking at us.'

Mr Maiden swerved to the right to avoid it.

'As we got alongside of it we were almost at a standstill. All of a sudden it was four feet away from the car. It rounded on us really quickly and I saw the face. It was totally horrific...very small, black beady eyes. It was like a wizened face. The worst thing of all was the mouth. It opened and was like an empty black hole.

'My mother was sitting directly behind me. At the same time I remember we said, 'Oh my God.'

With the figure turning on them, a hissing sound filled the car, even through the closed windows. The figure was carrying twigs. Mrs Maiden quickly engaged the central locking, instinctively bringing up her arm to protect herself. Mr Maiden was trying to get the car into gear, to get away. As he did so, and started to pull away, Mrs Maiden's mother turned round to watch the figure. It began to

Reconstruction of the Maidens' encounter of 6 January 1993

move towards the nearside kerb, but seemed to vanish before it got there.

'We then proceeded to drive home. My daughter woke up feeling a terrible atmosphere in the car. I couldn't talk; all you could hear was everyone breathing.

'I can't explain to you how it felt. I've never felt evil before and I've never been so terrified. I felt as if I had looked into the eyes of the devil.'

In a desperate attempt to find some rational explanation, Angela Maiden telephoned the cottage to find out if they had had a fancy dress party that night or seen anything strange. The lady who answered said 'no' to both questions, saying that she did not want to discuss it further; there had been enough strange things happening outside the house and she was quite frightened. Mrs Maiden did not believe it was possible for anyone to dress up to look like the figure. If they had, it was the sickest of jokes.

The Rayburns' experience, I would discover, when I telephoned them in June 1994,[7] actually took place the night *before* the Maidens' encounter, on 5 January 1993. While the family's real name had been used in the *Kent Today*, Mr Rayburn, who described the incident to me, said he preferred that it not be repeated in print here.

Their story is almost identical to the Maiden's, which, considering that they had read about it before Mrs Rayburn reported their own experience, doesn't appear to impress very much—until, that is, we consider that some of the matching details (the precise location, for instance, and the specific behaviour of the apparition) were *not* features of the newspaper accounts.

On the night in question (a damp, misty one), the family—Mr Rayburn, his wife Diane, and their two children, a girl, 11, and a boy, 14—were at a birthday celebration (Mr Rayburn's sister's) at The Windmill pub in Burham. They left the pub around midnight. Mr Rayburn hastened to add that neither he nor his wife had been drinking.

Mr Rayburn waved as his nephew pulled away ahead of them. His brother was to leave a few minutes after them. All were heading in the same direction home, eastbound along the Pilgrims' Way to Rochester Road and Blue Bell Hill.

At the bend-junction of the Pilgrims' Way with the Rochester Road (located at the foot of the trackway that leads up to Kit's Coty House, and very near the scene of the Greens' experience (Chapter 9), the Rayburns' daughter remarked aloud, 'I wonder if we'll see the ghost?' To which Mr Rayburn replied, 'Don't be bloody stupid.'

However, just a minute or so later, having rounded the bend at Kit's Coty Cottage, they sighted the figure of an old woman standing in the middle of the road. The figure was 'as described in the newspaper', except that her hair somehow did not look real. Her features were drawn. She wore a skirt made from a material that looked like tartan, and she wore a light-coloured top. She was holding what appeared to be a posy of heather, and she beckoned to the car as they approached. Mr Rayburn by then had slowed from around 30 mph (third gear) to around 5 or 6 mph. The figure shuffled sideways across the road from right to left before them, so that she faced them all the time, until she reached the opposite pavement. Mr Rayburn drove slowly by, and the figure turned to watch them pass, all the time continuing to beckon towards them.

The whole family was disturbed by the sighting. Mr Rayburn searched for a police car on the way home. Finding one further up, on the Maidstone Road, he reported the incident, thinking perhaps that this was a cruel hoax that could badly frighten someone, as indeed it already had. Like Angela Maiden, who had been unable to sleep following her family's experience, the Rayburns were awake all night. At around 3 a.m. Mr Rayburn telephoned Chatham Police, who told him that an inspection of the scene had yielded nothing. Mr Rayburn's brother, passing the same way only minutes after they had, had seen nothing unusual.

In time further accounts would emerge concerning what would variously come to be called the 'old woman', the 'hag', or the 'witch'.

Construction worker Donald Gallagher* saw the ghost in late September of 1983 or 1984, when on his way home to Aylesford from visiting an elderly aunt in Thanet. His daughter, Sarah, recalls that it was a Sunday night, sometime between 9.30 p.m. and 10 p.m. Her mother kept telling her to go to bed as she had

The Lower Bell crossroads (looking west)—scene of Donald Gallagher's sighting of an apparition of an old woman that glided uphill toward him

school the next morning, but she really wanted to wait up see her father. When he arrived, she could hear her mother asking him what was wrong as he was in 'a bit of a state', so she went out to see what was going on. He then described the unnerving experience he had just had at Blue Bell Hill.

Coming off the M2 at the top of the Hill, he had driven down the A229 and taken the turn-off for Aylesford, Eccles and Burham, which curves under the dual carriageway, becoming the Rochester Road as it bends left at the bottom of the hill towards Aylesford, a mile-and-a-half distant. As he emerged from the oasis of light at the Lower Bell crossroads and started down the dark tree-lined hill, he found himself almost immediately confronted by the figure of an elderly woman rushing toward him in the middle of the road. He swerved sharply to avoid her—his car, a Citroën Dyane, rocked madly on its suspension in the manoeuvre.

Shaken, he pulled up, to check that he had missed her, which he felt could only have been by a few feet. There were no cars following him, but he could see the woman 'racing up the hill behind'. She was illuminated by the headlights of cars travelling in the other direction and following her up the hill to the crossroads, where she turned up the Chatham Road and was lost to sight.

The woman was dressed in a dark, full length dress, and had on a bonnet and a shawl. The style at once suggested Victorian, but Mr Gallagher described her as most closely resembling Old Mother Riley, the popular post-war character of stage & screen originally played by Arthur Lucan. But while the dress and circumstances were unusual, it was the manner and speed of the woman that convinced him that what he had seen was not normal. He estimated her speed as 6 or 7 mph, remarking that no-one could walk that fast; that an athlete would struggle to achieve this on what is a short, but significant uphill stretch to the Lower Bell. Rather, she seemed to glide effortlessly up the Hill.

The figure had not been transparent; it had been lit up by his headlights as well as those of the cars that followed her up the road. When asked if she seemed aware of her surroundings, Mr Gallagher said he gained no impression of fear from the woman—she appeared oblivious of the cars around her and determinedly proceeding on her own business.

In conclusion, Mr Gallagher said: 'I was an absolute cynic before, but I saw what I saw.' He added that friends of his who worked at the Aylesford Paper Mill (formerly Reeds) would drive the longer route around the back roads on their way home to Chatham rather than go via Blue Bell Hill.[8]

The first thing to note about Donald Gallagher's experience is the location: near to the Lower Bell crossroads, which was the scene of Jack Woodger's and Malcolm Grant's experiences in 1934 and 1967/8 respectively, and not far removed from the bend of the Rochester Road where Darren and Christine Green encountered a vanishing teenager in 1984 or 1985 (Chapter 9).

In Donald Gallagher's encounter the outstanding question is what the drivers of the other cars made of her as they followed her up the hill? Could they even see her—and if so, what happened next? We can only wonder.

Roll on four years, to the spring or summer of 1988, and around 1 a.m. of one weekday morning. Nick Norris of Maidstone and several friends were driving through the former Sandling roundabout (at Junction 6 of the M20) onto the uphill section of the A229, when they spotted the crouched form of an old woman by the roadside. She was sitting a little back from the road on the left, against a bank below the site of the former Veglios Motel site (now occupied by an Audi car dealership—see Chapter 7). The spot, despite the modifications made to the junction from 1992 and the construction of the showroom, is preserved alongside the northbound slip-road leading off the updated roundabout/flyover complex, where it is marked by an old cedar tree near to the entrance to the dealership.

The figure seemed oblivious to their presence, sitting with her arms crossed, with a bundle of some sort at her feet. She was dressed in dark clothing, with a hood and what looked like a brown shawl.

The location of the former Veglios Motel on the A229 on the outskirts of Maidstone

On this occasion there was no encounter, nothing to alarm the car's occupants—merely the unexpectedness of seeing someone dressed in that fashion and at that spot at such an early hour. It was over very quickly, but the event stuck in their minds said Nick because '... it shouldn't have been so.'[9]

John Arnold owns Ormonde Garage in Robin Hood Lane, in Blue Bell Hill Village. John grew up in the village, and today lives with his wife and three daughters on Kits Coty Estate. John ventures out with his Border Collie, or to go riding, on most days—but never has he experienced a repeat of the sighting he made with a former girlfriend late one summer's evening around 1990.

The couple had been out for the evening at the Running Horse at Sandling, on the outskirts of Maidstone. His girlfriend was driving, and they had come up by the old hill (Chatham Road) in their Mk 2 Escort—'that shows you how long ago it was'—and were approaching the section of road where a public footpath descends via a set of steep steps (on the left) to the top end of Kit's Coty field, when they saw an old lady on the side of the road ahead. Again, it was late—'definitely after the pubs had turned out'—11 p.m. to 11.30 p.m. The section of road here is unlit, the only light the faint glow from Maidstone behind, and the overspill from the oasis of light near the entrance to Salisbury road and the dual carriageway slip-road 200 metres up the road.

Chatham Road, in the vicinity of the public footpath steps (below), where the figure of an old woman has been seen shuffling across the road

The figure stood in the gloom on the right-hand side of the road, opposite the footpath steps. She did not turn toward them as they approached (at 'normal speed', typically 30–40 mph or so for here), but as they closed on her position, without warning she started across the road into their path.

John's girlfriend braked, stopping the car in front of her. The woman, who he estimated to have been 'about seventy', simply stood in the car's headlights and 'looked at us.' She had straw-coloured or 'yellowy' hair. Her clothing he could not recollect, but he noted that she carried what looked like a bunch of heather or lavender. She stared at them, and then continued across the road and disappeared down the pathway steps.

At the time, John had regarded the woman as simply a strange old lady. Other than the unusual circumstances of meeting her, which he described as 'surreal', there was nothing otherwise ghostly about her. It was only years later, when telling his daughters about it, and they 'Googled' Blue Bell Hill's ghost, that he discovered other accounts that tallied so well with his encounter. Summing up his experience, whatever it represented, he did not believe it was someone dressing up for a hoax.[10]

Paranormal author Neil Arnold adds a brief account of a figure seen at the same location in the early 1970s. It was in the early hours of the morning. The informant (unnamed), then a lorry driver, had started up the old road from the Lower Bell. Up ahead, before meeting the dual carriageway, in the region of the footpath steps, he saw a figure in a black cloak and hood walk from left to right across the road and disappear. When Neil related tales of the Hag, the gentleman and his wife said they had never heard of anything other than the woman in white. There had been something about the figure's form that suggested a female—it had reminded him, in fact, of the woman in the Scottish Widows television adverts.[11]

It is said there is safety in numbers. Unfortunately for the victims of the old woman, her most terrifying appearances seem to be reserved for parties of witnesses. So it was in the case of James Shoebridge and several friends who had a particularly chilling encounter with this frightening figure in January of 1990 or 1991. The encounter has much in common with the Maidens' and the Rayburns' experiences: it took place in January, between midnight and 1 a.m., but two or three years earlier, and at the foot of Blue Bell Hill, on the Rochester Road towards Aylesford—which places it closer to Donald Gallagher's sighting.

The four, who were then college students, had been for a Friday night out in Maidstone, and were returning home late, into the early hours of Saturday. James recalls it was a bitterly cold night, with some icy conditions. The driver of the car (a Fiat) was a male friend, Paul, and two girls were in the back; one of them at the time was asleep. One of the girls lived in Aylesford, and they had taken the somewhat circuitous route of travelling via Blue Bell Hill and heading down the Rochester Road from the Lower Bell. At the bottom of this short downhill stretch, the road (a two-lane country road) enters a sweeping left bend where it crosses Pilgrims' Way before straightening out again to run forward into Aylesford. Approximately 150 metres along this stretch, on the left, stand the jumbled Neolithic stones of Little Kit's Coty House. It was on this stretch, after taking the bend that James and the driver spied a figure up ahead:

> I saw someone standing up on the bank, on my side of the car (I was the front passenger). My friend, driving, said 'what is this idiot doing?' Now this is the bit that sounds like nonsense and fantastical, but the car just cut out, just stopped dead—everything, lights, dashboard.
>
> At this point my mate was effing and jeffing as he thought his car was dead. We slewed to a halt, sliding a bit on ice I think. I looked up and saw the 'figure' had moved into the road and was in front of the car. Again this bit sounds unbelievable but I swear what happened next really did happen. It was clearly an ancient looking woman. I can recall vividly her features. Her face was nut brown and looked like a prune; it was the most wrinkled countenance I have ever seen (and I'm a nurse and worked in old people's homes!). The next thing I recall was her eyes; they bored into me. I got an overwhelming sense of evil and malevolence. I can recall she wore a shawl or hood, with lank white hair hanging free over her face. She was clutching a bunch of twigs and she had a mouth opened in a black maw. The whole apparition (?) was accompanied by a horrible hissing sound that seemed to fill up the inside of the car. She looked like she wanted to hit the windscreen with her bunch of twigs but as she went to strike, she simply vanished, gone, like in a split second! The car then just kicked in and started.
>
> The whole encounter lasted probably a couple of minutes. In this time one of the girls was hysterical, screaming and trying to get out the car. I was terrified and badly shaken. My friend driving was in a state and swearing. The lass who was sleeping was woken by the screaming and shouting. The girl who became hysterical had hurt herself and was inconsolable. We had to literally drag her back into the car and took her to Medway Hospital. The police were involved by concerned staff as obviously our story seemed 'odd' to say the least.
>
> This is as much as I can recall and haven't attempted to embellish anything. I still get quite upset recalling this. I still don't like driving down this way either. Time has helped lessen the impact of that night, but it changed me from a skeptic forever.[12]

Additional details emerged from further correspondence, in which I attempted to ascertain a clearer idea as to precisely where this took place and how the figure came to be in front of the car:

Rochester Road, toward Aylesford, scene of James Shoebridge's terrifying encounter

I recall the car just going dead, and my friend panicking to avoid swerving into the 'woman' and it sliding on the ice. At this time the girl was screaming and trying to get out the car because the thing was looking in the windscreen.

I think it was just a little bit past Little Kits Coty. She certainly seemed elevated before she approached the car. In fact she looked like she was in the hedgerow if that makes sense. I'm now almost certain it was above the road…the headlights really didn't illuminate it very much. When we spotted it, it was as far as I can recall standing facing the opposite side like she was watching out across the way; it turned as we approached. The car cut out and then she was in front of the vehicle. It didn't step into the road. It just kind of was there after we saw it in the hedgerow.

It was able to look right in the windscreen and appeared bent a little. As to what she was wearing, I don't want to embellish or give false information, but it seemed like shawl and dress were one, tatty and dark. Jem was sure she (it) wore a tartan shawl, but me and the driver swore it was black. Also I think Jem said she (the thing) had something like a little skull of a little animal hanging in a braid. This I neither recall or can confirm so kept it out of the account. I DO remember the hideous mouth and lank white hair. These are burned on my brain forever!

The hissing noise came before she went to strike the car. I don't know if she paused because of screaming girls, swearing blokes and utter panic. I do know that after it happened we were trying to drag Sarah back into the car. When she was in, Paul sped-reversed up the road and into another road that seemed to be split by a large bank. Then back up the way we came.

We took Sarah to the hospital as she was screaming and had fallen out the car trying to run nowhere. At this point the car had started and bucked and stalled. The girl had hurt her fingers and hand (I assume) falling out the door and scrabbling to open it.

The police were called I think because the nurses were concerned that a group of people had turned up in an agitated state with a girl screaming and shouting that we had crashed into an old lady who wanted to hurt us.

The police took statements and examined the car. We know we didn't hit anything because the car stopped clear before the thing got close. My friend was breathalysed and obviously passed. I think they had a patrol car drive down that way.

It's not a thing I enjoy recalling as it was a truly terrifying experience. What I can say with certainty is that it had very dark skin and a face that was unbelievably wrinkled. I'm not even sure it was an apparition *per se*; it felt far more ancient and chilling than the ghost of some old girl should do.

It sounds really silly, but it's been two decades plus, but the feeling that what 'it' was is something that bore malice and wasn't human. I have been forever changed by it, like I know evil exists. But maybe that's just the years and my imagination forming something that can be somehow rationalized and made tangible. Maybe the terror of that night's events has remained and grown into a disproportionate sense of evil, but I don't think so. I know it meant us harm.

I appreciate the sheer fantastical nature of what I have told you, but I assure you it happened. I have often thought of telling someone in the 'field' so to speak, but the sheer magnitude of what I'd be asking someone to believe has thus far prevented me from doing so.[13]

James Shoebridge's experience took place at precisely the same spot as Darren and Christine Green's encounter with a vanishing teenager in 1984 or 1985. The circumstances are also strikingly similar; the Greens having also come off the A229 at the same turn-off, bound for Aylesford, where Christine then lived (a warning perhaps to anyone residing in that village!). In their case, the girl was standing in the road just after the bend, giving Darren Green little or no opportunity to avoid her.

The circumstances and behaviour of the ghost, similar in most respects save for the description of the figure—rather than suppose that two distinct apparitions happen to favour a similar modus operandi at the same location—hint at a deeper connection between the different personas in the Blue Bell Hill phenomenon.

Alan Matthews saw the old woman late one Saturday night (between 11.45 p.m.

and midnight) in September 1994. Alan, of Ashford, had been visiting a lady friend in Gillingham, whom he had left around 11.30 p.m. His homeward journey brought him down Blue Bell Hill. Approaching the Aylesford turn-off, he saw an elderly lady walking hurriedly along the verge of the main road.

'As I came down the road I saw an old lady who I took to be a gypsy. She had an old shawl over her, and the thing that stuck most in my mind was the long twigs she was carrying.

'I must say, I did not see her face. I carried on driving past, but thought somehow the situation did not seem right. Anyway, I returned home and told my family and simply carried on with life.

'I really never knew about the hag until I looked on your [web] site, and was amazed to read that a family had seen this old woman too. I was absolutely gobsmacked and just had to write to you.'[14]

Sightings of the old woman inevitably gave rise to suggestions (and not for the first time) that Blue Bell Hill is haunted by more than one ghost. ASSAP investigator David Thomas (see Chapter 8) heard that the ghost might be that of 'Paraffin Lynn', an old woman said to fit the description of the apparition, who used to wander over the dual carriageway in the region of the modern (Shell) petrol station, near to the scene of Colin Eacott's (and Ian Sharpe's) encounters.

One Blue Bell Hill Village resident told *Strange But True?*'s Daniel Barraclough that her husband had seen the apparition on two occasions near here. On one of these she had walked through the concrete uprights of the footbridge over the A229 (which holds some meaning for the dark form 'hit' by Jacquie Hopkins at that spot).

The fact that the dual carriageway has only been in existence since 1972 (this area was previously occupied by chalk quarries and lime kilns) suggested that Lynn's demise, and the start of her posthumous peregrinations, were fairly recent events—the former, we might imagine, a possible subject of record or living memory. Indeed, a lady who had lived on Kits Coty Estate for thirty-eight years, told me in 1995 that 'a long time ago', an old lady had lived in the woods at Blue Bell Hill.[15] Other versions hold her to have been a gypsy woman who sold pegs, or a former village resident of whom local children tended to be wary.

The above find recognition in the recollections of an elderly informant who grew up around Blue Bell Hill, regarding a reclusive old lady who lived near the Upper Bell until the 1950s. Known to some as 'Dirty Dolly', the lady habitually wore black and ventured out only for paraffin. She had a house full of cats, and perished in a fire that gutted the property.[16]

These anecdotes almost certainly recall the habits and sad death of Mrs Emmeline King, an eccentric 76-year-old lady who lived in a shack ('Elmo') in woodland in Victoria Road, Weeds Wood, Blue Bell Hill, and was found burned to death there on Sunday 28 January 1951. At the inquest at Aylesford the following Thursday, it was proposed that one of her six cats may have knocked over an oil stove, starting the fire. Firemen later found a number of oil stoves and lamps in the debris, plus three one-gallon paraffin cans. Dr. R. C. Ponder, who knew her well, stated that Mrs King kept her door locked and the windows boarded out of fear of Borstal boys, and spent part of the time in her chair brooding—in one report '... rather like a witch casting spells.'[17]

In Mrs King's lifetime, Victoria Road extended either side of Kit Hill. On its westward side (which is no longer in existence) it extended through Taddington Woods to meet the Maidstone–Chatham Road a little above the old Mission Hall at the northern end of Blue Bell Hill village (approximately where the entrance to the Blue Bell Hill car park in Lord Lees Grove is now situated). Mrs King's home would therefore have stood somewhere in the area now occupied by M2 junction 3 interchange.

Mrs King evidently presented something of a mysterious and forbidding character to the area's youngsters, which, together with her suitably tragic death, might mark her as a fitting candidate for the Hill's ghostly old woman. But whether she could account for the sightings in the lower reaches of Blue Bell Hill, two kilometres or more from her home, where the encounters with the ghostly old woman are concentrated, was open to question. Certainly, toward the end of her life, she was enfeebled and, according to her doctor, could only move at a slow rate.

As it would transpire, a far more compelling candidate for Blue Bell Hill's dark ghost would eventually come to light, from the same decade, who lived and died right at the epicentre of the sightings.

As with the ghost girl, those instances involving the old woman in which the figure was directly observed to vanish would seem to preclude such prosaic and reassuring explanations as hoaxing; and, on the strength of the testimony offered by the witnesses, lead us to conclude that they had likewise seen a ghost—the obvious corollary of which is that it is assumed to be the spirit of a human being. But unless the descriptions given by the Maidens and Rayburns in particular were overstated, it seems hard to reconcile such a frightening caricature with the spirit of a departed person, no matter how odd their character and habits in life. Indeed, the figure resembles more the kind of dark, non-human entities portrayed in mythology and folklore.

From Folklore to...Folklore

Throughout this entire study of Blue Bell Hill's ghost, it has been impossible to escape the shadow of folklore—which has been one reason that has prevented me from committing to any one interpretation of what people report seeing on Blue Bell Hill. We have seen that the encounters with the ghost girl, while persuasive in terms of their correspondences in detail and behaviour (in either Phantom Hitch-Hiker or Spectral Jaywalker 'mode'), still quite clearly obey the conventions set out in the PHH folk versions—which begs some explanation. Intriguingly, a similar pattern and behaviour is repeated in the encounters with the old woman, which again suggests that there is more to it all than purely 'human' factors such as imagination or hoaxing, but a very strange game played out to a particular set of rules:

- These encounters (with the exception of Colin Eacott's and Donald Gallagher's experiences) occurred very late, between around 11.30 p.m. and 1 a.m.—approximately within the time-frame that describes the majority of encounters at Blue Bell Hill (and a number elsewhere).
- The locations described coincide with places where the 'ghost girl' has also been encountered—most significantly the Chatham Road in the vicinity of Kit's Coty Cottage; the footbridge area and the dual carriageway before the Aylesford turn-off; the Rochester road between Pilgrims' Way and the Lower Bell; and the foot of the Hill by the site of the former Veglios Motel.
- The figure attracts the attention of passing vehicles by standing in the middle of the road, but rather than seeking a lift and vanishing from the vehicle or running into its path, it occasions a deliberate and possibly more profound horror through its onslaught of the vehicle's occupants.

The principal difference is that, unlike the Phantom Hitch-Hiker or the Spectral Jaywalker, which vanishes without being directly observed, the old woman seems to have no objection in this regard, vanishing in full view of groups of witnesses.

It should not, then, be surprising to find that the old woman, like the girl 'accident victim', should have its Hitch-Hiker counterpart. Indeed, to take the converse (and perhaps, proper) view, the old woman and the young girl could be regarded as the pedestrian counterparts of the Phantom Hitch-Hiker.

In folk terms, our primary interest in this case has been restricted to Beardsley's and Hankey's Versions A and C Phantom Hitch-Hikers, which describe the habits of the young blonde woman in white. It may be recalled, however, that these were but two of the four types recognised by these workers. To take the last first, Version D was defined as a local deity (which will be seen also to have some relevance, as we shall see). Version B, however, is said to take the form of a darkly prophetic old woman, frequently dressed in dark clothing, who characteristically issues dire warnings before vanishing.

As his primary example of the Version B Hitch-hiker, Michael Goss cited a German case, the experience of a 43-year-old businessman at Greifnau (Grafenau) near the border with Austria in 1975. According to *The News of the World* of 13 April 1975,[18] the encounter caused a wave of hysteria in the local community, prompting the local police chief, Captain Siegfried Eismann, to threaten prosecutions and heavy fines for drivers who repeated the stories. The witness, who is unnamed in the newspaper account, told a local newspaper that he was stopped at midnight by a person he took to be a hitch-hiker.

'She was a weird-looking old woman, dressed in black. She waved at me. So I stopped the car and she asked for a lift.'

The woman took the seat next to him. Ignoring the driver's questions, she murmured that something evil would happen. When he looked next, the woman had vanished. The shock was so great he almost crashed into an oncoming vehicle. Others claimed similar experiences. Some reported that the woman had vanished as they opened the car door; others that she had sat silently beside them before vanishing.

The Griefnau encounter (which itself is strongly reminiscent of the German folktale of the basket-carrying old woman who climbs uninvited onto farmers' wagons as they drive home alone at night) leads us to ponder what might have befallen the Maidens and the Rayburns at Blue Bell Hill had they responded to the old woman's beckoning and stopped to offer her a lift instead of fleeing at the sound of her scalding hiss.

The old woman crops up elsewhere, in folklore and in 'fact'—for instance, in the figure described in Terence Whitaker's *Ghosts & North Country Legends* that is said to haunt the lanes around Longridge, in Lancashire. In this case, the old woman seen hobbling along in her shawl and bonnet, and carrying a basket under her arm, is said to be the masquerade of a 'boggart' (or *bargaist*—a term applied in the North of England to shape-shifting, mischievous and fickle sprites). Here, the old woman is said to walk quietly alongside persons trying to pass her, even listening politely to their conversation. Suddenly, she would turn on her companion, revealing the absence of a head inside her bonnet, which emerges from her basket as she pulls back its cloth, it 'shrieking with demonic laughter' as it chases the appalled and terrified victim down the lane.[19]

In 1905, in Birkenhead, the stooping figure of an elderly woman dressed in black and wearing a grey shawl and dark bonnet was seen on several occasions in Woodchurch Road; on two occasions a cyclist was forced to brake hard to avert a collision.[20] In the West Country, an old gypsy woman is said to stagger across the

A363 Bathford to Bradford-on-Avon road at the woody hill-section known as Sally-in-the-Wood, a spot known for vehicles plunging off the road and for rumours also of a ghostly girl in white who runs from the woods to be knocked down by passing vehicles.[21] While in Cumbria, a gypsy woman is occasionally seen in the house and grounds of, and on the road and bridge (A6) outside Levens Hall, near Kendal. On several occasions, members of the Bagot family, the hall's owners, have gone out to investigate the sound of heavy braking outside the hall to find drivers claiming they had to take evasive action when a figure had come out in front of their vehicle.[22]

While each of the above examples targets a single subject or witness as in the 'standard' Hitch-Hiker script, another fascinating facet of the encounters with the old woman at Blue Bell Hill is her habit of frequently appearing to multiple witnesses, to car loads of people and families—a feature, the reader may recall, that emerged in Beardsley's and Hankey's study of the Version B Hitch-Hiker (Chapter 5).

Removing the detail of the modern transport in the Greifnau case, we might easily be recounting an encounter with one of the Weird Sisters, that trio of withered supernatural hags that stopped the way of Macbeth and Banquo to prophesy to them on the heath road to Forres.[23] Indeed, Macbeth's witches are echoed in Blue Bell Hill's three legendary witches, who were said to have constructed Kit's Coty House (Chapter 2).

This mix of accounts demonstrates how the boundaries between 'fact' and 'fiction' can become blurred in such cases, often without the modern witness being aware of the significance of the recurrent 'folkloric' elements that feature in their reports.

The bizarre, negatively charged encounters with the old woman were bound again to raise ideas of a connection between the phenomenon at Blue Bell Hill and its ancient sites, or to arcane practices—which, as we have seen, is not a new one. In 1974, Nigel Nelson noted that the A229 runs across the sites of numerous prehistoric graves, 'several of which are known to be connected with occult practices.'[24]

One source told me that a cottage attached to Kits Coty Estate, which was located near to the flight of steps that provide public access from Chatham Road down into Kit's Coty field (close to the scene of the sightings of the old woman), had been built on the site of a former cottage, which in turn had been built over an arrangement of sarsen stones, which the owners were not permitted to disturb. The site was said to be so haunted that people would not go near it. An elderly gentleman, who, until his death the previous year (1993), had lived here and reportedly claimed it to be the 'oddest place'—an observation that tallies with the view of the Kit's Coty Cottage resident who told Angela Maiden that strange things happened outside her house. The gentleman's pet dog would never go outside in the dark.[25]

For the sake of completeness, it can be added that Diane Rayburn's uncle had apparently seen 'the ghost' in his field, which lies immediately behind Kit's Coty Cottage, and adjoins Kit's Coty field.

The impression that some of the unusual (and undefined) activity is the result of arcane practices was bolstered one night in May or June of one year when a local man heard noises emanating from Kit's Coty field. Making his way down to investigate he saw a group of people dancing around the stones, which 'shook him up a bit'.[26]

While such an unfamiliar sight might be unnerving to impartial onlookers, we need not look to witchcraft or sinister rites to find an explanation. Kit's Coty House, an English Heritage site, is visited by a surprising number of people, particularly in the spring and summer months. It is easy to misinterpret the largely innocuous activities of certain groups for something more sinister, particularly after dark, and since Blue Bell Hill's fame has been spread abroad.

Local religious groups known collectively as the Odinic Rite ('Odinists'), whose costume dress might very well give the wrong impression to outsiders, similarly identify with the Neolithic sites. In 1993, they spoke out in defence of one important site, the White Horse Stone (located behind the Cossington service station), which was threatened by one planned route of the Channel Tunnel rail-link.[27] Finally, there is Kit's Coty Morris, a Maidstone-based Morris dancing side (see Chapter 2), who take their name from Blue Bell Hill's ancient stone sites, and whose May Day custom might very well explain some of these 'sightings'.

As an aside, further back in time, in 1887, a correspondent to the *South Eastern Gazette* related the following strange story:

> Returning homeward on Jubilee night up Blue Bell-hill, I noticed a queer light around Kit's Coty House, and, approaching it curiously discovered, the figure of a quaintly draped, white-haired, long-bearded, old man seated thereon. How on earth he got over the railings and on to the top of the stone I have not the least idea; and if this were not sufficiently astonishing his subsequent antics were marvelous enough. He tugged his beard and cracked his fingers and kicked his heels against the stone in almost boyish fashion, and then exclaiming 'Old Times' jumped upon the top of the cromlech and began a grave and stately dance, making occasional obeisances to the beacon fires which were blinking around. Just as I was beginning to feel creepy he shouted 'The solstice! The solstice,' and, as I was about to speak to him, took a header right on to the top of me, falling like a waggon-load of flints. I became insensible and was discovered at sunrise by a

> member of the county constabulary.
>
> The officer looked suspicious, but was convinced by my later explanation of the phenomenon. I remembered that, by a curious coincidence, the Druids lighted their religious fires on the hill tops at the time of the summer solstice, June 21st, the very day of the Jubilee. I concluded, therefore, that I had met with an original member of the A.O.D., who had been made lively by the surrounding fires.[28]

The stones and the Hill have evidently attracted some odd ones in their time!

… to Fact

For years, it seemed possible to consider the sightings of the old woman only within the context of Folklore, as part of the Phantom Hitch-Hiker story cycle, and within the context of the wider pool of folk stories and myth—all of which is certainly relevant, perhaps even essential, to gaining any kind of meaningful understanding of the case as a whole. It is an idea we will return to shortly.

At the same time, it is possibly less satisfying to have to rely on what many of us might think of as a fiction to find meaning behind real, reported events. Unlike the ghost girl, whose sightings had found plausible connection with a real life tragedy (whether the 1965 crash or the murder of Emily Trigg), the sightings of the old woman (if we were to disregard the later identification of Emmeline King) appeared to lack such a real life foundation.

That all changed in 2006. In February of that year I received the first of several fascinating emails from a gentleman who related his childhood recollections of a former resident of the Hill, an old lady whose described appearance and habits bore an uncanny resemblance to the ghostly old woman. In that correspondence, Nigel D., of East Sussex, related his own experiences at Blue Bell Hill:

> Bluebell hill has certainly changed dramatically, though not unrecognizably so, since we used to live there with my aunts in the mid fifties. My two brothers and I spent many of the school holidays staying in an old Romany caravan that my aunts had bought for £16 and put at the bottom of their garden at Kits Coty Cottage. The caravan has long since gone and the character of the cottage and gardens has changed considerably since those days, but one can still see the spot where the caravan once stood, by the gate that leads directly onto the footpath that runs down to Kits Coty Stones. These holidays, between 1955 and 1961, will always rank as amongst the most enjoyable, and in one case, certainly the most memorable experiences in my life.
>
> I have no tales of a phantom hitch-hiker but certainly have a personal experience that I can only describe as supernatural and another that, after reading your most interesting website, although at the time we never considered supernatural

as such, certainly may have some relevance to some of the accounts recorded on your pages.

I shall start by telling of a rather weird woman who lived close by and whom I had all but forgotten until I read your account of 'Hekate'.[29] When my aunts first moved to Kits Coty, one of their first callers was a Mrs A----. She was a strange, almost deranged woman of about 60,[30] who had vividly dyed red hair, and long and flowing old-fashioned clothing. She knocked at the front door of Kits Coty Cottage and offered for sale some daffodils. She explained that she normally sold them for half a crown, but said that she was offering them to my aunts for one shilling as a welcoming gesture. My aunts were quite touched and bought the flowers. They were subsequently rather amused when they discovered she had picked them from their own front garden. They later learned it was her frequent habit to raise money by such means and with the funds she would walk into Maidstone and spend it at The Flower Pot, a pub on the northern outskirts of the town.

There were many rumours circulating about Mrs A---- : that she was to be seen standing on the top of Kits Coty Stones on the night of a full moon, wearing nothing but a long night gown and her dishevelled red hair blowing wildly in the wind. There were other tales of her prowling the local area at night and that she was guarding some dreadful secret. We certainly never saw her on the stones, although we waited and watched on more than one occasion. We did see her on one occasion, however, running across the Kits Coty field at night. I well remember the strange figure she presented silhouetted against the night sky-line.

On another occasion we encountered her in the disused quarries on the other side of the road. Several of us were rambling at dusk or thereafter and she was standing on a chalk promontory. When she saw us she screeched at us in an almost unworldly manner, '*Go home, go home, go home.*' We were really quite scared on that occasion.

One evening she was caught in a heavy shower whilst walking home from the Flower Pot, she apparently caught a chill and died of pneumonia soon after. There were no tales of her ghost haunting the area and, before long, we had all but forgotten her.

In 1960 I stayed at the caravan with a school friend quite late in the summer holidays. We spent our days catching lizards, slow worms and snakes, with which then the district well abounded, to sell to classmates when we returned to school. In the evenings we roamed the lanes and fields and quarries after maybe a half a pint of illicit ginger beer shandy at the Lower Bell.

It was on one of those evenings [that] I experienced the one certain supernatural experience of my life. We were in the same quarry that we'd once encountered Mrs A----; this was about adjacent to the Georgian red bricked building called Kits Coty House and quite certainly on the spot where the dual carriageway now runs. We had been roaming for some time and it was dusk, but not dark. My friend Malcolm was quite startled by a strange object, about three times the size of a football, which had passed across his vision, behind me and about two feet off the ground. We conjectured for some time as to what he had seen; shadow or lights from a passing car going down the hill?

We could think of no rational cause and soon continued on our jaunt. I think we would have completely forgotten this incident were it not for something happened some little while later. We had come to a chalk ledge with a four foot or so drop, which had a mass of soft gravelly chalk at the base. We discovered it was fun to jump from the ledge and slide on our bottoms down the soft chalk below. We had completed this procedure several times and were taking it in turns to run back up to the top to have another jump. It was when I reached the bottom for the fourth or fifth time that I saw it. Malcolm was at the top, awaiting his turn, and I had arrived, spread legged at the bottom. As I came to a stop he appeared in my vision, about four metres in front of me and three to the left: a figure, a man, a shadow of man, I can't quite describe. I could see not one feature of his face. Nevertheless I knew that he was running with his head turned looking over his right shoulder and looking behind him. I can only say it was conveyed to me that he was in mortal fear and was pursued by something or someone that threatened his life. He ran two, three or four stumbling strides; his arms seemed to lope loosely down by his sides. Then, about two or three metres to the right of my vision he seemed to stumble over a branch or some such and faded from my sight.

Malcolm had landed next to me and I was sitting there bemused and open mouthed. Though I lost touch with Malcolm some years ago, we recounted this experience many times. This was long before rumours of hauntings on Bluebell Hill and for some years after we would go back with friends on dark nights to try to replicate the experience. I never saw anything remotely strange again there or anywhere else!

I would finally like to refer to one other incident that happened before. This would have been 1955 or 1956. I should say first that the Hill, particularly just below the cottage was, even then, notorious for car accidents; 'though I don't believe I ever heard of any of them being fatal. But my aunts were always talking of selling up and leaving because they were so frequently distressed by the sound of screeching tyres preceding the inevitable crash during the night. Yet another motorist had misjudged the start of the long left hand bend that starts at the cottage and continues down to the Lower Bell.

On one such occasion when my brothers and I were in the cottage we heard the familiar sound followed some five minutes later by a knock on the door. A very distressed motorist had made the usual misjudgement whilst going down the road and had crossed the road and had hit a pedestrian who was walking up the road on the footpath; the problem was he couldn't find them down the embankment where they must have been thrown.[31] Several of us went out with torches and

> scoured the area but could find nothing nor any trace of an accident. I don't believe this happened as late as midnight but then, I have to say that this memory would have remained dormant forever if I hadn't read your pages. I don't believe I have thought of it once until this time. I hope that these accounts, which certainly predate the fatal car accident of the 1960s, will be of some interest even if the sum of the parts is better than the whole.[32]

In a subsequent email, and in answer to my request, Nigel gave Mrs A's surname. While the details presented here will enable determined readers to discover her true identity, as this has not previously been given as a matter of public record, I have chosen to withhold it here—even if, as Nigel believed, she had no children and therefore no direct descendants. As it is, her identification makes little difference to the accounts per se, but inevitably, the proof that there was such a person adds to the credibility of the later stories, and offers further clues toward our understanding of what may be happening at Blue Bell Hill. For ease of reading, I will from here refer to her by the pseudonym Ash*.

Since his first email, Nigel had contacted his two brothers to discuss their memories of Blue Bell Hill, which had yielded additional details. The first thing to come out of this was a correction to Nigel's estimated age for Mrs Ash. Nigel's brothers suggested that she had been nearer seventy than sixty. She was married to a kind old gentleman who did odd jobs, including some gardening, for their aunts, who got to know the couple fairly well. Not infrequently, their aunts gave Mrs Ash a lift into Maidstone when they saw her waiting at the bus stop at the Lower Bell or walking the few miles into town. Both were health visitors based at County Hall in Maidstone. Mrs Ash would have them drop her off on the Sandling road a little past the Flower Pot, or sometimes outside County Hall itself, at the head of Week Street. But her true destination was thinly disguised; they saw her double back in that direction or later emerge from the pub on several occasions.

> Although of a somewhat withdrawn and taciturn disposition, Mrs A. left my aunts in little doubt that she regarded herself as some sort of self-appointed guardian of Blue Bell Hill: by that we always assumed that meant Kits Coty and the Countless Stones further down the hill.
>
> There is one final slight mystery to relate which, although rather obscure, as it has some indirect reference to Mrs A., I shall mention it now. A year or two after her death (certainly no more) Mr A. called at our cottage rather late one night. He was a very nice old chap with a waxed moustache and always wearing leather gaiters; apparently his military excursion to South Africa was only time in his life that he had ever been outside Kent. He came up the back garden at Kits Coty Cottage

> and called at the kitchen door. He had apparently seen some lights down in the Kits Coty field and asked my aunts if any of 'the boys' were down there with torches. We weren't, but obviously we were into our Wellington boots in no time at all and following him back down to the field.
>
> He related as to how, when walking up the north side of the field he had heard what sounded like children's voices in the trees on the west side. He had then seen what had appeared to be a face (no body), as if a torch was being held directly under the chin. We stood with him a little way in at the north end as he described how this apparently disembodied face had made its way across the field and had disappeared behind the stones. We stayed there for half an hour or more but I'm afraid that there was no encore performance for us and it remained forever as a mysterious adventure and nothing more. The only remaining curiosity for us was that the course the 'face' took across the field was exactly that which we had seen Mrs A. take when we had witnessed her night-time capering in the field several years before.[33]

For a fitting conventional candidate to account for the sightings of the old woman (i.e. a deceased person with a proven connection to the area), we need surely to look no further than Mrs Ash. Her age, her style of dress, her bizarre behaviour, and such eccentric details as the clutch of flowers she sold for drinking money and the association with the Hill's ancient sites, find remarkable recognition in the ghostly encounters years after her death—and perhaps make some sense of those sightings reported some distance away down the Hill, as in Nick Norris's case near the junction with the M20 motorway (and to some degree, the associations with the early versions of the ghost story with Maidstone's Week Street).

But further investigation was to reveal further impressive correspondences. Mr and Mrs Ash lived at The Helm, a property that was located immediately to the right (north) of the steps down to Kit's Coty field. The steps themselves led down to the main entrance to the property. Mrs Ash died here on 7 February 1955, aged 72, from pneumonia, as my correspondent Nigel indicated.[34] Mr Ash lived there until his death in 1965 at the age of 80.[35] The property itself no longer exists; the site is now occupied by a new private residence of the same name.

Two former residents of the Hill were to later relate their memories of Mrs Ash. Mr Pat Sandford, whose family owned and operated the chalk quarries above the Lower Bell that were later exploited in the construction of the dual carriageway, recalled that she had flame-red hair and wore a black fur coat. Her husband was known as Teddy.[36]

Brian Culver moved back to the Hill, to Kits Coty Estate, in the 1970s after living away for a decade. Brian's family has a long history of residence at Blue Bell Hill. Kit's Coty Cottage, for instance, located on the bend approximately a hundred metres down the road from The Helm, was the Culvers' family home since the 1800s. His grandfather was born there. As a youth in the late 1940s, Brian knew the Ashs quite well, visiting them on many occasions on errands for his parents. He knew them as Ted and Annie. 'Annie', he said, 'was always known as 'old Ginger Ash' because she tried to dye her hair red—but she was not very good at it.' Their house then was a wooden construction, with a glass-fronted verandah, which, before the war, Annie had used to run as a tea-room.

Brian said that Mrs Ash was certainly eccentric. In their large garden, which ran down the footpath to Queenswood Road, she maintained a rockery full of old pieces of pottery, the centrepiece to which was a broken toilet pan. On one occasion, he recalled, she had 'a go' at his mother after he and a cousin had been throwing old apples at the rockery to try to knock the plates over. In his view, though, she was 'OK'.

Francies Moore contributes an anecdote from this period, which involved her parents who, on a visit to Kit's Coty in 1948 encountered a lady who can only have been Mrs Ash:

> My Mum and Dad visited Kits Coty in 1948. At that time it was not in the care of the Ministry of Works/Dept of the Environment/English Heritage and there were no railings. My mother actually stood beneath the capstone!
>
> She remembers Blue Bell Hill itself as just a narrow lane with trees on one side and just a high hedge on the dolmen side. She says it all combined to give it a creepy air.
>
> The path down to the dolmen was just an overgrown little track, and there was a gap in the hedge. There is (or was) a bungalow near the stones which when I went in the 1970s was inhabited by the Dept of the Environment curator. However at the time my parents went, it was obviously in private hands.
>
> As they approached the bungalow through the gap in the hedge this elderly lady appeared out of the bungalow. She had a bashed-in old hat on and was wearing a very large apron tied round her neck and completely covering her. She was wandering down her garden with a bucket which contained either cement or plaster of Paris. There was a grassy track between the bungalow and a bank, and on the bank were many statues. Mum can't remember what they actually were, but they were figures of some sort.
>
> She greeted my parents with: 'I makes 'em all meself!'
>
> And that was it. They didn't stop to converse and she was intent on her sculptures.[37]

Back to Brian Culver: 'Annie always dolled herself up on a Friday, complete with fox fur and bright red lipstick; then off to Maidstone where she frequented the

'Gin Palace', as it was known (real name: the Red Lion), which occupied the corner of Week St and High Street.'[38] Ted, and Brian's father and the Culver family, used the Lower Bell.[39]

Why it was that Mrs Ash chose the pubs of Maidstone over the local ones can only be conjectured, but it is not hard to imagine that had she been partial to a tipple, she may have chosen to remove herself from the scrutiny of her neighbours to the less conspicuous surroundings of the Flower Pot or the Red Lion. Or maybe this was not her choice. Regardless of the true reason, it would have been uncommon in the early 1950s for a woman to frequent pubs unaccompanied, and this detail adds another facet to the picture of quirkiness we can form of her.

One puzzling detail given by Brian Culver, however, is the name 'Annie'. Official records (including her marriage and death certificates) give Mrs Ash's first name as Elsie.[40] Brian could not account for this; to him, she was always Annie Ash. This discrepancy will likely remain unresolved, but the name has some passing significance in the Blue Bell Hill story. It may be recalled that it was one given by psychic Nella Jones during her brief sojourn on the Hill in 1992 (Chapter 8), and it will arise again for discussion later in this chapter.

Accident

Before we move on to discuss the implications and significance of the old woman within the Blue Bell Hill case as a whole (whether it is Mrs Ash or not), we will briefly return to Nigel D's own experience of the early 1960s in the former chalk pits near the Lower Bell.

The three main pits—roughly C-shaped in plan and resembling bite marks out of the chalk hillside—on the eastern side of the old road, together with their lime kilns, were closed in 1970 and were subsequently demolished to make way for the laying of the new A229 dual carriageway. Of the two located nearest to Kit's Coty House (the Georgian brick building, then owned by Pat Sandford's 'Uncle Ern' (Ernest) and now occupied by Kits Coty Brasserie), the lower (and largest) was the original pit. Its site is now occupied by the cliff-section of road that was the scene of Colin Eacott's sighting of the old woman in 1991 and Ian Sharpe's encounter in 1992. Its southern extremities extended to the western side of the new road to where the northbound Shell petrol station and Mickey's Diner now stand. Part of the second quarry survives above Kits Coty Brasserie, where it today houses Lower Bell Industrial Estate. The third, smaller pit was located further up, opposite Salisbury Road.

It was in one of the two older quarries that Nigel and his childhood friend Malcolm witnessed both the odd football-shaped object, and the shadow-like apparition of a stumbling man. It was also here that Nigel and his brothers had had the unnerving experience of Mrs Ash screeching at them.

The apparitional figure of a running man presents something quite different for Blue Bell Hill, although it might broadly be taken to relate to the general pattern of ghostly encounters. The location, for instance, could not be better, it being a familiar one with several later phantom encounters on the road; while the awkward, loosely hanging limbs are a sometime reported feature of other road ghost encounters.[41]

Mindful that in the long history of the quarries (over 130 years under the ownership of the Sandford family) it would be unusual if accidents or fatalities had not occasionally occurred, I asked Pat Sandford if anyone had ever been killed there. It transpired that a fatal accident had occurred there—the only such incident in the pits' history—in 1948.

The accident, which was reported by the newspapers on Friday 19 November (the same day and date that would prove fateful for a pre-wedding party of young women in 1965), happened on the morning of the previous Tuesday (16 November), when a man and a boy were killed when ten tons of chalk crumbled away from the quarry face above where they were working. The incident happened some distance away from the main workings, where a small section of quarry was used by private contractors to dig their own soft chalk, which was taken away to be used as lime on farms. The force of the chalk fall broke the back of the tipper truck on which they stood, burying them both. The man was William Edward Bellward, 41, a private haulage contractor from Sittingbourne, who was married with five children. The boy was 16-year-old Donald Ray Foster, a keen cyclist, also of Sittingbourne, who had been working with Mr Bellward for only a short time. Although nearby workmen freed the pair within minutes, both were found to be dead.[42]

At the inquest, held on the Friday (19 November), it was heard that contractors were forbidden to work in that part of the quarry, the north side, for danger of undermining the road into the main quarry, which ran close to the face here. Bellward had been so-warned by the quarry's foreman, Edward Goodayle, around ten minutes before the fall, and had been previously warned by the pit owner, Mr E. H. Sandford (Pat's father), only four days before. Bellward had been going to the pit since the start of the war.

On the morning of the tragic accident, another driver, William Henry Eddy, also of Sittingbourne, had arrived late at the quarry, and found the usual loading spots occupied. The prescribed manner of loading, attested Mr Sandford, was to make a chute from the top of the bank and work down to a ledge about the height of the lorry, with one man standing on the slope to shovel and scrape the chalk down. Bellward had called him over to work on the north side of the small quarry, where there was an overhang of chalk. He did so, but was wary of the face, but bowed to Bellward's longer experience. He had not been working long when he saw the foreman warn Bellward. Not long after, he decided to 'clear out'. Before he moved away, he heard Bellward shout, 'Look out!' Before he could turn, the chalk had collapsed. 'Bellward's working appeared to me to render it unsafe,' he said. Bellward died from multiple injuries, and Foster from head injuries. The jury returned a verdict of 'accidental death'.[43]

Pat Sandford placed the scene of the accident where Mickey's Diner now stands. Nigel D's sighting could not have been far away from this spot, and it does therefore seem conceivable that the two events are related.

Before leaving the quarry, there is one further incident that is worthy of mention. While it does not qualify as a pit accident per se, in that it involved a fatal fall from the quarry perimeter rather than an employee or contractor at work in the pit itself, it is one that may hold some significance for those sightings in the case's history that describe a figure of a young girl.

On the afternoon of Saturday 18 August 1900, a nine-year-old child was found at the bottom of the chalk pit after an apparent fall of around forty-five feet. She was Kate Olive Gadd, the young daughter of Stephen Horace Gadd, a resident of Blue Bell Hill. The child's grandmother told the inquest at West Kent General Hospital, Maidstone, the following Monday evening, that her son and the girl lived with her (Mr Gadd's wife was dead). She had been playing at home until around 3 p.m., and was found to be missing at 3.30 p.m. when Mrs Gadd wanted her home to run an errand. When she hadn't appeared by tea time, Mrs Gadd began a search, assisted by two other girls, one her own daughter, who spotted the girl at the bottom of the pit, just 150 yards from her cottage home.

The land above the quarry belonged to a Mr Brassey of Aylesford. It was confirmed that no part of the cliff had given way. A strip of fir wood separated the cottage from the pit, with several paths running through it, which evidently were made by children playing there. The edge of the pit itself was unprotected, as no-one had any right to be on the land. How the girl came to be there no-one could say. The bank above the pit had wild flowers growing on it. Kate would often play by herself and was fond of chasing butterflies.

The girl's father was found outside the Lower Bell at 6.30 p.m., and rushed to the spot, where he found her unconscious, but warm and breathing. At Maidstone Hospital, however, she was found to have severe internal head injuries, from which she succumbed.

The inquest recorded a verdict of 'accidental death', and stipulated that the owner of the land above the cliff should be requested to provide a fence, or to put up an appropriate warning notice.[44]

It is impossible to relate the death of this young girl at the turn of the twentieth century with any certainty to the sightings of a young female figure encountered by Maurice Goodenough and other motorists over seventy years later, but it is interesting that such a tragedy should have occurred in relatively close proximity to where the phantom figure was later encountered.

Daylight

Early in 2011, I received an email from Andy Reeds of Gillingham regarding an experience he had had around 2001 while he was driving southbound along the A229 Maidstone Road near to Rochester Airport towards Bridgewood, approximately a mile-and-a-half north of Blue Bell Hill.

Andy, of Gillingham, has a career background in the Army, and is a founding partner of a company that provides public relations training, consultancy and media-related services to a variety of governmental, military and corporate clients. He is therefore someone we might expect to be pragmatic and no-nonsense. At the time, he had not heard of Hill's ghost, and even later, after stumbling over my website, had discounted his sighting as related to it as it had happened some distance from Blue Bell Hill.

Andy's description of the figure, however, and its behaviour finds ready familiarity with the other accounts related in this chapter. But what makes Andy Reeds' sighting particularly interesting is that it happened on a busy road in broad daylight. The time of year is uncertain—anywhere between late spring and October (when the family moved for a time to Wiltshire). It was, however, most likely a Saturday. The road and the shopping complex he had just passed (the Horsted Retail Park) were very busy. The day was bright and clear. Andy had just crossed the roundabout southbound by the Tiger Moth pub at the corner of Shirley Avenue, and was driving forward in the outside lane when he realised there was an elderly lady walking toward him down the white line:

> I swerved and just missed her but when I looked up (probably one hundred yards or so later) there was no sign of her. It shook me and I thought that she was probably a bit gaga. However that evening when I sat and thought about it I realised that she was completely grey from head to foot. An elderly lady in the dress of the early 20th Century (I particularly remember the Mary Poppins type shoes), she was so solid that at the time I was convinced she was real.

In follow-up correspondence, Andy was able to provide additional detail:

> Thinking it through in more detail and discussing it with my wife and daughter, it was a bit further up the road than I initially remembered. I was travelling at a

good 40 mph when I saw her, which means I had gone at least 200 metres from the roundabout to have enabled me to have built up that level of speed. They both reminded me that I said at the time it was in line with a turn off to the left into a housing estate and before you get around the corner to the Asda superstore [this will be Watson Avenue, opposite the Holiday Inn Hotel].[45] I remember thinking it was such an odd spot to cross the road. However she wasn't crossing the road, she was walking down it towards the roundabout (and me), apparently unaware of the traffic flashing past her. She was about a quarter of the way into the fast line from the centre line of the road (I was in the right hand lane). Hence my shock and only just being able to swerve to avoid her (narrowly missing clipping the curb).

Having recovered control (probably within 5 seconds or so) I looked in the mirror and could not see her. The other thing that struck me was that for a moment I was sure that one of the cars behind me must have hit her but they seemed to all be driving normally.

She was probably only in my view for perhaps 10–15 seconds. I would have said that she was in her late sixties or seventies and was dressed in a way that I would associate with Victorian dress of the working or poorer class. I thought her elderly but relatively upright in stance. I think she had an odd hat (possibly a bonnet) and her hair was long but tucked up beneath whatever she had on her head. I thought that she had gloves and possibly a shawl. A fairly shapeless long dress

The A229 toward the Tiger Moth roundabout. Andy Reeds was driving southbound (towards the camera)

> and I distinctly remember her shoes which reminded me of Mary Poppins. Her feet were just visible below the hem of her dress.
>
> At the time it happened I was just shocked at such a near miss and thought that perhaps she was suffering from dementia or something similar and didn't realise where she was (she took no notice of the traffic at all). I watched the local papers and listened for news of an elderly lady being hit by a car but there was nothing reported.

When Andy recollected the incident to his wife prior to writing back to me, she told him she recalled it clearly as he had been so shaken up by it, and couldn't stop talking about it—a normal, understandable reaction whether the woman were real or supernatural. I asked him if he thought whether, her attire aside, the woman could conceivably have been a real flesh-and-blood person and somehow edged out of sight in the few seconds before he could look back. The location would seem to preclude this—here the road is a dual carriageway, straight, with a grassy central reservation and unobstructed views in both directions.

> Yes, somebody could pull off a stunt like that and dive back into the side of the road or the central reservation but it would be an incredibly reckless and dangerous thing to do, and I would have thought that I would have seen her.
>
> When I saw her she was very close, perhaps 20 metres in front of me, leaving me virtually no time to react. I had assumed that the other cars ahead of me had masked her from my view until it was almost too late but then thinking about it, they didn't swerve either, which was very odd. There was no easy answer such as 'the car went through her'. That would have made it much easier to work out what was going on.
>
> One of my first thoughts was that she could have been someone on her way to a fancy dress event in Rochester such as the Sweeps Festival, but it just didn't fit. For some time after it happened I just couldn't believe that somebody would do something so stupid, but by that evening I had calmed down and thought it through more rationally. Ideas and possibilities were discounted as my wife and I sat there talking about it but then I distinctly remember having a 'eureka' moment when I said, 'She was grey, that's weird'. You would think I would have noticed something that obvious at the time. The only thing I can put it down to is that I was totally focused on missing her and not wrecking the car and as a result I put that information to one side mentally.
>
> Even with the realisation that she was grey from head to foot, it took a lot longer before I finally concluded that she had to have been a ghost of some kind. The problem was that it contradicted what I know of ghosts. I just couldn't believe that something like that might be visible in full daylight. It was only later that I thought it through, discounted all the options and concluded that the only likely

answer was that it was some kind of ghostly manifestation.[46]

What should we make of Andy Reeds' sighting? His description of the figure and her behaviour finds ready comparison with Donald Gallagher's experience in particular, and with the known appearance and habits of Mrs Ash. In principle, it makes some sense to include this figure (taking it to be a real apparitional sighting) with those clustered at Blue Bell Hill than to suppose it represents an unrelated apparition. The road here, after all, is the A229, and we know also of Mrs Ash's penchant for travelling some distance from her home. Not far from the scene of Andy Reeds' experience—indeed he had passed it when negotiating the roundabout further back—is the Tiger Moth pub. The old woman was walking in that direction. Could she have been heading for the pub, which is less than two miles from her home? It might be considered characteristic of Mrs Ash to do so, given her habit of venturing for a similar distance or further, to the Flower Pot at Sandling, or to Maidstone's Week Street.

Alas, there is one snag to this idea: the Tiger Moth was not built until 1959, four years after Mrs Ash's death. So, unless she happened to be heading elsewhere, this link seems tenuous despite the otherwise meaningful correspondences, not least the nature of the encounter itself. Indeed, the following year, further information came to light that would seem to dissolve this link altogether—but, at the same time, strengthening the case for Andy Reeds' ghostly encounter.

In October 1980, two Kent newspapers (*Chatham Standard*, *Evening Post*) reported the death of a 71-year-old pensioner on this same stretch of road. The accident occurred on 16 October on the dual carriageway near to the Tiger Moth as the lady, a resident of Thorndale Close, Chatham, attempted to cross the road to the bus stop on the other side. One of the witnesses, the driver of a Transit van heading for Maidstone, had seen the old lady (who I shall call Mrs 'R') slowly crossing the road ahead and slowed down:

'When she got to the white line in the middle of the road I looked in my mirror and saw a car just overtaking me. She got one step off the line and the car hit her.'

In a statement to police, the driver of the car, from Brighton, said he did not see the woman before he hit her. His testimony was supported by the van driver, who said his van would have hidden her from view. The car was travelling at around 35 mph. Mrs R was thrown into the air by the impact, and she had landed on the bonnet of his car. She died two days later in hospital. The coroner for North Kent recorded a verdict of 'accidental death'.[47]

Remarkably, Thorndale Close links with Watson Ave, the road identified from correspondence as a marker for Andy Reeds' encounter at the same location some twenty years later. So, perhaps this incident relates more to this unfortunate lady than to Mrs Ash, even if we still have the same apparent discrepancy in style of dress—which, according to Andy Reeds, was more characteristic of the early twentieth century.

But the question as to whether this figure can be related meaningfully to Mrs Ash or to Mrs R is overshadowed to a large extent by the nature of the encounter itself, which is identical to those taking place at Blue Bell Hill, little over a mile south of this spot, on the same road, the A229. The incident, like those further down the Hill, does prompt the question as to what constitutes a haunted 'place'. Unlike a house, or a churchyard, with their clearly defined boundaries, a road is an open feature, which perhaps makes it harder to comprehend how the same figure could manifest miles away from its supposed 'centre'. But, in fact, for a non-material entity, the solid walls of a building should present little hindrance to its movement; and yet many manifestations appear to be confined to a given local geography—in the case of the Blue Bell Hill set, the section of the A229 between the M2 and the M20 motorways.

Why this is so appears to have as much to do with *notional* boundaries and features—those we perceive and label as such—as actual physical features. In this sense, a road, irrespective of its length, may be defined as a haunted place as much as any strictly defined local feature. This is a concept we will explore further in the closing chapters.

Wise Woman

Taking Nigel D's recollections of Mrs Ash's bizarre behaviour in the quarries and her self-styled guardianship of Kit's Coty, Mrs Ash could be seen to stand comfortably at the end of a long line of 'wise folk' or 'cunning (or 'uncannie') folk'—women and men who were a feature of rural life from medieval times until the early twentieth century.

Wise folk, eccentric in character and appearance were purveyors of folk magic and medicine—the equivalent of the tribal shaman in undeveloped cultures—and consequently were sought for a range of services that included healing, midwifery, herbal and other 'old wives' remedies, divination (including fortune-telling and prophecy), spells and charms for match-making, and the locating of missing objects (including stolen goods) or persons. By their craft, wise folk achieved a social standing and respect that they may have gained by no other means, which was sometimes reflected in their titles—in the case of wise women, 'Mother', 'Granny', and, in Cornwall—interestingly—'*An*' (Aunt).[48] The most famous example of an English wise woman is probably the North Yorkshire seer and prophetess, Old Mother Shipton.

An important role within this spiritual and magical sphere was in the area of what we might today call 'psychic defence'. Wise folk were often called upon to treat ailments and afflictions that were believed caused by malignant magic. In this role as 'witch doctor' or 'fairy doctor', wise folk might employ various means to neutralise or reverse the effects of spells and curses, or to break the bewitchment by direct counterattacks on the alleged witch by incantation and/or prayer, or by the use of physical devices such as witch bottles and voodoo-like effigies.

Some of the above functions are recognisably the domain today of modern fortune-tellers, clairvoyants and mediums. Like the latter, and the shamans of tribal societies, one aspect of the craft supposed that wise folk could communicate with spirits, familiar or otherwise, and were therefore consulted as mediators between the living and the dead, or to deal with supernatural disturbances such as haunted houses.

There is no doubt that the habits and actions of wise folk could lead them to be confused with witches. Their methods were often very similar. Both were known to have spiritual familiars, for instance. But to ordinary people, the distinction was clear: the cunning craft served for good, in contrast and opposition to the harmful effects caused by malevolent witchcraft. On this popular distinction many wise folk were spared prosecution during the witch hunts of the seventeenth century.

As with any human situation, however, things were never completely black and white, and wise folk (sometimes styled 'white witches') could at times be found using their powers for less than altruistic purposes, such as issuing curses or bewitchments for a fee (thereby blurring the distinction between the cunning art and witchcraft), or on personal whim—as illustrated by an account of Granny Boswell, a wise woman of Irish Romany birth who, for the latter half of her life, was feared by local people of Helston, Cornwall as an 'ill-wisher'. During the 1906 elections, it is said she emerged intoxicated from an inn, to be confronted by a strange contraption—a motor car—whose driver promptly honked its horn at her. This action invited a foul retort from the old woman, who cursed the vehicle to break down, which it promptly did so before it was out of the street.[49] (A similar disregard for motor vehicles, it seems, is exhibited by the old woman at Blue Bell Hill). Such a reputation for capriciousness perhaps explains the success of wise folk in locating stolen goods—which, one can imagine, were hastily returned once the accused came under the threat of curse!

The cunning craft gradually declined alongside the diminishing belief in malevolent witchcraft that came with the advance of scientific rationalism (which removed healing and medicine from the purview of mystics) that had begun with attempts to stamp out the vestiges of both crafts with the Witchcraft Act of 1736. Some historians have argued that the craft did not vanish, but its practitioners metamorphosed (it could be argued, devolved) into the astrologers and tarot readers of today, while elements of its magical practices became absorbed into new religious movements such as neo-pagan witchcraft (Wicca), which uses Neolithic sites as places of worship or to mark festivals in honour of the Mother Goddess.[50]

It is interesting to note that the services a wise woman offered did not necessarily end at her death. According to some traditions, she might continue to be honoured at her burial place or a sacred spot with which she was associated, where offerings were made in exchange for pleas for assistance. A predictable extension of this tradition is that the wise woman's spirit itself remained on earth, and either helped or hindered persons who encountered them.

The ghost of an old woman, for instance, reputedly a witch, was said to continue to be seen by residents of the village of Horseheath, Cambridgeshire, two years after her death. The woman, who died in 1926, and was known as 'Mother Redcap', had a sinister reputation in life, which she seemed intent on perpetuating after death. Her 'ghost' was said to shake its fist menacingly in the faces of those who encountered her at night.[51]

Macbeth's ghost-witches, the 'weird women' or 'weird sisters' (after *Wyrd,* the personified Anglo-Saxon goddess of fate), are the quintessential example, and we have seen that Blue Bell Hill preserves a similar, albeit less dramatic, legend. And we can see also how the description is an apt one for the strange, prophetic old woman that is the Version B phantom hitch-hiker, whose pedestrian counterpart we have met on the roads and back lanes of Blue Bell Hill.

So, what was it that Mrs Ash was up to during her night-time adventures on the Hill? If she was a self-styled guardian of some kind, was she trying to ward something off, or inviting it in for protective purposes? Was she even aware of the Hill's phenomenal history?

Nigel D.'s information (as I had also heard from others) suggests that events involving vanishing pedestrians were known at least as far back as the 1950s, so it seems reasonable to conclude that Mrs Ash may have heard some of these accounts. Was her behaviour, then, somehow connected to the phenomenon—or was she, after all, simply indulging her own private fancies? It is doubtful we will ever know.

While the descriptive overlap between the apparitional old woman and Mrs Ash is impressive, and her habits at least suggest a plausible motive for her continued appearances at Blue Bell Hill, it is, as we have noted, impossible to overlook the close resemblances also to a broader cast of legendary and mythological characters, of which the Version B hitch-hiker is one example. Nor should we forget that 'she' accounts for only one of the trio of female characters reported at Blue Bell Hill. Unless we are to suppose that Blue Bell Hill possesses special properties that give it the ability to ensnare human spirits and condemn them to the re-enactment of a very similar and nonsensical 'script', we are forced to look again to the complex role that folklore itself plays in these encounters to attempt to discern what, if anything, they mean.

... and Back to Folklore

We have seen that the Blue Bell Hill encounters are precisely reflected in Phantom Hitch-Hiker lore, even down to the description and character of their counterparts: the ghost girl for the pitiful Versions A and C Hitch-Hikers, and the old woman or hag for the gloomy persona of the Version B. This observation, together with the noted similarities in behaviour, suggests that the girl in white and the old woman are not distinct entities that just happen to haunt the same spots, at the same times, and in broadly similar manner, but are facets of the *same* phenomenon. It has even been suggested to me that what we might call the Version B character is the transmogrified form of the ghost girl—which is an interesting and, within the context of folklore, a not entirely irrelevant comment. This duality or polarity in form: the youthful appearance, white apparel and comparatively benign character of the ghost girl, in opposition to the frightening aspect and dark character and dress of the old woman—light and dark, positive and negative—is plainly demonstrated elsewhere, in the misty realms of folklore and myth (where the two, while sometimes appearing singly, are often portrayed as expressions of the *same* character, which is frequently hostile toward or beguiling of lonely travellers)—and indeed, in a case that hints at what the Blue Bell Hill encounters may (in part) be about.

Following the eruption of Mount St Helens in May 1980, police in Washington State, USA, received a number of reports concerning a 'ghastly old woman', who prophesied about a further cataclysm that was to occur a month to the day afterward. In later encounters, in which the disaster was postponed to the following October, the hitch-hiking phantom took the form of an attractive female in a white gown[52]—all of which have obvious repercussions for the ghost-as-spirit-of-the-dead case.

It is important to remember that ghosts themselves have emerged from the pool of folklore to gain some respectability through the associations we make between them and the spirits of the dead. The sightings of the ghost girl at Blue Bell Hill have plainly been interpreted in this light. But in viewing them as such, we are frequently at a loss to explain their apparently nonsensical behaviour, such as throwing themselves beneath the wheels of passing vehicles—which, as I have pointed out previously, hardly stands for the attempts at meaningful communication we perhaps expect from surviving human personalities.

What we appear to be confronted with in this case is not so much a local legend come to life in the popular guise—the ghost of a young woman killed on Blue Bell Hill some years before, or the restless shade of a girl murdered a hundred years ago, or even the spirit of an elder former resident (although features related to all three seem to be represented without conflict)—but a branch of impersonal folklore that plays out in real-life situations: something with a much deeper root than the Phantom Hitch-Hiker motif that largely describes its character and form.

The overarching question, of course, is the conundrum that has been posed in previous chapters—whether these encounters represent a real phenomenon (as we understand it) which came to be passed down as folklore, or a vividly portrayed fiction that is by some means unconsciously projected by the witness into a real situation. Or perhaps there are elements of both: of 'fact' informing 'fiction', and 'fiction' informing 'fact'. Whichever the case, the encounters as a whole make any kind of sense only when viewed within the context of folklore and its inherent symbolism, which appears to be unconsciously tapped by witnesses in the descriptions of their encounters.

It was noted much earlier that the main objective of all the behavioural types at Blue Bell Hill (and indeed, elsewhere) appears to be to quite simply scare the living daylights out of passing motorists—a terror that is generated to greatest degree in lone motorists, but is by no means confined to single witnesses.

Michael Goss points out that this is hardly a novel observation. In Swiss Protestant priest Louis Lavater's *Of Ghostes and Spirites Walking by Night* (1572),[53] from which he quotes, Lavater states that these 'walking spirits' habitually 'stoppe the way before men as they travell, and leade them out of their way,' and cause 'great feare'.[54] According to Lavater, those most prone to such experiences were 'carters'—unquestionably, notes Goss, the equivalent of modern motorists.

Similar entities are described in the folklore of the Netherlands, and across much of northern Europe. The Dutch historian Cornelius Kempius (1516–c.1587) relates that in the reign of the Lothair I (around the year 830) many spectres, particularly *witte vrouwen* (white ladies), infested Friesland in the north of the country. Residing in subterranean caves, they emerged to surprise travellers abroad at night.[55]

Closely related, if not identical, are the *witte juffers* (white damsels) of the Netherlands and Belgium, the *weisen frauen* of Germany, and the *dames blanches* (France). These ubiquitous White Ladies have a long pedigree. Kempius linked them to the nymphs (nature spirits) of the ancient Greeks.

In the Netherlands also are the *witte wieven* (or *witte wijven*), which translates literally as 'weird sisters' (or 'white wives')—said to be the spirits of wise women—which haunt hilltops, hollows, caverns, and other natural features and ancient burial places (dolmens and tumuli). The *witte wieven* are usually found together, usually in groups of *three.*

Three *witte wieven*, for example, are said to reside at Witte Wievenkuil (Weird Sisters' Pit), a sand pit located between two forested hills, the Lochemse Berg and Kalenberg near the village of Barchem, in the province of Gelderland, Achterhoek. According to legend, the sisters emerge at night to stalk the forest and hills in search of victims.[56] Also in Gelderland, at Eefde, near the town of Zutphen, there is a hillock known as Wittewievenbult (Weird Sisters or Wise Women hill) where, every Christmas Eve, *witte wieven* traditionally appear and dance on the mound. Excavations at this mound have proven it to be an ancient burial mound.[57]

The *witte wieven* are commonly depicted in white, in contrast to the dark apparel of the likes of Blue Bell Hill's senior ghost—which may arise from some confusion regarding the meaning of the word *witte.* 'Witte' can be translated as 'white', but may also be taken to mean 'wit', from the Dutch *weten* (*to know*, i.e. sagacity or wisdom)—much as 'brilliant' in English can mean 'brightly luminous', or 'clever' or 'knowledgeable'.

Like those other weird sisters, Macbeth's ghost-witches, the *witte wieven* have been linked to the white-attired *Moirai* (*Fates*),[58] the triadic sister goddesses of Greek and Roman mythologies that governed the measure and cycles of life; and to the *Matres* or *Matronae* ('Mothers'), a trio of goddesses venerated in north-west

The three *Moirai* (Fates). From a relief on the tomb of Alexander von der Mark, by Johann Gottfried Schadow, Old National Gallery, Berlin *(Andreas Praefcke CC BY-3.0)*

Europe between the first and fifth centuries. Traditionally, the *witte wieven* were fickle; they could be benign (if left alone), but could quickly turn hostile towards those who disturbed or derided them.

Similarly, in his summary of findings regarding the elemental spirits that were said to bedevil Scottish farmers, the Reverend and Professor Robert Kirk of Aberfoyle, Perth, in his *The Secret Commonwealth of Elves, Fauns, and Fairies* (1691), notes that it is during their travels from place to place that men are likely to have 'terrible encounters' with them, 'even on the great highways'.[59]

Kempius' White Ladies naturally invite comparisons with Blue Bell Hill's girl in white, whose habit of running or standing in the way of vehicles has the same effect of stopping travellers in their way. Similarly, the Phantom Hitch-Hiker, by enticing motorists to stop to offer a lift—especially in the evolved versions where the motorist continues on to a given address—clearly 'leads men out of their way' (as might a subsequent trip to the police station to report the incident).

A quite literal demonstration of this is found in an anecdotal and admittedly anonymous 'friend of ...' account at Blue Bell Hill that is dated to '35–40 years ago' (around 1970–1975). In this episode—one again heard by Neil Arnold—the witness (a friend of the informant, who was from Sevenoaks), was driving up the Hill at night when she braked to avoid a small animal, possibly a cat, that ran across the road. Suddenly, in front of the car, she saw a figure, which, although lacking distinguishing features, appeared to be a middle-aged woman. The woman reputedly had her hands on the bonnet, and seemed to be pushing against the car, as if to prevent it moving up the Hill.[60]

How this particular episode at Blue Bell Hill ended we do not discover, but it is one that echoes the legend of the white lady of Montferland, near Beek, in Gelderland, Netherlands, who upset the cart of a farmer who was disrespectfully loading it with heather sods at the foot of the hill. The cart was overturned 'in a moment', but without injury to the farmer or his horse.[61]

The White Lady of Montferland is said to carry a basket, inviting comparison to the Zeeland goddess *Nehalennia*, a protectress of seafaring commerce and travel, who is often depicted with a basket of fruits or loaves on her lap and a dog at her feet.[62] A basket, it may be recalled, was an accoutrement also of both the Hawaiian goddess *Pele* and the figure of the old woman seen by Nick Norris at the foot of Blue Bell Hill, as well as an item associated with the Version B Phantom Hitch-Hiker (Chapter 5).

It is noteworthy, in terms of tracing identifications with some of the classic figures of mythology, that one of the Greek *Matronae* is always depicted with a basket of fruit on her lap.[63] Baskets or cornucopias (horn-shaped containers overflowing with produce) are found in association with goddesses of various traditions, including *Demeter* (the Roman *Ceres*) and the Celtic/Roman goddess

Erecura. They have been interpreted variously as symbolising offerings to the gods (the first fruits of the harvest), but more often as representing the annual harvest itself, as symbols of the goddess's bountiful provision of the fruits of the Earth, typified by autumnal crops such as apples and cereals.[64] The basket-bearing goddess is thereby identified as an *earth* goddess, specifically one associated with autumn, the harvest and fertility.

Relief of the goddess Nehalennia 150-250 AD., with basket of produce and dog at her feet (National Museum of Antiquities, Leiden, Netherlands) *(Mystic Mabel CC-BY-SA-2.0)*

In certain instances, such as in the case of blonde-haired *Demeter*, the role of earth-goddess is fused with the concept of mother-goddess (*De-meter* is literally 'Earth-mother'), whereby (akin to the Matronae and the Fates) she presided over the customs and sanctity of marriage, law, and the cycle of life and death. Similarly, in Nehalennia (whose name has been interpreted as 'woman who steers'—a guide), and by her frequent accompaniment by a dog (a symbol of the guardianship of the dead and of divination), we find an extension to her role as goddess of nature, agriculture and commerce to include goddess of death—a guide not only to mortal ventures but also to the dead (and therefore a *psychopomp*), responsible for guiding the newly deceased in their journey to the otherworld.[65]

Thus, the mythological characters we find echoed in the encounters at Blue Bell Hill and in other modern road ghost cases hold symbolic associations with both fate and death, which are clearly meaningful to incidents of tragic and untimely death on our roads and the ghostly encounters associated with them. At the same time, the idea that modern ghostly encounters share as much (if not more) with mythology and symbolism as with the unfortunate victims of specific incidents, prompts further questions regarding what these manifestations truly represent.

Hekate on the Hill

The mythologies and folklore of many cultures are replete with such characters, many of which bear more than a passing similarity to the principal aspects and habits of Blue Bell Hill's 'ghost', particularly the figure of the old woman.[66] Possibly their best recognition, however, is found in Celtic and pre-Celtic mythology, in the *Cailleach* of the Scottish Highlands (or in Ireland and the Isle of Man, the *Caillaigh* or *Cailleac*), the tutelary earth or mother goddess; and in *Hekate*, the Dark Goddess of early Greek tradition.

The Cailleach ('old woman' in Gaelic) was an ancient figure of wisdom and supernatural power that was commonly depicted as a hooded crone or hag (*caille* meaning hood or veil)—the title itself lending itself to interpretation as 'hooded hag' or, interestingly, in terms of the PHH comparisons, 'veiled nun' (and therefore no longer merely associated with the Version B character, but now also Version D—representing the transition, through the influence of Christianity, from pagan goddess or semi-deity into nun).[67]

The Cailleach's common depiction as the personification of winter, and her triple form of Virgin-Mother-Crone (representing, like her counterparts in classical mythology, seasonality and the nurturing and hostile faces of nature) have clear relevance to the forms and timing of the appearances at Blue Bell Hill (which are often described as autumn or winter).[68]

In some traditions, she is depicted as transforming into a beautiful girl (her seasonal counterpart, *Brigid* or *Brìghde*), which traditionally takes place on 1 February (St. Brigid's Day, *Là Fhèill Brìghde,* or *Imbolc*—one of the cross-quarter days of the Celtic calendar). Thus, the Cailleach rules the winter months from its onset at *Samhain* (Hallowe'en) until summer commences under Brigid's rule from 1 May (*Beltane*, or May Day). By the mid-point, at the start of February, the Cailleach's wintry grip was seen to be weakening, and tradition indicates that if the day is sunny and bright, the Cailleach will be at large gathering her firewood in readiness for a prolonged winter; but if overcast, she is asleep and winter will soon be over. (Some readers, particularly those in the USA, will note the principle of the tradition extant in the Pennsylvanian custom of Groundhog Day, on 2 February).

But it is the Cailleach's role as a spirit of place (*genius loci*) that has particular relevance to our discussion regarding Blue Bell Hill. We can note for instance that many Scottish mountains, regarded as places of sanctity, where the veil between this world and the next was said to grow thin, had their own personal hag as guardian.

Other high places and sacred spots preserve similar traditions. In addition, in the Celtic world, we find her connected with caves, springs and rivers, plus dolmens and fairy mounds (today's Neolithic sites)—traditionally sites supporting tales of ghosts, fairies, and other elemental entities, and again something in common with Blue Bell Hill and its prehistoric hilltop 'necropolis'. Thus, in Ireland she goes by the ancient name of Áine or Ana or Anu; in other parts, such as the High Peaks, Th'Owd Woman; in still others, as Gentle Annie, Black Annis,[69] or simply The Mother. Again, we can note the significance of these name variations in relation to Blue Bell Hill's 'Ann' or 'Annie'. In other traditions, essentially the same character goes by other names—for instance, Pele, Hawaii's basket-laden mother goddess.

And it isn't all myth. The old lady has been encountered elsewhere in modern times. The old woman sometimes seen on a hilltop road near Bicknoller in Somerset, is known as the Woman of the Mist, who reputedly appears in the autumn and winter months, sometimes as a crone *gathering sticks*. She is reputed to have been seen in 1920, and again in the 1950s.[70]

And there is the experience of 16-year-old Christopher Christie on 1 January 1990 in Red Well Road, Whitehills, Aberdeenshire. As he hurried through the darkness of a miserable winter's evening along the narrow single-track road, an old woman in black appeared in front him and promptly walked straight through him with an icy chill. Horror-struck, he turned and fled back towards Whitehills, but the assault continued, with the woman reappearing and passing through him several times before he could reach the reassuring surroundings of the main road and home.[71]

Turning again to early Greek tradition, to the pre-Olympian earth goddess Hekate, we find further eerie echoes of Blue Bell Hill's dark ghost. Like the Cailleach, Hekate (*Hecate* in Latin) has been featured as one aspect of the primordial triple goddess: Maiden (Hekate), Bride (Persephone), and Mother (Demeter).[72] In the most ancient depictions, she is portrayed as a 'bright-coiffed' (light-haired) girl or young woman, in keeping with her function as attendant,[73] guide and guardian—a role demonstrated most famously by her leading Persephone out of Hades and back to her mother, Demeter, after hearing her cries from her cave dwelling.[74] As with the Cailleach, it is difficult to overlook here the apt comparison to Blue Bell Hill's own triple set of Young Girl (Maiden), Young Woman (Bride, or *Bride-to-be?*), and Old Woman (Mother or Crone).

Thus, Hekate's image and sanctuaries to her were erected at doorways and gateways to ward off outside evils.[75] Similarly—and significantly in terms of our interest—as 'goddess of the crossway' (crossroads)[76] and protectress of roads, her three-headed or three-faced likeness was set up to watch over and act as a guide to travellers.

But it is Hekate's transformed later guise that finds greatest recognition here for, from around 400 BC and particularly since Roman times, the darker aspects of Hekate's character became dominant. And along with her changed character and function came a wholly different and frightening image. Instead of the youthful and benevolent goddess, we find instead the quintessential expression of the supernatural hag: a terrifying chthonic goddess of magic, of the waning moon, of night and death. Known variously as the Crone Goddess, Goddess of Witches, the Veiled One, Goddess of Midnight, Queen of Crossroads, Queen of Death, and Queen of Restless Ghosts,[77] this Hekate was said to walk the highways of night, particularly at the dark of the moon, sometimes crowned with coils of wild snakes (connecting her to divination or prophecy—a Version B characteristic) and wielding terrible black torches.[78]

With her wandered a train of fearful ghosts: deceased humans, apparitions and phantom dogs. The human souls that accompanied Hekate were those who had died before their allotted time, the victims of violent or premature death, or those denied burial or its rites. Prominent among them were her *propoloi* (attendant spirits), which were all female. These spirits could not rest, but were to continually wander with Hekate and her pack of spectral hounds. Some of these spirits merely frightened men; others were said to bring disaster, bad dreams, illness or madness. Since crossroads were associated with her, these especially became the realm of these 'unquiet souls of the dead'.[79]

Offerings (the 'suppers' or 'banquets' of Hekate) were made at cross-ways to appease her and to keep these ominous spirits at bay. Significantly perhaps, Hekate's chief feast day is 16 November (the Night of Hekate)—a date, as much as the anniversary of the 1965 tragedy, that is neatly straddled by two of the principal ghostly encounters on Blue Bell Hill in 1992.[80]

The folklore and mythologies relating to these goddess figures have hidden depths and meaning for the real-life encounters at Blue Bell Hill and elsewhere. But while we should not be too specific and overlook the wider body of folklore that shares relevant features with our Phantom Hitch-hiker or Jaywalker accounts—and here I am thinking broadly of Professor Kirk's mischievous, sometimes malicious elementals, whose form and behaviour in today's fashion we might interpret as ghostly[81]—it is the Cailleach, or Hekate, or the Hag—call her what we will—and her role as an arch-spirit of nature, a personification of the Earth itself, that, at Blue Bell Hill at least, provides a key to understanding, if not the mechanism of what people see there (*why* they see the precise form and behaviour the phenomenon exhibits), then perhaps something of the 'why here' and 'why now' aspects of the appearances. For what emerged from my own research at Blue Bell Hill, and which became difficult to overlook in other examples was the correlation between 'road ghost' outbreaks and environmental disturbances. In 1992 and 1993, the supernatural disturbances at Blue Bell Hill were paralleled by physical disruption to the environment in the form of major construction and re-modelling work at the foot of Blue Bell Hill, at the junction of the A229 with the M20 motorway (junction 6). The works, which commenced in the spring of 1992, were in full swing by November, and continued through the sightings period.

Published rumours (and sightings?) similarly surrounded the construction of the current A229 over Blue Bell Hill in the early 1970s, and have been associated with other road-building schemes—for instance, at Stocksbridge (South Yorkshire, 1987) and Newbury (Berkshire, 1996)—which attest to a repeated and meaningful correlation between environmental factors and ghostly activity.

The point of these examples is to highlight these apparitional figures as much as symbols of a universal character as the real human personages that have traditionally been linked through circumstances to Blue Bell Hill and similar cases. These symbols, which are commonly expressed through the appellations of goddesses and gods of the ancient world, the noted psychologist C.G. Jung termed *archetypes*. These were recurrent, shared images and themes that emerged in mythology and dreams, in visions, and in paranormal experiences. Jung encountered them at the deepest levels of his patients' unconscious experiences, where they took on semi-autonomous lives of their own, outside of the conscious awareness and experience of the person concerned.

Likewise, apparitional encounters and other paranormal experiences frequently were found to feature these impersonal elements that pointed to a deeper origin than the personal experiences of witnesses; deeper also than the traditionally regarded 'causes', to something older and universal in character. Jung viewed these figures as personifications of a collective unconscious, the source and repository of the collective experience, knowledge and imagination of the entire human race. As a psychopomp, the role of the archetype is to act as a guide, mediator or messenger between the impersonal unconscious and the conscious mind (whether to an individual or collectively), bringing to conscious attention matters of import that otherwise are in danger of passing unheeded.

But what is the content of these messages—what are they trying to tell us? And what is it, after all, that shapes the forms and habits of these apparitions—why do they appear in the guises they commonly exhibit, and not in some other?

We will attempt to unravel some of the possible answers to these questions in the remaining chapters.

TWELVE

WALKIN' AFTER MIDNIGHT

> Heaven in its mercy loose me from my sins, and defend me from goblins and earth-creatures with the shapes of men and ghosts that walk in the unhallowed night.
>
> Oscar W. Firkins[1]

After 1993, events again petered out at Blue Bell Hill, at least as far as those reaching wider public attention. While the dramatic encounters seemed to fade away almost as quickly as they had arrived, the ripples sent out by the encounters of 1992 and 1993 continued to attract the interest of various media parties, from magazines to television, for some time.

In October 1994, the case was featured on the pilot episode of the BBC's *Out of This World*, hosted by Sue Cook. Alongside reconstructions of their encounters, both Ian Sharpe and Chris Dawkins appeared on the show to discuss their encounters. Also interviewed for the show were the two police officers from Maidstone, PC Roger Ginn and PC Steve Nelkin, who had accompanied Ian Sharpe back up the Hill to investigate his reported collision with a female jaywalker. On its heels, in 1995, came *Arthur C. Clarke's Mysterious Universe*, with Ian Sharpe again recounting his story on camera, plus the rather more shallow treatment by *The Magic & Mystery Show* with Brian Blessed and featuring psychic Nella Jones, which took a backward step to look at the legendary hitch-hiker and the unfounded rumours associated with it.

In the same period, I published articles about Blue Bell Hill's ghost(s) in the magazine *Fortean Times* ('The Journal of Strange Phenomena') which, in 1994, focused on Sharpe's and Dawkins' encounters; and in 1997 on the later encounters with 'the Hag'.[2]

All of the above contributed in their own way toward establishing Blue Bell Hill firmly on the Paranormal map.

The late 1990s saw the Internet's surge in accessibility and use, which was inevitably to transform communications, making it quicker and easier for information to be accessed and exchanged. In 2001, I launched a website (www.roadghosts.com) to share information on Blue Bell Hill and similar cases, and as a means of attracting new accounts. Some of the examples given in this book, not previously published, arrived by this channel.

The inevitable flipside to the Internet's usefulness would be the amount of regurgitated 'noise' it also generates. Anecdotal accounts arise quite naturally in the casual electronic culture, but, ironically, they do not always permit adequate follow-up, even in those cases suggestive of a genuine experience. The oral grapevine has been supplanted by an electronic version, and the rumours of old now take the form of postings on web forums, weblogs and other social media.

It is therefore difficult to imagine the Blue Bell Hill case again commanding anything like the same undiluted attention and relative lack of 'contamination' in its reporting as it did in 1974 and again in 1992. And in terms of the kind of interest held by folklorists, who at one time would have plotted the slow propagation of the Phantom Hitch-Hiker story through printed media and word of mouth, the Internet's ability to rapidly distribute and mix rumour and report seems to have largely seen off the PHH as a reported encounter in developed nations, where it is the phantom road accident scenario—the girl running into the path of the vehicle—that is the favoured modus operandi of contemporary road ghosts.[3] The electronic medium, though, has succeeded in bringing to light a few reports seemingly involving hitch-hiking phantoms from Blue Bell Hill's past.

The broadcast media of the day seem also to have shown some reluctance to part ways with the legendary aspects of the case, as some of the accounts that follow suggest. Before we proceed, I will add that in only one of the following cases did I have the opportunity to talk directly to the witness; hence these must be taken and assessed at face value.

Bob Vandepeer

In November 2003, the *Kent Messenger* ran a summary of the Blue Bell Hill story to coincide with the November anniversary of the 1965 car crash.[4] Reporter Emily Hall's closing appeal for further sightings prompted a handful of readers to submit their accounts. One of these was from James Skene (who we met in Chapter 9), which was printed on 5 December. Two others (which we will look at in the next chapter) were printed later that month.[5] The fourth (and last), which appeared in January 2004, came from Bob Vandepeer, of Strood.

Mr Vandepeer, who was accompanied by a friend, Paul Clarke, told the *Kent Messenger* that he had stopped for a girl who was thumbing a lift at the roadside at the bottom of Blue Bell Hill. The girl, who he estimated to be in her late teens or early twenties, asked to be taken to Rochester. Since they were heading to Rochester for an evening out, they offered her a lift, and she climbed into the back seat. Then, according to the report, 'the trio spent the rest of the journey in silence'.

After an undisclosed period of time or distance, Mr Vandepeer turned around to ask the girl where she wished to be dropped off, only to find there was no-one there. Fearing that the girl may have fallen from the car, the two men searched either side of the carriageway, but could find no trace of the girl. They then 'immediately' called officers at Rochester Police Station to report the incident.

'We didn't know what to do,' he said. 'I'd locked the car doors when she got in and they were still locked. The fellow at the police station told us not to worry about it because it was the fifth similar incident that week.'[6]

Bob Vandepeer's experience can be seen to broadly fit the familiar story: the lone female hitch-hiker; her desire to be taken to Rochester and her unobserved disappearance during the journey; the police statement regarding the number of similar reports, and so on. Where it differs from the established script is the year it is said to have taken place: mid-1962, three years before the commonly regarded 'cause', the 1965 tragedy.

It would not be the first time that ghostly events on the Hill have been placed earlier than 1965, but other than the notable exception of Jack Woodger's encounter, which we looked at in Chapter 10, these have been sparse and anecdotal at best, with few details to link them to the later rumours and reports. In these, the phantom hitch-hiker scenario is not represented, which features most prominently in both rumour and print between 1966 and 1974. Indeed, such details as the Rochester Girl and the nonchalance of the police response are hallmarks of the story of this period.

While it is nevertheless possible that Bob Vandepeer's experience *could* predate the 1965 tragedy, it can be seen to sit more comfortably with the post-1965 period, and therefore we might reasonably suspect that the witness's (or the journalist's) estimation of the year of his experience may be a little off.

But there are other reasons why, without the benefit of the witness's direct testimony, we might view the account with some caution. As we noted in the opening chapter, the police are obliged to follow up all reports made to them. It is therefore hard to imagine a report of a disappearing passenger being dismissively brushed off, no matter how many times they may have heard it before. We might also be a little wary of the detail about Mr Vandepeer locking the car doors after their passenger had boarded. While this adds a further 'proof' element to the account, in that only a ghost could depart a locked and moving vehicle, it hardly speaks well for the confidence of the passenger in the presence of two men—who, until she was found to have vanished, was naturally assumed to have been a normal human female.

And there are other points (or their lack) that raise further questions: The men were said to have searched both sides of the carriageway (which we will assume refers to the original two-lane road, since the dual carriageway did not exist before 1972) and then 'immediately' phoned the police. Telephoning in the 1960s would have meant finding a public call box or imposing on a nearby private or business address. In addition, we have no reference to the time of the encounter, which we can assume to be early evening, in keeping with the men travelling to Rochester for an evening out—a time that is atypical of most encounters. Also lacking is any description of the girl, or where she was picked up or vanished—although, in fairness, these details are perhaps less a commentary on the witness's recollections than the reporter's treatment of the piece.

Indeed, in time, a slightly different version of Bob Vandepeer's experience came to my attention from a former resident of Kent who knew him as a customer in the early 1970s. As well as providing some independent corroboration for his account, Rex Harvey's recollections help to address the apparent discrepancy of the year of Mr Vandepeer's encounter.

Mr Harvey owned and ran Pembroke Garage Ltd at HMS Pembroke at Chatham Dockyard between 1969 and the dockyard's closure in 1983. He came to know Bob Vandepeer early in 1972, when he had some car problems and a colleague at the Dockyard's design department referred him to the garage. Rex Harvey dates Bob Vandepeer's encounter to a few months after this, to the summer of 1972, as it was still 'fresh in his mind' when he recounted his experience to him. On the evening in question, Mr Vandepeer was returning from Maidstone and near to Kits Coty House he stopped to pick up a young female who was hitch-hiking up the Hill. As he had a lot of work papers and plans on the front passenger seat, the girl sat in the back. She asked to be dropped off at the top of the Hill, near Bridgewood. On arrival there, he found there was no-one else in the car.[7]

In this version, there is no mention of a second witness, or of a report to the police. What it *does* have is a more familiar time frame, and a pattern of behaviour and dropping-off point that is shared by at least one other encounter at Blue Bell Hill—Richard Studholme's experience, which, by this revised date, would take place the following year. Only in this instance the encounter ends in more typical and unequivocal fashion with the girl's unobserved disappearance.

But Bob Vandepeer's ghostly experiences were not to end there. According to the same *Kent Messenger* article, he claimed also to have had a road ghost encounter on Detling Hill later the same year (which we might now also date to 1972). In this instance, he was again accompanied by a friend, Peter Mantle, who was driving. The time of day (or night) is not specified, but as they approached the brow of the hill on the A249 for the descent to Maidstone, a man reportedly ran out in front of their car from a gate on the left. Mr Mantle 'hit him head on' and he made an emergency stop. Both men jumped out and ran back to look for the casualty—a man who was wearing a flat cap, grey trousers and a jacket. But there was no evidence of a body or any debris to indicate an accident—only what looked like a handprint on the bonnet of their car.

Mr Vandepeer said: 'There was no way he could have crawled off. He would have been lying in the road seriously injured. The fact that they were both ghosts is all I can put it down to.'

Two road ghost encounters in one year? Some people win the lottery twice, so it is not outside the realm of possibility that Bob Vandepeer had the misfortune (or privilege) to have had two such encounters. Detling Hill has thrown up its own sporadic claims to ghostly encounters, although these have usually described a female figure.[8]

The collision scenario in this instance is at least more plausible, by comparison to a host of similar encounters at Blue Bell Hill and elsewhere. The reader will have to decide for him- or herself whether this enables us to extend acceptance to Mr Vandepeer's claimed encounter with a hitch-hiking phantom at Blue Bell Hill.

John Dawkins (c. 1975)

A few days before Hallowe'en in October 2005, the *KM Extra* printed a brief report by former *Kent Messenger* senior editor Brian Paine. Mr Paine, who, with his wife, retired to Almeria in Spain the previous year, was the co-author of *Unexplained Kent* (1997),[9] which naturally had briefly featured Blue Bell Hill's ghost.

John Dawkins
(KM Group)

'I met the Blue Bell Hill ghost' relates the story of fellow retiree and neighbour John Dawkins, formerly of Gravesend. The 'interview' arose casually over a glass of cerveza in a local bar, when it transpired that Mr Dawkins (no relation to Chris Dawkins) had had an encounter at one of Kent's most notorious haunted locations. Unusually, the incident involved a female hitch-hiker who wished to be taken *to* Blue Bell Hill rather than being picked up from it.

The year of Mr Dawkins' encounter and where precisely he met his unusual passenger go unreported—put it down to the beer—but it was around 6.30 a.m. one morning around thirty years before (therefore around 1975) that Dawkins, who was on his way to work as a litho camera operator, stopped for a blonde-haired woman who flagged him down for a lift. Unlike the classic case where the girl sits in the back seat, John Dawkins' hitch-hiker took the passenger seat beside him.

Dawkins asked the girl what she was doing out at such an early hour. She told him she had been up all night spray-painting a motorbike with her boyfriend. Her hands were green—the 'colour you see on old, rusty gravestones'. She asked to be dropped off at a bus stop halfway down Blue Bell Hill. When they reached the location, he pulled into a lane opposite the stop 'where there were no houses, no gates, only grass verges and thick bushes either side'. He let the girl out of the car, and then he realised she had 'instantly vanished'.

'I drove to the top of the lane to see where she'd gone,' he said, 'but she was nowhere to be seen.'

At work the following day, a colleague told him: 'You know what you've done—you've picked up the ghost of Blue Bell Hill'.[10]

John Dawkins' experience differs even from other accounts that purport to involve a hitch-hiking ghost. The lack of specifics, together with the melodramatic touch of her strange green hands (albeit 'explained' by the spray-painting of her boyfriend's motorbike) would make it easy to dismiss his experience as either a hoax perpetrated on him, or an unusual but 'normal' event that he confabulated into a ghostly one by its association with Blue Bell Hill. The only detail that might defend against either (assuming Dawkins' own word is accepted as trustworthy) is the abrupt disappearance of the girl, with no place for her to hide.

If it was a hoax, the girl had picked an irregular time for her prank. She might also have selected a more conventional behaviour (within the bounds of the popular story) by opting for Blue Bell Hill as her pick-up point rather than the place she wished to be dropped off (where she was picked up is not stated). In a sense the reversal in habit, with the Blue Bell Hill as the destination adds some credibility to the encounter, whatever its true nature.

While it introduces a new detail—that of the girl working overnight with her boyfriend—Mr Dawkins' story tallies with those hitch-hiker encounters that identify the area of the bus stop halfway down the Hill as a place one is likely to encounter the girl, and those that vary the destination to which she wishes to be taken, which hearkens back to Tom Harber's belief that this simply demonstrated the ghost girl's volitional freedom, in this case returning to the spot where she died.

Hitching a ride ...?

The following two brief accounts are included more for sake of completeness than their contribution of anything further to our understanding of the Blue Bell Hill phenomenon. Apart from the named witnesses themselves, who came forward to recount their experiences for television, their accounts (as related) differ very little to the anonymous anecdotal versions of the classic story, and perhaps therefore do not convey that same sense of authenticity as the hitch-hiker accounts we examined in Chapter 9.

In January 1999, *The Why Files*, a paranormal show for British cable television company L!VE TV, aired an episode featuring Blue Bell Hill's ghost. Among various commentators, was a single witness, Bobby Parr.

Mr Parr said: 'Well, I picked up a young lady and she asked me if I could drop her off in Rochester, and mention to her father that she was OK, and that I'd dropped her off at home. And he nearly broke down, and said that was my daughter, and she died on the spot where you picked her up.'[11] The account is developed no further.

The other account, which followed in October 2000, was featured in a segment about Blue Bell Hill's ghost that formed part of a pre-Hallowe'en series ('Legends and Mysteries') for regional news programme *Meridian Tonight*, and was given by John Hippisley of Canterbury. According to the report, Mr Hippisley was driving up the A229 near to the Chatham Road at Blue Bell Hill when he pulled in to pick up a *male* hitch-hiker.

'He got in the car,' he said, 'and I put his seat-belt on for him, as he put his stuff in the back. And we drove up the hill, probably thirty or forty yards. I'd just turned to him to say 'whereabouts do you want to go', and he wasn't there anymore.

And it really was just like that. But the strange thing was, not only was he not there, but the seat-belt was still attached to the bracket. And it really was an unnerving experience for me.'[12]

John Hippisley *(Meridian Tonight)*

In both cases some allowance must be made for the tendency of television to pare accounts down to their bare bones—hence the absence of more meaningful information (locations, times, descriptions) that we might reasonably expect even in a newspaper article. We should not therefore automatically dismiss either account based on their fleshless form, which otherwise typify the essential phantom hitch-hiker story. What are often telling in some accounts, however, are certain lapses or inconsistencies in their internal logic or in relation to established facts of the case, which lead us to question their veracity or to suspect other than supernatural explanations.

In the former case, we might readily identify the young lady with Judith Lingham, the 'Rochester Girl' from the 1965 tragedy, and the only one from that party living at the time in Rochester. This would imply that Mr Parr's claimed encounter took place before 1982, which was the year Judith's father passed away. Judith's sister, Catherine, told me in 1992, however, that the family home in Albany Road was not vacated until 1983, and until that time no-one had ever knocked on the door claiming to have picked Judith up.[13] This was confirmed by the late Andrew Green, who once spoke to Judith's father, Charles Lingham, and told me that the only persons to call at the address about the ghost had been three journalists.[14]

Unless, of course, Bobby Parr's ghostly companion was some other victim of Blue Bell Hill, one also with a connection to Rochester *and* a father who may still have been living—or Parr may have been the target of a hoax based on the popular story. Alas, no such candidate has been identified. In any case, the visit to the father's address to inform him that she was alright makes little sense (although it is a feature in at least one other reported encounter, Richard Studholme's in 1973), particularly in the age of the telephone, when the device of the motorist making the onward visit to a relative (a staple of the folk version) is perhaps rendered redundant.

Passing over this account, to John Hippisley's claimed encounter with a male hitch-hiker, we face a different set of questions, not least related to the gender of his passenger. Taking the witness at his word, the conclusion that his passenger was a ghost would seem indisputable. The encounter is certainly characteristic of those that lack the neat and satisfying conclusions of the home-seeking Versions A and C hitch-hikers. Brief and fragmentary, it resembles more the fleeting and nonsensical experiences that Michael Goss indicated describe most reported ghost sightings. In the actions of the figure—the absence of speech, and its sudden disappearance shortly afterward—it resembles the hitch-hiker accounts at Blue Bell Hill, plus the few credible Phantom Hitch-hiker reports in the literature, particularly Roy Fulton's experience near Stanbridge in 1979 and Jean Clarke's encounter at Borley in 1949 or 1950 (Chapter 4), both of which also feature a male hitch-hiker.

But here again, the brevity of the report meant there was insufficient detail to permit a meaningful assessment. Even so, there were a couple of small but puzzling points that might be addressed in most everyday reports, but which seem to pass without question when dealing with claims of the paranormal. It might be more usual, for instance, for the motorist to establish the hitch-hiker's destination *before* the offer of a lift, in the event that it differs wildly from their own (although, in Roy Fulton's case also, it seems his passenger got in the car before the question was posed). More pointedly, in light of the claim to a supernatural encounter, we might wonder what became of his passenger's luggage. We can assume it vanished along with the hitch-hiker, but no further comment is made; the confirmatory 'proof' part of the story having instead been served by the passenger seat-belt found still locked in its clasp.

I traced Mr Hippisley via his website and interviewed him firstly by phone, and then briefly afterward in person.[15] His website, I discovered, promoted ghost tours in east Kent. Today called The Canterbury Ghost Tour, it advertises walking tours of that historical city conducted by the self-styled Ghost Hunter himself, theatrically garbed in a black top hat and cape.[16]

There are a number of persons today who make at least part of their living from the paranormal, so again this fact should not necessarily prejudice our judgment of Mr Hippisley's account. His first claimed ghost sighting was at the age of thirteen, which evidently piqued his interest. So, possibly he has an attuned sensitivity, or his interest has naturally placed him in locations where such experiences are more likely to be had. Even so, as a resident of Kent with a lifelong interest in ghosts and the paranormal, Mr Hippisley could hardly have been unfamiliar with Blue Bell Hill's ghost, Kent's most famous phantom—or perhaps also Roy Fulton's well-known Phantom Hitch-Hiker encounter, whose story his most resembles. In this regard, those who are better versed in ghost lore, ironically, do not necessarily make the best (that is, uncontaminated) claimants to sightings themselves.

But back to his encounter itself, which he told me took place in March 1983.[17] Mr Hippisley had been at a function in Maidstone, which he left at around 11.30 p.m. His estimate for the encounter fell between that time and 12.30 a.m. He was heading north on the A229 at Blue Bell Hill, where he intended to take the turn-off for the M2. However, before the turn-off loomed he saw, some way ahead, the figure of a man, thumb cocked in customary hitch-hiker style. Taking pity on him on what was a miserable night, Hippisley pulled over, and the man, who was dressed in contemporary clothes, got into the car. Fastening the seat-belt (an action the televised version suggests was aided by Mr Hippisley himself), he pulled away. Almost immediately he turned to his passenger to ask him where he wanted to go, only to find him 'simply not there'. In his shock, he nearly crashed the car, and brought it to a halt. There was no trace of the man; the only evidence he had been there was the seat-belt still fastened in place across the seat.[18]

What, then, of the gender of the hitch-hiker? I must say that the suggestion of a male hitch-hiker at Blue Bell Hill was not completely surprising, as difficult as it is to relate to its cast of female victims in the accepted story (or indeed to the strong bias toward female ghosts in the folk versions). But, as we shall see, there is cause to expect that male figures also might be part of the natural line-up of any road ghost 'set'.

The only question remaining is whether to regard these two reports as genuine, or as examples, perhaps, of the desire to be a part of the Blue Bell Hill legend? The reader is left to decide.

We stay with the Phantom Hitch-Hiker theme for the following two accounts. In each case, the account is second-hand, told by an acquaintance of the witness(es). What distinguishes them from the classic FOAF tale are the named witnesses, even if they are not themselves available to tell their own stories (due in large degree to the length of time that has elapsed since their encounters).

The Gowers (1968)

Frank Lynch recalls the time in the summer of 1968 when his employers, Mr and Mrs Kenneth Gowers, who owned the Queens cinema and bingo hall in Sittingbourne High Street, came in one morning to relate an unnerving experience that had befallen them the evening before:

> One morning, Bill, the other projectionist, and I were getting the films ready for an afternoon performance, when Mr and Mrs Gowers came into work. They told us a story of what happened to them the previous evening. They had been on their way to Maidstone where they were meeting friends for dinner. They were going down Bluebell Hill when they saw a young lady at the side of the road. They stopped the car and asked if she needed a lift. She replied that she did and gave them an address in Maidstone where she would like to be dropped off. She got in the back of their car, which at that time was a blue Mk 2 Cortina Estate. They proceeded to Maidstone, to the address they had been given and when they pulled up, Mr Gowers turned round to tell her they had reached her destination and there was nobody in the back of the car.
>
> They were really upset and went to Maidstone police station to report the strange event and were informed by the officer on duty about the accident a few years previous[ly], and their description matched that of one of the girls killed in a bad accident.
>
> Mr and Mrs Gowers were pillars of society and very Victorian in their outlook on life and were not the type of people to make up such a weird and frightening story.[19]

The Gowers' experience (albeit coming to us second-hand) is important in that it provides the first named witness account to identify Maidstone as the destination of the ghost girl. As such, it recalls the earliest published accounts of the story from 1967 and 1968 (Chapters 3 and 7) that also name the county town as the place to which the girl wishes to be taken, and where she vanishes. In particular, the account echoes the very first published story about Blue Bell Hill's ghost, Roy Plascott's *Kent Messenger* article of December 1967, which has the girl picked up at Blue Bell Hill by a motorist who is accompanied by a friend. Thus there is a plausible reason for the girl to take her characteristic place in the back of the car, from where she can vanish unobserved. That article attributed the ghost to a road accident that had claimed the life of a girl who used to live at the address where the men called after their passenger had vanished.

Six months later, in May 1968 (the same year as the Gowers' experience), Plascott reported again on the story, noting that the rumours that had been widespread in the Maidstone area several months earlier were once again in circulation. This time there was Tom Harber's involvement, which may have helped the rumours to crystallise into the nucleus of the legend as it became popularly known. In this summary, the ghost is identified with a road accident 'some time ago'—which, while not positively linked to Blue Bell Hill, is inferred.

If the Gowers' report to Maidstone Police is true, it would seem the 1965 crash was indeed being thought of as the probable origin of their experience as early as 1968. No other fitting accident had occurred on the Hill within the frame of a few years. The 1965 tragedy was also well publicised at the time, so it seems quite reasonable that police officers or other commentators might recall it with relative freshness a few years afterward. Whether that recollection might extend to descriptions of the victims, enabling one of them to be a suggested match for the ghost girl, is debatable.

Time, unfortunately, is against us in attempting to learn much more about the Gowers' experience. Frank Lynch was nineteen when he started work at the Queens cinema. He estimated that Mr Gowers was in his late fifties to early sixties at the time; his wife, a little younger; so it is likely that the couple, who were from Minster on the Isle of Thanet, have passed on by now. We can note, however, that if their encounter did indeed take place in the summer of 1968 and they were on their way to dinner in Maidstone as stated, it would very likely have been early evening—which would make it (unusually) a daylight event.

What we are left with is the testimony of Mr Lynch regarding the character of the couple, and the returning conundrum of Maidstone as the suggested home of the girl. While this does not fit well with the 1965 crash victims (other than this being their direction of travel on the night of the tragedy, and where two of them were to die), it compares favourably with the rumours in circulation at the time. We might speculate that a real report to the police by the couple may have provided the inspiration for at least some of these, which were only beginning to appear in print (hence it would be unlikely that the printed versions or rumours would have reached the couple beforehand). But we should remind ourselves that the couple's report does not stand alone as a named witness encounter in the same period with a female hitch-hiker at Blue Bell Hill. They are joined by Malcolm Grant's experience on the Maidstone-bound carriageway near to the Lower Bell in 1967 or 1968 (Chapter 9). Together they bring some unexpected credibility to the earliest tales surrounding the case.

Peter Leadbetter (c.1967–8)

In 2010, Mike Stevens posted a personal recollection about Blue Bell Hill's ghost on the *Kent History Forum* website. In a thread titled 'The Blue Bell Hill Vanishing Lady Hitch Hiker', Mike told of the morning a colleague came into work to report a disturbing experience he had just had at Blue Bell Hill:

> Back in the late 60s a friend and workmate of mine, Peter Leadbetter, of Bearsted, was driving to work at Elliott Automation at Rochester Airport when he gave this lady a lift in his Beetle at Blue Bell Hill, just after the Lower Bell. He was speaking to her after she got in his car when, near the top of the hill, before the Upper Bell, he turned to look at her, [and] she had vanished. I knew Peter well and he was shell-shocked when he arrived at work that morning. He was so stunned he did not even want to talk about it.[20]

Peter Leadbetter
(as printed in the GEC Avionics News Oct 1986)

In subsequent correspondence, Mike, who now resides in Lincolnshire, stated it would have been around 8 a.m. that Peter came into work that morning in 1967 or 1968. This was the start time at Elliot Automation (now BAE Systems Rochester) at Rochester Airport. Mike and Peter worked together in the Flight Instrument Department (FID). Peter at the time drove a blue Volkswagen Beetle.

'The expression on his face when he arrived at work that day told the story as he did not know if anyone would believe him—and believe me, he was shook up,' he said. 'At that time I only lived about a mile away in Walderslade and knew the stories of Blue Bell Hill well but unfortunately never experienced it myself in all the years I have travelled that road.

'Peter will be in his 70s now, as he would have been approximately 30 at that time. I was 23; now I'm 65. We lost touch in 1968 when I moved to another electronics firm in Rochester High Street making test gear for Elliots before moving on again.'[21]

In this account, the motorist, who is characteristically alone, meets the lone female hitch-hiker on the Hill, who in this instance, wishes to travel north towards Rochester and the Medway towns. We do not learn the girl's precise destination, but we can assume that she gave Mr Leadbetter at least some pertinent information in their short journey together to the top of the Hill (since his own destination would not be much further on). It seems the girl—who again goes undescribed—quite naturally took the passenger seat, but managed to vanish suddenly without being observed. Defying convention again is the unusual time for the encounter: some time before 8 a.m., therefore, like the Gowers' experience, likely to be in daylight (or in the twilight approaching sunrise, depending on the time of year).

More we cannot say, other than to note the features that tally with both the legend and the other accounts of the same period: the estimated year of the episode (no later than 1968, when Mike Stevens had moved on in his career); the picking up of the girl at Blue Bell Hill (in the area again of the Lower Bell) and the sudden curtailment of her journey shortly afterward (in this, and in Malcolm Grant's case, before even leaving the Hill itself). We can add to this the stated sincerity of the witness, who never sought publicity himself after his experience, but rather was inclined not to talk about it. Such details speak for the authenticity of the encounter, even if we are challenged in our acceptance by the absence of the witness himself to vouch for his own encounter, and by the very proposition itself: a vanishing passenger, judged initially to be have been a normal human female.

With these accounts we are, in a sense, brought full circle, to the case as it stood in the late 1960s involving a hitch-hiking phantom, and the variations in destination reported by Tom Harber's anonymous witnesses. We may have advanced to a point where the premise of a genuine haunting is more supportable, but the case overall still falters in the pursuit of the single satisfying 'explanation' found in the time-honoured 'cause' of that period, the 1965 tragedy.

An interesting adjunct to Mike Stevens' original post included his impression that the origin of the ghost girl was to be found in an accident with a horse-drawn cart back in the Hill's history, or so he recalled from his years growing up in Walderslade in the 1950s. While I have found no historical support for this,[22] as we noted in the cases of Bob Vandepeer and Jack Woodger, and in Nigel D.'s recollections in the last chapter, suggestions of a road ghost associated with Blue Bell Hill prior to the 1960s can certainly be found among senior residents of the area, even if these are little more than anecdotes without easy connection to the later reports. We can recall, for instance, Mrs Renee Hughes' remembered tale from the 1950s of a man in a snowstorm (Chapter 6). The one exception (which we looked at in detail in Chapter 10) is Jack Woodger's experience in 1934, and its possible connection with the tragic case of Emily Trigg in 1916.

But there is precious little reference to ghosts or mysterious happenings at Blue Bell Hill in the news archives of the intervening years, before 1934, or between 1934 and the 1950s. The closest we get is an initially promising-sounding snippet in the *Chatham Observer* for 8 August 1952—'Blue Bell Hill Mystery Solved'—which goes onto to relate how a pair of crutches found in a pool of blood on the Maidstone–Chatham road at Blue Bell Hill turned out to be the petrol-soaked appendages of an invalid carriage owner who had broken down.[23]

Other sources—from outside the archives—however, *do* place rumours of a ghostly female at Blue Bell Hill in this period, and these leave behind the Phantom Hitch-Hiker scenario for the more familiar territory of the modern encounters. One also makes a connection with Rochester Airport. In his book *Ghost Stations V,* Bruce Barrymore Halpenny talks about the ghost of Blue Bell Hill in relation to a German air attack on Rochester aerodrome in August 1940. Rochester Airport then housed the Short Brothers production facility for the four-engine Stirling Bomber. As such, it became a target of *Adler Tag* (Eagle Day), the Luftwaffe's planned sweeping destruction of the RAF as a prerequisite to an invasion of Britain. On 15 August 1940, the facility came under a bombing attack, which resulted in the destruction of six new Stirlings in their hangar, and set back the manufacture of the aircraft here for a year. This much is true.

According to the book, on the night of the raid a young woman set out from Maidstone to cycle to Rochester airfield, where her boyfriend was working. At Blue Bell Hill, the chain on her bicycle broke. Seeking assistance, she ran out to stop a lorry, but under wartime restrictions on dipped headlights the driver did not see her and she was knocked down and allegedly run over by its rear wheels. A few months afterward, it is said, a motorist ran over a young lady, only to find she had vanished when he got out to investigate.[24]

On the face of it, this would seem to point to yet another candidate for the ghost of Blue Bell Hill. The book itself, which was published in 1993 (and therefore after the much-publicised encounters of Sharpe and Dawkins), provides no reference. Nor have I found any record of such an accident in the newspaper archives for that date or for some time either side of it.

The air raid was a daylight one. It is known that a group of fighter-accompanied Dornier Do17 bombers crossed the English Channel towards Dover at around 3.30 p.m., and divided over Faversham to head for their respective targets, one of which was the Shorts factory at Rochester. Around 300 high explosive bombs were dropped, causing extensive damage to the airfield's buildings. Some also fell on the nearby Davis Estate east of the airfield, demolishing five houses and damaging others, with nine reported injuries.[25] A surviving flight log from one of the Dorniers involved in the raid records the aircraft departing Antwerp at 15.10 hrs for Rochester, and returning at 17.25 hrs.[26] Sunset on 15 August 1940 was at 20.23 hrs (8.23 p.m.). The girl in this story started her journey after the fall of darkness, which would make sense only if she had delayed her journey (perhaps out of caution of another attack) and had set out with some confidence that her boyfriend would be at the field at that hour.

This singular incident and its purported ghostly sequel are clearly anecdotal, and therefore without serious claim to a place in the Blue Bell Hill canon. Nevertheless we might concede some meaningful connection with Bob Fearne's brief encounter involving a girl on a bicycle (Chapter 9).

Leon Posner encountered an out-of-place female figure on Blue Bell Hill in 1957. At the time, he worked as a taxi and wedding driver, operating mainly out of the rank by Chatham's Town Hall, and would often work a late shift that ended in the early morning. In the spring of that year, he had picked up a fare outside the Army and Navy store to take two soldiers back to the barracks at Maidstone. The weather was clear, with good visibility. On his return journey, at around 1 a.m., and 'just past' Common Road in Blue Bell Hill Village, he saw a woman walking in the road towards him. She wore a long dress and her head was covered. He immediately swerved to avoid her, but believing he had caught her with his car, he stopped. But when he got out of the car, there was no-one there, and no evidence of a collision. He drove on to his home at Rochester, and woke his wife to tell her, but she simply told him to go to bed. The next day he contacted the local police to find out if there had been any report of an accident, only to be told (apparently) that he had seen the 'ghost' and to forget about it.

Mr Posner's son, Howard, who related his father's story, said: 'He would never tell this as a boast, or very often, but I certainly recall it was told with a sense of unease and no embellishment. I never heard him tell any similar experiences. I have no idea on the truth of what happened, but he was always convinced of what he had seen and done and he was normally sensible.'[27]

We remain in the realm of anecdotes for the next few accounts, which nevertheless are set at familiar locations.

In April 2010, 'JST' of Sutton Valence, Kent, posted his own account of an encounter on Blue Bell Hill on the same thread of the Kent History Forum website that Mike Stevens had recorded his recollections. This happened in the early hours, around 2 a.m., of one November morning in 1979 or 1980, when JST was working in Maidstone and had just bought his first car, a Mini 1275GT. He was heading home after an evening out at The Warehouse nightclub in Maidstone, and was driving up Blue Bell Hill, where he was to drop off the girl he had been out with in Robin Hood Lane (in Blue Bell Hill Village):

> The hill was patchily misty, and as we passed the Upper Bell the mist became thicker. I lifted off the accelerator and a fraction of a second later saw a young woman in a long hooded coat or cape standing in the road in front of me, illuminated by my headlights. I was still doing about 40 mph, but slowing quite quickly as the hill levelled out, and I hit the brakes thinking (selfishly) 'I've had this car a couple of weeks and I'm about to wreck it and it's my fault.' The girl with me screamed and I braced myself for the impact. But it never happened.
>
> I got out of the car shaking like a leaf, not helped by the girl with me yelling at me, 'you hit her, you hit her'. There was no-one there; the car was undamaged. I had hit nothing.
>
> Very scary moment, (I can feel my back tingling now as I remember this event). I had not heard the story of the 'ghost of bluebell hill' (and I don't believe in ghosts, etc), and it was some years later that I read about the legend. I like to think it was an illusion caused by swirling mist, but it scared me half to death and the girl with me that night refused to ever go out with me again![28]

It is possible JST was right in his assessment, although it would have to be an effect capable of fooling his companion also, to identical effect. We can note that the Upper Bell is also where Common Road begins, and is therefore the same area as Leon Posner's encounter over twenty years earlier. Likewise, it was outside the Upper Bell that Ann-Marie Austin and a friend passed a woman in white late one night in 1977 (Chapter 7); both being only a short distance from both Emily Trigg's former home and Chris Dawkins' encounter in 1992. It is also the spot at which a young woman died in childbirth in the late eighteenth century (Chapter 2), and the scene of a road accident in July 1939 in which a young Maidstone woman, Edna May Yearsley, sustained fatal injuries when the motorcycle on which she was the pillion passenger was in collision with a car outside the Upper Bell, throwing her over the car.[29] And this area would feature again in another curious incident in 2012.

In this round-up of anecdotal accounts, we might include the boy-racers, who, in an episode reminiscent of Peter Hedge's 1976 supernatural radio play *The Ton-Up Run* (which was set at Blue Bell Hill)[30] started out for home from the Malta Inn for a midnight race up the Hill: '... and going up the hill, where the [Shell] garage would be now I suppose, a lady in white appeared in the road from nowhere. They just managed to avoid her by swerving around her at 90-100 mph, but Clay's Alfa is so close he can see her eyes; he must surely have hit her.' They both braked hard and pulled over to go back to investigate but found nothing.[31] And there is the account given by 'Dave1970' of a figure encountered in the same area in 1990: 'I saw the lady standing with a white nightie with dark hair standing on the edge of the road where the Shell garage is now, going up the hill. The figure stepped out right in front of me whilst staring at me. No sign of a body afterwards. It was reported to the police; they advised me of the previous sightings and the story. When the police informed me of a possible ghost I changed my views of ghosts and spirits completely. And before you ask, I'm not mad and I wasn't drinking.'[32]

This same part of the Hill would feature in another very similar named-witness encounter around the same year (see the next chapter).

In 2003, an anonymous contributor to the BBC Kent website (identified only as an employee of the Bridgewood Manor Hotel), posted the following account, which, it was claimed, occurred in October of 2002:

> I travel daily down the A229 past Bluebell Hill, and into Aylesford. As I take the turnoff for Aylesford, across the motorway is a road leading from Aylesford onto the motorway. Here is a bus stop.
>
> One night as I was leaving Aylesford and coming up the same usual road to come onto the motorway, I saw a woman standing by the bus stop. I slowed down as this time buses had stopped running, and her attire was rather odd. As I have slowed the woman moved in front of my vehicle. We slammed on the brakes and suddenly, the woman was gone. We looked around the car yet, there was no sign of her or any kind of injured person.[33]

From the description, the bus stop in this case is inferred to be the one on the Chatham Road near Salisbury Road (i.e. near the scene of the 1965 crash; the 'motorway' actually being the A229 dual carriageway).

Meaningful as it is in terms of location and time frame (after the last bus would make it very late), plus the figure's behaviour and the absence of specific details such as the witness's identity or any elaboration regarding the 'odd' attire or age of the woman, prevents this account—like the others in this section—from being regarded as anything more noteworthy than an interesting aside to the better known encounters.

In April 2003, Blue Bell Hill's ghost was featured on the late night (10 p.m. to 1 a.m.) slot of the popular national radio show talkSPORT, which at that time accommodated phone-ins from listeners on a variety of subjects. The show, then usually hosted by James Whale, was on this occasion covered by a stand-in presenter, who received a call from a lady who appealed for listeners' accounts about the Blue Bell Hill road ghost. A gentleman subsequently rang in to claim that he had seen this ghost not once, but twice. The man (who gave his name, although this was not noted by my correspondent, who was listening to the show and summarised it for me by email the following day) said the first incident had taken place a month before Christmas in 1978. The location on Blue Bell Hill was not stated, but the incident is said to have occurred late at night, after 11 p.m.

The witness was driving via Blue Bell Hill when he noticed a young girl (between ten and thirteen years old) at the side of the road. He had scarcely time to register her before she strode out in front of his car and he struck her. In a state of shock he got out of the car to find the girl lying prostrate in the road.

'He couldn't tell whether she was alive or dead, but what he recalled after a very fraught initial inspection before getting a blanket from the boot of his car was that she had ginger shoulder-length hair, an old-fashioned style of clothing (even for the 1970s), of which details escape me, but I believe a blue cardigan were mentioned and some sort of frock or dress—not really in keeping with the winter season. She also appeared to have no marks of impact, no bruises or scratches.'

When the man returned from the car, the girl was still there. He wrapped the blanket around her and ran to the nearest house for help. When he returned, she had vanished.

The second occasion was a year later, and at a similar time of night, when he was again at Blue Bell Hill, and glanced into his rear-view mirror and saw for an instant the same girl sitting in the back of the car. The man stressed that it was only for a moment, and rationalised that it could have just been a trick of his mind. When he checked the back seat there was no-one there.[34]

The incident sounded very much like the Goodenough encounter of 1974, but my correspondent was certain this was not the man's name. Besides, the dates did not agree. So, superficially, we might have a similar incident to Maurice Goodenough's just a few years after his well-publicised encounter. It would be interesting to learn where this incident was said to have taken place.

This gentleman's experience a year later was perhaps an unconscious spillover from the first incident, which might understandably arise in someone who had had a prior personal encounter. But fears that the ghost might appear in the back seats of cars (already a feature of the legend at Blue Bell Hill) appear in relation to other road ghost cases also, and seem to be an instinctual expression of the innate fear related to them. In some instances this is not without justification, as in Rod Vecsey's case at Easton, Connecticut (Chapter 9) and Jean Clarke's at Borley in Essex (Chapter 4).

Encountering a ghost on the road is one thing (even if it involves the kind of shocking collision scenario featured in this book, in which there usually remains a degree of detachment from the figure). Finding it in close proximity within one's own vehicle is quite another, particularly if the invasion of this personal space is without invitation. Here it is much harder to avoid the notion that the

encounter is purposefully directed toward the witness, and he or she was not simply the next unlucky motorist to happen along.

Legends and folklore have their own say on the matter. In the lore of the Steubenville ghost, the hitch-hiking phantom of Route 7 south of Steubenville, Ohio (USA), it is said that those who stop to give her a ride are never seen again—which accords both with traditional folklore, which describes the propensity of some elemental spirits to abduct people, body and soul together, and with the claim of a Blue Bell Hill resident in 1992 who claimed that when he accompanied a research team to the Hill in the 1970s a medium ran off screaming saying the ghost wanted to take somebody to the 'other side'.[35]

Such ideas might be fanciful, but the primal fear that suddenly wells up in these encounters to overwhelm the rational faculties is very real. The perceived threat, however, is perhaps less a physical one than one posed to the conscious mind from its brush with the ineffable.

As business partners Kenneth Halbert and Clarence Coulter discovered when they met the Steubenville phantom on a drive through difficult wintry conditions on 30 December 1948. Coming into a place where the Ohio River valley flattened out and the road ran straight for some distance, the pair found their way blocked by a woman in a white gossamer gown and veil, who stood with her hand raised in halting gesture. Fearing she might be the bait for a gang of robbers, Coulter tried to gently steer the car around her, cautiously avoiding putting it into a skid on the icy road. The figure reacted by floating quickly back into their path. Again, Coulter steered back, trying to avoid hitting her, and again the woman glided quickly back to block their path, forcing them to a full stop, at which point the figure moved to her original position in the middle of the road.

> We were confused and scared, but completely lucid and in control. I rolled the window down about 4 or 5 inches. She sounded like someone in a complete alcohol or drugged stupor as if her tongue was very thick. She leaned down and her face was may be 18 inches from mine. She asked if we were going to Steubenville. She kept repeating it and I said 'any fool could see that we just came from there'. Clarence leaned forward to see her past me, and tried to get some sense out of her.
>
> I suddenly realised she was featureless. There were dark spots where there should have been eyes, nostrils and mouth, but she was like smoke. In back of her to the west against the foot of the hill, a house had been recently built. As we were both staring into her face, someone turned on a light in the front of that house, and we saw it—through her.
>
> We were suddenly very scared. He was a semi-pro fighter, and I was not a coward either. *I was afraid she might enter the car.* I'll never forget my exact words as I cranked the window closed: 'Let's get the hell out of here.' [italics–mine].[36]

Related to the instinctual fear of an unbidden appearance in the car is a belief found in other areas of ghost lore and investigation that these phantoms are capable of following the witness home. In some instances it appears intentional, as in the case of Christopher Christie at Whitehills, and in the example of the diminutive ghostly woman that terrorised the village of Coolock, near Dublin (Eire) late at night in the early 1930s with its weird, wild, unearthly cries. In January 1931, a Mr J. Connor met the ghost while cycling home at 12.45 a.m. in bright moonlight. The figure was standing in the middle of the road, and while he pedalled faster, it (and its ceaseless wail) kept pace with him until he reached home, where it disappeared in the shadows of some trees.[37]

That there is a sinister flip-side to the ostensibly benign and pitiful actions of the classic Phantom Hitch-Hiker is self-evident in the graphic encounters in which 'she' runs into the path of a car, and in the dark encounters with the crone—both of which must rank with the most dramatic and terrifying of ghostly encounters.

That these apparitions might be the cause of road deaths as well as a consequence of them is also well developed in folklore and belief, as befitting these typically ambivalent entities. In September 2012, I came across the following account by Nigerian writer Chioma Obiefuna, who had heard it directly from the witness, a Lagos businessman, whose encounter took place during his late night return from a cross-border trip to Cotonou (Benin). The coastal road crosses the border into Nigeria at Seme Border, where it becomes the F100. After Badagri, the F100 becomes the Lagos-Badagry road:

> I was on my way back to Lagos from Seme Border and it was almost midnight. Because of the lateness of the hour, our driver was driving at high speed and just before the popular Maza Maza area in Lagos, what looked like a middle-aged guy appeared in the middle of the road with his right hand raised. I tell you—the guy just mysteriously appeared in the middle of the road; I didn't see him walk out from anywhere and I'm very certain because I was awake, alert and sitting in front with the driver.
>
> Our driver saw him and hit the accelerator even harder. I screamed at the driver to stop but he told me that if he stopped, we would be in big trouble as it was a road ghost looking for blood to shed. When we passed and I looked back, there was nothing.
>
> He, along with another passenger in the car who travelled often and late at night, started telling many tales of road ghosts they'd come across in their journeys. The road ghosts came in many forms—some appeared as little children and some came in the forms of very old women bent over walking sticks and usually, they just appeared in the middle of the road, forcing drivers to stop. He said those that made the mistake of stopping usually found themselves in nasty accidents and few lived to tell the tale. I'd heard many stories of road ghosts but I saw one and it was scary. And now, I believe.

Chioma told me that businessmen that trade between borders often make these trips in hired cars with a driver. The witness, who is known to her, told her that others had claimed similar experiences, and some had hit these apparitions so hard they had dented their cars (echoes of Keith Scales' experience, Chapter 9)—but when they check, there is no evidence of anything there.

Chioma said: 'The driver's explanation for not stopping was due to tales exchanged by many other late night road users who have talked about the negative consequences of stopping for these apparitions, i.e. many experienced serious accidents and some were fatal. I guess it's the survivors that come back with these strange tales.'[38]

A popular theory in Nigeria is that such apparitions are the products of bad *Juju* (old voodoo) that are set abroad by their creators for harmful purposes or as a means to gaining magical power, but which may afterward gain some autonomy.

Similar encounters, and interpretations, are found across the African continent. In 2005, Kenyan journalist Kamau Mutunga, a feature writer for *The Nation* newspaper in Nairobi, penned a survey of the road ghosts that plague long distance drivers.

'I have seen many apparitions while driving at night,' said Nyangoro Mong'are, who had twenty years' driving experience on Kenya's roads. 'They are mostly children or naked women crossing the road. This happens near a bridge or during a misty night. But I usually hit or drive through them.'

Well, one can only hope that these *were* all apparitions, for his sake; more so for the plight of any real pedestrians foolhardy enough to risk crossing the road late at night!

But Mr Mong'are is not alone. In April 2004, bus driver Samuel Osiago was driving Easter travellers along the Nakuru–Kisumu Road when he saw a man roasting maize in the middle of the road—at 3 a.m.

'I had heard a lot about apparitions and I had been warned by other drivers never to brake or swerve. I was cruising at over 100 km an hour. So I just ran over him,' he said. There was no impact, no damage to the vehicle, and no man or maize cobs under the bus.

Other drivers have been involved in real accidents that they have attributed to the sudden appearance of apparitions, to which they have reacted by braking or swerving. It is easy to be cynical and assume it a natural tendency to try to avoid personal responsibility by blaming someone or something else in these situations. However, it is surely interesting that the figures they report they were trying to avoid were a 'child', a 'gorgeous beauty' or an 'old woman' in the road—precisely the character set found at Blue Bell Hill.

Peter Kisebu, 76, a tour driver for forty-nine years, said: 'Several of my colleagues have seen them near Mariakani on the way to Mombasa. Those who ignore and ran over them survived. Those who did not died and caused the death of others. I have lost several friends that way. But apparitions are nothing but genies.'[39]

While these ideas serve as explanations in parts of Africa, where reports of road ghosts may become readily assimilated into the cultural mindscape, in Western culture interpretations attempt to find meaning from the basis of its own heritage of beliefs. Here, ghosts are the restless spirits of the dead; or, increasingly today, where they have been pushed to the margins of a materialistic-scientific worldview, dismissed as dying vestiges of a superstitious past—which is why their continued occurrences in modern times and settings prompt an array of confused responses and interpretations among those confronted by them.

But in the West we seem to have forgotten our own folklore regarding ghosts. As Alan Watts reminds us: 'So, in the same way old folklore says, whenever you meet a ghost, don't run away. Because the ghost will capture the substance of your fear and materialise itself out of your own substance, and will kill you eventually, because it will take over all your own vitality. So then, whenever confronted with a ghost, walk straight into it and it will disappear.'[40]

But if we step away from cultural influences for a moment and look more closely at these African examples we find all the same recurring features found in Western accounts—indeed, in similar accounts the world over: the figure makes its appearance late at night; it assumes the middle of the road; not uncommonly, a hand is raised in 'stop' gesture (sometimes it assumes a pleading or supplicatory pose). In some instances, an overwhelming air of sadness emanates from the figure; in other examples, the figure's leering smile advertises a perverse, darker intent. Where the attempt at stopping the vehicle fails, the figure seems to deliberately move to be run over. Sometimes the collision is felt by the motorist; rarely, but not unheard of, some damage is registered by the vehicle. Most often there is no 'body' to be discovered and no evidence of a collision at all. Sometimes and again, rarely, the victim *is* found in the road (e.g. in Maurice Goodenough's case), only to be found to have vanished shortly afterward; or, as in one example associated with Chicago's Resurrection Mary, it melts away before the witness's eyes.[41]

In other instances, the figure achieves the same effect by assuming an equally disturbing stance: of lying in the road. Blue Bell Hill provides one example, albeit only in the form of a brief anecdote heard by Neil Arnold. The informant was an elderly lady who came forward after a talk in Rainham (Kent), to state matter-of-factly that 'around twenty years ago' her brother-in-law had been driving up Blue Bell Hill at night when, near the Kits Coty Restaurant (therefore on the Old Chatham Road), he saw, lying in the road ahead, a woman in a white dress. As he approached the figure stood up and literally floated away.[42]

The tale is, to be sure, a friend-of-a-friend one. In its defence it has the adamance of the informant, and its originality. It is not the kind of scenario one would likely think up to go alongside the more familiar behavioural styles at Blue Bell Hill. And, as indicated, it has the rare, but attested support of similar cases of prostrate phantoms from around the world.

Michael Fletcher met such a phantom in 1955, when he was fifteen. Returning home at about 9.30 p.m., he was pushing his bike up the steep Spring Hill in Lincoln (Lincolnshire), when he saw a man lying in the gutter. Thinking initially that the man was drunk, Michael was frightened, but noticed he seemed to be wearing old-fashioned clothing. He had his arm raised as if asking for help, and he appeared injured. His mouth moved as if trying to speak, but there was no sound. Hurrying past him a few paces, Michael turned around, thinking he should try to help the man, but the man had vanished.[43]

A very similar apparition is described by Edson C. Hendricks, who, together with his wife and another couple, encountered it in rural western Massachusetts (USA) in the autumn of 1969. Mr Hendricks was at the time a computer scientist for IBM, and was in fact the developer of the networking software that became known as VNET, which became the foundation for the Internet. The incident also took place between 9 p.m. and 10 p.m. on a dark and deserted two-lane road:

> I suddenly noticed a large middle-aged man lying on his stomach across the right shoulder, facing the road. As I drove by at about 40 miles per hour, he tried to raise himself using his left arm, and waved his right arm above his head as if gesturing for help. His dark clothing appeared ragged and soiled, and he seemed to be in severe distress. His restricted movements and facial expression suggested to me that he was seriously injured, and in substantial pain.

Mr Hendricks braked to a stop, and asked his friend, who was seated next to him, if he had seen the man. He said he had not. They both leapt out and ran back along the road to where he had seen the man.

> The shoulder was not very wide along that stretch of road, and there was a deep gravel embankment that dropped steeply off the road, down about twenty meters into a broad, flat brush and wooded area below. There was no significant vegetation on the shoulder or the embankment below it, and no other apparent place near our location where a person could have hidden. The embankment looked pretty treacherous to me; it seemed to me that it would have been no simple matter to move up, down, or along it. We reached what I thought was the place where I'd seen the man laying on the shoulder. I recall being quite confident that I'd gotten it right, but we found nobody there.
>
> Then, as we looked back behind us, we saw that apparently this same man had somehow gotten between us and our parked van. He was about half way be-

> tween us and the van and running back toward it, away from us.
>
> Fearing for the safety of the two women still in the van, my friend and I both ran back toward the parked van as fast as we could, following the running man from behind. We were running much faster than the mysterious man was moving; he still seemed somehow in poor physical condition, and we reached him just as all three of us converged on the parked van. I was shouting at the man to stop, but he made no sound that I can recall. I did not even hear sounds of his feet on the road shoulder. As I was just about to leap on the man to tackle him from behind, he abruptly veered to the right, over the edge of the very steep embankment, but extremely oddly, he did not go down the embankment. Rather, he appeared to float off the shoulder into the air over the embankment, briefly, rising slightly. Then he seemed to shrink abruptly and vanish, as if collapsing.
>
> This end to the chase transpired in just a second or two. We could neither see nor hear any further trace of the man, and I recall thinking in astonishment at the moment that there was no way he could simply have disappeared from our view.[44]

Such accounts are reminiscent of the habits of shrieking boggarts found in folklore. One such anecdote involves the story (collected in 1906) of a farmer who met a 'bullbeggar' at Creech Hill, Somerset. Making his way home late one night, the man came across a figure lying in the road. Going to its aid, it suddenly raised itself up to more than human height and chased him all the way home, where his family witnessed it cavorting up the hill, shrieking with laughter.[45]

Road phantoms have still other means of accosting, stopping, diverting, or delaying passing motorists. Thankfully, the kinds of event that follow are quite rare.

In 1998, the presenters of ITV's popular daytime show *This Morning* turned their attention (not for the first time) to the subject of ghosts. Richard Madeley (one half of 'Richard & Judy', the popular husband & wife team) and Julia Carling (standing in for Judy Finnegan) hosted a phone-in of personal experiences from the general public. Neither Richard nor Julia could have anticipated that they were about to hear a story that would so captivate them that it would result in an investigation that would span several shows. The story that was to prove so fascinating was Kevin Whelan's terrifying encounter just weeks earlier on a dark lonely stretch of the A15 near Ruskington, in Lincolnshire.

A fortnight prior to the show, Mr Whelan had been driving home from Lincoln to Sleaford (southbound) on the A15 at around 2 a.m. on a Sunday, when:

'Just before the Ruskington turn-off I saw, on the horizon, like a white shadow. I didn't know what it was. I thought it could have been car lights. I didn't give it much thought. When I got to that white shadow all of a sudden, from the driver's side of the car, a face appeared around the front pillar, and it was on my windscreen, with the left hand up. I had been travelling probably a little bit faster than I should have been, and it completely—well, it just got me by surprise.'

'It had dark hair. The skin was olivey-green. It had a pitted face. I could see the teeth. I could see everything. One hand was up. From the neck down was like when you photograph someone with a flash on—it's too bright, you get that white fluorescent sort of look.'

Mr Whelan estimated that the figure remained for forty or fifty seconds. In his panic, he did not stop the car, but accelerated to around 60 mph with the frightening figure still with him and staring in at him.

The figure '... didn't just go away; it [eventually] faded into obscurity down the side of the car.'

After this, Mr Whelan just 'bombed it' back home. When he arrived, he left his car unlocked and then locked the front door behind him ('which I never do') before waking up his wife. 'I looked in the mirror,' he said, 'and I was white. My skin looked like a turkey, it was all goose bumps. I was crying.'[46]

Inevitably, Kevin Whelan's experience prompted speculation over what he had encountered. Julia Carling suggested that it was because he had been driving too fast, and the figure may have been trying to warn him. Two other people called in to report having seen a figure along the same stretch, in one instance, with its hand raised.[47]

The location is certainly one where accidents might be expected to occur. The turn-off for the village of Ruskington sits atop an east-west ridge, which would have formed the horizon for Kevin Whelan when he first saw the figure. The A15 crests this ridge before descending on either side into a sinuous path across the lower ground. The bends are appropriately sign-posted to warn drivers. Even so, this section of road has no worse a fatality record (three incidents) for the decade following Kevin Whelan's encounter than others in the area; in fact, it has a far slighter record than the nearby A17 between Sleaford and Leadenham (11) for the same period.[48] But the location is quite characteristic of those favoured by road ghosts, which are frequently encountered on bends or hills on rural roads, befitting their liminal character.

Significantly, perhaps, the scene of these encounters is the site of a vanished medieval village. The remains of Dunsby St Andrews, which is recorded in the Domesday Book, is visible today only as crop marks and earthworks (particularly in aerial view) on the eastern side of the A15. A landmark named in identifying the scene by Kevin Whelan and other witnesses—'the house on the right'—known as Dunsby House, is said to stand on the site of the medieval church; hence the modern road runs through the site of this abandoned village.[49] Is there a connection between the sightings and the history of this location? We can only guess.

Noteworthy in this case is Kevin Whelan's reaction. Had it been the figure's intention to warn of danger, as supposed, then the action backfired when he understandably accelerated to try to rid himself of his unwelcome passenger. In so doing, Kevin Whelan's instinctive response resonates more with the African cases that recognise something inherently 'wrong' or even dangerous about road ghost encounters, in relative contrast to the intuitions that spring most readily to Western minds. Little wonder that road ghosts (among others—for instance, the frightful *Bean-sídhe* (banshee) of Irish Gaelic folklore) came to be interpreted as omens of death.

Julia Nash encountered a similar apparition in 1999 on a country road (the B2166) between Chichester and Pagham, West Sussex. It was around 8.30 p.m. on a November evening. The road was busy, with cars in front and behind hers, and a line of traffic coming the other way. After Runcton Nursery the road enters a sweeping S-bend section that is marked by warning chevrons and a white village sign for Lagness. The verge on the left is lined with trees and bushes; the right is flanked by a wide grass verge and a stream that flows parallel to the road. Julia takes up the story:

> I saw something black flapping at the corner of the front passenger part of the windscreen and then just a head and shoulders in a black hood and cloak came across the bonnet about half way and looked at me with dark amused eyes. The car didn't go through it; it was carrying it along on the bonnet. At first I thought it was a pheasant, then a human, so I was shouting at it to get out of the way. I had no option but to keep going because of the heavy traffic. I must have been travelling about 35–40 mph. We went into the bend and then down the road and got to the long hedge on the right side of the road [opposite the entrance to Roundstone nurseries, around 200 metres down the road] and then the ghost dissolved into that hedge in a kind of jagged way, having crossed the line of cars coming in the opposite direction. I remember it was still just the head and shoulders in the black hood and cloak, and the head turned to the left before it disappeared, as though it was looking at the traffic coming towards it. The whole incident must have taken only 10–15 seconds.
>
> As I've said, surely other drivers coming in the opposite direction must have seen it as it crossed in front of them, and of course the driver behind me. It was a solid ghost, not transparent at all, but the features were indistinct except for the eyes which were dark brown. The face in the hood was sallow and fairly long and I didn't see a mouth and nose. I'd say it looked like a 30-year-old man, but probably not a monk. I felt a bit stunned by it all but not exactly frightened. I accepted it was a ghost although I've never seen one before. But it must be fairly

unusual to see a ghost on a busy road?[50]

Julia indicated that the figure, which she thought resembled a poacher or smuggler from two centuries or so ago, had stared straight at her 'with dark eyes that were definitely amused'—as if, she reflected afterwards, he had hoped she would have a collision—which fortunately did not happen. Julia later heard that the figure had been seen previously and was known to some of the locals. She was sufficiently intrigued to look into the accident record of the area but this proved unremarkable.[51]

More significant is the location itself which, like Ruskington, has the familiar features: the rural location, the bend in the road; even the nearby water course may be significant. All are features of modern and historical road ghosts and the folklore behind them. Unusually, this incident occurred at a relatively early hour and in busy road conditions, and seems to combine the Phantom Jaywalker and the Phantom Hitch-Hiker habits. The figure emerged from undergrowth on the left, 'rode' on the car's bonnet for 200 metres, and continued on its way through a hedge on the other side of the road—a novel manoeuvre for a road ghost! One possible reason for this is the presence of a parallel-running stream on the road's west side, which veers away from it further down the road. Ghosts are traditionally said to be unable to cross water. Is this the reason the figure needed to deflect from its east-west course—to obey the convention?

While ideas among those accepting of ghosts tend to interpret them as the restless spirits of deceased humans, cases such as Keith Whelan's and the other accounts related here demonstrate that, much as we attempt to deny or rationalise them, the boggarts, bullbeggars and other ambiguous sprites that populate our folklore refuse to be left behind with a superstitious past. Rather, they appear to very much alive and vital as we stride into the twenty-first century.

THIRTEEN

MORE WHITE LADIES

I met a lady in the meads,
Full beautiful—a faery's child,
Her hair was long, her foot was light,
And her eyes were wild.

She took me to her Elfin grot,
And there she wept and sighed full sore,
And there I shut her wild wild eyes
With kisses four.

And there she lulled me asleep,
And there I dreamed—Ah! woe betide!
The latest dream I ever dreamt
On the cold hill side.

I saw pale kings and princes too,
Pale warriors, death-pale were they all;
They cried—'La Belle Dame sans Merci
Hath thee in thrall!'

I saw their starved lips in the gloam,
With horrid warning gaped wide,
And I awoke and found me here,
On the cold hill's side.

From *La Belle Dame sans Merci*
John Keats (1819)

Thus far at Blue Bell Hill we have concentrated on the two principal forms of ghostly encounter exhibited there: the Phantom Hitch-Hiker and the Phantom Jaywalker. But there is a third category belonging to this set that we have encountered along the way. These are the female figures that do not hitch lifts from passing vehicles or throw themselves beneath their wheels, but are seen either simply walking or standing passively by the roadside. Among the examples of this latter version is the female figure encountered at the bottom of Blue Bell Hill by Barry Collings and Steven Pope, and the one by Anne-Marie Austin and a companion near the Upper Bell (Chapter 7), both in the 1970s; plus the anecdotal examples in Chapter 10.

Such figures, where they fail to provide such evidences we might expect of ghosts, are naturally much harder to differentiate from living persons and we should rightly be more cautious in our assessments of them. But there is evidently something about these encounters that goes beyond merely the unexpected sighting of a lone female at a remote location at a late hour—something that whispers to the witness that they may have encountered a *ghost*.

In 2003, Ron Thomas wrote to me to relate his sighting of an unusual female at Blue Bell Hill in 1968:

> For many years I have wondered if a woman I saw on Blue Bell Hill at around 4.15 a.m. on the corner of [what is] now the old road and very near the accident site, was in fact the 'Ghost'. The passenger in the car with me wanted me to stop and talk to her but I drove on as it all happened so fast as we were travelling down the hill and in a hurry to get to Southampton.
>
> The year would have been around 1968 and I was very aware of the stories that surrounded the incident. Once in a while I take a guest on a recap of the 'sighting' and it still sends shivers down my back!

In subsequent correspondence, Mr Thomas confirmed his sighting to have been near the bus stop before Salisbury Road, a short distance from the old quarry entrance on the 'up' side of the Hill—as he indicated, very near the scene of the 1965 tragedy.

'It would have been in the autumn around mid-November, as my 6-month contract at Esso Fawley near Southampton was coming to an end, and I had started that in the May of that year.'

At the speed Mr Thomas was descending the Hill, around 45 mph to 50 mph, the sighting was over in a matter of seconds. This understandably limited the information he could gather, but he recollected that the figure was a female of average height; she wore a long, light-coloured coat and stood motionless at the side of the road, where his headlights picked her out as he swept around the bend.[1]

A lone female standing at a bus stop, even late at night at Blue Bell Hill wouldn't necessarily be unusual. After all, the placing of the bus stops here, and over the footbridge on the southbound side of the A229, was made to cater for those residents of Kit's Coty Estate who were without their own transport. However, the very early hour, long after the last bus of the previous night, and some time before the start of the next morning's service, would tend to rule out this explanation. Almost as unlikely (but not impossible) is the possibility that she was waiting by arrangement for a lift. Coupled with the strange stillness of the girl and the location, it is understandable that the figure might be taken for the ghost.

Wendy Lang saw a similar figure near the same spot in the late 1960s—certainly before 1970, as the dual carriageway had not yet been constructed. At the time, she worked for British Sisalkraft at Strood. A couple of times a month, on a Tuesday or a Thursday night, her partner would pick her up after work and they would drive up to the speedway at West Ham stadium in their old primrose-yellow Ford Zephyr. They would often return late, arriving home at Princes Park, Chatham, after midnight. On this occasion, which was late in the year, October or November, they started up the Hill from the direction of Burham.

A little further up, at a place they knew as 'the gap' (a wider point marked by a fence and fir trees where a footpath led down to Kit's Coty), Wendy caught sight of a 'young girl' in a long white dress standing back on the verge, illuminated against the backdrop by their car's headlights as they passed her. She stood quite motionless, 'as if in a bit of a dream'. She was around eighteen to twenty years old, with shoulder-length hair, and her dress was old-fashioned in style: ankle-length, with a square neckline, banded at the waist, and long sleeves—'definitely not a wedding dress'—but something from late Victorian times or the turn of the last century.

Wendy remarked, 'What's she doing here at this time of night?' But her partner, who hadn't seen her, turned his inside mirror to look back and, seeing nothing, said, 'Are you sure? Maybe she lives down there.' But the possibility it might be someone in need of a lift at that late hour prompted them to stop. Wendy's partner ran back down the hill to the spot, but could not find her. He had a look over the steep bank on one side, and in the strip of woods across the road, but came back to report that there was no-one there.[2]

In 2004, Nick Morgan, then living and teaching in Australia, added his own encounter with an out-of-place female on the Hill:

> I lived on the Davis Estate near Chatham for a few months in 1991 and walked from the bottom of Bluebell Hill at the motor-way exit to the Davis Estate in the very early hours of the morning. I think that it would have been July of 1991 and somewhere between 12.30 a.m. and 2.30 a.m. I can recount the events, but you must understand that I am a complete skeptic and it would scare [the] life out of me if I were to believe in this ghost story. What intrigues me is that years after walking up Bluebell Hill I read a chapter in the book entitled *The Haunted South,*

> and was staggered to read that this hill is haunted by the ghost of a young woman, because a young woman appeared and disappeared whilst I was walking. If this interests you in any way, shape or form, do not hesitate to get in touch.

Naturally, I was interested to hear more about Nick's experience, which he furnished by reply:

> I was dropped off at the motorway exit around 12.30 a.m., around mid-July in 1991, and commenced walking up the hill. It was still, and a little hazy, and the street lights were lighting up the road and a little of the fields and golf course. This is before the petrol stop was built on the left hand side as you travel up the hill. There was no traffic whatsoever and there were an amazing number of foxes out and think I recall counting 24 of them as I scaled the hill.
>
> When I was about 20 minutes into the walk, I heard the sound of high heels on the road behind me. About 60 metres behind me was a youngish woman, who was quite well dressed, who was walking in the same direction as me. I recall thinking at the time that as it was well after last drinks call at the pubs, that she must have gone somewhere and at this early hour decided to make her way home. I also thought to myself 'where on earth did she come from?' as I hadn't passed her and she hadn't caught up to me from further down the hill.
>
> She didn't make eye contact with me but was walking with haste and seemed a little upset. I didn't want to scare her so I made the gesture of crossing the road to walk on the other side, letting her know that I had seen her and was no threat to her.
>
> Her footsteps were audible for another reasonably long period of time and she remained the same distance behind me despite me walking pretty speedily. Suddenly the footsteps stopped and she was not there. At the time I thought of all the options that could have occurred, but I would have seen her if she had stopped or had walked off the road. I remembered being intrigued by this but was tired and nearly home so I continued without giving it any further thought.
>
> A good 2 years later I was in the souvenir shop at the White Cliffs Experience in Dover and picked up a book entitled 'The Haunted South' [by Joan Forman]. I read the chapter on the Ghost of Bluebell Hill, and although the basic story was different to mine, I remembered with a jolt that I had seen a young woman; she was well dressed, and that she seemed to appear and disappear without any simple explanation. The more I thought about it there was so much about this woman that just didn't make sense. She seemed so out of place.
>
> Please believe me that I am one hell of a skeptic, but I haven't got a clear explanation about this experience. I am a school teacher, and deal with facts all day every day, so to experience something that I cannot explain really bugs and scares me.[3]

Anyone with any knowledge of Blue Bell Hill will appreciate that it is not a location where you expect to see numbers of pedestrians late at night (other than the occasional ghost hunter perhaps); especially alone; especially female.

The Hill effectively occupies the mid-point between the M2 and M20 motorways and Maidstone and the Medway Towns, with the wide snaking ribbon of the A229 facilitating a fast and efficient link between them—which provides one clue as to why anomalous events might happen here. Road ghosts, as we shall see, are most often encountered in suburban or rural settings—where the street lights finish; where ordered society gives way to the barely tamed, unconscious landscape.

Even so, facility does exist to travel this route on foot or by bicycle. The Chatham Road is paved northward between the Lower Bell and Salisbury Road, where a footbridge spanning the A229 links to a designated cycle path on the road's eastern side that continues uphill into Blue Bell Hill Village. While keen cyclists are sometimes in evidence, even into the night, it is rare to find pedestrians attempting the two-mile slog (unless, perhaps, they have missed the last bus or lack the means or opportunity of a lift).

Where it may be that lone pedestrians *are* encountered on the Hill at night, females will naturally stand out, for reason of their gender or from the associations they evoke with the Hill's ghostly reputation. But for all this, those witnesses to a lone female have generally found in them incongruous features that have prevented them from easily dismissing their sightings as 'normal' events.

In December 2003, two further witnesses to a passive female figure at Blue Bell Hill wrote to the *Kent Messenger* with their sightings.[4] Tracy Boon, then of Boughton Monchelsea near Maidstone, reported that she had seen the figure of a young female standing on the above-mentioned footbridge on four separate occasions. She and her husband Simon regularly travelled up the Hill before 7 a.m. on the way to work in London.

'We used to go up Blue Bell Hill to get to the A2 and I used to see her in the morning on the pedestrian bridge in a long, white, frilly, flowery nightie, just standing there watching. She had longish hair, past her shoulder, and looked like she was holding something, possibly a toy, but Simon never saw her even though I pointed her out.'

Mrs Boon's initial thought was one of concern, since although it was summer, it was not warm and the girl was ill-dressed for the conditions and alone. Having recently moved into the area (from Bromley), her thoughts were not of ghosts, but that the girl might have absconded from a care home, as it was 'totally odd' that someone would be out in a nightgown so early in the morning. But after repeated sightings it was evident there was something strange about the figure, which she could not put down to an ordinary though unusual occurrence, such as the actions of a sleepwalking youngster. After 1999, she never saw the girl again.

The footbridge over the A229 and the Chatham Road at Blue Bell Hill

Joe Chester, of Chatham, met a strange female around 10 p.m. one inclement Friday night in October 1968 while on his way home from Maidstone. He was pushing his bike up the section of road below the Upper Bell (now a disused slip-road out of Blue Bell Hill Village) when '… this young girl in a nightgown or frock ran from the hedge. She was soaking wet, with hair hanging round her face, and she headed straight for my cycle. When she got to the front wheel she stared straight at me before heading off behind me down the middle of the road and disappearing into the hedge again.'

Mr Chester told the *Kent Messenger* that the woman was in her late teens or early twenties, about 5ft 2in tall, with brown shoulder-length hair. She wore a light-coloured dress with a flower print on it, and she did not appear to have anything on her feet.

'She looked like a normal person, he said, 'but I have never ridden so quickly home on a bike. I was wide awake and I know it happened.'[5]

Joy Gammon of Maidstone saw a figure in white on Blue Bell Hill one night in the mid-1970s—certainly after 1972, as her sighting was definitely on the new road. A friend had missed the last bus back to the Medway Towns from Maidstone, and Joy had gone out to collect her and drive her home. By the time she was making her return journey it was late, around midnight. She was in the near-side lane when, 'about halfway down the hill'—not as far as the pedestrian footbridge, but below the now defunct slip lane out of Blue Bell Hill Village, where the verge is close to the high bank of the cutting—a white figure suddenly loomed up from the grass verge, maybe ten feet away, and just as quickly vanished. It was grey-white in colour, but little other detail was evident, other than it was female in form, with a 'typical' kind of flowing dress ('that you expect of ghosts'). The sighting was only fleeting—Joy was travelling around 50 mph, but she is certain it was not her imagination.[6]

White Ladies

In description and habit, these figures (and we can include their hitch-hiker and jaywalker counterparts) can be identified with the ubiquitous White Lady (or Woman in White), the pitiable female apparition of legend who, as a consequence of a life cut unnaturally short, or from unrequited love or betrayal or unresolved angst or guilt, cannot find rest. In the words of Aniela Jaffé: '... there is generally some place—a house or castle—where she regularly appears. She is said to walk.'[7]

The ethereal, thinly shrouded form of the White Lady is encountered also along roads, and in cemeteries and woodlands and other obscure and timeless places. Examples include Chicago's Resurrection Mary, and the ghost that walks the roads around Chew Valley Lake, between Bath and Weston-Super-Mare, Somerset.

Among a number of witnesses who have encountered the ghost girl along the B3114 south of Chew Stoke, is hairdresser Carol Gillen, who was forced to slow down as the figure crossed the road in front of her.

'She had on a long, heavily embroidered Victorian style dress with 'leg-of-mutton' sleeves,' she said. 'They were billowing back with the breeze and the whiteness of her dress was very bright, as if electric. Her hair was loose, very thick, long-ish to the top of her shoulders and blowing off her neck.' She walked across the road with a 'confident stride', taking no notice of the approaching car—prompting Carol's realisation afterward that she must have been a ghost.[8]

Another chilling example is the experience of Adrian Moorfield*, a lorry driver from Yorkshire, who had parked up for the night at a remote rural spot in November 2007 on or near to the A487 near the small Welsh town of Penparc, near Cardigan, Ceredigion, South-west Wales. What transpired after a quiet night's sleep in his cab is related by his brother-in-law, who submitted his story:

> He awoke around 3.15 a.m., had a brew, smoked a cig[arette] and carried out his morning routine of getting washed, brushing his teeth, etc.
>
> He is not allowed to set off until 4.30 a.m. so took his time getting ready. When the time came to get going, he switched on the engine and headlights only to see a figure of a young woman looking in at him!

> Sat as he was in the cab, his eye level was around seven or eight feet from the ground yet the figure was level with him.
>
> He immediately pulled around the figure and drove off. Seeing the figure pass on his left he instinctively looked in his mirror to see if it was still there but it was not visible.
>
> I asked him to describe the figure and he said she appeared young, fair haired; light-coloured dress and bare feet which were not on the ground!
>
> My brother-in-law is a fairly level-headed bloke, not the type to make things up and he's remained consistent in his description of what happened.[9]

In a follow-up, my correspondent said: 'The only lasting effect of his encounter is that he prefers to park in less secluded spots these days, but seeing as he now drives for a different company, this is an easy thing to achieve. Adrian is a very down-to-earth bloke and doesn't make a habit of seeing ghosts or telling tall tales. He is pragmatic and practical, and sceptic though I am, I believe he genuinely encountered something out of the ordinary.'[10]

Resonating with the popularised story at Blue Bell Hill, in several examples of legendary white ladies the ghost is a bride who died on or near to her wedding day; the thwarted event explaining both the emotional charge that has tied her to this world and her white attire, her wedding dress, in which in some instances she was buried.[11]

Commonly, appearances of the White Lady are said to be connected with death—either directly with it, as the ghost of a person who has died; or they appear in an impersonal, elemental guise as presagers of death or ill fortune to the living. Various traditions maintain that it is bad luck to see a White Lady, which seems to be instinctively sensed by those that see them. Less comforting is the belief shared by disparate cultures that the appearance foreshadows a death—most disturbingly, the witness's own or a person closely related to them.

The classic example of the latter is the *Banshee*, which we touched on in the last chapter. Appearing as an old hag or a beautiful woman in white, her wailing, mournful cry is said to foretell the impending death of someone, particularly in old Irish families. For the witness, the foreboding of death might be figurative rather than literal, but nonetheless marking a death of sorts: the death of their previously held world view.

As Blue Bell Hill's ghosts can be regarded as a subset of apparitions of the White Lady, she in turn belongs to a wider set of night-walking apparitions, of which she is merely the most prominent.

Liminal Lemures

In Roman tradition, the *lemures* were the restless or malevolent spirits of the dead.

In contrast to the *lares,* the generally beneficent and guardian spirits of the home and family and the domains and utilities of organised society (such as property, cultivated land, roads and crossroads),[12] the lemures were the lawless, outcast spirits that haunted the wild outer reaches beyond the boundaries of civilisation, rite and order. These spirits were the shades of those who had died unnatural (violent) or premature deaths, or whose remains lay unburied and without a customary funeral, or whose crimes in life held them in punished reflection. Restless and fearful, they were fated to wander among the living, trapped in a limbo between this world and the next, their condition manifested in sadness or remorse, or in hostile or revengeful action toward the living.

The 'dead not yet at rest'—those that had died before their allotted time, and these included the murdered, the executed, and victims of self-murder (suicide)—were fated to *walk* until the span of their natural life was completed or their crime pardoned. As we saw in Chapter 11, some of these spirits were associated with Hecate (the Romanised Hekate) and her nightly roamings with a train of human spirits.[13] These unpredictable, untamed ghosts needed to be propitiated to prevent them from afflicting the living, which the Romans achieved through the annual festival of Lemuralia (or *Lemuria*), which was held in May.[14]

Particular places in the outlying landscape were said to be especially haunted by these spectres. Lonely roads and crossroads, bridges and fords, cemeteries, hills, caves, woodlands, water courses and sea coasts, plus moors and fens, stiles and gateways, and notional features such as district boundaries (e.g. parish or county lines)—all were places where these night-walking phantoms might be encountered, and which the superstitious would hurry past after dark.

These are all *liminal* places—marginal, boundary places ('limen' denoting 'threshold'), hence places of transition between one place (or state) and another—where, in the dark of the night, the conscious rational mind yields with trepidation to a primal, unconscious state in which imagination and mystery and the unknown take on a power of their own. And it is at these very locations, true to the traditions, we find the majority of road ghost encounters taking place.

There is really no better paradigm for understanding much of the enigma of ghosts, particularly those found at large in the landscape, than the concept of liminality. It doesn't tell us *what* they are, but provides us with a framework for understanding where they appear and under what conditions. (A related concept, Jung's ideas regarding *archetypes* and the unconscious, contributes another major piece of the puzzle).

Most of us are familiar with the expression 'subliminal', which refers to stimuli that are below the threshold of an individual's normal level of perception. Subliminal messages are implanted directly into the unconscious, from where they may subtly influence conscious action.

The concept of liminality itself was first coined early in the twentieth century by French ethnographer and folklorist Arnold van Gennep (1873–1957). The concept, which was later developed by British cultural anthropologist Victor Turner (1920–1983), was originally applied to rites of passage in small societies, whereby the liminal period was the transitional phase 'betwixt and between' two culturally defined states. Examples might include a child's passage from childhood to adulthood, where some event or ritual or test marks the means by which the subject is initiated into a new social status; or we might look to a couple's engagement, even their wedding day, as liminal periods, marking in this case the transition of the individual from single to married status. The Blue Bell Hill case, of course, in the wedding-eve death of a bride-to-be has this as a real, unforced element as part of the story.

Van Gennep noted the significance of these rites as forms of social regeneration, relating them to the natural cycle of death and rebirth, both literal and figurative. In the latter sense, something has to be given up (it might be said to die) to enable the initiate to be 'born' anew to the new status. We can begin to see how this facet of liminality can be seen to apply to our subject of interest. We have noted that the experience of seeing a road ghost may result in the death of the witness's prior-held beliefs concerning them and the hereafter; and we have seen how the ancient mythological figures and other symbols associated with the cycle of life and death resonate in the sightings at Blue Bell Hill and other road ghost cases.

Liminality has found meaningful application to every area of human interaction and experience. Applied to folklore, in particular to supernatural events and traditions, workers such as Jeremy Harte and Bob Trubshaw have demonstrated its compatibility and usefulness to this field. The measure of any good theory is how well it fits the range of data, and liminality in folklore and in paranormal experiences works very well. An analysis of the phenomenon of ghosts reveals them to be residents of the liminal: they occupy the narrow thresholds and intervals of human experience, including the twilight areas of perception and consciousness.

Liminal systems may have more than one aspect, and include spatial, temporal, and notional elements (which may also include symbolic features). Applied to road ghosts, the 'ghost' is often associated with linear and boundary features in the landscape, whether *physical* (e.g. natural ones such as hills, rivers or streams; or human-defined—roads, bridges, and so on), or *notional* ones (e.g. county or parish boundaries).

The spatial (physical) features where they are encountered are plainly evident. Roads themselves are liminal features; they link one place to another, particularly where they traverse the rural landscape. Crossroads and bends in roads are liminal points, marking changes in direction, where the unknown (perhaps in the guise of a standing figure) may be waiting out of sight. Bridges (commonly associated with ghosts) likewise are features that mark a transition from one place to another. (As an aside, we can include also the domestic environment, where we find ghosts commonly encountered in doorways, gateways and on stairs—features whose purpose is solely to facilitate passage from one space to another.)

Turning to the temporal and notional features, we can note that numerous road ghost encounters (including those at Blue Bell Hill) fall around the liminal time of midnight, which by Western reckoning at least, marks the transition between night and morning, one day and the next. Other liminal times include twilight (dusk, or before dawn), and the observed divisions in the calendar cycle—the annual equinoxes and solstices. As cardinal events in human observation and experience, these slender zones of transition came to be ritualised and imbued with meaning. Likewise, the so-called cross-quarter days, which mark the mid-points between the solstices and the equinoxes, and include 1 May (May Day) and 31 October (Hallowe'en), preserve associations that transcend their possibly original purposes (as practical markers for the beginning and ends of the growing seasons) to live on in the calendar and in our imaginations as times in the year when the veil between this world and the next was said to grow thin (see Chapter 2).

Likewise, we can appreciate that the liminal places of the physical landscape have notional dimensions to them as well. Nature's geographical barriers historically served also as ethnographic and political boundaries, as the borders between kingdoms, nations and empires. At the local scale, ranges of hills, streams, the margins of woodlands, and even remnant human artifacts such as the lines of ancient (e.g. Roman) roads, are features that have been adopted to delineate the borders of parishes and other administrative divisions.

The full demarcation of the boundary is usually a notional construct, an invisible line on the earth that we make by an agreement of minds and plot onto maps, but rarely (where it is not a natural feature) is it physically defined in the environment itself (exceptions might include places where roads cross the boundary, e.g. county borders, where the transition may be sign-posted). To cross such a border, physical or notional, is a liminal act.

A fascinating aspect of road ghosts encounters, and one that provides an important clue in our understanding, is their behaviour in relation even to these invisible boundaries. Not infrequently the ghost is encountered at or is respectful of a parish or a county border. What makes these particularly impressive is that this fact is rarely recognised by the witnesses themselves.

Andrew Cutajar's encounter in November 1981 with the figure of a tall man in a long coat, old-fashioned lace-up boots, and long straggly grey hair, who was standing in the middle of the road near Hopton, Norfolk, and who he was forced to swerve to avoid, took place near to the Suffolk-Norfolk border, which crosses the A12 immediately south of Hopton in a diagonal line (north west from Longfulans Lane). The notional line here then follows a water course that leads into Fritton Lake towards St. Olaves.[15]

In February 2003, 'Keeley' wrote to Roadghosts.com to report her and a companion's sighting of a female ghost on the A46 at Six Hills, Leicestershire, which had taken place twenty years earlier (around 1983). As they passed the Durham Ox Hotel (now the Six Hills Hotel), heading north at 5.45 a.m., Keeley and her passenger both saw the figure of a girl in front of them, her hands held up as if to ward off the collision. They skidded to a halt, and got out. There was no-one there. There was no damage to her car, and no thump as she hit the girl, whom she described as around twenty-three, with long hair, and very pretty looking.

There are a number of ancient boundaries at this location. There is the A46 itself, the ancient Fosse Way built by the Romans, and probably exploiting a pre-existing prehistoric track; as was the B676, which crosses the A46, forming a cross-road interchange at Six Hills. Additionally and perhaps most significantly, is Six Hills' position at the hub of a radial arrangement of eight parishes—a possible Anglo-Saxon meeting ('moot') site. Finally, Six Hills lies not far from the Leicestershire–Nottinghamshire county boundary.[16]

The final example is from the county of Essex. One Tree Hill is within the bounds of the elevated expanse of Langdon Hills Country Park, a 385-feet high crescent-shaped ridge which sits between Laindon and Basildon and the A13, and extends from Dunton to Vange. At around 6.30 p.m. one Saturday evening in late January or early February 2003, Lisa H. and her family took their usual northward short-cut via One Tree Hill towards Dry Street, a narrow ribbon of tarmac that meanders through hedgerows bordering open countryside. As they emerged from a strip of woodland toward a bend near to Dry Street Memorial Church, they all noticed a very unusual 'figure' in the road ahead.

'It was about a foot long, self-illuminated, and of a white-grey colour,' said Lisa. 'It was not a shape you could describe, not a human or animal shape. It was just 'bobbing' on the spot, as if it was content on being there. When it noticed us, it darted off towards the church, where it vaporised completely.' Later investigations by the family produced anecdotes that suggested that a woman had been killed by a car along that stretch of road, and a 'lady' had been seen at the same spot.[17] Most pertinent to our interest here is that a similar apparition was seen in 1969 less than a mile to the east along the ridge, where it peters out at Vange.

John Howard, the landlord of the Five Bells pub, described it as follows: 'It was pure white and coming down the A13 from the direction of Vange Church, and then it disappeared over in the direction of the Fobbing rail crossing.'[18] In this case, it is noteworthy that the boundary between Thurrock Unitary Authority and

One Tree Hill, near Basildon, Essex

the greater area of the non-metropolitan county of Essex (to which it belongs) touches the road at the One Tree Hill location. Remarkably, this same boundary crosses the A13 at Five Bells and the railway level crossing along the line of High Street, Fobbing. In other words, the 'ghost' witnessed by John Howard deflected southward at the invisible Thurrock boundary and followed it toward the railway line.[19]

As we noted in the previous chapter, there is a traditional cross-cultural belief that ghosts are unable to cross over water, but we might reasonably substitute any liminal boundary in the landscape. But why should ghosts respect such boundaries—why indeed should they be confined by *any* barrier, the walls of a house or castle, the cemetery grounds—particularly notional ones?

The answer again lies with the principle of liminality. It is not that they are incapable of crossing these boundaries—ghosts, after all, are observed passing through walls, or parading on bridges—but that it is simply of their nature to be found at such places. The geographical features therefore are perhaps not significant in themselves, possessing no special properties (other than perhaps historical ones), but are significant for what they *represent*. When a ghost is encountered at an invisible boundary of which the witness is not consciously aware, it hints at a connection between the mind and the environment. In this sense, all liminal boundaries are notional: they have only the significance that we ourselves apply to them. They are markers in a symbolic geography, simultaneously features of the physical landscape and the landscape of the mind.

The same principle of liminality applies to the very mechanism of ghost-seeing. Ghosts occupy the limits of perception: they are most often seen fleetingly, and within the frame of the unconscious mind. In road ghost sightings, it is difficult to overlook the common (although not exclusive) incidence of lone drivers who, as often as not, have fallen into the border 'auto-pilot' state of consciousness, particularly on practised, familiar routes, where the critical faculties of conscious thought are dulled into quiescence and it is the unconscious mind that steers the car. It is in this disconnected state that road ghosts tend to be encountered.

Finally, we should not overlook the obvious association ghosts have with the ultimate boundary or threshold: that separating life from death, so often recalled by memories or legends of tragedies, or by the close proximity of cemeteries or crematoria or other features of a funereal or memorial character—which may in itself offer some explanation as to why ghosts are seen at places that have been tainted by tragedy.

Where these characteristics come together: a liminal place, a road, a liminal time-frame, and the border mind-state of the motorist, the odds of a ghostly encounter are apt to increase. Blue Bell Hill has them all: the rural location (at the mid-point between two towns), the hill road, ancient funereal monuments, a burial ground (Medway Crematorium), bridges, and a history of accidents and fatalities—which makes it almost inevitable that it would develop a reputation as a 'haunted place'. Reflection on the record of sightings here finds a characteristically higher proportion of lone drivers (and male ones at that, the significance of which we will return to in the final chapter) and the liminal marches of time, with encounters frequently found between 11 p.m. and 1 a.m.

Interestingly, while this time-frame was arrived at by an analysis of a number of modern road ghost encounters from Blue Bell Hill and elsewhere, precisely the same frame—an hour before to an hour after midnight—can be found in certain traditions relating to night-walking phantasms. It was a rural superstition, for instance, that on the eve of St. Mark's Day (25 April), and on Midsummer's Eve (21–24 June), if one sat in the church porch and watched from eleven at night until one in the morning, one might see passing by the apparitions of those in the parish who are to die in the next year, and either enter directly into the church or knock first on the door before entering. The figures would be dressed in their usual style and appear in the order they were destined to depart.[20] While these were the shadows (*wraiths*) of the still-living, their appearances are nevertheless still clearly associated with the threshold of death.

Liminality as a consciously defined concept may be a fairly recent construct, but these threshold zones (as both a literal and figurative 'no-man's' land) have long been recognised, as attested by the above superstition, and by the practice in pre-nineteenth century Britain of burying corpses of executed murderers and suicides in rural highways and crossroads. Sometimes the execution itself of the criminal would take place at these locations.

Highway burials served both punitive and deterrent purposes. They extended the deceased's punishment into the next world by an 'ignominious burial in the highway, with a stake driven through his body', which served as a powerful deterrent against a plethora of offences that carried a capital penalty. But the latter indicates a superstitious motive also, this action catering for the belief that the restless spirit of the felon might be capable of returning to haunt the living. Since executed murderers and suicides were denied a Christian service and burial, it was commonly believed that their restless spirits might walk unless unchecked (even a murdered person was said to be so-fated until their body could be recovered and accorded a proper burial).[21] The four ways of the crossroads may also have played a part in preventing this, by offering a confusion of choice to the spirit of the deceased which, if it were to walk (it was hoped), it would be unable to find its way back to its community. Thus, said Montague Summers:

> He will be puzzled to know which way to take and will stand debating until dawn compels him to return to the earth, but woe betide the unhappy being who happens to pass by when he is lingering there perplexed and confused. Accordingly after sunset, every sensible person will avoid all crossroads since there are no localities more certainly and more fearfully haunted and disturbed.[22]

Sometimes the corpse might be buried face-down as a further precaution.

Hence the criminal deceased was outcast even in death, banished from society and deprived of all usual burial rites, including burial in consecrated ground.[23]

The practice of highway burials ceased with a Parliamentary Act of 1823, which permitted burials to be made in churchyards and burial grounds.[24] But discrimination continued even here. Interments had to take place within twenty-four hours of the inquest and between 9 p.m. and midnight, and without a Christian service. The north side of the churchyard was often reserved for the burial of murderers and suicides (plus the unbaptised and the unidentified corpses washed up by sea or river), and was accordingly left unconsecrated.[25] Despite some concession toward a customary burial, established beliefs and superstitions often held sway and the felonious dead continued to be displaced to the unhallowed margins of place and time.

Ghosts encountered on roads and at crossroads have customarily been connected with the consequences of human intrigue, justice and tragedy; hence we tend to look no deeper for our explanations than these assumed causal events.

Numerous 'ghost' books seem content to stay with the traditional interpretations and to recount the same romanticised tragedies for their origin without much in the way of historical or critical assessment.

Some of the assumptions are undoubtedly valid. Many ghosts appear to have a connection with death and dying (which seems to be stating the obvious), both as personal representations of (usually tragically) deceased persons, or as certain mythological characters (in particular those that symbolise death and fate). But there are as many cases where *no* causal event can be identified. Rather, the liminal factors themselves seem to be the reasons such figures are seen where they are.

We should also note here the distinction between 'ghost' and 'apparition'. The former carries the loaded interpretation of it as the spirit of a dead person, the surviving essence of that person's personality, which appears in a familiar form to persons or at places with which it had formed an emotional attachment in life. Apparition means 'an appearance' or the act of appearing, without any inference as to meaning. Apparitions of the living and of inanimate objects such as vehicles and aircraft have also been reliably reported, which collectively force us to reevaluate our ideas as to what they represent.

It is apparent from the liminal characteristics of road ghosts that they operate in virtually every sense on a *symbolic* level. Indeed, liminality itself is a symbolic concept, representing a place or a state of crossing over. The very state in which road ghosts are perceived is the twilight zone between consciousness and unconsciousness, the semi-trance state which seems most conducive to experiencing them.

Furthermore, the language of the unconscious (more familiarly rendered *sub*-conscious), and as expressed in dreams, is metaphorical. Likewise, the surreal experience of the ghostly encounter (which is heightened in lone night-drivers) echoes the symbolic nature of dreams themselves.

Liminal features likewise have a symbolic dimension. Bridges, in particular, are identified with apparitions and death, where they symbolise the crossing over between this world and the next, '… or in psychological terms, between consciousness and the unconscious.'[26] White Ladies, in particular, are closely associated with them, where they are often encountered in the literal and figurative act of 'crossing over'.

The young girl seen by Tracy Boon on the footbridge at Blue Bell Hill stands perhaps as one example. We might add Ian Sharpe's, Colin Eacott's and Jacquie Hopkins' encounters near the same footbridge, and Paul Lowing's and Ann King's sightings near the overbridges spanning the A229 at the top of the Hill; plus the bridge-section of the A229 at the Lower Bell and that accommodating the M20 at junction 6 at the foot of Blue Bell Hill.

But other cases in which the meeting of the ghost seems contrived to take

The footbridge over the A229 that is associated with sightings of Blue Bell Hill's ghost. Bridges symbolise the crossing over between this world and the next

place on or near to a bridge at a suitably liminal hour are plentiful—for example, at Northam Bridge (Southampton), Pearoyd Bridge (Stocksbridge, South Yorkshire), and Rickety Bridge, on the A34 at Newbury (Berkshire), to name a few.

We can recall also Bill Hopkins' experience near the railway bridge known as the Red Bridge near Llanidloes, Powys (Wales) in 1973, when a girl had suddenly stepped out of the hedge in front of his car and faced him, forcing him to brake hard. She seemed to pass through the car; he could see her in the road behind in his rear-view mirror, still facing him (Chapter 7).

In 2005, Andy Doyle, then a taxi-cab driver, had a similar encounter at another railway bridge, near Corringham, Essex. Remarkably, his route northward along the B1420 Southend Road leads directly towards One Tree Hill, which we visited earlier in this chapter:

> On the 29th of January this year I was out late at night, about 2 a.m. I was alone in my car. I live in Corringham in Essex and I was driving down Southend road over a railway bridge. As I was about to go over the brow of the bridge I saw a young woman walking over the bridge on the verge. I saw her in complete detail: she was wearing a red puffer jacket, jeans and a pair of moon boots. She had on a

The railway bridge on Southend Road, near Corringham, Essex

> pair of earphones and a rucksack. My first thought was: What on earth is this girl doing there at this time of night?' She then stepped in to the road and disappeared—and reappeared at the other side of my car! She looked as if she was walking above the ground on the other side of the car. Then she simply disappeared. I then went round a nearby roundabout and went back to see if I could see her, but there was no sign of her. The whole experience has shaken me up and I would like to know if anyone else in the area has had this experience.[27]

Andy told me that the girl was on the right side of the road, walking in the same direction when, without warning, she suddenly veered across in front of him. She seemed to pass through the front right wing of his car, and vanished and reappeared in the bushes of the verge on the left.

On his return trip from Basildon, where he had picked up a fare, he was apprehensive about going back over the bridge, but he did so, and looked again for her, saying nothing to his passenger, but saw nothing. He avoided the route for several weeks afterward.[28]

Of possible additional significance, the bridge shows evidence of repairs to its brickwork, and the structure has emergency notices attached requesting that any witnesses to a collision with the bridge (no. 172) immediately telephone Network Rail to report the incident and then call the police on 999. Is this another reason for the apparitional encounter here, as a warning of the danger (or, according to their contradictory nature, as a potential cause) of collision here?

The traditional white garb of the White Lady (who is generally depicted as a young female) has been eschewed also by some of the incongruous female figures seen at Blue Bell Hill in recent times (those other than the Old Woman, who, as we have noted, appears generally in darker attire). The description given by James Skene (Chapter 9) fits this profile. Another example might be found in the experience of James, a security systems engineer who contacted me in 2003 with his sighting, which had happened around a year earlier:

> I was driving down Blue Bell Hill late one evening heading towards Maidstone. It was pee-ing it down big time and really dark. I recall having to slow down as the rain made it hard to see ahead. I decided to pull into the Shell garage half way down on the left. I expect you'll know there's a small slip way on the entrance to the petrol station. Due to it raining so heavily I had to look hard to see where this slip road began. This is where I believe I saw her, 'the ghost of Blue Bell Hill'.
>
> The one thing that really struck me and still sticks in my mind: she looked so happy. She had shoulder-long blonde hair and a long black coat on. She was walking with a 'spring' in her step. I also recall thinking her mode of walking didn't go with the weather she was walking in. Her head was held high; she was smiling, and another feature I noticed: she had 'REALLY BRIGHT RED' lipstick on.
>
> I kept looking at her as I drove down into the petrol station. As I passed her I looked to see if she had a petrol can in her hand. I kept thinking perhaps it's someone who has broken down and their on their way back to the car having bought more fuel. She had no fuel can.
>
> Something to this day still tells me I'm sure it was the ghost! I asked the lady in the station who was the woman walking up the road in such bad weather and in such a dangerous location, given the poor visibility. The attendant joked 'you've seen the ghost!' I asked if she had seen anyone or served any one and told her I meant it. She said 'no'. It's the first time I have mentioned this to anyone but feel I really have seen her. I would love to know if anyone else has mentioned the bright red lipstick?[29]

The detail of the lipstick is but a minor one, and one not previously reported, but it is strongly remindful of Blue Bell Hill resident Brian Culver's description of Annie Ash* (Chapter 11), which included the 'bright red lipstick'—precisely the same expression—that, in her more youthful years, she would put on to go out on Friday nights. Quite probably this is only a coincidence, but is an interesting feature all the same.

The foregoing perhaps loosely claim a connection with the Blue Bell Hill phenomenon, with the witness again coming away with the impression that he may have just had a sighting of the Hill's ghost rather than merely a pedestrian in unusual circumstances.

More emphatic accounts come from the following witnesses.

Gillian Barry encountered a young female on the dual carriageway of the A229 at around 1 a.m. in January 1992. Gillian was driving home towards Maidstone on the downhill stretch between Blue Bell Hill Village and the Lower Bell when she was startled to see a figure ahead on the central reservation to her right, standing side-on to the road. As she closed on her, the girl turned to face her. She looked about nineteen or twenty years of age, with dark hair and pale features. Most notably, despite the very cold night, she was wearing only a black knee-length dress—'that's it', said Gillian—no jacket or coat, just a quite modern-looking black dress.

Instinctively, Gillian braked hard as she passed close by the girl, partly in a flash of concern for the girl's plight, and pulled up in the middle of the road, thinking she had just missed her (an otherwise dangerous manoeuvre for this busy road, but there was no other traffic around). She immediately checked in her rear-view mirror—only to see the girl looking in her direction, with a malevolent smile on her face that kind of said '*Got you*'.

Shaken, Gillian took her eyes off the mirror for a second. When she looked back the girl had vanished. There was nowhere she could have gone. Only at that moment, when met with the girl's strange expression and her disappearance did she realise the girl wasn't real and probably a ghost. 'It really did shake me up', she said. When she arrived home she was still shaking.[30]

Joan Masters* and her husband encountered a similar figure one night as they approached the roundabout complex at the top of the Hill:

> It was between fifteen and twenty years ago [around 1993 to 1998]. I was with my husband coming from Maidstone to our house in Hempstead.
>
> We approached the roundabout (which I'm sure has changed a lot since then) at about midnight—it was winter—when standing on the verge I saw a girl. What struck me immediately was the whiteness of her face: very gaunt, lost-looking. The girl was looking at me as we approached, almost as if she needed help but couldn't say so. I was so struck by her white face that I don't recall what she was wearing at all, just clothing that appeared darker. We were within a few feet then drove by and I said to my husband, 'Did you see her?' And he said that he had seen her. I told him I wanted to go back to help her, but as we were en route home and it was late he said 'No.'[31]

The darker clothing aside, this figure—which was encountered in the same general area that Paul Lowing and Ann King saw the walking figure of a young woman in a white dress—displays a similar passive, non-threatening demeanour. If anything, 'she' portrays the other extreme of character, in which it is the ghost that shows disquiet, fear or sadness, in an apparent appeal for help. In this she compares well with other female road ghosts that give out an affecting sorrow, as in Bill Hopkins' experience at the Red Bridge near Llanidloes, Wales, and Rod Vecsey's encounter outside Union Cemetery at Easton, Connecticut.

The Girl in Blue

In March 2006, I heard from Donna Maillie who, after visiting my website, felt she had to email me with her family's own brush with the ghost of Blue Bell Hill.

Donna had moved with her family to Lower Warren Road in 1999, when she was fifteen. Lower Warren Road is a narrow, single-lane road that runs between high hedgerows and fields along the foot of the North Downs east of the A229. The lane's entrance starts at the apex of the bend of the aforementioned Eccles-Burham-Wouldham (and Aylesford) slip-road off the A229, and, apart from providing access to Warren Road (the original Roman road that begins its steep northward ascent of the chalk escarpment) halfway along the lane, it serves a handful of properties dotted along its 500-metre length before narrowing into an unmade public footpath and bridleway. Donna and her family were unaware of anything paranormal about the area. When they moved in, a neighbour knocked to say 'hello':

> I remember the neighbour jokingly saying not to have a party, or the ghost will appear. Confused I asked what he meant. He explained that when they moved to the area, they decided to have a party. About 8 o'clock, a girl came to the door. She was a very pretty girl, and their son, who answered the door, invited her in. He chatted with her for a while, and they seemed to get on very well. He offered to get her a drink, but when he came back, she was gone. Confused, he asked everyone if they had seen where she went to, but no-one had noticed him talking to a girl! According to everyone, there was never a girl there.

The family had not lived there long when Donna's mother saw the girl in their own house: a young woman, in her twenties and dressed in blue, who walked past an open doorway. On another occasion, Donna's younger brother Daniel also saw the girl. He was changing a fuse in a plug and had turned to call out to their elder brother for some help, and in the doorway there was a young woman standing there watching him. 'He was so frightened he refused to sleep for a week afterwards.'

In addition to the apparitions, the family was beset with what might be termed poltergeist activity. Objects would vanish, only to reappear where they were last seen weeks afterwards. Lights would turn on and off by themselves (another common habit of poltergeists, with a liminal flavour), and the television and phone would unplug themselves. There would be knocks on the front door, but no-one would be there when it was answered, and at night footsteps would be heard going up and down the stairs.

The family only lived there for six months. 'I am not sure if this information is of any use to you,' said Donna, 'but all I can say is there is definitely something paranormal going on at Blue Bell Hill.'[32]

The neighbour referred to by Donna Maillie, I later discovered, was John Gear, who used to run a photographic equipment shop ('Camera Gear') in Maidstone High Street. Mr Gear, who passed away in 2000,[33] lived with his wife Georgina in a property adapted and restored from buildings belonging to the former Warren Farm. The original buildings, of solid lime-brick construction, are around 150 years old.

When I spoke to Mrs Gear in 2010, she said that the jocular warning about a party arose from the occasion of her husband's fiftieth birthday (1978), when they had had a number of friends over. All were around the same age, with one exception. One couple had brought their 17-year-old son, who was feeling a bit on his own there. He had a Jack Russell puppy, which he had to let out at one point. Before coming back in, he saw through the window a girl sitting on the settee. When he came in, she wasn't there. On a later occasion, he asked Mr Gear who the girl at the party had been, but was told there hadn't been anyone of that

Lower Warren Road (looking east)

age or description at the party.

John Gear had his own sighting of the girl in blue, which took place in the lane outside one cold winter around 1976 or 1977. He worked at the time at a photographic shop in Tonbridge, and usually returned home between 6 p.m. and 6.30 p.m. One night, he came across a young woman standing in the lane outside the Old Bell House (now a private residence owned by Chris & Janice Leigh). The weather was freezing, and yet the young woman wore nothing more than a blue summer-style dress. Mr Gear stopped his car beside her, and wound his window down. 'Can I help you?' he asked. The girl replied simply with 'No'. And so, there she remained as Mr Gear pulled away to trundle down the remainder of the snow-bound lane toward his house at the end. When he glanced back in his mirrors the girl had vanished.

Georgina Gear's own experience took place only a few weeks before my brief interview with her. She was dozing in a chair (in the same room as the teenager's sighting), and awoke with the feeling that someone was standing beside her. Fleetingly, she saw the legs and skirt of a female, which vanished.[34]

Fright Wood

The properties on the north side of Lower Warren Road bite into the lower boundary of Frith Wood, which occupies the scarp slope of the North Downs as far up as the array of television transmitters atop the ridge. 'Frith' is derived from the Old English for 'peace' (and, interestingly, also 'fate'). From Medieval times it, and its variations—*frithe*, *fright* and *firth*—came to mean a wild topographical feature: a woodland, forest, heath or moorland (the latter, *firth*, is applied most commonly in Scotland to denote the mouth of a river or an estuary). In whichever case, the term aptly describes a liminal place.

Until the last years of the eighteenth century this belt of woodland at Blue Bell Hill was known as Fright Wood, an appropriate name in appreciation of the old road's reputation as the haunt of vagabonds and highwaymen, and later, of course, its ghost(s). The reality, unfortunately, is more prosaic. The name *Fright* (later Frith) was applied to thin, scrubby woodlands of the type that characteristically cling through thin soils to the chalk downlands.[35] Even so, the thin scatter of creeper-festooned trees and tangled underbrush provide the perfect setting after dark, one might think, for a flitting lady in white (or blue). And yet the single track route that ascends the ridge as Warren Road, following the line of the original Roman road, has been devoid of ghost sightings—or at least that appeared to be the case up until March 2014, when a new sighting came to light at this location.

Glenn Jones

At the time of his sighting the previous month, Glenn Jones had been cycling to and from work for around three months. His preferred route on his way home to Walderslade from Maidstone was to pass under the A229 by the Lower Bell into Lower Warren Road, and then turn left into the hill-climb at Warren Road.

Warren Road ascends steeply to a hairpin bend where it turns westward to climb across the contours of the escarpment. Between here and the crest, a scattering of private houses hug the hillside. After these the road runs northward and bordered by woodland and fields for around 600 metres until again encountering private residences and businesses before merging into Mill Lane. The road tends to be quiet and infrequently travelled, especially after nightfall.

According to Glenn, this route is a steeper but quicker way home than the main road. In addition to the discomfort of having to push his bike up the steepest section of the road, his journey in the winter months is cloaked in darkness; his return trip usually bringing him to the Hill after dusk, around 6.50 p.m. or 7 p.m.

On some nights, he said, a thick mist would blow across the road, creating a decidedly eerie atmosphere. Even so, it never occurred to him that Warren Road might be haunted or connected with Blue Bell Hill's ghost. This he only came to question after his experience on the wet and windy evening of Friday 14 February 2014:

> I have been cycling down and up [Warren Road], to and from work, and on the way home in the dark I have witnessed some strange things. I only have a camping light on my head as I push my bike up the hill. The first thing that happened was, just as I turned the left hairpin at the bottom I heard footsteps behind me so I turned to shine the light down [there] but [there was] no-one there. Another ten feet up and I heard a definite foot scrape on the road behind, but undeterred I pushed on. The next thing was [two days later], as I reached the brow of the hill and [where] the woods open up on your left, through the trees I could see a woman in a white dress dancing around a tree. As I got further up the hill I turned my light over to where I saw her but she had gone and instead I could hear women laughing!

The scene of Glenn Jones's encounter on Valentine's Day 2014

The oak tree beside which he saw a dancing woman in white

Glenn was later able to identify the spot more precisely:

> Just before the brow on the left is a lay-by. She was in the woods right there, about 10 to 15 feet back off the road. It was the dress that caught my eye in the gloom of the woods. I didn't believe what I saw. That's when I stopped to get a better look and try to find a reasonable explanation, and could hear two or three women laughing.
>
> It was an old fashioned dress. I didn't see much when I [first] saw her—she was about 25 feet away—until I got level with the tree. She had her left arm in the air, I remember that.
>
> I could see her without shining a light, and when I got close enough to do so she had gone. It shook me up to see a woman in the woods at night but I was curious. The lay-by is my marker to get back on anyway and it was there that I turned my head and the light away from the road to look for her. I did pedal down the road toward the village a bit quicker that night.[36]

The woman's dress—long, with covered arms—was white or cream in colour and old-fashioned in style. The arm she held in the air had stood out against the dark wooded background. As well as Glenn could estimate from the few seconds she was in view, the woman was in her twenties.

Was she a ghost? She looked real. Glenn's thoughts at the time were concerned more with what the woman was doing at this spot, in the dark and in the rain, than anything else. The voices he heard, once he drew closer, seemed to come from the tree and sounded feminine—maybe two or three individuals, but there was no sign of anyone to account for them.

Glenn Jones was pragmatic about his experiences, not leaning in any particular direction regarding their interpretation; noting only that they were not within the scope of his normal experience. Subsequent examination of the spot, the said tree and the surrounding woodland, yielded no clues to suggest a prank—which, while it cannot be ruled out, seems an unlikely prospect in consideration of the relatively remote location (certainly one removed from the familiar haunts of the Hill's ghost), the conditions and the sparsity of passers-by.

The girl in blue (a literal *blue belle*?) and Glenn Jones's girl in white stand somewhat apart from the principal ghostly encounters at Blue Bell Hill. The colour of the former's dress notwithstanding, she is in both cases clearly related to, if not synonymous, with the figure of the young woman that walks the main roads of the Hill just a few hundred metres away. We perhaps then do not have to burden ourselves with a search for yet further candidates for the Hill's repertoire of ghosts—although inevitably I looked into a few possibilities. While this produced no new information, we can note several tentative connections from the case record. For instance, Emily Trigg was wearing a plain blue dress (a blue cloth jacket, and matching skirt) on the fateful last day of her life; while in 1976, a 24-year-old female Naval secretarial officer (Navy blue?) died in a three-car accident on the dual carriageway not far from the opening to Lower Warren Road (Chapter 8). Here also we may as well throw in an echo of the legendary murdered Blue Boy in the woods at the top of the Hill directly north of here: a Blue Girl instead of a Blue Boy? While the above are suggestive, there is, however, little else to connect any existing candidate to the appearances along this unfrequented lane.

An unusual feature of the sightings along Lower Warren Road is the girl's appearances inside two of the houses. Even so, we should not be too surprised by this. Road ghosts are so-named, of course, after the places they are principally encountered. But such labels, convenient as they are, may be overly restrictive. We should not overlook, for instance, that the essential theme of the Phantom Hitch-Hiker story is the homeward journey. In the Version C, to remind ourselves from earlier chapters, the girl is met at a social function, a dance or a party.

So here we have elements of the legendary scenario: the prospective hitch-hiker; the unfamiliar girl at the party. All that is missing is the onward car journey to another address, or to the cemetery.

Nor have we left behind the liminal and symbolic features. The spot where John Gear encountered the girl—the junction with the steeply ascending Warren Road—was until fairly recent times (around 1880) still a crossroads. It still has this appearance on maps, but the southern arm is represented now by a narrow bridleway that marks the line of the Roman road towards Maidstone. The interior manifestations likewise obey the rules of liminality: the girl is seen passing a doorway, or her footsteps are heard at night on the stairs; while light switches represent the boundary between the conditions of darkness and light.

Crossroads, as we have noted, share symbolic meaning with bridges as places where the two worlds meet, and where ghosts might be encountered in the liminal hours of night. They also, metaphorically as well as literally, represent a choice of direction and therefore of fate. True to the convention, we can note that crossroads feature in several other encounters and sightings at Blue Bell Hill: at the Lower Bell (Jack Woodger, Malcolm Grant, Donald Gallagher), and the crossroads at the Upper Bell in Blue Bell Hill Village (Anne-Marie Austin, 'JST').

In Glenn Jones's case also we find meaningful correlations with mythology and custom, plus the recurrent themes of fecundity and the cycle of life and death—even if Glenn Jones himself was not cognisant of them.
Is it mere coincidence that he met his phantom dancer on 14 February—Valentine's Day?

Valentine's Day traces its origin (at least by popular acceptance) to the ancient Roman festival of purification and fertility, *Lupercalia*, which was observed in Rome on 15 February (or 13–15 February). The festivities began with the sacrifice of goats and dogs by the priestly *Luperci*, who, after the feasting and drinking, cut the goat hide into thongs with which to strike the spectators (particularly women) as they cavorted naked or scantily clad in goats' skins around the Palatine Hill. The blows from the goatskin *februum* (a term applied to an instrument of purification (*pl. februa*); hence the name given to the month, *Februarius*) were reputed to impart fertility, or to ease delivery in childbirth.

Overlapping Lupercalia, from 13 to 21 February, was the festival of *Parentalia*, held in commemoration of the dead—principally the *Manes*, the souls of the ancestors and the familial dead (and linked therefore to the *lares* and *lemures*), who were honoured or appeased by ritual offerings at their gravesides at this time.[37]

Both festivals took place near the end of the Roman year (the New Year began on 1 March), and the timing of Glenn Jones's encounter can be seen to have this liminal aspect to it too. Also, we should not forget that this took place on the original Roman road. And there are other interesting correlations with mythology that we shall return to shortly.

Archetypes

'A ghost,' said writer and antiquary Francis Grose (1731–1791), is supposed to be

> … the spirit of a person deceased, who is either commissioned to return for some especial errand, such as the discovery of a murder, to procure restitution of lands or money unjustly withheld from an orphan or widow, or, having committed some injustice whilst living, cannot rest till that is redressed. Sometimes the occasion of spirits revisiting this world is to inform their heir in what secret place, or private drawer in an old trunk, they had hidden the title deeds of the estate; or where, in troublesome times, they buried their money or plate. Some ghosts of murdered persons, whose bodies have been secretly buried, cannot be at ease till their bones have been taken up, and deposited in consecrated ground, with all the rites of Christian burial.[38]

Grose neatly summarises the popular notions that are still often touted as to what ghosts are and why they appear to the living. In essence, they are taken to be *purposeful* manifestations, bound or intent to correct some unfinished business or injustice either perpetrated by them or suffered in life.

Within this traditional framework, the manifestations at Blue Bell Hill make some sense. The murdered Emily Trigg, whose killer or killers escaped justice (remaining unidentified to this day), has reason enough to walk still in silent protest at her stolen life. Likewise, Suzanne Browne, the tragic bride-to-be, who was so cruelly denied her wedding day, might have desperate reason for wishing to complete her last journey. But overarching these very reasonable and personal factors, and applicable to *all* of the young female victims of Blue Bell Hill, is the sense of each having being cheated of the full potential and opportunities of life, leaving emotional energies that might be supposed to lead to unsettled appearances beyond physical death.

But why *women*—why are so many *female* figures represented in the record of road ghost sightings? And why are they generally attired in pale clothing (and not only at Blue Bell Hill)? Of the fifty or so recorded road-related or other tragic deaths on Blue Bell Hill between 1790 and the present day, only a third are female.[39] And yet the ghostly sightings are almost exclusively of a female figure.

Grose noticed something else about ghosts, a distinction between particular kinds. 'Ghosts', he said, 'commonly appear in the same dress they usually wore while living, though they are sometimes clothed all in white; but that is chiefly the churchyard Ghosts, who have no particular business, but seem to appear *pro bono publico,* or to scare drunken rustics from tumbling over their graves.'[40] White Ladies.

Attired in pale clothing and walking sedately along the roadside in the dead of night, apparitions of the White Lady may appear to be aimless (other, perhaps, than to elicit wonder and fear in the witness, particularly if they should suddenly rush into the motorist's path). It is initially difficult to reconcile their actions with the stated purposefulness and individuality of 'ordinary' ghosts—the ghosts of departed persons that Grose suggested appear for more or less rational reasons, with the specific aim of communicating with the living. But are they really so different? At Blue Bell Hill, elements of the seeming personal are evident: in the young lady in old-fashioned dress; in the girl wearing the contemporary, summery outfit; and especially in the figure of the old woman in black. All seem to relate in some meaningful manner to particular deceased persons, each of whom had a strong emotional connection with the Hill in life or became related to it by their death.

It is equally difficult to deny that the locations of some of the sightings appear to be significant. But at the same time, we find that the generalised descriptions and behaviour and timings of these ostensibly distinct ghosts are subsumed to a script to which they all conform—which says little for their individuality or personal freedom in the hereafter. Rather, as we have discussed previously, each seemingly distinct age character appears to represent a facet of a *single* phenomenon, as symbolised by the triple-aspect goddesses of mythology to which they bear the most fitting comparisons.

These 'primordial images' or archetypes, which C.G. Jung identified as the personifications of the unconscious aspect of the psyche (of which the White Lady is a prime example) fit the data much better than any other single 'explanation' for road ghosts, whether it be hoaxing, misidentification, autosuggestion, or even the spirits of the tragically slain. These spontaneous and recurring forms represent principles that are rooted in the essential structure of the psyche. Jung used the analogy of a crystal that forms according to the molecular structure of its parent liquid. The outer form of the crystal may vary according to a myriad of factors, but its underlying structure remains the same. So it was, Jung believed, with the depths of the unconscious psyche—that these archetypal forms developed out of this latent ocean of potential and instinctual processes that underlie all conscious experience:

> The greatest and best thoughts of man shape themselves upon these primordial images as upon a blueprint. I have often been asked where the archetypes or primordial images come from. It seems to me that their origin can only be explained by assuming them to be deposits of the constantly repeated experiences of humanity.[41]

The roles and relationships and events and experiences that are shared by all people at all times—mother, father, birth, marriage and death—are archetypal. (We may note in passing that some are also liminal in character). And we can include other ingrained patterns or forms that find expression through and are reinforced by our mythologies, folklore and arts, and even in familiar characters or objects: phantom horses and black dogs, horse-drawn carriages and motor vehicles, plus trains, ships and aircraft—all have featured in the record of ghost sightings. While these largely fall outside of the scope of this book, we can pause to reflect that the archetypal model accounts more completely for the range of reported apparitions than most traditional concepts, which otherwise must seek also to explain how it is that inanimate objects, including the clothing and accoutrements of human apparitions, can possibly be accounted for in ghost sightings. The answer is that they in themselves are templates or patterns that become imprinted (or arise from) the collective unconscious in the same manner as the archetypes themselves. Thus, in recent times we have reports involving apparitions wearing the ubiquitous yellow hi-visibility vests of the health and safety culture, and apparitions clutching mobile phones reflected back to us as contemporary archetypes.

The idea of causality—whether the pattern inspired the archetype or vice versa—is meaningless when applied to the timeless, spaceless realm of the unconscious:

> Not only are the archetypes, apparently, impressions of ever-repeated typical experiences, but, at the same time, they behave empirically like agents that tend towards the repetition of these same experiences. For when an archetype appears

> in a dream, in a fantasy, or in life, it always brings with it a certain influence or power by virtue of which it either exercises a numinous or a fascinating effect, or impels to action.[42]

The archetypes within the context of road ghosts appear to enact the roles of their mythological counterparts, as messengers and guides. In psychological terms, the archetype acts as a *psychopomp,* a mediator—we might even say bridge—between the unconscious and the conscious mind, conveying to the latter a message or providing what might be interpreted as intuitive guidance or direction. In their guise as 'ghost', their forms and behaviour appear to draw on these same blueprint archetypes that are deeply rooted in the realm of the collective unconscious. They can therefore be seen to both embody and convey a message. But what is this message? How do we discern its content and meaning?

It is a convention that ghosts cannot speak until they are spoken to (if they speak at all)—which appears to be borne out by the few reported encounters in which such close contact has taken place, as exampled by Roy Fulton's meeting with a phantom hitch-hiker.[43] It is therefore necessary to pay close attention and to learn to decipher their native language: *symbolism.*

The most obvious association these apparitions have is with death. Road ghosts, then, are at very least symbols of death itself. In her insightful work *An Archetypal Approach to Death Dreams and Ghosts,* Jungian psychologist Aniela Jaffé (1903–1991) explores the phenomenon of the White Lady in relation to individual cases of personal tragedy, particularly those involving female victims.

White Lady ghosts interested Jaffé the most as they seemed unrelated to historical incident, or were supposed so long removed from their originating cause that their personal identity had become blurred or forgotten, leaving an anonymous, impersonal form that has assumed something of an autonomous existence. What remains, in effect, is a psyche stripped of the conscious, rational and emotional aspects of human personality (as Jung himself termed it, something resembling a fragmentary personality), which is why we perhaps find them uncanny, alien and disturbing. She has become an iconic figure, an archetype.

According to Jaffé, the archetype in operation in the legend of the White Lady is the 'female principle' itself. We can remind ourselves that the mythological characters to which the White Lady relates (both being derived from the same archetypal principle) are symbolically representative of the natural cycle of birth, life and death.

Jaffé identifies the motivational force behind appearances of the White Lady as a 'crime against love'—whether from love unrequited, from betrayal or tragedy; or, most extremely, from murder: 'A crime of this kind does not only destroy the life and soul of human beings, it breaks the archetypal laws of life. We might even say that a divinity has been outraged.'[44] But the question is posed: why is it the *victim* of a crime who is unable to find rest and not the perpetrator? As Jaffé observes, this apparent injustice occurs over and again in legends and in ghost stories—which, after all, are inspired of the same archetypal principle as our mythologies, and speak of a form of 'law' to which the archetype conforms. The victim as restless spirit

> … becomes comprehensible if we consider it is not the actual woman who is seen as a ghost, but an impersonal phantom, a deity. As a matter of fact it is the *female principle* which was outraged and wounded with the victim, an archetypal figure which by far exceeds the time-bound existence of the woman who suffered the crime.
>
> What has once outraged an archetype has outraged it forever. For the archetype belongs to a realm outside of time and space and exists just as much today as it did yesterday or years ago, and as it will continue to exist in all time to come.[45]

In effect, it is the natural order that is offended: Mother Nature (or in psychological terms, the unconscious), whose indignation is personified in the archetypal form of the apparition of the White Lady. Applying Aniela Jaffé's idea to Blue Bell Hill, any of the female victims there may potentially have served as the instigating tragedy—the one to prompt a response from the archetype, which, once set in motion, resonates forward (and back) through time.

Emily Trigg might seem the fitting candidate for the young woman in old-fashioned dress, and by the nature of her death perhaps the most likely to draw an archetypal response. But then there is the problem of accounting for the stylistic and age estimates for the phantom female reported in other instances—unless the archetype is capable of presenting aspects of *all* of the victims, past and future; the ghost in effect being all and none of them at once.

There is clearly a perceptual and psychological aspect to road ghost sightings. Archetypes, as they are encountered in depth psychology, shape many of our mythologies and folklore; they inspire art and fiction and manifest in the symbolic realm of dreams. It isn't surprising, then, to find archetypal features also in reported sightings of ghosts and in paranormal experiences. All are expressions of the same unconscious realm of the human psyche.

Jung himself compared supranormal experiences to the unconscious (dream) state: 'We know that something unknown, alien, does come our way, just as we know that we do not ourselves make a dream or an inspiration, but it somehow arises of its own accord. What does happen to us in this manner can be said to emanate from…the unconscious.'[46]

Like dreams, paranormal experiences arise spontaneously, and they have a similar quality of unreality about them. They may be inspired by and incorporate 'real' aspects or events and, as we have seen, they follow a symbolic narrative. And of course, they operate in the same sphere: the unconscious.

The crucial difference for our interest is that ghostly phenomena seem able to break out into the external world and perceptibly interact with our material environment, and in a uniform fashion irrespective of the social and scientific norms of the culture in which they manifest. Whatever their psychological characteristics, apparitions imply (at least in part) an outer, objective existence. The difficulty for us is to conceive how the principle of the archetype—even if it is accepted as a manifestation of a shared unconsciousness that underpins the individual psyche in us all—might appear to be exteriorised into actual forms capable of being seen by multiple witnesses, with consistencies in descriptions, locations, time-frames and specific behaviour; and arguably with the capability of achieving physical effects such as damage to vehicles or of interacting with the motorist in the interior environment of their vehicle. The relationship between the inner world of the psyche and the outer material world (which Jung came to some definite conclusions about in the latter part of his life) we will explore further in the final chapter.

For now, we can apply the psychological model to gain further insights into what might seem the paradoxical behaviour found in White Lady apparitions: at one moment she is sad, benign, pitiable; in the next, terrible and hostile, a figure of fear and foreboding. The latter has found its way into versions of both the Phantom Hitch-Hiker story and the Phantom Jaywalker in which the actions of the ghost have been attributed to her vengeful retribution for her untimely death, which is visited either on men in general, or a particular category (e.g. motorists, the unfaithful, and so on) as representative of the one whose actions led to her death.

The Jungian model, however, regards such ambiguity as simply a natural condition of the archetype, and therefore of the unconscious. The unconscious comprises all potential states (including opposites) without differentiation, and therefore without conflict. It is only the conscious mind that has the tendency to separate, to compare, and to make distinction between things.

The very colour of the White Lady's apparel is telling. On one hand, whiteness symbolises death. It is the colour of the traditional burial shroud, as worn by the spirit as it continues to walk in a state of unrest; and it reflects the pallor of the skin that ensues with the departure of life. But white also represents purity and wholeness (as symbolised by the wedding dress) and undifferentiated light, and can therefore be taken as representative of the unconscious itself and the liminal.

Jaffé points to the two-fold nature of the archetypal characters of mythology, the classical goddesses, who are at once goddesses of life and love and beneficence, and goddesses of mourning, despair and death. Aphrodite (Venus), the Nordic goddess Frigg (or Freyja), the Sumerian Inanna, and the Igbo (African) goddess Ani, plus other examples of goddesses that are associated with love are also naturally linked to death as part of the overall cycle of life and fate over which they preside. Like unconscious nature itself, which is ambiguous, comprising the passive and the aggressive, the gentle and the cruel, browser and predator, and, of course, human nature, the archetype naturally embodies this same dichotomy. As Jaffé notes: 'Love and death, grace and doom, form her being.'[47]

We see something of this two-fold nature displayed by Blue Bell Hill's ghost(s), in which the ghost appears passive and demure on the one hand, and in other instances behaves in what appears to be a cold, calculated manner as she steps in front of an approaching car and, with a twisted smile, turns to face the horrified motorist. Such an act could be interpreted as an intention to *cause* an accident. Indeed, in spite of the popular legend that depicts a lonely hitch-hiker seeking assistance from passing motorists, it has been speculated that some of the late night single-vehicle death accidents involving lone drivers may have been caused by the ghost. This idea is perhaps inspired by the kind of encounter reported by Ian Sharpe in 1992, but it is also one that resonates with the African perspective we looked at in the last chapter that sees such a sinister motive in all road ghost encounters. In the UK, an example is found at the roundabout junction of the A2021 with the A22 at Willingdon, near Eastbourne, where a phantom female is reputed to have been the cause of several near accidents, and a fatal accident at the spot in 1923.[48]

The Beckoning Fair One

The dualistic character of road ghosts is further exampled in the following case, which involves another white lady on Beacon Hill Road (the B1403), a rural road that rises to the village of Gringley on the Hill, Nottinghamshire. Beacon Hill itself is crowned by an Iron Age hill fort, which provides one clue perhaps for the sightings here. The village even has a pub named The Blue Bell Inn.

The encounter took place in the autumn of 1976. Ian M. had called his father to pick him up from work after he found that his moped had broken down. They set out together from his workplace at 6 p.m. Over to Ian:

> We were travelling from Misterton to Gringley (Notts). Just before the last corner leading up to Beacon Hill, in the headlights we saw a white figure about 3ft into the road. It was that of a young lady, beckoning us to come towards her with her left hand. My father slowed down. As he did she was smiling.
>
> At this point we noted that her flowing white gown was 8 to 10 inches from the floor with no feet visible. As my father accelerated past she retreated (floated)

> backwards at an angle in front of us with an angry scowling face, through a closed iron farm gate and quickened pace until almost a blur, across the field until she vanished into the hillside. Lengthy discussions followed on the way home with my father refusing to believe what he had seen.
>
> Over the past years since then, both my mother and father have seen the same apparition twice, years apart, but around the same autumn period in the same place.
>
> Discussions have ensued after each occurrence, my father now reservedly admits he has seen something; my mother, well, she would not mind seeing her again. Some years after our experience, a bus crashed at that same spot; he was coming down the hill and said he had swerved to miss a 'woman in white'. No one else was found around the crash.[49]

Beckoning ghosts, like those who raise their hands in exhortation or hitch-hikers that silently point ahead, do so again in symbolic gesture. Such actions may understandably come across as sinister, adding additional dimensions of fear through the ghost's focused attention on the witness—particularly where the motorist's refusal to stop is met with outward disapproval or reprisal, whether in the form of a reactionary shaking of the fist or a suicidal leap beneath the wheels of the vehicle.

Beacon Hill toward Gringley on the Hill. The gate is visible at centre-left

But, as always, the intent and symbolism of such encounters may operate on different levels. Recalling again the mythological roles of the archetype, the gesture may be inviting us into greater understanding of and interaction with the unconscious (or as Jung might term it, a greater integration between the conscious and unconscious minds). But as the above encounter demonstrates, a refusal is just as quickly admonished, and may even prove dangerous.

Like the Sirens, the Lorelei and the Rusalka of Greek, Germanic and Slavonic mythologies, the original archetypal *femme fatale*, the White Lady, is both beguiling and fatal (if only to the witness's prior world view). Those that are respectful and open-minded tend to be rewarded with a non-threatening encounter. Those that fail to stop or show respect are met with sadness, or hostility. One of the ironies of road ghost encounters is that it is those holding no belief or are outwardly most dismissive of them who may be in most 'danger' of a dramatic, mind-altering experience.

At Blue Bell Hill, the white lady with hand raised is exampled in one instance only, in the experience of Barbara Selwyn*. Barbara, now a resident of Blue Bell Hill Village, had moved from Bexley to Walderslade in 1987, and knew nothing of the Hill's reputation prior to her own encounter with a mystery woman on the Hill, which took place one autumnal night, around 10.30 p.m. or 11 p.m. while on her way home. She had just passed the Shell petrol station on the northbound carriageway of the A229 when she noticed, around thirty yards ahead, the figure of a young woman stepped out from the narrow grass and scrub verge with her left hand raised toward her, in a clear gesture for her to stop. Unusually for the Hill, there was no other traffic around at the time. Barbara braked to a stop around ten feet in front of her, thinking she had probably broken down and needed a lift. She immediately set about putting on her handbrake and hazard warning lights on this exposed section of road as the girl smiled and started toward the car. She was around five feet five inches tall, and dressed in a creamy white dress (no coat), and had dark eyes and brownish hair. The girl moved toward the car's nearside, but an instant later, when Barbara turned to greet her, she was nowhere to be seen. Barbara was surprised but not frightened, thinking the girl had changed her mind and slipped away unseen. She did not get out of the car to investigate; plus it was a dangerous spot and dark. So Barbara pulled back out and continued on her journey, giving the episode little further thought until some time later, when recounting it to someone, it was suggested she may have encountered the ghost.

Certainly the location (before the footbridge), the description and behaviour of the figure and the time of the encounter are consistent with others at Blue Bell Hill—even to being suggestive of a classic hitch-hiker encounter, with the girl (whose stopping gesture might stand in place of the stereotypical thumb-cocked pose of the hitch-hiking phantom) vanishing from view somewhere near the middle pillar of the car (where she had entered Barbara's blind spot), as if she were heading for the back seat.

The whole episode lasted only seconds, but the girl had seemed perfectly solid, with nothing unusual besides the spot she had chosen to hitch-hike (when the brightly lit forecourt of the petrol station was not far away). Musing over why the girl had 'changed her mind', Barbara said, 'She probably didn't like me!'[50]

Rusalka **(1934) by Ivan Yakovlevitch Bilibine (1876–1942). A female water spirit of Slavic mythology, the Rusalka was both beguiling and fatal to the unwary**

Appearances of road ghosts, and of white ladies in particular, have often been thought of as heralding a death—a situation that places the ghost *before* a tragedy, and therefore something of a reversal over our customary expectations. It is easy to appreciate why their appearances have instinctively been regarded in many cultures as omens of ill. But this, as we have seen, may simply be one aspect of their complex nature. Jung might observe that we ourselves are not so very different, pointing to the Shadow aspect of the personal psyche, which holds all the negative tendencies ever present in the unconscious that are capable of upwelling and overwhelming the individual's conscious volition.

But this perspective—their contradictory nature—makes room for another interpretation: that there may also be a positive side to their appearances ('for the public good', as *pro bono publico* is translated), as indicators of *potential* tragedy rather than as sinister predictors of death. From this perspective they may appear at accident black spots as supernatural versions of that superseded symbol and its modern equivalents, the personal floral commemorations, notices and white-painted 'ghost' bikes and 'ghost walker' signs placed by relations and friends; and the official signs, the speed or safety cameras. In essence, they may serve as markers or warnings (to those that heed them) that announce this as a dangerous road (as evidenced by its record of fatalities)—which is more in keeping with their original archetypal role as messenger and guide to the living; *lares* rather than *lemures*.

If a map of the sightings at Blue Bell Hill is superimposed on one of the history of fatalities, we find some favourable correlation in their distribution. The places with the greatest concentrations of ghost sightings are also those with the higher incidence of fatalities, which seems impressively to link the ghosts to the victims of these tragedies—until we remind ourselves that the vast majority of ghostly figures are female and the majority of death casualties are male. This includes locations on the Hill where the victims have been exclusively male, such as the stretch of the A229 between the short slip-road at the top of the Hill that features the turn-off for Common Road and the Picnic Site, and the new slip road for Buckmore Park and Borstal (which has only been in existence since 1983, and was the scene of Paul Lowing's and Ann King's sightings of a female pedestrian in a long, flowing pale dress).[51]

While there may be a good deal to Aniela Jaffé's ideas about the nature of the White Lady in many road ghost encounters, the archetype clearly represents *all* of the deaths at Blue Bell Hill, not solely the female victims that resonate most meaningfully with its symbolic form.

The connection between female road ghosts and certain arch figures from our ancient mythologies seems well founded, particularly those associated with death and fate and/or those that served as guides or protectors. But there may be other reasons why female ghosts are most often encountered, and this seems to have as much to do with the gender psychology of the witness as external factors such as the accident record.

There are naturally exceptions to any rule, but often it is a lone male motorist that encounters a female ghost, or the ghost is of the opposite gender to the driver. Jung's ideas regarding the complementary nature of the individual's own unconscious psyche, that are laid out in his concepts of the *anima* and *animus*, add an additional component to the mechanism of ghost-seeing, which we shall look at in more detail in the next chapter.

In other cases of road ghosts, a different archetypal figure is featured. For instance, a virtually identical figure of a middle-aged or old man with grey straggly hair and wearing a long grey overcoat, and sometimes waving a torch, has been reported along both the A38 in Somerset and the A12 from Essex to Norfolk. In the former case, as a hitch-hiker, the figure would utter morbid descriptions of the accidents that had occurred along the stretch of road. On other occasions, he would jump out in front of lorries and other vehicles, only to reappear unharmed and shaking his fist at the driver (Chapter 4).

Holding up the mirror of mythology, we again find this character meaningfully reflected by certain familiar characters: for instance, by Hermes, the male counterpart of Hekate in classical mythology. Hermes, brother of Apollo and messenger of the Olympian gods (Mercury, to the Romans), shared many functions and attributes with Hekate. Hermes was a fertility god and a god of roads (who was venerated at crossroads) and a guardian of travellers. Like Hekate, Hermes was a deity of liminality, of boundaries, occupying and traversing the borderlands between the known and the unknown, between safety and danger, life and death—or, in the physical realm, between the trodden and untrodden, such as caves, forest paths or lonely trails, where the road or trackway is the very boundary between the 'safe' known and the wild unknown. Like Hekate, Hermes was a psychopomp, an escort to the dead on their journey to Hades, and likewise also a rescuer of Persephone from the Underworld. Among still other attributes, Hermes was the inventor of language and speech, of fire, a bringer of dreams, and had some ability in the area of prophecy. On his flip side, he was a god of cunning and fraud; the prince of tricksters, and father of Pan (the source of irrational fear (panic), who, with occasional ill temper, loved to frighten unwary travellers).[52] In place of a lighted torch, Hermes carried a winged staff (his *caduceus*) with facing serpents coiled around it, a herald's staff that signified his role as a divine messenger. Sometimes he was depicted wearing winged sandals, symbolising his swiftness of travel as well as the supernatural and immortal nature of their wearer.

Where male ghosts predominate, and taking Aniela Jaffé's principle of an instigating tragedy, it may be that that figure becomes incorporated into the equivalent archetype as the primary symbol for that stretch of road—in effect, as the Romans termed it, the *genius loci* (spirit of place, or guardian spirit) of the location.

Other prominent male figures from Greek mythology find passing recognition in road ghost encounters—and here I am again thinking of the male hitchhiker of the A38. Thanatos, the personification of death itself, who was associated with Hermes and shared his function as a psychopomp, was also depicted as a winged figure. In early depictions he was portrayed as a mature individual, sometimes bearded; later as a clean shaven youthful figure. In some representations he is shown holding a lowered torch, its extinguished tip downturned to signify the ending of a life.[53]

Thanatos and his twin Hypnos (Sleep), were the sons of Nyx (Night) and brothers to the Moirai (Fates) and the Kêres (the ruthless, blood-thirsty female spirits of sudden or violent death) and other personifications of the unconscious and its darker aspects.[54]

Associated with the Kêres was Akhlys (Achlys), the female personification of woe and the mist that clouds the eyes on death. The Greek poet Hesiod describes her chillingly as a decrepit shrunken figure, withered from despair and the incessant streaming from her eyes and nostrils. She stands on the sidelines of violent and bloody death, grinning horribly with blood dribbling from her cheeks. Noteworthy is the dismal green pallor of her skin (the colour of disease and decay)—a detail, we might add, that is echoed in John Dawkins' description of the strange green hands of his hitch-hiking passenger at Blue Bell Hill, and Kevin Whelan's unwelcome passenger on the A15 near Ruskington, Lincolnshire (Chapter 12).[55]

Overstepping the claimed encounter with a male hitch-hiker at Blue Bell Hill by John Hippisley (Chapter 12), I have on record only one other eyewitness sighting of a *male* road ghost at Blue Bell Hill. Significantly perhaps, it was reported by a lone female witness.

In 2004, Stephen Watts wrote to me to relate the story of his then-girlfriend's sighting, which took place in the winter of 1987, not long after they had moved to Walderslade from Clapham (London). New to the area, neither at the time had heard of Blue Bell Hill's reputation or any other local ghost story. Sarah M. had been visiting a friend in Tonbridge and was returning home alone when, at around midnight, while travelling up Blue Bell Hill:

> … a MAN ran across in front of her waving his hands in a criss-cross fashion in front of him. He was wearing a white butcher's style coat, buttoned double-breasted. As he stared at her she went straight over him driving fairly fast. She then looked in the mirror and there was nothing there. She came home shaking and crying; she was sure she had run over someone and [suggested we] should go back. I calmed her down and said that maybe she imagined it. We only found out about the sightings a couple of weeks later when I mentioned it to the landlord of the Upper Bell pub.[56]

In consideration of the history of casualties on the Hill, it seems reasonable to expect male ghosts to feature in the line-up. The suggestion of a butcher's uniform recalls the legend of the 'murdering butcher', and also the tragic real-life case of butcher John Wildash who was crushed by his own cart on Blue Bell Hill in January 1848 (Chapter 2). But while a white coat might be characteristic of an old-time butcher's or shopkeeper's outfit, its colour and the behaviour of the figure (one of warning or of trying to gain the attention of the witness) also bear comparison to the archetypal female ghost, and therefore could be regarded equally as the *animus* (male) aspect of the phenomenon.

Variations

By extension, while particular characters seem to dominate at given locations, representatives of the full themed 'set'—the set of archetypes that represent liminality and guidance (both in life and in the afterlife) and the cycle of life itself—cannot be ruled out from making their appearance.

A hint of one such variation from Blue Bell Hill comes in the form of an anecdote linked to an alleged encounter in the early 1970s. A male witness by the name of Parkinson is said to have picked up a young woman in white who was holding a baby. The woman asked to be taken to the top of the Hill, but she and the baby vanished before reaching the destination.[57]

While the above *is* only an anecdote, and a singular one for Blue Bell Hill, it does find some meaningful connection with at least one historical tragedy on the Hill that we looked at in Chapter 2—when, in 1793, a young woman and her newborn child died for lack of assistance outside the Upper Bell. It finds meaning also in certain depictions from various mythologies, in which the goddess is holding or nursing an infant. In Chapter 11, for example, we looked at the *Matronae* (the 'Mothers'), one of whom was usually given a youthful appearance, with loose flowing hair. In addition to their associations with baskets of produce, the *Matronae* were also depicted with babies, napkins or scrolls, linked to the aspects of their role that presided over fertility, childbearing and midwifery. Other examples include the Egyptian goddess Isis (with Horus); Eirene (or Irene), a Greek goddess of peace (and one of the three *Horai*), who is linked also with the spring and shown holding a cornucopia, plus either an olive branch or the staff of Hermes; and the Greek messenger goddess Iris, who has been depicted holding the infant Hermes.[58]

This iconography is expressed in at least one other road ghost encounter, where it was combined with the familiar phantom jaywalker scenario. In April 2003, I received a fascinating email from a gentleman whom I shall call Gerry. Gerry was prompted to write to me after stumbling upon my website, whose content resurrected memories of an incident that had taken place late one night in a street in West Bromwich, Birmingham, and which had bugged him ever since:

> In September 1980 my wife and I had just returned from a 4-year stay in the USA where I was working. At the time we were living with my parents in Perry Barr, Birmingham, while we looked for a house to buy.
>
> My wife's parents lived in Gladstone St, West Bromwich. On the night in question I had been to see some friends while my wife was visiting her parents, where I'd dropped her earlier that evening.

> It would have been a Friday as I was visiting a club that met on Friday evenings. At around 11.30 p.m., I left Bilston to collect my wife at her parents' and I headed for West Bromwich via the Holyhead Road. I turned off Holyhead Road at, I think, Greswold Street [and then Milton Street].
>
> The street-lighting was not good. Given the late hour there was very little traffic. I was driving slowly, not sure of my bearings, when without warning, within sight of The Merry-go-Round [a pub on Garratt Street], I slammed on my brakes to avoid hitting a woman crossing the road.
>
> She was tall, youngish, gaunt, and (this I will never forget) carrying a child. It must have been a baby or a very young child as she carried it in her arms as though it was asleep. She seemed to be wearing a long, light-coloured coat, almost reaching her feet.
>
> I remember seeing her face in my headlights—her expression was ghastly, as anyone's would be if they were about to be hit by a car. I was certain I had hit her, and got out. I could smell burning rubber. There was no woman, no child, in fact no-one at all. No pedestrians, nobody. I even looked under my car. To say I was shaken is an understatement.
>
> I continued to my wife's parents' house, said nothing, collected my wife and told her what had happened as we drove to Perry Barr. By the time we reached my parents' house I was in something of a state, and I went into my parents' bedroom to tell them what had happened. Naturally, they thought I was drunk (I was 34 at the time and still their 'young' son) and I received a real piece of you-know-what from my father. So completely convinced of what I had seen I contacted the *Express & Star* newspaper during the next few days, to inquire if there had been any fatal accident at some time in the past, but didn't get very far with my inquiries. They suggested I contact the local police station, but I never did.
>
> A long time later I happened to mention to someone I knew in West Bromwich what had happened and he said that I wasn't the first driver to experience what had happened to me on that particular street. He could tell me no more. This has bugged me for 23 years. Can you throw any light on my experience? I can't say that I've been permanently affected by what happened that night, but I can still see the woman's face quite clearly and I sometimes think I could pick her out on an identification parade! This is my only experience of such things. I am a rational, hard-headed person with a passing but slightly cynical interest in matters paranormal.[59]

As we have noted, birth and motherhood are both archetypal and liminal events. Until relatively recent times, giving birth carried significant risk to the mother. Joseph Hall, Bishop of Exeter (1564–1656), said: 'Death borders upon our birth, and our cradle stands in the grave.' In the nineteenth century, up to seventy maternal deaths were recorded for every thousand births.[60] Hence death was an ever present prospect, waiting patiently in the wings even at the start of new life. And the circle here is complete. This perhaps throws some light on Gerry's experience, even if it fails to account precisely why it manifested to him on this particular occasion.

Phantom Dogs

Other variations of road ghost take a different form. Phantom black dogs with glowing coals for eyes are associated with many English counties, where they prowl the liminal spots such as churchyards (as the Church Grim), crossroads and ancient roads and boundaries. Their counterpart in Greek mythology is *Kerberus* (*Cerberus*), the triple-headed hell-hound that guarded the gates of the Underworld (where it was his function to prevent souls from escaping). Hence phantom black dogs are also regarded as symbols and portents of death. But like their human-form counterparts, the actions of phantom dogs show the same polarity in attitude, acting as guides and protectors as well as in a fearsome, hostile manner.[61]

There have been no reports of phantom *black* dogs at Blue Bell Hill, but in 2004 I received an email from Mervyn, who came across my website on a rainy day in Tauranga, on New Zealand's North Island, where he had lived for thirty years after emigrating from Kent. In 1965, Mervyn was twenty-two years old and recalled, among other things, the fatal accident of that year on Blue Bell Hill.

> But what I wanted to mention was the story that my grandmother would tell me when I was small: about the white dog Garm who was sometimes seen between Tunbury and Aylesford along the length of that hill. Sometimes he was seen with a young woman supposedly. (She was talking of the 1890s–1900s). Have you ever in that area encountered people speaking of Garm, or Hell's hound? From the Lower Bell there was a farm road that came off to the left, and went way back into the woods [Lower Warren Road]. Tunbury was off in that direction.[62]

Garm (or *Garmr*) was the monstrous hound of Norse mythology that (like its Greek equivalent Kerberus) guarded the approach to Helheim, the realm of the dead, and similarly, devoured those souls that tried to escape.

Interestingly, this anecdote of the late nineteenth century recalls also the association of a dog with a goddess figure—particularly Hekate from Greek mythology (Chapter 11), who, in her youthful guise as depicted on late classical pottery, stands with raised torches over the three-headed Kerberus, who is being restrained by the hero Heracles (Hercules). In this particular example, in the collection of the Antikensammlungen in Munich, Germany, the figure of Kerberus is distinctly pale in appearance, with upright pointed (prick) ears. In other examples also, Kerberus is rendered in pale shades, which may be an intentional feature rather than an artifact of the limited palette of the pottery's glaze.[63] (Oc-(Occasionally, we find road ghosts accompanied by a dog, as in Peter Leslie's experience near Stanmore in 1985, which involved a male figure described as around fifty years old, five feet four inches tall and wearing a mac (a somewhat familiar description), who had a Doberman dog with him (Chapter 9).)

The spectral hounds of other myths and legend are sometimes described as white (in opposition to their usual black colouration). Examples include the bullock-sized *Gally-trot* of English (Suffolk) folklore, and the white dog that sometimes accompanies the Hawaiian goddess Madame Pele (who herself appears in various forms, from a young girl to a haggard old woman). Then there are the *Cŵn Annwn* (the hounds of Annwn) of Welsh mythology, a pack of ghostly white dogs that accompany the hunter king Arawn (which in turn recall the Wild Hunt of northern European myth, the baying supernatural night-hunt in search of the souls of criminals and wrongdoers).[64]

On 22 January 2001, Rick Flynn of Maidstone was returning home from Bluewater, near Dartford, Kent. He started the run down Blue Bell Hill at around 10.35 p.m. The conditions were windy and wet.

> I was just about to go under the footbridge that crosses near to the Aylesford turn-off, Maidstone bound. I saw what looked like a white coloured Alsatian dog run across the road in front of me, causing me to brake rather quickly, my front wheels locked slightly. I released them just as soon to avoid any skidding. There was another car coming down the hill in the fast lane. I don't even know how the driver managed to miss this dog as he was going faster than me.
>
> The dog, if this is what it was, went under the central reservation then straight over the Chatham bound carriageway, on which there was no traffic near enough to be worried about.[65]

An ordinary dog, a supernatural one, or something else? Whatever it was, its appearance and the location of the encounter are noteworthy, even if we have no other accounts associated with the immediate area (other than Mervyn's recollection of a matching legend).[66]

The Hooded Ones

If it were not too much to expect further ghosts at Blue Bell Hill we return to the environs of Lower Warren Road and the line of the former Roman Road for the final aspect to Blue Bell Hill's ghostly manifestations.

Janice and Chris Leigh live in Lower Warren Road, in what was the original Lower Blue Bell inn on the old Roman road, a remnant of which survives in

Warren Road, which descends to meet the lower road opposite the house. Southward from here, the line of the old road is marked by a narrow bridleway that passes beside the house.

Prior to the start of excavation work that began near here late in 1998 in preparation for the laying of High Speed 1 (the Channel Tunnel rail-link) and the boring of the North Downs Tunnel beneath Blue Bell Hill, the bridleway and footpath traversed a corner of the field directly southward to Cossington service station, where the former Maidstone–Chatham Road meets the modern A229. The works (during which the archaeological survey uncovered the footprint of a Neolithic longhouse) forced the pathway to be temporarily displaced to the eastern side of the line of the railway.

Janice would regularly walk her dog of an evening in a circuit of the footpaths, which were usually uneventful. One evening they had some friends over to visit with their children. It was Hallowe'en. On a whim they decided to go for a 'ghost walk' (possibly the inspiration for the annual ghost walk around Blue Bell Hill they would later start in support of funding-raising toward the preservation of the village). The group visited the White Horse Stone, and as they were returning on the temporary path, they could see three figures coming across the field. It was a moonlit night, and the field was ploughed. Janice said to her husband, 'Oh, look, three people, like hooded monks or something.' To which Chris replied, 'Oh, don't be ridiculous.' But their dog, which wasn't on a lead, ran after the figures, barking, and when she got to the three figures, they vanished. Speculating over what they had seen, Chris believed they had simply lain down out of sight. Janice insisted he go over and find out. So, he did, but when he stumbled over to the spot, there was nothing there.

'I searched everywhere,' added Chris. 'I thought that they'd gone back and were hiding in the footpath, which is sunken. But nope—[they] weren't there either.'

Then, a few years later, on a November evening, Janice was again walking her dog on her usual circuit:

> It was dusk, about half-past-five, and I was just walking back, having done my circuit with my dog, and once again this crazy dog of mine saw a figure, which was walking along the path further up here. The figure was hooded, and the dog charged off again—didn't take a blind bit of notice of me—and went up to this figure barking, and then turned around and came running back to me. So I thought, well actually, this time I'm going to find out what's going on here; so I put her on the lead and I legged it across the path and…this figure was just gliding along in front of me, and I was stumbling on the bumpy path; and as I got close to my house, I saw the figure go onto the tarmac, onto the road, and in fro-

The North Downs Tunnel under construction beneath Blue Bell Hill. Completed in December 2001

The southern end of the North Downs Tunnel today. Lower Warren Road runs along the foot of the wooded scarp

> nt of my eyes it disappeared. And I don't even know what it was. Well again, it can't have been human.[67]

It is easy, rightful even, to be sceptical, to suppose the figures to have been other walkers or perhaps hoaxers out for a spot of Hallowe'en harum-scarum. Blue Bell Hill, in common with other reputedly haunted locations inevitably draws some thrill seekers at Hallowe'en, and on the anniversary of the 1965 tragedy. But if this were a hoax, the location and the form of the 'ghosts' stand as a puzzling choice.

Janice Leigh's less equivocal second sighting would seem to rule out conventional explanations, and her husband Chris indicated that similar figures had also been seen by neighbours.

> I'm not looking out for these things; I don't go out looking for them. It's just twice it's happened: once there was a group of us and we all saw it; and this time I was on my own. At the time I thought, well there's nobody here around; it was a horrible evening and anyone else would give me a long rebuke since she went up them barking and carrying on; but these figures just disappear. The one on the path just glided—carried on gliding—and didn't take any notice. I can't explain to you what I saw, but it must have been some sort of ghost or something like that. And as Chris said, we've had other sightings from neighbours of hooded, monk-type people gliding along the road, which goes up to a stony lane at the top. And it used to be quite a busy road that used to go from Aylesford Priory to Lidsing Abbey. So, many centuries ago it was a very busy place.

St. Mary Magdalene's Chapel-of Ease at Lidsing, Gillingham (a chapel rather than Abbey) was demolished in the 1880s after centuries of under use. Dating to the eleventh century, it is possible there was a connection with Aylesford Priory via the former pack-way that is now Lower Warren road—if only as a wayfare taken by pilgrims on the Way to Canterbury, which crosses the Roman Road at Cossington service station and ascends past the White Horse Stone and on to Boxley.

We do not have to venture quite so far, however, for what was certainly an active Abbey and monastery near to Blue Bell Hill, just two kilometres (1.5 miles) south of here.

Boxley Abbey (or the Abbey of St. Mary, Boxley, to give it its full name) was established in the twelfth century. For four hundred years, until 1538, when it was disbanded with the Dissolution of the Monasteries by the decree of King Henry VIII, the abbey and its grounds were home to around forty monks of the Cistercian order. Little today remains of the original buildings: the granary and vestiges of the original buildings and boundary wall still exist (which include the remnant gateway at the southern end of Tyland Lane), but the site and grounds are now privately owned.

Again, it is hard to envisage a meaningful connection with the fields below Lower Warren Road, other than as a way-point on the Roman road for any travelled correspondence that may have taken place between the monastery at Boxley and the Carmelite friars at Aylesford. Even so, it may be noteworthy that the Abbey's official seal of the early fourteenth century included as part of its motif the upper-half profiles of three upward gazing monks.[68]

But if this were the case, the Leighs' description of the costumes of the monk-like figures (dark, or at least not conspicuously coloured) is less encouraging. The Cistercians were also known as the White Monks in reference to the colour of their habit (white, with a black scapular worn over the shoulders)—in which case we might have expected a more fitting description of the monk-like figures, particularly ghostly ones.

Anecdotal accounts of hooded figures place sightings in the same area, on the Old Chatham Road below Cossington service station in 2001 and, in 1965, on the main road further up the Hill, when a couple returning home to Medway late on a winter's night saw a figure in a black cloak and hood float across the road from right to left and vanish in front of them.[69]

The latter is remindful of the *female* figure in a hooded cloak that crossed the path of an unnamed lorry driver on the Chatham Road in the vicinity of the steps down to Kit's Coty field. In this instance, the location hinted at an association more with the old woman character (see Chapter 11).

A very similar figure was the subject of a dramatic and shocking encounter involving two gentlemen returning to Maidstone in early hours of one autumn morning in the late 1970s or early 1980s. Neville Butteriss was at the time a freelance courier for a coach company. He and the driver had taken a group of people to London, and were returning to their depot in Armstrong Road, Maidstone. The courier's position was the low middle seat next to the driver, so that when seated, Neville's knees were level with the base of the coach's windscreen. The driver and he were smoking as they started down the dual carriageway at Blue Bell Hill, which at the time was not artificially lit. It was between 1.00 a.m. and 1.30 a.m., and there was little other traffic on the road. They had just crossed the overbridge level with the Lower Bell when a woman suddenly appeared in their headlights. The driver hit the brakes immediately, but it was too late to avoid her. Neville instinctively raised his arms in front of his face, expecting a collision. The woman seemed to raise an arm also, as if to protect herself. But instead of the anticipated impact, 'it was like we'd gone through nothing,' said Neville.

The coach slewed to a stop diagonally across the carriageway before the end of the southbound slip-road that starts at the entrance to Warren Road. Both men remarked, 'What the bloody hell was that?' They hopped out of the coach to walk back to where they had seen the woman. There was sufficient light (from lights on the overbridge or from moonlight—Neville cannot recall which) to see the long skid marks on the road made by the hard braking 13.5-ton coach, but no sign of the woman. They even looked over the side of the bridge in case she had been knocked to the side, but there was no evidence at all. The coach was undamaged, and it was as if the woman had vanished beneath it without a trace. The whole episode had lasted just seconds, but Neville gained an impression of her as she faced him as they closed the short distance to her at 50–55 mph: a female figure wearing a long reddish dress (her lower legs were not visible), with a dark hooded cape covering her top half. The hood covered the top half of face, obscuring her features, making it impossible to judge her age, but her upright posture suggesting a younger woman. Her head was at a level where, had she been a real person, it would have impacted with the lower part of the windscreen, and Neville feared she would come straight through it. She vanished from view beneath the bottom edge of the windscreen.

The two men did not report the incident, but did recount it later to workmates, who said simply that they 'must have been seeing things'. But both men, who had reacted to it simultaneously, and despite trying to rationalise the experience, maintained they had definitely seen a figure.

When asked if there had been any opportunity to swerve around the figure, Neville said that if they had tried, the manoeuvre might have rolled the coach, with disastrous outcome.[70]

We may remind ourselves that Neville Butteriss's encounter took place a little further down the same stretch of road from Ian Sharpe's and Gillian Barry's very similar experiences in 1992, plus Colin Eacott's sighting of an old woman in dark clothing (whom we have compared to the cailleach, the hooded crone of Celtic mythology).

Whenever and wherever they are reported, hooded ghosts tend to find interpretation as monks (or perhaps nuns). Hooded figures, taken to be monks, have been observed in proximity to the restored Neolithic long barrow known as Belas Knap, on the high Cotswolds overlooking Winchcombe, Gloucestershire; while the single track road at the foot of the ridge between Winchcombe and Charlton

Pearoyd Bridge over the A616 at Stocksbridge, scene of terrifying encounters with a hooded figure during the construction of the bypass

Abbots was the scene of a road ghost encounter in 1956 when an RAF liaison officer witnessed a glowing cloaked male figure that came up through the trees on his right and passed through the bonnet of his car before continuing up the hill in the direction of the barrow.[71]

Likewise, the terrifying figure witnessed on separate occasions by security guards and by police officers (both around midnight) at Pearoyd Bridge on the A616 Stocksbridge bypass (South Yorkshire), has been linked to a legendary monk whose grave was allegedly disturbed during its construction.

It is natural when faced with spontaneous and inexplicable events to look for some kind of logical framework into which to fit them. It is not surprising, then, that in this case, an 'explanation' should have arisen in the form of a vague story about a monk who, having grown disillusioned with the monastic life, departed the order and was later buried in unconsecrated ground, which the bypass eventually disturbed. But while such anecdotes may provide emotionally satisfying bookends to the reports, rarely do they tend to stand up to scrutiny by finding support either in an actual discovered grave or from historical information that will permit any kind of plausible link to the location.

This particular stretch of the A616 which overlooks the steel town of Stocksbridge has also generated reports of a woman in white, plus a circle of dancing phantom children (as witnessed by security guards beneath the electricity pylon beside Pearoyd Bridge)—which underline this book's latter argument that a complex of archetypal figures can be expected to be encountered at such locations. *Why* they should make their appearances when they do is explored in the next chapter. For now, we can continue to draw comparisons to their mythological counterparts with which they are undoubtedly related.

Of the two police officers, PC Dick Ellis and Special Constable John Beet, who underwent their own terrifying encounter with the hooded figure at the uncompleted bridge section at Stocksbridge on 12 September 1987, three days after the security watchmen's sighting, only Beet obtained a close view of the upper part of the figure, which after ten minutes of waiting in their patrol car suddenly appeared beside the driver's window. Its appearance was accompanied by a paralysing feeling of coldness and helplessness. Instantly it vanished and reappeared on the passenger side. From his clear view, Beet might have been describing Blue Bell Hill's ghostly hag from 1993, even using the same word—'wizened'—to describe its features, which included a sharp nose and piercing eyes.

Alarmed, but jumping out of the vehicle, PC Ellis found no trace of anyone or anything to account for the experience. The officers withdrew a little way before radioing for assistance. At this point, something took place that also has its parallels with Blue Bell Hill. A loud bang came from the back of the car, followed, as the pair quickly got out, by a series of thuds and crashes that sounded like an angry attack on the vehicle. Later inspection revealed no damage or marks on the vehicle.[72]

An account from Blue Bell Hill describes what the motorist concerned felt was distinct from the usual kinds of creaks, rattles and bangs that might be expected from vehicles at times. In November of 1973 or 1974, a gentleman from Larkfield, whose mother had been knocked down and killed the previous evening, was returning home in the afternoon (a Saturday) after visiting her body, and 'about halfway down' the Hill the car 'came over freezing cold' and he heard three very loud thuds on the back of the seat, definitely inside the car. On this occasion, the correspondent made no claim that his experience was connected with the Blue Bell Hill ghost (which he only heard about much later)—only that it was something new and unnerving for him which, under the circumstances, he connected more with the passing of his mother.

The Stocksbridge incident involving the initial sighting by the two security men—of a group of children in old-fashioned clothing dancing in 'ring-o'-roses' fashion beneath the struts of an electricity pylon—also finds counterparts at Blue Bell Hill and in other cases. The presence of the children, who vanished before the men's eyes and were later conveniently accounted for by a story of an overturning cart that claimed the lives of a number of children near the spot some 150 years ago, is remindful of another 'incident' at Blue Bell Hill, albeit one that received no independent confirmation. In the summer of 1994, ASSAP investigator David Thomas directed a group to Blue Bell Hill, where they subsequently carried out a night-time vigil, which seems to have passed without incident—apart from, that is, a sighting of a young girl dancing around the stones of Kit's Coty House.

Similar accounts arise from elsewhere. At 1.30 a.m. on 9 August 1977, David Swift, a police officer in Hull (Humberside) went to investigate a strange bank of fog on a playing field in Stonebridge Avenue. There, he observed three figures dancing in the mist. One was a man dressed in a sleeveless jerkin; the other two were women in bonnets, shawls and white dresses. Each held an arm in the air as if dancing around an invisible maypole. All three vanished as he approached within fifty feet of them.[73]

As absurd as these accounts may appear in isolation, collectively they begin to add up to something more. Readers acquainted with folklore will perhaps already have connected these events with the fairy folk's habit of dancing hand-in-hand in circles, particularly at megalithic sites. In one account recorded by the anthropologist and writer Walter Evans Wentz at the turn of the twentieth century, the 'fair folk' sometimes seen at a hilltop cromlech appeared as little children in clothes resembling soldiers' outfits.[74]

***Dancing Nymph* (*Nymphe Danseuse*) by Walter Crane (from *L'Estampe originale, Album IX*, 1895)**

The characters of European Fairy (or *Faerie*) lore share many similarities with those of the older mythologies, principally Celtic and Graeco-Roman, from which they are arguably derived. The lares and the nymphs find recognition both in these tales and in modern road ghost sightings. The lares are frequently depicted as youthful dancers that hold a horn cup in one hand and a bowl in the other (symbolising plenty). Likewise, the nymphs, often described as beautiful maidens, were inferior divinities of nature, usually associated with specific natural features such as hills, groves, springs, pools or forests (or even individual trees)—in other words, *genii loci*: spirits of place.

As personifications and animators of a numinous nature, they are often depicted as joyfully dancing or frolicking, sometimes hand in hand or with hands raised high. (The experience of Glenn Jones at Warren Road at Blue Bell Hill in 2014 springs immediately to mind—to which we might add the penchant of the fair folk to vanish, leaving the sound of their laughter hanging in the air around their victims).[75]

We can recall also the female figures described by Joe Chester and Adrian Moorfield, and recognise in them the same characters, whose bare feet symbolise their intimate, unfettered connection with the earth (marking them as nature spirits).

The lares were usually regarded as guardian spirits, protectors variously of the family (*lares familiares*), the countryside (*lares rurales*), travellers (*lares viales*) and crossroads (*lares compitales*). But as we have noted, their fickle nature meant their beneficence could turn by whim to hostility when justly provoked. The nymphs also, when threatened (as when their habitat is endangered), could appear to frighten solitary travellers.[76]

The nymphs of trees (*dryads* and *hamadryads*), whose lives were intimately linked to the tree they inhabited or were associated with, would take retribution on mortals who wilfully damaged their abode. Again, it may perhaps be significant that in the disturbed ground beside the large oak tree that was the focus of Glenn Jones's sighting lay the cut and broken remains of another.

Returning to the monk-like apparitions, we again find a deeper resonance with certain figures from mythology, particularly the *genii cucullati* (hooded spirits) of Romano-Celtic religious iconography (named for the *cucullus* (Latin for cowl)), which were represented across northern Europe by carved religious reliefs or sculptures of dwarf-like deities in hooded capes. In Britain, they are uniquely shown in triplicate, sometimes associated with a mother goddess, or found in the same regions in which the *Tres Matres* (the three Mothers) were venerated (as at Hadrian's Wall, for example). The gender of the figures is disputed, but the bias of opinion is toward males; the softer features depicted in some renditions interpreted as child-like rather than adult female, which might be more consistent with their smaller stature. Sometimes the figures appear to hold what has been interpreted as an egg in one hand; in other cases they carry swords, suggesting they served both as fertility totems (the egg symbolising the cycle of life and rebirth), and as protectors or guardians. In Kent, singular examples are known from fragments found at the small Roman town of Springhead at Southfleet, near Gravesend, and at the Roman coastal fort of Reculver (*Regulbium*), a location where hooded apparitions have been seen in recent times.[77]

Finds of such carved reliefs at wells and springs—as exampled by the three genii cucullati associated with the Roman god Mercury and his consort Rosmerta (a Gaulish goddess of abundance and fertility, herself sometimes depicted in a hood or veil) at the Temple and extant Roman baths of *Aquae Sulis* (modern day Bath, Somerset)—seem to identify them (in part) with health or healing, related to the curative powers of the mineral-rich spring waters that issued from the beneficence of the divinities associated with them.

It has been postulated that there is a connection between the genii cucullati and Telesphorus, the son of Asklepios, the Greek god of healing and medicine. Telesphorus (whose sister was Hygieia—the three are sometimes depicted together) was a child-god of convalescence and dream healing. Depictions of him share many characteristics with the genii cucullati: a small, hooded, cloaked figure, shown sometimes clutching a scroll or a tablet (possibly denoting wisdom or the secrets of the healing arts—or perhaps a record of accounting, of judgement). In some versions, he is shown carrying a lantern,[78] inviting comparison again with the male archetype of the A38 whose mackintosh and torch are the contemporary accoutrements. Telesphorus is therefore believed by some to have been a god of Celtic origin who was later adopted into a minor role in the Greek and Roman pantheons.

Both the singular (Telesphorus) and the triadic forms of the genius cucullatus are clearly linked with health, recuperation and regeneration. But inevitably in the sphere of the unconscious, there is a flip side.

Wells and springs have been regarded as sacred places from ancient times as channels to the gods and to the otherworld. Their sweet waters, miraculously issuing from the earth, were linked to healing and symbolised life itself. The Celts, the Greeks and the Romans all venerated deities at natural springs and made their votive offerings and supplications to them there. In the Christian era, many of these sites were taken over as holy wells and shrines connected with often Christianised versions of the original pagan god or spirit. These too, then, were liminal places. Not infrequently holy wells have legends or sightings of white lady apparitions and black dogs associated with them.

Often, offerings of coins or items of practical or sentimental value were made as entreaties to the gods for some positive purpose, a cure for a disease or ailment, or for infertility. Vestiges of these votive offerings survive today in the custom of depositing coins into wishing wells and fountains, albeit mostly without the conscious regard for any guardian goddess.

The supplications made to the gods, however, were not always positive or altruistic in intent. So-called *curse tablets* have been found at a number of 'wet' sites such as the Temple springs at Bath or Uley in Gloucestershire. A single example was found in a possible temple building at a newly discovered Roman farmstead at East Farleigh, near Maidstone, Kent, in 2009.[79] Usually consisting of small squares of lead sheet that were inscribed and then rolled into a scroll-like configuration before they were deposited, curse tablets often called on the god(s) for justice or retribution to be meted out to the named person for some committed wrong (theft being the leading example)—or they might be employed as appeals for gainful purposes such as the hindering of a rival in love or trade, or the ruination of an enemy or an unrepentant thief.

While many wells and springs are associated with female deities, in Britain the subject god for many of the curse tablets was Mercury, the Roman equivalent of Hermes and the Celtic god Lugus, who in the Romanised world became syncretised with Mercury. Mercury and Hermes share many attributes in addition to their respective role as messenger of the gods. Each was a god of commerce, of roads and protectors of travellers, a trickster, and a psychopomp (guide to the dead).

The association between the genii cucullati and Mercury, and in turn between Mercury and spring sites and the rites performed at them, suggests not only a connection between the genii cucullati and roads (the Roman road), but also, through Mercury's role as pyschopomp, a subsidiary role in the ministrations of death.

Archaeologist Miranda Green has cautioned that the hooded cloak (the Gallic *caracalla* or Roman *paenula*) was a common and practical form of overgarment worn by travellers and pilgrims alike, particularly in Britain (indeed, one curse tablet found at Bath is made concerning the theft of just such a garment) and some caution therefore should be applied in the interpretation of the depictions of genii cucullati.[80] Their supernatural nature, however, is hinted at by their triplicate form and by their close relationship with deities, and by other associations. In the relief of Mercury and Rosmerta found at Bath, carved beside the genii cucullati at the feet of the gods is the likeness of a dog. Dogs also were symbols of protection, guidance, healing and fertility; but also of death and the hereafter. In other examples, the genii are depicted with ravens, which were symbols of ill omen, the dead and the Underworld. Green concurs: 'The cult of the cucullati would appear, then, to be sophisticated, embodying elements of fertility, healing, death and renewal.'[81]

Modern culture is not devoid of their influence, as it cannot be where expression is given to the inspirations of the unconscious. Hooded ghosts themselves are stereotypical: we stylise them as hooded or veiled forms—arcane figures whose features are hidden from us—possibly because, as personifications of the unconscious, they have no personal face to show. The quintessential hooded spirit of Western cultural heritage must be the Grim Reaper, the black-cloaked

The picturesque springhead pool at Great Tottington Farm, with sarsens evident at its margin.

Cossington, toward the springhead and Blue Bell Hill – once regarded as 'the most delightful glen in the district'

personification of death and psychopomp to the newly deceased. Images of hooded figures associated with death, illness or foreboding occur also in dreams, and in near death experiences,[82] and emerge also in popular culture as icons of mystery, wisdom, or as the embodiment of dark powers or death.[83]

Related (in principle) to the cursing tablets are the *Bullaun* stones, or 'cursing stones' as they are known in Ireland, where they are chiefly found. These are rounded stones or pebbles that were ritually turned by hand on a larger flat stone (the bullaun), whose action eventually wore one or more bowl-shaped depressions into the lower stone. The turning of the stone would have been accompanied by the recital of a prayer (to 'cure'), or (usually in a counter-clockwise rotation) when uttering a curse. The stones tend to be found at holy wells and springs, or at old church sites and burial grounds. These generally date from early Christian times, but may have a much earlier origin.

Similar markings are found at megalithic sites, and on megaliths themselves. The worn cup-like depressions naturally collect rainwater. Folk traditions imbue this water with healing or magical properties, such as a reputation for never drying out. At Blue Bell Hill, Kit's Coty has such a legend attached to it: a hollow on the top of the capstone is said to never dry out; or if it is ladled out it refills immediately.[84] Kit's Coty's (and Little Kit's Coty's) megaliths also display rounded depressions, some quite deep; but these appear to be a consequence of deep weathering of pits naturally found in the sandstone.

In the valley immediately below Blue Bell Hill, on either side of the Rochester Road between the Lower Bell and the village of Aylesford lie the ancient manors of Great Tottington (now Great Tottington Farm) and Cossington. Both lie on the spring line along the foot of the ridge of the North Downs, where the upstanding chalk meets the underlying Gault Clay of the valley, and are distinguished by extant spring-fed pools and streams.

We looked briefly at Tottington in Chapter 2 in relation to its mooted name association with the Celtic god Teutates (variously rendered *Toutates* or *Totates*, or abbreviated sometimes as *Tot*), a deity of protection, healing and war who was venerated in Gaul and Britain and identified by the Romans with the gods Mercury and Mars.

The wood-shrouded spring at Cossington, still marked today on maps as Wellhead, is located a little east of Tottington and just 600 metres from the line of the former Roman road on the eastern side of the A229 where the Leighs sighted their hooded figures.

In his book *In Kentish Pilgrim Land* (1925), Kent engineer and historian William Coles Finch speculates over the root meaning of the name *Cosenton*, as it was rendered from medieval times when it was the estate of a knightly family of the same name. The estate encompassed the field where the figures were seen plus all of the land to the north-east as far as the area above the escarpment between Frith Wood and the M2 motorway (an area distinguished now by a television transmitter array and still known today as Cossington Fields). Coles Finch reminds us that *cursian* in Anglo-Saxon signified 'to curse', '… therefore Cussing-ton is the cursing-field of Druidic times.'[85] In light of the foregoing, perhaps *Cursing-ston(e)* might be more fitting?

The etymology of the name may be little more than a play on words, but there is every possibility that these spring sites served a religious as well as a practical purpose for the peoples of the ancient past. Both the Tottington and Cossington springs preserve relict sarsen stones of disputed provenance. The scattering of stones at Tottington (numbering up to a hundred) were reported in some instances as being as large as those comprising Kit's Coty House.[86] A rough semicircular arrangement of stones that outcropped above the springhead, as noted during a survey by E.H.W. Dunkin in 1871, may have been the inspiration for various antiquarians of the eighteenth and nineteenth centuries that saw in them the remnant of a stone circle and traces of avenues. Dunkin concluded that many of the stones were natural (periglacial deposits) that had been removed from the farm's surrounding fields. Some later workers, however, still entertained the possibility that the substantial stones around the Tottington springhead were from a purported Coffin Stone long barrow, evidencing some megalithic activity nearby if not actually originally associated with the spring.[87]

A similar collection of sarsens was also reported for the Cossington springhead, which were later removed (by, Coles Finch assumed, the 'Water Company'—the Maidstone Waterworks Company, which took control of the springs to tap its groundwater source for municipal supply in the 1880s). Prior to this, when the spring and its brook were still in full flow (its sound reputedly giving its name to nearby Pratling Street) the springhead sat in what 'was without doubt the most delightful glen in the district.'[88] John Thorpe's description of Cossington in his *Custumale Roffense* (1788), from his visit to the springhead in 1776 (as quoted in Coles Finch), imbues it with idyllic, almost sacred, qualities:

> At a corner of a field above the hop-ground north of the house, between two hills, is a hollow almost perpendicular, except at the bay-like entrance, which is very wet to approach. The sides are covered with coppice-wood and bushes, and above the bay are one or two large walnut trees. At the bottom issue several springs, which are so cold and sharp that the water is said to cramp and kill young ducks, and the flints which lie in it are tinged red as blood, and to try the experiment stones have been marked and put in, which, in less than a year's time, were of the same colour.[89]

The source of the red tinge (dissolved iron salts), which Coles Finch regarded as probably exaggerated, was nevertheless a real property of the Cossington waters. The small paper mill downstream of the Cossington brook at nearby Pratling Street was among those of north Kent that closed in the mid-nineteenth century, in part because of their reliance on the chalybeate waters that rendered them unable to produce the whiter grades of paper produced elsewhere by new processes.[90] Today, while its trickling stream and pools are still in evidence around the site of the original manor of Cossington in the still picturesque lower section of the glen, the springhead itself is now a forbidding dry hollow, its headwaters tapped directly from the substrata by the pumping station here that is operated by Mid-Kent Water. It seems inconceivable, though, that in its time, the Romans and the area's earlier inhabitants would not have utilised (and perhaps venerated) the springs here and at Tottington—even if direct evidence for this is lacking.

Both sites, however, have a later religious connection that provides a tenable through-line to their ancient past. In medieval times the springs served as waypoints and refreshment opportunities, both physical and spiritual, for pilgrims travelling the nearby Pilgrims' Way to Canterbury. Free chapels were established on the lands of both estates: St. Stephen's Chapel, located near to the Coffin Stone at Great Tottington, and another (dedicated to St. Michael) established at Cossington by Sir Stephen de Cosenton. Both are long vanished.[91]

St. Michael was the patron saint of high places—for example, St. Michael's Mount in Cornwall (UK) and Mont Saint-Michel (Normandy, France)—and is associated with a number of medieval pilgrim routes. Curative springs were also dedicated to him, and he therefore has a connection with healing. Other familiar attributes include messenger, protector, warrior, and a conductor of souls to Heaven (psychopomp). Both Western and Eastern iconography portray St. Michael with the requisite halo and wings of an angel, carrying a flaming sword (or staff), and sometimes a scroll or scales (denoting judgement)—features all that echo the attributes of Mercury-Hermes-Teutates.

Tellingly perhaps, like England's St. George, St. Michael is frequently shown slaying a dragon in symbolic defeat of Lucifer in the great cosmic battle—but also as a symbol of the triumph of the new religion of Christianity and its saints over the pagan beliefs, divinities and holy shrines that it supplanted.

Considering the close connection between apparitions of white ladies at holy wells and sacred springs and their associations with hooded spirits, it would not be surprising to hear of sightings at these less frequently visited, off-road liminal spots. At very least, the hooded figures seen a little distance away below Blue Bell Hill, at first seemingly inconsistent with the cast of female apparitions seen there, are by no means out of place.

That many of the ghostly figures exampled in this book appear to take on symbolic forms from our mythologies—particularly those of the Greeks, the Romans and Celts—seems natural considering the founding influence these have had on European historical and literary culture, and therefore their ingrained availability to the collective psyche. In like fashion, operating as they appear to do, in symbolic acts, the messages they embody are likely to be absorbed (if only subliminally) and reintegrated into the modern psyche. In modern times, we are more likely to interpret them in light of our own cultural conditioning, as the personal ghosts of road accident victims rather than the goddesses, demi-gods, and elementals of old that occupied the impersonal spheres of nature and the collective imagination—but the 'messages' they convey are essentially the same.

It may be that road ghosts spring forth spontaneously in relation to untimely or violent death purely because, as denizens of the liminal, it is in their nature to do so. An example of this at Blue Bell Hill might be found in the experience of Clare Bush of Maidstone, who, on the afternoon of 18 October 1990, around 3 p.m., a month before her eighteenth birthday, was in a serious crash on Blue Bell Hill when a rear wheel sheared off her car (a red VW Polo) at 70 mph on the sinuous section of the Maidstone-bound carriageway of the A229 below Cossington service station. The incident and her reaction to it threw the car into a severe spin, which was brought to a jolting stop as it collided with a roadside lamp-post. The car crumpled in the collision. When the emergency services arrived they expected to find a seriously injured young woman. Instead, Clare miraculously escaped with just cuts and bruises to her legs. 'When my parents saw the state of my car they said there was no way I could have come out alive.'[92]

Clare remembers being thrown heavily one way by the force of the impact. When she stopped, she closed her eyes and all she could see (as a strong mental impression) was a figure of woman with lank black hair standing about twenty feet behind her car, staring at it as it spun out of control (with Clare in it)—almost like an out-of-body experience.[93]

Was Clare Bush's experience but a flash impression born of shock and an unconscious association with the Hill's reputation, or one brought about by a close shave with death akin to the theme developed in this chapter?

There may be deeper, more complex reasons for the appearances of archetypal road ghosts. Death itself is a liminal state; either the final threshold at the end of life, or it is perhaps a transitional state to a new order of existence. In some examples of road ghosts (see Roy Fulton's and Jean Clarke's experiences with the Phantom Hitch-Hiker (Chapter 4)), the ghost, in enacting the role of its mythological counterparts as guide, literally raises an arm and points to the way ahead.

Is this what the appearances of these archetypal figures are trying to impart—what we already know deep inside but, in Western culture at least, we seem intent to forget—that liminal states and events always lead somewhere else, and that coupled with death is a renewal of life? In some measure, we might intuit that ghostly encounters (where the ghost itself symbolises death) are directing us to this ultimate question.

FOURTEEN

THE ESSENTIAL QUESTION

'The earth hath bubbles, as the water has,
And these are of them. Whither are they vanish'd?'

Banquo (*Macbeth*: Act I, Scene III (William Shakespeare))

Part I

Together, Jung's concept of the archetypes and the principle of liminality provide a satisfying framework for understanding the symbolic nature of road ghosts. They help to explain the principal forms they take, the locations, time-frames and circumstances in which they are most likely to appear, as well something of the 'why' of their appearances.

What they do *not* provide is an answer to the question most apt to be posed by the modern Western mindset (if it is considered at all): Are ghosts 'real'? Are they an objective phenomenon, as this is commonly understood, or are they a purely psychosocial phenomenon? Might they conceivably be both?

So, what exactly *are* people encountering at Blue Bell Hill, and at numerous other locations where road ghosts are periodically and repeatedly reported? The easiest thing in the world (and what for many might be the preferred option) would be to dismiss it all as a combination of imagination, hoaxing and mistaken identity. But while particular witness events may remain open to such criticism—particularly single-witness cases, based on the Roman maxim *testis unus testis nullus* (one witness is no witness)—when taken collectively, and taking into account the vivid, sometimes matching witness descriptions, plus the correspondences in the style and timings of encounters and their close resemblance to cases reported elsewhere and in the historical and folkloric record, they begin to add up to something not so easily explicable.

There can be little question that people *have* seen apparitions at Blue Bell Hill—that is, human figures in some cases so life-like in appearance that the witness has afterward unhesitatingly rushed to report the incident to the police, firm in the belief that they have struck and quite probably killed a real person.

Accepting that people sometimes see apparitions should come with no great difficulty. The incidence of such encounters throughout history, and universally, in quite separate societies and cultures is testament to the reality of the phenomenon—a conclusion that would come to be shared by the first critical study of the phenomenon, which was instigated by the Society for Psychical Research (SPR) in 1882, even if this found reason to question the customary beliefs of apparitions as the spirits of the dead—and indeed, whether apparitions were really an objective phenomenon at all.

Today, more than a century after the inception of the SPR's pioneering work, there exists a prodigious body of evidence to the effect that certain unexplained and repetitive phenomena *do* occur. The fact that a proper understanding still eludes us is more a reflection of the subtlety and complexity of the subject matter (which is demonstrated in microcosm at Blue Bell Hill) than a deficiency in the evidence—although much of this rests, admittedly, on human observation and testimony. But times are changing. Some branches of scientific enquiry are beginning to turn their attention to the paranormal field. We find, for instance, more universities offering courses in Parapsychology, reflecting some recognition that the existing data, and the very persistence of the respective phenomena, describes an area of human experience that is worthy of proper study—and which, irrespective of the conclusions that might be reached in specific cases, can only add to our understanding of ourselves, and possibly teach us something about our fundamental nature.

The real question then is not whether people actually see ghosts, but one of interpretation: What *are* they? What conditions, if any, are conducive to their appearance, or to seeing them? Why do some people see apparitions while others do not?

Naturally, given that a century or more of formal study and conjecture has so far failed to come up with a definitive explanation, it would be unreasonable to expect to arrive at any firm conclusions here regarding the case at Blue Bell Hill, or about apparitions in general (although it is my hope that this work contributes, if only in small measure, to our understanding). In this time a host of theories and 'explanations' have been proposed to account for ghosts and related phenomena, and include hoaxing, autosuggestion and hallucination (including Charles Bonnet syndrome), telepathy (ESP), time-slips, the stone tape theory, infrasound and electromagnetic anomalies; even the presence of toxic mould in old buildings! No single theory, however, can be said to persuasively account for the full range of reported phenomena. Rather, each tends instead to focus on a selective area of the data, and some merely substitute one mystery for another. Ironically, one that is rarely prominent today is the possibility that ghosts might indeed be what they have always been purported to be: an aspect of human personality that transcends death.

What we *can* say is that there does appear to be a genuine case to answer at Blue Bell Hill. But can we, in face of what is evidentially a strong case, still find a completely rational, everyday explanation for the events there?

Just an illusion?

The majority of encounters at Blue Bell Hill have been of the 'spectral jaywalker' type, in which the motorist has encountered a figure ambling or, in some cases, running into the path of their vehicle. It is fair to say that the majority of road ghosts encountered everywhere are of this type.

One possible explanation—and one that will be favoured by those resistant to the very idea of ghosts—is that proposed in the *Hampstead Local Advertiser* report on the experience of Peter Leslie on the A41 near Stanmore in 1985 (Chapter 9).

Referring to a spate of similar sightings which accompanied the opening of the M1, Britain's first motorway, over which Mr Leslie's route carried him, an 'expert' (who was not identified) attributed such experiences to the hypnotic effects of driving along open stretches of road at twilight. Under such conditions, it was said, motorists might be fooled into misinterpreting bold features such as bridges and junction markers as smaller objects (human figures) in the path of the vehicle. Such images, which could last for several seconds, would form the basis of the brain's attempt to rationalise the illusion and to prompt evasive action. As soon as the brain has had the chance to recompose and reinterpret the image, and perhaps with disaster averted, the figure would be found to have vanished.

That the eye is capable of being momentarily fooled in all manner of circumstances is not disputed. Short-lived optical illusions of this nature may certainly be generated under the right circumstances—but more particularly, I would argue, late at night on dark, deserted roads when the visual field is muted and illuminated features stand out with greater contrast. Signposts and other roadside features, particularly those in line-of-sight over sweeping bends and visible over rises, may give the illusion of something in the road itself, whose apparent movement is produced by a combination of the road configuration and the forward motion of the motorist's own vehicle.

Left bends and offside objects (in Britain), generally produce 'figures' that cross from the left, while right bends with nearside objects give the impression of movement from the right. The illusion lasts but a few seconds, and what might be taken momentarily to be a vague figure crossing the road is quickly resolved for what it is as the vehicle closes on its apparent position. But it is possible that someone failing to recognise the cause of such an illusion might come away with

The A15 at Ruskington, illustrating the apparent movement across the road of a fixed feature (a roadside pole) with the forward motion of the vehicle

the impression that they had seen a ghost, albeit at a distance, particularly if that person's mind has been primed by that locality's reputation for being haunted.

What we may term the 'M1 hypothesis' may explain a few road ghost sightings, but such 'tidy' explanations tend to run into difficulties when we try to apply them to cases like Blue Bell Hill. By it, we might expect to find these encounters confined to long, essentially unvarying stretches of road, which according to the hypothesis provide three of the vital components that lead to the hallucinatory experience: monotony, speed, and, at the roadside or spanning it, a steady supply of bold physical structures to act as 'trigger' objects.

At Blue Bell Hill, only the motorway-grade dual carriageway of the A229 itself compares to the open stretches of road most likely to draw the motorist into the semi-hypnotic state by which the motorist is liable to—for want of a better word—hallucinate. But even this (up to the time of Ian Sharpe's encounter in November of 1992) ran unbroken for no more than three miles (or three minutes at a typical 60 mph) before encountering changes in road layout (a roundabout at either end) that would prompt the driver into reduced speed manoeuvres that would tend to break such a state even before it had really developed. Added to this is that the A229 between Maidstone and the Medway towns has been fully lit since 1989, making arguments relating to effects of highly contrasting light and shadow largely void. In other instances, a variety of low-speed settings are represented, from dark hedgerow-lined back lanes to the well-lit built-up area of Blue Bell Hill Village itself.

While sightings of road ghosts tend to cluster along particular stretches of road, such encounters are not always location-specific, as we might expect if the cause of the illusory figure were a fixed feature, artificial or otherwise. Often an appropriate 'trigger' object is absent or the apparition comes from the 'wrong' direction to the one the road layout might predict. Perhaps most significantly, in a number of cases the assumed purpose of the vision, to prompt evasive action, is defeated by the vehicle apparently striking the figure!

In general terms the hypothesis fails also to explain why it is that many more 'fitting' roads do not have reputations for being haunted. It is therefore difficult to imagine quite how these characteristically short-lived and obscure episodes could be transformed into the kind of vivid, close-up experiences of, say, Ian Sharpe or Chris Dawkins. And as an explanation for Maurice Goodenough's experience, which continued outside of his vehicle, or for any accepted Phantom Hitch-Hiker encounter or historical case, it seems completely inadequate.

Having said that, I do believe the M1 hypothesis is on the right track. While we can generally discount several of the predicted features of the hypothesis at Blue Bell Hill and in other cases, it does point to a particular condition as an important factor in these experiences—the state of consciousness of the driver.

Trance states (today more commonly referred to as altered states of consciousness) have long been recognised as a factor in many, although certainly not all, instances of ghost-seeing. Driving, as we are well aware, accounts for a number of apparitional experiences, but someone is just as likely to see a ghost upon looking up from a book, on absent-mindedly entering a room; or, as is frequently the case, waking in the night (the so-called 'bedroom visitor' experience).

Most drivers will be familiar with that detached state of consciousness that tends to set in during long or overly familiar journeys, particularly those conducted in the dark, quiet hours. When there is little demand for conscious input in the form of manoeuvring or navigating, the mind has a tendency to switch into 'autopilot' mode. In this state the driver's full conscious awareness disengages to follow other trains of thought, leaving the practised act of driving under unconscious control. Various labels are applied to this trance-like state—'white line fever', 'highway hypnosis'—and the mind *is* effectively hypnotised. Often the lapse into this altered state is recognised only after the driver finds him- or herself arriving at their destination to find they cannot recollect portions of the journey, or when they are jarred back to alertness either by their wheels running over the 'cat's eyes', or by some other stimulus that re-engages full conscious attention. (Occasionally this condition can and does lead to the driver falling asleep, with predictably disastrous results. Up to 20 percent of road accidents and one in every four fatal or serious road accidents are attributed to drivers falling asleep behind the wheel.)[1]

As we have noted, this effect is likely to occur less frequently under the low contrast conditions of twilight (which may or may not have been detailed in the report of Peter Leslie's encounter as a means of linking the hypothesis with the timing of his experience, around 6 p.m.), but late at night when traffic volumes are much reduced, and particularly to persons travelling alone or without the wakeful company of others. Under these conditions, it is the added sensory isolation, coupled perhaps with fatigue, and the fixation of the dominant, visual sense by the narrowed field of view that may lead to the induction of the trance state.

In this respect, and in some agreement with the hypothesis, the arresting appearance of a figure in the road ahead might come as a necessary jolt to the driver's lapsing consciousness to stir and take evasive action—the 'ghost' in this instance symbolically representing a threat to the life of the driver rather than to the figure in the road. This is an idea, of course, that is consistent with road ghosts appearing as warning symbols at locations with significant accident records, as we have explored in earlier chapters.

What remains unanswered is if such apparitions are purely a psychological phenomenon, by what mechanism do they occur (even to persons unaware of a given location's reputation for either death accidents or ghosts) and in a consistent, repeatable fashion; and why do they not feature at many other locations marred by poor accident records?

Day dreams / Night dreams

Night-driving, particularly by lone motorists, ironically creates virtually ideal conditions for inducing hypnotic states. While the precise conditions and circumstances naturally vary in every road ghost sighting, the cognitive state of the witness at the time of their encounter can often be described in similar terms: relaxed, unchallenged, idle, and so on. Whatever label we attach to it—altered state, trance, daydream—it is a state that is characterised by the suspension of critical, decision-making thought, which, when coupled with the right circumstances, seems conducive to the experiencing of apparitional and other kinds of paranormal phenomena.

As particular stimuli might be screened out as a consequence of the preoccupation with a single activity, so can the unchanging or repetitive nature of this activity lead to a further reduction in conscious attention, which has the effect of putting the percipient closer in touch with the unconscious—that inexhaustible wellspring of our imagination and creativity, our dreams…and Jung's archetypes.

The process becomes clearer when we consider that the function of the conscious mind is to analyse, to compare and to make sense of new data presented to it; to apply labels, and so on. In everyday life the conscious mind is fed with a sufficiently variable and challenging stream of stimuli to sustain active, purposeful thought, to the extent that we commonly regard it as the primary state of awareness. But what we see on the screen of the conscious mind only hints at the unseen activity and abilities of the unconscious processes underlying it. At times when we are at rest or engaged in tiresome or repetitive activities during which no fresh stimuli are presented, the conscious mind's critical faculties become suspended. We become inattentive or distracted. We daydream. Being the efficient organ it is, the brain finds it unnecessary to constantly re-evaluate information it has already examined, so any repetitive or ready-learned stimulus passes out of conscious awareness and is tended by the unconscious mind. Examples include playing a musical instrument or catching a ball. Such actions are best performed when we simply let them happen. If we try to do these things consciously, the fluidity of the experience falters.

When we permit ourselves to be so absorbed, active analytical thought is dulled and routine or practised functions like night-driving become virtually autonomous, involving little or no conscious guidance. Under such circumstances, the mind becomes open to the full flood of sensory input, experience and imaginative potential of the unconscious. In effect, a trapdoor to the unconscious is thrown open and 'reality' may then potentially be constructed from both real and imaginal sources, with the subject unable to distinguish between the two.

This principle is well understood by hypnotists, who exploit the unconscious mind's susceptibility to suggestion to guide a subject into trance, which is achieved by directing the subject's attention to an object of fixation. As the subject concentrates on this, other sensations are gradually introduced into their conscious awareness, which are continually fed back to the subject, engaging their attention on a broader sensory front, and focusing their attention inwardly. As physiological changes are noticed—in the pattern of breathing, in the relaxation of the muscles, indicating a shift in consciousness—so these sensations too are incorporated into the hypnotist's feedback routine. After a while, the conscious mind reaches a point of overload, where it loses attention to all the repeated stimuli it is trying to monitor, and the subject slips into trance. At this point, the hypnotist is free to deliver suggestions which, implanted directly into the subject's unconscious, bypass their normal critical abilities and inhibitions, and are responded to spontaneously and in an appropriate manner. In effect, the subject's mind has become a *tabula rasa*, a blank slate for the hypnotist to write new things on.

Of particular interest and obvious relevance to the study of apparitions is the remarkable ability of the mind, in response to suggestion, to conjure up realistic images of objects, which are known as *positive* hallucinations (a negative hallucination being one in which a real object in the percipient's visual field is rendered invisible to the percipient). With respect to human 'objects', the hypnotist need only suggest to the subject that they can see a human figure, broadly defined with regard to, say, age, sex and dress, and the subject's own imagination will accommodatingly furnish the details, projecting the figure convincingly (with full parallax) into three-dimensional space, applying light and shadow, and so on. The resultant image is what appears to be a normal human being. So long as the figure stays within the expected framework of the percipient's model of reality—for instance, occluding objects as it passes in front of them; avoiding physical obstructions like tables and chairs—it could be difficult to convince the witness that it is, in fact, a construct of their own mind.

Viewed in another context, particularly one in which the figure is seen to do something impossible like appear or disappear spontaneously, or walk through walls or other physical barriers, that same image becomes the perfect ghost.[2]

Following a personal experience in 1961, Sidney Russ (1879–1963), medical physicist and Emeritus Professor at London University, became convinced that ghosts were nothing more than this: illusions manufactured by the unconscious under certain conditions of trance—in his case, the near-sleep state. While his theory[3] maintained that ghosts were subjective experiences, Russ did concede that they may be more than imaginary forms realised only in the mind, but real images, invented by the dreaming mind and projected onto the retina in a reversal of the usual direction of communication between eye and brain that is found in the wakeful, conscious state. The conscious mind, stirred by the alarming content of the dream (perhaps with the sure knowledge that they are being watched, or there is something in the room with them), would awaken to find the aberrant image on the retina, and the percipient would see before them an apparition, an apparently objective form that would last as long as it would take their conscious faculties to re-coordinate and take grasp of 'true' reality. This, according to Professor Russ, was the reason why ghosts were commonly seen by persons in bed, as either a hypnagogic (one seen just before the onset of sleep) or a hypnopompic illusion (seen just before full wakefulness).

The difficulty with Russ's hypothesis is that it cannot account for the forms the apparitions take or the consistencies in descriptions and behaviours between different witnesses.

But while direct hypnotic suggestion can be ruled out as an explanation for most haunting cases, in that it is an artificially induced state that depends on deliberate guidance by a third party (and in this sense differs to the kind of casual trance states into which we all occasionally lapse in everyday situations, including driving), might an *indirect* form of suggestion produce a similar effect, in the form, say, of a widely known reputation for being haunted?

Earlier in this book, I made the point that the power of suggestion should not be underestimated or ruled out in any haunting case—a point that was illustrated by an experiment conducted on an unwitting public in 1970 by journalist Frank Smyth. In the summer of that year Smyth fabricated his own and published it in the magazine *Man, Myth and Magic* with the intention of gauging the effect of people's gullibility and inventiveness in response to ghost stories. Supported by a number of credible details and witness accounts, the story in the forthcoming months was replicated and uncritically sold in a number of books. The most intriguing point came in 1973 after Smyth's published confession to the *Sunday Times*, when a BBC television programme featuring the invention included a number of persons who claimed to have actually seen Smyth's ghostly vicar at the Ratcliffe Wharf location in London's docklands, with at least one account predating 1970.[4]

Overlooking one attempted rebuttal to Smyth's invention that suggested that Smyth himself may have unwittingly acquired unconscious knowledge of a real haunting, Smyth's experimental case demonstrates the impact a ghost story or haunting reputation can have on the public imagination—either as a prompt toward the unconscious construction of fresh sightings ('autosuggestion'), or as a means by which witnesses might re-interpret prior experiences.

And so to Blue Bell Hill: what do we have here if not a perfect combination of absorptive state (the night-driving experience) and suggestion (Blue Bell Hill's reputation for being haunted)?

While it cannot be said for every witness, it is often true that a number of the Blue Bell Hill witnesses had some prior awareness of the Hill's reputation—which, in the first chapter, I decided should not lead to an automatic dismissal of their accounts on the basis that the story is widely known in the area, but it is a point which nevertheless demands consideration. Is it possible that witnesses, in response to an unconscious awareness of the haunting, might be creating their own apparitions in the visual field as dream-like images—something akin to a hypnagogic illusion? This is certainly possible in view of what we have seen of the potentials of suggestion under formal hypnotic trance. The question is whether Blue Bell Hill's reputation by itself is a potent enough source of inspiration for the generation of images of the same quality as those achieved by hypnotic suggestion, and whether it can possibly account for the close correspondences in descriptions and details between numbers of non-publicised sightings.

If we look at the Blue Bell Hill encounters collectively, we find some common and telling features. Most occurred late into the night, generally between 10 p.m. and 1 a.m. Most witnesses were on their way home, some from work, some from social events. What is probable is that each was somewhat tired, in a process of mentally 'winding down'. Significantly, the most important and impressive accounts come from lone drivers—those we would expect to be most susceptible to trance states. Now add to the sense of fatigue the familiar journey, the monotony of the night-driving field, the comfortable conditions inside the vehicle. All of these factors combine to lead the driver into the detached state of mind that, as demonstrated by the statistics attached to driving accidents, tends to be deeper than the light, daydreamy states that develop in other situations. It is a state that, if not quite comparable to that achieved by direct hypnosis, is really quite close to the next best thing: the self-hypnotised state.

In this, we find the familiar sensory feedback routine, except in this case, the percipient serves as his or her own hypnotist. In the driving experience we find that the senses are occupied and overloaded in a similar way: the visual sense by the road ahead; hearing is frequently served by the constantly changing but harmonious input of music or radio (or simply by the hum of the engine), and the body by the warm interior of the car and the moulded comfort of the car seat. Under these conditions the visual sense is often the one experiencing the least variance in input, and may therefore be the field most susceptible to modification by the brain's creative musings. Unconsciously acknowledging their presence at Blue Bell Hill, and triggered by that fact, what the witness sees is perhaps an externalisation of the primary association he or she has for that location. The reason some accounts might appear to be similar in terms of the description of the apparition might lie with some preconceived or popularised notion of what the ghost girl should look like, explaining to some degree, perhaps, why 'she' often resembles the young, light-attired Phantom Hitch-Hiker of folklore and media fame?[5]

In each case, the encounter would end with the breaking of the hypnotic spell, most notably with the driver striking the figure and getting out of the car. Returned suddenly to a normal, alert and fully conscious state of mind, the driver inevitably finds no-one there, and no sign of damage to their vehicle.

Mirror of the Soul

One other feature about which we may gain some insight by this mechanism is the not infrequent and chilling habit some phantoms have of staring into the eyes of the driver as they are run down. While this undoubtedly achieves an increase in horrific effect (particularly when accompanied by an incongruously benign expression or even a smile), could another reason the gaze of a phantom seems so penetrating be that the eyes of the percipient offer, as is said, a window and a mirror to their own soul—a case of the unconscious recognising itself, or at least an acknowledgement of its function in apparitional experiences? This of course is speculation, but to those who have experienced it the phantom's eyes are often the most lingering and literally haunting impression the witness takes away from the experience.

Carl Jung, father of modern analytical psychology *(photo attribution not known)*

This idea finds support and elucidation from Jungian Psychology (after Carl Gustav Jung (1875–1961)). Jung recognised that the unconscious of the individual often manifests itself symbolically in dreams as a figure. This figure, which Jung stressed is a spontaneous product of the unconscious, he termed *anima* (or *animus*). Which is encountered depends on whether the dreamer is a man or a woman. For a man, the personification of his unconscious is generally in the form of a female figure. The Swiss poet Carl Spitteler (1845–1924) called her 'My Lady Soul'.[6] Jung preferred a less emotive term: Anima.

For a woman, the converse is true: her unconscious is reflected as a male figure (animus). Without venturing too far down what could be a convoluted path, it can be simply noted that the anima/animus is seen as the figurative representation of all the contrasexual traits inherent in the human genetic makeup and psyche. As Jung stated, the character of the anima/animus is always compensatory to the outer persona, so if the conscious personality is masculine, the inner, unconscious side will be feminine in character. Likewise, strong outward traits such as extroversion or aggression tend to be balanced by an inner timidity, and so forth. When the qualities of the anima/animus become projected onto another person, finding connection with their persona, it might be said that we have discovered our *soul mate.*

The anima has the same role in the personal psyche as the archetype (the personification of the collective unconscious)—as a mediator or a psychopomp between the unconscious and the outward conscious state. It brings to the latter vital information that has either escaped its attention or has been suppressed. Furthermore, this personal 'soul-image' can be said to be synonymous with the archetypal feminine image (the impersonal or objective psyche) that we met in the context of white lady apparitions in the last chapter. As such, there is a plausible relationship between the 'inner' and the 'outer' experiences, whereby the witness's mind-state at the time of their encounter (which provides access to the internally-realised anima) forges a connection with the ostensibly objective form of the archetype.

While we have to be mindful to avoid extending this idea too far, the above might provide some explanation for the preponderance of female 'ghosts' and male drivers in both folklore (the Phantom Hitch-hiker) and 'fact' (the related but more commonly reported phantom jaywalker scenario). Inevitably, we might ask whether such events (or at least their interpretation) are predominantly a part-product of the male psyche?

Looking a little closer at the anima we see one or two other characteristics that are reflected in the habits of the female road ghost. In Phantom Hitch-Hiker lore its positive aspects are found in passive, demure figures and kindly old women (sometimes taken as nuns or angelic beings) who, as spectral travelling companions, reflect the role of the unconscious as guide and protector. However, while the positive attributes of the anima (that is to say, the unconscious self) are manifold, the effects of its negative side can be detrimental, leading the individual away from reality, toward unrealistic pursuits and, in extreme cases, to their own destruction—a course, Jung noted, that is much more likely to be followed by men than by women.[7] This habit of 'leading men out of their way' is one with which we are familiar, having already noted it of Phantom Hitch-Hikers and certain other 'night-walking' spirits in folk tradition, and in the apparent desire the ghost has in some cases of exacting revenge on the motorist responsible for her death, or on motorists in general.

Interestingly, in its most frightening and malevolent form, the anima is sometimes depicted as an ugly hag, which naturally invites comparison to the dark character of the crone-hag-witch of Blue Bell Hill and the Cailleach or Hekate of mythology (Chapter 11). It shows itself also in the oppressive and terrifying *nightmare* of the Old Hag Syndrome, which frequently manifests as a symptom of anxiety and stress, signifying an imbalance in the psyche.[8] Jung's therapeutic approach to the anima saw its role as leading the individual back to healthful re-integration of the whole psyche, its conscious and unconscious aspects together.

Since we are to regard the personal anima as a splinter aspect of the universal female archetype, the question naturally arises as to what the externalised figure may be attempting to impart to the collective psyche (which represents our shared identity and experience)—what is it that may be out of balance and requires our conscious attention to redress?

A further clue might be found in the anima's regard for nature. Where it is carried over into mythology and folklore, the anima is frequently represented as a spirit of nature. We have seen some of the associations between these archetypal figures and features in the landscape, particularly those that came to be regarded as sacred.

Within the context of the Phantom Hitch-Hiker we can recognise the dark aspect of the anima in the Version B, who characteristically possesses the power of prophecy (an attribute of the unconscious), which is directed to both the individual and to wider environmental issues. In a number of road ghost cases the correlation between spates of sightings and environmental factors is hard to overlook. As we saw in Chapter 11, the manifestations in 1980 of both the 'ghastly old woman' and an attractive female in white near Mount St. Helens closely followed an eruption of the volcano. More often, though, the warnings tend to be of a more personal or local concern, which might be expected if the phantom is in some aspect a reflection of the protagonist's own persona and experience.

The ghost-as-anima is not, I am sure, the whole of it with regard to Blue Bell Hill, or to Phantom Hitch-Hiker and other haunting events elsewhere, but from this perspective the anima/archetype model certainly provides a possible explanation as to why we see descriptively the same figures and patterns of behaviour again and again—not as the repetitive habits of particular road accident victims who are doomed to repeat the same actions ad infinitum (which reflects our need to find some kind of logical understanding for these events)—but as symbolic carriers of messages not recognised or acknowledged by the conscious mind.

In this chapter we will take a closer look at the apparent link between road hauntings and environmental disturbances. At Blue Bell Hill, for instance, the coincidence of the dramatic encounters of November 1992 with the commencement that same year of a major refurbishment of junction 6 of the M20 with the A229 at the foot of the Hill may be significant. In these instances it is reasonable (within the frame of the archetype) to postulate that the road works late in 1992 and into early 1993 may have prompted a form of symbolic protest by the collective unconscious at the despoilment of the local environment—a campaign that became increasingly hostile as the scheme progressed?

Meanwhile, it could be said that in many encounters the ghost was just about the last thing on the witness's mind at the time (at least in the conscious frame). The best advice, then, I can offer anyone who wishes to avoid an apparitional encounter at Blue Bell Hill or elsewhere (other than to simply avoid the place) is to remain alert, deliberate and critical when driving there. The danger, if you like, lies where the unconscious mind is given the opportunity to elaborate on reality.

The objective/subjective debate

While the above provides us with some means of understanding the role played by the unconscious and its ability to override or dupe our conscious faculties, the hallucinatory theory of apparitions, like any single proposition over the years (even one based on the anima/archetype model) cannot on its own account for all of the reported data. The 'ghost', for instance, is not always of the opposing gender to the witness; nor does the theory account for the encounters involving multiple witnesses or those rare instances in which a collision with the figure has seemingly left physical evidence in the form of damage to the witness's vehicle. It also fails to account for the specific pattern of behaviour at Blue Bell Hill, which is reflected in similar encounters the world over. Nor, as Michael Goss posed in relation to the Phantom Hitch-Hiker habit, does it tell us why one particular mode of behaviour should be consistently displayed to the exclusion of others. If such encounters are simply the play of the imagination on conditioned or unconsciously buried ideas, we might reasonably expect a relatively larger proportion of the encounters at Blue Bell Hill to reflect the hitch-hiking habit (and the figure of a young woman, as inspired by the original story) rather than the phantom jaywalker scenario that characterises the majority of the later encounters.

What is more, the hallucinatory theory doesn't hold up very well if we try to apply it to instances such as Maurice Goodenough's encounter, which had him carry to the roadside a young girl he had knocked down. Few might dispute that he must have been alert and consciously engaged at this point (assuming, of course, that the girl was indeed a phantom).

Somehow it is more disturbing to suppose that in response to little more than rumour or suggestion an individual's unconscious mind might be capable of spontaneously inventing and sustaining a hallucinatory event so convincing that they would race off to involve the authorities in their delusion, or drive miles out of their way to drop off a non-existent passenger.

In his reply to the suggestion made to him by psychologist Susan Blackmore in the BBC's 1994 pilot paranormal programme *Out of This World* that he may have hallucinated the ghost, Ian Sharpe said: 'I couldn't be a coach driver if I hallucinated.'[9] While we have seen that people can indeed be made to hallucinate to a convincing degree, Ian raises a very pertinent point. If such experiences can befall even very experienced drivers like him, the roads are even less safe than we suppose. This being the case, we might be grateful for the fact that these apparitional events are not more common than they are; their failure to appear randomly on our roads resting with the absence, in most cases, of an appropriate trigger to which the unconscious mind of the percipient might respond.

Standing more firmly in the way of the hallucination theory as a wholesale explanation for apparitions are those cases that the SPR, in its original study, termed 'veridical'—that is, those events for which there were various kinds of independent corroboration. These might take the form of multiple witness events; or, in haunting cases, instances in which the same figure had been reliably sighted at the same locality on a number of occasions and by different witnesses (preferably individuals who had no prior awareness of the case).

While some criticism has been levelled at collective sightings with respect to mass hallucination or some kind of 'psychic contagion' that spreads between witnesses either during or after a given experience (by which a whole other speculative mechanism must be entertained), these accounts are perhaps more persuasive in terms of suggesting an objective phenomenon as we understand it—particularly, as at Blue Bell Hill, where they find further support through overlapping circumstantial details such as locations and timings. At Blue Bell Hill we have no less than fifteen shared experiences, the most impressive being (according to the criteria outlined) the Maidens' and Rayburns' experiences with the old woman in 1993 at precisely the same location, just one night apart—which support the idea that what is active in many cases is more than simply individuals' imaginations or mental trickery, but something associated with the haunted locality itself.

Theories

The most commonly held view of apparitions, of course, is that they represent the spirits of the dead. Even those disbelieving in ghosts are familiar with their supposed characteristics and habits, which were succinctly summarised by Francis Grose in the last chapter. Implied by any of these appearances is that the faculties, personality and consciousness that made up that person remain intact after death, preserved in some kind of astral counterpart to their earthly body. Moreover, and unfortunate for those individuals who died in infirm or grisly circumstances, this is a 'body' very much alike their own at point of death. Whatever its precise nature, the astral body was one that was capable of definite if tenuous physical presence. This describes what is essentially expounded by what some have termed the 'animistic' or spiritualist theory of apparitions.

What the SPR discovered, however, was that the traditional view of apparitions was not well supported by the evidence. Instances in which apparitions imparted prolonged or meaningful communications were rare. Neither did they display the warmth or roundedness of character or intelligence we might expect of them—not enough, in most cases, to convince us that we were dealing with complete, though non-corporeal human personalities. This painted a very poor picture of any prospective afterlife, inspiring the theories that suggested that if survival does take place, it may do so only on a fragmentary level, where ghosts were the animated but soulless husks of former personalities: psychic automatons capable only of repetitious acts and limited, thoughtless interactions.

Even less encouraging was that apparitions seemed curiously dependent in many cases on the state of mind of the percipient for their appearances, suggesting that there was a hallucinatory aspect to their nature. Some of the reasons cited in favour of this viewpoint highlight popularly recognised habits and characteristics of apparitions, some of which will be familiar from our brief look at hypnotic suggestion. There were instances in which of two persons present, one could see the apparition while the other could not. Apparitions seemed to have little effect on their environment: they displaced no air in their spontaneous appearances or disappearances. Sometimes they were witnessed to pass effortlessly through solid objects. And then there were reports describing phantom inanimate objects, such as carriages and, in modern times, phantom engine-driven vehicles and aircraft (an observation that could be extended to clothes or other paraphernalia worn or carried by the ghost). Further complicating the picture was a significant body of evidence depicting apparitions of *living* persons.

While the foregoing might have appeared to threaten not just the survivalist position, but the very idea of apparitions as an objective phenomenon, the existence of a significant number of good veridical cases made it difficult to dismiss all reports by this means.

In practice, it may be impossible to arrive at a single, definitive explanation for ghosts and apparitions. Ambiguities exist even in individual veridical cases, making it possible to arrive at a variety of conclusions based on these alone. This need not represent a weakness in the evidence so much as an indication of their complex nature. At Blue Bell Hill, for instance, the collective sightings of the old woman, together with the fact that in two cases at least the figure held the headlights of the car, seem to points to an actual objective presence; whereas the Painter episode, in which only one of the two people in the car could see the girl, tends to suggest the play was conducted at least partly in the mind of the percipient.

Following the SPR's lead, many researchers today, I believe, tend to view apparitions as images that are realised in the mind of the percipient but whose source or inspiration is some stimulus outside of them. On a general level, this concept works fairly well for many, if not all cases. The problem lies with deciding what the source of that information is and the mechanism by which the percipient obtains and composes it into an image identical to that described by independent witnesses.

One such idea attempts to explain apparitions in terms of 'place memories', psychical recordings that are somehow recorded at the haunted locality that, under certain conditions, might be activated ('played back') by a properly attuned human mind. In an age of video, digital and holographic technology we are in a far better position to appreciate how this might work than our predecessors could have imagined (what, after all, are television pictures if not apparitional replays of persons and events past?).

The brain's ability to compose hallucinatory images is quite well evidenced, even though it has only been demonstrated satisfactorily in the context of subjectively produced images. How the environment might store such information, and whether the mind might be capable of picking it up, is a different matter. But apparitions of this nature are certainly described in the literature, even in relation to road ghosts. The well-known case involving the late Harry Martindale, who saw a troupe of Roman soldiers emerge from a wall of the cellars of the Treasurer's House in York in 1953 fits this category.

What has become known as the 'stone tape' theory, however, encounters evident difficulties in those rare but intriguing cases in which the figure reacts to or even acknowledges the presence of the witness—as for instance when the apparition has paused to look the observer in the eye (a particularly unnerving habit we have seen sometimes favoured by the Blue Bell Hill girl). If we interpret such actions as intelligently motivated (as opposed, say, to some modification of the image imposed by the percipient's mind) then the phantom's otherwise tiresomely repetitive behaviour seems more a kind of perverse and wilful charade than a looped recording or a pattern of senseless habit. And, of course, it is this kind of apparently pointless and nonsensical behaviour, reflected in all the encounters at Blue Bell Hill and consistently through many other reported cases, that often prevents the subject from being treated seriously (although we have seen that this may simply be a function of the conscious mind's failure to grasp the symbolic language and nature of the unconscious).

Interactive phantoms clearly present a problem for any kind of recorded image theory. In trying to reconcile a solely hallucinatory mechanism with veridical sightings (and thus holding out against acceptance of ghosts as a discrete phenomenon), other theories have considered the problem in terms of an innate ability of the human mind to communicate directly with others. The idea that apparitions might result from telepathic contact between sympathetic human minds is an idea that goes right back to the SPR's founding studies, in particular to its Census of Hallucinations in 1889, which revealed that apparitions of living persons outnumbered apparitions of the dead ('ghosts' proper) by two-to-one. The theory supposes that the preoccupation of thought regarding a person, living or dead, could result in another at the scene of a tragic event or other place that holds some strong association the 'sender' has for the subject of their thoughts, hallucinating an appropriate apparitional form there—one person acting as a transmitter, another as a receiver. The purported mechanism might have some bearing on anniversary ghosts. People very often think of loved ones near the anniversary of their birth or their death. In the latter case, the image we prefer to hold is of that person as they were when they were last alive. In actuality, I suspect that true anniversary ghosts are a most rare phenomenon (despite the apparent conformity with regard to the Sharpe and Dawkins incidents and the 1965 tragedy at Blue Bell Hill).

But again, telepathy—or to use a more up-to-date expression, extra-sensory perception (ESP or Psi)—really only explains one enigma in terms of another, and in its only way stretches credibility as far as the idea of objective ghosts.[10] Nevertheless, for some it is an attractive mechanism, not least because it removes the need for discarnate personalities.

But for F.W.H Myers (1843–91), one of the SPR's founders and leading lights, the leap from so-called phantasms of the living to those of the dead was not a very great one to take. If apparitions could be realised from the minds of the living, why should not they also be derived in similar manner from the random thoughts of the dead? Myers, however, felt that what was being projected in some cases was more than simply a telepathic 'signal' to be randomly picked up by a receptive mind, but some essential aspect of self that was capable of achieving some kind of actual if tenuous presence. This capacity for involuntary detachment of personal energy, occurring often without the conscious awareness of the sender, he termed 'psychorrhagic diathesis'. Many postmortem cases, he felt, suggested that this energy, generated by a person while alive could, in some fashion, persist for some time after their death. The apparition it generated might result from the deliberate attempt of a deceased person to communicate with the living. Myers did not completely rule this out. Instead, he preferred to view them as 'veridical afterimages' of past habits or events—the lingering dreams of the dead.

The further problem with respect to road ghosts is that any aspect of human personality that may persist after death appears to be subsumed under a very specific form and behaviour that finds some understanding only through our examination of the roles of the unconscious archetypes.

More tangible support for an objective aspect to ghostly phenomena comes from various physical effects that are associated with them. It has long been noted that poltergeist ('noisy ghost') activity tends often to be associated with persons (especially the young) who are experiencing disturbed emotional states. Consequently, it has come to be regarded as quite a separate phenomenon altogether, a supposed latent human ability dubbed psychokinesis ('PK' for short). But what is often overlooked is that these cases are not nearly as clear cut as some would like to believe. Some poltergeist cases exhibit features more usually characteristic of hauntings, including apparitions. Conversely, while certain physical effects in haunting cases—the sounds of phantom footfalls, doors opening and closing—might be attributable to auditory hallucinations in the same manner that images might be generated, there are occasions where physical events (the displacement of objects, measurable temperature drops) are documented.

While the question of intelligent motivation remains unanswered, what these effects provide by their recurrence and habits is some evidence of an objective aspect to the phenomenon, and clues to its nature.

Ghostly activity sometimes shows an affinity with electrical devices. Light switches and dials seem to be a favourite, but we can include any device that is dependent on electrical power and itself generates an electromagnetic field—including cars. And, of course, human beings themselves, in terms of the workings of the heart, brain and nervous system, are essentially electrical in nature. A logical inference, then, is that ghostly energies may themselves be, in some aspect, an electromagnetic phenomenon.

Viewing apparitional sources as discrete packets of energy might account for some of their observed habits and characteristics. Occasionally the phenomenon may appear strong enough to cause localised ionisation, producing visible forms, and in extreme cases, giving rise to the kind of disruptive effects found in poltergeist cases. Thus the form the apparitional experience might take, whether apparently psychological in nature, perceived only by virtue of the unmasked faculties of the unconscious mind, or unequivocally objective in nature, may very much depend on its *intensity*—an idea in which might lie a resolution to the objective/subjective paradox of ghostly phenomena.

Part II: Transients & Tumuli

Ghosts are notoriously unpredictable. There seems to be little rhyme or reason to their appearances, which in the majority of cases seem to be truly random. But are they? Do they conform to any kind of pattern that may permit a better understanding of them, if not to predict when and under what circumstances they are likely to manifest?

In respect to road ghosts, we do have some clues in this area, as outlined in Chapters 11 and 13 in reference to outbreaks of sightings that appeared to coincide with major road building schemes. At Blue Bell Hill, 1992 was a significant year for reasons other than the dramatic reappearance of its ghost after years of little more than rumour and dubious press reports. 1992 was also the year that saw the largest construction project there since the present dual carriageway was driven through its scarp face in 1971–72. At that time, as the reader may recall (Chapter 7), John Huffam, writing for the *Evening Post*, idly (or perhaps intuitively) speculated that the ghost girl's latest rumoured appearances might be a result of the massive earth-moving programme antagonising the spirit world.

With the new works at the base of the Hill (a major refurbishment of junction 6 of the M20 with the A229) begun in the spring of 1992 and well under way by November of that year, it was difficult to overlook the correlation between Ian Sharpe's vivid encounter and those that followed the start of this project.

Likewise, Chris and Janice Leigh's sightings of hooded figures in the field be-

The major roadworks below Blue Bell Hill in 1992 that coincided with vivid new encounters with its ghost

hind their house coincided with the construction (from 1998) of the Channel Tunnel rail-link (High Speed 1) and the North Downs Tunnel beneath Blue Bell Hill (see Chapter 13).[11]

We have noted a similar correlation at Stocksbridge, Yorkshire. In another case, the A34 Newbury bypass construction site in October 1996, security personnel began to report a 'grey hazy thing' with discernible head and shoulders but no features. The first witness, Scott 'The Prof' Aggarwal, who saw it at around 1.30 a.m. on 21 October, described it as having come up out of a hole and entered a nearby portakabin (without opening the door). A historical cause for the haunting was quickly identified in the English Civil War battles of 1643 and 1644, which took place nearby.[12]

Switching back to 1992, to March, reports began to come out of the village of Castledawson in County Derry, Northern Ireland, of a figure that came to be known as the Tamnadeese Ghost—a woman with long flowing blonde hair, who screamed wildly as she staggered out of the centre of a roundabout outside the village.

According to Neville Chambers, a churchwarden who lived near the roundabout, one man had been alarmed to see her appear in front of him on the roundabout in chains. He was not sure if he had struck her. And Mr Chambers had himself heard the screams the month before: 'The hair stood on my head. I don't know what it was but the screams I heard, I'll take to my death.'

Another witness, Harriet Hudson, swerved to avoid the woman as she appeared abruptly from the right into the path of her car. 'The most striking feature was her long straight blonde hair,' she said. 'As I was driving round, she walked from my right into my path. She was waving her arms and staggering. She looked to be drunk. I got alarmed because she came out on me so abruptly and I had to swerve violently to the left to avoid her.'

One possible explanation put forward was that the construction of the A6 Castledawson bypass, which runs from the roundabout onto the Toome Road, may have disturbed an old grave.[13]

Here we can recognise the symbolic elements from our consideration of Jung's archetypes: nature personified, shackled in chains (of concrete and tarmac) and bewailing her plight like a screaming banshee—but on the present theme we can note also that alterations to the environment are a recognized factor in the triggering (or termination) of haunting events.

When modifications made in the strictly localised surroundings of the home set off a haunting, the activity is often taken to reflect the displeasure the changes have provoked in a former resident. When alterations are made in the wider environment we are more likely—as the Castledawson case demonstrates—to look to the disturbance of places of burial for their cause. Likewise, the haunting at Blue

Bell Hill has been linked to the desecration caused to ancient burial places destroyed or overbuilt by the A229 modernisation, despite the fact that much of the activity predates the construction.

It seems absurd to think that the disturbance of a relatively small area of land could be responsible for sightings of apparitions, let alone for there to be the kind of similarities we observe between them. All we can say, I think, is that the reported phenomena seem in some way to be symptomatic of the nature or scale of the physical disturbance itself. But if the correlation is valid, should we not expect to see similar cases wherever and whenever extensive roadworks and excavations are made? To some extent we do. Some locations—particularly those of a permanent or semi-permanent nature such as quarries—often have histories of strange phenomena attached to them. But, as a rule, most work proceeds uneventfully. So what is it about places like Blue Bell Hill that sets them apart?

Window area?

In 1965, the late American researcher and journalist John A. Keel coined a phrase that soon earned a place of prominence in the lexicon of the paranormal: *window area*. Keel made the astute observation that small areas all over the world seem particularly prone to the occurrence of anomalous phenomena—in some cases, as attested by records and legend, extending back centuries. This focus of activity, he felt, was linked to certain geological and geomorphological factors. They were areas often characterised, for instance, by concentrated faulting or geomagnetic anomalies (areas of high magnetic potential, such as metallic ore bodies). At given times, he proposed, the electromagnetic conditions associated with these features permitted them to act as gateways to forces intent on entering our level of reality. Prime among these intruding forces were the UFOs, which often seem to originate or hover around these sites. But included in this gamut of invading entities were ghosts, fairies, and the angels and devils of old. For Keel, these were all expressions of fundamentally the same phenomenon—one that existed to sow bedevilment and confusion among human beings, which it achieves through its ability to tailor its actions and appearance according to whatever belief structure exists at the time.

Whatever one may make of Keel's conclusions,[14] his observations have found some support by later work, notably from Canadian scientists Michael Persinger and Gyslaine Lafrenière, who in the late 1970s analysed UFO and other anomalous events across the USA, finding both confirmation of the geographical clustering described by Keel's window concept, and a calendrical distribution that compared favourably to foreign studies. Independent studies have also shown that such events tend to cluster around the same time of night, with the largest peak at around 10 p.m. to 10.30 p.m., with a smaller one in the early hours, towards 3 a.m.[15]

Persinger and Lafrenière's theory was, in the first instance, based on an assumption: that the respective phenomena were based on a recognisable form of energy, and that that energy was of natural origin. The question was what was capable of providing this energy, and how was it localised? The researchers considered a number of possible sources, including thunderstorms, tectonic processes, and solar and lunar influences. When they began to look for correlations, it was the tectonic mechanism that emerged as the most prominent candidate.

The key to this correlation was seismic electricity. Colossal forces of mechanical energy can build up in the Earth's crust, whose energy and destructive force we are made acutely aware of when it is released catastrophically as earthquakes. What is not so well known is that highly stressed rocks are also capable of generating significant quantities of piezoelectric energy.[16] What results, according to Persinger and Lafrenière, is that a transient electromagnetic field—an 'electric column'—develops above the stress zone, particularly in the vicinity of faults and/or mineral concentrations in the crust. The 'normal' radius of such a column may be between 3 and 30 metres, but could be much larger. At given strengths, this field may be capable of ionising the air above it into visible 'luminosities' (dubbed 'earth lights'),[17] which, suspended in the otherwise invisible column, would appear to hover—or (if the field itself is dynamic and variable, moving along lines of fracture or other paths of least resistance) seem to 'fly', giving rise to reports of glowing UFOs. These events are transient in nature, they argue, simply because the forces themselves are transient. Luminosities and other effects of the field, such as the possible affect on biological systems, can only exist during periods when the stress itself is present. With its relief, most obviously with an earthquake, the column and the activity would disappear, only to start over with the onset of a new phase of strain. The cyclicity of phenomena in these areas is therefore an important aspect to bear in mind.

Luminous effects of various kinds—aerial glows, streamers, unusual lightning displays, and discrete balls of light, have long been observed in relation to earthquake activity, and have naturally given rise to their share of legends and folk tales. In the modern day, the impact of so-called 'earthquake weather' is demonstrated by the interference with radio transmissions that is sometimes noted just prior to the quake itself, resulting from the disruption of the ionosphere. While these effects have obvious value in the warning against earthquakes, they also demonstrate something that is only beginning to be properly appreciated: that the Earth is a very dynamic system, with its various components—land, sea and atmosphere—interacting in unusual and surprising ways.

In the months leading up to the eruption of Mount St Helens in 1980 there were reports of luminous displays (which included an 'eerie blue lightning' observed by two geologists that arced between the volcano's main vent and a subsidiary one that had developed during the activity) and other anomalous phenomena, which were collected by a co-worker and associate of Michael Persinger's, Lynn Henry, who was in the area at the time.[18]

The events associated with the Mount St Helens episode are typical of a three-part pattern of effects that emerged from Persinger's data. During phase one, in the initial build-up of strain, six months or more before the event (eruption or quake) straightforward electromagnetic effects predominate. Interference takes place with electronic equipment and power failures are more common. Various effects on human beings are also noted, which we will look at in a little more detail in due course. With increased levels of strain, phase two is entered, which is characterised by the appearance of luminosities in close proximity to the strain which, in the modern day, are likely to be popularly interpreted as UFOs. If the strain increases further, there is a tendency for the luminosities to disappear—at which point, in the words of Persinger, 'the very unusual things begin to occur.'[19]

Now, Blue Bell Hill is not known for its earthquakes. An important point of the Tectonic Strain Theory, which Persinger and Lafrenière were at pains to point out, was that earthquakes themselves were not necessary to the production of light and other phenomena. Major tectonic events provide the most obvious, most energetic sources giving rise to localised electromagnetic conditions, but the associated phenomena need not necessarily be concentrated in earthquake-prone areas. Conditions of strain may extend over relatively great distances, into what are regarded as tectonically inactive or stable regions, where it is peculiarities in the local environment—remnant faulting, mineralisation, hilly or mountainous terrain, and areas of high resistivity, to name a few—that provide the focus for the development of the electromagnetic column and the associated phenomena. Where tectonic pressures are applied and relaxed non-catastrophically over relatively long periods, giving very low level or no seismicity, such activity might occur in some places for little apparent reason. Overlying this, there are other factors, such as the lunar-induced patterns of strain, and the Earth's own geomagnetic field. The Earth's magnetic field may be modified locally by surface or subsurface features (whereby aerial magnetic surveys, for instance, can help to identify buried mineral deposits). And, in turn, the geomagnetic field of the Earth and its meteorological systems can be influenced by variations in the Sun's own magnetic field. Magnetic outbursts from its surface can result in the sending out of streams of charged particles that can have a significant impact on the Earth's magnetic field, energising the system to degrees where power lines and electronics/communications systems can be overloaded.

Taking into account the scale and complexity of the forces that play within and across the surface of the Earth, it isn't difficult to appreciate the idea that, from the perspective of the whole planet, minute points and features at its surface might act as foci for these transient energies, which occasionally reach potentials capable of sparking earth light displays and other unusual phenomena. It might also give us some basis for understanding how significant alterations in the environment (particularly those prone to such phenomena) and therefore to local electromagnetic conditions, could result in fresh outbreaks of activity *à la* Blue Bell Hill.

If we zoom in to examine one of these window areas, what characteristics are we likely to note? The first, which is responsible for drawing our attention to them in the first place, is a history of strange phenomena, particularly light phenomena, which are very often reflected in folk tales and legends attached to the area. Famous earth light phenomena such as the Bodhisattva Lights on the North China Plain, and the Marfa Lights, which manifest regularly over the prairie near the small town of Marfa, Texas, have attracted religious and ghostly connotations respectively. In both cases, the variably coloured balls of fire that float lazily across the terrain are said to represent spiritual entities—in the former, enlightened souls that have passed the ten stages to spiritual perfection; in the latter, as spirits of the dead ('ghost lights' or 'spook lights'), traditionally recognised as such by both the native peoples and white settlers alike (although the latter have attached a variety of other meanings to them as well, such as guardian lights of hidden treasure). In other places and other times, these same light phenomena have found interpretation as fiery dragons, fairies, and, in the modern day, as UFOs.

A few of these characteristics were noted earlier. High on the list are geological faulting, and areas of high mineralisation. They show an affinity for hilltops, rocky ridges and mountain peaks, and other projections such as pylons, transmitter towers, and other metallic constructions. They regularly occur near power lines, along roads (where Earth mysteries writer Paul Devereux adds, they might be attracted to metallic vehicles),[20] railway lines and bodies of water. They also like to haunt caves, quarries and mines. Persons coming into close proximity to them have reported buzzing, humming or whistling (and hissing?) sounds.[21]

Comparisons have naturally been made between these terrain-related lights and so-called 'ball lightning'—that similarly rare, exotic, but marginally accepted by-product of some thunderstorms. Modern instrumentation has enabled us to study the interactions that occur between the land and the atmosphere. For instance, when the negatively-charged base of a thundercloud passes over the land, positively charged ions are sucked out of the ground. A person standing in the area is likely to feel the effects of the build-up of static electricity as a literally hair-raising event. A comparatively recent discovery, captured in rare instances on film, highlights how objects come to be 'selected' by lightning strikes. Potential strike subjects extend a 'positive streamer' toward the descending 'stepped leader' (the lightning bolt's pathfinder). The streamer, a faintly luminous filament of positively charged particles up to a few metres in length, in effect advertises itself as a strike candidate. If one succeeds in attracting the bolt (which all happens in a fraction of a second), a circuit link is immediately established between sky and ground, and the lightning's return stroke discharges its massive 10,000 ampere charge to the ground.

One theory of earth lights is that this process works more or less in reverse, with the Earth, under certain conditions, discharging energies into the air. Most often, during a lightning strike, little resistance is offered by the ground, and the charge spreads out in all directions and is absorbed by the rocks and earth. Under the conditions postulated by Persinger, where electromagnetism is sustained and finely focused, certain features of the land, its geology and structure, acting as foci, could precipitate the 'sparking' of earth lights.

One possible mechanism involves the presence of water as a contributor to resistivity of underground minerals, particularly in conjunction with fractures and fissures in the rocks. German biophysicist, Helmut Tributsch's idea is that earth currents leaping across air-filled fractures into thin linings of water could result in a glowing discharge.[22] Whether we can extend this idea to larger fractures and air-filled spaces in rocks—to caverns and artificially produced discontinuities such as mines and tunnels, is open to question. The fact that these appear to be haunted by light-form and ghostly phenomena, suggests a plausible connection.

While on this subject, it is for a moment worth casting our recollections back to the characteristics attributed to the elementals by Professor Kirk, particularly their cave-dwelling habits and their ability to pass unimpeded through the interstices of the rocks. Large underground cavities (particularly the poorly-supported excavations made by humans) add additional points of stress into the local environment—something that is also true of quarry workings and unsupported cuttings and cliff faces—all of which we can postulate as providing foci for the generation of light phenomena.

Is Blue Bell Hill and its environs a 'window area'? It certainly qualifies in a number of respects. The most obvious characteristic is, of course, the hilltop location itself. But added to this we have the former quarry workings that cut into the Middle and Upper Chalk that make up the scarp of the Hill. The chalk is sufficiently rigid to support the sheer cliff and bench section of the 'haunted section' of road east of the A229 between the Lower Bell and Blue Bell Hill Village. Like the workings which lie abandoned a little west and north of here, this section is a former quarry site. Any unsupported feature such as the 150 ft eastern face of the section is naturally subject to low-level, gravitationally induced stresses that might contribute to or serve as a focus for the postulated electromagnetic conditions. Furthermore, chalk is an 'aquifer' rock which, as a consequence of its numerous joints and fissures, allows it to transmit and store large quantities of groundwater. The presence of this water may have the effect of increasing resistivity of the rocks, but it might also add to stresses at given surface points and potentially give rise to local conditions of ionisation—all of which, if there is anything to the theory, makes the cliff-section of the A229 between the Lower Bell and the footbridge appear a promising area for the generation of such phenomena.

Researchers such as Paul Devereux believe that some megalithic sites may have served a different purpose than has hitherto been assumed—as permanent markers for places revered for possessing special energetic properties. Such sites show the same kinds of correlations with unusual phenomena as fault zones, as reflected by the stories and traditions attached to them. In Britain and Ireland, and in much of Europe, these sites were frequently associated with fairies and other elementals, a commonly reported phenomenon being 'fairy lights'. Such lights are subject of eyewitness accounts even in the modern day, the difference being that they are likely now to attract a different interpretation. While their strongest association is, perhaps, with aerial light phenomena, Devereux also noted that such places often support reputations as places of apparitions (his 'Spook Road' associated with Oxfordshire's Rollright Stones comes to mind),[23] and it is here we find the greatest relevance to Blue Bell Hill and other road ghosts.

So far purposefully overlooked is that outbreaks of earth lights are said sometimes to be accompanied by a low-level or ground-based phenomenon—roughly human-sized gaseous columns that often find interpretation as white lady ghosts. Devereux provides several examples of this phenomenon, and it is indeed easy to see how these short-lived 'vaporous luminescent columns' drifting about the countryside or perched beacon-like on the crests of hills late at night (when they are most visible) might be seen as 'shining spectres'.

Of particular interest are those instances in which the 'figure' is seen in closer proximity, in or at the side of the road. At Castle Hill, a mound at Newton-le-Willows, Lancashire, a 6 ft tall 'white shape' has been seen flitting, gliding, or stationary on a nearby road, which has been interpreted at various times as both white lady and monk. Some claim to have seen a figure detailed within the light. Significantly, its appearance is said to have been the cause of at least one traffic accident.[24]

Other examples describe such columns emerging from hedgerows ahead of vehicles; in one case floating ahead of a van for a while before disappearing into a gateway.[25] And in another, at a location in Leicestershire reputed to be haunted by the ghost of a nun, a bus stopped one night for a white figure only to find it

Floated out and came at me

APPARITION as Allan Neilsen, 14, schoolboy, described it, emerging from the concrete wall of the railway subway in Victoria Park on Saturday night . . . bluish-grey, luminous, and transparent.

A SCHOOLBOY, Allan Neilsen, 14, of Bowral Street, Enoggera, last night relived his encounter with the Ghost on Saturday.

He was taken to Brisbane General Hospital for treatment after his sighting of the ghost on Saturday.

He said: "I was standing about 10ft. from the subway under the railway line.

"This thing . . . it was a misty, bluish, white floated out from the wall.

"I turned and ran, for about 30 yards, and stopped to look back.

"It was floating in the middle of the subway and it came towards me."

The Victoria Park ghost: The railway cutting location, scene of Allan Neilsen's encounter in November 1965 (*Courier-Mail*, Brisbane)

was the 'ghost'—a softly glowing misty column of light that drifted off across a field.[26]

A similar apparitional form has been seen several times in Victoria Park in Brisbane, Australia. On the night of 20 November 1965 (the same day, coincidentally, that an Australian bride-to-be and her fiancé were to have been married in the UK), 14-year-old Allan Neilsen went to the park with some friends. There they saw the apparition, which they described as a 'misty, bluish-white' thing of roughly human proportions, float out of the brick wall of a railway arch.

'I turned and ran,' he said, 'for about 30 yards, and stopped to look back. It was floating in the middle of the subway and it came towards me. It had the body of a child of about seven years. As it got near me, I froze. The next I remember is being in the hospital and asking, 'Where am I?'' [27]

As with similar tales, it was not long before the cause for the 'haunting' was found: the suicide of a man beneath a train near Victoria park in 1960. Others, though, claimed that the park was renowned for ghosts as far back as 1903.

In March 1999, 'tjohns' posted his own encounter with the Victoria Park Ghost. The sighting, which took place in 1964, describes a very similar scenario to Allan Neilsen's sighting. Accompanied by his mother, sister, his brother and his girlfriend, they waited at the underpass:

> On the far side of the underpass a streetlight was throwing its light through the branches of a tree on the left hand wall. This had a vaguely human shape. Mum walked up to it and said, 'This is what people think is the ghost'. As she said this

> from out of the wall directly behind her came rushing out a ghost, shaped very nebulously, rather bright and glowing but giving off no light itself. What was terrifying about it was the PURPOSE it seemed to have as it suddenly exited the wall. Everybody either screamed and ran back, or just ran back to the traffic barriers, about 20 feet.
>
> I remember the girls actually shrieking in terror, particularly my sister who was now hanging around my neck and screaming into my ear. We ran back to the posts and automatically turned around. The bloody thing was standing about two feet away as if looking at me. I was certainly looking at it. As they say, for what seemed an eternity but was probably no more than a second, it floated in front of me, opaque and I think very pale bluish white, gently rocking side to side. It hung there for a few seconds more then it shot back into the underpass at great speed straight through and out the other side where it suddenly disappeared instantly as if at the flick of a switch.[28]

Within the context of an electromagnetic phenomenon, it is tempting to view these forms popping out of the cliff face, or rising out of the ground in the fashion noted above and, depending on the conditions at the time, to remain static, or, if it can gather sufficient stability, to drift off along whatever plane of weakness may have facilitated its birth in the first place.

At Blue Bell Hill, the predominant trend of such planes is likely to be roughly east-west, in accordance with the fold-axis of the Wealden Anticline, and, in most cases, at right-angles to (i.e. across) the road. It is easy to appreciate that with the approach of a vehicle, with its metal skin and own electromagnetic field, the column might be attracted to it—an effect that Devereux suggests would imbue it with an apparent sense of purposefulness.

Might a motorist interpret such an action as a figure running out in front of or towards their vehicle; a figure that cannot then be found? We have already looked at the possible influence that foreknowledge or expectation may play in the interpretation of such events—a process of unconscious elaboration known as confabulation. But if the witness fails to interpret what they saw, then others, particularly the media, may be relied upon to do so.

Maurice Goodenough's encounter in 1974 hints at another feature in common between these vaguely human columns and road ghosts—their sometimes observed habit of rising up out of the ground before taking off cross country. We may recall Tom Harber's interview with Maurice Goodenough, from which it was said the girl had seemed to spring out of the earth from beneath the car (Chapter 7). In this instance, we might speculate that the presence of the car itself may have been the catalyst in the encounter, having the effect of drawing up the column before it—as exampled perhaps also by Joy Gammon's fleeting sighting of the ghostly figure that sprang up from the roadside at Blue Bell Hill in the mid-1970s (Chapter 13).

The comments of others regarding the disappearances of the girl are also noteworthy, in particular those of Ian Sharpe and Chris Dawkins, who both remarked on the unnatural way the girl seemed to sink beneath their car rather than being thrown over the top or to the side. The impression given to Dawkins was that it was as if the ground had moved apart to swallow her up.

The outstanding problem with this whole idea, though, is how these misty columns of ionised gas, or whatever they are, could be mistaken for detailed human figures. Confabulation will play some part, but can it possibly be extended to the likes of Maurice Goodenough's close contact, or to those Phantom Hitch-Hiker encounters judged to be genuinely reported experiences?

As a neurobiologist, Persinger's particular area of interest lay with the effects such electromagnetic fields might have on the human brain, in particular in relation to the induction of temporal lobe seizures. Persinger managed to reproduce some of the low intensity effects described earlier (feelings of unease and so forth) by artificially stimulating the temporal-proprietal area of the brain with mild but complex electromagnetic fields applied via an experimental helmet.[29] While the fields applied in the laboratory were necessarily mild to avoid risks of seizures, the stronger field strengths postulated as accompanying visible luminosities, Persinger believed, might create a temporary state of neuronal misfiring that could result in the incorporation of elements of memory and fantasy into the waking moment, that would continue for a short time after exposure for as long as the instability lasted. The result would be that the witness experiences and remembers an elaborate event which was real only so far as its contextual framework, and the fact that they encountered a rather exotic phenomenon of nature.

Could this possibly explain Maurice Goodenough's sustained experience—how he believed he had carried the injured girl to the roadside, making her comfortable before driving off to seek help? Might it also account for how motorists apparently pick up hitch-hikers who subsequently vanish from their cars—not as a result of the ionised column somehow entering the car, but from the temporary exposure to an electromagnetic source that makes them believe they have done so—until a little way along the road, the effect wears off and the passenger is found to have inexplicably vanished?

Perhaps. It is difficult, of course, to accept the encounters themselves at face value; but then it is almost as difficult to accept exotic substitute explanations, which have a tendency to stretch credulity almost as far in a different direction. Experimentally induced feelings of dizziness, dissociation, or of presence,[30] are a world away from apparitional visions, especially of the kind of vivid encounters found in real world situations. For these, it is postulated a hugely more energetic field would be required—and therein lies part of the problem, particularly in relation to road ghosts.

Persinger's experiments necessitated wiring up the subject inside a Faraday cage, which isolates the subject from the influence of extraneous electromagnetic signals. Cars likewise act as crude Faraday cages, and tend to conduct electricity preferentially around its occupants (which is why sheltering in a car is the safest place in a thunderstorm)—meaning that a motorist would be largely insulated from the effects of a postulated geoelectric column. In short, it is questionable if the field could operate on the motorist directly (although there is no strong objection to the idea that a visible column might be the inspiration for a confabulated sighting). But if it were possible, the onset of a temporal lobe seizure in a motorist might just as well cause them to crash the car as conjure up a vivid archetypal image from deep within their unconscious.

The other difficulty is to conceive how a similar process could account for most other apparitional encounters, particularly those in domestic situations—inside buildings or at locations with a history of detailed veridical sightings. Nor should we overlook the premise we looked at earlier—that ghosts themselves might bring or utilise the electromagnetic effects, rather than being a product of them.

Ultimately, the idea is untestable in the real world. Nor have these transient columns been observed and studied outside of the kinds of reports described in these pages. Furthermore, Persinger's findings, while interesting, have not been reliably replicated by other workers.[31]

I would not presume to suggest to Ian Sharpe (or any witness) what he saw that night. The very detailed figure he saw under good observational conditions (and the strong impression of sentience) begs an explanation beyond what is presented here, but these features are noteworthy all the same, and we should not overlook their possible significance. And it would be folly to completely disregard the possible significance of the apparent correlation between outbreaks of road ghosts and environmental disturbances such as those at Blue Bell Hill.

There is one other factor of possible relevance to these cases that we have so far only touched upon, and which, under the right circumstances, brings significant transient boosts to the Earth's geomagnetic state: the influence of the Sun's own magnetic cycle. A number of researchers have noted the correlations between increases in UFO activity and rises in the Earth's geomagnetism, which in turn is directly influenced by the Sun. Swedish researcher Ragnar Forshufvud found that these apparent rises in activity correlated well with times of sunspot maxima—the peaks in the roughly 11-year magnetic cycle of the Sun, that are indicated by increased densities of sunspots. Sunspots, which are relatively cooler (and thus, darker), transient features of the Sun's photosphere are localised re-

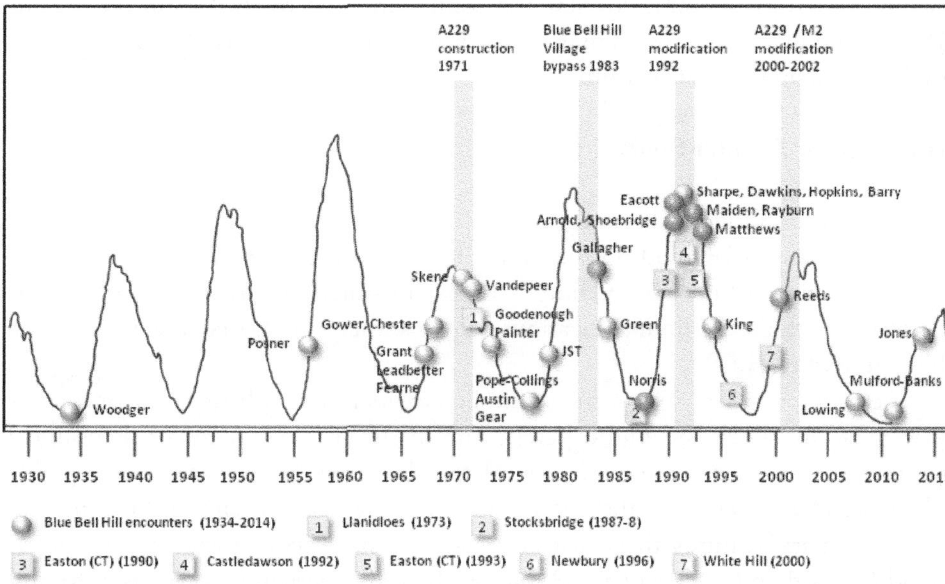

Blue Bell Hill sightings and other road ghost cases plotted against Sunspot maxima data

gions characterised by intense looping magnetic fields. They are the most obvious of the Sun's active regions, which together with solar flares, faculae and prominences indicate periods of increased activity and energy output from our parent star.

At these times the effects of the highly energised solar wind, and especially of impacting coronal mass ejecta (or CMEs—immense clouds of charged particles and tangled magnetic fields thrown off by eruptions on the Sun) can be highly disruptive to natural and artificial systems on Earth, producing both atmospheric and ground-level magnetic disturbances. Considering the reported increase in UFO activity at such times, it seemed reasonable to suppose that there would be a corresponding increase in other kinds of paranormal occurrences.

What I noticed from Forshufvud's graph data for the period c.1950-1970[32] was that a period of sunspot maxima corresponded with the period of initial press interest in the Blue Bell Hill ghost, around 1968–69. On a graph with a wider range (1900 through to 2012),[33] peaks were shown for c.1970–1972 (coincidental with the main construction phase of the A229), for 1980, and for the period c.1990–1993 (the actual peak occurring in July 1989, a year that witnessed one of the most dramatic outbursts on record from the Sun, a massive X-ray flare).[34] Although these correlations were based principally on the press reporting (which may bear little relationship to actual numbers and the time distribution of sightings), it was tempting to view the combination of roadworks in the area in 1992–3 and increased solar activity in the same period as a possible trigger for the outbreak of sightings at that time.

Inner Space / Outer Space

The geocentric model will clearly appeal to those who prefer a naturalistic (if exotic) explanation for road ghosts and other paranormal phenomena. But what should we make of the observation that these postulated transient columns are to be found at the same liminal locations as our archetypal ghosts (albeit for arguably different reasons)?

We have previously noted the symbolic factors in road ghost sightings, particular those in which the figure perches meaningfully on bridges or at notional features such as parish or county boundaries. It is much harder to assign a purely objective phenomenon in the latter instances: how does a natural phenomenon come to mark features that exist only as consensual constructs of the human mind (other than by coincidence)? Rather, the full experience would seem to hint at an interaction between the mind, the phenomenon, and the environment itself.

There is a tendency in Western thinking to separate mind and matter— the inner space of conscious thought and experience from the outer space of the world and universe at large, which we flatter ourselves we evaluate as objective, rational and logical observers. What is more, within the context of this Western scientific worldview the psyche itself has tended to be reduced to little more than a biochemical effect (or as Jung termed it, an epiphenomenon) produced in the human brain that merely gives the illusion of a free-thinking ego-identity. More so, the faculties of the mind's unconscious aspect are relegated in importance beside the conscious discursive mind that we fancy rules our psyche and, because it largely works in comprehending the macro world, is taken to be a reliable yardstick by which to measure the universe.

We tend to think of the unconscious as the same stuff as some of its products. Like dreams, its territory is regarded as unreal, insubstantial, fanciful, and irrelevant. But the unconscious is much more than this. Jung himself stated that the unconscious is the mother of consciousness,[35] which bloomed in early humans out of unconscious nature (which itself is not self-aware, at least in a manner we can recognise). But the unconscious, said Jung, is more than a remnant part of the psyche, but a dynamic and persistent aspect 'which goes on functioning together with it or even in spite of it.'[36] It exhibits a different kind of consciousness and intelligence: the body regulates and repairs itself; the heart beats; we breathe—all without our conscious direction or even awareness. And the dreaming mind follows narratives we might scarcely invent in wakeful consciousness. In effect, it is a super-consciousness.

What we like to think of as the objective world is actually and unavoidably a subjective representation. Everything we experience inevitably comes to us through our senses. Even where we develop instrumentation to operate beside us, its scope and the data it generates are nevertheless defined by and interpreted by our conscious faculties. As both Jung and science itself might state, the object itself is unknowable directly. Everything we perceive, everything 'out there', is really modelled from interpreted signals inside our heads. Ultimately everything is imagined—imag(e)-ined. In a sense, we could say the world itself is to a significant degree a construct of the mind. From this perspective a ghostly image is as valid as the material environment in which it appears; only the stimulus for it is less readily identified and its existence cannot be verified empirically.

But we can take this further: 'We call the unconscious 'nothing," said Jung, 'And yet it is a reality *in potentia*. The thought we shall think, the deed we shall do, even the fate we shall lament tomorrow, all lie unconscious in our today.'[37] In other words, *everything* arises from the objective unconscious: our capacity for intuition, our imagination and creativity, and what might be termed our irrational tendencies—our moods and emotional impulses, plus our dreams and premonitions. But also the ego-centre itself and its rational functions: all of our thoughts and ideas and creative achievements emerge like temporary islands from this vast sea of latent potential. The chair you are sitting on, the book you hold in your hand, all creations of human beings, must first have been conceived and formulated in our imaginations (the realm of the unconscious) before they were made 'real' by a conscious manipulation of matter.

If we doubt the power and importance of the unconscious in our supposedly rationally directed lives, Jung observed that consciousness all too often succumbs to unconscious influences, which may override rational thought and will, often to the detriment of the individual. 'Indeed,' he said, 'the fate of the individual is largely dependent on unconscious factors.'[38]

What this underlines is that the real and the imaginal, the physical and the notional, outer and inner space, are in fact inextricably linked and everything therefore in our experience ultimately arises from the same source. Where they meet, at the liminal threshold of human perception and experience, is of course of vital interest to us in our pursuit of an understanding of ghosts, which characteristically occupy the border state between the boundless unconscious and the conscious mind. Said Jung: 'The place or medium of realisation is neither mind nor matter; but that intermediate realm of subtle reality which can adequately be expressed only by the symbol.'[39] In the context of this book, that symbol is represented by the archetypal ghost.

As we have noted, the reason it seems we have so much trouble in accepting ghosts and the paranormal is the irrational behaviour, the unpredictability and the shadowy, immaterial nature of the phenomena. These, of course, are also characteristics of the unconscious, but this realisation does little to persuade a mind governed by conscious processes that what is seen and experienced by a significant sector of the population is indeed 'real' in any sense we can understand. But how can consciousness be expected to make sense of something that is, by its nature, the antithesis of it? The unconscious operates in a completely different manner to the conscious mind. Its scope and timescales are vastly protracted, and therefore seemingly meaningless to the limited ego-dominated psyche.

The conscious and the unconscious are opposite sides of the same coin: connected and co-dependent but never coming face to face. If consciousness inhabits the wakeful daylight hours, the night belongs to and symbolises the unconscious, accounting for why ghosts and apparitions seem most active after dark.

By its nature, then, the unconscious cannot be directly explored by consciousness, although its contents, as we have seen, may rise to conscious awareness in the form of symbols or mythic narratives or as synchronicities. To explore the workings of the unconscious we need to surrender all normal processes of reason, logic, and causal thinking. 'This,' said Jung, 'is the great difficulty'.[40]

When they intrude into the 'real' world, apparitions are like soap bubble, fragile and short-lived. When the harsh spotlight of the conscious mind is turned on them, they evaporate. In the psychological terminology of Aniela Jaffé, the apparition could be said to sink back into the dark substrate of the unconscious—which again provides a symbolic parallel with the literal behaviour of road ghosts that are observed sinking into the earth.

Science itself is beginning to recognise a fundamental link between mind and matter, in what could be termed unconscious properties at the frontiers of current knowledge, most notably in the field of quantum theory. While it is undeniably a reliable and useful tool for describing the physical universe on the macro and super-macro scales, science, as an expression of rational conscious thought, inevitably struggles at the liminal boundaries—best exampled at the subatomic (quantum) level where, along with the breakdown of matter into energies and states of probability, are thrown out such familiar concepts as space, time and causality.

Since the famous and paradoxical 'double-slit' experiments of the twentieth century, in which light was first noted to exhibit either the characteristics of waves or particles depending on whether or not they were being observed (the act of measurement or observation seemingly causing the collapse of the wave function to produce particles), the further findings and hypotheses of quantum physics and cosmology have gone on to read like the most far-fetched science fiction, in which 'impossible' events regularly occur: where particles pop into existence from nowhere and as quickly vanish, or exert influence retroactively across time; where entangled pairs of particles instantaneously affect the state of one another irrespective of distance and in apparent contravention of known physical laws. And then there are the theories of multiple dimensions and universes, plus the theory that the known universe may be a holographic projection from a lower dimensional space. And, of course, there is cosmology's most audacious theory: that the whole physical universe inflated out of a pin-prick of absolute nothingness in the Big Bang that started the whole deal.

All of the above are the result of serious observation or conjecture. It is ironic then, that the materialistic scientific culture that dismisses such notions as ghosts scarcely bats an eye at a revealed universe that is every bit as mysterious and ephemeral as any ghost.

The abundant void

Far from being something outside or above nature (as the terms 'paranormal' or 'supernatural' infer), ghostly phenomena, as representative of the workings of the unconscious, appear to have a greater affinity with the quantum world than with the macroscopic, physical one we inhabit. In both fields we have to deal with insubstantialities and probabilities, where rational understanding of space, time, causality and predictability break down. Jung himself came to realise this connection as he observed the fields of microphysics and analytical psychology developing concepts that displayed remarkable analogies. 'If this trend should become more pronounced in the future,' he said, 'the hypothesis of the unity of their subject-matters would gain in probability.'[41]

Jung's former secretary and protégé Aniela Jaffé stated that before the end of his life Jung had concluded that at their deepest level the psychic and the physical were but different expressions of the same fundamental background reality.[42] As we plumb their depths, the 'inner' (psychic) and the 'outer' (quantum) worlds merge and show themselves to be part of a unified and interdependent whole. Thus the sphere of the psyche is connected intrinsically with the physical world: as without, so within—and vice versa.

If we think about it, this shouldn't be so surprising—we and everything, including our own consciousness and experiences, plus all possible phenomena, are all part and product of the same universe and therefore all are natural expressions of it, even if parts are beyond the measure of the conscious rationale of finite human beings.

In search of a name for this transcendent psycho-physical background—the ultimate level of reality—Jung borrowed a term from Gnostic theology: *Pleroma.* The pleroma is:

> … a thing that is infinite and eternal hath no qualities, since it hath all qualities. This nothingness or fullness we name the Pleroma. Therein both thinking and being cease, since the eternal and infinite possess no qualities. In it no being is, for he then would be distinct from the pleroma, and would possess qualities which would distinguish him as something distinct from the pleroma. In the pleroma there is nothing and everything.[43]

Other terms have been adopted to describe essentially this same state. The theoretical physicist David Bohm (1917–1992) called it the *Implicate Order.* Quantum physicists refer to *Zero-Point Energy*, the plenum state of latent quantum energy, a property of the absolute vacuum that underlies the quantum universe. From these perspectives, the material universe might be analogous to the foam whipped up by the waves on the surface of a dark simmering ocean.

In Gnostic terms, the pleroma was the abode of God and the source and totality of the divine: a state of pure, limitless power and creative potential. Whatever the preferred label, this avenue of thought inevitably leads to deeper philosophical questions regarding the nature of consciousness itself, and to matters of spirituality (which inevitably have been alluded to in this book but any further discussion about which necessarily falls outside its scope). Suffice to say that philosophy and science have met at similar conclusions regarding the unitary nature of the universe and the interconnectedness of all things.

From this perspective, psychic abilities and supranormal events become less paradoxical, and it becomes more comprehensible how apparitions might manifest simultaneously in the media of the mind and in external reality within a single event—as well as accounting perhaps for those instances (although still barely imaginable) by which psychic events, including apparitions, might be capable of leaving lasting physical effects such as damage to vehicles. We can't answer how this happens, only that it sometimes appears to.

In the material, conscious world we are programmed by experience to expect events to make ordered sense: a rock tossed at a window results in a broken pane, and so on. Cause precedes effect within a framework of advancing time. Causality and repeatability are outwardly so dependable they enable us to establish a logical foundation for our comprehension of the world.

In the subatomic realm, and in the unconscious, however, events are antithetical to familiar order: they are spontaneous, acausal, and defiant of our usual notions of time and space. According to Jung, the relational factor, the 'inner logic' of the unconscious, is not causality but *meaning.* Jung called this acausal connecting principle between psychic and physical events *synchronicity*.[44]

In the last chapter we saw how meaningful connections emerge with the mythological characters of the archetypes and the liminal features of their ghostly appearances at Blue Bell Hill and elsewhere—as warning markers at the threshold of death; as psychic eco-warriors defending the sanctity of nature; or as bridges, guides or mediators between the realms of the conscious and the unconscious, and between life and the afterlife.

The search for meaning and understanding is a natural human response to mystery. It is the impetus for inquiry into all the important areas of human interest, whether philosophical, spiritual or scientific. It is in our nature to seek answers to puzzling or unusual events. In the ancient past the awe-inspiring natural phenomena of Earth and the heavens found their explanation in the manifestations, actions and whims of gods and spirits. Hence a natural order developed in human culture that made sense of the world based on practical knowledge and experience *and* our imaginative faculties—in other words, one that engaged and satisfied *both* aspects of the human psyche.

With the increases in knowledge that have come about through the scientific method many of the wonders of nature have become demystified. Hence there has been a progressive tendency in modern culture to throw out prior beliefs and attempts at understanding as archaic and redundant. But in the process we may be losing something. Our attempts to understand the universe and our place within it through the reductionist tendencies of science, which sees everything dissected, divided and deconstructed, threatens also to diminish and devalue what and who we are; in the process withering our capacity for wonder, reverence and awe. Cold science would have you believe that you are nothing more than a biochemical machine, an accidental consequence of a billion random events to produce one of the most complex organisms in existence: an adaptive, inventive supercomputer that came about by happy accident, for no essential purpose, and ultimately a by-product of dead nature. By this reckoning you and I do not really exist, not in any meaningful sense. Our thoughts and ideals of friendship, altruism, self-sacrifice and love—all the things that make life worth living—are merely processes in the game of the selfish, mindless gene. But by imbuing sequences of proteins with sentiment, all we are doing is exchanging one scale of intelligence and purpose for another, with no advancement in understanding.

But reductionism misses the bigger picture too. Jung lamented that we have turned the gods into neuroses[45]—by which he was not proclaiming a longing belief in the ancient gods, but commenting on the loss of the sense of the transcendence and spiritual aspects of the unconscious psyche that they represented. And he was keen to stress that there may be a penalty to be paid for this loss.

One of Jung's central ideas, which he developed out of a long career in analytical psychology, was the principle of *individuation*, whose essential goal is to regain balance within the psyche and consequently achieve wholeness of *self.* Jung's professional career placed him in an ideal situation to observe the dysfunction and disablement that can result from an imbalance between the conscious and unconscious aspects of the mind. Problems arise when one is injured or suppressed by the other.

On the one hand, the fullest vent given to unconscious impulses may swamp the rational processes, resulting in psychosis (the delusional mental state in which the subject is overrun with chaotic thoughts and fantasies and is generally said to experience a loss of contact with reality). On the other, the forceful nature of the ego-consciousness may create its own imbalance as it belittles the importance of the unconscious and strives to expunge or ignore the numinous and the divine. 'But,' said Jung, 'if we understand anything of the unconscious, we know that it cannot be swallowed. We also know that it is dangerous to suppress it, because the unconscious is life and this life turns against us if suppressed, as happens in neurosis.'[46]

In modern secular culture we do not have to look far to notice its effects, to rising levels of anxiety and depression linked to a faltering sense of significance and purpose that becomes expressed outwardly in obsessions and phobias, and in impulsive, aggressive and anti-social behaviour. We might call this a loss of *spirit.*

But the unconscious doesn't go away; it needs to be acknowledged. To compensate, we seek out awe and deity and meaning and purpose in other ways, in different kinds of veneration, in the dissipations and idolatries of celebrity worship, hedonism and consumerism. But these pose a new kind of danger: the materialistic suppression of the unconscious, which may itself amount to a collective psychosis, since it diverts the individual and society itself away from the healthful balance of both aspects of our true and complete nature. 'Both are aspects of life,' said Jung. 'Consciousness should defend its reason and protect itself, and the chaotic life of the unconscious should be given the chance of having its way too—as much of it as we can stand. This means open conflict and open collaboration at once. That, evidently, is the way human life should be.'[47]

One further interpretation of archetypal ghostly encounters, therefore, is that they represent an attempt by the unconscious to halt our slide into material unconsciousness, by stopping us in our way; to shock us into reflection. The sorrow the ghost girl sometimes exudes might be a reflection of this neglect and the state of the human condition.

Ultimately, the psychological archetype (whose motives Jung noted are often truer and wiser than our conscious thinking) leads the individual to the reintegrated self, back to a healthy psyche based on the balanced contribution of both its conscious and unconscious aspects, and to the realisation of our complete nature (mind, body and spirit), and consequently to an expanded consciousness and a life enriched. *This* may be the treasure guarded by the ghost in all those folktales and legends that is the reward of those who follow her to where it is concealed—after which the lady is seen no more.

The world of materiality and conscious thought is not all there is. Which should be self-evident. We spend a third of our lives in the unconscious, when we go to sleep and dream. This is at least as much of who we are as our wakeful selves. We need a little of its salt in the diet of our waking lives too.

Human beings have always instinctively believed in ghosts, and will continue to do so regardless of what they are 'taught' by those who profess to know better. Ghosts and our fascination for them are, at very least, a reflection of our own mortality and our hopes for its continuation beyond the apparent finality of death. The popularity of the Blue Bell Hill story surely lies with this, but it also has an added dimension—a lesson, one that is embodied by the Phantom Hitch-Hiker tale at its heart, but found particularly in the real, tragic, and premature deaths of a young bride-to-be and two of her companions in a car crash here in 1965, and in the murder of a young woman a century ago, and in all of the tragic deaths suffered on the Hill: that life, for all its hopes and expectations, is ultimately a walk along a precipice, with the possibility of its ending at any moment, and we should therefore strive to savour every moment.

Meanwhile, the tale with which this book began, the Phantom Hitch-Hiker, can finally be seen as the journey itself—one that is literally enacted, but figurative in intent, and actually intended for the witness (and, by extension, us all)—a journey to who or what we really are; a journey perhaps into the limitless and timeless realm of the unconscious and its limitless possibilities. A journey home.

So, should you ever one night encounter a phantom standing thumb raised at the roadside, or rushing out in front of your car, remember that with the experience you have been posed a choice: either to continue on and try to convince yourself that it never happened—or, you can stop and begin to ask yourself some searching questions.

Epilogue

Blue Bell Hill Village. 12.15 a.m. Sunday 10 June 2012

It was spitting with rain as 17-year-old friends Dan Mulford and Ryan Banks turned into Blue Bell Hill Village. Five minutes earlier they had dropped another friend off at his home, and now Ryan was driving Dan back to Barling Close in the village before himself heading home to Rochester.

Moments later the southbound road dog-legs left-then-right and continues past Robin Hood Lane and Laurie Gray Avenue before reaching their destination, on the right.

Just before Laurie Gray Avenue, Ryan steered around a parked car. At that moment, a young woman suddenly ran out in front of them. She turned quickly to face them and stretched her arms wide to block their path. Ryan braked immediately (from about 20 mph), and stopped the car in front of her. The woman placed her hands on the bonnet of the Ford Fiesta, preventing them from going forward.

'She was stood in the middle of the road; wouldn't move,' he said.

Dan started to wind his window down, and the woman moved around to his side of the car. She was around 22 or 23, fairly attractive, and smartly dressed in a

Ryan Banks (left) and Dan Mulford (right) at the spot they encountered a strange young woman just after midnight in June 2012

white blouse (with exposed arms) with something dark underneath, and a dark skirt. Her attire suggested she had been for a night out or at a party. She had shoulder-length brownish hair, which framed an ashen face. But most striking of all were her eyes—she had dark eyes, with what looked like mascara smudged down her face. Her eyes (the pupils) were large and black.

'Can you help me?' she pleaded. Her speech seemed slurred, and she seemed dazed, as if drugged—or, said Dan, 'when you look at someone when they've just woken up and they don't know where they are.'

'Then she kept saying, 'Can you help me?' And we said: 'What with?' And every time we said that, she said: 'Can you help me?'

'And then she asked where she was. And we said 'Blue Bell Hill', and she was like: 'Why the hell am I here? Where is Blue Bell Hill?'

'We kept trying to say 'Where do you live?' said Dan. 'And she said 'Sultans Road'. And every time we said 'Where's Sultans Road?' she said 'Can you help me?''

Finally she said: 'Snodland'.

'And then,' said Ryan, 'she said 'I need you to help me'—and tried getting in the car!'

The dilapidated Upper Bell, in June 2012, less than a year before it was demolished. Scene of several ghostly encounters before Dan Mulford's and Ryan Banks' experience

With relief they realised the car's rear doors were locked. At this, the teenagers' patience and nerve understandably broke: 'So I drove,' said Ryan. 'I just went. I wasn't staying there any longer.'

They drove off, past Barling Close, and continued to the end of the road, and turned right at the derelict Upper Bell pub into Common Road and up as far as the entrance to the picnic area, where they waited, reflecting on what had just happened and trying to decide what to do.

Initially they had thought the woman to be just a confused and lost soul; her flustered, disorientated state and dilated black eyes the result perhaps of intoxication. But the setting of the encounter didn't escape Dan. Both knew of the Hill's reputation.

'I didn't even click,' said Ryan, 'until he went like, 'Why does it have to be here, where the Blue Bell Hill ghost is?''

'I was joking about it,' said Dan. But then, said Ryan: 'It was like: 'What would a girl dressed up like for a party be doing in the middle of Blue Bell Hill at half-twelve at night?'

'I phoned my mate. I said thank you for locking my door—because he'd locked the door in the back before he got out.'

Ryan recalled that in this time, another car had come up that way but there was no evidence to suggest they had seen anything.

After five minutes or so they decided to drive back down. But as they approached the bottom of the dip toward the Upper Bell, Dan said, 'Ryan, stop'. The woman was in the road near the Upper Bell. So they turned around and went back up and parked again.

This time they thought: 'This isn't going anywhere. We're going to have to go past.'

'So we sat there,' said Dan, 'and then we drove right down to the Robin Hood [pub] and drove back.'

This time, as they crossed the bridge over the A229 and started down the dip toward the Upper Bell, they saw her standing in the bushes by the disused slip-road. As they approached, she stepped forward on the pavement with her right hand out as if to flag them down again.

'And we just went,' said Ryan. 'I swerved a little bit, just in case she stepped out again, but I don't think she did.'

Ryan drove them to the car park at Asda, a mile north on the A229. 'We got one of our mates to come and meet us, and we came back in his car. We went round looking everywhere.' But she was nowhere to be found.

Both were left shaken by their encounter. Later they looked up the ghost on the Internet. On 13 June, Dan Mulford's mother contacted Neil Arnold, who in turn alerted me, and an arrangement was made for us to meet at the location for an interview the following Friday (15 June), from which the account above is constructed.[1] That same day their story (as given by Neil) was carried in the *Kent Messenger*[2] in the hope that it might yield further information, perhaps even the identity of the girl.

On the face of it, it seemed that Dan Mulford's and Ryan Bank's initial assessment was the most likely explanation. The girl's slurred speech, her dilated pupils, her run mascara and general confusion and disorientation suggests intoxication, or perhaps some physical or emotional trauma. But for her bizarre behaviour the pair may have been more inclined to help. At one point they had suggested calling a taxi for her, but this went unanswered amid the girl's pleas for help. As for giving her a lift, this might not have been ruled out had she been capable of stating what was wrong instead of creeping them out.

Only after longer reflection did they realise how very odd their encounter had been. Blue Bell Hill Village is not a place you expect to meet anyone on the streets very late at night. Since 2003, the village has been closed to through-traffic to Maidstone by a barrier-gate across the former slip-lane outside the Upper Bell. The consequent demise of the Upper Bell and the small post office has left the village much quieter to both traffic and pedestrians, particularly at night. Even the buses serving the village stop hours beforehand.

The only social venue in the immediate area is the Robin Hood pub, 1200 metres westward along Common Road. It is possible she had been at the pub that Saturday night and despite the pitch darkness of the long tree-shrouded lane had ended up in the village, perhaps to seek a lift or wait there for a taxi—but then this might have been achieved as readily from the pub. But if this were the case, or there was some other reason for her distress (and as the two witnesses indicated), she might have just said so. As it was, no recognition was found among the evening staff at the pub on subsequent inquiry.

The girl had no handbag, no purse, and evidently no mobile phone. Her smudged mascara, which blackened her cheeks like marker ink, suggested she had been crying, although she was not visibly upset at the time of the encounter (the light rain not itself able to account for it). Her confused state and condition, however, might as readily have been explained by intoxication. This in itself might make sense of her failure to recognise where Blue Bell Hill was, or to knock at any of the houses in the village for assistance. Snodland is only 2.5 miles (4 km) directly across the River Medway. Most residents of Snodland would certainly be familiar with Blue Bell Hill as part of their local geography.

It is one of the features of unusual or unexpected situations that the kinds of questions that one might have asked only seem to arise when it is too late—to take the girl's name for instance, or a telephone number to call on her behalf. But, given the unusual circumstances and the frustration of trying to get her to say anything meaningful, plus the youthfulness of the witnesses themselves, their reaction is understandable.

There is a *Saltings* Road in Snodland, which is likely what the girl was trying to say (although it has to be noted, there is a Sultan Road in nearby Lordswood). It did occur to the pair subsequently that it might have been possible to go there and check to see if anyone knew of her. Alas, as Ryan said, 'I wish we'd asked for a number or something, or what number in Saltings Road.'

But such speculation doesn't really address how a well-dressed, though evidently upset girl, came to be in Blue Bell Hill Village in the first place, or how she managed to remove herself afterwards.

It may perhaps be significant that in September 2012 it was reported that squatters had moved into the derelict Upper Bell. The report, by the *Kent Messenger*,[3] indicated that they had moved into the premises (which had been boarded up since 2003) at the beginning of the month—which happened to coincide with a change in the law (from 1 September) that made it illegal to squat in residential properties. The action prompted Tracey Crouch, MP for Chatham and Aylesford, to highlight the increases in the occupation of empty commercial properties and to campaign for an extension of the amendment to include these.

In December, the *Kent Messenger* reported that six people had been arrested at the Upper Bell on suspicion of drug offences and reports of antisocial behaviour at the property. The six included three women: a 33-year-old from Rochester, and a 41-year-old and an 18-year-old from Maidstone.[4] Coincidentally, on the same day the *Kent Messenger* carried the Mulford–Banks encounter, newspapers elsewhere were reporting an incident involving a 19-year-old Lincolnshire woman who had taken an amphetamine-like 'legal high' called Benzo Fury and had marched spaced-out and naked into a supermarket. On her 'terrifying trip' she had bitten into a pen which blackened her teeth and she had drawn all over her body.[5]

Might this account for the presence and the confused state of the woman encountered a few months earlier by Dan Mulford and Ryan Banks? It would rather depend on how long the Upper Bell might have been used for such purposes, and by what variety of people.[6]

As it was, the arrests and the dilapidated state of the Upper Bell provided its owner with the justification he needed to persuade the council's planning department to grant his new application (made that December) for its demolition as a 'solution' to the problem. Consequently, a few months later this well known local landmark, which had otherwise been long protected within earlier planning decisions, was irrevocably lost, and with it (as one half of the reason the Hill came by its name) a part of Blue Bell Hill's heritage.[7]

While the above offers a plausible and natural explanation for the presence of the girl that night, it is impossible to overlook the close, even uncanny, correspondences with the ghost sightings at Blue Bell Hill, including those in the village itself: there is the broad description and age-estimate of the girl, her behaviour (in both its aspects, as jaywalker and attempted hitch-hiker), the time-frame of the encounter, and the location itself. If it were a 'normal' encounter the girl could hardly have chosen a more apt spot or behaviour for her appearance, which was identical to Chris Dawkins' encounter in November 1992, save for the difference that there was no collision between her and the vehicle. But that could easily have been the same too: 'If I'd been going any faster,' said Ryan, 'that would have been it. I would have hit her.'

As in Dawkins' encounter, the girl had come out suddenly from the left, from behind a parked vehicle. Of note also (which before this book was published could not have been generally known) is that the spot, which is marked by a red post box outside the former post office,[8] is virtually outside the site of Emily Trigg's 1910 home.

And there are other parallels. The encounter itself and the reaction of the witnesses is reminiscent of Pope and Collings' meeting with a mystery female at the foot of Blue Bell Hill in 1977; while the road outside the Upper Bell features in several reports: in Ann-Marie Austin's sighting around the same year, and JST's two years later, both of which involved pairs of witnesses. And there is Joe Chester's encounter in 1968, which took place on what is now the disused slip-road below the site of the Upper Bell, which saw the girl emerge from the foliage toward him as he pushed his bicycle up the Hill.

Such small details are impressive. Even the disorientated state of the girl, so easily attributed to drugs or alcohol (although in the latter case, we might have expected Dan Mulford to have noticed this from his closer proximity to her through the open passenger window), has its precedents in other cases. The same has been said of Resurrection Mary (Chapter 4), and is exhibited in such cases as the Steubenville ghost (Chapter 12) and the female ghost that staggered across the road at Castledawson (Chapter 14)—as if in each case she had stepped out of nowhere to find herself confused and struggling for consciousness and identity.

Neil Arnold's appeal in the *Kent Messenger* for further information failed to produce a resolution—although it did result in one piece of correspondence that introduced an interesting and possibly significant aside to the Blue Bell Hill story. The gentleman concerned wrote to Neil a week after the *Kent Messenger*'s article to draw his attention to an incident on the Hill in October 1981 that resulted in the death of a young woman, which he claimed matched some of the details given in the newspaper account.[9]

He cited the tragic case of Sarah Burnley*, a 19-year-old supermarket assistant, who was run over and killed while walking home in the pouring rain to Old

Chatham Road, Blue Bell Hill. It was an incident I was aware of from newspaper records but had not explored in detail. The accident occurred on the A229 at the foot of the Hill on the outskirts of Maidstone, and much later than the established legend and sightings; hence it was somewhat disconnected from the main story.

As reported by the *Kent Messenger* (Maidstone) of 30 October 1981,[10] Miss Burnley, who worked at the Tesco stores in Farleigh Road, Tovil (Maidstone), was killed as she crossed the A229 just north of Tyland Lane the previous Wednesday evening (28 October).

Reports on the inquest the following February provided further details on the circumstances of the tragedy. The inquest heard that a 54-year-old doctor from Wrotham, whose car had struck and killed Miss Burnley, had no chance of avoiding her. He had been driving on the Chatham-bound carriageway of the A229 at around 6.50 p.m. It was raining hard and he had his headlights on. 'Suddenly,' he said, 'a figure appeared to dash at me. Within seconds there [was] a horrifying thud at the front of my car and my windscreen shattered.' He stopped and was expecting to walk back on the road to find someone lying there and the traffic stopped. Instead, on checking his vehicle he was shocked to see the body of the girl on his car's roof. He moved her to the ground and examined her for a pulse, but found none.

Another witness testified that he had passed a figure dressed in white who was trying to flag him down as if in distress: 'I assumed that the figure I had seen had broken down and was asking for assistance.' He had pulled in to see what she wanted when another car ran into him from behind. The driver of this vehicle, who was accompanied by his girlfriend, said he had the impression that the girl had been in front of the car in front, and had moved quickly from left to right. Neither driver witnessed the collision that killed her.

The victim's father told the inquest that his daughter usually caught the bus to and from work. Inquiries showed that she had been dropped off by a friend at the Archbishop's Palace in Maidstone, but on this night she had no money and evidently had decided to walk home. The family had only moved to Blue Bell Hill from Nettlestead a week before the accident. But why she seemed distressed and tried to cross the busy road at that point could not be determined. The coroner, Mr Gerald Coombe said: 'It is really totally inexplicable why she ran across the road at this point.' A verdict of accidental death was recorded.[11]

The parallels with the Mulford–Banks incident are self-evident, but the fact of another tragic young woman with ties to Blue Bell Hill (albeit of only a week), plus the circumstances of her death, will also not be lost on the reader. Is it merely coincidence that the actions of a young woman who happened to be dressed in white and who met her death by running into the path of traffic at Blue Bell Hill should so uncannily reflect the style of the ghostly encounters at that location years afterward—a chance instance of true life mirroring ghostly 'fiction'? It would seem so.

Chronologically, the victim's death occurred years after Blue Bell Hill's reputation became established. All the same, it may be noteworthy that the majority of the dramatic 'jaywalker' incidents post-date this young woman's tragic demise. But if there is anything to Aniela Jaffé's idea regarding archetypal effects transcending the normal temporal frame, then this might not be unrelated after all.

Sarah Burnley's story enters late into the Blue Bell Hill saga, but it is one that resonates with the earliest historical candidate, Emily Trigg. Of all the tragic deaths that have occurred on the Hill it is uncannily apt that among them we should find two young women, both residents of Blue Bell Hill, who in description (Emily was twenty; Sarah was just shy of her twentieth year) and by tragic circumstance (both losing their lives on their homeward journey) should accord with the tenets of the classic Phantom Hitch-Hiker story.

One outstanding difficulty with the Mulford–Banks encounter is in trying to reconcile the girl's stated objective (Snodland) with Sarah Burnley's destination on her fateful last evening—her new home in Old Chatham Road, further down the Hill near to the Lower Bell.[12]

It is easy to say from the outside, but one can't help wishing that Dan Mulford and Ryan Banks had stayed a while longer, or had at least obtained the girl's name.

But there is a postscript to this incident. A couple of months after their encounter, on 25 August 2012, Neil Arnold visited the Hill with an investigative team from Thanet. Just after midnight they asked if they could see the spot where the recent incident had taken place. It was an unplanned extension to their visit. They drove to the Upper Bell and parked at the barrier by the disused slip road. They were standing there talking when a taxi (Express Cabs of Maidstone) came out of Mill Lane beside the Upper Bell. Seeing them, the driver pulled up, but two of the party waved him off to indicate that they hadn't called a cab. The driver looked baffled. Neil walked over and asked him who he was picking up. He said someone had called for a taxi from the Upper Bell to the Bridgewood (Manor) Hotel (just over a mile to the north). Then Neil asked the driver what name he had. He replied 'Burnley'*. Neil was stunned. The driver then called the despatch office, only to discover that there was no record of a fare from that location. Nonplussed, he drove away.

'I wish I'd asked if it had been a woman,' said Neil. 'But again, I found it odd that someone would get a cab from the Upper Bell. If we'd got there five minutes earlier or later we wouldn't have seen the cab. Very strange.'[13]

Blue Bell Hill is indeed a strange place. Until next time.

Published History

THE 1965 TRAGEDY

'Doctors fight for death-crash bride', *Evening News*, London, Saturday 20 November 1965, fp (late extra edition).

'Battle for crash bride's life', *Evening News*, London, Saturday 20 November 1965, fp (late extra final).

'Bride-to-be injured in death crash', by Bill White, *Evening Standard*, London, Saturday 20 November 1965, fp & back.

'Fight for bride-to-be's life', *The News of the World*, Sunday 21 November 1965, p. 11.

'Bride-to-be hurt in death crash', *The Observer*, London, Sunday 21 November 1965, fp.

'Bride fights for her life on wedding day', *The People*, Sunday 21 November 1965, p. 10.

'Bride in eve of wedding death crash', *The Sunday Express*, London, 21 November 1965, p. 17.

'Tragedy ends bride's 'hen party', *The Sunday Mirror*, 21 November 1965, p. 7.

'Bride-To-Be "Critical" After Crash', *The Sunday Post* (Glasgow), 21 November 1965, fp.

'Bride's injury halts wedding', *Sunday Telegraph*, 21 November 1965, p.3.

'S.A. bride-to-be injured in U.K. car smash', *The Advertiser* (Adelaide), Monday 22 November 1965, fp.

'Wedding day in hospital', *The Australian*, Monday 22 November 1965, p. 3.

'Girl injured on eve of wedding', *The Courier Mail* (Brisbane), Monday 22 November 1965, p. 4.

'Adelaide girl still serious', *The Herald* (Melbourne), Monday 22 November 1965, p. 12.

'Girl in wedding eve smash', *Newcastle Morning Herald* (Newcastle, NSW), Monday 22 November 1965, fp.

'Girl fighting for life', *The News* (Adelaide), Monday 22 November 1965, p. 3.

'Adelaide girl, 22, critical', *The Telegraph* (News-Pictorial) (Brisbane), Monday 22 November 1965, p. 17.

'Wedding Plan Upset By Road Smash', *The West Australian* (Perth), Monday 22 November 1965, p. 21.

'S.A. girl still critically ill', *The Advertiser* (Adelaide), Tuesday 23 November 1965, p. 3.

'Wedding-eve crash: bride critical', *The Australian*, Tuesday 23 November 1965, p. 3.

'Two die in smash drama: bride-to-be in a coma', *Chatham Standard*, Tuesday 23 November 1965, fp.

'Still critical', *The Courier Mail* (Brisbane), Tuesday 23 November 1965, p. 4.

'Australian girl still 'critical'', *The Examiner* (Launceston), Tuesday 23 November 1965, p. 29.

'Girls die in wedding eve smash', by Peter Rimmer, *Maidstone Gazette*, Tuesday 23 November 1965, fp.

'Weekend Picture Special' (photo feature), *Maidstone Gazette*, Tuesday 23 November 1965, p. 22.

'Bride-to-be is dead', *The Herald* (Melbourne), Thursday 25 November 1965, p. 3.

'Bride-to-be badly hurt in death crash', *Hunts Post*, Thursday 25 November 1965, fp.

'SA girl dies in Britain', *The News* (Adelaide), Thursday 25 November 1965, p. 2.

'Wedding tragedy', *The Telegraph* (News–Pictorial) (Brisbane), Thursday 25 November 1965, p. 33.

'Bride-to-be dies', *The Sun*, Thursday 25 November 1965, p. 7.

'Bride-to-be dies after crash', *The Times*, Thursday 25 November 1965, p. 7.

'Injured S.A. woman dies', *The Advertiser* (Adelaide), Friday 26 November 1965, p. 8.

'Bride dies in UK', *The Australian*, Friday 26 November 1965, p. 5.

'Bride-to-be dies', *The Canberra Times*, Friday 26 November 1965, p. 12.

'Death roll three with bride-to-be', *Chatham News*, Friday 26 November 1965, fp.

'Bride-to-be dies after crash', *Chatham Observer*, Friday 26 November 1965, fp.

'Fight for life: then wedding eve crash girl dies', Chatham Observer, Friday 26 November 1965, p. 3.

'Tragedy of a bride-to-be', *The Courier Mail* (Brisbane), Friday 26 November 1965, fp.

'Prelude to grief ...', by Peter Rimmer, *Kent Messenger*, Friday 26 November 1965, fp.

'Smash Death', *Newcastle Morning Herald* (Newcastle, NSW), Friday 26 November 1965, p. 5.

'Aust. Girl Dies In U.K.', *The West Australian* (Perth), Friday 26 November 1965, p. 20.

'Last Minute News', *Chatham Observer*, Friday 3 December 1965, fp.

'We will Remember', *Chatham Observer*, Friday 3 December 1965, p. 10.

'Deaths crash survivor improving', *Chatham Standard*, Tuesday 7 December 1965, fp.

'Acknowledgments', *Chatham Standard*, Tuesday 7 December 1965, p. 18.

'Survivor in crash horror improves', *Chatham News*, Friday 10 December 1965, p. 7.

'Acknowledgments', *Chatham Standard*, Tuesday 14 December 1965, p. 16.

'Crash killed three girls, inquest jury told', *Chatham Observer*, Friday 25 March 1966, p. 50.

'Blue Bell Hill triple tragedy 'accident'', *Kent Messenger*, Friday 25 March 1966, p. 7.

'Death crash of three girls still remains a mystery', *Chatham Standard*, Tuesday 29 March 1966, p. 5.

THE GHOST

'Maidstone Comment', by District Editor Roy Plascott, *Kent Messenger*, Friday 8 December 1967, p. 3.

'Hitch-hiking spirit' (in 'Talk of the Town'), by Roy Plascott, *Kent Messenger*, Friday 10 May 1968, p. 3.

'Riddle of the phantom girl', *Evening Post*, Monday 9 September 1968, p. 3.

'Have you met the ghostly hitch-hiker?', *The Gazette*, Tuesday 10 September 1968, p. 3.

'Blue Bell Hill - the driver's nightmare!', *Evening Post*, Thursday 27 February 1969, p. 5.

'Words in brief' (in 'Listening Post'), by John Huffam, *Evening Post*, Wednesday 9 December 1970, p. 2.

'Riddle of the phantom on death hill', *The News of the World*, Sunday 14 July 1974, p. 5.

'Ghost on the A229..', *Sunday Mirror*, 14 July 1974, p. 13.

''Ghost walks' after crash', *Sunday People*, 14 July 1974, p. 9.

'Ghost riddle of 'injured girl'', *Evening Post*, Monday 15 July 1974, fp.

''Ghost' mystery of injured girl', *Chatham Standard*, Tuesday 16 July 1974, bp.

'Hunt for phantom schoolgirl road victim', *The Gazette*, Tuesday 16 July 1974, fp.

'Riddle of injured girl who 'disappeared'', *Chatham News*, Friday 19 July 1974, p. 20.

'Drivers beware of the phantom on the hill', by Nigel Nelson, *Evening Post*, Friday 19 July 1974, p. 7.

'Bluebell Hill's phantom girls', *Kent Messenger*, Friday 19 July 1974, p. 4.

'Spectre of Bluebell Hill', by Nigel Nelson, *Kent Messenger*, Friday 26 July 1974, p. 8.

'Memories of Judy' (in 'Letters to the Editor'), *Kent Messenger*, Friday 9 August 1974, p. 2.

'Phantom on the TV screen' ('Haunted Kent') by Jenni Balow, *Kent Messenger*, Friday 30 August 1974, p. 8.

'Ghost hunters discover surprise spirit', by Phil Dalton, *Kent Messenger*, Friday 10 January 1975, fp.

'Hauntings' (Letters to the Editor - letter of appeal by Andrew Green), *Kent Messenger*, Friday 14 February 1975. p. 2.

'I gave ghost a lift, says pop star', *Reveille*, May 1975.

The News (now *Fortean Times*) No.10, June 1975, p. 5.

'Two in 'haunting' encounter on Blue Bell Hill', *Evening Post*, Tuesday 30 August 1977, p. 10.

'Ghostly experience', *Evening News* (London), Monday 12 September 1977, p. 9.

'Ghosts and Visions', by Steve Moore, Fortean Times No.24, Winter 1977, pp. 13-14.

'Tales of phantom hitch-hikers', by Paul Screeton, *The Mail*, Hartlepool, Friday 31 October 1980, p. 27.

'What a story - if it's on the level!', by Roy Plascott, *Kent Messenger*, Friday 26 September 1980, p. 6.

'On the road again', by Michael Goss, *Fortean Times* No.34, Winter 1981, pp. 14-16.

'Taken for a ride?', by Michael Goss, *The Unexplained* (1986), pp. 1706-09.

'Collecting UFO facts' (in 'Letters'; letter of appeal by Sean Tudor), *Adscene*, W/E Friday 10 November 1989, p .M4.

'Have you met phantom hiker?' (in 'Starpost'; letter of appeal by Sean Tudor), *Maidstone Star*, Thursday 25 January 1990, p. 2.

'Search for the ghost' (in 'Postbag'; letter of appeal by Sean Tudor'), *Evening Post*, Friday 20 July 1990, p. 6.

'Ghost girl seen again', by Emma Cooper, *Kent Today*, Tuesday 10 November 1992, fp.

'Driver runs over a ghost', *Daily Mirror*, Wednesday 11 November 1992.

'Driver told girl he hit 'was ghost', *The Sun*, Wednesday 11 November 1992, p. 9.

'Crash girl gives up the ghost', *Today*, Wednesday 11 November 1992, p. 17.

'Terror as ghost girl reappears', by Emma Cooper, *Kent Messenger*, Friday 13 November 1992, p. 3.

'Resurrection of ghost story can create pain for living' (in 'Messenger letters'; by Sean Tudor), *Kent Messenger*, Friday 20 November 1992, p. 2.

'Briefly' (in 'Local News'), *KM Extra (Ma)*, W/E Friday 20 November 1992, p. 6.

'Accident victim vanished', *The Weekly News*, Saturday 21 November 1992, p. 12.

'Blue Bell Hill ghost seen again', *Kent Today* (Maidstone), Monday 23 November 1992, fp.

'Ghostly vision 'appears again'', by Clare Blackburn, *Kent Today* (Medway Towns Final), Monday 23 November 1992, fp.

'Horror of driver who hit a spook', *Daily Sport*, Tuesday 24 November 1992, p 7.

'Driver tells how he 'hit' ghost girl', by Helen Sissons, *Kent Today* (Maidstone), Tuesday 24 November 1992, p. 2.

''Ghost looked me in the face' says teenage driver', by Helen Sissons, *Kent Today* (Medway Towns Final), Tuesday 24 November 1992, p. 2.

'I ran over ghost of tragic bridesmaid', by Paul Hooper, *The Sun*, Tuesday 24 November 1992, p. 7.

'Our psychic hears tragic tale of bridesmaid ghost', by Mike Ridley, *The Sun*, Thursday 26 November 1992, pp. 12-13.

'Ghost claims latest victim', *Adscene*, W/E Friday 27 November 1992, p .MS3.

'Second driver 'knocks down' ghost', *Kent Messenger*, Friday 27 November 1992, p. 3.

'Is this the ghost of Blue Bell Hill?', *The Sun*, Friday 27 November 1992, p. 17.

'Join The Sun psychic tour: Let medium Nella speak to spooks in your home', *The Sun*, Wednesday 2 December 1992, p. 11.

'Briefly' (in 'Local News'), *KM Extra (Ma)*, W/E Friday 4 December 1992, p. 6.

'Bridesmaid's ghost haunts highway where she died', by John Cooke, *The National Enquirer*, 15 December 1992, p. 44.

'Spirit sightings of car crash girl on the increase', *Psychic News*, 26 December 1992.

"Wizened road horror is ruining our lives", by Claire Ogley, *Kent Today*, Friday 8 January 1993, p. 13.

'Cabbie confirms 'ghost' sighting', by Claire Ogley, *Kent Today*, Thursday 14 January 1993, p. 12.

'Blue Bell Hill spectre puzzles historian', by Claire Ogley, *Kent Today*, Friday 22 January 1993, p. 11.

'Ghostly figure fails to show', by Claire Ogley, *KM Extra* (Medway), W/E Friday 29 January 1993, p. 56.

''Bizarre creature' causes motorists miles of misery', *Psychic News*, February 1993, p. 5.

'Is this the most haunted road in Britain?', by Alison Legh-Jones, *Woman*, 8 March 1993, pp. 28-29.

'Blue Bell ghost picks on Paula', by Emma Cooper, *Kent Today*, Wednesday 23 June 1993, p. 7.

'Ghost reappears', *Kent Messenger*, Friday 25 June 1993, p. 13.

'Briefly' (in 'Local News'), *KM Extra (Ma)*, W/E Friday 2 July, 1993, p. 2.

'Hit and Myth' (in 'Road Ghosts'), by Sean Tudor, *Fortean Times* 73, February/March 1994, pp .27–31.

'TV appeals for police witnesses to ghostly events', *Kent Today*, Wednesday 18 May 1994, p. 8.

'TV company needs help to nail ghost', *Kent Messenger*, Friday 20 May 1994, p. 5.

'Spectral jaywalkers' (in 'Dear FT...' (letter by Anthony Bell of Leeds)), *Fortean Times* 75, June/July 1994, p. 57.

'Obsessive Compulsion' (in 'Dear FT...' (letter by Jeffrey Vallance of Portland, Oregon)), *Fortean Times* 76, August/September 1994, p. 55.

'Good guide scores with five ghouls!', by Carol Davies, *Adscene*, W/E Friday 9 September 1994, p. MS5.

TV guide/review references to the BBC's *Out of This World* (7 October 1994): 'I had premonition of death, says TV Sue', by Peter Willis, *The Sun*, Thursday 6 October 1994,

p. 13; 'Watching Brief: *Out of This World* (BBC-1, 9.30pm)', *The Guardian*, Friday 7 October 1994, in '28 Television'; 'Pick of the Day: *Out of This World* (BBC1, 9.30pm)', by Liz Jarvis, *Today*, Friday 7 October 1994, p. 33; 'Pick of the Day: *Out of This World*, BBC1, 9.30pm (N Ireland 10.25pm)', by 'NA', *Daily Mail*, Friday 7 October 1994, p. 56; 'Aerial views: Spotlight on spooks', *Kent Today*, Friday 7 October 1994, p.21; 'Choice: *Out of This World* BBC1, 9.30pm', *The Times*, Friday 7 October 1994, in 'Television 43'; 'The ghost in the scheduling machine', by Jasper Rees, *The Independent*, Saturday 8 October 1994 (Television & Radio); 'Catering for the wrong medium' (in Stephen Pile's 'On TV'), *The Daily Telegraph*, Saturday 8 October 1994, p. 24.

'Tortured bridesmaid haunts the hill', *EVA*, 19 October 1994, p. 21.

'101 Ghosties, Ghoulies and Scary Monsters', by Murray Davies, *Yes! Magazine (The People)*, 30 October 1994, pp. 24–25.

'Road ghosts' (in 'Dear FT...') (letter by Sean Tudor)), *Fortean Times* 77, October/November 1994, p. 56.

'The Unexplained: Phantom hitch-hikers', by Harry Hinde, *ME*, December 1994.

'Tell us about those spooks', *Maidstone Star*, Wednesday 5 July 1995, p. 3.

'Let me have your ghost stories' (in 'You Say...' (letter of appeal by R.A. Stevens-Bassett of Eastbourne)), *Kent Today*, Friday 20 October 1995, p. 6.

'Ghostly goings-on in North Kent' (see '9. Blue Bell Hill: Chatham'), *Kent Today*, Tuesday 31 October 1995, p. 20.

'Students out to lay pub's ghost', by Louise Kirby, *Kent Today*, Thursday 16 May 1996, p. 4.

'Haunted Blue Bell Hill', by David L Thomas, *Anomaly* (Journal of research into the paranormal (ASSAP), No.19, November 1996), pp .2–8.

'Phantom's £3,000 bill', in Mirror Motoring, with Ken Rogers, *Daily Mirror*, 1 November, 1996, p. 28.

'The Ghosts of Bluebell Hill', by Alison Legh-Jones, *The Virginian* No. 10 (Spring 1997), p. 7.

'The Spook Map of Britain', *Sunday Mirror*, 19 October 1997, p. 17.

'Mind out who you bump into', by Sean Keeley, *Kent Today*, Thursday 30 October 1997, p. 5.

'Hell's Belles', by Sean Tudor, *Fortean Times* 104, November 1997, pp. 36–40.

'Hell's Belles' (in 'Letters' (by Neil Arnold of Chatham, and Lenna Mahoney)), *Fortean Times* 108, March 1998, p. 54.

'News in brief', *Kent Today*, 27 April 1998, p. 2.

'We'll haunt you with a spirit of good value' (advertisement feature), *Kent Today*, Tuesday 28 April 1998, p. 7.

'Kent's Ghost Cat' (in 'Cats in the Hats' ('Strange Days')), *Fortean Times* 111, June 1998, pp. 14–15.

'They came from Kent', by Jonathan Sale, *The Guardian*, Thursday 31 December 1998.

'UFO adds to spooky spot's mystery', by Geoff Maynard, *Kent Today*, Thursday 8 April 1999, p. 5.

'Atomics power UFO?', by Geoff Maynard, *Kent Today*, Wednesday 14 April 1999, p. 5.

'It's our very own Blue Bell Witch Project...', by Geoff Maynard, *Medway Today*, Friday 5 November 1999, p. 24.

'Blair Witch!' What about the hag of Blue Bell Hill?', by Geoff Maynard, *Kent Messenger*, Friday 12 November 1999, p. 53.

'Ghost Stories' (in 'WI: A page in support of WI' (Bearsted Green)), *Downs Mail*, March 2000, p. 43.

'Chilling legend at fire station', *Medway News*, Friday 27 October 2000, p. 9.

'Los fantasmas de Blue Bell Hill', by Sean Tudor, *Enigmas* 12 (Spain), December 2000, pp. 8–13.

'SUPER NATURAL—GHOSTS: Blue Bell Hill, Kent', *Bizarre* 46 (Summer 2001), pp. 88-89.

'Weird accolade for local haunt', *Medway Today*, Friday 4 May 2001, p. 4.

'Visions from the past', by Peter A. McCue, *The Scots Magazine*, Vol. 154, No. 6, June 2001, pp. 648-652.

'A scarier side to All Hallows Eve', *Medway Messenger* (KM) Friday 26 October 2001, p. 20.

'Landscape Spirits' (Letter by Sean Tudor), *Fortean Times* 155, February 2002, pp. 54–55.

'Can you help?', *Kent Messenger (Maidstone)*, Friday 3 May 2002, p. 40.

'Kentonline WebWATCH: www.roadghosts.com', *Kent Messenger (Maidstone)*, by Pauline Green, Friday 10 May 2002, p. 21.

'GHOSTLY GOINGS ON'; 'Triple death crash began riddle of Blue Bell Hill', by Emily Hall, *Kent Messenger* (Maidstone), Friday 14 November 2003, p. 2 & p. 18.

'Was my hitchiker [sic] a girl or a ghoul on the hill?', by Emily Hall, *Kent Messenger* (Maidstone), Friday 5 December 2003, p. 15.

'Wet hair, big eyes and bare feet: Two more readers tell of their ghostly sightings on Blue Bell Hill', by Emily Hall, *Kent Messenger* (Maidstone) Friday 19 December 2003, p. 18.

'Ghostly hitch-hiker who vanished into thin air...', by Emily Hall, *Kent Messenger* (Maidstone) Friday 30 January 2004, p. 52.

'Our haunted highways', by Natalie Dye, *Fate & Fortune magazine*, February 2004, p. 27.

'I met the Blue Bell Hill ghost', by Brian Paine, *KM Extra* Friday 28 October 2005.

'Stories of the paranormal', *Kent Messenger* (Maidstone), Friday 25 November 2005, p. 61.

'Haunted hills and highways', by Anna Stephens, *Kent Messenger* (Maidstone), Friday 16 November 2007, p. 44.

'Haunted', *Daily Star*, Tuesday 30 October 2007, p. 3.

'Ghost Writer', by Lee Wilmot, *Adscene*, W/E Friday 23 January 2009.

'Haunted Highways', by Paul Devereux, *Paranormal Magazine*, Issue 31, January 2009), pp.32-37; 'Hill of Horrors', by Neil Arnold (same issue), pp. 38–39.

'The truth is out there', *Kent Messenger*, Friday 30 October 2009, pp. 42–43.

'Fright Night', *Daily Star*, Saturday 31 October 2009, pp. 26–27.

'Have you seen big cats in the county? (Letters), *Kent Messenger* (Sittingbourne) Friday 4 June 2010, p. 38.

'Strange Stories from Burham and Wouldham', by Neil Arnold, *Burham and Wouldham Parish Magazine*, September 2010, p. 19.

'Ghouls, ghosts and Hythe's moth-man', by Marijke Cox, *Kent on Sunday* (Mid North Kent Edition, No.421), 17 October 2010, p. 10.

'The Phantom Hitchhiker of Blue Bell Hill', by Brian Haughton, *Ghost Voices*, Issue 11, October-November 2010.

'Renovation Hauntings', by Peter A McCue, *Fortean Times* 268, November 2010, pp. 30–35

'Winter's Tales', by Jim Keoghan, *Kent Life*, November 2010, pp. 50–52.

'Author's ghostly tales set to scare', *Medway Messenger*, 29 October 2010, p. 30.

'All in the right spirit: The 'true' tales of things that go woof in the night (A review of Peter Ackroyd's 'Spectres Through Time' by Suzi Feay in Arts & Books, *The New Review (The Independent on Sunday),* 31 October 2010, p. 39.

'The English Ghost: Spectres Through Time' (in Books and Arts: Haunted Britain - Spooky), *The Economist,* 20–26 November 2010, p. 101.

'Creepy Kent', by Neil Arnold, *Paranormal Magazine,* Issue 55, January 2011), pp. 70–75.

'Woman in white gives men a fright on midnight drive', by Chris Hunter, *Kent Messenger* (County) Friday 15 June 2012, p. 19.

'Traffic Stopper', *Daily Star,* Saturday 16 June 2012, p. 17.

'Was ghostly woman the Blue Bell Hill phantom?', by Chris Hunter, *Medway Messenger* (Monday edition), 18 June 2012, p. 13.

'Haunted Maidstone: A ghost hunter's guide to the area', by Andy Gray, *Kent Messenger* (Maidstone), Friday 22 June 2012, p. 22.

'Film Launch Success', *Medway Messenger* (Monday edition), 10 September 2012, p. 6.

'Second spookiest road in the world', *Kent on Sunday* (North & West Kent) 14 October 2012 (p. 22); (East Kent edition, p. 25); 'Second spookiest road in the world', *Your Maidstone* (and other district versions) w/e 14 October 2012 (p. 22; p. 25).

'Scary News', *Medway Messenger* (Monday edition), 22 October 2012, p. 10.

'Clubs and Societies', *Sittingbourne News Extra,* 24 October 2012, p. 26.

'Second spookiest road in the world', *Your Maidstone* (and other district versions) w/e 14 October 2012 (p. 22; p. 25).

'Halloween: Blood will fall from the skies as haunted night draws near', by Marijke Cox, *Kent on Saturday* (East Kent), 27 October 2012. p. 3.

'Halloween: Blood will fall from the skies as haunted night draws near', by Marijke Cox, *Kent on Sunday* (North & West Kent), 28 October 2012, p. 3.

'Halloween: Blood will fall from the skies as haunted night draws near', by Marijke Cox, *Your Maidstone* (and other district versions), 28 October 2012, p. 3.

'Blood rain to hit "spooky" Kent ahead of Halloween', by Marijke Cox, *Your Maidstone* (and other district versions) w/e 28 October 2012, p. 3.

'Ghosts? Rush hour is the real nightmare', *Medway Messenger* (Friday edition), 2 November 2012, p. 24.

'Danger! Haunting Ahead', Take A Break's *Fate & Fortune,* October 2012, p. 41.

'Book reveals the power of urban legends and other creepy tales', by Joe Bill, *Kent on Saturday (East Kent edition),* 16 March 2013, p. 3; 'Book reveals the power of urban legends and other creepy tales', by Joe Bill, *Kent on Sunday (East Kent Edition & Mid-Kent edition)* 17 March 2013, p. 3.

'Chronicle of the creepiest local legends', by James Scott, *Kentish Express (Ashford & District)* (and other district versions), 11 April 2013, p. 21.

'Kent Urban Legends: The Phantom Hitch-Hiker and Other Stories', by Neil Arnold (in Books, *What's On (Kent Messenger),* 12 April 2013, p. 11.

Medway Messenger (Friday edition), 20 September 2013, p. 24 (in 'Mouth of the Medway').

'Spooked by ghostly blobs', by Alan McGuinness, *Medway Messenger* (Friday edition), 4 October 2013, p. 4.

'Blue Bell Hill ghost story being turned into a film', by Claire McWethy, *Kent Messenger* (Maidstone edition), 11 October 2013, p. 24.

"Blue Bell Hill ghost saved my life', says crash survivor Clare', by Nick Lillitos, *Kent Messenger* (Maidstone/Weald/County editions), 18 October 2013, p. 31.

"Blue Bell Hill ghost saved my life', says crash victim, *KM Extra* (Medway edition), 23 October 2013, p. 9.

'Clubs and Societies: Tunstall WI', *Sittingbourne News Extra*, 23 October 2013, p. 14.

'Good Samaritan Ghoul', Take A Break's *Fate & Fortune,* April 2014, p. 23.

'Ghostbuster's tales of the unexplained', *Kent on Sunday* (Mid-Kent) w/e 2 November 2014 (p. 24); (North & West Kent edition, p.24; East Kent, p. 26).

'Anniversary of tragic crash is marked by ghost hunters', by Mike Thompsett, *Medway Messenger* (Friday edition) (and *Sittingbourne Messenger),* 20 November 2015, p. 37.

'Haunting tale of crash that claimed three lives', by Mike Thompsett, *Kent Messenger* (Maidstone), 20 November 2015, p. 14.

'Most Haunted', *Kent Messenger What's On*, 14 October 2016, p.11 ('Blue Bell Hill').

BOOKS

G. Weaver, *Kent Ghosts* ((Viewing Kent series); James Pike Ltd, St Ives, Cornwall. First Edition 1977; ISBN 0-85932-181-9), The Open Road, p. 22.

Alan Bignell, *Kent Lore: A Heritage of Fact and Fable* (Robert Hale, London, 1983; ISBN 0-7090-1013-3), Chapter 8 - Spirits of the Lore, pp. 102–3.

Ghosts (a compilation of *The Unexplained,* Orbis Publishing, 1980-84), edited by Peter Brookesmith (Book Club Associates, London, 1984), Ghosts and Legend ('Taken for a ride?', pages 63–66), p. 66.

Michael Goss, *The Evidence for Phantom Hitch-Hikers* (The Aquarian Press, 1984; ISBN 0-85030-376-1). In particular, see Chapter 6—The Haunted Hill.

Lorrie Mack, Eric Harwood & Lesley Riley (eds), *The Unexplained* (Orbis Publishing, 1985, for Marks and Spencer plc), p. 135.

Peter Underwood, *Ghosts of Kent* (Meresborough Books, 1987; ISBN 0905270-86X), p. 93.

Janet and Colin Bord, *Modern Mysteries of Britain: One Hundred Years of Strange Events* (Grafton Books, 1988; ISBN 0-586-06529-6), Chapter 16 - Phantom hitch-hikers, p. 160 & p. 306.

Joan Forman, *The Haunted South* (Jarrold Colour Publications, 1989; ISBN 0-7117-0359-0), pp. 16–18.

The Best of Fortean Times: The Journal of Strange Phenomena (Selected and edited by Adam Sisman) (Futura Publications 1991; ISBN 0-7088-5335-8), Phantom Hitch-hikers, pp. 146–7.

Adam Sisman, Hunt Emerson & Lyall Watson, *The World's Most Incredible Stories: The Best of Fortean Times* (Avon Books, 1992; ISBN-10: 0380767546; ISBN-13: 978-0380767540), p. 147.

Fortean Times 1–15 (compilation: 'Yesterday's News Tomorrow', Fortean Tomes, London, 1992, for John Brown Publishing Ltd; ISBN 1-870870-26-3), issue 10, p. 5.

John and Anne Spencer, *The Encyclopedia of Ghosts and Spirits* (Headline Book Publishing plc, 1992; ISBN 0-7472-0508-6), Chapter 11—Phantom Hitchhikers, pp. 212–14.

Ted Wright, *One Dog and Her Man: The Life of Police Dog Bess* (Meresborough Books, 1992; ISBN 0948193-719), The Ghost of Bluebell Hill (Chapter 3), pp. 68–69.

Bruce Barrymore Halpenny, *Ghost Stations V* (Casdec Ltd, 1993; ISBN 0-907595-81-2), pp. 141–2.

Fortean Times 31–36 (compilation: 'Gateways to Mystery', Fortean Tomes, London, 1993, for John Brown Publishing Ltd; ISBN 1-870870-37-9), issue 34, p. 14 & p. 16.

Jenny Randles, *The Paranormal Year: 1993 Edition* (Robert Hale, London, 1993; ISBN 0-7090-4955-2), Ghosts, pp. 93–94.

Anne Bradford & Barrie Roberts, *Midland Ghosts & Hauntings* (Querrus, 1994; ISBN 189813605X), p. 121.

John Brooks, *The Good Ghost Guide* (Jarrold Publishing, 1994; ISBN 0-7117-0669-7), Southern England, p. 38.

Sarah Hapgood, *The World's Great Ghost & Poltergeist Stories* (Foulsham Books, 1994: ISBN 0-572-02049-X), The Phantom Hitch-Hiker of Blue Bell Hill, pp. 100–101.

John Spencer & Tony Wells, *Ghost Watching: The ghosthunters' handbook* (Virgin Books, 1994; ISBN 0-86369-719-4), p. 47 & pp. 229–31.

Tony Wells & Melanie Warren, *Ghost Stories of the South West* (Broadcast Books, 1994; ISBN 1874092257), p. 7.

Harry Ludlam, *Ghosts Among Us: Eye-witness Accounts of True Hauntings* (Janus Publishing, 1994, reprinted 2009; ISBN 978-1-85756-158-6), pp. 157–158.

Fortean Times 16-25 (compilation: 'Diary of a Mad Planet', John Brown Publishing Ltd, 1995; ISBN 1-870021-25-8), issue 24, p. 14.

Peter Hough, *Supernatural Britain* (Judy Piatkus (Publishers) Ltd, 1995; ISBN 0-7499-1406-8), p. 63–64.

Jenny Randles, *Strange But True?* Casebook (Judy Piatkus (Publishers) Ltd, 1995; ISBN 0-7499-1558-7), Chapter 9 - Phantom Hitchhiker, p. 118.

Tony Allan, *Tales of Real Haunting* (Usborne Publishing Ltd, 1997; ISBN 07460 23596), Chapter: Haunted Highways (pp.53-55) (Bluebell Hill), p. 53.

Brian Paine (Ed.) with Trevor Sturgess, *Unexplained Kent* (The Breedon Books Publishing Company, 1997; ISBN 1-85983-104-4), pp. 63–64.

John and Anne Spencer (eds), *The Unexplained* (Simon & Schuster, 1997; ISBN 0-684-81985-6), p. 169. Book version of the Flagtower CD-ROM (see below).

Fortean Times - Issues 102–106, John Brown Publishing, 1997. A compilation of issues, including *Hell's Belle's*, by Sean Tudor, issue 104, November 1997.

Michael Wilson, *Performance and Practice: Oral Narrative Traditions Amongst Teenagers in Britain and Ireland* (Ashgate Publishing Ltd, 1997); ISBN-10: 1840141123; ISBN-13: 978-1840141122).

Robert Anton Wilson with Miriam Joan Hill, *Everything is under Control,* (HarperCollins, 1998; ISBN-10: 0062734172; ISBN- 13: 978-0062734174, p. 183.

Ursula Bielski, *Chicago Haunts: Ghostlore of the Windy City* (Lake Claremont Press, 1998; ISBN-10: 0964242672; ISBN-13: 978-0964242678).

Fortean Times 73-77 (compilation: 'Mouthful of Mysteries, John Brown Publishing Ltd, 1998; ISBN 1870-870-662), issue 73, pp. 28–31; issue 75, p. 57; issue 77, p.56.

Alan Baker, *Sci-Fi Channel True Life Encounters: Ghosts and Spirits* (Orion Books Ltd, 1998; ISBN 0-75281-766-3), The Ghost of Blue Bell Hill, pp. 198–202.

Lionel Beer (ed.), *TEMS News* 19 (ASSAP area newsletter), May 1998), The Bluebell Hill Ghosts p. 6.

Janet and Colin Bord, *The World of the Unexplained* (Blandford, 1998; ISBN 0-7137-2746-2), Phantom Hitch-hikers, p. 69.

Anthony North, *The Supernatural: A Guide to Mysticism and the Occult* (Blandford, 1998; ISBN 0-7137-2728-4), Ghosts ad ESP, p. 20–21; p. 32).

Jenny Randles, *Truly Weird: Real-life Cases of the Paranormal* (Collins & Brown Ltd, 1998; ISBN 1-85585-442-2), Blackspots: The Local Stories, p. 116. See also p. 114 for misplaced photograph of the 1965 crash.

Anna Claybourne, *The Usborne Book of Ghosts & Hauntings* (Usborne Publishing Ltd, 1999; ISBN 07460 37163), Ghostly Girl/Second Sighting, p. 76.

Ghosts (pocket reference digest) (Geddes & Grosset, 1999: ISBN 185534-237-5), pp. 33–34.

John Guy, *The Unexplained: GHOSTS Haunted Houses and Spooky Places* (a snapping-turtle guide; Ticktock Publishing Ltd, 1999; ISBN 1-86007-103-1), 'Caught in the Beam', p. 28.

Andrew Green, *Haunted Kent Today* (S. B. Publications, 1999; ISBN 1-85770-181-X), pp. 51–53.

Natalie Osborne-Thomason, *The Ghost-Hunting Casebook* (Blandford, 1999; ISBN 0-7137-2768-3), Case 99: The Belle of Bluebell Hill, pp. 186–187.

Valerie Hope & Maurice Townsend (eds), *The Paranormal Investigator's Handbook* (Collins & Brown, 1999; ISBN 1-85585-703-0), p. 55.

Terry Deary, *True Mystery Stories* (Scholastic Children's Books, 2000; ISBN 0-439-01437-9), Chapter: What Did the Driver See? (Kent, south-east England, 1992), pp. 99–106.

Hilary Evans and Patrick Huyghe, *The Field guide to Ghosts and Other Apparitions* (Avon Books, 2000; ISBN-10: 0380802643; ISBN-13: 978-0380802647), pp. 70–71.

W.H. Johnson, *Kent Stories of the Supernatural* (Countryside Books, 2000; ISBN 1-85306-650-8), pp. 37–41; p. 121.

John and Anne Spencer, *Ghost Hunters' Guide to Britain* (Collins, 2000; ISBN 0-00-448964-0), pp. 48–49.

The Unexplained: Strange Encounters (Parragon, 2000; ISBN 0-75253-597-8), pp. 304–306.

Dennis William Hauck, *The International Directory of Haunted Places* (Penguin Books, 2000; ISBN 0-14-02.9635-2), Section 1, p. 31.

Dennis William Hauck, *The International Directory of Haunted Places: Ghostly Abodes, Sacred Sites and Other Supernatural Locations* (Penguin Books Australia, 2001; ISBN-10: 0140296352; ISBN-13: 978-0140296358), p. 31.

Jonathon Sutherland, *Ghosts of Great Britain and Ireland* (Breedon Books, 2001), p. 41.

Karen Hurrell & Brenda Ralph Lewis, *The Unexplained: A Source Book* (Flame Tree Publishing, 2003; ISBN 1-9040410-41-8), pp. 86–78.

Brad Steiger, *Real Ghosts, Restless Spirits, and Haunted Places* (Visible Ink Press 2003, ISBN 1-57859-146-5); Chapter 20—Phantoms on Roads and Highways.

Janet Sanger (ed.), *Scary Shorts for Halloween* (Accent Press Ltd, 2004); ISBN-10: 0954489942; ISBN-13: 978-0954489946), 'Blue Bell Hill', by Nina Tucknott, pp. 29–38.

Brad Steiger, *Out of the Dark: The Complete Guide to Beings from Beyond* (Kensington Publishing Corp., 2005; ISBN-10: 1575668963; ISBN-13: 978-1575668963), p. 34.

Jason Karl, *Jason Karl's Great Ghost Hunt* (New Holland Publishers, 2005; ISBN 1-84537-43-4 (paperback), 1-84330-735-9 (hardback), p. 36.

Rupert Matthews, *Ghost Hunter Walks in Kent* (SB Publications, 2005; ISBN-10: 1857703006; ISBN-13: 978-1857703009), Walk 2: Blue Bell Hill, pp. 14–19.

Edward Slee, *A Few Memories of Little Moment* (Authors OnLine Ltd, 2005; ISBN 0-7552-0159-0), p. 79.

Steve Dewey, John Ries, *In Alien Heat: The Warminster Mystery Revisited* (Anomalist Books, 2005; ISBN 1933665025), pp. 100–101.

Vikas Khatri, *True Ghosts and Spooky Incidents* (Pustak Mahal (Delhi), 2006; ISBN 81-223-0943-7), p. 72. (58. Vanishing Girl).

John Michell, Bob Rickard, Robert J. M. Rickard, *Unexplained phenomena: a rough guide special* (Rough Guides, 2nd ed., 2007; ISBN-10: 1843537087; ISBN–13: 978-1843537083), Chapter 7: The Haunted Planet.

Jennifer Westwood and Jacqueline Simpson, *The Lore of the Land:* A Guide to England's Legends, from Spring-heeled Jack to the Witches of Warboys Penguin Books, 2006; ISBN-10: 0141021039; ISBN-13: 978-0141021034), pp. 371–374.

Leslie Rule, *When the Ghost Screams* (Andrews McMeel Publishing, 2007; ISBN-10: 0740761757; ISBN-13: 978-0740761751), p. 177.

Melvyn Willin, *The Paranormal Caught on Film: Amazing Photographs of Ghosts, Poltergeists and Other Strange Phenomena* (David & Charles, 2008; ISBN-10: 0715329804; ISBN-13: 978-0715329801), p. 120.

Jennifer Westwood and Jacqueline Simpson (ed. Sophia Kingshill), *The Penguin Book of Ghosts* (Allen Lane (an imprint of Penguin Books), 2008; ISBN-10: 0276445457; ISBN-13: 978-0276445453), pp. 187–188.

Brian Haughton, *Lore of the Ghost: The Origins of the Most Famous Ghost Stories Throughout the World* (New Page Books, 2009; ISBN-10: 1601630247; ISBN-13: 978-1601630247), 'The Vanishing Hitchhiker', pp.95-97.

Peter Ackroyd, *The English Ghost: Spectres Through Time* (Chatto & Windus, 2010; ISBN-10: 0701169893 ISBN-13: 978-0701169893).

Neil Arnold, *Paranormal Kent* (The History Press, 2010; ISBN 978-0-7524-5590-7), pp. 7–14.

Jennifer Westwood, *Haunted England: The Penguin Book of Ghosts* (Penguin, 2010; ISBN-10: 0141039744; ISBN-13: 978-0141039749).

Reader's Digest, *The Most Amazing Haunted and Mysterious Places in Britain: More Than 1000 British Ghosts, Eerie Haunts and Enduring Mysteries* (Reader's Digest (29 Jan 2010; ISBN-10: 0276445457; ISBN-13: 978-0276445453), p. 67.

Gregory Branson-Trent, *Believe: Stories of Ghosts and Hauntings* (CreateSpace Independent Publishing Platform, 2011; ISBN-10: 1463597266; ISBN-13: 978-1463597269), p. 157.

Gregory Branson-Trent, *Return to the Cemetery: More Ghosts and Hauntings* (New Image Productions, 2011; ISBN-10: 0578041529; ISBN-13: 978-0578041520), p. 52, p. 166.

Gregory Branson-Trent, *The Dark Side of the Cemetery: Ghosts, Hauntings, and More* (CreateSpace, 2011; ISBN-10: 1466404337; ISBN-13: 978-1466404335), p. 43.

Michael Pye and Kirsten Dalley, *Exposed, Uncovered, And Declassified: Ghosts, Spirits & Hauntings: Am I Being Haunted?* (New Page Books, 2011; ISBN-10: 160163174X; ISBN-13: 978-1601631749), p.172, p. 176.

Neil Arnold, *Haunted Maidstone* (The History Press, 2011; ISBN 978-0-7524-5922-4), pp.22-34, with a Foreword by Sean Tudor.

Brian Haughton, *Famous Ghost Stories: Legends and Lore* (The Rosen Publishing Group, 2011; ISBN 978-1-4488-4840-9), pp. 93-95.

Mike Hanagan and Pat Cox, *Legends of Kent* (CreateSpace, 2012; ISBN-10: 1470174243; ISBN-13: 978-1470174248), p. 159.

Martin Latham, *Kent's Strangest Tales: Extraordinary But True Stories* (Portico, 2012; ISBN-10: 1907554335; ISBN-13: 978-1907554339).

Peter A. McCue, *Zones of Strangeness: An Examination of Paranormal and UFO Hot Spots* (AuthorHouse, 2012; ISBN-10: 1456778420; ISBN-13: 9781456778422), Chapter 15: Other British Hot Spots.

Melvyn Willin, Jim Eaton, *The Best of Ghosts Caught on Film: The Paranormal and the Supernatural Caught on Camera* (David & Charles, 2012; ISBN-10: 1446302717; ISBN-13: 978-1446302712), p. 122.

Brad Steiger, *Real Ghosts, Restless Spirits and Haunted Places* (Visible Ink, 2nd ed., 2013; ISBN-10: 1578594014; ISBN-13: 978-1578594016), p. 480.

Paul Adams and Eddie Brazil, *Extreme Hauntings: Britain's Most Terrifying Ghosts* (The History Press, 2013; ISBN-10: 075246535X; ISBN-13: 978-0752465357), pp. 130-134.

Neil Arnold, *Kent Urban Legends: The Phantom Hitch-Hiker and Other Stories* (The History Press, 2013; ISBN-10: 0752481460; ISBN-13: 978-0752481463), pp. 28-57.

Michael Pye, Kirsten Dalley, *Ghosts, Specters, and Haunted Places* (Rosen Publishing, 2013; ISBN 978-1-4488-9250-1), p. 172, p. 176.

Jill Amar, *Reincarnation Angels, Demons and Ghosts: According to the Zohar and Kabbalah* (Trafford Publishing, 2013; ISBN-10: 1466979828; ISBN-13: 9781466979826), p. 78.

Mary Devey, *True Stories on Road Ghosts & Phantom Hitchhikers* (2013, Kindle edition, 85 pages).

Paul Adams, *The Little Book of Ghosts* (The History Press, 2014; ISBN 978-0752498683), p. 149.

Jon Fordham, *Thanks For The Memories* (PublishNation, 2014; ISBN-10: 1291869360; ISBN-13: 978-1291869361), p. 364.

Richard Holland, *Kent Ghost Stories* (Bradwell Books, 2014; ISBN-9781909914056), pp. 69–70.

James Warrender, *The Paranormal Principle: A Real True Myth* (CreateSpace Independent, 2014; ISBN-10: 1500168297; ISBN-13: 978-1500168292), pp. 45-46.

Michael Goss, *The Evidence for Phantom Hitch-Hikers* (reprint: Coronet, 2015; ISBN 9781473606326). In particular, see Chapter 6—The Haunted Hill.

TELEVISION

1982: Middle English (series): *The Hairy Hand and The Phantom of Bluebell Hill* (Thames (London). Written and presented by Dave Arthur. Produced/directed by Peter Tabern, and featuring Tilly Vosburgh and Diana Payan. Broadcast 9 November 1982 (16 mins).

Thames TV programmes are now owned by Freemantle Media Enterprises (www.fremantlearchivesales.com), where the programme segment is archived under Thames catalogue number 61023. The piece may be viewed in person courtesy of the National Arts Education Archive (Trust), at the Lawrence Batley Centre, Bretton Hall, West Bretton, Wakefield WF4 4LG (archive no. BHTVFV00372). (www.artsedarchive.org.uk).

1992: Television South (TVS) *Coast to Coast* (regional news programme) item ('Ghost?' - Ian Sharpe's encounter)), introduced by Mike Debens, and reported by Hugh Kirby. Broadcast 11 November.

23 November: TVS News reports (1 p.m. and 3.15 p.m. (highlights), by Mike Debens, and Liz Wickham, respectively) on the Chris Dawkins encounter.

1994: *Out Of This World* (BBC1), presented by Sue Cook, with Dr Susan Blackmore and Dr Lyall Watson, featuring Ian Sharpe and Christopher Dawkins. First broadcast 7 October 1994, 9.30 p.m.

1995: *The Magic and Mystery Show* (CST Productions (East) Ltd for Anglia Television/Meridian Broadcasting Ltd, 1995), presented by Brian Blessed, with Lynn Picknett and Toyah Willcox, featuring Nella Jones. First broadcast 12 July 1995, 10.45 p.m.–11.15 p.m.

1995: *Arthur C. Clarke's Mysterious Universe* (a Granite Production for Yorkshire Television), 'Spirits of Place', featuring Ian Sharpe.

1998: *The Why Files*, episode 10, Part 2, 'The Ghost Bride' (02.10.98, File no.78877), (L!VE TV (Cable)), presented by David Barrett, featuring Sean Tudor, Peter Parvin, Bobby Parr, Lawrence Walker. First broadcast 25 January 1999.

2000: Meridian. *Meridian Tonight* (regional news programme (South East)). 'Legends and Mysteries—the Hitch-Hiker on the Hill'. 3-minute feature presented by Derek Johnson, and featuring Chris Dawkins, Dennis Chambers, David Thomas, John Hippisley. Broadcast 26 October 2000, 6 p.m. (feature start 6.20 p.m.).

2002: *In Search Of*, presented by Mitch Pileggi (a KAOS/USA Cable Entertainment production for the FOX Network). Season 7, Episode 2: Ghost Hitchers. Series began to air on the Scifi Channel in the USA from 4 October 2002. Featuring Ian Sharpe, PC Roger Ginn, and Sean Tudor. The show was not broadcast in the UK.

2002: *Scream Team*, episode 2, 'Blue Bell Hill in Kent' (a Making Time production for the UKLIVING (Cable) Channel. Featuring the 'Scream Team', which included Phil Whyman, later of *Most Haunted*; plus Ian Sharpe, Sean Tudor, Mike Ridley, John E. Vigar. First broadcast on 1 October 2002, 9 p.m.; repeated 6 October 2002, 9 p.m.

2002: *Paranormal Files*, episode 6, 'Blue Bell Hill and Cricklewood' (a JUST About production for the UK Horizons (Cable) Channel). Featuring Ian Sharpe, Sean Tudor, John Spencer, Albert Budden, Clare Bond. First broadcast 11 December 2002.

RADIO

1976: SABC (South African Broadcasting Corporation). *The Ton Up Run*: a radio drama written by Peter J. Hedge, and based on Blue Bell Hill's phantom hitchhiker. (See Chapter Twelve notes (30.) for further details.)

MULTIMEDIA

1996: *The Unexplained* (Flagtower). Released Spring 1996. Written by Ed Fenton, Keith Tutt, John & Anne Spencer. Narrated by Monica Buferd. Subject matter consultants: John Spencer and Anne Spencer). *See* Ghosts & Spirits/Modern Ghost Mysteries/Phantom Hitchhikers/Phantom Accidents (single page description of Ian Sharpe's and Maurice Goodenough's encounters).

MUSIC & AUDIO

1996: 'Bluebell Hill' (Band of Pain), on the album Seedmouth (Cold Spring Records), an instrumental track,, the inspiration for which I can only suppose *is* the Blue Bell Hill case.

1997: *Fortean Times 1* (Polygram Spoken Word cassette; produced by Steve Deakin-Davies for The Ambition Company). 2 cassettes featuring 2 hours of some of the best stories from the archives of the *Fortean Times*, including dramatisation of 'Road Ghosts Hit & Myth' (side 4).

2012: 'The Ghost on Bluebell Hill' (Sally Ironmaker (Duo)), on the album *Cheap Day Return*. This folk track gives a musical overview of the Blue Bell Hill's mysterious and historical heritage, that is reminiscent of Willott & Snyder's 'Bluebell Hill' (Albert Snyder, Stanley Willott; Albey Road, 2009), on their album *Something About the Night*.

INTERNET

A number of paranormal-based sites contain references to Blue Bell Hill. The author's own site can be visited at: www.roadghosts.com.

FICTION OFFSHOOTS

Josephine Cox (writing as Jane Brindle), *The Seeker* (Headline Feature, 1997, ISBN 0-7472-5570-9; and BCA, 1997, CN 4576; by arrangement with Headline Book Publishing): 'an unforgettable tale of haunting suspense', whose inspiration, and named setting is 'Bluebell Hill'.

Author's note: Although the above is the most exhaustive listing of references to the Blue Bell Hill case, I am nevertheless sure it is incomplete. I would therefore welcome details of any omissions. Please e-mail me at sean@roadghosts.com.

Notes & References

Introduction

1. A practice that continued until 1823, when a Parliamentary Act (4th George IV. cap. 52) was passed (on 8 July) 'to alter and amend the Law relating to the Interment of the Remains of any Person found *Felo de se'* (Latin for 'felon of himself'—a self-murderer, a suicide). (See expanded notes for Chapter 13 (24)).

2. Tracey Crouch, MP for Chatham and Aylesford (Con), made her inaugural speech in the Hansard Debates (House of Commons) on 10 June 2010, in which she gave an overview of her constituency, which included Blue Bell Hill. In her words: 'Nearby is Blue Bell hill, well known to many motorists in Kent as a key intersection between the M20 and M2. However, I mention Blue Bell hill today not for its historical or transportation value, but for its supernatural element. The ghost stories are legendary, and sightings have been reported in the local papers on numerous occasions—including, I was amused to see, by a current member of the Press Gallery, Mr Nigel Nelson, whose article, which was written for the local paper before I was born, is still cited by today's paranormal investigators.'(www.publications.parliament.uk/pa/cm201011/cmhansrd/cm100610/debtext/100610-0012.htm. See Column 516).

3. *The Evidence for Phantom Hitch-Hikers*, by Michael Goss (The Aquarian Press, 1984 (part of the Thorsons Publishing Group)). Reprinted in 2015 by Coronet (an imprint of Hodder & Stoughton), and by Weiser Books (USA). References in this book relate to the original 1984 version.

Chapter One: 'Ghost Girl Seen Again'

1. 'Ghost Girl Seen Again', by Emma Cooper, *Kent Today* (a *Kent Messenger* group newspaper), 10 November 1992, fp. While this was the first occasion the Blue Bell Hill ghost had achieved a front page *headline*, it was a front page feature of the *Evening Post* of 15 July 1974 and *The Gazette* of 16 July 1974. It also found brief mention at the foot of another front page article describing another haunting in the *Kent Messenger* of 10 January 1975.

The article's introductory paragraph took for granted public familiarity with Blue Bell Hill's sinister reputation: 'Tales of the ghost of Blue Bell Hill have taken a chilling new turn ...' But whether this 'chilling new turn' referred to the unexpectedness of a convincing named witness encounter after so many years of spurious (or at best, anomalous) reports, or to the noted departure the 'ghost's' behaviour took from her traditional habit of seeking lifts from unwary motorists in typical hitch-hiker fashion, is uncertain. Suffice to say that this phantom needed no formal introduction.

2. 'Bluebell' Hill is often used (and sometimes signposted as such) in place of the correct *Blue Bell* Hill.

3. 'What a story—if it's on the level!', by Roy Plascott, *Kent Messenger*, 26 September 1980, p. 6.

4. According to the report 'Ghost?' in TVS's regional news programme *Coast to Coast*, broadcast on 11 November 1992.

5. Sources disagree as to whether Maurice Goodenough covered his victim with (or wrapped her in) a tartan car rug (Nigel Nelson's articles for the *Evening Post*, 19 July 1974; *Kent Messenger*, 26 July 1974) or a car blanket (all other sources: *The News of the World*, 14 July 1974; *Sunday Mirror*, 14 July 1974; *Sunday People*, 14 July 1974; *Evening Post*, 15 July 1974; *Chatham Standard*, 16 July 1974; *The Gazette*, 16 July 1974; *Chatham News*, 19 July 1974; *Kent Messenger*, 19 July 1974; *Kent Messenger*, 30 August 1974). Nelson's articles actually use both terms to describe the coverlet.

6. *The News of the World*, 14 July 1974; *Chatham Standard*, 16 July 1974; *Evening Post*, 19 July 1974; *Kent Messenger*, 26 July 1974.

7. Sources also disagree as to whether the Goodenough incident took place just *before* midnight (*Chatham Standard*, 16 July 1974; *Chatham News*, 19 July 1974; *Evening Post*, 19 July 1974; *Kent Messenger*, 26 July 1974) or soon *after* midnight (*Evening Post*, 15 July 1974; *The Gazette*, 16 July 1974; *Kent Messenger*, 19 July 1974). For the record, *The News of the World*, 14 July 1974 states 'at midnight'.

8. Quote from: "Ghost' mystery of injured girl', *Chatham Standard*, 16 July 1974, back page; *Chatham News* ('Riddle of injured girl who 'disappeared", 19 July 1974, p. 20)—apparently sourced from the *Chatham Standard*—states also that the collision was 'with a hell of a bang'.

9. 'Riddle of the phantom on death hill', *The News of the World*, 14 July 1974, p. 5.

10. *Chatham News* & *Chatham Standard*, *op.cit.*

11. The search employed a single tracker dog, rather than the reported *dogs* (a fact established by Michael Goss through correspondence with the Kent County Constabulary, dated 19 February 1980). See also Chapter 7.

12. *The News of the World*, *op.cit.*

13. From tape-recorded interview with Ian Sharpe at his home, 13 March 1993.

14. *The News of the World*, *op.cit*: 'Riddle of the phantom on death hill'; *Sunday Mirror*, 14 July 1974, p. 13: 'Ghost on the A229.'; *Sunday People*, 14 July 1974, p. 9: "Ghost Walks' After Crash'.

15. 'Drivers beware of the phantom on the hill', *Evening Post*, 19 July 1974, p. 7; 'Spectre of Bluebell Hill', *Kent Messenger*, 26 July 1974, p. 8.

16. *Evening Post*, *Ibid.* Not only did it reproduce material on the 1965 crash, but the phraseology was similar: 'TALES of the ghost of Blue Bell Hill have taken a *chilling* new turn ...' is reminiscent of Nelson's *Evening Post* article, which stated: 'The *chilling* story of the phantom girl that haunts a lonely stretch of Bluebell Hill took a bizarre new turn this week.' [*italics* - mine]

17. Unless we consider the account of David Smith's ghostly pedestrians ('Blue Bell Hill—the driver's nightmare!', *Evening Post*, 27 February 1969, p. 5).

18. Emma Cooper subsequently provided a description (very probably taken from the TVS broadcast of 11 November, which she told me was about to go out) in her article for the *Kent Messenger* of 13 November 1992 ('Terror as ghost girl reappears', p. 3). Included is a detail not produced elsewhere—that the girl had been wearing a white coat.

19. 'Maidstone Comment', by District Editor Roy Plascott, *Kent Messenger*, Friday 8 December 1967, p. 3; 'Hitch-hiking spirit' (in 'Talk of the Town'), by Roy Plascott, *Kent Messenger*, Friday 10 May 1968, p. 3

20. See 14.

21. 'Girls die in wedding eve smash', by Peter Rimmer, *Maidstone Gazette*, 23 November 1965, fp.

22. Letters dated 19 & 24 July 1990.

23. "Ghost' Mystery of Injured Girl', *Chatham Standard*, 16 July 1974, back page.

24. 'Hunt for phantom schoolgirl road victim', *The Gazette* (formerly the *Maidstone Gazette*) 16 July 1974, fp. Two other sources place Goodenough's encounter at the same spot as a fatal accident which took place 'eight years ago' (*Evening Post*, 15 July 1974, fp), or 'in 1967' (*Sunday People*, 14 July 1974, p. 9.).

25. Correspondence with PC Elvy dated 3 July 1998.

26. Although the scene was pictured in various newspapers, aiding, perhaps, in the identification of the scene (as, indeed, they had helped me).

27. 'Driver tells how he 'hit' ghost girl', by Helen Sissons, *Kent Today* (Maidstone), Tuesday 24 November 1992, p. 2; 'Ghost looked me in the face' says teenage driver', by Helen

Sissons, *Kent Today* (Medway Towns Final), 24 November 1992, p. 2. (A follow-up version appeared in the *Kent Messenger* (27 Nov.).

28. 'Our psychic hears tragic tale of bridesmaid ghost', by Mike Ridley, *The Sun*, 26 November 1992, pp. 12–13. See Chapter 8.

29. Telephone contact 25 November 1992.

30. 'Driver told girl he hit 'was ghost'', *The Sun*, 11 November 1992, p. 9.; 'Crash girl gives up the ghost', *Today*, 11 November 1992, p. 17.

31. Jenny Randles' *The Paranormal Year* (1993 edition), Robert Hale, London, 1993, pp. 93–94. What I have come to call 'The Police Inspector Story' was featured in 1994 on CST Productions' *The Magic and Mystery Show*, presented by Brian Blessed. The 5-minute feature, which names Judith Lingham and reconstructs the occasion she reputedly hitched a lift from a passing police inspector, repeats the account given in the *Psychic News*. This, together with its attribution to 1992 (the year the article was published (mistakenly taken as the year of the 'incident'?), and the involvement of Nella Jones (who repeats on camera 'findings' she made known to *The Sun* and *Psychic News* in November and December of 1992) leads me to believe that the *Psychic News* article formed the sole source—one that, as I have indicated, provides no evidence to support the claim.

32. 'I ran over ghost of tragic bridesmaid', by Paul Hooper, *The Sun*, 24 November 1992, p. 7.

Chapter Two: A Special Place

1. Michael Goss *op.cit.*, p. 100; (Coronet edition 2015, p. 91).

2. Blue Bell Hill retains much of its natural beauty in untouched chalk down and woodland atop the ridge west of Blue Bell Hill Village. Blue Bell Hill Picnic Site, with its panoramic views over the Medway Valley, is designated a Site of Special Scientific Interest (SSSI). The slopes of Blue Bell Hill today also support vineyards. The 112-acre Kit's Coty vineyard, belonging to Tenterden-based Chapel Down, occupies the south facing slopes below the Pilgrims Way.

3. As a cat, the simulacrum aptly symbolises Blue Bell Hill's other modern claim to fame in the strangeness stakes: the *Beast* of Blue Bell Hill. So-dubbed in 1997 (no doubt for its alliterative ring) by a KM Group journalist, the Hill is but part of a wide tract of the North Kent countryside where large black felines (black panther or melanistic leopard) have been regularly observed. For a full accounting of the Beast, see Neil Arnold's *Mystery Animals of the British Isles: Kent* (CFZ Press, 9 Mar 2009), ISBN-13: 978-1905723362.

The sheer rock face here has been in existence here since at least 1828, when it was described as 'a considerable cliff occasioned by the chalk having been dug in large quantities from below.' (Sylvanus Urban,* *The Gentleman's Magazine,* Vol. XCVIII (July-Dec. 1828 (London: J.B. Nichols and Son, 1828)), p. 512.

A sketch of the section of road by F.G. Kitton, which includes Kit's Coty House, appears as a frontispiece in the book *Round About Kits Coty House: An Essay in Popular Topography* (London: Bell and Daldy; Maidstone: C. J. Cooke, 1861), and in William R. Hughes' *A Week's Tramp in Dickens Land* (London: Chapman & Hall, 1891), p. 315. In the latter, a footnote (p. 314) states: 'Mr. Kitton's illustration [annotated 'Kits Coty House and Blue Bell'] (from the painting by [J.J.] Gegan, a local artist, executed many years since) gives a good idea of the scenery of this beautiful district. It also reproduces the profile of a huge chalk cliff not now visible, but which existed about half a century ago, having a curious resemblance to the head of a lion, and forming at the time a conspicuous landmark to travelers.' (*Sylvanus Urban was the *nom de plume* of Edward Cave (1691–1754), the founder and editor of *The Gentleman's Magazine*).

4. The large chalk pits, Upper and Lower Culand, resembling two huge ice-cream scoops made in the escarpment and slopes of the North Downs between Burham and Blue Bell Hill, were opened to meet the increasing demand for chalk by the burgeoning cement

industry along the river Medway between Frindsbury and Burham following the discovery, in the 1830s, of a way to make 'Portland Cement'. On the Ordnance Survey map (1:2500) of 1876 the quarries are absent, but 20 years later (1896) both are present and well developed, indicating a rapid expansion of activity, with lines of tramways linking the quarries to the lime works on the river front at Burham and Wouldham. During this period, the population of Burham increased accordingly, and the whole village relocated to its present position, with a new church (1881), school, and workers' cottages nearer the source of employment. By 1937 the quarries had been abandoned following a decline in the industry—although smaller scale quarrying and lime-burning continued at the older pits immediately east of the Maidstone–Chatham road at Blue Bell Hill right up until their demolition in 1970 to make way for the new A229.

Additional sources: John E. Vigar, *Church of St Mary the Virgin (Burham, Kent)* (a booklet by The Churches Conservation Trust, 2009); 'Memories of Blue Bell Hill', a talk given by Mr Pat Sandford at Blue Bell Hill Village Hall, 24 May 2010. Pat's family had been in the lime-burning business (E.H & E.G. Sandford Ltd) at Blue Bell Hill since before the 1850s. In 1894 his grandfather and his grandfather's brother purchased the eastern side of Blue Bell Hill from the Lower Bell almost as far as the Upper Bell (for £500).

5. A Messerschmitt ME 109 crashed between Aylesford and Burham in 1940; while in October 1941, a Spitfire (Serial no. AD255 Vb, 401 Squadron) crash landed at Blue Bell Hill (www.spitfires.uk.net).

6. Or *Andreds-Wald*, or, by the Britons, *Coit-Andred* (the Forest of Andred). The words *Weald* and *Coit* are from the Saxon and Celtic for 'woody country' or forest. According to Lambarde, the early Weald was a wilderness '... not planted with Townes, or peopled with men, as the outsides of the shyre were, but stored and stuffed with heards of Deere, and droves of Hogs only.' (William Coles Finch, *In Kentish Pilgrim Land—Its Ancient Roads and Shrines* (The C.W. Daniel Company, London, 1927), pp. 53–55; William Lambarde, *A Perambulation of Kent* (written 1570; published 1576), this edition published by Baldwin, Cradock and Joy (London, 1826), pp. 189–191).

7. Established in 1998, the stone (the brainchild of author Nigel Nicolson) is located on the bank of the Medway opposite Snodland Church, and accessible via a track beside the disused Church of St Mary the Virgin, Burham. The inscription reads: 'This stone commemorates the battle of the Medway, AD 43, when a Roman army crossed the river and defeated the British tribes under Caractacus.'

8. Bede (St. Bede, *Beda Venerabilis* or the Venerable Bede), was a Northumbrian monk and author of the *Historia ecclesiastica gentis Anglorum* (*The Ecclesiastical History of the English People*, completed in AD 731), which was to earn him the title 'The Father of English History'. The site of Horsa's burial place has traditionally been associated with Horsted, a mile north of Blue Bell Hill, which Lambarde rendered as the 'Place of Horsa' (Lambarde *op.cit.*, p. 327). Horsa's burial here after the battle of AD 455, alas, is a tradition that appears to extend back no earlier than the 16th century, and is based on the said discovery of large stones or a mound of cairns here (Coles-Finch *op.cit.*, pp. 33–34).

Lambarde provides an alternative site for Horsa's burial: *Horsmundene* (Horsmonden), 10 miles south of Aylesford, which he interprets in the Saxon script as 'Valley of the monument (or memoriall) of Horsa' (Lambarde *op.cit.*, p. 327).

9. Also *Ægelesford* or *Aegels-threp* (*The Anglo-Saxon Chronicle*). According to Nennius, the 9th century Welsh monk and author of the *Historia Brittonum*, the Britons called it *Sathenegabai*, and the Saxons, *Episford* (or *Elesford* (Domesday Book), and later, *Aillesford* or *Ailesford* (Camden and Leland), *Ailesforde* or *Angleford* (Lambarde). (Charles Knight, *The English Cyclopædia* (Vol. 1, London: Bradbury & Evans, 1854), p. 764).

10. Coles Finch *op.cit.*, p. 297. According to the Megalithic Portal (www.megalithic.co.uk), the first time Kent was linked with the white horse emblem was in Richard Verstegan's *A Restitution of Decayed Intelligence in Antiquities, concerning the most noble and renowned English Nation* (Antwerp 1605; London 1634), in which he describes Hengist's and Horsa's landing with a banner depicting a white horse. A woodcut in the book (p.117) depicts the rampant white horse that was later adopted for Kent's own emblem ('Invicta'). 'However,

armorial emblems were not used until the 12th century, so it is highly unlikely that there is any validity in the link between the white horse emblem and the Saxons.'

11. Coles Finch *op.cit.,* pp. 298–299. See also: *Murray's Handbook for Travellers in Kent and Sussex* (3rd edition, London: John Murray, 1868), p. 183. This latter reference states the boulder to have been located 'on the top of the hill'.

12. Josiah Colebrooke, *An Account of the Monument commonly ascribed to Catigern* (Read at the Society of Antiquaries, June 12, 1766) (in *Archaeologia*, Vol. 2, 1773), p. 107.

13. The earliest writers covering this period, and whose work has informed all later commentators, are Gildas, Bede, and Nennius. The earliest source is Gildas's *De Excidio et Conquestu Britanniae (Of the Ruin and Conquest of Britain)*, written in the mid-6th century. Gildas (c.AD 500-570) is the only near contemporary of the events described, but is scant on detail. Bede, writing around AD 731, is regarded as the most trustworthy of the three sources; whereas Nennius—the first to give the name Arthur to a heroic British king—has been described, in the words of Gerhard Helm in his book *The Celts*, as 'unrestrainedly inventive.' Later commentators have come to doubt the literal existence of some of the principal participants of this period. 'Hengist' (*Hengist*) and 'Horsa' (*Ross*) for instance, are said to be the Teutonic names for stallion and horse (Coles Finch *op.cit.,* pp. 32–33)—the inference being that these are mythical personages invented as founding figures with alliterative names like Romulus and Remus, in order to glorify the lineages of later Kentish kings (Anglo–Saxons.net).

14. See 9.

15. One of the possible origins for the name given by Lambarde (Lambarde *op.cit.*, p. 368).

16. Historical sources differ over the reason the Saxons first came into Kent, some stating that were invited (as a mercenary force) by Vortigern, the British King (Gildas, Bede); others that they arrived opportunely, possibly as exiles (Nennius). Whichever the case, the first wave of ships arrived in AD 449 (*Anglo-Saxon Chronicle*) or AD 450, landed at Ebbsfleet, on the Isle of Thanet, at the eastern shore of the former Wantsum channel, which then separated it from the rest of Kent. (Sharon Turner, *The History of the Anglo-Saxons* (Vol. 1 (7th ed.), London: Longman et al, 1852), p. 219; Revd Francis Thackeray, *Researches into the Ecclesiastical and Political State of Ancient Britain under the Roman Emperors* (Vol. 2, London: Thomas Cadell, 1843).

17. David Hume, *The History of England*, Vol. 1 (Dublin: United Company of Book-Sellers, 1775, p. 17.).

18. *Dolmen* and *Cromlech* are interchangeable terms to describe prehistoric 'portal' tombs consisting of three or more upright megaliths capped by a large flat horizontal stone.

19. *The Bristol Magazine*, Vol. I. (Sept. 1857–June 1858) (London: Simpkin, Marshall, & Co.), p. 253.

20. *The Diary of Samuel Pepys*, 1669 (The Project Gutenberg EBook #4199; www.gutenberg.org); Coles Finch, *op.cit.*, p. 297.

21. Dickens himself makes mention of 'Kits Coty House' on Bluebell Hill in his *A Child's History of England* (Boston: Hickling, Swan & Brown, 1856). (See Chapter 1—*Ancient England and the Romans*, p. 18.).

22. William R. Hughes, *A Week's Tramp in Dickens-Land* (London: Chapman & Hall, 1891), p. 310.

23. Various sources (*The National Review*, Vol. 15., p. 539; *The Living Age,* Vol. 186, p. 163 (both 1890)); Percy Fitzgerald, *The Life of Charles Dickens* (*as revealed in his writings*), Vol. 1. (London: Chatto & Windus, 1905), p. 118. 'The Lower Bell Inn, where they were suspected of having stolen the horse, is minutely described, with its 'signpost in front, one or two deformed haystacks behind, kitchen-garden at the side, and rotten sheds and mouldering outhouses, jumbled in strange confusion, all about it.' It is a nice idea that the

Lower Bell and Blue Bell Hill should be immortalised in a Dickens tale, but it has to be said that other candidates have been offered for the identity of the inn in the *Posthumous Papers of The Pickwick Club* (to give it its full original title), including The Falstaff Inn, at Gad's Hill, Higham; and The Running Horse at Sandling, near Maidstone (now a Harvester restaurant). Maidstone itself is commonly taken to be the Muggleton of *Pickwick*.

24. Similar constructions to Kit's Coty House are found as far afield as Cornwall, Carnac (Brittany) and the Middle East. Estimates vary as to when Kit's Coty House and the other members of the eastern group of the 'Medway Megaliths', were constructed. The English Heritage sign at Kit's Coty itself gives the period 3000–2800 BC. Other sources push the date back to between 4300 BC and 3000 BC. Stonehenge dates from around 3100 BC.

Excavations carried out along the route of the Channel Tunnel rail link, which began in October 1998 have yielded numerous archaeological finds. At Blue Bell Hill, near the entrance of the North Downs Tunnel, the site of a rare Neolithic longhouse was discovered (October 1998), dated to between 4000 and 2000 BC. The find, originally a building of wood and wattle, is thought to be the oldest example in the country, and almost certainly connected with the ancient monuments in the area ('Stone Age house on link route', *Kent Messenger*, 16 October 1998, p. 3; 'Anger over block on ancient site', *KM Extra (Ma)*, 11 December 1998, p. 24; 'Lining up a few surprises', by Alan Watkins, *Kent Messenger*, 19 November 1999, p. 46.)

The same area, but around 200 metres south and east of the Neolithic longhouse site, on the higher ground of a chalk spur at the extremity of Westfield Wood (near to the White Horse Stone), has given up a Late Bronze Age / Early Iron Age settlement. In addition to post holes of the buildings, a number of deep pits were discovered (presumed to have originally been for corn storage, but later filled with pottery and animal bones). Two of the pits contained human burials, and another contained a cremation deposit, in which were found a collection of pots (one full of grain) and iron artefacts (early Iron Age). The site also yielded evidence for metal working in the form of furnace bases and pits of slag. The excavation was carried out by the Oxford Archaeological Unit. (*White Horse Stone: A Neolithic Longhouse*, Current Archaeology, No. 168, Vol. XIV No.12, May 2000, pp. 450–453).

25. In 1885, Kit's Coty House was one of the first sites in Britain to become a Scheduled Ancient Monument. The iron railings, installed at the suggestion of Augustus Pitt Rivers, were added a few years afterward for its protection. The monument is today under the care of English Heritage.

26. Stukeley's sketch, 'A Prospect of the Country from Kit's Coty house' (dated 15 October 1722), showing its remnant barrow and the now-lost General's Tomb, appears in his *Itinerarium Curiosum* (1724). See also Coles Finch, *op.cit.*, p. 289). A University of Birmingham excavation of the mound in July 2011 (part of the 5-year Medway Valley Prehistoric Landscapes Project (2008–2012)), led by Dr Paul Garwood, found no evidence of a peristalith (kerb perimeter), and questioned whether the mound itself would have reach the height of the capstone.

27. Kit's Coty House has been variously rendered over the centuries, from the *Cit's Cotihouse* of Stow, to *Citscote house* or *Citscotehouse* (Lambarde), Keith-Coty-house (Camden), *Kits-Cotehouse* (Phillpot), and later as Kets *Coity* House *(Grose)*; *Kits Cotty-House* (Harris), *Kit's Cotty House* (Pegge), *Kits-Cotty House* (Wright) and finally *Kits Coty-house* (Rudge) and *Kits Coty House* (Wright (again)). A writer for *The Mirror* made this statement in 1825: 'The name of Kits Coty House baffles all research and ingenuity to discover the real title from this vulgar corruption.' (*The Mirror of Literature, Amusement, and Instruction*, Vol. 5, (London: J. Limbird, 1825), p. 41).

28. 'Kit' being a common (Elizabethan) contraction of Christopher before 'Chris' became popular (Thomas Dyche, William Pardon, *A New General English Dictionary* (London: C & R Ware, 1768); Josiah Colebrooke, *op.cit.*, p. 114; *The Kentish Coronal*, by H.G. Adams (ed.) (London: Simpkin & Marshall, 1841, p. 177); Edward Rudge, in *The Gentlemen's Magazine*, Vol. XCIV, Part 1, by Sylvanus Urban (London: John Nichols and Son, 1825, p. 125); Samuel Pegge, *Observations on Kit's Cotty House, in Kent*, *Archaeologia*, Vol. IV (1777), p. 112.

Rodney Castleden refers to Kit's Coty as the 'Hut of St Christopher', 'presumably because it stands above what was an important fording-place.' (Rodney Castleden, *Neolithic Britain* (Routledge, 1992), p. 134). It is possible the Christopher reference is so derived, as Kit's Coty overlooks Aylesford and Snodland, both important fords over the Medway on the Pilgrims' route from Winchester to Canterbury. The Pilgrims' Way hugs the foot of the North Downs below Blue Bell Hill.

29. The early antiquarians, John Stow (c.1525–1605), William Lambarde (1536–1601), and William Camden (1551–1623) promulgated the idea that Kit's Coty was raised as a monument over Catigern's burial place. By the 18th century, Kit's Coty's name was being interpreted as derived from Catigern's, as in the works of Edward Hasted (1732–1812) and Francis Grose (1731–1791), who continued to popularise the tradition of Catigern's burial here.

30. Thomas Wright, *Wanderings of an Antiquary* (London: J. B. Nichols and sons, 1854), p. 175. Wright mentions the finding of 'fragments of rude pottery' beneath Kit's Coty House, but it is clear that this is a discovery not made by Wright himself, as sometimes reported.

31. Lambarde, *op.cit.*

32. Taken from the *Story of 'Kit's Coty House'* (George Clinch), Aylesford, Kent (printed and published by R.E. Thomas & Co., London, 1907)).

33. *The Penny Cyclopaedia*, Vol. III (London: Charles Knight, 1835), p. 192.

34. From *coeten* in the Celtic languages of Wales and Cornwall (William Spurrell, *An English-Welsh Pronouncing Dictionary* (Carmarthen & London, 1850), p. 58. To see 'a coit's cast' in context, see *The Penny Cyclopaedia*, Vol. III, *op.cit.*, p. 192. According to Borlase's *Cornish Vocabulary*, a Quoit or *Koeten* is 'a broad thin stone.' The term has also been applied to the monument as a whole, as in 'Koeten-Arthur' (Quoits of Arthur), a term applied to cromlechs or dolmens in Wales and Cornwall.

35. *Murray's Handbook for Travellers in Kent and Sussex* (London: John Murray, 1858), p. 77. 'Kitt's Hill' is Kit Hill, near Callington, the highest point (334m) of Hingston Down, preserves Neolithic and Bronze Age barrows. Kite's House has been more difficult to locate.

36. Aubrey L. Parke, *The Folklore of Sixpenny Handley, Dorset*, Part I, Folklore, Vol. 74, No.3. (Autumn 1963), pp. 481–487. Variations on the story, found in Edith Olivier and Margaret K S Edwards' (*eds.*) *Moonrakings: a little book of Wiltshire Stories* (Warminster: Coates & Parker, 1930), suggest the site, at meeting point of three parishes, is named after a female suicide, either a young woman or an old gypsy woman who drowned herself in a well near the churchyard, the lane beside it being known as 'Skit's Lane'. The old woman was buried at the crossroads at night with a stake through her heart.

37. Jabez Allies, *On the Ancient British, Roman, and Saxon Antiquities and Folk-Lore of Worcestershire* (London: J. H. Parker, 1852), pp. 242–243; John Dudley, *Naology: or A Treatise on the Origin, Progress, and Symbological Import of the Sacred Structures of the Most Eminent Nations and Ages of the World* (London: F. and J. Rivington, 1846), p. 274.

38. For instance, Drizzlecombe Kist, Roundy Hill Kist, and Grim's Grave on Dartmoor.

39. Known also as the Warren Farm Chamber. *Round About Kits Coty House: An Essay in Popular Topography* (London: Bell & Daldy, 1861), p. 100 (Author anon—attributed to Alfred Pryer); William Coles Finch, *op.cit.*, p. 293 & p. 297; Rodney Castleden, *op.cit.*, p. 134.

40. Variously rendered *coit* and *coeten*. (See also 34.). Revd John Bannister, *A Glossary of Cornish Names* (Truro: James R. Netherton, 1869), p. 78; William Spurrell, *op.cit.*, p. 58; Jonathan Forbes-Leslie, *The Early Races of Scotland and their Monuments*, Vol. I (Edinburgh: Edmonston and Douglas, 1866), p. 188.

41. William Cartwright (1611–1643), dramatist and playwright. *The Ordinary* (c.1635) is reprinted in Robert Dodsley's *Old Plays* (Vol. 10) (London: J. Dodsley, 1780), p. 265.

42. Rev. Samuel Lysons, *Our British Ancestors* (Oxford and London: John Henry and James Parker, 1865), p. 197; *Transactions of the Philological Society, 1868–9* (London: Asher & Co.), p. 156; *The Gentleman's Magazine,* (ed. Sylvanus Urban), October 1784, Vol. 54 (London: John Nichols, 1784, p. 768); Revd John Bannister, *op.cit.*, p. 33.

43. As preserved in place names such as *Bettws y Coed* in Snowdonia. One source (*Murray's Handbook for Travellers in Kent and Sussex, op.cit.*, p. 182), gives the interpretation the 'Tomb in the Woods' to Kit's Coty (from the term *Kêd-coit*, where the Celtic word *kêd* in this case is said to mean 'a hollow', conceivably taken as 'hollow-stone', i.e. a tomb).

Another claimed (although spuriously connected) origin of the name is found in the works of several 19th century writers who saw Kit as a corruption of Ket or Kêd, the preeminent female divinity of the early Celts, known also as Keridwen (or Ceridwen), the celebrated sorceress or goddess of Welsh medieval mythology. Accordingly, Kit's Coty House becomes the 'House of Ceridwen', a temple rather than merely a sepulchral monument. For these mythology-inspired authors, cromlechs were the 'halls of Ceridwen' described in the late medieval *Hanes Taliesin* (Tale of Taliesin). This in itself has been suggested as an allegorical death-and-rebirth poem that recounts arcane initiatory rites performed in the 'dark chambers of probation' within them by aspirants to the Druidic priesthood (see Edward Davies, *The Mythology and Rites of the British Druids* (London: J. Booth 1809, pp. 255–256).

44. *Proceedings of the Society of Antiquaries of Scotland* (Sessions 1860–1, 1861–2), Vol. 4 (Edinburgh: Neill and Company, 1863), pp. 157–8); Edward O'Reilly, *An Irish–English Dictionary* (Dublin: A. O'Neil, 1821), p. 9.

45. Revd Mr Whitaker, *The History of Manchester* (London: 1775), p. 38; Daniel H. Haigh, *The Conquest of Britain by the Saxons* (London: John Russell Smith, 1861), p. 285.

46. Thomas Wright, *op.cit.*, pp. 62–63; T. Eric Peet, *Rough Stone Monuments and Their Builders* (London: Harper & Brothers, 1912), p. 9. Examples from elsewhere include *Robin Hood's Ball*, a Neolithic causewayed enclosure on Salisbury Plain, near Amesbury, Wiltshire, (England).

47. Donald Maxwell, *Unknown Kent* (London: John Lane, 1921), p. 105.

48. John H. Evans, 'Notes on the Folklore and Legends Associated with the Kentish Megaliths', *Folklore*, Vol. 57, No.1 (March 1946), pp. 36–43.

'The Witches' Stone …' was reviewed in the *Theatrical Times*, No. 99, of 25 March 1848: 'On the road between Maidstone and Rochester the traveller will see a curious antiquarian remain known as Kit's Cot House, this is the subject of various traditions, one of which has served for the ground work of a very interesting drama which has been produced here with considerable effect, it is called the 'The Witches' Stone, or the Battle of Blue Bell Hill.' The piece was very well put on the stage and played excellently. Mr. Melville, Mr. Young, and Miss Palmer particularly distinguishing themselves.' (*Theatrical Times*, Vol.III (London: S. Grieves, Jan–Sept. 1848), p. 104. The last performance at this theatre was on 11 March 1884. The Theatre Royal buildings are now incorporated into the Royal Function Rooms, Star Hill, Rochester.

49. Frederick Evans and HJ Anderson, *Kit's Coty. A Musical Fairy Play (In Three Acts)* (London: Lincoln Williams, 1932). I have found no evidence to suggest the play was performed publicly. Later still, Kit's Coty would feature in the finale of the popular children's book, *Stig of the Dump*, by Clive King (Puffin Books, first published 1963). While unnamed, the stones described can only be Kit's Coty House.

50. Thomas Wright, *op.cit.*, p. 63.

51. John H. Evans, *op.cit.*, p. 39. Another tradition related to Kit's Coty House by Evans is that if a person climbs on to the capstone at full moon, and places a hand into a natural cavity in the stone, they will find five iron nails (the number to secure a horseshoe). Evans notes that a similar, more fully preserved tradition is associated with Wayland the Smith's Forge (Wayland's Smithy) in Berkshire.

Further examples include the idea that Kit's Coty House cannot be measured, since the surveyor forgets the values before they can be written down (Evans, *op.cit.*); and that water contained in a hollow on the top of the capstone never dries up (EHW Dunkin, in *Notes and Queries*, Oxford University Press, January 8, 1870, p. 32) or refills as soon as it is ladled out (William White, in *Notes and Queries*, Oxford University Press, Vol. 60, July 26, 1879, p. 66).

52. Robin Hood Farm is indicated on pre-1900 Ordnance Survey maps, but is detailed as Robin Hood House on later maps.

53. John H. Evans, *op.cit.*, p. 38. The collapsed state of the Lower Kit's Coty stones has been attributed to excavation by would-be treasure-hunters and to exploitation by the landowner, who intended to send them to pave the garrison at Sheerness at the beginning of the 17th century. (Eneas Sweetland Dallas, *Once a Week,* Vol. XIII (London: Bradbury & Evans, June–Dec. 1865, p. 418. The tradition of the baker of Aylesford is recounted in Coles Finch, *op.cit.*, pp. 296–297.

54. 'Ghost riddle of 'injured girl'', *Evening Post*, 15 July 1974, fp.

55. Thomas Wright, *The Celt, the Roman, and the Saxon, op.cit.*, p. 64; *Round About Kits Coty House: An Essay in Popular Topography* (London: Bell and Daldy; Maidstone: C. J. Cooke, 1861), p. 99. While anonymously penned, it has been supposed that the latter is the work of Alfred Pryer (Coles Finch, *op.cit.*, p. 280).

56. Coles Finch, *ibid*, p. 28.

57. *The Archaeological Journal*, Vol. I, published by The British Archaeological Association (London: Longman, Brown, Green, and Longman, 1845), pp. 263–264. The pit at Ryarsh, which was 20 feet in depth, opened into a chamber cut into the chalk. (Thomas Wright, *Wanderings of an Antiquary*, *op.cit.*, pp. 175–8).

58. James Fergusson, *Rude Stone Monuments* (London: John Murray, 1872), p.117; Coles Finch, *op.cit.*, p. 295.

59. John Stow, accompanied by William Lambarde and two others, described his impressions of Kit's Coty House and the General's Tomb during a visit to Blue Bell Hill on 4 September 1590: 'And about one quoyts cast from this monument [Kit's Coty] lyethe one othar very greate stone, moche part therof in the erthe.' (Quoted in *Stow and the Contemporary Antiquarian Network*, by Oliver D. Harris (in Ian Gadd and Alexandra Gillespie (eds), *John Stow (1525–1605) and the Making of the English Past* (London: British Library, 2004), pp. 27–35. According to Josiah Colebrooke *(Archaeologia*, Vol. 2, 1773, p. 115), the General's Tomb lay around 70 paces north-west of Kit's Coty House and measured approximately 11 ft by 7 ft.

60. Coles Finch, *op.cit.*, p. 301.

61. Tottington is found in the Domesday Book as *Tot-in-tune* (the Field of Mercury) (Coles Finch, *ibid*, p. 299, referencing John Thorpe's *Custumale Roffense*, p.67). Tot, said to represent the Celtic god Teutates (equated with the Egyptian Thoth, the Greek Hermes, and the Roman Mercury), who stood as a guide over the hills and track ways (Jabez Allies, *op.cit.*, p. 234.

62. Coles Finch, *op.cit.*, p. 35, p. 163 (map), ps. 164, 279 & 287. According to Coles Finch (p. 164): 'This is the local name for the huge sarsens or Druid sandstones which abound here, the name being derived from the resemblance of the stones to a scattered flock of wether sheep.' The same term and comparison in relation to megalithic sites is found in various parts of the UK.

63. Edward King, *Munimenta Antiqua* (G. Nicol, bookseller to His Majesty, 1799, Vol.1, Chapter 5, p. 210 (taken from the *Story of 'Kit's Coty House'* (George Clinch), Aylesford, Kent (printed and published by R.E. Thomas & Co., London, 1907)).

64. Paul Devereux, *Places of Power* (Blandford, 1990), pp. 154–155; p. 142. The wispy 'spirit' mists sometimes captured on camera by enthusiasts are in fact easily reproducible,

being attributable to exhaled breath (unintentionally or otherwise) illuminated by the camera flash in cool conditions.

65. 'Flashing lights above field, then crop circles appeared', by Helen Greener, *Kent Messenger* (Maidstone), 10 August 2005, p. 41. The crop circle pictured in the article appears poorly made, and may have been there prior to the appearance of the lights. Crop circles have been recorded below and in the vicinity of Blue Bell Hill since at least 2003.

66. Devereux, *op.cit.*, pp. 190–192.

67. Coldrum is Kent's best preserved long barrow. While absent of its capstone, Coldrum's rectangular mound and peristalith (stone revetment kerb) are still largely intact. See also 23.

68. See Devereux, *op.cit.*, p. 37. The alignment detailed here takes in Trosley Church, west of Coldrum (whose Saxon foundations are said to incorporate megaliths), Snodland Church and Burham St. Mary's. A different alignment was indicated by the observations of surveyor and historian Doug Chapman in 2007. Mr Chapman, the owner of the former church at Dode, near Snodland, plotted a ley alignment from Dode through the Coffin Stone and Little Kit's Coty, and on through Boxley Church and Thurnham Church. The line follows the NW–SE trend of the North Downs, so may be an artifact of that alone ('Surveyor could have a line on ancient history', by Nathan Rao, *Kent Messenger*, Friday 4 May 2007, p. 14).

69. *The Archaeological Journal*, Vol. I, *op.cit.*, pp. 263–4); Thomas Wright, *The Celt, the Roman, and the Saxon, op.cit.*, p. 64; The chalk hills above Ryarsh and Trottiscliffe, which form the western continuation of the North Downs across the Medway valley west of Blue Bell Hill, were referred to by Wright as the White Horse Hill. Today, a White Horse Road hugs the ridge 2 km north of Ryarsh.

70. Thomas Wright, *The Celt, the Roman, and the Saxon, ibid*, p. 61.

71. Alfred Watkins, *The Old Straight Track* (Abacus, 1993 reprint), pp. 165-166. To this we can add a Blue Bell Hill in Huddersfield, and in Nottingham. See also the earlier work (1852) of Jabez Allies *op.cit.*, pp. 232–6. *A Fourth Kentish Patchwork, 'Hunting, Shooting and Fishing'* (p. 49.), by Robert H. Goodsall, refers to the capture of a marten cat at *Upper Blue Bell* reported in a Maidstone journal of 2 February 1802.

72. Alfred Watkins, *ibid*; Charles Dickens, 'Beltane, or May-Day', No.477, May 14, 1859) in *Household Words*, Vol. XIX (London: Ward et al, 1858), pp. 557–561. Patricia Monaghan's *The Encyclopedia of Celtic Mythology and Folklore* (Facts on File Library, 2004) indicates that connections with the Semitic god Ba'al have long been disproven, but Belenus and Belisama have been related to the bonfires of spring and the Beltane celebrations. On Beltane Eve, hearth fires were extinguished and relit from bonfires made on the nearest signal hill.

73. See 60 (for Coles Finch, *op.cit.*, p. 299.

74. Jabez Allies, *op.cit.,* p. 234. See also 60. (Like Kit's Coty House, cromlechs are often found at elevated locations affording views across hills, rivers or coastal districts (Thomas Wright, *The Celt, the Roman, and the Saxon* (London: Arthur Hall, Virtue & Co., 1861), p. 63).

75. 'Toot Hills', by Penny Drayton, *At the Edge* (www.indigogroup.co.uk). Or 'Tut' or 'Tutt', as in Tutt Hill, Westwell, Kent, where Bronze Age remains have been recovered ('Human remains from Tutt Hill, Westwell, Kent', by Annesofie Witkin, *CTRL Specialist Report Series 2006* (Channel Tunnel Rail Link / London and Continental Railways / Oxford Wessex Archaeology Joint Venture)).

76. 'Beacons and Coastal Defences' (www.somerset.gov.uk/archives).

77. 'A Carde of the Beacons, in Kent', Lambarde (2nd ed (1596)), *op.cit.*, (See 6.). A reproduction of Lambarde's map can be found in Nigel Pennick's and Paul Devereux's *Lines on the Landscape* (Robert Hale, London, 1989), Fig. 3.12 (p. 149).

78. J. M. Russell, *The History of Maidstone* (Maidstone: William S. Vivish; London: Simpkin, Marshall & Co., 1881), p. 373. See also: *The Morning Chronicle* (London), Monday, 3 October, 1803, issue 10723.

The late Edwina Kissick, in her book *A Steep High Hill: Blue Bell Hill Village* states this as having stood where the car park of the Blue Bell Hill picnic area is now located. It remained in existence until at least 1812 (Ms Kissick's source: *Maidstone Journal and Kentish Advertiser*, 5 May 1812). (*A Steep High Hill*, First Edition: Imagic Design, Chatham, April 1996; printed by Scarbutts Ltd, West Malling). (Second edition, April 2011, p. 110).

In 1841, a telegraph system from London to Dover was announced, which was designed to give early news of ship arrivals to their owners in London. Among the intermediate stations, all located at elevated points, was Blue Bell Hill (*The Times*, 26 Nov. 1841, p. 5). Signal lamps were also tested as a military communications device in the 1860s, when signals were flashed between Sheerness, Blue Bell Hill and Chatham (Capt. Schaw, R.E., 'On Military Telegraphs', *Papers On Subjects Connected With The Duties of the Corps of Royal Engineers*, Vol. XI (Woolwich: W.P. Jackson, 1862), pp. 111–124.

79. Paul Devereux, Robert Forrest, 'Straight lines on an ancient landscape', *New Scientist*, Vol. 96, 23/30 December, 1982, pp. 822–826.

80. Raven Grimassi, *Beltane: Springtime Rituals, Lore & Celebration* (Llewellyn, 2001), p. 5. Belenus was said to be a god of the Continental Celts. Dickens (*op.cit.*, p. 557) states Bel or Belis to be one of the names for the sun in Gaul.

81. Dickens, *op.cit.*, p. 557.

82. *Ibid*, p. 558.

83. Patricia Monaghan *op.cit.*, p. 41; Francis Lieber (ed.), *Encyclopædia Americana*, Vol. XIII (Philadelphia: Thomas, Cowperthwaite & Co., 1838), p.60; *The European Magazine*, and *London Review*, Vol. 80 (July-Dec. (London, 1821) (October 1821 edition) p. 314.

84. Patricia Monaghan, *ibid*, p.42.

85. The May Queen and her attendants were traditionally dressed in white, and crowned with garlands of flowers. The Queen was the living representation of *Flora*, the Roman goddess of flowers, who was celebrated at the ancient May Day festival of *Ludi Florales* (28 April to 3 May). In the 16th century, it was still customary for ordinary folk 'to go a-Maying', whereby wild flowers and Hawthorn branches were collected at dawn on May Day to decorate home and village in merriment and celebration at the return of summer. (R. Chambers (ed.), *The Book of Days*, Vol. 1 (Edinburgh: W & R Chambers, 1864). p. 571.

86. Allen W. Wright, Robin Hood Tales (website), *No. 125: Robin Hood and Little John*, from *The English and Scottish Popular Ballads,* Vol. III, by Francis James Child).

For other sources for the Robin Hood games, see: R. Chambers (ed.), *The Book of Days, op.cit.*, p. 580 & p. 573 (May Day customs); George Ritchie Kinloch, *Ancient Scottish Ballads* (London: Longman et al, 1827), pp. 65–68; P. Hume Brown, *Scotland in the Time of Queen Mary* (London: Methuen & Co., 1904), pp. 165–166; Stephen Knight, 'Robin Hood: The Earliest Contexts', in *Images of Robin Hood: Medieval to Modern*, Lois Potter, Joshua Calhoun (eds), (NJ: Associated University Press, 2008), pp. 2–34.

87. The 1:10,560 Ordnance Survey map of 1961 details the pub's name in full as *The Robin Hood and Little John.* It was certainly known as this in 1851 (see *Colburn's United Service Magazine*, Part III (London: Colburn & Co., 1851), p. 144). From 1964 onward, it is simply given as *The Robin Hood.* The current address notation is: Common Road, Chatham, Kent ME5 9RJ.

88. *Archæologia Cantiana*, Vol. LXV (1952) (Kent Archæological Society, 1953). See Miscellaneous Notes: 'Kentish Fairs and Prehistory', p. 196. The handbill, printed by J. Blake of Maidstone, included these other diversions: 'A chemise to run for by young ladies', 'A pound of tobacco to be smoked for'; 'A hot hasty pudding to be eat by boys, for a new hat.'

89. Alan McCrerie, *Knowing Aylesford* (Hadlow, Kent; published on the press of John Hilton, 1965).

90. The source for this is Frederick W. T. Sanders' *Psychical Research in Haunted Kent* (unpublished MS, written c. 1945–1946) held in the Private Collection at Medway Archives and Local Studies Centre, Strood, Kent. See 'The Third Investigation'. The story is recounted in Peter Underwood's *Ghosts of Kent* (Meresborough Books, 1987, p. 93. Credit to Neil Arnold for the find.

91. John Bell's nickname, 'Any Bird', is possibly accounted for by an alternative rendition that is given alongside the familiar appellation in the summary record of his trial and execution at the 1831 Summer Assizes (Kent): *John Henebar Bell*, which is phonetically similar (Henebar /Any Bird). (England & Wales, Criminal Registers, 1791–1892 (Class: HO 27; Piece: 41; p. 381) (National Archives / www.ancestry.co.uk).

92. See the entry for 29 July—'Singular Case. Murder. Maidstone', *The Annual Register* (for 1831) (London: Baldwin and Cradock, 1832), in *Chronicle* (section) for July, pp. 111–116, specifically p.113 for Henry Lewington's account. The *Blue Bell* is specifically mentioned as Lewington's destination in the *Maidstone Gazette and Kentish Courier*, 2 August 1831 ('Trial of John Any Bird Bell')—probably the most comprehensive account of John Bell's trial).

93. Bridge Woods, which then extended on both sides of the Nashenden Valley and the Rochester–Maidstone road (today's B2097), which runs along its northern side, was the scene of another murder—that of Emily Maria Trigg in August 1916 (see Chapter 10).

John Izard's (or Izzard's) testimony places the scene of his discovery in the wood on the north side of the Rochester–Maidstone road (*The Annual Register*, *op.cit.*, p. 113). A later source (A. Wells of Rochester, c. 1942) names the location as Delce Woods, an extension of Bridge Woods (Medway Local Studies, ref. DE53/1/58/5).

The site of the murder is given on a sketch map of 1831 in the *Gordon Ward Collection* (ref. U442/Z10) held at the Kent History and Library Centre, Maidstone. The site of Great Delce Woods is now occupied by Rochester aerodrome, which locates the two murders very close to one another, Emily Trigg's remains having been found in the undergrowth of Bridge Woods below the Rochester–Maidstone road. The map is reproduced in the *Maidstone Gazette and Kentish Courier* of 2 August 1831, *op.cit.*

94. Minor variances in the descriptions of the clothing found on the deceased are reported by the eyewitness accounts as compared to Taylor's father's, which chiefly differed in respect to the colour of the trousers ('blue', 'brown', or 'dark'). (*The Annual Register*, *op.cit.)* Probably the most reliable source, the *Maidstone Gazette and Kentish Courier* (2 August 1831, *op.cit.*, describes them as brown cloth trousers.

95. 'Summer Assizes. Maidstone, Friday, July 29', *The Times*, Saturday 30 July 1831; p. 4; 'Trial of John Any Bird Bell', *Maidstone Gazette and Kentish Courier*, Tuesday 2 August 1831. Henry Lewington's surname is rendered in some sources as 'Newington'; John Izard as 'Isard' or 'Izzard'; and Constable Tupp's as 'Tuff'. The arrest of the Bell brothers, given as 17 May by *The Times*, is stated as 19 May by the *Maidstone Gazette*. Chatham cage probably gives its name to Chatham's Cage Lane (now Upbury Way).

96. *Maidstone Gazette and Kentish Courier*, Tuesday 2 August 1831, *op.cit. The Times* (Saturday 30 July 1831, *op.cit.*) and derived sources attribute the idea to murder Richard Taylor to John Bell himself. I tend to trust the local source, demonstrably more detailed, as the more reliable.

97. At 14, John 'Any Bird' Bell was the youngest person to be executed at Maidstone, and the last ever child to be executed in Britain. For his crime, the heartless murder of Richard Taylor, whom he had lured into the woods on pretence of showing him a shortcut home), only to cut his throat for the 9 shillings he was carrying, the judge at the Maidstone Assizes pronounced the death sentence, and announced to the prisoner that his body would afterward be dissected, at which point 'he dropped a solitary tear.' (*The Times*, Saturday 30 July 1831, *op.cit.*; *The Annual Register*, *op.cit.*, 'Maidstone Prison' (www.kent-opc.org/Parishes/Court/Maidstoneprison.html); V.A.C. Gatrell, *The Hanging Tree: Execu-*

tion and the English People 1770–1868 (Oxford University Press, 1994).

Dissection was indeed his body's fate, and it was passed to military surgeons at Fort Pitt, Chatham, whose elaborately-named *Catalogue of Preparations in Morbid, Natural, and Comparative Anatomy contained in the Museum of the Army Medical Department* (London: Richard Taylor,* 1833) includes, under 'Casts' (plaster death masks), the following entry (no. 10) (p.236): 'Head of John Any Bird Bell, *aet.* 14, executed for Murder, at Maidstone, 1831—*Presented by Mr. Blythe, Assistant Surgeon, Royal Marines.*' (*in an ironic twist, the name of the murdered youth being the same).

The *Annual Register* for 1831 describes John Any Bird Bell's appearance thus: 'The prisoner was remarkably short in stature, but thick-set and strong built, with an almost infantine countenance, being of exceedingly fair complexion, rather sunburnt, and flaxen hair' (*The Annual Register 1831* (Chronicle (July 29, p.115), London: Baldwin and Cradock, 1832)).

John Bell's death mask was for a while exhibited at the Edinburgh Anatomy Museum (Edinburgh University) alongside the remains and impressions of the famous and infamous (M. H. Kaufman, Robert McNeil, 'Death masks and life masks at Edinburgh University', *British Medical Journal*, Vol. 298. 25 February 1989, pp. 506–507). It is currently in the care of the Scottish National Portrait Gallery's Granton Centre for Art in Edinburgh (Scotland's purpose-built store for paintings, drawings and sculptures from the national collection), where I had the privilege of a personal viewing on 12 December 2011. The mask (in reality, a complete cast of the head in plaster) confirms John Bell's youthful features: with a full face and a seemingly peaceful expression, his is truly the visage of a baby-faced killer. A sketch of John Bell can be found in Henry Smetham's *History of Strood* (Parrett and Neves, 1899), p. 333 (reproduced in this book, p. 62).

See also: 'The Murder Near Rochester', *The Morning Post* (London), Friday 27 May 1831; 'Murder Near Rochester' (From the *Maidstone Journal*), Jackson's Oxford Journal (Oxford), Saturday, 28 May 1831; 'Execution Of John Any Bird Bell, For Murder' (from the *Kent and Essex Mercury*), *The Times* (London), Tuesday 2 Aug 1831, p. 4; 'Execution of John Any Bird Bell, For Murder. Maidstone, Aug. 1, 12 o'clock', *The Standard* (London), Tuesday, 2 August 1831 (based on original articles in the *Maidstone Journal, The Kent and Essex Mercury,* and *The Kentish Gazette*).

98. Peter Underwood, *op.cit.*, p. 93.

99. 'I don't believe it myself, but local folk say...', by Ted Harrison, *Kent Messenger*, 26 March 1971, p. 8.

100. No sighting of either is known from record, but history does record that prior to the Battle of Maidstone on 1 June 1648, several thousand Royalist troops under the Earl of Norwich, were encamped 'on the bluff of the hill east of Kit's Coty House' (i.e. on Blue Bell Hill) in defence of the approach to Maidstone by Parliamentarian forces led by Sir Thomas Fairfax. When it came, Fairfax's attack on the smaller force at Maidstone came via the backdoor of East Farleigh and Barming, and reinforces despatched from the Royalist main force were sent too late to hold the town. (J. M. Russell, *The History of Maidstone, op.cit.*, pp. 58–59). Edwina Kissick (*op.cit.*, p. 116 (second edition, p. 111) states that musket balls from this period were found in Frith Wood (woodland on the eastern side of the old Roman road) in 1833.

101. A tale given some small measure of support from a supposedly true account by three male friends who were walking to Kits Coty at around midnight (said to be 21 June; year unspecified, but 'a good few years ago' (Nov. 2000) when a horseman appeared, travelling at speed and forcing them out of the way. The figure neither responded to them when they called after it, nor made any sound. The story, while anecdotal, has two named informants (withheld here) to back it up, one of whom was a personal friend of the witnesses.

102. Source: Mr and Mrs David Ashmore of Sittingbourne (23 Nov. 2013). At a family funeral, an elderly relative of Mrs Ashmore's, on hearing that she used to live in Rochester Road, said that he wouldn't live there as he had once seen a Roman army complete with chariots coming down the road there toward Aylesford. As an anecdote, the story

has limited value, but it is certainly a logical route for the Roman invaders under Vespasian to have taken, to cross the River Medway by the ford at Aylesford.

103. One of these, in fact, would in time crop up in the complex development of eyewitness accounts at Blue Bell Hill (see Chapter 11), indicating that any proposed solution(s) to the mystery would be far from straightforward.

104. *The Archaeological Journal*, *op.cit.*, p. 264. Wright interpreted his find as indicative of a destructive event associated with the Roman withdrawal from Britain. Finds reportedly made by the cottagers included Roman pottery and coins. On pre-1980s Ordnance Survey maps, the site is marked as a Roman Temple. Other references have referred to it as a shrine, or a villa. In respect of Wright's work, it seems more reasonable to suppose that the latter is more likely to be correct. The precise site of the villa is now uncertain; as it must lie perilously close to the edge of the chalk-cliff, on now-private property overlooking the entrance to Lower Warren Road and the A229. Finds of Roman tiles and pottery are still made in this area by today's residents.

105. Anno 1° Georgii II Cap. XII (1728): 'An Act for repairing and enlarging the Road leading from the House called the *Sign of the Bells* in the Parish of Saint *Margaret* in *Rochester* to *Maidstone*, and other Roads therein mentioned, in the County of *Kent*.' (*The Statutes at Large, of England and of Great-Britain*, Vol. IX. From I George II A.D. 1727 to 15 George II A.D. 1742. (London: George Eyre and Andrew Strahan, 1811), p. 35. The total length of the turnpiked road was 11 miles. Original records for the Rochester–Maidstone turnpike trust are held at the Centre for Kentish Studies, Maidstone (NRA 7551; Ref. T12).

106. A petition read in the House of Commons in 1773 on behalf of the trustees of the Rochester–Maidstone Turnpike Trust, raised again the poor state of the road, and requested an extension of the terms and powers to carry out repairs and enlargement of the road from Crow Lane, Rochester, to Maidstone—which sets an earliest date for the Blue Bell Hill section to the mid-1770s (*Journals of the House of Commons, op.cit.,* pp. 69–70. A later source (1839) states the new road was built—and the side of the hill 'much sloped' in 1800 (*Topography of Maidstone and its Environs* (Maidstone: J. Smith, 1839), p. 106). The new route appears on Mudge's one-inch map of Kent (1801), but not on Hasted's map of The Hundred of Rochester and Larkfield (in *The History and Topographical Survey of Kent*, published in 12 Volumes from 1797–1801).

107. Kissick (*op.cit.*, p. 6) inferred from historical sources that the road was diverted between 1782 and 1786.

108. 'An Entirely New & Accurate Survey Of The County Of Kent, With Part Of The County Of Essex 1801, by Captain William Mudge', for which the survey of north and west Kent was conducted in 1799. First published in 1801 by William Faden, and later (in 1819) as the first Ordnance Survey map (one inch to the mile). The Mudge Map gives the name 'Fright Wood' to what is now known as Frith Wood, immediately east of the haunted section of the A229 at Blue Bell Hill.

109. Kissick, *op.cit.*, Chapter 3 (Second ed., p. 24).

110. See for instance: *A New and Accurate Description of all the Direct and Principal Cross Roads in England and Wales* (15th ed.), by Lt.-Col. Paterson (London: Longman et al, 1811), p. 327 (reprinted as *Paterson's Roads* (16th ed.), by Edward Mogg (London, 1822), p. 9; William R. Hughes, *A Week's Tramp in Dickens-Land* (London: Chapman & Hall, 1891), p. 311; *A Handbook for Travellers in Kent and Sussex* (London: John Murray, 1858), p. 77 ('The Bell' (Lower Bell)).

111. See, for instance *The Whitehall Evening-Post* (*Or London Intelligencer*) for 5–7 July **1759**, which includes the following snippet: 'By the violent Lightning and Thunder which happened on Friday last, a Barn and Stable were burnt down by the Upper Blue Bell at Boxley Hill near Maidstone.' (Recounted also by *The London Chronicle*, Vol. 6 ('Upper Blue Bell' (see 17 July)); *Journals of the Hon. William Hervey, From 1755 to 1814* (Suffolk Green Books, No. XIV, (Bury St. Edmund's: Paul & Mathew, 1906), p. 252 (**1775**: 'Blue Bell' (the inn atop Boxley Hill); 1802: *The Sporting Magazine*, Vol. 19 (London, 1802), p. 293 (**1802**: 'Upper Blue Bell'); George M. Arnold, *Robert Pocock, the Gravesend Historian, Natural-*

ist, Antiquarian, Botanist, and Printer (London: Sampson Low, Marston, Searle, & Rivington, 1883), p.134 (**1822**: 'Upper Blue Bell'); *The Christian Miscellany, and Family Visiter (for the year 1848),* Vol. III (London: John Mason, 1848), p. 17 (**1848**: 'Blue-Bell inn'); *Round About Kits Coty House, op.cit.*, p. 60. (**1861**: 'Upper and Lower Blue Bell'); *Kirby's Wonderful and Eccentric Museum,* Vol. VI. (London: R.S. Kirby, 1820), p. 143 (**1816**: 'Old Upper Blue Bell'); The Annual Register (for the year 1816) (London: Baldwin, Cradock, and Joy *et al,* 1817), p.168 (**1816**: 'Old Upper Blue Bell').

The new Lower Bell inn is depicted in a drawing of 1828 (by George Sidney Shepherd (1784-1862)) of 'Kitts Cotty', which also includes another sometime inn, *The Kit's Coty House.* (W. H. Ireland, *A New and Complete History of the County of Kent,* Vol. III (London: G. Virtue, 1829), p. 557. Built within sight of the dolmen around 1812, and described in 1865 as a 'commodious roadside inn' (Eneas Sweetland Dallas, *op.cit.*, p. 418), the latter is now Kits Coty Brasserie (15 Old Chatham Road). The Lower Bell is described in 1852 as the 'Lower Blue Bell Inn' in an advertisement placed in the *South Eastern Gazette* (13 April 1852, fp) by new publican John Green.

The former Lower Bell inn, in Lower Warren Road is now a private residence; while both the old Upper Bell and new Upper Bell no longer exist.

112. See: *Topography of Maidstone and its Environs, op.cit.*, p. 106 (**1839**: 'Old Blue Bell Hill'); Sylvanus Urban, *The Gentleman's Magazine,* Vol. XXIII (January to June **1845** (London: J. B. Nichols and Son, 1845)). p. 184 ('the Blue Bell Hill'); *The Archaeological Journal,* Vol. I (**1845**), *op.cit.*, p. 263 ('the Blue Bell Hill'). Eneas Sweetland Dallas, *Once a Week, op.cit.*, p. 418 (**1865**: 'Blue-bell Hill'); Alfred Elwes, *Guy Rivers* (London: Griffith and Darran, 1862), p. 40. ('Blue Bell Hill').

113. References to Blue Bell Hill as *Boxley Hill* include: **1753**: *Index to the Additional Manuscripts preserved in the British Museum* (acquired in the years 1783-1835) (London, 1849). See: 'Swinhow (Dr Francis) p. 442. Letter to Dr. Ward concerning a pile of stones in the neighbourhood of Kit's Scot (Coity) House, Boxley Hill, 30 June, 1753. 6211. f. 113'; **1759**: The *London Chronicle,* Vol. 6., *op.cit*; **1775**: *Journals of the Hon. William Hervey, op.cit.,* p.252; **1797**: Edward Hasted, *The History and Topographical Survey of the County of Kent,* Vol.1 (Canterbury: W. Bristow, 1797), p. 58; **1784**: Francis Grose, *The Antiquities of England and Wales* (London: Hooper & Wigstead, 1784), p. 56; **1802**: *The Sporting Magazine,* Vol. 19, *op.cit.*, p. 293; **1802**: William Granger, *The New Wonderful Museum and Extraordinary Magazine,* Vol. 1 (Printed for R.S. Kirby, London: M. Allen, 1802), p. 448 (includes a depiction of Kit's Coty House). Advertisements for the auction of timber in **1804** and **1807** refer to 'the Upper Bell, Boxley Hill' (*Kentish Gazette,* 13 November 1804, p. 4; and 14 April 1807, p. 4. **1811** (& 1822): Edward Mogg, *Paterson's Roads, op.cit.*, (1811 edition, p.327; 1822 edition, p. 9.). Blue Bell Hill was sporadically referred to as Boxley Hill, for instance, in Rev. Arthur Hussey's *Notes on The Churches in Kent, Sussex and Surrey* (London: John Russell Smith, **1852**), p. 25; and *Baily's Magazine of sports and pastimes,* Vol. 34 (London: A. H. Baily & Co., 1879), p. 291 ('Boxley or Blue Bell Hill').

114. *Journals of the Hon. William Hervey, From 1755 to 1814* (Suffolk Green Books, No. XIV, (Bury St. Edmund's: Paul & Mathew, 1906), p. 252. Or the Hill was located simply by reference to the inns themselves, particularly the Upper Bell. In February 1833, land 'near to the Upper Bell, on the road to Rochester', was the venue for a bare-knuckle boxing match before a gathered crowd of around 2,000 (*Kentish Gazette,* 5 February 1833, p. 3).

115. For example, the *Bluebell Inn,* Farnah Green, Belper (Derbyshire); *The Blue Bell Inn,* Tissington (Derbyshire); *The Bluebell,* Gateshead (Tyne & Wear).

116. See also: *Ye Olde Blue Bell,* Preston; *Blue Bell Inn,* Tattershall Thorpe, Lincoln; *The Blue Bell Inn,* Arkendale, N. Yorkshire; *The Blue Bell Inn,* Dogsthorpe, Peterborough; *The Blue Bell Inn,* Tushingham, Cheshire, and numerous other inns named 'Blue Bell' or 'Bluebell'—which include *The Bluebell Inn* at Hempstead, Essex, which, in 1705, was the birthplace of John Palmer, *aka* Dick Turpin, the notorious highwayman.

117. Jacob Larwood and John Camden Hotten, *The History of Signboards* (London: Chatto & Windus, 1900).

118. Thomas Miller, *Rural Sketches* (London: John Van Voorst, 1839), p. 297. Among his round-up of 'sterling English names', Miller includes 'The Old Blue Bell'.

119. The most common colours found in combination with the most popular inn names were red, black, white, blue, gold, and green. Hence there are, for example, numerous Black, Red, White, and Brown Bears; and Red, Blue, Golden and White Lions.

120. For instance, *The Blue Boy Inn*, Clapton, Crewkerne, Somerset; *The Blue Boy Hotel,* Farnham, Surrey. The Blue Boy is interesting in light of references to the legendary Blue Boy ghost of Blue Bell Hill. Prior to the advent of the Mail Coach in the 18th century, post boys (in reality, diminutive men as well as youths) capable of fast-riding the mail horses carried the mail in relays between established Post inns. Post boys often wore coloured jackets, denoting the political leaning of the inn that employed them—blue for Tory, red or yellow for Liberal (*The Badminton magazine of sports and pastimes*, Vol. 8 (Longmans, Green and Co., 1899), pp. 384–5; Athol Mauslay, *Highways and Horses* (London: Chapman and Hall, 1888), p. 227. We might speculate that the Blue Boy could conceivably refer to a post boy.

121. George M. Arnold, *Robert Pocock, the Gravesend Historian, Naturalist, Antiquarian, Botanist, and Printer* (London: Sampson Low et al, 1883), p. 134. From the roof of the Upper Bell, Pocock he could see the road climbing up Shooter's Hill (Greenwich, London) (24 miles), and Brentwood, Essex (30 miles).

122. Emily Maria Trigg, 20, a quarryman's daughter, who lived at Blue Bell Hill, and was found murdered in Bridge Woods in September 1916 (see Chapter 10).

123. *London Journal*, Saturday 24 April 1725, Issue CCC.

124. *Mist's Weekly Journal* (London), Saturday 24 July 1725, Issue 13. See 'Maidstone, July 17'.

125. *Public Advertiser* (London), Friday 3 May 1776, Issue 14536. See 'Country News. Maidstone, April 26'; *Morning Chronicle and London Advertiser* (London), Friday 3 May 1776, Issue 2169.

126. 'Maidstone: The Thimble-Rig Gentry', *Kentish Mercury*, Saturday 3 May 1834, p. 3.

127. *Morning Post and Gazetteer* (London), Thursday, 16 August 1798, Issue 9238; *Bath Chronicle*, 23 August 1798. Other sources suggest that victim had been married for only four days (*True Briton* (London), Thursday, 16 August 1798; Issue 1762.

128. 'Dreadful Accident on Blue-Bell Hill', *West Kent Guardian,* 29 January 1848. Another butcher, a Mr Igglesden, also had a carting accident, with two friends, on Blue Bell Hill, 15 years previously (virtually to the day), on 20 January 1833. The party's horse took fright and ran down Blue Bell Hill, throwing them out. None were severely hurt (*Kentish Gazette*, 29 January 1833). A similar night-time death occurred in when drayman Ernest Addy, 26, on his way to Aylesford from Blue Bell Hill, died when his pair-horse van rode up the bank of a bend and overturned on him at the foot of the hill ('A Drayman's Sad Death: A Dangerous Corner on Blue Bell Hill'; *Kent & Sussex Courier*, 28 November 1902, p. 6.

Not surprisingly for a location where animal-drawn transport met sloping ground, records of accidents involving horse-drawn carriages fairly abound at Blue Bell Hill. Not all were fatal, but overturning or runaway carts were capable of inflicting every bit as much horrific injury or death as modern accidents. Another noteworthy example underlines the point, as well as providing another example of the synchronicities the historical record can throw up. On 9 September 1840, James Blake, a young gentleman who was proceeding from Maidstone to Rochester on the 'Wonder' omnibus, alighted from the carriage when it slowed on the ascent at Blue Bell Hill to walk up alongside. When he tried to reboard the moving carriage, he missed his footing and fell beneath a rear wheel, which badly lacerated his knees. He was carried to Rochester, but despite doing well for ten days, he contracted lock-jaw (tetanus) and died on 2 October (*Kentish Mercury*, 10 October 1840). Five years later, in 1845, another James Blake, a 3-year-old child was thrown from a cart and a wheel ran over his left arm. Likewise, his injury led to tetanus and he too died of it ('Death from lock-jaw', *Kentish Gazette*, 30 Septernber 1845, p.4).

As well as the Phantom Hitch-Hiker, other urban legends associated with the dangers of the road (which may well have originated with the fears instilled by the highway robberies of the 18th and 19th centuries) include 'The Hairy-Armed Hitch-Hiker', 'The Hatchet in the Handbag', and 'The Knife in the Briefcase'—all variants of the same premise.

129. *Kentish Gazette*, Friday 14 June 1793, p.4; *Sun* (London), Friday 21 June 1793, Issue 227. See 'Summer Circuit'; *Star* (London), Wednesday, 26 June 1793, Issue 1612.

130. *Kentish Gazette*, Friday 28 September 1810, p.4.

131. 'Curious Case of Sudden Death', *Maidstone Telegraph, Rochester and Chatham Gazette*, Saturday 19 February 1859 (in 'Local Intelligence'–Burham), p. 4.

132. *The Morning Chronicle* (London), Tuesday 15 October 1816, Issue 14806; *The Derby Mercury* (Derby), Thursday 17 October 1816, Issue 4406 (see 'Saturday and Sunday's Posts'); *Trewman's Exeter Flying Post* (Exeter), Thursday 17 October 1816, Issue 2667; *Royal Cornwall Gazette, Falmouth Packet & Plymouth Journal* (Truro), Saturday 19 October 1816, Issue 695. (All reports sourced from the *Kentish Gazette* ('Dreadful Circumstance'). The 11 days that Ann lay at the spot would refer to the period 16-26 September (which excludes the Sunday (15 Sept.) she first lay down and the Friday (27 Sept.) she was rescued). Death Indexes for England and Wales (1837–2005) for September 1873 record the death of one Ann Martin of Lewes, aged 80. If this is indeed the Ann Martin rescued on Blue Bell Hill, this would have made her 19 in 1816, a comparable age at the time to another tragic young female, 20-year-old Emily Trigg, whose murdered remains were discovered at Bridgewood almost precisely a 100 years later, on 21 September 1916 (See Chapter 10).

133. *The Morning Post* (London), Saturday, 20 October 1821, Issue 15787 (sourced from the *Maidstone Gazette*). Blue Bell Hill has proven to be quite a popular suicide spot over the years. In 1935, Frank Hanshaw (30), a male nurse from Chatham, who had been having an affair with an 18-year-old woman, shot himself dead 'in some tea rooms at Blue Bell Hill' ('Husband in Tragedy of Remorse', *Western Daily Press*, 13 February 1935, p. 8.); while in 1938, the second of two managers of the same Chatham shop, Frederick Butt (42) of Postley Road, Maidstone, was found dead in woods at Blue Bell Hill, just days after his predecessor had committed suicide in his car at Frindsbury ('Two Managers of Same Shop Found Dead', *Gloucestershire Echo*, 26 November 1938, fp.). In 1998, 60-year-old Barry Markham of Gravesend, who had been a long sufferer of depression, walked in front of a lorry at Blue Bell Hill (*Kent Messenger*, 13 November 1998, p.27).

134. 'Uphill work' (in 'Comment'), by Roy Plascott, *Kent Messenger*, 16 September 1966, p. 3.

135. 'Maidstone Comment', by Roy Plascott, *Kent Messenger*, 13 October 1967, p. 3.

136. 'Bluebell link-up' (in the 'Talk of the Town'), by Roy Plascott, *Kent Messenger*, 5 July 1968.

137. 'Snow wreaks its fury', by Andrew Moss and John Couzens, *Kent Messenger*, 6 March 1970, fp.

138. 'Black spot road plan: at last the go ahead', *Kent Messenger*, 20 February 1970, p. 4. Although Blue Bell Hill had been described as a 'black spot', formal recognition of the Maidstone–Chatham Road here as such applied to the junctions with Sandling Lane and Forstal Road at the base of the Hill, on the outskirts of Maidstone. In later years, the accident spotlight has focused on the 70 mph stretch of the A229 between Cossington service station and The Bluebells housing estate which had claimed (according to Alan Veitch, the farmer of the adjacent Great Cossington Farm) up to six lives since 1970, and over 40 serious accidents in total ('Road safety call after fatal crash', by Beth Mullins, *Kent Messenger*, 22 October 1993, p. 5). Of the 22 reported death crashes at Blue Bell Hill since 1990, six have occurred at this spot. While, however, the author's files record 39 deaths at Blue Bell Hill and Bridgewood between 1965 and 2017 (with 15 since 2000), considering the large daily volumes of traffic that use the A229, Blue Bell Hill is certainly not outstanding as far as death accidents are concerned.

139. 'Serving a jam free recipe for Blue Bell Hill', by Alan Bignell, *Evening Post*, 10 December 1970, p. 6.

140. 'Hill road opens ahead of time', *Kent Messenger*, 3 March 1972, p. 10.

141. See Epilogue notes (6.).

142. 'Now girl dies on hill of fear', *Kent Messenger*, 5 November, 1971, fp. Christine Spencer, of Benenden Road, Frindsbury, died in West Kent Hospital, Maidstone. The driver of the van, Paul Larkin, of Columbine Road, Strood suffered a broken arm and leg and cuts.

143. Roger Pen, *Portrait of the River Medway* (Robert Hale, London, 1981), p. 143.

144. 'Lights all the way to Chatham', *Maidstone Star*, 23 November 1989.

Chapter Three: Early Days

1. A girl in her early teens—a little too young to be getting married?

2. Goss, *op.cit.*, pp. 12–13 (Coronet edition 2015, pp. 2-3).

3. *Ibid.*

4. The southern half of Week Street was converted into a pedestrian precinct in 1970.

5. On 2 February 2011, 'NigelH' posted the following anecdote on the forum pages of the S.P.I.R.I.T Norwich website (topic: 'Road Ghost-Bluebell Hill, Maidstone, Kent'): 'Before moving to Norfolk, my family lived in Kent. My dad was an ambulance driver back then. One night, he was returning back to the station after attending a call. In the ambulance with him was his crewmate Don. It was quite late, about 1.00-1.30 a.m. They were driving up Bluebell Hill, when they saw a lady stood at the side of the road waving them down. It was pouring with rain, and the lady looked distressed. They pulled over, and Don wound the window down, and shouted to the lady. They decided to check her over, and take her into Maidstone. Don got out to open the side door, so the lady could get into the ambulance. When he turned to ask her to get in, she had gone.' The date of the encounter is not given, but we may speculate that the incident may have been one of Tom Harber's lost witness accounts, the one involving 'an ambulanceman'. Unfortunately no further information was forthcoming from correspondence.

6. Michael Goss, *op.cit.*, p. 102 (Coronet edition 2015, p. 92).

7. 'Maidstone Comment', by Roy Plascott, *Kent Messenger*, 8 December 1967, p. 3; 'Hitch-hiking spirit' ('Talk of the Town'), by Roy Plascott, *Kent Messenger*, 10 May 1968, p. 3; 'Riddle of the phantom girl', *Evening Post*, 9 September 1968, p. 3.

8. 'Have you met the ghostly hitch-hiker?', *The Gazette* (Maidstone), 10 September 1968, p. 3.

9. *Ibid.*

10. A figure that would increase to 14 by 1974 ('Spectre of Bluebell Hill', by Nigel Nelson, *Kent Messenger*, 26 July 1974, p. 8).

11. Goss, *op.cit.*, p. 120 (Coronet edition 2015, p. 106).

12. *Ibid.*, p. 107.

13. A situation that circumstances changed with the widespread public naming of the victims of the 1965 crash following the renewed phase of appearances in November 1992 and the subsequent correspondence I received from relatives of Judith Lingham, which, I decided, necessitated setting the record straight with regard to the 1965 tragedy (see Chapters 7, 8, and 9).

14. The 'Rochester Girl', usually associated with Judith Lingham, but also possibly identified with another tragically slain young woman, Emily Trigg, a candidate from the beginning of the 20th century (see Chapter 10).

15. There was never any intention, when I began my research, to try to contact any of the relatives of the deceased. Eventually I would talk to some of them—Judith's sisters—but only after I had first been approached. Later I would have opportunity also of talking with the groom, and the bride-to-be's brother in Australia.

16. 'Maidstone Comment', by Roy Plascott, *Kent Messenger*, 8 December 1967, p. 3.

17. Goss, *op.cit*, p. 108.

18. Or Gillingham or Rochester.

19. An observation made by author Joan Forman in her *The Haunted South* ((first published in Great Britain by Robert Hale Ltd, 1978); Jarrold Colour Publications, 1989), p. 17, and referred to by Goss (p. 108).

20. There have been four Maidstone-based researchers who have more than cursorily investigated the Blue Bell Hill case. These are: Tom Harber, Dennis Chambers, ASSAP's David Thomas, and of course, myself.

21. The car was, in fact, heading south towards Maidstone (see Chapter 8).

22. The bride-to-be was not from Maidstone, but *was* staying in Gillingham just prior to the wedding (see Chapter 8). However, the fact that she was staying in Gillingham and heading towards Maidstone on the night of the accident satisfies this interpretation just as well.

23. The Electoral Register entry for this period suggests a second name preference by the witness to that detailed in the article, the other (forename) here withheld.

24. 'Blue Bell Hill—the driver's nightmare!', *Evening Post*, 27 February 1969, p. 5.

Chapter Four: The Phantom Hitch-Hiker

1. Otherwise known as Urban Myths, Whale Tumour Stories, or Friend-of-a-Friend stories.

2. Goss, *op.cit.*, p. 13.

3. See Published History, pp. 445-446. The Phantom Hitch-Hiker (even a few actual cases), and variations on the theme (including the familiar road ghost stance, standing in the middle of the road) have inspired a number of entertainment media productions, from Country Music hit 'Bringing Mary Home' (J. Duffey, C. Mank & J. Kingston, first recorded by The Country Gentlemen in February 1965; 'Laurie (Strange Things Happen)' (Milton 'Mitt' Addington), recorded by Dickey Lee, also in 1965; and Ritchie Blackmore and Candice Night's 'I Guess It Doesn't Matter Anymore' (2006)—all of which were inspired by the story of Resurrection Mary; to TV play 'Ride, Ride', in *Tales of Unease*, by Michael Hastings and featuring Susan George (LWT, 1970), and films *Resurrection Mary* (2005 and 2007), and *Die Spook van Uniondale* (South Africa, 2014); plus *Ghost Story* (1981), *What Lies Beneath* (2000), *Gothika* (2003), and *Dead End* (2003).

4. One convention holds that the hitch-hiker is likely to be of the opposite sex to the motorist. Why, in most instances the motorist appears to be male and the hitch-hiker female is addressed further in to Chapter 4 and in Chapter 11.

5. Jan Harold Brunvand, *The Vanishing Hitchhiker: American Urban Legends and their Meanings* (W.W. Norton & Co., 1981); also (Picador (published by Pan Books), 1983).

6. While historical sources describe a number of accounts of spectral travelling companions that we might today group under the Phantom Hitch-Hiker umbrella, some examples are clearly comparable to the modern types, such as the Swedish story dating back to 1602 cited by Goss, and referred to him by Swedish researcher Sven Rosèn (Goss, *op.cit.*, p. 46–47).

7. Based, in turn, on the observations of Andrew Lang (see Goss, *op.cit.*, p. 49).

8. Beth Scott & Michael Norman, *Haunted Heartland* (Warner Books, 1987), p.3. The renovation or alteration of a site is believed by some to be a factor in triggering hauntings (see Chapter 11).

9. *Arthur C. Clarke's World of Strange Powers* (Yorkshire Television: 'Ghosts, Apparitions and Haunted houses'). The account of Resurrection Mary presented here is derived from various sources: John Fairley & Simon Welfare, *Arthur C. Clarke's World of Strange Powers* (Collins, 1984, pp. 101–104; Book Club Associates edition, 1985, pp. 126–128); Beth Scott & Michael Norman, *op.cit.*, pp. 1–4; Richard Winer & Nancy Osborn, *Haunted Houses* (Bantam Books, 1979), pp. 75—76; *Mysteries of the Unexplained* (The Reader's Digest Association, 1982), pp. 180—181; 'Tales of phantom hitch-hikers', by Paul Screeton, *The Mail* (Hartlepool), 31 October 1980, p. 27.

10. *Unsolved Mysteries* (Television series), 'Resurrection Mary', Episode 179 (Season 6, Episode 19), hosted by Robert Stack. First aired 1994.

11. A term donated, I believe, by Michael Goss. The Spectral Jaywalker or encounters with it have been variously described in the literature: the *phantom road accident victim*, the *suicide simulation*, or in this text, the *knock down scenario.*

12. Richard Winer & Nancy Osborn *op.cit.*, p. 76.

13. Joan Forman, *The Haunted South* (Jarrold Colour Publications, 1989), pp. 100–101.

14. A different spelling of the witness' surname is given in Jenny Randles' *Strange But True? Casebook* (Piatkus, 1995), p. 117: Legrange.

15. Jenny Randles' account (*op.cit.*, p.117) differs, suggesting the witness, noting the girl to be pale and in need of help, offered to take her the 12 miles into Uniondale to find some food, to which the girl's mumbled reply was taken as agreement (which had also been her response when asked for her address).

16. Other sources describe the duffle coat as green, or the coat or top to be simply dark in colour.

17. From the witness' own account, given on London Weekend Television's *Strange But True?*, 1995.

18. This account of the Uniondale case derived from various sources: Michael Goss, *op.cit.*, pp. 121–128; Jenny Randles, *op.cit.*, pp.115–124; LWT's *Strange But True?* (TV series, presented by Michael Aspel), 1995; Janet & Colin Bord, *Modern Mysteries of the World* (Grafton, 1989), pp. 87–89.

Maria Roux (18 September 1945–12 April 1968) is buried in Old NG Kerk begraafplaas, in her home town of Riversdale, Western Cape, S. Africa. Cause of death: Vehicle Accident ('Died as result of a vehicle accident on the road between Uniondale and Williowmore, Cape Province' (Source:www.geni.com). The suggestion that Maria Roux is the ghost of Uniondale has understandably proven wearying and frustrating to her family over the years. Maria's eldest brother, Frans Roux, speaking in 2006, dismissed the reports that had been linked with his sister, of whom he said: 'People need to know, Ria was a happy girl and she was a compassionate person. She loved jokes, loved music, liked animals, and she had a bubbly personality.' ('Laat Uniondale se 'spook' rus' ('Let Uniondale's' ghost 'rest'', by Gerhard de Bruin, *Rapport* (Johannesburg), 6 Augustus 2006, p.11.

19. 'Ongelukke toon groot ooreenkoms: Twee spoke loop dalk' ('Accidents show great agreement: Two ghosts may be walking', *Die Burger*, 23 July 2004.

20. 'Die spook van Uniondale maak weer haar verskyning' ('The ghost of Uniondale makes her appearance again'), *Beeld*, 21 May 1994; 'Spookvrou van Uniondale gooi weer duim' ('Ghost woman of Uniondale hitch-hikes again'), *Die Burger*, 21 May 1994.

21. *Foaftale News* (No. 13, March 1989; the newsletter of the International Society for Contemporary Legend Research (ISCLR)), from 'Will the Uniondale Ghost Strike Again?', by David Barritt, *Sunday Times Magazine*, 29 March 1987, pp. 22-23.

22. 'Gaan Uniondale se spook dié Paastyd weer loop?' ('Will Uniondale's ghost walk again this Easter?'), by Ludwig Olwagen, *Die Burger*, 17 April 1987 (attributed to a former police chief, Capt. PE Barkhuizen in 1980 in a letter to *The Citizen*).

23. 'Female ghost terrorises Bulawayo motorists', *The Zimdisapora*, 25 June 2012.

24. From an account sent to David Thomas by Swiss researcher Andreas Trottmann, and based on details given in a locally published booklet (unidentified) on legends and traditions.

25. The original source for this story is the *Dunstable Gazette* of 18 October 1979. The witness was subsequently interviewed by Michael Goss for *The Evidence for Phantom Hitch-Hikers*, *op.cit.*, pp. 90–99. Roy Fulton passed away in 2002 at the young age of 49 (Paul Adams, Eddie Brazil, *Extreme Hauntings: Britain's Most Terrifying Ghosts*, (The History Press, 2013)). This account taken from various sources: Goss, *ibid*, pp. 90–99; 'Night Ride Riddle of Hitch-Hike Ghost!', by Anne Court, *Dunstable Gazette*, *op.cit.*, p.7; John Fairley & Simon Welfare, *op.cit.*, pp. 119–120; 'On the Road Again', by Michael Goss, *Fortean Times* (The Journal of Strange Phenomena), No.34 (Winter 1981), pp. 14–16; 'Taken for a ride?', by Michael Goss.

26. 'The night I took a ghost for a drive…', by Peter Hopkirk, *Sunday Express*, 15 January 1956, p. 5.

27. From Goss, *op.cit.*, pp. 82–86; Andrew Green, *Our Haunted Kingdom* (Fontana, 1974), p. 254; Terence Whitaker, *England's Ghostly Heritage* (Robert Hale, London, 1989), pp. 131–133; *Exeter Express & Echo* ('Western Ways by Dexon': 'The Night a Ghost Hitched a Lift'), 12 August 1970, p. 6.

28. *Strange But True? Encounters* (TV series, presented by Michael Aspel), LWT Productions, 1996; first broadcast 13 September 1996.

29. From correspondence dated 22 July 1990.

30. 'Spectre of Bluebell Hill', by Nigel Nelson, *Kent Messenger*, 26 July 1974, p.8. Whereas it turns out that the author was basically correct with respect to the weather on the night of the 1965 tragedy, he was definitely in error in giving 19 November as a Thursday. It was, of course, a Friday.

31. 'Wet November', *Chatham News*, 3 December 1965, p. 28. The Medway Water Board's Luton pumping station recorded 2.5 inches of rainfall for the month, with the heaviest being 0.68 inches on the 28th.

32. Attributing the appearances and behaviour of Phantom Hitch-Hikers to sudden death on the road is one thing; trying to account for the 'suicide simulation' by similar logical means is another entirely. The behaviour surely cannot relate to the manner of death in so many cases. Suicide by this means is unusual, although not unheard of. An open verdict was given on the death of a pensioner who apparently ran towards a vehicle on the M20 in Kent in 1980 (*Kent Messenger* of 31 October 1980, p. 41). See also notes to Ch.2 (133.).

33. Janet and Colin Bord, *Modern Mysteries of Britain* (Grafton, 1988), pp. 36–37. Similar encounters have been reported by named witnesses on the A12 at Rackham's Corner, and at the Beccles turn-off, and the stretch at Kelvedon.

34. For instance, the Sevenoaks by-pass in Kent, between Gracious Lane Bridge and Chipstead flyover, scene of a number of fatalities (*Fact or Fantasy* (Macdonald & Co (Black Cat imprint)), 1991), pp. 419–420.

35. 'Ghost Walks' After Crash', *Sunday People*, 14 July 1974, p. 9.

36. Terence Whitaker, *England's Ghostly Heritage* (Robert Hale, London, 1989), pp. 129–131.

37. *Reported road casualties: by severity: Great Britain, quarterly and annual from 2000* (Table RAS30003) (https://www.gov.uk), While the average number of fatalities (2,704) seems

high, the annual figure has been progressively reduced, with 2012's figure (1,754) halved (51%) compared to the number of deaths in 2002 (3,431).

Chapter Five: Against the Lore

1. Summarised from a paper by Richard K. Beardsley and Rosalie Hankey: 'The Vanishing Hitchhiker', *California Folklore Quarterly, Vol.1* (October 1942), No.4, pp. 303–335.

2. Beardsley and Hankey provide contradictory data in their first paper regarding the number of Version A disappearances: 53/60 or 88% (p. 312), or 47/60 or 78% (p. 313).

3. Detling Hill, characterised by steep, deceptive bends, even after its conversion to a dual carriageway in 1963, earned blackspot status following a number of fatalities there. In 1974, a 28-year-old pregnant mother and a 17-year-old hitch-hiker were killed when their car crashed in heavy rain (*Kent Messenger*, 10 May 1974, p. 3). The hill appears to have acquired its own Phantom Hitch-Hiker. Two individuals came forward with the familiar story, in June 1993, and the other in January 1995. In the latter case, the informant, from Chart Sutton, claimed a friend had encountered the Detling Hill girl on no less than three occasions. She usually appears, I was told, on Tuesdays at around 7.30 p.m. Needless to say, no further information was forthcoming. Nevertheless, it is interesting that just as the story at Blue Bell Hill should stray from the hitch-hiker script, another nearby location should take it up. (Source: unnamed informant at a talk by Andrew Green at Sandling Village Hall, 24 January 1995).

4. Personal correspondence dated 22 July 1990.

5. 'In search of news' (under the 'Talk of the Town' column), by Alan Bignell, *Kent Messenger*, 22 August 1969, p. 17.

6. Phantom Hitch-Hiker tales appear to have enjoyed something of a revival with the national press around the early to mid-1970s.

7. 'Maidstone Comment', by Roy Plascott, *Kent Messenger*, 8 December 1967, p. 3.

8. In some cases, the researcher's expressed wish to follow up the story can lead to an awkward avoidance of the whole thing!

9. Phantom Hitch-Hikers are often to be found or wish to be dropped off at culverts, streams, rivers, and other water courses, not to mention their preference for rainy conditions.

10. Janet & Colin Bord, *Modern Mysteries of the World: Strange Events of the Twentieth Century* (Grafton, 1989), pp. 86-87.

11. Or indeed, by disappearing even before she gets in the vehicle.

12. Goss, *op.cit.*, ps. 20, 27 & 55)

13. Beth Scott & Michael Norman, *op.cit.*, pp. 3–4.

Chapter Six: The Overgrown Path

1. 'Rail link valley viaduct sparks angry protest'; *Kent Messenger* (Maidstone), 21 September 1990, fp. 'Plans for second parkway station' & 'Action group leader fears city invasion', *Kent Messenger* (Maidstone), 21 September 1990, p. 8; 'Pylon would be 'eyesore'', *Kent Messenger*, 2 June 1995, p. 12.

2. 'Girls die in wedding eve smash', by Peter Rimmer, *Maidstone Gazette*, 23 November 1965, fp.

3. 'Prelude to grief...', by Peter Rimmer, *Kent Messenger*, 26 November 26 1965, fp.

4. The blue Mark 1 Ford Cortina (reg. APG 825B), belonged to the bride-to-be.

5. The West Kent Hospital, in Marsham Street, Maidstone, was demolished in 1988. The site is now occupied by maisonettes (Hengist Court, Friars Court) that offer private re-

tirement apartments. Interestingly, rumours that the original hospital was haunted have now been transferred to the modern accommodation, with sightings of ghostly figures reported by residents in recent times.

6. The spelling of the bride-to-be's name, and her age, as given by some of the sources reporting on the 1965 crash, is inaccurate—Susan Browne rather than the correct *Suzanne Browne.* Her age was actually 24. (See Chapter 8; p.181.)

7. It was later established that the women were not on their way home, but heading towards Maidstone at the time of the crash (See Chapter 8).

8. In addition to Aylesford, Blue Bell Hill and the location of the crash have been variously described as coming under Burham, Wouldham, Maidstone, Rochester, and Chatham. The correct—that is to say, the current—Post Town address is Chatham, but the village is located within the parish of Aylesford, in the borough of Tonbridge and Malling.

9. The original newspaper reports were also found to be in error here. In fact, it was Judith Lingham who died instantly, with Patricia Ferguson expiring later in hospital. (See Chapter 8.)

10. Real name withheld.

11. Erroneously given as Chatham in the *Maidstone Gazette* version.

12. The correct name of the church is 'Our Lady of Gillingham', located in Ingram Road, Gillingham. (See Chapter 8.)

13. 'Girl dies in car driven by her fiance', *The Gazette* (Maidstone), 18 February 1975, fp.

14. 'Fiancée tells of wedding plans before fatal crash', *Kent Messenger*, 20 October 1967, p. 3. Another that is worth mentioning is that footnoted in *The People*'s coverage of the 1965 crash ('Bride fights for her life on wedding day', 21 November 1965, p. 10), which, in a reversal of roles over Blue Bell Hill, tells of a bride-to-be's wait by the hospital bedside of her fiancé, on the day they were to have been married—20 November—the same day as the Blue Bell Hill couple.

A haunting case with more of a direct resemblance to Blue Bell Hill's tragic bride-to-be is that of the 'Ghost Girl of Fifth Street Hill', outside Huntington, West Virginia—a young woman who stands in the rain at the top of the hill (usually after midnight), thumbing lifts from passing motorists, whom she rewards after a few minutes by vanishing from the car. In November 1958, a newspaper described the ghost in similar terms to the Blue Bell Hill girl: 'she never says a word and she always disappears from the car like a puff of smoke when it reaches the stoplight at the bridge.' An 'explanation' is found in the story of a young bride killed after her wedding when the vehicle she was travelling in with her fiancé and parents overturned in wet conditions at the foot of the hill. ('Ghost Stories' by Joseph Platania, *Huntington Quarterly Magazine* (Issue 36), www.huntingtonquarterly.com).

15. 'Collecting UFO facts' (Letters), *Adscene*, 10 November 1989, p.M4; 'Have you met phantom hiker?' (Starpost), *Maidstone Star*, 25 January 1990, p.2; 'Search for the ghost' (Postbag), *Evening Post*, 20 July 1990, p. 6.

16. *Maidstone Star, Ibid.*

17. The dark shapes witnessed by Mrs Hughes and Jacquie Hopkins have another possible explanation: Blue Bell Hill, in the 1990s, was the assumed hub of numbers of reports of black panther-like big cats (dubbed by *Kent Today*'s Geoff Maynard the 'Beast of Blue Bell Hill' (a subject of rigorous investigation by Medway researcher Neil Arnold)). Whether, in particular, Mrs Hughes' experience in 1934 can be 'explained' in this fashion is open to debate. Renee Florence Hughes passed away in 2005, aged 89.

18. This was also the time period identified by the mother of one informant for her first hearing of a female ghost on Blue Bell Hill, a ghost said to be dressed in red (a detail

found also Neville Butteriss's account, p.371). Others have stated that they believe they heard similar rumours of a female ghost long before 1965.

19. From (undated) letter received 23 August 1990.

20. Here, I'm thinking of a report on a young lady who was killed as she tried to cross the A229 near the Tyland Lane junction ('Girl, 18, killed as she crosses road', *Kent Messenger*, 30 October 1981, fp). (See Epilogue).

21. Oakwood specialised in the treatment of mental health problems. While we have no means of deciding for sure, the anonymous nature of this story points to it being apocryphal; its use but a device employed by the narrator to bolster its acceptance as a true event (ref. Goss, *op.cit.*, p. 52.).

22. Agreeing with the postscript to my first hearing of the Blue Bell Hill story, where it was said the girl would continue to hitch-hike until such time as she successfully reached her destination. The reader may also recall this being said for the ghost of Maria Roux in the Uniondale case (see Chapter 4).

23. A popular post-encounter drink, it would seem! (see Roy Fulton's encounter, Chapter 4).

24. Eccles is a village lying a little over a mile south and east of Blue Bell Hill, and features in a first-hand witness account collected by researcher David Thomas (see notes Chapter 9).

25. See Chapter 7 ('Brief Encounter'—the Collings/Pope encounter).

26. Dennis also pointed out what I would hope is an uncharacteristic error in detail on my part, when I remarked that November 1989 would mark the 25th anniversary of the 1965 crash (which, of course, was not until 19 November 1990).

27. Reporter Emma Cooper also mentioned to me that it was understood that motorists had visited Judith's home in Albany Road. However, Judith's youngest sister, Catherine, told me that no-one had ever knocked on the door claiming to have picked Judith up (see Chapter 12).

28. An exorcism has never been confirmed, although Steve Moore, in an article for *Fortean Times* 24 ('Ghosts and Visions' (Winter 1977), pp. 13–14), states that churchmen had exorcised the Hill, but reports continued to come in.

29. A common hair covering of the 1960s, a headscarf features also in the description of a mature female hitch-hiker in a white mackintosh encountered close to midnight by four people at a bridge near Palavas-les-Flots, near Montpellier, France in 1981 (see Goss, *op.cit.*, pp. 24–25).

30. Probably Southern Television. The *Kent Messenger* of 10 January 1975 ('Ghost hunters discover surprise spirit', by Phil Dalton, fp) reported that a film crew had gone to Blue Bell Hill to film a reconstruction of a Phantom Hitch-Hiker encounter for a half-hour programme on ghosts. My attempt to obtain a copy of the programme in 1990 via TVS proved fruitless. It is possible the programme was never completed. Andrew Green reported that he was interviewed on the Hill in the 1970s for a programme that was never subsequently aired (telephone conversation 23 November 1992).

31. A former colleague.

Chapter Seven: Published History 1967–80

1. 'Maidstone Comment', by Roy Plascott, *Kent Messenger*, 8 December 1967, p. 3.

2. 'Hitch-hiking spirit' ('Talk of the Town'), by Roy Plascott, *Kent Messenger*, 10 May 1968, p. 3.

3. 'Riddle of the phantom girl', *Evening Post*, 9 September 1968, p. 3; 'Have you met the ghostly hitch-hiker', *The Gazette*, 10 September 1968, p. 3.

4. 'Blue Bell Hill—the driver's nightmare!', *Evening Post*, 27 February 1969, p. 5.

5. 'Riddle of the phantom on death hill', *The News of the World*, 14 July 1974, p. 5; 'Riddle of injured girl who 'disappeared'', *Chatham News*, 19 July 1974, p. 20.

6. 'Words in Brief' (in 'Listening Post'), by John Huffam, *Evening Post*, 9 December 1970, p. 2.

7. 'Work begins on £1.75m road scheme', *Kent Messenger*, 31 July 1970, p. 18.

8. The start of construction of the North Downs Tunnel (part of the £4.2 billion Channel Tunnel high speed rail link) was marked on 6 May 1999 with a ceremony at the site in honour of St. Barbara, the patron saint of miners, which included the placing of a statue of the saint in the entrance of the 3.25 km long tunnel ('Work starts on tunnel', *Kent Messenger*, 7 May 1999, p. 3; '24-hour tunnelling under hill begins', *Kent Today*, 7 May 1999 p. 5. The completed tunnel—the first high-speed and largest single-bore rail tunnel in the UK—was handed over in July 2001.

9. 'Warning of traffic delays', *Kent Messenger*, 10 January 1992, p. 53.

10. 'Riddle of the phantom on death hill', *The News of the World*, 14 July 1974, p. 5; 'Ghost on the A229..', *Sunday Mirror*, 14 July 1974, p. 13; ''Ghost Walks' After Crash', *Sunday People*, 14 July 1974, p. 9; 'Ghost riddle of 'injured girl'', *Evening Post*, 15 July 1974, fp; ''Ghost' mystery of injured girl', *Chatham Standard*, Tuesday 16 July 1974, back page; 'Hunt for phantom schoolgirl road victim', *The Gazette*, 16 July 1974, fp; 'Riddle of injured girl who 'disappeared'', *Chatham News*, 19 July 1974, p. 20; 'Drivers beware of the phantom on the hill', by Nigel Nelson, *Evening Post*, 19 July 1974, p. 7; 'Bluebell Hill's phantom girls', *Kent Messenger*, 19 July 1974, p. 4; 'Spectre of Bluebell Hill', by Nigel Nelson, *Kent Messenger*, 26 July 1974, p. 8.

11. 'Schools slammed as girls vanish', *The Gazette*, 2 April 1974, fp.

12. ''Ghost' Mystery of Injured Girl: Youngster disappears after accident at Bluebell Hill', *Chatham Standard*, 16 July 1974, bp.

13. Which, Goss was told in this correspondence dated 19 February 1980 (copy seen), occurs after records have lain dormant for 5 years.

14. Taken from notes made by Michael Goss following his interview with Tom Harber on 28 November 1980.

15. From correspondence (letters) with Mr Elvy in 1998. PC Elvy's father (Snr) was involved in the 1974 investigation, and Mr Elvy himself interviewed the families who met the 'hag' character that joined the scene in 1993 (Chapter 11). The detail about the police house (although small) is disputed by the testimony (memory) of police dog-handler Ted Wright, who was also at the scene. In this case, Wright was puzzled as to why Goodenough had driven like 'hell's bells' to Rochester when at the top of the Hill, in Blue Bell Hill Village, the police house had been open, with light showing, *and* there had been a telephone kiosk there, which Ted himself ascertained was in working order. However, it is possible that Goodenough was unaware of their existence, or that they were overlooked in his panic following the accident. Under the circumstances, he likely decided that it would be quicker to drive directly to a place where he was sure help could be obtained rather than waste time searching for a phone.

16. *Evening Post*, 15 July 1974; *The Gazette*, 16 July 1974; *Kent Messenger*, 19 July 1974.

17. See Goss, *op.cit.*, pp. 113–114.

18. *Chatham News, op.cit.*

19. There were, of course, three girls who died as a result of the accident.

20. Only the tabloids (*The News of the World*, the *Sunday Mirror*, and the *Sunday People* (all dated 14 July 1974)) give 1967 as the year of the accident; the *Evening Post* (15 July) and *The Gazette* (16 July) state 'eight years ago'; while the *Chatham News* gives the correct year and number of victims, but incorrectly describes the bride-to-be as a 17-year-old.

21. Telephone conversation 25 August 1990.

22. In the case of Chris Dawkins, barely a year old in 1974, the degree of matching detail would necessarily have had to be derived from a review of the newspaper coverage of the time or, most likely, from the recent coverage of Ian Sharpe's own encounter. But from the paranormal perspective, American writer John A. Keel has observed that such phenomena frequently appear to be 'reflective' in nature—that is, they have a tendency to mirror our own beliefs, attitudes and expectations. Whether this is an aspect of a real, objective phenomenon, or simply a function of the interpretations we ourselves apply to it is addressed in Chapter 14.

23. *The County Times and Express* (Mid-Wales), 2 June 1973 ('Ghostly Girl Gives Teacher a Fright', by Graham Breeze), fp; 30 June ('The night I saw the Red Bridge ghost'), fp; 14 July ('Saga of the Red Bridge ghost—Chapter 4'), fp; 21 July ('Letters to the Editor'), p.4; Janet and Colin Bord, *Modern Mysteries of Britain* (Grafton, 1988), pp. 35–36; Andrew Green, *Phantom Ladies* (Bailey Brothers & Swinfen Ltd, 1977), pp. 149–150. The Red Bridge, which was located on the A470 over a dismantled railway line between Llanidloes and Llanidam, was itself finally demolished.

24. See 14.

25. 'Driver tells how he 'hit' ghost girl', by Helen Sissons, *Kent Today* (Maidstone), 24 November 1992, p.2; "Ghost looked me in the face' says teenage driver', by Helen Sissons, *Kent Today*, 24 November 1992, p. 2.

26. Goss, *op.cit.*, pp. 105–106.

27. An inset picture of Judith Lingham appears on the front page of the *Maidstone Gazette* (23 November 1965), while Patricia Ferguson's picture accompanies front page reports by the *Chatham News* (26 November 1965) and *Chatham Standard* (23 November 1965), the latter of which also features an upper torso shot of Judith.

28. Maurice Goodenough is reputed to have later moved to the West Country (*The Sun*, 26 November 1992).

29. Ted Wright, *One Dog and Her Man: The Life of Police Dog Bess* (Meresborough Books, 1992), pp. 68–69.

30. This detail obviously differs significantly over the press versions of the incident, although it is perhaps consistent with a collision with a vehicle at a fair speed. Having said that, a person thrown clear over a vehicle in this manner would surely have sustained injuries too severe to allow a speedy departure from the scene, or to evade proper medical attention (unless, of course, she was a ghost). A similar case involving a phantom road accident victim that was thrown over the top of the car is recounted in Chapter 9 (the experience of Peter Leslie).

31. Unless, of course, it had rained and stopped before Ted Wright's arrival.

32. Placing the injured girl on the blanket rather than covering her with it would make more sense if she were being left there while the driver was off seeking help. It is interesting to note that a car blanket features in Beardsley and Hankey's leading story of a Phantom Hitch-Hiker in their paper 'The Vanishing Hitchhiker' for the *California Folklore Quarterly* (Volume 1 No.4 (October 1942), pp. 303–335). In this, set in San Francisco, a girl picked up by two men on a street corner on a cold and wet night is wrapped in a car blanket. When she is found to have vanished at her mother's address, the pair find only the crumpled blanket where she sat.

33. Correspondence with Mr Nelson, 19 & 24 July 1990. At time of writing, Mr Nelson is the Political Editor for *The Sunday People.*

34. Probably Fred Johnson, the front counter man at Rochester at the time (correspondence from David Elvy, dated 10 March 1998).

35. Again, from Michael Goss's interview with him of 28 November 1980. See 13.

36. 'Drivers beware of the phantom on the hill', by Nigel Nelson, *Evening Post*, 19 July 1974, p. 7.

37. 'Haunted Kent—Phantom on the TV screen', by Jenni Balow, *Kent Messenger*, 30 August 1974, p. 8; 'Ghost hunters discover surprise spirit', by Phil Dalton, *Kent Messenger*, 10 January 1975, fp (see notes Chapter 6). This ignores a letter ('Hauntings') of appeal for witnesses of the Phantom Hitch-Hiker by author Andrew Green that appeared in the *Kent Messenger* of 14 February 1975.

38. 'I Gave Ghost A Lift, Says Pop Star', *Reveille*, 9 May 1975.

39. The article incorrectly spells the witness's name: Stodholme instead of Studholme. It also states (erroneously) that Studholme was the lead guitarist for the (Maidstone) band *Chicory Tip*—who he certainly played with and is credited as a guitarist on their 1972 no. 1 hit 'Son of My Father'. At time of writing, Richard Studholme is still working as a musician (see www.richardstudholme.com).

40. 28 September 1994.

41. With the year of the incident reliant on Studholme's admittedly hazy recollection, it is possible that his experience took place sometime before Maurice Goodenough's. The *Reveille* article, attributed to 9 May 1975 by Michael Goss, states his age as 19—which, if accurate, would date the article or the event to around 1971–2 (in which case the events he read about a few months later could not refer to the Goodenough incident). The article's questionable accuracy regarding the story as a whole, however, leads us to question this detail also.

42. Michael Goss, *op.cit.*, p. 40.

43. 'We will Remember', *Chatham News*, 3 December 1965, p. 10.

44. 'Now girl dies on hill of fear', *Kent Messenger*, 5 November 1971, fp. The article names the victim as Christine Spencer of Frindsbury.

45. 'Crashes mar the holiday', *Kent Messenger*, 16 April 1971, fp.

46. 'Two in 'haunting' encounter on Blue Bell Hill', *Evening Post*, 30 August 1977, p. 10.

47. 'Ghostly experience', *Evening News (London)*, 12 September 1977, p. 9. An Audi showroom and dealership now occupies the former Veglios Motel site.

48. *The Running Horse*, now a Harvester Restaurant & pub.

49. 'What a story if it's on the level', by Roy Plascott, *Kent Messenger*, 26 September 1980, p. 6.

Chapter Eight: Primary Candidates

1. Letter received 17 November 1992.

2. 'Our Psychic Hears Tragic Tale of Bridesmaid Ghost', by Mike Ridley, *The Sun*, 26 November 1992, pp. 12–13.

3. Nella Jones, of Bexley, passed away in 1998, aged 66 (*Death Index, England & Wales* 1916–2005).

4. 'Prelude to grief...', by Peter Rimmer, *Kent Messenger*, 26 November 1965, fp.

5. 'Girls die in wedding eve smash', by Peter Rimmer, *Maidstone Gazette*, 23 November 1965, fp.

6. The victims' death certificates, which detail the date and place of death. Judith Lingham died on 19 November 1965 on Blue Bell Hill, Burham, Kent. Patricia Ferguson died on 20 November 1965 in the West Kent General Hospital, Maidstone. Bride-to-be Suzanne Browne is detailed as having died on 24 November 1965, also in the West Kent General Hospital, Maidstone.

7. Obtained from the groom, Bryan Wetton, in October 2001, with whom I started corresponding following a Google find of his tribute to his fiancée that also mentioned rumours that linked her name to the Ghost of Blue Bell Hill. In all, Bryan kindly sent me photographs showing Suzanne and her tragic companions, some of which are reproduced in this book.

8. 'Terror as ghost girl reappears', by Emma Cooper, *Kent Messenger*, 13 November 1992, p. 3.

9. This feature of Chris Dawkins' description was given almost two years after his encounter, on the BBC's one-hour special on the paranormal, *Out Of This World*, presented by Sue Cook, and broadcast on 7 October 1994—which also featured Ian Sharpe and a reconstruction of his experience.

10. 'Death roll three with bride-to-be', *Chatham News*, 26 November 1965, fp.

11. Full name: Charles Eric Lingham.

12. Mr Richard (Dick) Ferguson. Source: *Chatham Observer*, 26 November 1965, p. 3 ('Fight for life: then wedding eve crash girl dies'). It is worth also noting in passing that Bryan Wetton's father, Eric Lionel Wetton (1903–1943) was a Royal Navy Lieutenant.

13. 'Three die in horror crash', *Kent Messenger*, 20 August 1976, p. 5.

14. Although it might be argued that Nella had picked up on some association with the bride-to-be's birthplace, Port Pirie, South Australia. If, instead of a maritime connection, Nella had named the RAF (with which three of the four in the 1965 party had connections), any suggestion that she had made genuine contact with one or more of the crash victims might have prompted more serious attention.

15. We could, for instance, recall the 1816 case of Ann Martin, who had given up in despair and lain down to die on the Hill (see Chapter 2). Meanwhile, author Neil Arnold has heard the names 'Anne' or 'Annie'; and 'Annabelle' from other 'psychics' (correspondence 14 November 2010 and 26 August 2011).

16. 'Bridesmaid's ghost haunts highway where she died', by John Cooke, *The National Enquirer*, p. 44.

17. 'Crash killed three girls, inquest jury told' (subtitled 'Wedding Eve Horror'), *Chatham Observer*, 25 March 1966, p. 50. Nella Jones's repeated her 'findings' regarding the 'true' cause of the crash in 1995 on CST Production's *The Magic and Mystery Show* (for Anglian Television/Meridian Broadcasting, presented by Brian Blessed), declaring that at the time of her visit to Blue Bell Hill (November 1992) no-one knew what had caused the crash—no-one, that is, apart from the original newspapers that I suspected had served as the source of *The Sun*'s (and Nella's?) information, plus the inquest, the families of the victims, and of course myself!

18. The article states that the body of bride-to-be Suzanne Browne, an orphan of Adelaide, Australia, was to be flown home to her uncle and brother. Added to this, *The Advertiser* (Adelaide; 26 November 1965, p. 8) states that Ms Browne's parents died when she was only a few years old.

19. As detailed in Nella's autobiography, *Nella: A Psychic Eye*, by Nella Jones with Mandy Bruce (Ebury Press, 1992).

20. Photographs taken at 10.20 a.m. on Saturday 28 November 1992.

21. 'I ran over ghost of tragic bridesmaid', by Paul Hooper, *The Sun*, 24 November 1992, p. 7.

22. Association for the Scientific Study of Anomalous Phenomena.

23. 'Is this the ghost of Blue Bell Hill?', *The Sun*, 27 November 1992, p. 17.

24. In actuality, hedgerow foliage whose hairy grey-white buds, when backlit by the sun, gave the impression of a ghostly form (with a triangular road sign for her head). *Clematis Vitalba*, commonly known as Old Man's Beard or Traveller's Joy, can be seen all along the lane, and is a common feature of hedgerows throughout this part of Kent.

25. 'Join The Sun Psychic Tour' (subtitled 'Let medium Nella speak to spooks in your home'), *The Sun*, 2 December 1992, p. 11.

26. *Scream Team* (2002), Episode 2, 'Blue Bell Hill in Kent'. See Published History: Television.

27. *Scream Team* also featured two psychics: June Elleni Lane (psychic artist), and psychic medium Terri Andrews-Dunne. Lane made a roadside sketch of the features of a girl she sensed, giving the name 'June' or 'Jude', who had been part of a group of 3-5 people, then suddenly wasn't with them anymore, and was said to not like the idea that she had been left on her own. Shown the picture, Ian Sharpe found some recognition in the eyes and hair, but the inferred identity (Judith Lingham) was not the member of the party picked out by Ian from photos of the victims I had shown him in 1993. Inevitably over time, all three victims of the 1965 crash have been linked to the ghost. By contrast, Terri Andrews-Dunne, who was taken to Kit's Coty field, could only see 'loads and loads of bones', and sensed a lot of blood, pain, fear, and terror, which was imprinted into the landscape of which she described as an ancient burial site.

28. 'Blue Bell Hill triple tragedy 'accident'', *Kent Messenger*, 25 March 1966, p. 7.

29. Wednesday 24 November 1965. The bride-to-be's full name was Suzanne Ingrid Browne (see p. 181).

30. 'Bride-to-be badly hurt in death crash', *Hunts Post*, 25 November 1965, fp.

31. Held at the Office of Population Censuses and Surveys at St. Catherine's House, London.

32. As also summarised by Dr. P. Farnan, consultant pathologist at the hospital ('Death roll three with bride-to-be', *Chatham News*, 26 November 1965, fp).

33. Patricia Ferguson was born on 9 April 1942 at the Royal Naval Maternity Nursing Home, Barnsole Road, Gillingham. At the time of the crash, she was in her third year as a teacher at Fair View Junior School, Wigmore (*Chatham News*, 26 November 1965, fp). While the extent of Patricia's own personal association with Dunfermline is unknown, the *Chatham Standard* of 23 November 1965 hints that it was a one-time home for her in stating that her parents were living there at the time of the accident.

34. 'Two Die in Smash Drama: Bride-to-be in a Coma', *Chatham Standard*, 23 November 1965, fp.

35. Letter dated 16 November 1990.

36. *Chatham Observer*, 25 March 1966, *op.cit.* (see 17). This source provided a more detailed report on the inquest than the *Kent Messenger*'s, including the circumstances of the crash itself.

37. Personal correspondence (letter, received from Fr. Augustine Kinnane), dated 6 February 1992. While in my own mind I am satisfied that the scene of the 1965 crash is where it is described, it can be noted for the record that the *Chatham Standard* of 23 November 1965 (the only source to relate it to an easily identifiable landmark) states that the collision occurred near the Lower Bell. This, however, in no way contradicts the placement as given, the Lower Bell simply being the closest such feature in the vicinity of the crash scene.

38. The *Chatham Standard* of 29 March 1966 (p.5, 'Death crash of three girls still remains a mystery') states that Suzanne Browne arrived in Britain in May 1965, when she bought the car in which in November she would sustain her fatal injuries (from testimony given by her fiancé, at the inquest on 23 March 1966).

39. Arthur Patrick Porter (1912–1988) served as the Parish Priest of Our Lady of Gillingham for over 25 years prior to his death in 1988 at the age of 75. Father Porter was succeeded by Father Augustine ('Gus') Kinnane. *See*: www.ourladyofgillingham.org.

40. For the full published accounting of the 1965 tragedy, see Published History (pp. 433-

434).

41. Ingrid Alice Browne died on 24 January 1946 (aged 38) at Sister Pope's Hospital, Adelaide, SA. Suzanne Browne's father, Patrick Sylvester Browne had died the year before, on 26 July 1945 (aged 45), in the same hospital. (*The Advertiser*, Adelaide, 25 January 1946, p. 16; and 27 July 1945, p. 14). The couple's remains rest together in the Port Pirie Cemetery.

42. Rosary School: Gladstone Road, Prospect, SA 5082. St Aloysius College: Wakefield Street, Adelaide, SA. The *South Australian Countrywoman* was the 'official organ' of the South Australian Countrywomen's Association Inc. (est. 1929).

43. From a letter (of reply) from Patrick Browne, hand-delivered to my hotel during a visit to Adelaide in April 1993. Subsequently, I telephoned him and had an interesting and informative conversation regarding his sister. Patrick Browne could only decry the standards of the British popular Press, while at the same time commenting that he and Suzy's uncle '... always knew she would be famous.' Patrick Browne passed away in 1998.

44. Some sources (mainly Australian) state that Suzanne Browne met her fiancé, while he was stationed at the Woomera rocket range, some 500 miles NNW of Adelaide (*The Advertiser*, (Adelaide), 22 November 1965; *The News* (Adelaide), 22 November 1965; *The News* (Adelaide), 25 November 1965; *The Sunday Mirror*, 21 November 1965; *The Sunday Express*, 21 November 1965). As this book indicates, and confirmed by other sources and by the groom himself, he was actually stationed at Edinburgh airfield, near Elizabeth, to the north of Adelaide, but was connected to the military tests conducted at Woomera.

45. Bryan Wetton, in his summary history of Blue Steel and 4 JSTU, indicates that, with the wind up of the project from late 1964, the remaining personnel (of whom he was one) were released and repatriated in three stages: in November 1964, March 1965, and June 1965 (http://beesoft.soho.on.net/4JSTU). Another source, posting on the Key Publishing Ltd Aviation web forum in Oct. 2010 (as 'WV-903') stated he left 4 JSTU 'on closedown in April 65' (http://forum.keypublishing.com).

Three sources report the couple to have become engaged before leaving Australia, around 6 months before the accident (*The People*, 21 November 1965; *Evening News* (London), 20 November 1965; *The West Australian* (Perth), 22 November 1965). The latter two attribute this information to the groom himself.

46. The journey by sea between Australia and the UK in the 1960s typically took around a month. Suzanne and her party (which included the daughters of Mrs. R. P. Gosling (Anne and Helen), of Chain of Ponds, near Adelaide) arrived in England in May 1965. One of the Gosling sisters was at Suzanne Browne's bedside after the accident ('Girl fighting for life', *The News* (Adelaide), 22 November 1965, p. 3).

47. *Sunday Mirror,* 21 November, 1965, p. 7 ('Tragedy ends Bride's 'Hen Party''); *The News (Adelaide),* 22 November 22, 1965, p. 3 ('Girl Fighting for Life'); *The News (Adelaide),* 25 November 22, 1965, p. 2 ('SA girl dies in Britain').

48. The Good Companions Club occupied a Grade II listed building at the top of Star Hill, in New Road, Rochester (now occupied by the Rochester Independent College). The 'G.C.s' was founded in 1935 by Frank Taylor, who died in 1997. The Good Companions closed its doors at Star Hill for the last time in 1993 ('Social club founder dies', *Kent Today*, 23 July 1997, p. 7). Ironically, the driver of the Jaguar in the collision was also a Good Companions member.

49. Correspondence (email) from Bryan Wetton, dated 16 October 2001.

50. The close friends here were Peter Howes and Tony Bunting (*Chatham Standard.* 23 November 1965, fp ('Two die in smash drama: bride-to-be in a coma'); *Chatham News*, 26 November 1965, fp ('Death roll three with bride-to-be'). *Evening News* (London) (late extra final), 20 November, 1965, fp ('Party Girls Die On Bluebell Hill: Battle for Crash Bride's Life'). For the record, Judith Lingham's mother, in an interview the day after the accident, offers a slightly different picture, reportedly stating: 'The four girls were having a hen party before Susan got married.' She also said that she had last seen them at 9 p.m. the previous evening when she dropped Judith ('Judy') at her friend's home. (*Evening*

News (London), 20 November 1965, fp ('Doctors fight for Death-Crash Bride').

Richard Williams added some further information from the recollections of his mother, who had been a school colleague of Pat Ferguson's: 'My Mum said that she had spoken to her on the day that she died and that she was apparently making the bridesmaids dresses and said something along the lines that she thought she'd never get the dresses finished on time for the wedding as she had so much marking to do.' (By email 28 September 2006).

51. *Chatham Standard*, 23 November 1965, *op.cit.* Tony Bunting later married Dee Smith, ex-girlfriend of Tony Stone. Tony Bunting died in 1991, at the young age of 49.

52. Judith Lingham was born on 14 June 1943.

53. *Chatham Standard*, 23 November 1965, *op.cit.* Judith Lingham's two sisters, who I met in December 1992, believed the party may have been on their way to *The Malta*, a little over half-a-mile west of the *Running Horse* on the north bank of the River Medway, at Allington Lock. Bryan Wetton also indicated that he thought it might have been a venue other than the *Running Horse*. I am inclined to think that the *Running Horse* was the most likely destination, based on it being named in the *Chatham Observer* of 26 November 1965 —although it is quite possible that both establishments were on the girls' 'search list'.

54. *Chatham Observer*, 25 March 1966, p. 50 ('Crash killed three girls, inquest jury told' ('Wedding Eve Horror'); *Chatham Standard*, 29 March 1966, p.5 ('Death crash of three girls still remains a mystery').

55. *Chatham Observer*, 19 November 1965 ('Your Weekend Weather'), fp.

56. *Chatham Observer*, 25 March 1966, *op.cit.*

57. *Ibid.*

58. The former time of 10.45 p.m., is given in Bill White's report for the *Evening Standard* (London) of 20 November 1965 ('Bride-to-be injured in death crash', fp). The later time of 11 p.m. appears in the *Chatham Standard* (23 November 1965, 'Two die in smash drama::bride-to-be in a coma', fp)—a time, the reader will have noted, that tallies with Tom Harber's stated time for Blue Bell Hill's ghostly encounters.

The only other newspaper report to give a time was *The People* (21 November 1965, p. 10), which stated the crash had occurred at midnight. While this time agrees more closely with the general timing of recent sightings of the 'ghost', it is some way off the time given by either the *Evening Standard* or *Chatham Standard*, which are more consistent with the estimates given by PC Parvin and that inferred from crash survivor Gillian Burchett's testimony at the inquest on 23 March 1966 (See the *Chatham Observer*, 25 March 1966, *op.cit.).* Supporting the contention that these sources are the more reliable is the general accuracy of their reports. The *Evening Standard* piece, in fact, was the only pre-inquest article (that covered this aspect) to get the facts right concerning the location and timing of the deaths of Judith Lingham and Patricia Ferguson. The *Evening Standard* piece stands also as one of the earliest reports on the tragedy (the other being the *Evening News* (London), published the same day), appearing a day ahead of the Sunday nationals (for which it/they, like the Australian Associated Press reports published on 21 November in Adelaide, probably served as the source), and a few days ahead of any of the regional papers.

59. Peter Parvin's account to the 1996 inquest is supplemented by his testimony on 1999's *The Why Files*, Episode 10, Part 2, 'The Ghost Bride' (see Chapter 12 (9.)), and correspondence with him (February 1995).

60. A number of the initial newspaper reports indicate that Suzanne Browne underwent emergency surgery on arrival at hospital. Several of these (mainly Australian sources, based on a few of the London papers (*Evening Standard*, 20 Nov., *The Observer* (21 Nov.), and *The People* (21 Nov.)) further indicate that her fiancé waited outside the operating theatre throughout. Bryan Wetton himself, in his own recollected account ('Requiem for a Princess' (2001, *unpub*), indicates that Suzanne was lying peacefully when he saw her shortly after his own arrival. Considering the time interval between incident and his recollected awakening in the early hours of 20 November, it may be that his personal

recollections are the more reliable, and that surgery had been completed by the time he saw her—although it is also quite possible that the surgery, which would undoubtedly have been involved, was still ongoing when he arrived. The point is a moot one, but may perhaps say something about the way press accounts have a propensity to construct elements for dramatic effect, even where reporting starkly real situations.

61. 'Tragedy ends bride's 'hen party', *The Sunday Mirror*, 21 November 1965, p. 7.

62. At 126 Week Street, Maidstone. Fr Moore served at St. Francis' for 13 years.

63. *Chatham News*, 26 November 1965, fp; 'Injured S.A. Woman Dies', *The Advertiser* (Adelaide), 26 November 1965, p. 8.

64. *Chatham News*, 3 December 1965, fp ('Last Minute News'), p.10 ('We will Remember'). The former reports that the body of Suzanne Browne had been flown to Australia for burial in her hometown of Adelaide. 'We will Remember' records the funeral of Judith Lingham on 29 November [at Medway Crematorium, Robin Hood Lane, Blue Bell Hill]. For the record, it can be noted that Patricia Ferguson's funeral took place the same day, 29 November, at Gillingham's Woodlands Road Cemetery.

Suzanne Browne was finally laid to rest in the beautiful surroundings of Enfield Memorial Park, in Clearview, in the northern suburbs of Adelaide, a mile from where she had grown up (Blair Athol).

By way of postscript, Bryan Wetton remained in the UK until after the inquest in March 1966, and emigrated to Australia on 5 May 1966, arriving back in Adelaide a year to the day after he left. Two of his close friends, Tony Stone and Peter Howes, emigrated at the same time.

65. *Maidstone Gazette*, 23 November 1965, fp (Judith Lingham); *The News* (Adelaide), 25 November 1965, p.2 (Suzanne Browne); *Chatham News*, 26 November 1965, fp (Patricia Ferguson); *Chatham Standard*, 29 March 1966, fp (Patricia Ferguson and Judith Lingham), and later, *The Telegraph* (Brisbane), 25 November 1965, p. 33.

Chapter Nine: The Witnesses (1992–1994)

1. From notes made by Michael Goss following his interview with Tom Harber on 28 November 1980.

2. Michael Goss, *op.cit.*, p. 104 (Coronet edition 2015, p. 95).

3. 'Is this the most haunted road in Britain?', by Alison Legh-Jones, *Woman*, 8 March 1993, pp. 28-29.

4. A number of reports describe Ian Sharpe's car as having skidded to a halt. Ian, however, pointed out that his car was equipped with anti-lock brakes.

5. *Out Of This World* (BBC1), broadcast 9.30 p.m., 7 October 1994.

6. *Out Of This World, op.cit.* Stephen Nelkin passed away in 1998 at the young age of 46.

7. My first interview with the Greens took place on 23 November 1992, just a few days after Chris Dawkins' experience.

8. Such a speed, if accurate, would suggest the encounter took place much further down the Rochester Road towards Aylesford than was estimated in my first interview with the couple.

9. Something that tallies with the description later given by Chris Dawkins on the BBC's *Out Of This World* (see 5 & 6).

10. Letter dated 14 November 1992 (received 24 November 1992).

11. A feature in common with Ian Sharpe's description. While conceding this may have been a genuine feature of the description given by Mrs Brooks' mother in 1974, it has to be borne in mind that this was a prominent characteristic of Ian Sharpe's own much-publicised description.

12. Account courtesy of *Mysterymag.com*; personal correspondence with witness. In July 1988, French lorry driver Didier Chassagrande, ran over an elderly cyclist on the A12 at Kelvedon, Essex. When the shocked driver returned 10 minutes later with police, the man, who had been unconscious and bloodied when he was dragged to the roadside, had vanished, along with his bike ('By gum! Flattened cyclist vanishes', by Kieron Saunders, *The Sun*, 15 July 1988).

13. Personal correspondence with witness (email), 2004.

14. Personal correspondence with witness (email), Oct. & Nov. 2011.

15. *The Manchester Courier and Lancashire General Advertiser*, 7 September 1908, p. 3 (col.7).

16. 'Tragedy on Bluebell Hill', *Maidstone and Kentish Journal*, 10 September 1908, p. 8. A 26-year-old motorcyclist, Alfred George Thompson, was fatally injured after a collision with a car on this same stretch on 23 January 1939 ('Gillingham Motor Cyclist's Death', *Chatham News*, 3 February 1939).

17. 'Blue Bell ghost picks on Paula', by Emma Cooper, *Kent Today*, 23 June 1993, p.7. See also 'Ghost Reappears', *Kent Messenger*, 25 June 1993, p.13; 'Local News' ('Briefly'), *KM Extra (Ma)*, WE 2 July 1993. p.2.

18. Telephone call to Emma Cooper on 24 June. A subsequent letter to Paula Cooper detailing my interest, and requesting answers to a short list of follow-up questions went answered.

19. 'Phantom's £3,000 Bill' (in 'Mirror Motoring' with Ken Rogers), *Daily Mirror*, 1 November, 1996, p. 28.

20. 'Crash girl saved from fire', *Kent Messenger* (North Kent), 28 February 1975, p. 3.

21. 'Accident mystery baffles police', *Hampstead Local Advertiser*, 17 October 1985.

22. Sources for these accounts is a segment ('Lady in White') of the popular American series on the paranormal, *Sightings* (a trademark of Paramount Pictures), and 'Rod Vecsey—The White Lady' on *Seekers of the Supernatural*, a weekly cable show in the Connecticut area between 1998–1999 by Ed & Lorraine Warren, and hosted by Tony Spera.

23. Age as given by the *Evening Mail* (Birmingham), 2 & 3 January 1996. The *Birmingham Post* (3 January), however, gives the witness's age as 31.

24. A description that closely resembles Ian Sharpe's state as described by Emma Cooper in her original report for the *Kent Today* (10 November 1992). If these encounters seem to be uncannily close in pattern and detail, so too do the subsequent press reports recounting them.

25. 'Plumber spooked in ghostly run-in', *Evening Mail* (Birmingham), 2 January 1996, fp; 'Phantom crash will haunt me', *Evening Mail* (Birmingham), 3 January 1996, p. 14; 'All shook up after spooky encounter', *The Birmingham Post*, 3 January 1996, p. 5; 'I hit a ghost claims driver', *The Sun*, 3 January 1996, p. 11; 'And finally...', *Kent Today* (Maidstone & district), 3 January 1996, fp. Moor Lane features also in Andrew Green's *Ghosts of Today* (1980), pp. 167–168: At an undisclosed date, Arthur Spencer was driving along Moor Lane at 7 p.m. when he saw an airman walking slowly across the road toward the cemetery, before which he vanished. Two years previously, two factory workers returning home along the canal towpath saw, near the bridge, the figure of 'a young, handsome man 'about 27' with *fair, wavy hair* and dressed in RAF uniform, walk across the water and vanish. (*Italics*—mine).

26. 'Coach driver's ghostly collision', by Sally Yonish, *Kentish Express* (a *Kent Messenger* group newspaper), 13 January 2000, p. 3. While Keith Scales is probably right in believing that he was not specially selected for his experience, it is fascinating to consider the very close comparisons his encounter bears to Ian Sharpe's at Blue Bell Hill in 1992: both were coach drivers, one year different in age at the time of their encounter (Sharpe, 54; Scales, 53), and each with over 30 years' driving experience (Sharpe, 33; Scales, 32). Sharpe: 'When I walked into the station my face was white and I was shaking like a leaf.'

(*Kent Today*, 10 November 1992); Scales: 'I was shaking like a leaf.' (Sally Yonish, it should be noted was completely unaware of Blue Bell Hill's repute and its coverage by the *Kent Messenger* and *Kent Today*, and was surprised by the close comparison her report bore to Ian Sharpe's account in particular (see 17).

We must also consider the description of the girl (allowing for her estimated age) and the settings themselves: Blue Bell Hill, White Hill—both lying on the same chalk ridge of the North Downs. Putting it all together leads to some speculation that we may be dealing with the *same* figure? Indeed, the possibility exists that the same archetypal figure is involved wherever and whenever 'she' appears.

Finally, it may be significant that the early part of January features in Keith Scales' experience (6 Jan.). Compare this to Blue Bell Hill in 1993 (Rayburn, Maiden, 5 & 6 Jan. (see Chapter 11)), and Birmingham (Bingham, 2 Jan. (Chapter 9)). The first week of January correlates with the Earth's nearest approach to the Sun ('perihelion'). In years when the Sun is most energetic (every 11.1 years, according the Solar Cycle), it is hard to overlook the possible influence this additional energy impacting the Earth has on the environment and ourselves. Keith Scales' encounter came just three days after perihelion on 3 January 2000, in a year that was experiencing the build-up phase toward solar maxima in mid-2000 (See Chapter 14).

27. Female or male, the figure frequently has blonde hair—a small detail, but a common feature of the 'script', both in folklore and actual reports.

28. 'Ghostly figure' terrified driver', *Kent Messenger*, 2 July 1999, p. 51).

29. 'Was my hitchiker [sic] a girl or a ghoul on the hill?', by Emily Hall, *Kent Messenger* (Maidstone), Friday 5 December 2003, p. 15.

30. When I interviewed Jim Skene (by telephone) in 1994, he did not claim the girl had appeared before him (the inference here that she materialised rather than being 'just there'); nor did she vanish in view when he dropped her off in Chatham. Otherwise, the account stands up pretty well to the decade gap between tellings. James (Jim) Skene passed away on 23 January 2013, aged 83 (*Kent Messenger* (Maidstone) 1 February 2013, p. 41).

31. Back in 1965 at least, Chatham had two cinemas: the Ritz, and the ABC, both in the High Street, diagonally opposite one another, at 324 and 385 respectively. The ABC became a Cannon cinema for a short period in 1985, and closed in 2002. It was demolished in December 2003. The Ritz closed in May 1972, and the building converted into a bingo club. We can suppose that it was the Ritz that was being thought of by James Skene, as, at time of his recollections, this would have been the 'old cinema', since the ABC was still open up to 2002. The site is now occupied by the new Gala Bingo Club. Neither site has any known connection to any of the victims of the 1965 crash—but there is a tentative connection with the nearby site of the former Chatham Mortuary, which comes into the story of an alternative candidate for the ghost (see Chapter 10).

32. The *Kent Messenger* report (*op.cit.*) paints a less ambiguous picture of the disappearance: 'There were some gates so I backed up and she got out of the car and just vanished.'

33. See 29.

Chapter Ten: The Wood Murder

1. (Alfred) Jack Woodger passed away in 1994, aged 81 (England & Wales Death Index 1916–2005 (Birth date 8 December 1913). Registered Feb 1995 at Chatham, Kent, no. D7A. Entry no. 174.

2. The Bridgewood Café was located on the Maidstone-bound side of the A229 near to the Bridgewood roundabout. Like the other businesses along this section of road (which included a petrol station), the café succumbed to the road improvements here in 2002.

3. Not entirely true. I have an account from researcher David Thomas who, in November 1993, conducted an interview with 'John', a friend and resident of Eccles who had

had an 'encounter' one night the previous autumn with a young woman (judged to be in her twenties) standing alone at night several hundred yards along a trackway outside the village, who was staring out across the fields towards Blue Bell Hill. Back home, he mentioned it to his wife, who joked about the Blue Bell Hill ghost. The witness, however, while having no reason to think the woman to be anything other an ordinary human being, nevertheless could not help but reflect on the strangeness of the incident.

4. 'Murder Mystery at Chatham', *Chatham, Rochester & Gillingham News*, 30 September 1916, p. 5. Another report on the inquest (*Chatham Observer*, 30 September), gives the distance as a *half-mile* from the Bridgewood junction ('Servant Murdered in a Wood', *Chatham, Rochester and Gillingham Observer*, 30 September 1916, p. 8), approximately opposite the current Laker Road's junction with the B2097. Other sources more broadly state the location as between Stoney Lane and the junction of the Chatham and Rochester Roads (see 11.).

5. The Victorian church of St. Mary the Virgin, built in 1881, was located at the north end of Church Street, on the corner with Rochester Road. The church, deemed unsafe, was demolished in 1981. (See: John E. Vigar, *Church of St Mary the Virgin (Burham, Kent),* a booklet by The Churches Conservation Trust, 2009). The church is pictured in *Maidstone in Old Photographs*, a collection of old postcard images, by Irene Hales (Alan Sutton Publishing, 1990), p. 151. But this, in fact, is not where Emily Trigg was buried. Emily Trigg's remains almost certainly lie in an unmarked plot in the original St. Mary's churchyard of St. Mary's near to the river Medway opposite Snodland.

6. Gerald Hinks, *Crimes That Shocked The Medway Towns* (Parrett & Neves, 1973), pp. 53–56.

7. 'Is it Murder?', *Chatham News*, 23 September 1916; 'A Wood Tragedy', *Chatham Observer*, 23 September 1916, p. 5; 'Servant Murdered in a Wood', *Chatham Observer*, 30 September 1916, p. 8; 'Murder Mystery at Chatham', *Chatham News*, 30 September 1916, p. 5; 'The Wood Mystery', *Chatham Observer*, 14 October 1916, p. 3; 'Maidstone Road Murder', *Chatham News*, 14 October 1916, p. 3; 'The Wood Murder', *Chatham Observer*, 21 October 1916, p. 5; 'The Murder in a Wood: Artillery Man Discharged', *The Derby Daily Telegraph*, 24 October 1916; 'The Wood Murder', *Chatham Observer*, 28 October 1916, p. 12.

See also: 'The Skeleton Murder Mystery', *Chatham News*, 26 September 1941, p. 4; 'The Unsolved Mystery of Poor Little Emily' (in *Crimes That Shocked the Medway Towns*), by Gerald Hinks, *Chatham Standard*, 21 December 1941, pp. 22–23.

8. Michael Jennings, grandson of John Jennings, offers some correction to the newspaper accounts, stating that his grandfather's greengrocer shop was actually at 29 John Street, with a store in Hooper's Road, both nearby. At the time of Emily's death, he was living at 45 Princes Street, but subsequently moved to St Williams Way, where he died on 31 May 1957, aged 75. (via Neil Arnold, email 30 June 2016).

By remarkable coincidence, the discovery of Emily Trigg's remains came a hundred years, virtually to the day (just a day before), since the woeful discovery of Ann Martin, of Lewes, in the woods at Blue Bell Hill, on 22 September 1816 (see Chapter 2). Death Indexes for England and Wales (1837–2005) for September 1873 record the death of one Ann Martin of Lewes, aged 80 (Vol. 2B, p. 88). If this is indeed the Ann Martin rescued on Blue Bell Hill, this would have made her 19 years of age in 1816, a comparable age at the time to Emily Trigg.

9. *Chatham Observer*, 30 September 1916, *op.cit.*

10. *Chatham News*, 30 September 1916, *op.cit.*

11. *Ibid.* The *Kent Messenger* of 30 September 1916 ('The Mystery of the Wood', p. 3) gives the location broadly as between Stour Lane (meaning *Stoney* Lane) and the junction of the Rochester and Chatham roads from Maidstone.

12. 'The Mystery of the Wood', *Kent Messenger*, 14 October 1916, p. 3. The Nashenden Valley, through which the M2 passes, is very different than it was in 1916. The widening of this section of the motorway (between junctions 1 and 4) began in 2000, converting

the two lanes of the motorway to 4 lanes each way. The spoil from the excavation of the North Downs Tunnel beneath Blue Bell Hill (which was completed in July 2001) was used to form a new embankment for London-bound traffic from junction 2. The widening, which was completed in July 2003, included a complete remodelling of the junction 2/A229 interchange above Blue Bell Hill (see also Chapter 2 notes).

13. *Chatham News*, 30 September 1916, *op.cit.*

14. Most sources that describe Emily's hat, state it to have been white, and trimmed with pink roses (and pieces of black velvet). One source only (*Chatham Observer*, 30 September 1916, *op.cit.* mentions a *black* hat, which is almost certainly erroneous.

15. *Chatham News*, 14 October 1916, *op. cit.* The Mortuary, on the Brook, was located on the south side of Batchelor Street, approximately where the Iceland store and its car park are now located (the mortuary is marked on the 1932 Ordnance Survey (1:2500)). It is possibly noteworthy that the spot where Jim Skene dropped of his female passenger in 1971 (see Chapter 9)—the area of the 'old cinema' in Chatham (the Ritz, at 324 High Street) is only around 500 feet from the site of the mortuary. A tenuous connection, to be sure, but perhaps the only one that makes any sense of the Jim Skene episode (assuming, of course, that his passenger was indeed ghostly). (See also Chapter 9 notes (29 & 30.)).

16. See 42 & 43.

17. *Chatham Observer*, 30 September 1916, *op. cit.*; *Chatham News*, 30 September 1916, *op. cit.*

18. *Chatham Observer, Ibid.*

19. *Chatham News*, 14 October 1916, *op. cit.*

20. *Chatham News*, 23 September 1916, *op. cit.*

21. *Chatham News*, 30 September 1916, *op. cit.*

22. *Chatham Observer*, 30 September 1916, *op. cit.*

23. *Chatham News* & *Chatham Observer*, 30 September 1916, *op. cit.* Both sources confuse matters, however, by stating (in the same report) that the bullet had been brought home from France in January by Mrs Trigg's youngest son, Frederick. Emily's brother, William, was pictured in a recounting of her murder in the *Chatham Standard* of 21 December 1971 (pp. 22–23). William, 85 at the time, and still living in a cottage at Blue Bell Hill, reported that he had first learned of his sister's murder when a sergeant showed him the news in a copy of the *News of the World.* It was six months before he could return to England.

24. *Chatham News*; *Chatham Observer*, *Ibid.*

25. *Chatham News*, 30 September 1916, *op.cit.*

26. *Chatham News* & *Chatham Observer*, 30 September 1916, *op. cit.* In one of those strange coincidences, Emily's fiancé, George Harris, was mentioned in the same column of the *Chatham News* ('St Nicholas' Guild Sidelights: Providential Escapes and Re-Unions') that announced the discovery, the previous day, of Emily's remains (22 September 1916). The brief report notes that three chums from Rochester, including one Private G. Harris, had each arrived back home within a few hours of one another from different hospitals.

27. *Ibid.*

28. *Chatham Observer*, 14 October 1916, *op. cit.* (See also: *Chatham News*, 14 October 1916, *op. cit.*).

29. See 26.

30. *Chatham Observer*, 14 October 1916, *op. cit.*

31. See 26.

32. *Chatham Observer,* 30 September 1916, *op. cit.*

33. *Chatham News*, 14 October 1916, *op. cit.*

34. *Ibid.* The burial of Emily's remains is recorded in Church Register for Burials in the Parish of Burham (1883-1925), held by Medway Archives (P52/1/35), p.81. Entry No. 648 for 7 October 1916 states: 'An Unknown female person supposed to be Emily Maria Trigg'. (http://cityark.medway.gov.uk). The same register records the burial of Emily's father, John Trigg (no. 572) on 30 March 1912 (p. 72), and her mother, Kate Trigg (no. 717) on 23 August 1921 (p.90).

35. *Chatham Observer*, 21 October 1916, *op. cit.* Other sources that reported on the arrest of Charles B. Hicks include the *Kent Messenger* of 21 October ('The Blue Bell Hill Murder: An Arrest', p. 8). Before this, on 14 October, a special correspondent to *The People's Journal* (Dundee) ('Clue to the Slayer of Emily Trigg', fp) provided a description of the man that had reportedly been circulated all over the country: 'Age between 25 and 30, height about 5 feet 8 inches, rather thin with prominent cheek bones, darkish in general appearance, and wears coloured glasses, and an ugly birth mark on nose. This man is wearing khaki, has a 'funny walk."' But despite the quite specific description, it is not known whether Charles Hicks, once arrested, fit this description.

36. *Chatham Observer*, 28 October 1916, *op. cit.*

37. 'The Blue Bell Hill Mystery: Arrested Soldier Discharged', *Kent Messenger*, 28 October 1916, p. 5. Among the nagging questions that remain unanswered are what it was that Hicks reputedly said in his sleep in barracks in Winchester that would connect him to a murdered girl from Medway—unless he perhaps hailed from the area or even knew Emily Trigg. Whether this train of thought was also followed by the detectives we can only speculate. It may be telling, however, judging by the newspaper reports, that Hicks did not protest his innocence at his arrest, and did so only at his remand at Chatham.

38. By the almost methodical method by which Emily Trigg was gagged, and her body then dragged a distance and carefully concealed with cut lengths of grass, suspicions arise that she may have been the victim of more than a single assailant. Three sources even suggest as much: *The Yorkshire Post* ('The Kent Wood Tragedy' of 10 October 1916 (p. 7), and *The Swindon Advertiser* ('The Mystery of a Lonely Wood') of 13 October 1916 (fp) state: 'Probably more than one person was concerned in the crime'; while the *People's Journal* (Dundee) ('Wood Gives up its Grim Secret') of 30 September 1916 (fp) states: 'Her assailant or assailants (the police believe there were two)...'

39. See 5.

40. John E. Vigar, *op. cit.* (see 4.); www.burhamvillage.com. The website of the Churches Conservation Trust can be viewed at: www.visitchurches.org.uk.

41. Inland Revenue Record of Valuations 1910 (Duties on Land Values), held at the Kent History and Library Centre, Maidstone (Ref. IR4-15-1 & 2 (ledgers); Parish of Burham). The Trigg home is assessment no. 920, under the name of John Trigg, which is also handwritten on the 1:2500 scale survey map, 1908 edition, sheet XXXXI.2 (archive ref. 31/2). The Trigg's immediate neighbours are detailed under entries 918 and 919, the latter being a Mrs Gower (probably Elizabeth) who is cross-referenced in the 1911 Census according to the order (north to south along Maidstone Road): Miss Smith (Post Office); Mr Trigg; Mr Dadson; Mrs Gower; Mr Featherstone; Mr Larter; Mr Culver; Mr Mitchell (Upper Bell Inn) (See: Census of England and Wales 1911 (Enumerator's Summary Book): Rural District (Malling); Registration Sub-District: Aylesford; Ecclesiastical Parish: Burham St Mary the Virgin; Civil Parish: Burham (Schedule nos. 300–307, p.14; John Trigg is no. 301). (It is quite fortunate (for us) that the surveys (both Census and Land Duties) appeared then to be conducted door-to-door, which enable us to be reasonably confident of the sequences they portray, and their correspondences to the Land Duties maps).

42. One source differs, in giving the address as 4, Providence Row (*Chatham News*, 30 September 1916, *op. cit.*). All others give it as 3, Providence-row (or Providence-cottages).

43. The site of the Bridgewood Cottage pub is preserved on a triangular wedge of scrubland, marked by trees, at the north end of the village.

44. See: Census 1891: Rural District (Malling); Ecclesiastical Parish: Burham St Mary the Virgin; Civil Parish: Burham—Schedule no 221 (Public Record Office ref. RG12/668).

45. In the 1891 Census, the Bridgewood Cottage (pub) is schedule no. 220; James Broomfield (at no. 2 Bridgewood Cottages), is schedule no. 222, and Frederick Greenfield (no. 4 Bridgewood Cottages) is no. 224. No. 3 Bridgewood Cottages (later, 3 Providence Row), next to the Zion Chapel (Mission Hall) was occupied by William Mitchell and his family; a blacksmith who had a blacksmith's shop opposite the Upper Bell pub. Still here in 1901, by 1911 Mitchell had moved to the Upper Bell, and the cottage re-occupied, probably by a Miss Bassett. Evidently, it became vacant after 1912, enabling Kate Trigg to move in, most probably after her husband's death in March 1912.

46. Personal correspondence with Paul Lowing.

47. Initial source: Neil Arnold, who heard it from the witness in person on 4 April 2013 and summarised the account to me by email. I conducted my own brief telephone interview with Ann King on 8 April 2013.

48. Correspondence (email) dated 26 March 2011.

49. Correspondence (email) dated 12 September 2011.

50. Correspondence (email) May 2010.

51. It has to be said that when Mr Green tried to verify it on my behalf, the gentleman could not recall the comment about the motorway appearance (letter dated 28 January 1993). Andrew Green passed away on 21 May 2004, aged 76.

52. 'Walderslade Woman attacked', *Chatham Standard*, 5 July 1950, fp; Attacker wore red beret and gloves (*Newcastle Sun* (Australia) 18 December 1950, p. 2.

53. *Fortean Times* 108 (March 1998, p. 54). Quite how it was determined that the figure was a bridesmaid was unstated. In more recent correspondence (email, dated 13 September 2011), Neil indicated that this may have been an assumption based on the appearance of a longish 'gown' and the familiar legend (the 1965 crash story). This later recounting, though, relocated the sighting to the Lower Bell area of Blue Bell Hill itself).

54. Correspondence (email) dated 19 January 2002 and 20 & 21 December 2010.

55. Initial source: Neil Arnold, who heard it from the witnesses (who did not leave their name) at Chalk on 8 August 2015 and summarised for me the same day by email.

56. Michael Goss, *op.cit.*, p. 22.

Chapter Eleven: Hekate on the Hill

1. From *The Oxford Book of the Supernatural* (Oxford University Press, 1994), edited by D.J. Enwright, pp. 152–153.

2. 'Blue Bell Hill spectre puzzles historian', by Claire Ogley, *Kent Today*, 22 January 1993, p. 11.

3. 'Wizened road horror is ruining our lives', by Claire Ogley, *Kent Today*, 8 January 1993, p. 13.

4. *Ibid.* It should be stated for the record that it was always the view of some involved in the Maiden incident that their experience was the result of a hoax—for instance, ex-police employee Alison Bowers, who was on duty in the Maidstone control room that night, and the first person Mr. Maiden spoke to after the encounter (correspondence from PC David Elvy, dated 3 July 1998). When I spoke to Alison in July 1998, she told me that the response to the report was weighted toward someone paying a frightening prank—the impression being that Mr. Maiden himself seemed to be of this opinion (which came to be her opinion also, and also of at least one of the investigating officers). She also told me that there had been unconfirmed reports that someone in a costume had been seen in Blue Bell Hill village sometime afterward.

What we *can* be clear about is the physical and mental trauma suffered by the witnesses that night, as attested to by David Elvy (from previous correspondence by Mr Elvy to *Fortean Times*, dated 20 October 1997, and copied to myself). What to make of the above stands with the reader. No evidence of a hoax, however, has been forthcoming in the years following the encounter. And there are other reasons that leave the question open: the record of other sightings, the observed disappearance of the figure (if reported accurately), and the whole weight of folklore, some obscure, that stands behind the creature here reported, requiring the 'hoaxer', at least, to be one very knowledgeable of this branch of folklore/mythology.

5. 'Cabbie confirms 'ghost' sighting', by Claire Ogley, *Kent Today*, 14 January 1993, p. 12.

6. Given erroneously in the *Kent Today* report as Folkestone. From September 2011, the former *Great Danes* Hotel, which thereafter became the *Ramada Jarvis*, and now the *Mercure*, Maidstone.

7. 28 June 1994.

8. Telephone interview with the witness 7 January 2012, following initial correspondence (email) from his daughter 7 December 2011.

9. Private communication from the witness 25 April 1994.

10. Telephone interview with the witness 25 June 2010. The internet reference regarding other sightings of the 'the Hag' was almost certainly my own website (www.roadghosts.com).

11. Correspondence (email) dated 12 June 2011.

12. Initial account by email via Neil Arnold (14 September 2013).

13. Assembled from further correspondence (email) with witness (19–23 September 2013). One of the features hard to reconcile with the circumstances and my own knowledge of the location is to understand how the woman's complexion could be accurately determined once the car's headlights had gone out. The road here is unlit, and would be quite dark, especially on moonless nights, and despite any overspill from the lights of Aylesford or Maidstone.

14. Correspondence (email) with witness, 5 October 2003 & 29 August 2005. In the latter, Mr Matthews described the figure as giving off a menacing atmosphere, and disappeared in view—details which were not given in the original report.

15. After a lecture on ghosts given by the late Andrew Green at Sandling Village Hall in the evening of 24 January 1995, which included brief mention of Blue Bell Hill, a lady, who had lived on the Kit's Coty estate for some 38 years, told me that 'a long time ago' an old lady lived in the woods at Blue Bell Hill (a probable reference to Mrs Emmeline King, who is discussed later in this chapter).

16. Source: Neil Arnold via email 23 May 2013, from a conversation with the (unnamed) informant the previous evening. A different informant told Neil she had heard about the hag during her youth in the 1950s, and she and friends would cycle out to Chatham Road in search of her.

17. 'Old Woman Sat "Like Witch Casting Spells"', *The Newcastle Sun* (NSW, Australia), 10 May 1951, p.9. (Find credit: Neil Arnold, Nov. 2015). Other sources: 'Cat to blame for death of recluse?', *Chatham Observer*, 2 February 1951, fp; 'Aged Recluse Died in Fire', *South East Gazette*, 6 February 1951, p.6. Emmeline King is listed in the electoral register for 1950, in the parish of Aylesford, polling district Blue Bell Hill (D) under no. 226.

18. 'Thumbs down to ghostly hiker', by George Edwards, *The News of the World*, 13 April 1975, p. 5.

19. Terence Whitaker, *Ghosts & North Country Legends* (Grafton Books, 1988), pp. 313–314.

20. 'Vanishing Lady's Ghost', *Evening Express and Evening Mail*, 29 April 1905, p.4.

21. Roger Boar & Nigel Blundell, *The World's Greatest Ghosts* (Hamlyn, 1991), p. 130.

22. 'A ghostly tale for Christmas', by Emma Lidiard, *The Westmorland Gazette* (online edition), 24 December 2011.

23. William Shakespeare, *Macbeth*, Act 1, Scene 3. Shakespeare based his scene on Raphael Holinshed's *Chronicles of England, Scotland and Ireland* (1577). In Shakespeare's time, the Weird Sisters were portrayed as nymphs and fairies; only later devolving into the familiar guise of witches (*'We Three': The Mythology of Shakespeare's Weird Sisters*, by Laura Annawyn Shamas, Peter Lang Publishing, 2006).

24. *Evening Post*, 15 July 1974; *The Gazette* (Maidstone), 16 July 1974.

25. Telephone conversation with Mrs G. Beever, of Sheerness, 22 April 1994 (see also Chapters 6 & 7). The new cottage was built by Mrs Beever's father-in-law, and was named The Helm, after the original. The stones were said to lie beneath the original's kitchen.

26. See 25.

27. The 'Odinists', who worship the old Norse gods, took their plea to new heights in 1996 when they declared it their intention to appeal to the House of Lords to defend the setting of the White Horse Stone, their most sacred religious shrine, from being destroyed by the passage of high-speed trains on the Channel Tunnel rail-link. The Odinists, numbering between 3,000 and 4,000 nationwide, proposed extending the tunnel under Blue Bell Hill beyond the site of the White Horse Stone ('Plea to save pagan shrine', by Steve Hedges, *Kent Today*, 7 June 1996, fp; 'Worshippers' plea to save a pagan place', by Stephen Hedges, *Kent Messenger*, 7 June 1996, p. 3). The following month, a group calling themselves the Lords of the Forest wrote to the *Kent Today* pledging their determination to defend the site. Their forefathers, they said, had fought and died there (the battle of AD 455), and they had sworn to do the same! ('This stone is sacred' ('You Say...' – Reader's letters)), *Kent Today*, 4 July 1996, p. 6. The line passes approximately 100 metres south of the site.

28. Town and Country Notes, *The South Eastern Gazette*, 27 June 1887, p. 5. The A.O.D. stands for the Ancient Order of Druids, an organisation founded in London in 1781 and formed around contemporary notions of ancient Celtic druidism. The summer solstice, would appear to be an inopportune time to visit Kit's Coty. Undergraduate student Gerald Francis Buncombe, 19, visited the stones with a friend on 21 June 1906, and climbed the stones to have his photograph taken. On trying to get back down, he slipped and impaled his chest on the railings, and later died of his injuries at West Kent Hospital in Maidstone ('The Kits Coty Accident', *South Eastern Gazette*, 7 July 1906, p. 7.

29. Reference to 'Hekate on the Hill', a page then on my website, www.roadghosts.com.

30. Mrs Ash* was, in fact, nearer 70 at the time—as Nigel himself corrected in his next email to me, and as attested by her death certificate (see 29.).

31. A possibly interesting aside to this location is the loop of white footprints observed and photographed here by the author around 1990, which were small and feminine in style, and resembled whitewash, which emerged from a point on the grass verge onto the tarmac pavement in a short loop and back onto the grass. This was the area where psychic Nella Jones claimed her contacts with the ghosts in 1992 (see Chapter 8).

32. Emails 10 & 23 February 2006. Further correspondence with Nigel on 1 April 2006 recorded the following interesting and possibly significant snippet: 'Mrs Ash* quite frequently used the garden of Kits Coty Cottage as a short cut. Rather than walk up as far as the footpath (and then back down to turn off right along to her home) we sometimes saw her cut through the front garden and down to the back garden gate; thus saving herself a walk of a quarter of a mile or so. She certainly had no inhibitions about crossing our land and my aunts, I remember, believed Mrs Ash regarded it as a right of passage.'

33. Email 23 February 2006.

34. Registered at Maidstone (sub-district of Malling), 8 February 1955; certified by R.G. Ponder MRCS. Place and date of death: 'Seventh February 1955, 'The Helm', Blue Bell

Hill, Aylesford.' Wife of Edward Charles Ash* (a farm labourer). Cause of death: hypostatic pneumonia.

35. England & Wales, Death Index: 1916–2005: Edward C. Ash*, aged 80, registered at Maidstone, Jan-Feb-Mar 1965, Vol. 58, p.824.

36. Personal communication with Pat Sandford 24 May 2010 at a talk given by him at the Blue Bell Hill Preservation Group AGM. Edward George (Pat) Sandford passed away on 23 June 2016, aged 87.

37. Account received by email (via Neil Arnold) 31 January 2014.

38. At 1–2 High Street & 1 Week Street. The pub closed in the early 1960s, and the Grade II listed building was converted into shops in 1964.

39. Correspondence (email) with Brian Culver, dated 16 November 2011.

40. Elsie Ash's maiden name was Grigg. She married Edward Charles Ash* in 1918 (England & Wales, Death Index: 1916–2005: Malling, Oct-Nov-Dec 1918, Vol. 2a, p. 1805.

41. For example, the experience of David and Judi Simpson, in July 1992, at Stocksbridge, South Yorkshire. The couple were crossing the by-pass via an over-bridge when they both noticed off to their left a grey, featureless apparition apparently running across the field towards them, apparently above ground level, with its arms and legs flailing about in an uncoordinated manner. It came up the embankment, across the road and disappeared into the car. (*Strange But True?* TV series, presented by Michael Aspel), LWT Productions, 1994; Jenny Randles & Peter Hough, *Strange But True?* (Piatkus, 1994), Chapter 6 ('Highway of Horror?'), pp. 70–82).

42. 'Two Men Killed: Buried by Fall of Chalk', *Chatham Standard*, 17 November 1948, p. 2; 'Man and Boy Killed by 10 Tons of Chalk: Tragedy at Blue Bell Hill', *Kent Messenger*, 19 November 1948, fp; 'Buried by Chalk: Two Men Killed by Fall', *Chatham News*, 19 November 1948, p. 4; 'Man and Boy Killed by 10 Tons of Chalk: Tragedy at Blue Bell Hill', *Chatham Observer*, 19 November 1948, p. 2. In the earliest report (17 November), the driver's surname is given incorrectly: Belwood instead of Bellward.

43. 'Men Buried by Chalk Fall: Inquest Story of Disregarded Danger Warning', *Chatham Standard*, 24 November 1948, fp; 'Man and Boy Killed by Fall of Chalk: Tragedy at Blue Bell Hill', *Kent Messenger*, 26 November 1948, p. 5.

44. 'A Child's Shocking Death', *Kent & Sussex Courier*, 24 August 1900, p. 2; 'Fatal Fall Over a Chalk Cliff', *Chatham and Rochester News*, 25 August 1900, p. 2; 'Fatal Accident at Blue Bell Hill: Fall Over a Chalk Cliff, *Chatham, Rochester & Brompton Observer*, 25 August 1900, p. 6; 'Maidstone: Fatal Fall Over a Chalk Cliff', *Whitstable Times & Herne Bay Herald*, 25 August 1900, p. 7. Kate Gadd was born in 1891 (England & Wales, Birth Index: 1837–1915: Registered at Malling, Apr-May-Jun 1891, Vol. 2a, p. 647).

45. The Holiday Inn is rumoured to be haunted by a young female that some staff members have connected to a murder that took place on wasteland near the original building—a possible association with the murder in 1916 of Emily Trigg (see Chapter 10), who was found not very far from here directly west across the aerodrome field; or some other victim of misdeed? (Credits: *Paranormal Database* website ('Pale Woman in Blouse') / Neil Arnold).

46. Correspondence (email) with witness 4 & 9 & 11 February 2011.

47. 'Pensioner died after car hit her', *Chatham Standard*, 16 December 1980, p.17; 'Old lady did not see car coming', *Evening Post*, 15 December 1980, p.11. (Credit to Neil Arnold for the initial find of the *Chatham Standard* article).

48. Philip Carr-Gomm & Richard Heygate, *The Book of English Magic* (John Murray, 2010 (paperback edition), pp. 316–317. See also: Dublin University Magazine, Jan-June 1871, Dublin: George Herbert; London: Hurst & Blackett, 1871 (*Legends and Traditions of Cornwall* (May 1871, p. 491) for 'An' used as a title for a wise woman.

49. Carr-Gomm & Heygate, *Ibid.*

50. Willem de Blécourt, Ronald Hutton, Jean Sybil La Fontaine, *The Athlone History of Witchcraft and Magic in Europe: Twentieth Century* (Vol. 6), 1999. See Part 1: Modern Pagan Witchcraft (Ronald Hutton), p. 14.

51. 'Witch and Her Imps', *Falkirk Herald*, 12 September 1928, p. 6, and 15 September 1928, p.4.

52. Goss, *op.cit.*, p. 141.

53. Originally published in Zürich in 1569, the first English translation was in 1572, by Henry Benneyman (London) for Richard Watkyns. Available in full in *Lewes Lavater: Of Ghosts and Spirits Walking By Night 1572*, by J. Dover Wilson and May Yardley (eds) (University Press, Oxford, 1929). See Michael Goss *op.cit.*, p. 128.

54. In this instance, from the English translation (*Of Ghostes and Spirites, Walking by Night*, by Lewes Lavaterus of Tigurine), printed in London by Thomas Creede (1596). (See 'The First Part').

55. *De Origine, Situ, Qualitate et Quantitate Frisiae, et Rebus A Frisiis olim praeclare gestis* (1588).

56. 'De sage van de Witte Wieven' ('The saga of the Weird Sisters'), by John Damen, *De Kampioen* (magazine, Netherlands) Jan 2003, pp. 62–64: Witte wieven in de Achterhoek.

57. 'Prehistorische grafvelden en tumuli rondom Zutphen' ('Prehistoric burial sites and tumuli around Zutphen'), by Gerre van der Kleij, Michel Groothedde, *Volume 3 of Zutphense archeologische publicaties* (Gemeente Zutphen, Sector Ruimte, afdeling BMA/Archeologie, 2006).

58. The Moirai were also sometimes depicted as ugly hags (Lotte Motz, *The Faces of the Goddess* (Oxford University Press, 1997).

59. *The Secret Commonwealth*, by Robert Kirk, is available as a reprint from Element Books (*Robert Kirk: Walker Between Worlds*, by R.J. Stewart, 1996).

60. Source: Neil Arnold (email) 16 October 2010.

61. 'Een Weinig Bekend Hoekje Van Mooi Nederland' ('A Little Known Corner of the Beautiful Netherlands'), by Scheltema Gan (*Elsevier's Geïllustreerd Maandschrift* (*Elsevier's Illustrated Monthly Scripture*), Vol. 11, Part XXI, no. 6, 1901).

62. Scheltema Gan, *Ibid*; Patricia Monaghan, *The Encyclopedia of Celtic Mythology and Folklore* (Facts on File, 2004), pp. 351–2.

63. The *Matronae* (or *Matres*)—'mothers', usually depicted in groups of three, were venerated in NW Europe between the first and fifth centuries AD. One of the figures sometimes has a youthful appearance, with loose flowing hair (symbolising maidenhood) in contrast to the two older figures wearing head dresses or caps. In addition to baskets of produce, the *Matronae* are also depicted with babies, napkins or scrolls—hence are associated with (as protectors of) fertility, childbearing and midwifery, and the cycles of life and the harvest. (Dr Hilda Ellis Davidson, *Roles of the Northern Goddess* (Routledge, 1998).

64. Symbolism that is carried into contemporary times in the form of the Harvest Festival (held in Europe in September, on or near the Sunday of the Harvest Moon—the full moon closet to the autumn equinox), and in its equinoctial opposite, Easter, at spring time, where the laden basket (and its eggs) symbolises the renewal of life.

65. Patricia Monaghan, *op.cit.* The 'otherworld' is said to have been associated by the Celts with an island in the western sea (i.e. Britain).

66. A number of supernatural entities of Celtic, European and world folklore find familiarity with Blue Bell Hill's ghost and the Phantom Hitch-Hiker. In classical mythology, we find the *nymphs*, spirits of nature who were envisaged as young, beautiful women. The nymphs possessed the power of prophecy, and were generally kindly toward humans, although they could also be dangerous. Various classes of nymph have been distinguished: *dryads* and *hamadryads* (tree nymphs, *naiads* (nymphs of lakes, rivers, and springs);

oreads (nymphs of mountains and hills). Maria Leach and Jerome Fried, editors of *Funk & Wagnalls Standard Dictionary of Folklore, Mythology, and Legend* (HarperSanFranciso, 1984, p. 806), note that the nymphs probably developed into the fairies of general European folklore.

On the darker side, there are variations in the character of the hag in the *Cailleach Beará* of Irish and Scottish folklore, and in the *Cailleach Bheur*—in some versions a loathly lady who transforms herself into a beautiful young woman as a reward to kind-hearted young men. The Cailleach as goddess is in keeping with the idea that Blue Bell Hill, like many other sites distinguished by Neolithic artefacts, was a place held sacred by their builders. And then we have the *bean nighe*, also of Ireland and Scotland; the *Washer of the Ford*: an ugly hag that sometimes appeared in the guise of a beautiful young woman—and, akin to the banshee (*bean sidhe*, the 'woman of the fairies' (or 'woman of the hill'), similarly a hag or a young woman), who portended death by her appearance. In some descriptions of the banshee, we find an old woman with glowing red eyes (from the constant weeping) set in hollow sockets, with long flowing white hair (compare this to the blonde hair of Blue Bell Hill's hag, as described by Diane Rayburn).

In European lore, there is the *Rusalka*, a water spirit of Slavic lore said to be the spirit of a dead female (in some parts, a bride who died on her wedding night)—who, like the *Sirens* of Greek mythology, lure men to their drowning by sweet song; the *Vila*, another hostile spirit of Slavic lore, the spirit of an unbaptised child or an earthbound virgin. The vila dances in circles, condemning any who disturb them to join them unto death; the *Nocnitsa*, a hag of Eastern European lore; the *Berchta*, an ugly old woman of German folklore, thought to have originally been a goddess (the German equivalent of the Cailleach); the *nix*, a German equivalent of the Rusalka, and so on.

It is interesting to note that powers of prophecy are most commonly attributed to the darker (and by time-honoured interpretation, evil) characters of this lore, frequently old crones wizened by age, much like the Version B/D Phantom Hitch-Hiker in some examples.

67. *Funk & Wagnalls Standard Dictionary of Folklore, Mythology, and Legend* (eds. Maria Leach & Jerome Fried), HarperSanFranciso, 1984), p. 180 & pp. 473–474.

The Version D Hitch-Hiker which, in terms of discussion has really fallen outside the scope of this book, for sake of completeness can also be noted to take a more positive role. In some witness-attested cases, the Hitch-Hiker takes the form of an angelic being whose role generally appears to be a benevolent one (in accordance with some deeper strands of folklore and tradition), providing protection or guidance to travellers. Prophecies, when given, involving broader, less personal issues, similarly tend to be beneficial or optimistic, in opposition to the gloomy forecasts of the old women in black.

68. Some witness accounts at Blue Bell Hill, for instance, describe a young (teenaged) girl rather than the young woman reported by others. James Shoebridge, whose account is featured in Chapter 11, insightfully concluded that his experience was of something elemental in nature on account of the intense sense of malevolence emanating from it, which he identified with "The Crone', the winter embodiment of Mother Earth who is said to be as cold and deadly as the winter. That is common in pagan lore.'

69. The hag of Peak and Leicestershire tradition, a creature of the Dane Hills. See David Clarke and Andy Roberts' *Twilight of the Celtic Gods* (Blandford, 1996), Women of the Mists (pp. 70–74).

70. *Ibid*, p. 71; Katherine Mary Briggs, *The Fairies in English Tradition and Literature* (University of Chicago Press, 1967, 1989).

71. Norman Adams, *Haunted Scotland* (Mainstream Publishing, 1998).

72. Hekate is featured more familiarly in other triple-goddess sets: Artemis (virgin)–Persephone (nymph)–Hekate (crone); Persephone (daughter)–Demeter (mother)–Hekate (grandmother). As an aspect of the ancient triple-goddess, who presided over heaven, earth, and the underworld, and the cycle of birth, life and death, Hekate found a special place in the Greek pantheon as the only one of the ousted pre-Olympian deities, the Ti-

tans, to be so honoured by Zeus (see Hesiod (*The Theogeny*, 7.403–404). While not formally included in the Olympian family (in her early forms she is often found in subordinate roles), as a functionally all-encompassing goddess, it is not surprising that some of her manifold attributes should be shared or syncretised with other deities, such as Persephone, Demeter, Rhea, Artemis (the Roman Diana), and Selene—giving rise to a confusing picture of her status and role(s).

Hekate, as an aspect of the Triple/Mother Goddess can be related back to the earliest forms of the Mother Goddess, to: Astarte, Cybele; Ishtar, Inanna), Aphrodite, and the Biblical Ashtoreth. (Maria Leach & Jerome Fried (eds.), *Funk & Wagnall's Standard Dictionary of Folklore, Mythology, and Legend*, *op. cit.*, p. 84).

73. Early depictions of Hekate had her as a maidenly attendant and guide (*Propolos*) to the Olympian gods—notably Persephone (Queen of the Underworld), Demeter (the Earth Goddess/Mother), and Artemis (a mother deity and goddess of nature and the hunt). Later also a goddess of fertility, marriage and childbirth, she became linked to the Moon, magic, and the night. In common with Artemis, Hekate was also attended upon, both having attendants (*propoloi*) consisting of deceased humans and dogs. Both are linked to legends concerning female supernatural guardians, who died at their own hand or were sacrificed by others to enact this protective function on the behalf of their people. (Maria Leach, *op. cit.*, p. 76.).

Interestingly, the Romans continued traditions of veneration at crossroads, with their festival of *Ludi Compitales* (17 December to 5 January, at which they set up altars to the *Lares* (guardian spirits, possibly the ghosts of the dead), designed to retain or capture them to serve as supernatural guardians of place or property. The 5 January end-of-festival date overlaps favourably the dates (5 & 6 January) of the 1993 hag encounters on Blue Bell Hill. It does seem strange that two festivals connected with Hekate (this example by the association between Hekate and guardian spirits established by sacrifice or the entrapment of 'lost' or wandering spirits of the night) should be found to correspond to prominent encounters of the Blue Bell Hill series. ('The metaphors and rituals of place and time—an introduction to liminality', by Bob Trubshaw, *At the Edge*, (www.indigogroup.co.uk). Whether, at Blue Bell Hill, the manifestations of the girl or young woman character represent the youthful guise of the goddess herself, or members of her *propoloi*, or such guardian spirits, is open to interpretation.

74. A feature also in common with the Cailleach, marking her dominion and ease of passage in both the worlds of the living and the dead.

75. I. Robert Von Rudloff notes the dualistic functions of many Greek deities: to be both beneficial and destructive. With regard to Hekate, her ability to govern fearful ghosts might be the 'flip side' of her ability to protect against them. (I. Robert Von Rudloff, *Hekate in Early Greek Religion*, Horned Owl Publishing (July 1999)).

76. Also known as the 'three ways'. In ancient times, crossroads were fearful places, frequently un-signposted, and therefore liable to lead to confusion and the attendant fear of taking the wrong path or of being misled—a fear heightened at night, especially around the 'dread hour of midnight' ('The Mystery of the Cross-Roads', by Martin Puhvel, *Folklore* (1976, v. 87, p. 168). No wonder, as a result of the later perversion of Hekate's role as guide, these 'pauseless places' came to be regarded as the abode of fearful ghosts and demons, dedicated to leading people astray—and, in turn, to the later belief among Europeans that witches held their festivities at crossroads (which also came to serve as the burial places for certain 'undesirables', such as suicides, and/or the place of execution for murderers, witches, and outlaws). (See 'Hermes', by Ron Leadbetter, Encyclopedia Mythica (www.pantheon.org); Bob Trubshaw, *op. cit.*).

77. Hekate was referred to in the 7th century BC *Homeric Hymn to Demeter* as the goddess 'who wore a delicate veil'—a title also used to describe Rhea, Demeter's mother and Persephone's grandmother (whom Hekate ousts as the Crone/grandmother aspect in one version of the Triple-form containing the daughter and mother). Interestingly, in another of those similarities in detail between Mother Goddess figures and their Phantom Hitch-Hiker counterparts, we can recall the *caille* in reference to the Cailleach meaning 'hood' or 'veil'.

78. Inviting comparison to the Blue Bell Hill hag's bundle of twigs? One of Hekate's common titles was 'light-bringer' (*Phosphorus*). In art, she is frequently portrayed as carrying a pair of torches, which, according to the popular view, symbolises her as Moon-Goddess. Others differ, seeing the title and the torches as representative of her original function as guide or attendant. Hekate's other titles or epithets include: *Hekate Triformis* (three-formed (Triple) Goddess), *Hekate Prytania* (invincible Queen of the dead), *Hekate Nyktipolos* (night-wandering), *Hekate Skylakagetis* (leader of the dogs).

79. 'The Hosts of Hekate', by Erwin Rohde, in *Psyche: The cult of Souls and the Belief in Immortality among the Greeks*, Routledge, 2000). Dreams brought on by Hekate were not restricted to bad dreams, but included the vivid and terrifying 'personal' experience of her in the form of the original nightmare—the 'Old Hag' experience—a universal, often wakeful experience involving 'sleep paralysis' that, in other cultures, has been attributed to Hekate's Dark Goddess counterparts. 'Old Hag' experiences are named for the preponderance of cases in the folk record (and in 'real' situations) depicting wizened female attackers and male victims. The psychology of this relationship is addressed in Chapter 14. Having noted the same pattern and bias in Phantom-Hiker lore and reported Road Ghost 'fact', the re-stated question underlying these cases is whether these archetypal characters—seen or experienced in waking nightmares, in lucid dreams, or (as at Blue Bell Hill), at large in the physical environment—are an expression of a deep-seated but unconscious recognition of ancient (and diabolised) Mother Goddess traditions; or whether there is something else at play: real entities or forces that have found their place in tradition and folklore? Certainly, on the latter point, there are those who believe fervently in such dark powers, and regard *all* ghostly manifestations (including the Phantom Road Accident variety) as the work of demons. For the definitive study of the Old Hag experience read David J. Hufford's *The Terror That Comes in the Night* (University of Pennsylvania Press, 1982).

80. Carried over to the Wiccan calendar as 'Hecate Night'. 16 November marks also the Festival of Bast or Bastet, the ancient Egyptian cat goddess (meaning 'Devouring Lady'). Bast has much in common with Hekate and other goddess figures. Ancient artwork typically depicts Bast with the body of a girl and the head of a cat (or sometimes fully in the form of a cat). Interestingly, she is sometimes portrayed as a light-skinned girl with long blonde hair and bright blue eyes—inviting comparison to early depictions of the 'bright-coiffed' Hekate, and paving the way, perhaps, for later associations with the goddesses Artemis/Kore Artemis (Greek), and Diana (Roman). Black cats are said to especially sacred to her (Maria Leach (Ed.), *op. cit.*), raising interesting comparisons to the coincidence of sightings in the Blue Bell Hill area of a large panther-like feline, dubbed the 'Beast of Blue Bell Hill'.

Although caution must be maintained with regard to other possibly significant coincidences or proximities between certain festivals or commemorations and encounters at Blue Bell Hill, the following are nevertheless noteworthy:

8 November (date of Ian Sharpe's encounter): The day in Celtic tradition when *Gwynn ap Nudd*, king of the fairies, opened the door to his kingdom.

22 November (Chris Dawkins)—*24 November*: Three days sacred in the Greek and Roman calendar to the goddess Artemis/Diana in her aspect as divine Huntress and Destroyer.

5 January: Twelfth Night marks the feast of the old Roman goddess Befana, the 'Great Grandmother' (or St. Befana), an ugly but good-natured hag who rides her broomstick through the world on this night to deliver gifts to the stockings of good children. Descriptively similar, but contrasting in character, there is Berchta, of German folklore, whose feast day is also Twelfth Night, who stands as a diabolical opposite, hostile to naughty children. Like Hekate, Berchta has been said to 'ride the storm' leading a howling pack of dogs. Her children, likewise, are either the souls of dead children or the spirits of the unborn. (Ref: Maria Leach (Ed.), *op. cit.*)

81. We see the character and habits of Blue Bell Hill's and other phantom hitch-hikers reflected also in Kirk's elemental spirits. While the modern, popular conception of the fairy folk has been prejudiced by the likes of the infamous Cottingley case and Disney's

'Tinkerbell', our forebears saw them as quite different creatures, far removed from the often sanitised offerings made to children. The 'Good People' or *Sleagh Maith* (a name, Kirk explained, arising from the habit of the Irish to bless that which they feared) were not all they seemed. Frequently mischievous; occasionally malignant, these creatures are found in the folklores of cultures around the world, going by a host of names. For instance, a common prank of pisgies (pixies) is to lead astray and bewilder travellers (being 'pixie-led').

The habits and characteristics of Kirk's elementals that we might today interpret as ghostly include: their residence in the earth, or in caves; the light, semi-material nature of their bodies (like 'congealed air'), that enables them to pass through the fissures and interstices in rock; they are most visible at twilight; they are able to appear or disappear at will, and to change their form or appearance (an ability known as 'glamour'); they sometimes show themselves or speak to natural people (whose customs and language they adopt for the discourse), only to vanish in full view; their own language is a peculiar whistling sound, and they have a propensity to abduct people (particularly children), taking body and soul together (which is reminiscent of the claim of a Blue Bell Hill resident (unidentified) who told the *Kent Messenger* that when he accompanied a research team to the Hill in the 1970s, a medium ran off screaming saying the ghost wanted to take somebody to the 'other side' ('Terror as ghost girl reappears', by Emma Cooper, *Kent Messenger*, 13 November 1992, p. 3). (Alison Jones, *Larousse Dictionary of World Folklore* (Larousse, 1995); R.J. Stewart, *Robert Kirk: Walker Between Worlds* (Element Books, 1990); Jacques Vallee, *Passport to Magonia* ((Tandem, 1975); reprinted by Contemporary Books, Chicago, 1993).

Chapter Twelve: Walkin' After Midnight

1. Oscar W. Firkins, Richard Burton, Netta White Wilson, *Memoirs and letters of Oscar W. Firkins* (University of Minnesota Press, 1934), p.128.

2. 'Hit and Myth' (in 'Road Ghosts'), by Sean Tudor, *Fortean Times* 73, February/March 1994, pp. 27–31; 'Hell's Belles', by Sean Tudor, *Fortean Times* 104, November 1997, pp. 36–40.

3. It is interesting that the transition from the hitch-hiking habit to the phantom jaywalker habit should keep pace with the supportable level of public credulity. Where Western culture has become more sophisticated and knowledgeable about matters paranormal (not to say cynical), the hitch-hiking habit could be said to hold less conviction than in the decades before mass communication. Its replacement, the pedestrian accident victim, is arguably the more plausible alternative for the contemporary age. In so doing, the phenomenon gives up nothing of its core principle, as we have seen. Indeed, rather than simply representing an unconscious response to its time—a blindly reflected cultural or sociological phenomenon—the persistent counter argument, in light of the well-attested witness testimonies we have examined, is that there is something to the phenomenon in both cases that is more deeply reflective, matching itself adroitly to its time and circumstances—which might explain why the Phantom Hitch-Hiker can seemingly be alive and current in some parts of the world, while becoming virtually unheard of in Britain and the West after the 1970s.

4. 'Ghostly Goings On'; 'Triple death crash began riddle of Blue Bell Hill', by Emily Hall, *Kent Messenger* (Maidstone), Friday 14 November 2003, p. 2 & p. 18.

5. 'Wet hair, big eyes and bare feet: Two more readers tell of their ghostly sightings on Blue Bell Hill', by Emily Hall, *Kent Messenger* (Maidstone) Friday 19 December 2003, p. 35.

6. 'Ghostly hitch-hiker who vanished into thin air...', by Emily Hall, *Kent Messenger* (Maidstone), 30 January 2004, p. 52.

7. Correspondence (email) with Rex Lane Harvey (now resident in South Africa) 5 & 7 October 2015.

8. See Chapter 5 (note 3.). Detling Hill's tally of victims include a man called Shield who, in April 1914, was found dead near his bicycle, apparently the victim of a hit-and-run collision with a motor vehicle ('Two Motor Mysteries—Man Found Dead By his Cycle on Roadside', *The Manchester Courier*, 15 April 1914, p. 3); and two Maidstone women and the children (a boy, 6, and a girl, 7) of one of them, who died in September 1925 when a charabanc swerved into the hedge and overturned at the top of the hill; 'Road Crash Victims', *Western Daily Press* (Bristol), 14 September 1925, p. 7; 'Motor Charabanc Overturns', *The Western Morning News and Mercury*, 14 September 1925, p. 3.

9. Brian Paine (Ed.) with Trevor Sturgess, *Unexplained Kent* (The Breedon Books Publishing Company, 1997, pp. 63-64.

10. 'I met the Blue Bell Hill ghost', by Brian Paine, *KM Extra*, W/E 28 October 2005. Sadly, Brian Paine passed away suddenly in March 2006, aged 65 ('Ex-KM Group senior editor Brian Paine dies', by Trevor Sturgess, *KentOnline*, Monday 20 March 2006).

11. *The Why Files* (1999), Episode 10, Part 2, 'The Ghost Bride'. See Published History: Television.

12. *Meridian Tonight* (2000), 'Legends and Mysteries—the Hitch-Hiker on the Hill'. See Published History: Television.

13. At an evening meeting with Judith's two sisters 14 December 1992.

14. Telephone conversation 23 November 1992.

15. Telephone interview 30 October 2000; meeting on 31 October 2000. An email to John for further comment in 2012 went unanswered.

16. www.canterburyghosttour.com.

17. When, according to his personal resumé (LinkedIn), he would have been a student at Thanet College at Broadstairs (now East Kent College)).

18. Providing the essential and tangible 'proof' as to the intangibility of the passenger.

19. Initial contact with Frank Lynch was made via a student media project in March 2004. Further email correspondence between Mr Lynch and the author took place over 17-18 November and 31 December 2012. The Queens Cinema was located off the High Street, Sittingbourne, opposite St. Michael's Church.

The England & Wales Death Index 1916-2007 records the death of Kenneth Harry Gowers (b. 27 May 1911) at Thanet in June 1974, aged 63 (vol. 16, p.1785). His wife, Joan Harriet Gowers (née Thomas) (b. 22 June 1920), died in 1994, aged 74; registered at Thanet in November 1994 (B12D, 5751B).

20. www.kenthistoryforum.co.uk: 'The Blue Bell Hill Vanishing Lady Hitch Hiker', 25 April 2009.

21. Correspondence 12 & 15 May 2010; 22 November 2012. The photo of Peter Leadbetter is from the October 1986 edition of *GEC Avionics News.*

22. There are a number of preserved accounts of accidents, including fatalities, from the days of horse-drawn carriage (see Chapter 2), but none involving women.

23. 'Blue Bell Hill Mystery Solved', *Chatham Observer*, 8 August 1952, p. 6.

24. Bruce Barrymore Halpenny, *Ghost Stations V* (Casdec Ltd), pp. 141–142.

25. www.rochester-airport.co.uk/history. The damage to the Davis Estate and casualties is detailed in 'City of Rochester, Incidents 1939–1945', preserved in Medway Council Archives (http://cityark.medway.gov.uk).

26. Source: 'Fred', a German guest on the Kent History Forum, 9 January 2010 (Thread: 'Rochester airport myths or fact and bomb holes!'), whose uncle's surviving flight logbook records the sortie.

27. Howard Posner's account of his father's experience furnished via email (5 February 2016) from Neil Arnold.

28. www.kenthistoryforum.co.uk: 'The Blue Bell Hill Vanishing Lady Hitch Hiker', reply #22, 9 April 2010.

29. 'Woman Thrown Over Car', *Chatham, Rochester & Gillingham News*, 14 July 1939, p.6.

30. *The Ton-Up Run*, by Peter J. Hedge, was originally written in 1973 in Tehran, and broadcast by the South African Broadcasting Corporation (SABC) in 1976. The fictional story of Jacintha Alexander, the hitch-hiking phantom of a motorcycle accident, was inspired by the real-life rumours associated with Blue Bell Hill. Peter, who hailed originally from Medway and who now lives in British Columbia (Canada), actually attended schools with several of the protagonists of the real-life 1965 tragedy, including Judith Lingham, who was a classmate at Balfour Road School (Primary and Junior in Balfour Road, Chatham) until 1954—only he was not aware of the connections when he penned *The Ton-Up Run*; this only coming to light in later years, in 1988, after his daughter sent him a copy of Joan Forman's *The Haunted South*. The realisation that he had known the girl who later became tagged as the ghost literally gave him goose bumps.

31. www.kenthistoryforum.co.uk: 'The Blue Bell Hill Vanishing Lady Hitch Hiker', posted by 'iconic' (reply #9, 20 November 2009) and recounting the experience of two acquaintances.

32. Posted in the readers' comments section on 09 Oct. 2014 footnoting Kentonline (*Kent Messenger*) article ('Phantom spotted as Blue Bell Hill ghost story turned into spooky film by Rochester actress'), by Claire McWethy, 24 October 2013.

33. 'Ghost sightings—your story', Weird Kent (BBC Kent website), 9 December 2003).

34. Correspondence (email) 25 & 28 April 2003. The talkSPORT broadcast was probably on 23–24 April.

35. 'Terror as ghost girl reappears', by Emma Cooper, Kent Messenger, 13 November 1992, p. 3).

36. Source: 'A Ghostly Hitchhiker in Steubenbille', www.forgottenoh.com. The site owner, author Andrew Henderson, indicates on his pages that the account, among others, was submitted as a personal encounter (taken, with reason, to be Kenneth Halbert). The business of Halbert and Coulter Construction Co., Inc. that is referred to in the full report, and founded by these two men, still operates out of Wheeling, West Virginia. In the full account, in a tale reminiscent of the Blue Bell Hill story, the ghost is attributed to the death of a young woman of Rayland (Ohio), who was killed on her way to her wedding when the horse drawing her buggy became spooked and threw her from the carriage.

37. 'Haunted Village', *The Devon and Exeter Gazette*, 6 January 1931, p. 5.

38. http://chiomaobiefuna.blogspot.co.uk; correspondence (email) 16–19 September 2012, 4–5 January 2013.

39. 'Genies On the Road', by Kamau Mutunga, *The Nation* (Nairobi), 2 December 2005 (web version 1 December 2005). Also known as *Jinn* or *Djinn*, Genies are spirits in Muslim mythology, that were created before humans from smokeless fire, and of assuming temporary human or animal form and materiality. Like humans, they are capricious, capable of good and evil; most are hostile to humans.

40. Alan Watts: from taped lecture 'Face Your Problems Head On' (Youtube). Watts (1915–1973) was a British-born philosopher, writer and speaker who popularised Eastern philosophy and religion for Western audiences. The quoted excerpt was in the context of the need to confront our personal terrors in order to master and outgrow them.

41. The incident referred to occurred in the evening of 12 August 1976. Police officers responding to a call about a reported hit-and-run at the intersection of 76th Street and Roberts Road on the east side of Resurrection Cemetery, found a girl in her vehicle in tears and holding a CB handset. The girl pointed to the spot where a body had lain on the grass verge (presumably of a female; presumably after the witness had struck her). She told the police that the body had vanished just as the squad car had turned off 79th street

in her direction. ('Resurrection Cemetery (Home of 'Resurrection Mary') at www.ghostresearch.org (site created by Dale Kacmarek)).

42. Correspondence (email) 9 & 11 September 2010.

43. 'Vanishing Man' (in 'It happened to me'), *Fortean Times* issue 265, August 2010, p. 72.

44. 'Ghost by the Road', by Edson C. Hendricks (24 December 2003), on the website www.sunstar-solutions.com/ghoststories. Used with permission of the site owner, Sharon Cornet, and the witness/author himself (correspondence (email) January 2013).

45. Jennifer Westwood, *Albion* (Grafton, 1992), pp. 18-19.

46. 'Living With Ghosts', 'The Ruskington Horror', *This Morning* (ITV) 1998; *Lincolnshire Echo*, 6 February 1998; Fortean Times no. 137 (August 2000), p.8. A Greek god? The green skin echoes the description given by John Dawkins from his encounter at Blue Bell Hill (Chapter 13 and notes (56.)) and of certain characters from Greek and other mythologies. In Egyptian mythology, Osiris, the god of the dead, the afterlife and rebirth, was commonly depicted as a green-skinned pharaoh, symbolising the cyclicity of life and regeneration.

47. Rob Burkett (approx. 1984); Sarah Martin (1996).

48. The three incidents, in 1999, 2001 and 2010 all occurred north of the Ruskington turn-off. Source: 'Every death on every road in Great Britain 1999-2010' (www.bbc.co.uk/news/uk)—an interactive map based on official data recorded by police in Great Britain between 1999 and 2010 (a total of 36,371 fatalities) derived from the Economic and Social Data Service (www.esds.ac.uk).

49. www.heritagegateway.org.uk. HER number 60734; Grid. Ref. TF 039 512; Map sheet TF05SW (Parish: Brauncewell, North Kesteven, Lincolnshire). At the time of Domesday, this manor in Ruskington belonged to Geoffrey Alselin (c. 1055–1129), a Normandy-born feudal baron and tenant-in-chief of lands in the Midlands in the years after the Norman invasion of 1066.

50. Correspondence (email) 6 February 2013.

51. Correspondence (email) 18 January 2005. Only one road death (a 20-year-old male) is recorded a little north of the location, from a five-car accident, at 7.55 a.m. on 1 September 2000 (see source in 48.).

Chapter 13: More White Ladies

1. Correspondence (email) 4 November 2003 & 24 February 2004.

2. From email referral from Neil Arnold 10 October 2014, and telephone interview with witness 11 October 2014.

3. Correspondence (email) 16 & 17 November 2004.

4. 'Wet hair, big eyes, and bare feet', by Emily Hall, *Kent Messenger*, Friday 19 December 2003, p. 35.

5. *Ibid.* Further details added by correspondence (email) with journalist Emily Hall, 9 December 2003. Joe Chester passed away at the start of 2012.

6. From email correspondence with Neil Arnold 4 November 2009; Neil Arnold having first heard it from Mrs Gammon after a talk at Barming Women's Institute (Maidstone). I subsequently heard Mrs Gammon's directly from her in a brief telephone interview on 25 June 2010.

7. Aniela Jaffé, *An Archetypal Approach to Death Dreams and Ghosts* (Daimon, 1999), p. 95; ISBN 3-85630-580-7.

8. 'New sightings of 'Lady of the Lake', by Ros Anstey, *Standard & Guardian*, 9 September 1999; 'Ghostly Goings-on Down by the Lake', by Andrew Jefferson, *Bristol Evening Post*, 9

September 1999. Chew Valley's ghost girl was featured on London Weekend Television's 'Britain's Most Terrifying Ghost Stories' (broadcast 23 November 2001; narrated by Ian McShane).

9. From a post on the *Fortean Times* website forum 8 October 2008.

10. Correspondence (email) 15 January 2010; 13 July 2013.

11. For instance, the white lady of the Old Mill Hotel, Motherwell, in North Lanarkshire (Scotland); the white lady of Willow Park, Newton-le-Willows, Merseyside (England); and the lady in white of Tolamato Cemetery in St. Augustine, Florida.

12. Virtually synonymous with the *Lares* were the *Manes* (or *Di Manes*), the souls of the dead, which were often associated with deceased loved ones and deified ancestors, who maintained an interest in and protective function over the home and family. As the 'good dead', there was little to fear from them as long as they were continued to be worshipped and revered by their prescribed rites and festivals (such as the *Parentalia* or *dies parentales* ('ancestral days'), held in February). (Lacy Collison-Morley, *Greek and Roman Ghost Stories* (Oxford: B.H. Blackwell; London: Simpking, Marshall & Co., 1912)). The practice of placating the manes with offerings at their graves or memorials is echoed in the modern custom of placing wreaths or personal items on the deceased's grave, and in the simple 'paying of respect' by attendance at the funeral.

St. Augustine refers to Apuleius's belief that after death the souls of the deceased become *daemons* (or, in the Greek, *daimones*)—that is, sub-divine spirits of nature, messengers or other servile spirits—the benevolent guardians of the living (*City of God*, Book IX). Stephen A. Diamond notes that whereas all daimons were originally ambiguous, potentially good or bad depending on how mortals related to them, Xenocrates, a pupil of Plato, distinguished them from the divine, setting in train a developing concept of them as embodying only the negative aspects of the daimonic character. The *Lemures* (and the closely associated *Larvae*), then—the wandering, bad, disturbed or dangerous manes (or *di manes*) became transformed in concept and name in later Christian interpretation of the Greek into distinctly evil spirits—*demons*. (David A. Leeming, Kathryn Madden, Stanton Marlen (eds), *Encyclopedia of Psychology and Religion* (Springer, 2010), pp. 197-199).

13. Lacy Collison-Morley, *op.cit.*, p. 11.

14. The *Lemuria* involved the head of the family going abroad at dead of night to offer black beans while repeating an incantation to the haunting spirits in propitiation for his home and family. The feast days have been given as 9, 11 and 13 May. Marriages held in May were thus said to be unlucky—a superstition that has survived into modern times.

15. Janet and Colin Bord, *Modern Mysteries of Britain* (Grafton, 1988), pp. 36–37. For similar reports of the Man-in-Grey along the A12 in Suffolk and Essex, visit www.roadghosts.com.

16. Correspondence (email) with witness 20 February 2003; 'Six Hills, Leicestershire—an Anglo-Saxon moot site', by Bob Trubshaw. *At the Edge* (www.indigogroup.co.uk/edge—originally published in Mercian Mysteries No. 23 May 1995). The Six Hills Hotel is located at: Fosseway, Six Hills, near Leicester LE14 3PD.

17. Correspondence (email) February & March 2003 & February 2004.

18. Source(s): Jessie K. Payne, *A Ghost Hunter's Guide to Essex* (Ian Henry Publications, 1995), p. 117; *Thurrock Gazette*, 26 September 1969.

19. A misty white figure is reputed to have been seen at the railway crossing on other occasions (www.paranormaldatabase.com).

20. John Brand, M.A., *Observations on the Popular Antiquities of Great Britain* (revised (third) edition by Sir Henry Ellis), Vol. I. (London: Henry G. Bohn, 1853), p. 192, p. 327.

21. Francis Grose, *A Provincial Glossary, with a Collection of Local Proverbs, and Popular Superstitions* (London: S. Hooper, 1787), Superstitions, p. 7; Montague Summers, *The Vampire: His Kith and Kin* (London, K. Paul Trench, Trubner, 1928), p. 154.

22. Montague Summers, *op.cit.,* pp. 154–155. Various traditions contend that the night-walking spirits fly away (vanish) at the sound of cock-crow early in the morning. Hence we find the scenario played out, for instance, in the verse of Spenser, and Shakespeare (Hamlet Act 1, Scene 2).

23. That such fears existed is evidenced, for instance, by an entry in *The Gentleman's Magazine* (1784) in which a woman who had poisoned a man of Aberystwyth, and then herself, was buried on the seashore through fear that her revengeful spirit might join a band of ghosts that had terrorised a nearby village. The coroner had suggested burying her at a crossroads with a stake through her heart, but the seashore was deemed a more secure option. (See: *Criminal graves and rural crossroads*, by Robert Halliday, *British Archaeology*, no. 25, June 1997)).

24. The Parliamentary Act (4th George IV. cap. 52) was passed on 8 July 1823, 'to alter and amend the Law relating to the Interment of the Remains of any Person found *Felo de se* (Latin for 'felon of himself'—a self-murderer; a suicide). (See: *Criminal Law III*, pp. 549–551), *The Gentleman's Magazine* (1823) (Vol. 93, Part 2).

The 1823 Act was itself superseded in 1882 by the Interments (*Felo de se*) Act, which overturned all of the previous restrictions in accordance with the Burial Laws Amendment Act 1880—except the with-holding of the rites of Christian burial (in place of which now could be held a special form of service). The act of suicide itself remained a criminal act until its eventual repeal by the Suicide Act 1961.

25. Christine Quigley, *The Corpse: A History* (McFarland & Co. (USA), 2005); Walter Johnson, Byways in British Archaeology (Cambridge University Press, 2011).

26. Aniela Jaffé, *op.cit.*, p. 30. We could abstract liminality still further, finding meaning in other boundaries that the road ghost phenomenon inhabits: light/dark, benign/hostile, young/old, beautiful/ugly, life/death, fact/fiction, spirit/matter, belief/disbelief.

27. From Andy Doyle's initial email of 3 Feb 2005 to a New Zealand website (www.nzghosts.co.nz). Used with permission.

28. From my own correspondence with the witness (1–3 Feb 2013). Eight years on, and Andy Doyle's recollection has the girl first seen a hundred yards ahead, and interpreted as a jogger in a shell-suit, as he travelled at 40 mph. Following the 'collision', she is seen lying in the bushes of the verge before he stopped to find no-one there.

Of possible additional significance, the bridge shows evidence of repairs to its brickwork, and the structure has emergency notices attached requesting that any witnesses to a collision with the bridge (no. 172) immediately telephone Network Rail and the Police to report the incident. Is this another reason for the apparitional encounter here, as a warning regarding (or, according to their contradictory nature, as potential cause of) danger by collision here?

There is also the following account related to the footbridge at Blue Bell Hill, as heard by Neil Arnold: 'A sceptical old fellow came up to me yesterday at St Mary's Island and said that about 10 years ago he was driving a lorry down the dual carriageway, 3 a.m., and saw a figure dressed in all black standing on the footbridge above. Although the witness couldn't be sure if the figure was male or female he seemed to think it was dressed in the garb of a coachman—but when I asked him if it could have been a woman he said, 'I guess so, but they were dressed head to toe in black and when I drove under the footbridge then looked back there was no-one there." (Neil Arnold, by email, 21 February 2013.)

29. Correspondence (email) 28 August 2003.

30. Initial source: Neil Arnold, who heard it from the witness on 29 May 2013 and summarised the account to me by email. I conducted my own telephone interview with Gillian Barry on 4 June 2013.

31. Initial source: Neil Arnold, who heard it from the witness on 5 August 2013 and summarised the account to me by email the next day. The lady requested that her real name be withheld.

32. Correspondence (email) 19 & 30 March 2006. Donna indicated that her parents split up shortly after they moved out of the property. In view of the fairly well accepted causative factors in poltergeist phenomena, one wonders whether any evident tensions in the household may have contributed to a spike in activity.

33. The Death Index, England & Wales 1916–2005 records the death of John Thomas Gear (born 25 November 1928) in 2000, aged 73 (Medway, Kent, Register no. A39A, Entry no. 97).

34. Telephone interview with Georgina Gear 27 June 2010.

35. Fright Wood at Blue Bell Hill is referenced in *General View of the Agriculture of the County of Kent,* by John Boys (P. Norbury, Brentford, 1794), p. 96. For definitions of Frith/Fright woods, see: John William Horsley, *Place Names in Kent* (South Eastern Gazette, 1921), p. 40; Walter Jerrold, Highways and byways in Kent (Macmillan, 1920), p. 253; P.H. Reaney, *Dictionary of English Surnames* (Routledge, London, 1991 (3rd ed.).

36. Glenn Jones's account by email via Neil Arnold, 11 & 15 March 2014).

37. Rev. John Peter Bernard et al, *A General Dictionary, Historical and Critical (Vol. VII)* (for G. Strahan, J. Clarke, *et al*, London, 1738), pp. 244–245; William Smith, PhD, Charles Anthon, LLD (eds), *A Dictionary of Greek and Roman Antiquities* (Harper & Brothers, New York, 1870). For *Parentalia*, see p. 462; for *Lupercalia*, pp. 603–604; W. Warde Fowler M.A., *The Roman Festivals of the Period of the Republic* (Macmillan & Co., London, 1899), p. 298.

38. Francis Grose, *op.cit.,* Superstitions, pp. 6–7.

39. A probably conservative figure that is based on the incidents reported in newspaper sources and archives in the course of the research for this book.

40. Grose, *op.cit..*, pp. 9–10.

41. Anthony Storr (Ed), *Jung: Selected Writings* (Fontana Press, 1986), p. 70. From the essays 'On the Psychology of the Unconscious'; ISBN-0-00-686126-1. Reprinted by permission of HarperCollins Publishers Ltd © (C. G. Jung) (1983).

42. *Ibid*, p. 71.

43. Grose, *op.cit.,* pp. 11–12.

44. Aniela Jaffé, *op.cit.*, p. 96.

45. *Ibid*, pp. 97-98.

46. Aniela Jaffé (Ed), *C.G. Jung: Memories, Dreams, Reflections* (Fontana Press, 1995), pp. 368–369; ISBN-0-00-654027-9. Reprinted by permission of HarperCollins Publishers Ltd © (Random House Inc) (1961, 1962, 1963).

47. Aniela Jaffé, *An Archetypal Approach to Death Dreams and Ghosts* (Daimon, 1999), p. 99; ISBN 3-85630-580-7.

48. Andrew Green, *Ghosts of Today* (Kaye and Ward, London, 1980), p. 36.

49. Account by email via Neil Arnold, 15 August 2002. Used with permission. The header for this section, 'The Beckoning Fair One', is the title of a novella by English writer Oliver Onions (1873–1961), in his collection of horror stories, *Widdershins* (1911).

50. From telephone interview 15 October 2015, following referral and email summary of the witness's account by Neil Arnold (14 October 2015). Real name of witness withheld on request.

51. Two fatal incidents took place here between 1999 and 2010. A 26-year-old male driver died at 9.10 a.m. on 18 November 2002. No other vehicles were involved. The second took place at 12.05 a.m. on 15 November 2001, and involved two cars. The driver of one, a male of unknown age, died. (Source: 'Every death on every road in Great Britain 1999–2010' (www.bbc.co.uk/news/uk). See Chapter 12 notes (45.)).

52. Maria Leach and Jerome Fried (eds), *op. cit.,* pp. 493–4). Pan (as Faunus) was one of the gods associated with the Roman *Lupercalia.*

53. In addition to symbolising life, the torch also represents guidance, knowledge and illumination (enlightenment). The original 'torch-bearer' in Greek mythology was Prometheus, who stole fire (an invention of Hermes) from the gods to give to humanity.

54. Hesiod, *Theogony* (211) (translation by Hugh G. Evelyn-White, 1914).

55. Hesiod, *Shield of Heracles* (264) (www.theoi.com); P.E. Easterling & Bernard M. W. Knox (eds), *The Cambridge History of Classical Literature: Volume 1, Greek Literature* (Cambridge University Press, 1989), p. 62. The sickly pale green colour is also that of Death's pale horse of the Apocalypse in Revelation 6:1–8; also the British water hag *Jenny Greenteeth*, the Slavic *Rusalka* and similar water-dwelling creatures of folklore.

56. From correspondence (email) with Stephen Watts, 31 August & 1 September 2004.

57. As told to Neil Arnold by an informant following a talk at Maidstone on 6 September 2013. Neil heard another 'friend-of-a-friend' anecdote on this occasion from a different gentleman, which dates to October or November of 1972 and involved a police officer named Ashwood, who was driving up Chatham Road when he came across a woman at the side of the road who was wet through (the evening was dry) and caked in mud and clearly in distress. She asked to be taken to Chatham, but the officer insisted he take her instead to Maidstone police station, but en route she vanished from the car.

58. The *Horai* were sister goddesses of the seasons and the keepers of the gates of heaven. The depiction of Iris and Hermes is found on Attic Red pottery (v.500–450BC) in the collection of the Antiken-sammlungen, Munich, Germany (Cat. No. Munich J291). The iconography of the Mother Goddess with infant, of course, is exemplified most famously by the Madonna and Child in early Christian and Renaissance art.

59. Email correspondence with witness (real name supplied): 22 & 27 April 2003; 29 December 2010; 5 & 7 January 2011. The streets in the immediate area of this sighting are named after famous literary personages, e.g. Greswold St. (Samuel Griswold (1793–1860)), Garratt St. (Edward Garratt, the *nom de plume* of Isabella Fyvie Mayo (1869–1935)), and Milton St. (John Milton (1608–1674). It is unclear whether Gerry was still on Milton Street or had turned onto Garratt Street when he encountered the figure. If on Milton Street, it may be noteworthy that both Milton's first and second wives died during childbirth.

60. Source: Journal of the Royal Society of Medicine, November 2006; 99(11): 559–563.

61. See 'Black Dogs in Folkore' and 'Black Dogs: Guardians of the Corpse Ways', both by Bob Trubshaw, *At The Edge* (www.indigogroup.co.uk/edge); originally published in Mercian Mysteries No. 20, August 1994.

62. Correspondence (email) 2 February 2004.

63. T16.2 *Herakles & Kerberos*, Antikensammlungen, Munich; Cat. no: Munich 3297 (c. 330–310 BC).

64. Elizabeth Mary Wright, *Rustic Speech and Folklore*, Oxford University Press, 1918, p. 194; Rosemary Ellen Guiley, *The Encyclopedia of Ghosts and Spirits* (2nd Edition) (Checkmark Books, 2000), pp. 277–278; Miranda Green, *Animals in Celtic Life and Myth* (Routledge: Taylor & Francis e-Library edition 2002), p. 186; 'Black Dogs: Guardians of the Corpse Ways', by Bob Trubshaw, *op.cit.*

65. Correspondence (email) 24 January 2001.

66. There is, however, an account of the 'The Great Dogg of Trottiscliffe' that, in their *Folkore of Kent* (Tempus 2003, pp. 105–106), Fran and Geoff Doel attribute to early 20th century writer Charles Igglesden, who is said to have collected it in the course of his *Saunters in Kent* series, and refers to a large phantom dog seen in 1654 and 1745 between Trottiscliffe and the Medway. In the latter instance it reputedly attacked and killed a traveler. It next appeared before two Victorian gentlemen on the Pilgrims' Way between

Boxley and the White Horse Stone. I am, however, not the only one who has failed to locate these accounts in Igglesden's 34 volumes of his 'A Saunter Through Kent with Pen and Pencil'. Correspondence with Geoff Doel in June 2013 failed to identify the source without his original notes being to hand.

67. Chris and Janice Leigh, on their Blue Bell Hill Ghost Walk, 27 October 2011.

68. The seal is attached to a charter of 1336. (J. Cave-Browne M.A., *The History of Boxley Parish*, (Printed by E.J. Dickinson, Maidstone, 1892), pp. 40–41).

69. Correspondence via www.roadghosts.com, 2001. The second account was heard by Neil Arnold after a talk at Upchurch in January 2014, when he was approached by a lady named Carol, who saw the figure with her husband further up Blue Bell Hill toward the Medway Towns (Correspondence (email) with Neil Arnold, 8 January 2014).

70. From a telephone interview with the witness 8 November 2014 and email referral from Neil Arnold (7 November) following a Radio Kent interview on ghosts, which Mr Butteriss called in on to relate his opinion and experience.

71. Paul Devereux, *Haunted Land* (Piatkus, 2001), pp. 176–179; Vivienne Rae-Ellis, *True Ghost Stories of Our Time* (Faber, 1990), pp. 212–214.

72. 'Road Ghosts: Haunted Highway', by David Clarke (2011, 'http://drdavidclarke.co.uk); 'The Haunted Highway', *Strange But True?* (TV series, presented by Michael Aspel), LWT Productions, 1994 (air date: 2 December 1994); Jenny Randles & Peter Hough, *Strange But True?* (Piatkus, 1994), Chapter 6 ('Highway of Horror?'), pp. 70–82.

73. Janet Bord, *Fairies: Real Encounters with Little People* (Dell, 1998) (citing the *Hull Daily Mail* of 10 August 1977), pp. 53–54.

74. Jacques Vallee, *Passport to Magonia* (Tandem, 1975), p.53. (Reprinted by Contemporary Books, Chicago, 1993, p. 53.)

75. Janet Bord, *op.cit.*, p. 16.

76. William Smith, LL.D., Dictionary of Greek and Roman Biography and Mythology, Vol. II. (Boston: Little, Brown, and Company, 1867), p. 1217.

77. Reculver: The fragment of a genius cucullatus (from the Royal Museum, Canterbury, No. 1952/10), is described *Archaeologia Cantiana* 66, (1953): pp. 86–91 (Frank Jenkins). Reculver's reputation for being haunted extends back as far as 1732, when it is mentioned in the October edition of the *Gentleman's Magazine* ('Of Ghosts, Demons, and Spectres', pp. 1001–1002. The sound of a crying baby is joined by the apparitions of a Roman soldier and phantom monks. Around 1994, the *Kent Today* published a report of hooded figures that were seen moving high above ground level between the remnant towers of the ruined St. Mary's Church which, with its graveyard, sits inside the eroded remains of the Roman fort.

78. Aniela Jaffé (ed.), *C.G. Jung: Memories, Dreams, Reflections* (Fontana Press, 1995), p. 254.

79. 'Roman 'curse tablet' found in Kent', BBC News England (online), 15 August 2012 (www.bbc.co.uk); 'Mysteries of East Farleigh's Roman 'curse scroll' (The Historical Association, 22 July 2012 (www.history.org.uk). The two greatest concentrations of curse tablets are from the sacred springs of Aquae Sulis (130), and at Uley (140).

80. Tablet 65 (from Bath) reads, 'To Minerva, the goddess Sulis, I have given the thief who has stolen my hooded cloak ...' ('Cultural Hybridization: the Case of the Curse Tablets', by Carly Silver (http://wp.chs.harvard.edu); Miranda Green, *Symbol and Image in Celtic Religious Art* (Routledge: Taylor & Francis, 1992), p. 187; ISBN 0-415-08076-2; used with permission).

81. Miranda Green, *op. cit.*

82. For an example of hooded figures associated with illness, there is the case of Erika Seetzen-Woods in Shrewsbury (Shropshire) in 1969, who saw a hooded figure on three occasions in close association with impending surgery and its complications ('The hooded

figure of Garmston Road' (www.bbc.co.uk/shropshire). Hooded figures connected with Near Death Experiences (NDEs) are exampled by former air force pilot Alan Pring's impressive experience, as told on LWT's *Strange But True? Encounters: Life Beyond Death*; in which the cowled figures led him through a process of self-judgment (air date: 18 October 1996).

83. As famously portrayed, for instance, in the fantasy epics of *Star Wars* (the Sith Lords), *The Lord of the Rings* (ring-wraiths and wizards) and the *Harry Potter* series (the dementors). In 1973, a hooded Grim Reaper-like figure was featured in a British public safety film that was designed to warn children away from playing near deep waters. 'Lonely Water' depicted the figure (voiced by actor Donald Pleasence) appearing near a group of children. It begins: 'I am the Spirit of Dark and Lonely Water, ready to trap the unwary, the show-off, the fool, and this is the kind of place you'd expect to find me.'

84. A cursing/curing stone that fits a known bowl-shaped lower stone was discovered in an old graveyard in Scotland in 2012, making the first complete set known from Scotland ("Cursing stone' found on Isle of Canna', BBC News: Highlands & Islands, 20 May 2012). See also 'Cursing Not Curing: The Darker Side of Holy Wells', by Janet Bord (University of Bath: http://people.bath.ac.uk). For the legends attached to Kit's Coty House, see EHW Dunkin, in *Notes and Queries*, Oxford University Press, January 8, 1870, p. 32; William White, in *Notes and Queries*, Oxford University Press, Vol. 60, July 26, 1879, p. 66.

85. William Coles Finch, *In Kentish Pilgrim Land* (London: The C.W. Daniel Company, 1925), p. 166.

86. 'Great Tottington's Sarsen Stones', by Paul Ashbee, Paper no. 0001-02 (Kent Archaeological Society; www.kentarchaeology.ac). In 1946, Ashbee himself counted 'about a hundred stones'. Hercules Ayleway, who visited Kit's Coty House and Tottington in 1722 found numbers of large stones in 'Tottenden rivulet', some as large as those of Kit's Coty.

87. Paul Ashbee, *op. cit.*

88. Coles Finch, *op.cit.*, p. 166. *The London Gazette* of 30 November 1880 published a public notice announcing an application by the Maidstone Waterworks Company to 'take, use, and appropriate the waters of certain springs, respectively called or known by the names of the Springhead, upon Springhead Farm, and the Cossington Spring.'

89. Coles Finch, *op.cit.*, pp. 165–166; Alfred John Dunkin, *The Chronicles of Kent*, Lib. I (Dover: Reprinted by William Fenton for J.R. Smith, London, 1844), pp. 31–32.

90. Alan Armstrong (ed), *The Economy of Kent 1640–1914* (The Boydell Press, Woodbridge, and Kent County Council, 1995), p. 117.

91. Coles Finch, *op.cit.*, pp. 164–165; Edward Hasted, *The History and Topographical Survey of the County of Kent*, Vol. IV (Canterbury, 1798), p. 432 & p. 434. The locations of the chapels of St. Stephen (founded at Tottington by Richard de Poynings, and St. Michael (founded by Sir Stephen de Cosenton) are plotted on a sketch map in Coles Finch (p. 163).

92. "Blue Bell Hill ghost saved my life,' says crash survivor Clare', by Nick Lillitos, *Kent Messenger* (Maidstone), 18 October 2013, p. 31; "Blue Bell Hill ghost saved my life,' says crash victim', *KM Extra* (Medway) 23 October 2013, p. 9.

93. From telephone interview with Clare Bush 30 November 2013.

Chapter Fourteen: The Essential Question

1. 'Driver Fatigue and Road Accidents' (2011), The Royal Society for the Prevention of Accidents, www.rospa.com.

2. If we accept that appearances of ghosts are dependent on certain states or processes of mind of the percipient, then it is natural to expect certain limitations, perhaps explaining,

among other things, why a number of apparitions appear to lack facial features. Whereas any number of witnesses might be able to unconsciously project broad descriptive features based on rumour, expectation, or simply the setting of the experience, it could be argued that the requirement for very specific features (which could in some cases conflict with descriptions of the person reputedly represented) might place too great a strain on the imaging process. The mind, therefore, would simply omit this information.

3. The 'Cerebro Retinal Reciprocation Theory of 'Ghost' formation' (see *Arthur C. Clarke's A–Z of Mysteries*, by Simon Welfare and John Fairley (HarperCollinsPublishers, 1993), pp. 162–163)—a theory which finds expression as 'back-projection' (Humphrey, 1992), or the running in reverse of the visual machinery (V. S. Ramachandran & Sandra Blakeslee, *Phantoms in the Brain* (Fourth Estate, 1999). And there are various neurological conditions giving rise to visual hallucinations, such as Charles Bonnet Syndrome, which describes the tendency of visually impaired persons to hallucinate unfamiliar persons or objects that range from the bizarre to the completely real in appearance. These images may interact with the normal surroundings so that the percipient cannot differentiate what is real and what is not, but which may vanish with a blink or a nod of the head. Relevant to our discussion is the observation that poor lighting conditions or the changing tones at dusk are conducive to such hallucinations, which interfaces with the commentary on the M1 hypothesis.

As studies are beginning to show, human perception is a hugely more complex process, in which our 'reality' is a kind of virtual simulation arising from the interplay between visual signals and high-level stored information in the brain. (see V. S. Ramachandran & Sandra Blakeslee, *op. cit.*, p. 109 and pp. 274–5). But before we decide that this provides a satisfactory explanation for road ghost sightings, we must note that Charles Bonnet Syndrome is largely confined to *visually impaired* subjects—the elderly or accident victims, the latter of which commonly experience their visions in the 'blind spots' or *scotomas* in their visual field arising from their medical condition. We would suppose that the ordinary motoring public is *not* similarly disposed (although this has not prevented Ramachandran from speculating that a host of paranormal visions may be attributable to Charles Bonnet hallucinations (V. S. Ramachandran & Sandra Blakeslee, *op. cit.*, p. 106)), nor us from conceding the possibility that similar image feedback *may* occur in states in which no real input is coming from the retina, such as against the monotonously dark and repetitive night-driving field.

4. *Great Hauntings* (a compilation of *The Unexplained* (Orbis Publishing, London, 1984)), p. 74.

5. In this respect, BBH's apparitions (at least as relating to the girl in white) are not strictly veridical since they convey features that the percipients have in some cases been conditioned to expect (although, as we have seen, the specific pattern of events, not recognised in individual witness cases, does display the kind of correlative detail we might expect of true, objective events).

6. See 'Aion: Researches into the Phenomenology of the Self', by C.G. Jung (translated by R.F.C Hull), Bollingen Series XX (New York: *Pantheon Books*, 1959), p. 13.

7. Anthony Storr (ed.), *Jung: Selected Writings* (Fontana Press, 1986) p. 102. (from 'Definitions', Psychological Types—Collected Works 6, paras. 797-811); ISBN-0-00-686126-1. Reprinted by permission of HarperCollins Publishers Ltd © (C. G. Jung) (1983).

8. The ultimate archetypal *femme fatale* was, perhaps, Medusa, one of the Gorgons, the three hideous sisters of Greek myth with serpents for hair and a paralysing gaze. The only safe way to view Medusa was as a reflection in a mirror, else her direct gaze was capable of turning men into stone. Similarly, in dream symbolism, the mirror is said to represent the ability of the unconscious to reflect a true, undistorted view of the self—one which the conscious mind, if confronting it directly, might find uncomfortable or shocking. In addition to the psychological analogies, however, the turning of men into stone might serve as an apt description for the effect the staring eyes of the ghost girl have on the petrified motorist.

9. *Out of This World* (BBC1), presented by Sue Cook, with Dr Susan Blackmore and Dr Lyall Watson, broadcast at 9.30 p.m. on 7 October 1994. This one-hour special served as a pilot for a new series by the same name that commenced in July 1996.

10. The term 'Psi' is used more frequently today, representing not only telepathic/ESP powers, but a range of psychic talents.

11. Excavation work began on the North Downs Tunnel section (part of the first phase of the entire CTRL project) in Oct. 1998. The 2-mile long tunnel is the UK's largest volume rail tunnel since completion of the Channel Tunnel in 1994. Breakthrough was achieved on 8 June 2000 ('Light at the end of rail link tunnel', by Stephen Hedges, *Kent Messenger* 9 June 2000, p. 2), and the work completed in December 2001. An estimated one million cubic metres of chalk were excavated and taken by local cement companies and to construct the widened M2 motorway between junctions 2 & 3.

12. *Mysteries* (TV series, presented by Carol Vorderman), BBC, 1997); 'Spooked out on the ghoul carriageway', by John Kay, *The Sun*, 27 December 1996, p. 3.

13. 'Drivers Spooked by By-pass Ghost', by Tommy Walls, *Sunday Life*, 29 March 1992; 'Ghost busters flock to see the by-pass spook', by Tommy Walls, *Sunday Life*, 5 April 1992.

14. As 'way out' as some of Keel's ideas perhaps seem, a proper judgment of his work should only follow a reading of his work. See, for instance, *Operation Trojan Horse* (Souvenir Press, 1971), and *Strange Creatures from Time and Space* (Sphere, 1976).

15. J. Allen Hynek and Jacques Vallee, *The Edge of Reality* (Henry Regnery Company, Chicago, 1975), Figure 5., p. 20.

16. Paul Devereux (with David Clarke, Andy Roberts and Paul McCartney), *Earth Lights Revelation* (Blandford Press, 1989), p. 23.

17. A term coined by Paul Devereux.

18. *Fortean Times* 42–46 (compilation: 'If Pigs Could Fly', John Brown Publishing, London, 1994), issue 42, p. 54; Paul Devereux et al, *op.cit.*, p. 54.

19. *Fortean Times* 42–46, issue 42, p. 53.

20. Paul Devereux (with David Clarke, Andy Roberts and Paul McCartney), *Earth Lights Revelation* (Blandford Press, 1989), p. 221.

21. *Ibid.*, p. 163.

22. *Ibid.*, p. 51.

23. Paul Devereux, *Places of Power* (Blandford Press, 1990), p. 190.

24. Paul Devereux et al, *Earth Lights Revelation* (Blandford Press, 1989), p. 219.

25. Paul Devereux (with Paul McCartney), *Earth Lights* (Turnstone Press, 1982), p. 209.

26. *Ibid.*, p .208.

27. *The Australian*, 25 Nov. 1965, p. 3; *The Courier Mail* (Brisbane), 22 Nov., fp., 23 Nov., fp and p. 3; *The Age* (Melbourne), 23 Nov., p. 3; *The West Australian*, 22 Nov., p. 21., 26 Nov.. p. 20; *Sydney Morning Herald*, 23 Nov., p. 10; *The Herald*, 22 Nov., fp; *Telegraph*, 22 Nov, fp., 23 Nov., p. 18., 24 Nov., fp.

28. Posted on the www.anomalies.net website (March 1999).

29. The so-called 'God Helmet'. See: 'Enhancement of Temporal Lobe-Related Experiences During Brief Exposures to MilliGauss Intensity Extremely Low Frequency Magnetic Fields', by Ruttan, L., Persinger, M. & Koren, S. (*Journal of Bioelectricity*: 9 (1), 1990), pp. 33–54.

30. This includes the experiments of Professor Olaf Blanke and Dr Giulio Rognini of the Ecole Polytechnique Federale de Lausanne (EPFL) in Switzerland ('How to make ghosts

in the lab: scientists trick volunteers into reporting 'feelings of presence'', by James Vincent, *The Independent* (online), 7 November 2014).

31. Swedish workers Larsson, M., Larhammarb, D., Fredrikson, M., and Granqvist, P. (2005) attempted to replicate Persinger's findings but failed to do so, proposing instead that the suggestibility of the participants and other factors might be responsible for its effects.

32. As reproduced in Paul Devereux's *Earth Lights Revelation, op.cit.,* p. 48.

33. Source(s): NASA; David H. Hathaway, 'The Solar Cycle', Living Rev. Solar Phys., 7, (2010), 1. The Sun's magnetic field flipped on schedule in February 2001. The next peak reversal was expected in 2012 (the year of Dan Mulford's and Ryan Banks' encounter in Blue Bell Hill village—see Epilogue), but in fact this was confirmed in late December 2013.

34. An X20 flare of 16 August 1989, which followed the famous flare of 6 March 1989 that caused disruption to the power grids in Canada.

35. Anthony Storr (Ed), *Jung: Selected Writings* (Fontana Press, 1986), p. 218; ISBN-0-00-686126-1. Reprinted by permission of HarperCollins Publishers Ltd © (C. G. Jung) (1983).

36. *Ibid.,* p. 218.

37. *Ibid.,* p. 216.

38. *Ibid.,* p. 219.

39. *Ibid.,* p. 331.

40. Aniela Jaffé, *An Archetypal Approach to Death Dreams and Ghosts* (Daimon, 1999), p. 187; ISBN 3-85630-580-7.

41. Anthony Storr (Ed), *op. cit.* p. 335.

42. Aniela Jaffé, *op. cit.* p. 182–3.

43. Anthony Storr (Ed), *op. cit.* p. 342.

44. Aniela Jaffé, *op. cit.* p. 176.

45. From Jung's 'Commentary on 'The Secret of the Golden Flower'' (*Collected Works*, Volume 13, para. 54).

46. Anthony Storr (Ed), *op. cit.* p. 225.

47. *Ibid.,* p. 225.

Epilogue

1. From the on-site interview with the witnesses at 6 p.m. on 15 June 2012.

2. 'Woman in white gives men a fright on midnight drive', by Chris Hunter, *Kent Messenger* (County) Friday 15 June 2012, p. 19. The story was recounted also the following editions and publications: 'Was ghostly woman the Blue Bell Hill phantom?', by Chris Hunter, *Medway Messenger* (Monday edition), 18 June 2012, p. 13; 'Danger! Haunting Ahead', Take A Break's *Fate & Fortune,* October 2012, p. 41.

3. 'Squatters move in to derelict Chatham pub', www.Kentonline.co.uk (*Kent Messenger*) 13 September 2012.

4. 'Arrests at derelict pub in Blue Bell Hill, Chatham', www.Kentonline.co.uk (*Kent Messenger*) 11 December 2012.

5. '£10 legal high made me parade naked through Tesco', by Rob Cooper, MailOnline (www.dailymail.co.uk) 15 June 2012.

6. In June 2014, I corresponded with one of the women reported by the *Kent Messenger* as removed from the Upper Bell in December 2012. Marcia Wheeler, of Maidstone, said she

had not been the woman concerned and did not know who it may have been. Interestingly, though, she confirmed that the occupants had been holding squat parties there each month on the full moon (correspondence 26 June 2014), raising the possibility that the girl concerned had indeed been another partygoer around this time (although the KM had reported the squatters had moved in after this time, in September). Incidentally, the full moon in June 2012 was on 4 June—which doesn't tie up.

7. Tonbridge and Malling Borough Council (TMBC) received an application in December 2012 from the owner of the derelict Upper Bell to demolish the former pub on account of it having fallen into a poor state of disrepair and become occupied by squatters, who, it was rumoured, were involved in drugs. This was a situation that attracted some commentary from Medway Conservative MP Tracy Crouch, and the squatters were evicted and arrested in early December 2012. TMBC appear to have rubber-stamped the proposal following a limited public consultation, and despite the objections raised by Aylesford Parish Council and other interested parties. Thus, TMBC came to grant the demolition of a building that had long otherwise been protected within previous planning decisions, ostensibly to resolve a simple squatting issue. After the removal of the building, the site became a visual mess, giving rise to additional concerns and uncertainties for local residents, and remains so to date (February 2017).

8. Occupied today by no. 277.

9. Correspondence (email) received by Neil Arnold 23 June 2012.

10. 'Girl, 18, killed as she crosses road', *Kent Messenger* (Maidstone) 30 October 1981, fp. See also: 'News around Kent', *Evening Post* 29 October 1981, p.5. Sarah Burnley* (real name withheld) was 19 when she died (21 Dec 1961–28 Oct 1981) (England & Wales Death Index 1916–2005. Registered (Maidstone) Jan-Mar 1982 (Vol. 16, Page 1508).

11. 'Riddle of girl's fatal road dash', *Evening Post* 15 February 1982, p. 5; 'Teenager's road death in the rain', *Kent Messenger* (Weald) 19 February 1982, p. 25.

12. The inquest reports give the address name: *Bladon.* Previously this was occupied by Pat Sandford, who sold it to Sarah Burnley's father. The property today, at 33 Old Chatham Road, is called *Morningside.*

13. Correspondence (email) with Neil Arnold 26 August 2012.

Index

G

L

M

Printed and bound in the United Kingdom
11/03/2026
02069508-0006